Land Legislation in
Mandate Palestine

Land Legislation in Mandate Palestine

VOLUME 7

OFFICIAL REPORTS AND MEMORANDA,
PART III

Editor: Martin Bunton

CAMBRIDGE ARCHIVE EDITIONS

an imprint of

CAMBRIDGE
UNIVERSITY PRESS

CAMBRIDGE UNIVERSITY PRESS

Cambridge, New York, Melbourne, Madrid, Cape Town, Singapore, São Paulo

Cambridge University Press
The Edinburgh Building, Cambridge CB2 2RU, UK

Published in the United States of America by Cambridge University Press,
New York

www.cambridge.org
Information on this title: www.archiveeditions.co.uk

© Copyright in this edition including research, selection of documents, arrangement, contents lists and descriptions: Cambridge Archive Editions Ltd 2009

Cambridge Archive Editions is an imprint of Cambridge University Press.

Facsimiles of original documents including Crown copyright material are published under licence from The National Archives, London, England. Images may be used only for purposes of research, private study or education. Applications for any other use should be made to The National Archives Image Library, Kew, Richmond, Surrey TW9 4DU. Infringement of the above condition may result in legal action.

Subject to statutory exception and to the provisions of relevant collective licensing agreements, no reproduction of other parts of the work may take place without written permission of Cambridge University Press.

Every reasonable effort has been made to contact all copyright holders; in the event of any omission please contact the publisher.

First published 2009

Printed and bound by CPI Group (UK) Ltd, Croydon, CR0 4YY

British Library Cataloguing in Publication Data
Land Legislation in Mandate Palestine.
  1. Land tenure–Law and legislation–Palestine–History–
20th century. 2. Land tenure–Law and legislation–
Palestine–History–20th century–Sources. 3. Palestine–
Politics and government–1917-1948.
  I. Bunton, Martin P.
  346.5'6940432-dc22

ISBN-13:   978-1-84097-260-3 (set) (hardback)
            978-1-84097-306-8 (volume 7)

Land Legislation in Mandate Palestine

CONTENTS

VOLUME 7:

OFFICIAL REPORTS AND MEMORANDA, PART III

Section 7: Land Legislation and Development 1929–1933   1

7.01 "The land problem", in 'Report of the Commission on the Palestine Disturbances of August, 1929' (Shaw Commission, 1930, pp. 213–235. Maps were not available for inclusion. [CO 733/177/4]

7.02 'Report on Immigration, Land Settlement and Development',   27
Sir John Hope-Simpson, 1930. [Cmnd Paper 3686] [Maps referred to are reproduced in facsimile in the map box (Cmnd 3687)]

7.03 J. Hope-Simpson, Refugee Settlement Commission, Athens, to Lord   215
Passfield, Secretary of State for the Colonies, 18 August 1930, elaborating on his report [CO 733 193/1]

7.04 A. Wauchope, High Commissioner for Palestine, Jerusalem, to   225
Secretary of State for the Colonies, January 1931, forwarding report entitled 'First Report on Agricultural Development and Land Settlement in Palestine, December 1931', by L. French, Director of Development, Jerusalem, with appendices [CO 733/214/5]

7.05 'Palestine: Commitments in connection with land settlement and   377
development' [CO733/214/7]

7.06 Sir P. Cunliffe-Lister, Secretary of State for the Colonies, London,   391
to A. Wauchope, High Commissioner for Palestine, Jerusalem, 19 January 1932, sending, for his criticism, Cabinet memorandum, 'Cabinet. Palestine. Memorandum by the Secretary of State for the Colonies'; with response from A. Wauchope dated 5 March 1932 [CO 733/215/2]

7.07 'Supplementary report on agricultural development and land   465
settlement in Palestine', April 1932, by L. French, Director of Development, Jerusalem, with appendices [CO 733/214/8]

7.08 'Report by the Financial Adviser to the Director of Development on   595
the financial aspects of the proposals in the Director's first and supplementary reports on agricultural development and land settlement in Palestine', 20 April 1932 [CO 733/214/8]

Contents

7.09 Memorandum entitled 'Palestine – Land Legislation', by H.F. Downie, 19 May 1932 [CO 733/217/4]   625

7.10 Extract from a private and personal letter from Sir P. Cunliffe-Lister to Sir A. Wauchope, 3 June 1932, regarding the growing weariness with white papers, letters and reports [CO 733/214/9]   645

7.11 'Revised draft memorandum for Cabinet: land policy for Palestine', with appendices; A. Wauchope, High Commissioner for Palestine, Jerusalem, to Sir P. Cunliffe-Lister, Secretary of State for the Colonies, London, 22 December 1932, with observations on same, and extract from letter of 2 December 1932 [CO 733/217/6]   649

7.12 A. Wauchope, High Commissioner for Palestine, Jerusalem, to Sir P. Cunliffe-Lister, Secretary of State for the Colonies, 15 April 1933, providing recommendations on the reports submitted by L. French, with four enclosures: Awni Abdul Hadi, for Arab Executive Committee, Jerusalem, to A. Wauchope, High Commissioner for Palestine, Jerusalem, 10 March 1933, outlining the observations of the Arab Executive Committee on the two reports by L. French; Dr. Ch. Arlosoroff, for the Executive of the Jewish Agency, to A. Wauchope, High Commissioner for Palestine, Jerusalem, dated 10 March 1933, also in response to the two reports by L. French, (two items: a dated letter and an undated 'Memorandum on the Reports on Agricultural Development and Land Settlement in Palestine'); L. Andrews, Acting Director of Development, Jerusalem, to Chief Secretary, Jerusalem, 24 March 1933, responding to the observations of the Arab Executive Committee; L. Andrews, 'Comments of the Department of Development on the Memorandum of the Jewish Agency on the First and Supplementary Reports on Agricultural Development and Land Settlement in Palestine by L. French' [CO 733/230/7]   689

Section 7: Land Legislation and Development 1929–1933

7.01

-214-

CHAPTER VIII.

THE LAND PROBLEM.

As stated elsewhere in this Report the question of land, its ownership, occupation and colonisation is, perhaps, one to which more than to any other matter, importance is attached both by the Jews and the Arabs. Both in evidence which was submitted to us in Jerusalem and in the speeches which were addressed to us by the spokesmen of the many deputations which we received in every part of the country the fears of the Arabs, that the success of the Zionist policy meant their expropriation from the land were repeatedly emphasised. As an example of evidence of this character we would cite that of the Mayor of Nablus who told us that:-

> "In the early days the Jew who came worked on his land and employed Arab labour. Since immigration commenced in large numbers these Jewish employers have turned away the Arab labourers and have employed Jews in their place thereby throwing out of work a large number of Arabs .... Great harm has been caused to the country by the sale to Jews of large estates - for instance the Sursock family in Beirut who owned large areas of land in Palestine and the Wadi el Hawareth - and this throws out of employment a large number of Arabs. I understand, as all Arabs understand, that the Zionist policy is to dispose of the Arabs in every possible way and to replace them with Jews."

There is no doubt that the fears so stated by the Mayor of Nablus are deeply seated in the Arab mind and from whatever angle it is examined the land problem is a serious one, of great complexity and difficulty. Before expressing any opinion as to

whether

whether the Arabs are or are not justified in their point of view, it is necessary to examine in some detail the sequence of events which has led up to the present position.

According to the estimates supplied to us by the Director of Lands, the area of cultivable land in Palestine is approximately eleven million dunoms[x] of which approximately nine hundred thousand dunoms are recorded in the land registers of the Palestine Government as being in Jewish ownership. The figure for the total area given to us by the Director of Lands does not include that part of the Jordan Valley north of Jericho and south of Nablus where there is practically no rainfall and no cultivation. The soil in this area has so far been unproductive. Nor does Mr. Stubbs' figure include the large area south of Beersheba, occupied by Beduin, where the rainfall is very slight. But, we are informed, his figure includes, with these exceptions, the whole cultivable land of Palestine wherever situate.

Other figures were supplied to us by Dr. Ruppin, a land expert, who was deputed to give evidence before us on behalf of the Palestine Zionist Executive. According to Dr. Ruppin's figures twelve and a half million dunoms of land in Palestine are cultivable and of this area 1,200,000 dunoms are in Jewish ownership. It should, however, be noted that in Dr. Ruppin's calculations the dunom has been taken as having an area of 919 square metres. If his figure for the total

cultivable

---

[x] A dunom is 1,000 sq. metres or approximately a quarter of an acre.

cultivable area is reduced by 8% in order to express it in the standard dunom of 1,000 square metres, the difference between it and the figure furnished by the Director of Lands to the Palestine Government is not material.

Jewish colonisation is mainly concentrated in the Plain of Esdraelon and the Coastal Plain. We annex a map, kindly supplied to us by the Palestine Zionist Executive, which shows the distribution and size of the Jewish holdings. Inasmuch as the map distinguishes between high and low ground it gives a rough indication of the geographical distribution of the fertile land in Palestine. Of the land purchased by the Jews, so Dr. Ruppin informed us, relatively small areas not exceeding in all 10% ~~of the total purchased~~ were ~~by Jews direct from~~ acquired from peasants. The other areas have been acquired from the owners of large estates most of whom live outside Palestine and, in consequence, leased their land or allowed it to be worked on various conditions of tenure. Most of the Jewish purchases from peasants occurred in the coastal zone while in the Plain of Esdraelon all land was bought from absentee landlords.

It is clear from documents to which we have been referred that soon after the institution of civil government in Palestine the Administration became anxious lest the interests of tenants and occupiers should be prejudiced by the sales of large estates. That this is the case is shown by the following extract from the Minutes of the
Advisory

[Map not available for inclusion here.]

Advisory Council on the Land Transfer Ordinances of 1920 - 1921:-

"Third Meeting. 7th December, 1920.

Dr. Sahib Salem asked what measures were being taken to safeguard the rights of cultivators, etc., as he understood that in several villages cultivators had been expelled from their holdings.

His Excellency quoted the following extract from the Land Transfer Ordinance, and the terms of reference to the Land Commission, to illustrate the precautions taken by the Government to prevent such expulsions:-

Extract from Land Transfer Ordinance - paragraph 6.

"The Governor shall also withhold his consent unless (from a proposed disposition) he is satisfied that in the case of agricultural land the tenant in occupation, if the property is leased, will retain sufficient land in the district or elsewhere for the maintenance of himself and his family. The Governor may refer to the High Commissioner any case in which he withholds his consent."

Extract from Instructions to Land Commission.

"The Government of Palestine, while desirous to promote in every possible way the closer settlement of the country, is at the same time anxious that the interests of the present tenants and occupants of land, whether Government property or private property, should be properly protected. It will be necessary on the one hand to take steps to prevent the eviction of tenants by the landlords on a sale of the land, and on the other to secure for those who have exercised customary rights of cultivation and grazing, without full legal title, a sufficient area for the maintenance of their families ...."

The deliberations of the Advisory Council were followed in due course by the promulgation of an Ordinance, known as the Land Transfer Ordinance of 1921, from which the following sections are taken:-

Section 5 (1). Any person wishing to make a disposition of immovable property must first obtain the consent of the Government.

Section 8 (1).

-218-

> Section 8 (1). The consent of the Government to a disposition shall be given by the Director of Lands to the Registrar of the District or Sub-district who shall be satisfied only that the transferor has a title; provided that in the case of agricultural land which is leased, he shall also be satisfied that any tenant in occupation will retain sufficient land in the District or elsewhere for the maintenance of himself and his family."

The second of these sub-sections reproduces in a modified form a provision from an Ordinance passed in the previous year. The Ordinance of 1921 remained in force until the 31st of July, 1929, when it was repealed by the Protection of Cultivators Ordinance to which reference is made hereafter. The Ordinances of 1920 and 1921 were designed to avert the danger which appears now to be imminent, namely, that large numbers of Arab tenants and cultivators for whom no alternative land is available would be deprived of their holdings. These Ordinances failed to achieve the objects which those who framed them had in view and the Director of Lands offered the following explanation of their failure to do so. When asked as to the number of cases in which the provisions of Section 8 (1) of the 1921 Ordinance had been applied and sufficient land had been retained by tenants over whose heads an estate was being sold, he replied that he did not think that there was any case and that the Ordinance had in fact proved unworkable. This he explained in the following terms:-

> "A vendor would come along and make a contract for sale and purchase with the Jews. We would know nothing of this until 4, 5 or 6 months later when the transaction would come to the office. We then instructed the District Officer to report on the tenants. He would go out

-219-

> go out to the village and in some cases he would find that the whole population had already evacuated the village. They had taken certain sums of money and had gone, and we could not afford them any protection whatever. In other cases it was found that a large percentage of the population had already gone before the transaction came to us, and we could not find out who the tenants were, they had no written contracts, and we did not know what compensation they were getting and that was a reason for the introduction of the Ordinance of 1929, so that we would be able to supervise their compensation to be settled by an organised body; a Board under the Ordinance.
> (i.e. the Ordinance of 1921)
> The object of this Ordinance/was to retain the cultivator on the land but he had gone immediately the contract of sale and purchase was made. He was getting a certain sum of money, and away he went, and when the transaction came to us we found no tenants in the village."

At the beginning of 1927 Lord Plumer appointed a Committee under the Chairmanship of the Attorney General and with the present Commissioner of Lands as one of its members to consider (1) whether legislation for the protection of tenants from eviction would be effective and beneficial; (2) if such legislation is considered effective and beneficial to report what form it should take. The following is an extract from the communique in which the Government brought to the notice of the people of Palestine the substance of the recommendations of this Commission:-

> "It has been generally recognised that the present law for the protection of agricultural tenants from eviction is inadequate. The Transfer of Land Ordinance, 1920, which was issued at the beginning of the Civil Administration, contains a provision designed to secure the protection of such tenants when land is transferred by the landlord. The provision, as amended in 1921, is to the effect that the consent of the Government to a disposition of agricultural land which is leased shall be given only after the Director of Lands is satisfied that any tenant in occupation will retain sufficient land in the district or elsewhere for
>
> the maintenance

the maintenance of himself and his family. In a number of the larger land transactions which have taken place an attempt has been made to give effect to this clause, but experience has shown that where existing tenants of land which has been transferred are given a lease by the purchasers, they do not normally stay on the land, but dispose of their rights in a short period to the purchasers, and in most cases they have elected to contract out of their rights of receiving land in consideration of money compensation.

Save where land is transferred by the landlord while the tenants are still in occupation, the tenants have no legal protection from eviction, however long they may have cultivated the land on which they are living. Written contracts of tenancy are rare and there is no customary provision as to notice of eviction.

The Committee recommended that legislation should be introduced on the lines of that in force in England and elsewhere -

(a) To protect agricultural tenants from sudden eviction by requiring a due period of notice save in cases where the tenant fails to pay the rent or misuses the land, and

(b) to secure the tenant compensation for improvements which he has carried out during his tenancy and which are not exhausted;

(c) to secure further compensation for a tenant of long standing who is required by the landlord to leave his holding.

As a result of these recommendations there was enacted on the 31st of July last an Ordinance, entitled the Protection of Cultivators Ordinance, which repealed the provision in the Ordinance of 1921 whereby certain Government officials were required to satisfy themselves that tenants in occupation retain sufficient land for the maintenance of themselves and their families. The Ordinance of 1929 provided for the payment to certain classes of tenants of compensation for disturbance or for improvements on their receiving a valid notice to quit the holding of which

of which they had been in occupation. It
further provided for the constitution of Boards to
decide disputes as to whether or not compensation
for disturbance or compensation for improvement
was payable and as to the amount of any such
compensation. In the case of tenants who had
cultivated their holdings for a period of five years
and more the landlord who terminated the tenancy
was required to pay as additional compensation a
sum equal to the average annual rent paid by the
tenant during the five years preceding the
termination of the tenancy.

It is a matter of some surprise to us
that so long a time was allowed to elapse before
an effort was made to amend legislation which
had proved to be ineffective for the purpose
for which it was passed. The Ordinance of 1929
gives rights to a tenant who is dispossessed
which are very different from the rights which
by the Ordinance of 1921 it was contemplated
should be given to such persons. The new law
does nothing to secure to those dispossessed
"a sufficient area for the maintenance of their
families". In other words it is unlikely
that this law will have the effect of diminishing
the numbers of those rendered landless or
divorced from the soil in consequence of the
purchase over their heads of the holdings on
the cultivation of which they now rely for their
subsistence.

It is

It is necessary here to refer to two large sales of land which were brought to our notice on frequent occasions as illustrating the failure of the Palestine Government to prevent the creation of a large landless class. These sales of land were cited by the Arabs in support of their contention that the fears which they expressed were justified.

Between 1921 and 1925 various Jewish land organisations made large purchases by auction of areas in the Vale of Esdraelon. The area in question amounted to rather more than 200,000 dunoms. Twenty-two villages were included in the sales and the purchase price was £726,000. The lands in question were purchased from the Sursocks who, we were informed, are a large and wealthy family of Christian Arabs established in Beirut.

At the time of the sales the cultivators had no written agreement with the landlord to whom they paid annually one fifth of the produce of the land. After the sales, the Arab cultivators, having received compensation, left all these villages with the exception of Mahloul. Those who remained in this village were given 2,000 dunoms of land by the Sursock family and were offered by the purchasers a further area of 3,000 dunoms on a six years lease at a rent of six per cent on the purchase price paid for that land with the option to purchase at the same price. Consent was in due course given by the Government to the purchases and the transfer was recorded in the Government registers. According to Dr. Ruppin, who, as we have already stated gave

expert

expert evidence on behalf of the Palestine Zionist Executive, the number of tenants who had to leave the land purchased by the Jewish Organisations was between seven and eight hundred but, he added, nearly all of them remained in the same District and found other land which they could cultivate. According to Mr. Farah, who gave expert evidence on behalf of the Arab Executive/, the total number of Arab families who were displaced in consequence of these transactions was about 1,746 and the number of persons affected, on the basis of five per family, was about 8,730. Dr. Ruppin stated that these persons were moved to neighbouring villages of which he gave us a list but Mr. Farah told us that a large number emigrated to America, that others are employed for the time being as stone cutters and lime burners in connection with the construction of new buildings but that they have no other occupation to which they can turn when these are completed. Others, Mr. Farah added, are "scattered all over"; they cannot live there because "nothing was left to live on". He added that, so long as the villages were inhabited by Arab peasants, the Beduin, who through the winter months live in the hilly land around, were accustomed to come down after harvest and pasture their flocks on the lands which have now been sold. When the villages were transferred the Beduin, like the peasants, were "cut off." Dr. Ruppin stated that the Jewish land companies although not legally obliged to pay compensation to the tenants dispossessed in consequence of these sales, in fact paid more than £30,000 and that such

compensation

compensation was paid in order to facilitate the acquisition of land or leases elsewhere by those who through the sales had to remove from the Esdraelon Valley.

We think that the Jewish companies are not open to any criticism in respect of these transactions. In paying compensation, as they undoubtedly did, to many of the cultivators of lands, which they purchased in the Plain of Esdraelon, those companies were making a payment which at the time of the transactions the law of Palestine did not require. Moreover they were acting with the knowledge of the Government.

The second case to which we will refer is the recent purchase of land known as the Wadi el Hawareth. We do so because the sale of this land was made the subject of many protests addressed to us during our stay in Palestine and because this transaction serves to illustrate the extremely difficult position in which the Administration of Palestine are liable to be placed. The lands in question which belonged to Arabs were mortgaged in 1882 to a French subject. Between 1882 and 1923 there were two transfers of the mortgage without the consent of the mortgagor. After

After litigation in the course of which the validity of the mortgage was disputed judgment was given in favour of the heirs of the mortgagee and an order for sale was duly made.

The area offered for sale was 30,826 dunoms and the Jewish National Fund purchased the property for £41,000. The land was registered in its name on the 27th of May, 1929; the persons occupying the lands which have been sold number about 1,200 and own between two and three thousand head of stock. About a third of the land is used for grazing purposes; among the crops grown on the remaining areas are melons and the tithes paid in the year 1928 indicate that crop was worth at least £7,000.

Among the persons now occupying the land are actual cultivators who received in August 1928 notice to quit expiring on the 1st of October, 1929.

On

On the 30th of November, 1929, an order of eviction was made against a large proportion of the occupiers. At the time when we left Palestine we understood that the police had not executed the order of eviction and that the reason for their failure to do so was that they did not know of any locality to which they could move the present occupants and their flocks. We were informed that this action on the part of the police might at any time result in proceedings for contempt at the instance of the purchasers who are not disposed to abandon any of the rights which they possessed under the orders of the Courts or to postpone the enforcement of those rights. The purchasers have, however, offered to put approximately 5,000 dunoms of land in the Beisan area at the disposal of the occupiers for a period of three years on the condition that they are paid one fifth of the produce of that land. We were informed that this land is irrigable but that the present occupants of the Wadi el Hawareth land know nothing of irrigation and that furthermore the Beisan lands contain no grazing area. When we left Palestine no State or other land had been discovered to which the persons to be evicted could be transferred.

If, by some fortunate circumstance, it were found possible to place a certain number of these people in villages adjacent to the lands which they now occupy, this remedy would not, we were informed, meet the needs of those among them who are who are graziers and for whom there is no other land in the districts on which they could graze their flocks. Even if some suitable place could be found for the graziers and some other available land for the cultivators, it seems likely that the tribe will lose its identity as a tribe and become a scattered community.

These then are the instances which were put before us as justifying the state of extreme apprehension which was said to exist not only in the minds of those threatened with eviction but among occupiers of the soil in other parts of Palestine who fear lest the fate of those who live in the Wadi el Hawareth may also be theirs.

It is noteworthy that both the Sursock and the Wadi el Hawareth lands were the property of absentee landlords and in their absence were being cultivated by persons who paid as rent a percentage of the produce yielded by their holdings. The sale of lands over the heads of occupant tenants and the consequent dispossession of those tenants with or without compensation are not peculiar to Palestine but the position there is complicated by two factors which can seldom obtain elsewhere. In the first place the dispossessed tenant in Palestine is unlikely to be able to find alternative land to which he can remove. Secondly, in some cases, the cultivators who were or may be dispossessed have a strong moral claim to be allowed to continue in occupation of their present holding. Under the Turkish regime, especially

in the

in the latter half of the eighteenth century, persons of the peasant classes in some parts of the Ottoman Empire, including the territory now known as Palestine, found that by admitting the over-lordship of the Sultan or of some member of the Turkish aristocracy, they could obtain protection against extortion and other material benefits which counterbalanced the tribute demanded by their overlord as a return for his protection. Accordingly many peasant cultivators at that time either willingly entered into an arrangement of this character or, finding that it was imposed upon them, submitted to it. By these means persons of importance and position in the Ottoman Empire acquired the legal title to large tracts of land which for generations and in some cases for centuries had been in the undisturbed and undisputed occupation of peasants who, though by the new arrangement they surrendered their prescriptive rights over the land which they cultivated, had undoubtedly a strong moral claim to be allowed to continue in occupation of those lands.

Having discussed in detail the two land transactions of which frequent mention was made in the course of our Enquiry, we will now proceed to set out the salient facts, as they appeared in evidence given before us, of the land problem in Palestine.

Excluding the Beduin who occupy the desert area to the south-east of Palestine, the Arab rural population of that country is approximately 460,000. Taking an average of
five

five persons per family there are, therefore, 92,000 familes in Palestine dependent upon the soil for their subsistence. The available land in non-Jewish ownership, including State domain which falls under that description, is approximately 10,100,000 dunoms or an average of 109 dunoms per family. Now the area of land required to support the average family must vary with the fertility of the soil. From evidence given before us it would appear that where the land is used for the purpose of growing cereals the area which will provide a living for an Arab family varies from 100 to 150 dunoms. ~~[illegible struck-through text]~~ No other figures were put forward from the Arab side, but Dr. Ruppin informed us that "the average area of a Jewish colonist in the old wheat growing colonies in Lower Galilee is 250 dunoms, in the Zionist settlement in the Plain of Esdraelon with dairy farming it is 100 dunoms and in the Coastal Plain, where orange growing is the principal occupation, it is from ten to twenty dunoms".

From the figures given by the experts who were appointed by the Joint Palestine Survey Commission and who visited Palestine in 1928, it would seem that the average Jewish holding of land in the Zionist colonies is today 130 dunoms. These gentlemen found that few of the Jewish colonists were able to make a satisfactory living on their present holding. The experts were of opinion that in many districts the area of the average holding should be increased and we gather
from

from their reports that, in their view, the area required varies from 160 dunoms per family in good soil suitable for dairy farming to 320 dunoms in the less productive of the cereal growing districts.

Be that as it may the position seems to be that, taking Palestine as a whole, the country cannot support a larger agricultural population than it at present carries unless methods of farming undergo a radical change. It is no doubt true that the effects of agricultural research, capital expenditure and credit facilities offer in certain districts considerable opportunities for more intensive methods of cultivation and that ultimately it may be possible for the land of Palestine to support a larger agricultural population. We were told that experiments had shown that in the Valley of Esdraelon the introduction of more intensive methods depends largely upon the presence of water in much larger quantities than have so far been found available. For the present at all events it must be assumed that this part of the country is at least as closely populated as its productivity warrants.

In the Coastal Plain the prospects of intensive cultivation are much better. We were informed by Dr. Ruppin that "the productivity of one dunom of land under irrigation is estimated in Palestine as five times that of unirrigated land; in the Coastal Zone alone out of an area of 1,750,000 dunoms of light irrigable soil not more than 100,000 dunoms are actually under irrigation."

It is, however, doubtful whether water is
available

available for irrigating a large portion of the Coastal Plain. That the presence of water in sufficient quantities, and not the amount of land available, is the condition which limits the possibilities of ~~irrigation~~ intensive cultivation in this area is clearly stated by one of the experts who reported to the Joint Palestine Survey Commission.

We propose to refer to other aspects of the problem of introducing a system of more intensive cultivation in the Coastal Plain but before doing so we would cite the evidence of Mr. Smilansky as showing the benefits which such a system, if practicable, might bring.

Mr. Smilansky told us that Rehovoth, which today supports a population of 2,500 persons, was thirty eight years ago a waste area occupied by about a dozen Arabs. This extraordinary improvement has been effected by the introduction of machinery for providing an ample water supply and by utilising water so obtained for the growing of various kinds of fruit. There can be little doubt that, given capital, initiative and an adequate water supply, developments of a similar character can be effected elsewhere in the Coastal Plain.

On the other hand it may be doubted whether it is possible, even if it would be wise, to introduce the most intensive form of cultivation - namely the growing of fruit and of market garden produce - over large areas unless this were done gradually and with regard to local requirements for the perishable produce and world requirements for the variety

the varieties of fruit which it was intended to grow.
Up to the present the demand for the Jaffa orange
and for other fruits grown in the Coastal Plain
has kept pace with the supply but the conversion
of large tracts of land in that area to fruit
plantations might lead to difficulties, if not
to economic disaster, if the change were too suddenly
produced.

It must also be remembered that any form
of intensive cultivation, wherever it may be adopted,
requires capital expenditure to an amount which no
ordinary cultivator can afford. In particular this
is true of orange growing which, in addition to
requiring a large initial outlay of capital, does
not yield any return for some years after the
planting of the trees. The cultivator must be
assured of some means of support while he is
waiting for the orange trees to mature and to bear
fruit. It is therefore a matter for consideration
whether the Government should not provide for the
needs of the poorer people in this respect either
by granting them loans or by reviving the
Agricultural Bank or by some other means through
which the peasant cultivator can be enabled to
borrow money at a reasonable rate of interest for
the development of his property. This is a problem
which should be examined by the local Government;
we would only remark that, since the object in view
would be the improvement of methods of cultivation,
some safeguard should be employed to ensure that
loans made by the Government or through a bank are
used expressly for such purposes. The reconstitution
of an

-233-

of the Agricultural Bank would have the further advantage that it would in some measure remove a grievance which was put forward to us by the Arabs during our enquiry.

A third consideration is that even if intensive cultivation - whether for horticultural or agricultural purposes - is possible in the Coastal Plain it is important that the changes which it involves should be so introduced as to avoid the disturbance and dispossession of the present agriculturalists unless, of course, alternative land elsewhere can be found for them. Perhaps the most striking feature of Mr. Smilansky's evidence was his account of the way in which, through living in the midst of the Jewish new comers to whom they had sold a part of their land, the Arabs of the district around Rehovoth learned to improve their methods of cultivation, succeeded in freeing themselves from debt and today, by comparison with their former state, enjoy prosperity and a high standard of living. To those who in future may introduce intensive cultivation in the other parts of the Plain of Sharon we would commend a system of agricultural co-operation with their Arab neighbours similar to that followed by Mr. Smilansky and his fellow settlers in pre-war days.

The advantages of such a system and the improtance of providing alternative land are readily recognised by some Jewish leaders, such as Mr. Rutenberg, who gave evidence on the point in camera.

A fourth and last, but most important, point is that, even with improved methods and intensive cultivation, the Government of Palestine, in deciding the rate at which new comers are to be admitted to agriculture, should have regard to

the certain

the certain natural increase of the present rural population. The British Administration has brought improved sanitary conditions and with them a lower death rate. The net excess of births over deaths may be expected within the next thirty years to increase the population of the country by some 300,000 people of whom, in the absence of staple industries, most must look to the land to provide them with a living.

Having thus set out the four considerations which, in our view, must be taken into account, we would record the opinion that the possibility of intensive cultivation in the Coastal Plain and perhaps in other parts of Palestine should be carefully investigated by the Government of that country or by experts appointed by the Government. If this survey be sufficiently comprehensive, the field of possible development in the immediate future would be covered and for a period of years at least land policy could be regulated in the light of facts ascertained by scientific investigation.

Any complete survey of the whole country must take a very considerable time. In the meantime the Palestine Government are confronted with the prospect of repetitions of the situation now existing at Wadi el Hawareth and of further calls upon the police to carry out evictions of large bodies of cultivators with no alternative land to which they can be moved or upon which they

can

can settle. In the past persons dispossessed have in many cases been absorbed in the neighbouring villages; we were, however, told that this process, though it may have been possible four or five years ago, is no longer possible today; the point of absorption has been reached. The plain facts of the case are, so we are advised, that there is no further land available which can be occupied by new immigrants without displacing the present population.

We are only concerned with the land problem in so far as an examination of it was necessary to enable us to estimate the extent to which the difficulties involved in it were either a contributory cause to the recent disturbances or are likely to be a cause of disturbances in the future. But for this purpose such an examination was clearly essential. We think that there can be no doubt that a continuation, or still more an acceleration, of a process which results in the creation of a large discontented and landless class is fraught with serious danger to the country. If it be accepted that the conversion of large sections of those who are now cultivators of the soil into a landless class be, as we think, not only undesirable in itself, but also a potential source of disturbance, it is clear that further protection of the position of the present cultivators and some restriction on the alienation of land are inevitable. The Protection of Cultivators Ordinance of 1929 does nothing to check the tendency to which we have referred. The

mere

mere provision of compensation in money may even encourage it. Whether the object in view can best be achieved by some adaptation of the Ordinance of 1921 or by the introduction in Palestine of legislation based upon the "Five Feddan Law" in force in Egypt or by the restriction of the transfer of land now in Arab hands to others than Arabs or by some other means is a question which can only be decided after full examination and consideration by the advisers of the Palestine Government. In view of the obligation placed upon the Mandatory by Article 6 of the Mandate to "encourage close settlement by Jews on the land" on the one hand and on the other to ensure "that the rights and position of other sections of the population are not prejudiced" the solution of the land problem is obviously a difficult and delicate task, but some solution is essential in the interests of the whole population irrespective of creed and unless one be found to deal with the situation that we have described the question will remain a constant source of present discontent and a potential cause of future disturbance.

7.02

PALESTINE.

Report on Immigration, Land Settlement and Development.

By

Sir JOHN HOPE SIMPSON, C.I.E.

1930.

Presented by the Secretary of State for the Colonies to Parliament by Command of His Majesty.
October, 1930

LONDON:
PRINTED AND PUBLISHED BY HIS MAJESTY'S STATIONERY OFFICE.
To be purchased directly from H.M. STATIONERY OFFICE at the following addresses:
Adastral House, Kingsway, London, W.C.2; 120, George Street, Edinburgh;
York Street, Manchester; 1, St. Andrew's Crescent, Cardiff;
15, Donegall Square West, Belfast,
or through any Bookseller.

1930.
Price 8s. 0d. net.

Cmd. 3686.

To The Secretary of State for the Colonies,

MY LORD,

In accordance with Your Lordship's instructions I proceeded to Palestine in order to examine on the spot the questions of immigration, land settlement and development on which you desired that I should report.

I reached Jerusalem on 20th May, 1930, and at once commenced my enquiry. I was in constant consultation with the High Commissioner, who was thereafter kept in touch with the enquiry as it proceeded.

2. Much information has been obtained from official sources, and, in addition, both Arab and Jewish authorities and organisations have been consulted. Material has been obtained from the most varied sources, and has often been volunteered. In addition, as many tracts and villages of Palestine have been visited as the time available permitted. On Map No. 1, attached to the Report, both the tours and inspection of the villages visited are marked.*

3. In addition to local enquiry in Palestine itself a visit was paid to Trans-Jordan, where the British Resident, Lieutenant-Colonel C. H. F. Cox, C.M.G., D.S.O., very kindly arranged a tour throughout the northern part of the territory. His Highness the Emir of Trans-Jordan also accorded to me the favour of an interview.

4. I desire to acknowledge invaluable assistance received in many quarters. The High Commissioner, Sir John Chancellor, G.C.M.G., G.C.V.O., D.S.O., and Sir Spenser Davis, C.M.G., Officer Administering the Government after the departure of Sir John Chancellor, afforded me every possible help, and in consultation the benefit of their knowledge and experience. I had access to the records of all Departments of the Government. The enquiry inevitably entailed upon them heavy additional work, and I express my sense of the obligation under which the Heads and staffs of those Departments have placed me by the information which they collected and supplied.

The Supreme Moslem Council and the Arab Executive gave valued aid in the enquiry. Specially I am indebted to Jamal Effendi Husseini, who accompanied me on tours in some of the Arab villages.

The Jewish Agency supplied a very large amount of information on every subject investigated. I record my gratitude specially to Dr. Ruppin, whose aid was invaluable, and to Mr. Victor Konn, of the P.I.C.A. These gentlemen arranged my tours through the Jewish settlements.

---

* *See* Note on page 3.

3

Dr. Wilkansky, of the Agricultural Experimental Station at Tel-Aviv, not only placed his large technical knowledge of agricultural matters at my disposal and accompanied me on some of my tours, but has placed me under a particular obligation by allowing me to use the proof-sheets of his book, which is about to appear, on " The Fellah's Farm ".

Air-Commodore Playfair, M.C., very kindly arranged for an aerial test survey of the Hill Districts for the purposes of my enquiry. It has been a deciding element in the conclusions which have been reached. To him and the members of the Air Force who carried out the survey, my very sincere thanks are due.

Special recognition is also due to Mr. C. H. Ley, O.B.E., Director of Surveys, and his staff, who not only did a large amount of work in determining the areas but also prepared special maps which are attached to this report.

It is impossible to acknowledge in detail the innumerable sources from which help was drawn. It may be said generally that all concerned united to make my enquiry as complete as was possible in the time at my disposal.

I acknowledge with thanks the courtesy of the " Geographical Review ", published by the American Geographical Society of New York, and of Dr. Strahorn, in generously permitting me to use the soil map appended as Map No. 4* to the report.

Finally, I desire to record my deep obligation to Mr. Maurice C. Bennett, who served throughout as my secretary and accompanied me to Athens, where the report was written, and to Mr. C. L. Horton, my assistant secretary. Had it not been for the devoted service and untiring labours of these two gentlemen, the report could not possibly have been prepared by this date.

I now forward for your Lordship's information the Report on the matters included in the terms of reference.

I have, etc.,

J. HOPE SIMPSON.

22nd August, 1930.

NOTE.—The maps referred to in this Report, with the exception of No. 3 (not reproduced), will be published later in the form of an Appendix to this Command Paper.

* See Note on this page.

4

SYNOPSIS OF CHAPTERS.

Chapter I: Palestine: The Country and the Climate.
(Pages 12 to 20.)

The total area of Palestine—the natural divisions of Palestine—*The Hill country*: its area—its soil and agriculture—irrigation—development—*The Five Plains*: *The Maritime Plain*—its character—*The Acre Plain*—its area—its character—Haifa Harbour—*the Vale of Esdraelon*—its area—its fertility—results of Jewish settlement—its past—soils—*The Huleh Plain*—its area—its character—its marsh area—*The Plain of Jordan*—its area—its character—*The Beersheba Region*—its area—its possibilities—Palestine—the Rainfall.

Chapter II: Palestine: The Agricultural Land.
(Pages 20 to 24.)

Total area of Agricultural Land—Mr. Jabotinsky's Estimate—Dr. Ruppin's Estimate—Lord Stanhope's Statement in the House of Lords—Estimate of Commissioner of Lands—Estimate of Director of Surveys—Dr. Strahorn's figures in the report of the Experts to the Joint Palestine Survey Commission—the estimate of the Director of Surveys to be accepted for purposes of this Report—Area of Agricultural Land held by Jews—Area available for non-Jewish cultivators.

Chapter III: Palestine: The Population.
(Pages 24 to 29.)

Census of 1922—Population in 1930—Distribution of Population—Vital Statistics—Comparative Infantile Mortality figures—Size of average family of cultivating Fellah—Health—Anti-malarial measures—Ophthalmic Hospital—Government Health Service—Voluntary and Jewish Medical work and probability of extension of Government Action—Necessity for Continuation of Anti-malarial work—Poverty of the population—Jewish Medical Organisation—the extent to which Palestine Health needs are met—Main concentration in towns—the number of Medical Practitioners.

Chapter IV: Land Tenure in Palestine.
(Pages 29 to 38.)

Categories of Land—Mulk—Miri—Waqf—Metruké—Mewat—Mesha'a—Partition—Expense of partition—Unofficial Partition—Partition by agreement—Mesha'a—its extent and effect—Government action in regard to Partition—Partition under Land Settlement—Acceleration of partition—*The Law governing Agricultural*

5

Tenancies—Landlords—Tenants—Land Transfer Ordinance, 1920—Restriction on sale of land—Complaints against restrictions—Transfer of Land Ordinance, 1920-21—*Protection of Cultivators Ordinance*, 1929—its practical effect—*Occupancy Right*—Position of Jewish agricultural tenants—Its effect—Register of tenants—Palestine Survey—Land Settlement—Land Registration Fees—Land Registers—Maintenance of Record of Occupancy Right.

Chapter V: Jewish Settlement on the Land.

(Pages 38 to 60.)

Agencies of Jewish Settlement—Private Agencies—The Benei-Benjamin—Amount of land held by Jewish organizations:

(i) *The P.I.C.A. Settlements.*—The P.I.C.A.—the Kabbara concession—Pardessana—Benjamina—Colonies in Galilee Bitania—Relation of P.I.C.A. colonists with Arabs.

(ii) *The Zionist Settlements.*—The Jewish National Fund—Zionist settlements—Principle of " self-labour "—Expenditure by Keren Kayemeth and Keren Hayesod—Population of Settlements—Area of Settlements—Reserve Area—Emek Colonies and contagious abortion—Experts' opinion as to completion of establishments—Self-supporting Zionist Settlements—the Consolidation Budget—Kfar Yeheskiel—Cost of Settlement—Keren-Hayesod Budget—Influence of Federation of Labour—Kvutzoth Colonies—Small-holding Colonies—Emek and Upper Jordan Colonies—Nahalal—Regulating Societies Kfar Yeheskiel—Degania " A "—Kiryath Anavim—Jewish Rural Population—Zionist Settlements not self-supporting—Excessive cost of Zionist Settlement—Jewish Settlement in Russia—Settlements of Refugees in Greece—Expenditure on Settlement and Effect of non-payment.

(iii) *The Effect of the Jewish Settlement on the Arab*—P.I.C.A. and Arab relations—Zionist Colonization—the P.L.D.C.'s attitude towards Arab cultivators—Government responsibility towards Arab cultivators—the Constitution of the Jewish Agency—Land holding and Employment clauses—Keren Kayemeth Draft lease—Employment of Jewish labour only—Keren Hayesod Agreements, Employment of Labour—Zionist policy in regard to Arabs in their Colonies—The Effect of the Zionist Colonization policy on the Arab—Reasons for the exclusion of the Arab—Policy contrary to Article 6 of the Mandate.

(iv) *Government Lands.*—The question of the Government Lands—Huleh and Beisan—Chiftlik Estates—Only small areas available until developed—Possibility of additional Mewat land.

6

Chapter VI: The Position of the Fellah.

(Pages 60 to 74.)

Available information—Area of cultivable land occupied by the fellah—" Lot Viable "—Alteration of the " Lot Viable " by means of improved methods of Cultivation—Economic position of the Fellah—Distribution of available areas—The requirements and Standard of Life of the Fellah—The Fellah's capital—The Fellah's plough—The Fellah as a cultivator—The Return from the Fellah's Farm—Deductions from figures supplied by 104 villages—The Fellah's debts—Legal Rate of Interest—Commutation of the Tithe and the result of the fall in prices—Diminution of the size of holdings—Rise in rents—Financial situation of the Fellah—Warrants and imprisonment for debt—Taxation—Tithe—House and Land Tax—Animal Tax—Recovery of taxes—Remedial measures—Government action to relieve the burden of taxation—The Beduin Population.

Chapter VII:—Agricultural Development.

(Pages 74 to 91.)

A. Existing Agencies.—Jewish agencies for Agricultural Development—The Experimental station—the Extension Division—The Hebrew University—the Department of Agriculture of the Palestine Government—Expenditure—Relations with Jewish Agencies for Agricultural Development—Insufficiency of budget allotments—its budget—its Development activities—the Stock-breeding Service—Poultry husbandry—the importance of the Demonstration Plot—Scientific Services—the Distribution of Trees —the Forest Service—Jewish Plantations.

B. Education.—The Jewish Schools—the State Schools—the Budget—the Necessity—its importance to agricultural development —Agricultural Schools—the Village School and Agriculture—Need for additional Expenditure Technical Education in Agriculture—Agricultural certificated schoolmasters—Collaboration between Departments of Agriculture and Education.

C. Irrigation.—The existing waste of Water—the Aujha Concession—Nebi Rubin—The Acre Plain—The Huleh area—the Beisan area—the Beisan Agreement—the Jordan Valley—other possibilities—the Draft Irrigation Ordinance—constitution of a separate Irrigation Service.

D. Co-operation.—The Jewish movement—Information available—Rates of interest on deposits and loans—Activities of certain co-operative Societies—Co-operative Industrial Producers' Societies —Land-purchasing Societies—Membership of Societies—Necessity for extension to Arab population—Treatment of existing debts—Desirability of joint action between Jews and Arabs.

Chapter VIII: Agricultural Produce.

(Pages 92 to 106.)

(a) *Citrus Cultivation.*—Origin of orange cultivation—Area available—Area under Citrus cultivation—Future of the Orange Trade.

(b) *The Grape Fruit.*

(c) *The Banana.*—Area under cultivation—Cost of production and yield—Marketing possibilities.

(d) *Melons.*—Exports to Egypt and Syria—Adverse effect on Export due to imposts in Egypt and Syria.

(e) *Almonds.*—Production and Export figures—Area under Almond cultivation—Replacement of Almonds by Oranges—Pests—Markets.

(f) *Grapes.*—Export of Wine—Exports of Table-grapes—Competition in the markets—Trial consignments to London—Complaints against the Excise duty and Licence fees.

(g) *Tobacco.*—Extent of the Tobacco trade—Local leaf—Necessity for instruction in improvement of methods—Complaints in regard to the Tobacco Ordinance—Minimum area of two dunams—Prohibition of use of home-grown Tobacco.

(h) *Olives.*—Grade of Oil—Methods of culture—Introduction of improved methods—Extension of area under Cultivation.

(i) *Sesame.*—Imports and Exports—Value as a summer crop—Cultivation.

(j) *Barley.*—Export Trade—Possible reasons for reduction of overseas trade—Proposals for revival of the trade.

(k) *Minor Agricultural Products.*— The Silkworm—Present position of Sericulture—Bees—Prevalence of Foul-brood—Expansion of the Industry.

(l) *Dairy and Stock-breeding.*—Contagious abortion—Stall-feeding of Dairy Stock.

Chapter IX: Palestinian Industry.

(Pages 106 to 118.)

Census of Industries—Summaries—Food, Drink and Tobacco—Chemicals and Allied Trades—Cement, Brick, Stone and Clay Trades—Census of Jewish Industry—Principal Industrial Undertakings—" Nesher " Cement Works—Effect of Protective Tariff—Eastern Oil Industries, Ltd.—Tobacco—Messrs. Karaman Dick and Salti—Grands Moulins de Palestine—the Wine Industry—Other Industries—Printing—Smaller Industries—Fancy Leather Industry—Textile Industry—Fruit juice and Fruit Products—The Development of Industry—Industrial enterprises before the War and subsequent Increase—Industry in the past—Small Industries

8

—Number of persons employed—Future Development of Jewish Industry—Possibilities of an Extension of Industry—Future of Palestinian Industry—Immigration as a solution of Industrial Problems—Progress of Industry—Industries likely to succeed—Danger of Unemployment—Concentration on Industries showing Vitality—Arab Industries—Mineral Deposits.

Chapter X: Immigration.

(Pages 119 to 140.)

Early History—Pronouncement of June 3rd, 1921—Immigration Ordinance, 1925—Categories of Immigrants—Unrecorded Immigration—Procedure in regard to the issue of Immigration Certificates—The influence of the General Federation of Jewish Labour over Immigrants and Immigration—Preparation of Labour Immigration Schedules—Procedure after Schedule approved by High Commissioner—Authorization of visas—Failure of the System—Weakness of and responsibility under the present System—The selection of Immigrants abroad—Government control abroad—Travellers remaining in Palestine—Evasion of the Frontier control—Discouragement of Illicit Entry—Immigration and the General Federation of Jewish Labour—Settlement of cases in which members are concerned—Jewish labour as Key-stone of the Jewish National Home—The sources of Immigration—Immigration and Unemployment—Figures in regard to the number of unemployed—Arab Unemployment—Further Immigration and its probable Effect on Arab Unemployment—Recent increase in Jewish Unemployment—Duty of Government in regard to Immigration—Employment of Arabs in Jewish concerns—" Derived Demand "—Unemployment Statistics and Government Employment Exchanges—Seasonal and Occasional Labour—Importation of other than Jewish Labour—Prevention of illicit Immigration—Arab Unemployment as a political Pawn—Article 6 of the Mandate and its Effect on Immigration—Suspension of Labour Schedule—Preparation of the Labour Schedule—Proposed Change in Method—Formation of a Department of Immigration Labour and Travel.

Chapter XI: Conclusion.

(Pages 141 to 153.)

Land: Land available for settlement—Government Land—Present Agricultural Policy—Jewish and Arab advantages and disadvantages—Compensation of Beduin for loss of grazing rights—Alteration of terms under which J.N.F. purchases and leases Land—Government's duty under the Mandate.

9

Agricultural Development Scheme.—Improvement of the Fellah's Methods—Development of Intensive Agriculture—Development of Irrigation—Jewish reserves of Land—Control of Disposition of Land—Powers of Government to purchase Land—Development Commission—Responsibilities of the Development Commission—Available areas in Plains—Cost of Settling a Family—Distribution of Developed Land—Co-operation between Jewish Agencies and the Development Commission—Artificial Inflation of Land Values—Ascertainment of the Number of Landless Arabs—Migration—Its difficulties—Hydrographic Survey—Urgency of Irrigation Legislation—Formation of an Irrigation Department—Occupancy Right—Partition of Mesha'a—Acceleration of Land Settlement—Abolishment of Imprisonment for Debt—Redistribution and Reduction of Taxation—Reduction of Land Registration Fees—Co-ordination of Agricultural Scientific Services—Increase of Department of Agriculture's Budget—Demonstration Plots—Distribution of Trees—Separation of the Forest Service.

Education.—Increase of the budget of the Department of Education—Agricultural Course for Schoolmasters—Co-operation—Encouragement of Co-operation between Arab and Jew in Orange Industry—Constitution of Co-operative Credit Societies—Mr. Strickland's Mission.

Agricultural Development.—Government acquisition of The Huleh Concession—Limitation of Orange Cultivation—Development of other Fruit Crops—Import Duty on Melons in Egypt—Improvement of Grades of Tobacco—Amendment of Minimum area of Tobacco—Improvement of Quality of Olive Oil and Pruning of Trees—Steps to revive the Barley Export Trade—Encouragement of Sericulture and Production of Honey—Possibility of a Canning Industry for Dairy Produce.

Palestinian Industry.—Reduction of Excise on Wines—Position of Industries—Encouragement of Arab Industries.

Immigration and Labour.—Preparation of Labour Immigration Schedules—Immigration Officer at towns abroad—Expulsion of illicit Immigrants—Registration of Unemployment and Labour Exchanges—Constitution of a separate Department of Immigration, Travel and Labour—Part of Expenditure of Development Commission recoverable—Intensive Development of rural Palestine essential—Introduction of Settlers possible if Development carried out—Necessity for joint Endeavour.

10

GLOSSARY.

Arab Executive	Moslem and Christian body representing the Arabs of Palestine.
Supreme Moslem Council	Directs the religious affairs of the Moslems of Palestine.
Fellah	Arab peasant cultivator.
Effendi	Arab landlord.
Mesha'a	Unpartitioned land in customary joint ownership.
Jewish Agency for Palestine	Body directing the affairs of the Jewish National Home, and formed for the purpose of advising and co-operating with the Administration of Palestine.
Executive of the Jewish Agency.	Carries out the current executive business of the Agency, with offices in Jerusalem and London.
Keren-Kayemeth	Jewish National Fund (J.N.F.) The medium of the Agency for purchasing and holding land.
Keren-Hayesod	Palestine Foundation Fund. The main colonization instrument of the Agency.
Waad Leumi	National Council of the Jews of Palestine.
Agudath Israel	The representative body of Orthodox Jewry.
P.I.C.A.	Palestine Jewish Colonization Association.
P.L.D.C.	Palestine Land Development Company.
Histadruth	General Federation of Jewish Labour.
Tnuvah	Jewish Co-operative selling agency for agricultural produce.
Chalutz	Chalutzim (p.m.) Chalutzot (p.f)—Pioneer.
Kvutzoth	Kvutza (pl.) — Communal settlements.
Kushan	Title Deed.

11

TABLE OF EQUIVALENTS.

Exchange.

Palestine Pound (LP)	= Pound Sterling (£).
	= 1,000 mils.
	= 97½ Egyptian Piastres (Pt) or 975 milliemes (mm).
Pound Egyptian	= 1,000 milliemes (mm) or 100 Piastres (Pt).
	= Lp 1.02564.

Measures.

Standard or metric dunam	= 1,000 square metres.
	= ¼ acre.
	= .000386 square mile.
Turkish or old dunam	= 919.3 square metres.
Acre	= 0.40 hectares = 4 metric dunams
Square Mile	= 2.590 metric dunams.
Mile	= 1.60 kilometres.
Kilometre	= 0.62 mile.

Weights.

Kilogram	= 2.20 lb.
Ton	= 1,016 kilograms = 1.01 metric tons.
Metric Ton	= 1.000 kilograms.
Kantar	= about 3 to a ton = ⅓ ton.

Measures of Capacity.

Litre	= 1.75 pints.
Gallon	= 4.54 litres.

CHAPTER I.

Palestine: The Country and the Climate.

The total area of Palestine.

Palestine is a small country generally stated to be about the size of Wales. There have been many estimates of its size and varied statements and arguments based thereon. The size of Palestine, and especially the cultivable area of the country, are so highly relevant to the matters under enquiry and to the deductions which must be made, that it is necessary to examine the more important of the statements and the estimates with some care.

The " Handbook of Palestine " prepared by Messrs. Luke and Keith-Roach, puts the total area at 10,000 sq. miles, practically 26,000,000 metric dunams. The Report of the Experts submitted to the Joint Palestine Survey Commission (p. 18) recorded 8,800 sq. miles. They do not offer any information as to the authority for this figure.

On May 20th, 1925, a statement was made by Lord Stanhope in the House of Lords, which has frequently been quoted as authoritative. In that statement he said that the total area of Palestine was approximately 27,000,000 Turkish dunams; this is equal to 8,528 sq. miles.

On July 4th, 1927, the Chief Secretary of the Palestine Government wrote a letter (No. 10,566-27) to the address of Dr. Ruppin, Head of the Colonisation Department of the Zionist Organisation, in which he said that the total area of Palestine was 9,570 sq. miles.

The Statistical Abstract for 1929 published at Jerusalem by the Keren-Hayesod (Palestine Foundation Fund) records the area as 10,170 sq. miles.

Finally, the Director of Surveys in Palestine reported to the Commissioner of Lands in July, 1929, that, excluding the Beersheba sub-district and the southern desert, the area of the rest of Palestine was 13,760,000 dunams, and that the area of Beersheba sub-district and the southern desert was 12,398,000 dunams, making the total area of Palestine 26,158,000 dunams or 10,100 sq. miles.

In forwarding this estimate to the Chief Secretary the Commissioner of Lands wrote :—

> " . . . . I would emphasise in the first place that pending completion of the topographical cadastral survey, any estimates submitted of the cultivable and uncultivable areas of Palestine can be little more than guess-work based on insufficient data."

13

On the 20th July, 1930, the Director of Surveys forwarded to me the revised area estimate, and wrote in his letter :—

" . . . . The estimate for Beersheba is quite unreliable, and any figures must be misleading, since we have no sufficient data and what can be done there in cultivation is entirely dependent on a most unreliable rainfall."

It may be accepted that the total area of Palestine is in the neighbourhood of 10,000 sq. miles. The question of the cultivable area of the country will be discussed later in this Report.

The Natural divisions of Palestine.

The natural divisions of the country are— :

(a) The hill country of Galilee and Judæa.

(b) The five plains, including that lying in the rift which contains the Jordan Valley and which, from the north of Lake Tiberias to the Dead Sea, is actually below the level of the Mediterranean.

(c) The Beersheba area, different in character and population from the rest of the country.

(d) The desert areas.

The Survey Department has prepared a map showing these divisions of the country. It is appended to this Report as Map No. 2.*

(a) THE HILL COUNTRY.

Area.

The area of this tract is estimated by the Commissioner of Lands at 8,064,000 dunams, of which 5,376,000 dunams are cultivable. The area classified as cultivable was admittedly guess-work, the Commissioner of Lands having accepted that of the total area, two-thirds only were cultivable and one-third uncultivable. By the courtesy of the Officer Commanding the Air Force, a test photographic survey of the Hill country was made for the purpose of this enquiry. The area so surveyed, which covered about one-tenth of the Hill country, is shown in blue lines on Map No. 2 attached to this Report. This survey established that the cultivable area of the hills was not, as had been assumed, 66.6 per cent., but only 40 per cent. The photographs of the aerial survey have been very carefully examined by the Director of Surveys in the latest estimate submitted, which is by far the most reliable estimate hitherto prepared of the hill country in Palestine. It records the total area, including the Hill Wilderness, as 8,862,000 dunams, of which nearly 2,450,000 dunams are cultivable. Excluding the Hill Wilderness the inhabited Hills are estimated at

---

* *See* Note on page 3.

14

6,124,000 dunams. The difference between the figures quoted by the Commissioner of Lands and those of the Director of Surveys, whether the Wilderness is included or omitted, is very large. The estimate of the Director of Surveys, based as it is in part on results obtained by aerial survey, will be accepted for the purpose of this Report.

Soil and Agriculture.

The cultivated land in the Hills varies very largely both in depth and quality of the soil. In the valleys there are stretches of fertile land, which will grow sesame as a summer crop. On the hillsides the soil is shallow and infertile, and the extent of land hunger is evident from the fact that every available plot of soil is cultivated, even when it is so small that the plough cannot be employed. There cultivation is carried on with the mattock and the hoe. The harvest of such plots, even in a favourable year, is exceedingly small—in general it seems doubtful whether such cultivation can pay. On the other hand, even the most rocky hillsides support trees, especially olives, and if capital were available, many of the cultivators of these exiguous and infertile plots would be able to gain a livelihood by cultivation of fruit trees and of olives. These cultivators have, however, no capital, and cannot afford to forgo even the meagre crops obtained, for the four or five years which are required before fruit trees render a return. In the case of the olive, the period before a return may be expected is much longer.

Irrigation.

There is little irrigation in the hill country. Here and there are springs which afford a supply for the irrigation of a small area, but, taken as a whole, the country is arid and the crops depend on rain. It is possible that a hydrographic survey might disclose further water supplies, and scientific treatment might also improve the yield from existing springs. It is stated that during the War the Engineers of the Army of Occupation were able very largely to increase the supply from springs in certain places.

Development.

In the best case, however, it is impossible that the general character of the cultivation in the Hill country can be radically changed, except in so far as fruit can be made to replace grain. Something might be done to improve the soil and to reform agricultural methods, were capital available. The use of manures and provision of better seed would doubtless result in some improvement of the yield. But from the point of view of agriculture, the Hill country will always remain an unsatisfactory proposition.

15

(b) THE FIVE PLAINS.

1.—THE MARITIME PLAIN.

Character.

A reference to Map No. 2 will show that the Maritime Plain is taken to be the area between the coast and the hills up to the 150 metre contour, running from Rafa in the south up to Haifa in the north. Ordinarily the Maritime Plain is treated as running from Rafa to Ras-en-Naqura, on the Syrian border. The reason for the present division lies in the difference in the class of soil of the plains north and south of Haifa. The latter portion of the plain is the tract which contains the great mass of wind-blown sand, so suitable for orange cultivation. The former is in the main a heavy black soil quite unsuited for oranges.

The Maritime Plain as shown in Map No. 2 is estimated by the Director of Surveys to extend to 3,218,000 dunams, of which 2,663,000 dunams are cultivable. This estimate agrees very closely with that made by the Experts and printed on p. 22 of their Report to the Joint Palestine Survey Commission. They record the cultivable areas :—

Irrigable	2,251,500 dunams
Non-irrigable	410,000 dunams

giving a total of 2,661,500 dunams. It is true that they estimate the non-cultivable area at a higher figure than that adopted by the Director of Surveys. It is not clear how they calculated this area. In any case the difference has no great importance, for in the uncultivable area no question of development arises.

2.—THE ACRE PLAIN.

Area.

This is the coastal plain lying north of Haifa and running up between the sea and the hills as far as the Syrian border. Its total area is given by the Director of Surveys as 550,000 metric dunams, 379,000 of which are judged cultivable.

These figures differ materially from the analogous figures recorded by the Experts. In the Report of the Experts on p. 22, this plain is divided into the plain north of Acre and the Haifa-Acre plain. The total area of the two amounts to 183,000 Turkish dunams, i.e., 168,000 metric dunams. The cultivable area is shown as 103,000 Turkish dunams, i.e., 94,500 metric dunams. The cultivable area is also shown as all irrigable. It is not known whence the Experts obtained the estimate included in their Report.

16

Character.

This plain is in the main composed of an alluvial deposit, rather heavy in character. There is a small area of wind-blown sand suitable for plantations, but, generally, the type of developed cultivation will be mixed farming with irrigation. There is ample water from springs and streams. A large area in this plain is held by the Bayside Land Corporation—a Jewish corporation.

Haifa Harbour.

The future of this tract will be advantageously affected by the construction of the Haifa Harbour. Work is already in progress and is advancing rapidly. The harbour will greatly assist the development of the export trade in oranges, and perhaps other agricultural products. It is understood that the question of the pipe-line from 'Iraq is not yet decided, and that there are hopes that it may be constructed to Haifa. If this development occurs the Acre Plain will of course benefit still further.

3.—THE VALE OF ESDRAELON.

Area.

In the division of the plans made by the Director of Surveys and included in Map No. 2, the Vale of Esdraelon has been separated from the Valley of Jezreel, the latter being included with the lands of the plain of the Jordan. The total area of the Vale is reported as being 400,000 metric dunams, of which 372,000 metric dunams are cultivable. Dr. Strahorn, in his report on soils, printed in the Experts' Report, records, on p. 151, that the Plain of Esdraelon has an area of 475,800 Turkish dunams, i.e., 437,400 metric dunams. This is not very far removed from the estimate made by the Director of Surveys.

Fertility.

The evidence as to the fertility of the Vale of Esdraelon and the state of its prosperity in the hands of the Arabs, before the extensive purchases made by the Jews, is conflicting. In his report* on the administration of Palestine, 1920-25, at p. 35, Sir Herbert Samuel wrote :—

> " . . . . The whole aspect of the valley has been changed. The wooden huts of the villages, gradually giving place to red-roofed cottages, are dotted along the slopes; the plantations of rapidly growing eucalyptus trees already begin to give a new character to the landscape; in the spring the fields of vegetables or of cereals cover many miles of the land, and what five years ago was little better than a wilderness is being transformed before our eyes into a smiling countryside . . . . "

---

* Non-Parliamentary Publication (Colonial No. 15, 1925).

17

On the other hand, Dr. Strahorn writes in his report, p. 152 :—

".... Up to within recent years the land was cultivated from the Arab villages, located round the rim of the Plain. Cereals together with minor garden areas around the villages constituted the Arab cropping system. In very recent years considerable areas of land have passed under the control of Jewish colonies and villages; gardens and orchards are now dotting the former expanse of grain-fields . . . ."

Results of Jewish Settlement.

The results of Jewish colonisation of the Vale of Esdraelon are varied. In some villages there are clear signs of success; in others, the opposite is the case. The village of Afuleh, which the American Zionist Commonwealth boomed as the Chicago of Palestine, is a sea of thistles through which one travels for long distances. A plague of field mice, which has done extensive damage to both Jewish and Arab cultivation in the Vale during the present year was officially stated to be due to the fact that 30,000 dunams of the land held by the Jews are derelict and covered with weeds. It is also a fact that in a number of villages the tithes paid by the Jews are considerably below those paid by the Arabs who formerly cultivated those villages.

Its Past.

It is a mistake to assume that the Vale of Esdraelon was a wilderness before the arrival of the Jewish settlers and that it is now a paradise. A very large amount of money has been spent by the various Jewish agencies, and great improvements have been made. The work that has been done, especially in the direction of drainage and the introduction of new and improved methods of agriculture is highly valuable. There can be little doubt that in time, the application of capital, science, and labour will result in general success. It is, however, unjust to the poverty-stricken fellah who has been removed from these lands that the suggestion should continually be made that he was a useless cumberer of the ground and produced nothing from it. It should be quite obvious that this is not the fact.

In ancient times Esdraelon was the granary, and by the Arabs is still regarded as the most fertile tract of Palestine. The soreness felt owing to the sale of large areas by the absentee Sursock family to the Jews and the displacement of the Arab tenants is still acute. It was evident on every occasion of discussion with the Arabs, both effendi and fellahin.

Soils.

The soil of the valley is generally an alluvial clay, highly suitable to cereal cultivation. Across the Vale at one place there is a belt of residual soil, even heavier than the alluvial of the rest of the valley. Both in the cultivation of cereals and in that of fodder crops the soil responds to high farming.

4.—THE HULEH PLAIN.

Area.

The Huleh Plain is the most northerly part of Palestine, to the east of the country, and lies to the north of the Lake of Tiberias. Its area is reported by the Director of Surveys as 191,000 metric dunams; of this extent 126,000 dunams are cultivable. As in the case of other tracts there are wide variations in the estimates of area. The Experts, in their Report, p. 22, put the area at 150,000 Turkish dunams, i.e., 138,000 metric dunams, and the cultivable area at 120,000 Turkish dunams, i.e., 110,300 metric dunams. Dr. Ruppin has submitted on behalf of the Jewish Agency for Palestine a memorandum relating to the land and agricultural development. In the course of that memorandum he says that the area of the Huleh district is approximately as follows :—

Government land	47,000 dunams
Private land	110,000 do.
Lake Merom	18,000 do.

but does not specify whether the dunams used are the Turkish or metric dunams. As in the rest of the memorandum the Turkish dunam is habitually used, it is fair to assume that he has also employed it here. In that case the estimate, which totals 175,000 (Turkish) dunams, would represent 161,000 metric dunams.

Character.

The Huleh Plain may be divided into three parts. In the north there is rich alluvial cultivable land; south of this there is a large marshy area covered with papyrus reeds, the haunt of the wild boar and the grazing-ground of numerous water-buffaloes which are the property of the Bedu tribes of the neighbourhood. South of this again is the Lake of Merom, through which the Jordan flows southwards to Lake Tiberias. The Lake and marsh are caused by a ridge of basalt across the Jordan Valley. If this ridge were cleared away or the river deepened, the whole valley could be drained and considerable areas of land made available for irrigated cultivation.

Marsh Area.

There are widely varying estimates of the extent of the marsh and of the extent of the lake. Possibly one of the best is that recorded on a French plan dated 1321 Hijra (1903 A.D.) which is attached to this Report as Map. No. 3.* According to that map, the areas of the concession are :—

Marsh	36,844 dunams
Lake	11,921 do.
Cultivated land	1,824 do.
Cultivable land	353 do.

---

* See Note on page 3.

19

The figures are all Turkish dunams, and, reduced to metric dunams, the areas are :—

Marsh	33,871 metric dunams
Lake	10,958 do.
Cultivated land	1,677 do.
Cultivable land	325 do.

The concessionaire estimates the marsh at 41,400 metric dunams and the Lake at 13,800 metric dunams. Of the former some 9,200 metric dunams are, he says, cultivated by Arabs. In the Experts' Report (p. 154) Dr. Strahorn says that the area of the marsh north of the Lake is not less than 52,000 Turkish dunams, i.e., 47,800 metric dunams.

No survey of the marsh area has been made, nor is one possible, except by air, until the marsh is drained. It will be safe to assume that, excluding the cultivation of the Arabs in that area, there is still an area of some 25,000 to 30,000 metric dunams of marsh land available for reclamation. Were the Lake also drained a further 9,000 or 10,000 metric dunams would be rendered cultivable. The soil of the whole Huleh Plain is exceedingly fertile. It is indeed said to be the most fertile soil in Palestine.

5.—THE PLAIN OF THE JORDAN.

Area.

The Director of Surveys estimates the area of the Valley of the Jordan, in which he includes the Vale of Jezreel (*vide* Map No. 2 attached to this Report) at 1,065,000 metric dunams, of which 554,000 are cultivable. It is very difficult to obtain any comparable figures from other sources. Such as are available are examined in Appendix I.

For the purposes of the present enquiry a committee, consisting of the Government Geologist, the chief Agricultural Officer, the Irrigation Officer and an agricultural chemist, was appointed to enquire into and report upon the extent of irrigable lands in the southern part of the Jordan Valley. They report that there is an area of roughly 100,000 dunams which may profitably be irrigated, in addition to the present irrigated area, between the Dead Sea and the southern boundary of the Beisan area. Of this 28,500 dunams is land included in the Beisan chiftlik. The balance is 71,500. Already some 54,000 metric dunams are under irrigation in the lower Jordan Valley. Adding to this latter area the 71,500 dunams of the Committee's report and the 388,517 dunams of the Beisan Agreement areas, the total cultivable area of the whole Jordan Valley reaches 514,017 dunams.

20

Character.

The land in the north of the Jordan Valley is very fertile; in the south, with irrigation, it will grow all kinds of tropical fruits, and early vegetables. Properly developed the Jordan Valley might prove a great source of wealth to the country. In ancient times it undoubtedly supported a large population.

(c) THE BEERSHEBA REGION.

Area.—This is estimated at 3,200,000 dunams, of which 1,500,000 are cultivable. The figures are in fact pure guesswork, as is admitted by the Director of Surveys.

Possibilities.—Given the possibility of irrigation there is practically an inexhaustible supply of cultivable land in the Beersheba area. Without irrigation, the country cannot be developed. Up to the present time there has been no organised attempt to ascertain whether there is or is not an artesian supply of water. If there prove to be such a supply the problem of providing agricultural land for the Palestine population and, indeed, for a large number of immigrant settlers, will be easy of solution.

RAINFALL.

The rainfall varies largely from district to district in Palestine. In the Beersheba area it averages six inches and provides an exciting gamble for the cultivators. On the coast from Gaza to Acre its average is from fifteen inches in Gaza rising to about thirty inches at Acre. In the hills of Galilee thirty to forty inches may be expected, in the upper Jordan Valley twelve to sixteen inches, while at Jericho the average is five inches. On the map appended to this Report as Map No. 5* the average fall for the last ten years in shown graphically.

CHAPTER II.

Palestine: The Agricultural Land.

Total Area of Agricultural Land.—In the previous chapter an attempt has been made to provide an estimate of the extent of the Hill country, the areas of the Five Plains and of the Beersheba Tract. It remains to offer an estimate of the total area of agricultural land, cultivable and uncultivable, in Palestine. The whole question of the immigration of agricultural settlers depends of course on the amount of land which can be made available for them. This again depends on the difference between the total area and the area required for the existing agricultural population, Arab, Jewish

---

* *See* Note on page 3.

and other. No exact statement as to these areas is possible until the cadastral survey now in progress has been completed. It is, however, essential to the present enquiry that a definite figure, as reliable as possible, should be adopted for this purpose.

Mr. Jabotinsky's Estimate.—Many estimates have been made of the total agricultural cultivable area of Palestine, of which some have been rather in the nature of guess-work than of estimations. Mr. Jabotinsky has stated that the cultivable area is from 16,000,000 to 18,000,000 dunams. It is not known on what facts this suggestion is based nor whether the dunams mentioned are metric or Turkish. It is perhaps founded on a statement published in the Review of the Agricultural situation in Palestine, 1922, in which Colonel Sawer writes : " We are dealing with a total exploitable land surface not exceeding 4,500,000 acres." Colonel Sawer pointed out, however, that half of this area had been " written off as uncultivable."

Dr. Ruppin's Estimate.—In his evidence before the Commission on the Disturbances, Dr. Ruppin, head of the Colonisation Service of the Zionist Organisation, gave an estimate of the total area of Palestine as from 25,000 to 27,000 sq. kms., of which 12,500 kms. are cultivable. Of this latter area he described 20 per cent. as entirely uncultivated, that is to say, that in his opinion there are 2,500 sq. kms., or 2,500,000 metric dunams available for settlement. As an annex to his statement he filed a paper showing the total of cultivated and uncultivated land in Palestine. Here again the area described as " tillable but uncultivated " is given as 2,500,000 dunams. The statement was based on the figures quoted by Lord Stanhope in the House of Lords of May 28th, 1925. These dunams were Turkish dunams, and the area was therefore not 2,500 sq. kms. as stated in the body of the statement, but 2,298.4 sq. kms.

Lord Stanhope's Statement in the House of Lords.—Lord Stanhope's statement in the House of Lords, on which Dr. Ruppin relied, was in its turn based on figures submitted by the Palestine Government. It is unfortunate that these figures have been widely quoted and frequently accepted as accurate. They are in fact far from accurate, as there were no statistics available at that time from which anything in the nature of an exact estimate could have been framed.

Estimate of Commissioner of Lands.—Two recent estimates have been made in an attempt to determine more accurately the cultivable area of Palestine. Of these, one was submitted on April 30th, 1930, by the Commissioner of Lands, and in his letter forwarding the estimate, he discusses the question of the meaning of the term " cultivable land." He includes in that term land which is actually cultivated or which can be brought under cultivation " by the application of the labour and financial resources.

of the average individual Palestinian cultivator. This definition would therefore exclude marshes, the coastal sand-dunes between Rafa and Acre, the rocky hills, the wilderness of Judaea and extensive areas in the larger part of the Beersheba sub-district south of Beersheba town." It appears to include the wind-blown sands in the maritime plains which are suitable for orange plantations. On this basis the Commissioner of Lands estimates the cultivable area of Palestine as follows :—

	m.d.
Plain of Beersheba sub-district	1,641,000
Five principal Plains north of Beersheba sub-district	5,216,000
Hill country	5,376,000
	12,233,000

Estimate of Director of Surveys.—The cadastral survey of Palestine is now in progress and the Director of that survey has submitted a careful estimate of the total cultivable area of the country, based in part on the area already surveyed and in part on the results of the aerial survey to which reference has already been made.

He arrives at the following conclusions :—

Type of Country.	Cultivable.	Uncultivable.
	Metric Dunams.	*Metric Dunams.*
Inhabited hills	2,450,000	3,674,000
Hill wilderness		2,738,000
Five Plains :		
(a) The Maritime Plain	2,663,000	555,000
(b) The Acre Plain	379,000	171,000
(c) The Plain of Esdraelon	372,000	28,000
(d) The Huleh Plain	126,000	65,000
(e) The Plain of the Jordan	554,000	511,000
	4,094,000	1,330,000
Beersheba area	1,500,000	1,700,000
Southern desert		8,672,000
Total M.D.	8,044,000	18,114,000

Further details of the above areas are given in Appendix 3. The Director of Surveys states that this estimate is based on actual results so far as these have been reached, namely, in an area of 4,047,000 dunams, chiefly in the Maritime Plain. The Director of Surveys has applied to whole cartographic areas as measured on small-scale maps, the same percentage as has been found by large-scale survey in the large fractions of those areas already surveyed.

He also states that the cultivable area in the Hills, which has not yet been surveyed, has been calculated from the percentages obtained by close detailed examination of aeroplane photographs specially made by the Royal Air Force on cross-country flights over a number of tracts selected as representative. The results have given an average percentage of cultivable land in the tracts photographed which has been applied to the whole area of the inhabited hills as measured on a small scale cartographically. The cartographical measurements of whole areas have necessarily in each case been made upon previously existing maps and the figure so obtained is of course far from exact; nevertheless, it is probably much nearer to the actual than the figures hitherto suggested, which were in fact based on guess-work more or less intelligent.

Dr. Strahorn's figures in the Report of the Experts to the Joint Palestine Survey Commission.—During the enquiry of the Experts who reported to the Joint Palestine Survey Commission, a soil survey of nearly the whole of the area included in the Five Plains was made by Dr. A. T. Strahorn, whose report is found on pages 143-236 of the volume of Reports of the Experts. On page 231 he gives the areas of the Plains, excluding the Huleh and the Beersheba areas and a small portion of the Jordan Valley, viz., that portion lying between Wadi-es-Sherar and Jisr-ed-Damieh. The total area which Dr. Strahorn gives for the plains included in his soil examination is 4,873,354 dunams, of which 490,387 dunams are uncultivable. He uses Turkish dunams. Converting into metric dunams, the cultivable area according to his measurements is 4,029,262 metric dunams. The Huleh area, which is accepted as 80,000 Turkish dunams of which 52,000 dunams are marsh, would give 25,740 metric dunams of cultivable land. The total estimate for the Five Plains, excluding a small area in the narrowest part of the Jordan Valley, would thus be 4,055,002 metric dunams of cultivable land. This compares with the figure of 4,094,000 calculated by the Director of Surveys for the same area, including the portion of the Jordan Valley omitted by Dr. Strahorn.

The estimate of the Director of Surveys to be accepted for purposes of this Report.—For the purpose of this report the estimate of the Director of Surveys will be accepted. The important areas are those of the cultivable land of the Hills and of the Five Plains. The Beersheba region need not enter into consideration for the present. It is not an area in which settlement is possible at the present time. The total area in which settlement might be possible, if there be land to spare, amounts to 6,544,000 dunams in the Hills and in the Five Plains.

Area of Agricultural Land held by Jews.—According to Dr. Ruppin's statement before the Commission on the Disturbances, the total area held by the Jews was at that time 1,200,000 Turkish dunams, of which 1,000,000 was cultivable. Of the cultivable area of Palestine, excluding Beersheba, the Jews therefore held at that time 14.04 per cent. Since Dr. Ruppin made his statement a further 50,000 metric dunams have been purchased on Jewish account, and, in addition, some 80,000 to 85,000 dunams are under option of purchase. Thus the total percentage either in Jewish possession or under option amounts to over 16 per cent. of the whole cultivable area in these two regions.

Area available for non-Jewish cultivators.—Of this total, which is not less than 1,300,000 Turkish dunams, 20 per cent. may be deducted to allow for areas possibly uncultivable. The balance will be 1,040,000 Turkish dunams equal to 956,000 metric dunams. Deducting from the estimated cultivable area of 6,544,000 metric dunams a round figure of 900,000 metric dunams on account of Jewish holdings, an area of 5,644,000 metric dunams remains available for non-Jewish cultivators at the present time.

Soil Map.—By the courtesy of the "Geographical Review," published by the American Geographical Society of New York, and with permission kindly accorded by Dr. Strahorn, a map showing the distribution of the soils of Palestine is attached to this report as Map No. 4.*

CHAPTER III.

Palestine: The Population.

Census of 1922.—The last census was taken in 1922, and showed the total population as being 757,182, of whom 590,890 were Mohammedans, 83,794 Jews and 82,498 Christians and others. The division between the town and agricultural population was as follows:—

Town areas:
Mohammedans	139,074
Jews	68,622
Christians and others	56,621

Rural areas:
Mohammedans	451,816
Jews	15,172
Christians and others	25,877

Population in 1930.—There has been a very considerable increase of the population since that census was taken. In Appendix 4 are given the figures of population year by year, taken from the records of the Department of Health of the Government. The totals for mid 1930 may be accepted as approximately the following:—

Mohammedans	692,195
Jews	162,069
Christians and others	91,727
	945,991

---

* See Note on page 3.

25

Distribution of population.—In this estimate the Bedu population has been taken at the same figure as in 1922. The local distribution of this population is as follows:—

Urban population	340,962
Rural population	501,968
Tribal population	103,331

The total gives an average population of 94 per sq. mile, and, omitting Beersheba and the Southern Desert, about 155 per sq. mile. In Appendix 2 the figures of Jewish and Arab population have been examined, and it has been calculated that the rural Arab population of the Hills and the Five Plains is 478,390.

Vital Statistics.—The following figures give the average birth, death, and infantile mortality ratios according to religion during the period 1923 to 1929 inclusive:—

	Moslems	Jews	Christians	Others	Whole country.
Births	56·59	35·54	38·57	49·42	50·97
Deaths	31·24	13·10	18·03	25·51	26·52
Infantile Mortality	199·49	110·25	157·99	137·59	185·06

Appendix 5 gives the detail for each year. The figures are interesting and important and that from more than one aspect. In the first place it is noticeable that the excess of births over deaths is most marked (25.35) among the most numerous section of the population, namely the Moslems. The corresponding figure for the Jewish population is 22.44. The next noticeable point is the very low death rate among the Jewish population. This is without doubt in part due to the vigorous and young immigrants, of whom that population is composed to a material extent. Finally the figures of infantile mortality are interesting. The Jewish average for the past seven years is 110.25 per thousand, but during the years 1928 and 1929 the figures were 95.8 and 89.78. In England the corresponding figure for the year 1929 was 74, in Germany 97.

Comparative Infantile Mortality figures.—The following table gives some comparative figures:—

Year.	Country.	Infantile Mortality Ratio.
1926	New Zealand	39·76
1926	Netherlands	61·1
1925	U.S.A.	71·7
1927	Egypt	152·00
1926	Poland	174.75

26

Size of average family of fellah.—Enquiry has been made as to the size of the average family of the fellah. A return from the various district authorities and the Director of Health indicates that this average is 5.5. Applying this figure, the number of families resident in the Hills and the Five Plains is 86,980 this year.

Fellah families cultivating —An enquiry has been made by a Commission appointed by the Palestine Government into the economic condition of agriculturists in 104 representative villages. In these villages there reside 23,573 families, of whom 16,633 have holdings and 6,940 have not, that is to say, that there are in these villages 29.4 per cent. of families who live, not directly by cultivation, but by labour either in the village or outside and in other ways. Everywhere there is the complaint that many of the cultivators have lost their land. Doubtless this 29.4 per cent. includes these landless men who previously were cultivators. If a deduction of 29.4 per cent. is made from the total of 86,980 families reached above, the balance is 61,408 families actually cultivating the land in the Hills and the Five Plains. In addition, there are a large number of families which should be, but are not, cultivating the land.

HEALTH.

At the time of the Occupation Palestine was a country saturated with malaria. Since that time much good work has been done, not only by agencies of the country, but also with the help of outside scientific enquirers. The Rockefeller Foundation, the League of Nations, the Jewish Joint Distribution Committee have all rendered invaluable assistance in investigation, in research and in advice. Very much has been done in the drainage of swamps and marshes, in great part by Jewish agency and in great part by the Government. The Supreme Moslem Council has also taken a share, and its work in the drainage of the extensive and very malarial swamp at Wadi Rubin, under the advice of representatives of the Rockefeller Foundation, has been a complete success. A similar work of even greater magnitude which is now nearing completion is the drainage of the Kabbara Swamp by the P.I.C.A. The Zionist Agency was responsible, among other works, for the drainage of considerable areas in the Vale of Esdraelon. The Government Department of Health revolutionised certain areas of the Jordan Valley at comparatively small cost, by draining of marshes.

Much, however, still remains to be done. Huleh is a plague spot. The malaria of that part of Palestine will not be finally overcome until the Huleh Lake is drained and there is a free flow of water out of the Basin into the Jordan River. There are wide areas in the neighbourhood of Acre where drainage is necessary. There are still swampy areas in the Maritime Plain.

27

The second of the preventable diseases which are common in Palestine is trachoma. This disease is being combated with great vigour all through the Jewish Settlements and in the towns. In the village schools of the Government the eyes of the children are examined periodically by competent physicians. The work of the hospital of the Order of St. John at Jerusalem is famous even beyond the boundaries of Palestine.

Generally speaking, the health of the population of Palestine is the object of more attention than is the case in the great majority of Oriental countries. Once the malarial swamps are drained, and when the Arab villages become more accustomed to demand medical care than is the case at present, the position will be completely satisfactory.

It is the good fortune of the Government that Jewish organisations provide such an effective service for their own people. It would be impracticable for the Government to supply anything on a similar scale with the funds at its disposal. In its report* for the year 1928 on the administration of Palestine, submitted to the Council of the League, His Majesty's Government wrote the following :—" It has been the policy of Government to rely as far as possible on private and Municipal Hospitals and Dispensaries to furnish general medical relief to the population, and to devote Government funds to such services as isolation hospitals for serious infectious diseases, special clinics for trachoma and epidemic ophthalmia, the treatment of the endemic syphilis which exists in many of the villages and of malaria in rural areas. For certain sections of the population, however, such as the Beduin tribes, which would otherwise lack medical attention altogether, Government establish special clinics, and circumstances arise from time to time in which assistance to voluntary organisation for general assistance is necessary."

The country is fortunate that there is so much of voluntary help in Palestine. It is questionable whether with the large growth of the Jewish population, which is proceeding by natural increase, apart altogether from immigration, it will be possible for the Jewish agencies indefinitely to maintain expenditure on its present scale. It will be impossible for the Government ever to undertake medical services to the Jewish population on a scale more liberal than that applied to the rest of the population, but a time will surely come when the services of the Government will be compelled to extend their radius of action, so as to include Jewish settlements as well as Arab villages.

Meanwhile such funds as can be made available will doubtless be applied to the drainage of the malarial swamps which still remain. There is a distinct relation between the economic efficiency of a people and its health. Its vigour is seriously affected by malaria. If the country's agriculture is to be developed, that

---

* Non-Parliamentary Publication (Colonial No. 40, 1929).

development will be easier and more efficient if the rural population can be freed from the scourge of malaria.

The following is an extract from the report of the Department of Health for 1929, an advance copy of which has been furnished by the Director. It is interesting apart from considerations of health :—

> "The Village and Colony population both Arabs and Jews was clearly in financial difficulty. The Arab, though not starving, is beginning to feel the effects of the normal increase in population, which has been so remarkable a feature in Palestine during the last few years. He has no money to spend on his village, and so there has been little public health development. The situation in the Jewish Colonies continues to show a certain stagnation, and the sanitary conditions in the Colonies, particularly those in which the old huts have not given place to masonry buildings, have clearly deteriorated on account of the poverty of the colonists. More especially is this marked in the newer colonies in the Haifa Plain and in the Emek . . . ."

In considering the figures for the Jewish population, it should be borne in mind that this section of the population of Palestine enjoys the services of a highly efficient Jewish medical and Health Service in addition to the normal services afforded by the Government. It is served by the Kupath Cholim, a branch of the Jewish Labour Organisation, which maintains dispensaries, a hospital and a convalescent home for the working classes. It is served by the Jewish Hadassah Medical Organisation, which not only maintains five hospitals at various centres staffed by 34 doctors and surgeons, male and female, but also has a very efficient service which takes care of the child from its infancy and follows it through the kindergarten into the school and from the school into the home. The activities of the Organisation are widespread and highly laudable. But some of the credit for the remarkable figures dealing with the health of the Jewish population must be accorded to the children's houses in the Kvutza, the communal colonies, where the care of the child is entrusted to the hands of competent trained nurses. Whatever view may be taken of the principles which govern communal societies such as the Kvutza represent, no two opinions can be held as to the efficiency with which the children are treated in these colonies. In inspecting them one could not but be struck with the obvious vigour and health of the rising generation.

The Health Department of the Government is staffed by a Director, a Deputy-Director, an Assistant Director, six Senior Medical Officers, a specialist surgeon, a Government analyst, 40 junior Medical Officers. There are Government Hospitals at Jerusalem and Haifa, and Municipal Hospitals, assisted and administered by the Government, at Nablus, Gaza, Beersheba and Acre.

In all, including the hospitals administered by the Hadassah and the Government, there are 38 hospitals in Palestine. Of these, five are special hospitals—(two mental hospitals, 117 beds; one tuberculous diseases hospital, 53 beds; one ophthalmic hospital, 45 beds; one leper hospital, 60 beds)—and the remaining 33, with 1,692 beds, are available for the general needs of the population. This gives one bed for 559 persons.

It is noticeable that the main concentration of medical assistance of all kinds is in the towns. Private medical practice does not extend to the Arab villages. These are chiefly dependent on the services of the Government Medical Officers. The Jewish settlements are, however, well provided for in this respect, and that population, probably more than in any other country, has ample medical assistance at its door.

Among the complaints made by Arabs one had reference to the enormous influx of Jewish doctors into the country, an influx which was stated to have deprived a number of Arab qualified practitioners of their practices. The population of Jaffa is about 33,000; of Tel-Aviv, the Jewish suburb of Jaffa, which is now a separate Municipal area, 40,000. In 1922 there were registered 25 medical practitioners in Jaffa and 24 in Tel-Aviv. In 1929 the respective numbers were 32 and 147. That is to say, that for 73,000 people there are 179 medical practitioners, or one to every 408 inhabitants. It is clear that the number of new practitioners cannot but have affected the practice of the existing Arab doctors, the more so as it is very rare for a Jewish family to call in an Arab doctor. On the other hand, it is said that the Arabs have no aversion to the employment of Jewish medical men.

For the whole of Palestine there are 631 registered medical practitioners; of these there are 147 in Tel-Aviv, 140 in Jerusalem and 75 in Haifa.

CHAPTER IV.

Land Tenure in Palestine.

Categories of land.—Agricultural land in Palestine falls into one of five main categories, namely :—

(1) Mulk.
(2) Miri.
(3) Waqf.
(4) Metruké.
(5) Mewat.

1. *Mulk.*

Mulk represents English freehold. The absolute ownership rests in the private individual, who can dispose of it as he likes, except for a restriction on disposition by will. The amount of agricultural land held as Mulk is small and for the purposes of this enquiry is negligible.

2. Miri.

Agricultural property is commonly held by Miri title. Miri is property over which the right of occupation or of tenure can be enjoyed by a private person, provided that such right has been granted by the State. The absolute ownership remains vested in the Government, but the grant is in perpetuity, subject to certain conditions. Of these, the chief is continuous cultivation. If the land remains unproductive for three consecutive years it may revert to the State. In that case it may be redeemed by the possessor on payment of the unimproved capital value. If not so redeemed it is sold at auction to the highest bidder (Land Code, Article 68). It is not thought that the area of Mahlul* land is material. Freedom of disposition is allowed in the case of Miri land, with the exception that land of this character may not be bequeathed by will or constituted as Waqf.

3. Waqf.

The following is abstracted from a note furnished by Mr. Justice R. C. Tute :—

> " . . . . Both mulk and miri lands gave rise to dedications known as Wakfs. A wakf is a transfer of ownership to the Deity for a purpose which is, or may become, charitable or religious. Some Wakfs were charitable or religious foundations from the start. The majority however were, and are, made as a means of securing the use of the land to the founder and his heirs along a line of inheritance laid down in the Wakfiah or instrument of dedication. In these Wakfs the charitable or religious object does not materialise till the founder's line becomes extinct.
>
> " Wakfs are broadly classified into Sahih, or true Wakfs, and Ghair-sahih, or imperfect. The former arise from the dedication of mulk property; the latter from the dedication of miri. As miri property is owned by the State, dedication can only be made by its head. It took the form of setting aside some benefit attaching to the land, generally the tithe, for the use of the object of the dedication. The mulk owner had of course the power to dedicate as and when he pleased, and he still retains that power . . . . "

The area of agricultural land dedicated as " true Waqf " is comparatively insignificant. In the whole of Palestine it is not claimed to extend to 100,000 dunams, and, in fact, the extent is probably much smaller. The revenue from over one hundred villages, in addition to shares in many others, had prior to the occupation been dedicated by or on the Sultan's authority. These fall under the category Waqf Ghair-Sahih (imperfect) and the result is that a sum in the neighbourhood of £30,000, representing the Tithe in respect of these village lands, though collected by the Government, is diverted from the Treasury to the Waqf administration of the Supreme Moslem Council. The land itself in all cases remains Miri and is subject to all Miri dispositions.

---

* i.e., Miri land which has reverted to the Government.

31

4. *Metruké.*

Land left for roads, or assigned as the common land of the village, as, for instance, for pasture, is known as Metruké. Such land cannot be sold by an individual nor is any disposition possible.

5. *Mewat.*

Mewat has a certain importance in that its area, which is not yet determined, may be considerable. It is the waste land (which has not been left or assigned to the inhabitants or held by Kushan) at such a distance from the village site, that the voice of a man shouting there cannot be heard. This has been interpreted by judicial decision as one and a half miles. The land is vested in the Government. Cultivation with permission entitles to the issue of a title-deed (Kushan) free of charge. Cultivation without permission under the old Mohammedan law entailed payment of the unimproved value. Now, under the provisions of the Mewat Land Ordinance of 1921, any person breaking up Mewat land without permission is treated as a trespasser.

The area of Mewat will only be finally determined when the settlement operations now in progress are completed.

Mesha'a.

A common feature of the proprietary right in agricultural land is the existence of the system known as Mesha'a. In villages where this system prevails, the whole of the property held in the village is held in common. Each shareholder owns a fractional share in the village, but has no separate parcel of land allotted to him in proprietary right. The village as a whole belongs to the body of the proprietors as a whole. The individual's share is usually expressed in terms of various measures; a sharer may own a fedan (an area so large that a pair of cattle can plough it in one day), or a karat, that is 1/24th of the whole, or a fraction of the whole, called a sehem. But none of these represent defined plots or parcels of the village; they represent an undivided share of the total.

In the Mesha'a villages there is usually a permanent distribution among the Hamulahs—the tribal divisions of the village. Within these large areas individual shares are as a rule divided every two years, with the result that no development is at all possible. No cultivator will proceed to manure or improve his holding, which he knows will pass to some other cultivator in the course of the next two years.

This Mesha'a system is a constant cause of complaint among the fellahin.

Its partition.—Partition can be made in one of two ways, either by agreement among the parties and acceptance of that agreement by the Courts, or by the Courts themselves. In the former case there has to be unanimous agreement of all the shareholders. In the latter case the Courts act on the petition of the individual shareholder, but the cost to him is exceedingly heavy, for several reasons. In the first place, it has never been the custom to register changes of title upon transfer of property or succession. Most of the titles now held by proprietors are not actually in their name. Very frequently they are in the name of a father, or a grandfather, or other relation who is long dead. Before partition can be effected it is necessary that the title should be clear.

Expense of partition.—Apart from the difficulty in establishing the title, the registration of the amended title costs 3 per cent. of the value of the property by way of registration fees. Again, before the Courts will proceed to a partition they demand a map prepared by a qualified surveyor. This map has to be furnished by the applicant for the partition. In addition, there are the Court fees for the partition, which are themselves not negligible. In sum, the applicant for partition by action of the Courts is put to very serious expense as a preliminary, and is quite uncertain how long the proceedings may last and what the ultimate result will be.

Unofficial partition.—There are a large number of villages in which *de facto* partition has been carried out, although no official sanction has yet been given. In the majority of cases these partitions are unsatisfactory from the agricultural point of view. As in all Oriental countries there is in Palestine a universal desire that each shareholder should have a share, however small, of each distinctive class of land. The result is that the plots of individuals are scattered here and there throughout the village, and are frequently either of ridiculous shape or too small for effective exploitation. Cases are known of fields being so divided that a share is 2,000 metres long and 4½ metres broad. There are cases of this kind even where partition has been made by Government officers, as, for instance, in the Beisan area. This is exceedingly unfortunate.

Partition by agreement.—It is desirable that partitions should be made by agreement, in which case the procedure is simple and inexpensive, and the cost of the Courts is avoided. As a preliminary a survey of the area to be partitioned is necessary. In sanctioning these partitions it is essential that the influence of the sanctioning officer should be used to correct the tendency to diffuse and uneconomic partition. It is said that this is difficult. One case has been cited in which the fellahin were persuaded to re-distribute the land so as to amalgamate the holdings, thus constituting economic blocks. It was a long and tedious process, and the officer concerned was of opinion that it had taken three times as long as an ordinary partition case. The matter is of such extreme importance that it is well worth while to spend a large amount of trouble to ensure satisfactory partitions.

33

Its extent and effect.—A return of the year 1923 showed that of the villages in Palestine at that time 56 per cent. were Mesha'a and 44 per cent. Mafruz (i.e., divided). A return of the present year shows 46 per cent. Mesha'a and 54 per cent. Mafruz. This is an indication of the number of cases in which private partition has been carried out. The majority of these partitions are not final. They will doubtless become so by prescription, after a lapse of a considerable interval of time. This is not a satisfactory position.

Mesha'a is described by the Committee on the Economic Condition of Agriculturists as "perhaps the greatest obstacle to agricultural progress in Palestine." They record that the system misses alike the advantages of individualism and of co-operation; while it remains, they say, it is useless to expect that land will be weeded or fertilised, that trees will be planted, or, in a word, that any development will take place. These opinions are held generally by the Area Officers and District Officers of the Palestine Government and by the fellahin concerned.

Government action in regard to partition.—In the year 1923, a Commission was appointed by the Government to consider the whole question of Mesha'a. It made certain radical proposals, including the recommendation that legislation should be introduced empowering the executive authorities to enforce partition. It suggested the appointment of local committees to carry out partitions, and a reduction of taxation in respect of fees of registration and of survey in partitioned lands. It also suggested that the Werko tax should not be increased on newly partitioned lands until a general assessment of the tax is undertaken.

Nothing appears to have been done as a result of the enquiry and report of this Commission. This is to be regretted, as it is essential that every possible step should be taken to encourage the development of Arab holdings.

Partition under land settlement.—At present there is a settlement in progress, but its proceedings are complicated and difficult and many years will pass before they are completed. The Settlement Officers have power to deal with these cases. It would be advantageous to put on a special staff of selected officers to deal with Mesha'a and partitions, or to empower the Area and District Officers to deal with these cases on the spot. One of the essential pre-conditions of development is that the land shall be partitioned and that partitions shall be effected on reasonable principles.

Acceleration of partition.—The matter should form the subject of immediate and serious consideration by the Palestine Government. In passing legislation it would be well, if at all feasible to avoid the nomination of committees. These are notoriously ineffective, both as executive or as quasi-judicial bodies. It would be preferable to grant to Area Officers, and, under their supervision and control, to District Officers, the power to enable them to deal with partition cases. Some right of appeal will be necessary in case of

34

parties who feel themselves aggrieved, but resort to the civil courts should be discouraged as far as possible. It is preferable, if feasible, that appeals in partition cases from decisions of Area Officers should lie to the District Commissioner, from District Officers to the Area Officers.

The Law Governing Agricultural Tenancies.

Landlords.—Though it is known that very large areas are held by resident and non-resident landlords, the total area cultivated by tenants has not yet been ascertained. It will only be known when the survey and settlement at present in progress have been completed, and if the proposals on this subject contained in this report are accepted.

Tenants.—No occupancy right exists in favour of the Arab tenant in Palestine. As a rule he holds his land on a yearly tenancy, terminable by his landlord at will.

Land Transfer Ordinance, 1920.—Several attempts have been made to improve the position of the agricultural tenant in this respect. In September, 1920, soon after the establishment of the Civil Government, the Land Transfer Ordinance, 1920, was issued. The Preamble of that Ordinance recites :

(a) in order to meet the needs of the people it is desirable that transactions having in view the immediate use and cultivation of land be permitted;

(b) it is necessary to take measures to prevent speculative dealings in land and to protect the present occupants;

(c) a Land Settlement Court is shortly to be established, which will adjudicate all titles, and in the meantime no guarantee of title can be given by the Administration;

(d) it is intended to introduce legislation to secure orderly planning of the towns and the erection of buildings, subject to the control of the Administration;

(e) the Administration is taking measures to facilitate the establishment of Credit Banks in Palestine, which shall have power to grant loans on the security on immovable property; pending the consideration of the establishment of such Banks, it is desirable to continue the prohibiton of the sale of land in satisfaction of a mortgage or in execution of a judgment.

Restriction on transfer of land.—The Ordinance then proceeded to provide for the control of all land transactions. To all such transactions the consent of the Administration must be obtained; this consent was given through the District Governor, where he was satisfied that the person about to acquire the property (1) was resident in Palestine, (2) would not obtain property exceeding in value £3,000 or in area 300 dunams, (3) intended himself to cultivate the land immediately. It was also a condition (4) that the

35

transferor, if in possession, or the tenant in occupation of the property leased, would retain sufficient land in the district or elsewhere for the maintenance of himself and his family.

If an application were rejected by the District Governor, an appeal lay to the High Commissioner, whose decision was final.

The High Commissioner also had the power to consent to the sale of large areas of land, if he were satisfied that the transfer was in the public interest, or he might refer an application for any such disposition to a Commission which existed at that time, and whose duty it was to report upon closer settlement of the land.

Complaints against restrictions.—From the beginning there was general protest on the part of the Arabs against these restrictions on the sale of the land. They alleged that they were designed to impoverish the Arab population and to compel the sale of their land to the Jews at an inadequate price. These complaints were formulated before the Commission of Enquiry which reported on the riots of 1921. That Commission wrote as follows:—

> "The Arabs have regarded with suspicion measures taken by the Government with the best intentions. The transfer of Land Ordinance, 1920, which requires that the consent of the Government must be obtained to all dispositions of immovable property, and forbids transfer to other than residents in Palestine, they regard as having been introduced to keep down the price of land and to throw land which is in the market into the hands of the Jews at a low price . . . . "*

Transfer of Land Ordinance, 1920-21.—The Ordinance was amended, and was replaced by the Transfer of Land Ordinance, 1920-21. The Director of Lands was constituted as the authority to grant permission for dispositions of land, and he was bound to grant that consent if satisfied that the transferor had a title, " provided that, in the case of agricultural land which is leased, he shall also satisfy himself that any tenant in occupation will retain sufficient land in the district or elsewhere for the maintenance of himsel˜ and his family . . . ."

This Ordinance in fact remained a dead letter. It was circumvented in one of two ways; either the landlord, who desired to dispose of his land, ejected his tenants as a preliminary operation, and so sold the land with vacant possession to the purchaser, or the landlord or the purchaser induced the tenant to withdraw on payment of compensation. In both of these cases there was no tenant in occupation, and the conditions of the Ordinance consequently failed to operate.

Protection of Cultivators Ordinance, 1929.—The latest attempt to protect the tenant in cases of sale by the landlord is the Protection of Cultivators Ordinance, 1929. This cancelled the provision of the Ordinance of 1921, which required that, on sale, arrangements should be made to provide a tenant in occupation with land in lieu of the holding from which he was dispossessed.

---

* Cmd. 1540, page 51.

36

It aims at protecting the cultivator who has been at least two years in a holding, by requiring the landlord to give him a full year's notice before the tenancy can be terminated or before the rent may be increased, and by providing for compensation for the tenant for disturbance and for improvements, which he has carried out himself. It provides further that where the tenant has cultivated a holding for five years or more, the landlord shall pay him as additional compensation a sum equal to one year's average rent.

Its practical effect.—This Ordinance is of little value in preventing the displacement of tenants from the soil. There is no record of tenancies in Palestine, as there is, for instance, of agricultural tenancies in India. It would be extremely difficult for any tenant to establish a tenancy of five years on the same holding. In any case, at its best, the ordinance would only provide money compensation, while what is eminently required is, not compensation for disturbance, but a provision against disturbance.

Agricultural Tenancies.

Occupancy right.—One of the requirements of agricultural Palestine at the present time is an effective provision for occupancy right in favour of the tenant. The pressure on the soil is so great that, as will be shown later, rents are rising to a height which threatens to preclude the tenant from producing sufficient from a holding to pay the charges thereon and at the same time to maintain a standard of life that is even tolerable. Under these conditions any provision short of occupancy right is of little value. And if occupancy right be granted it must be secured by a provision preventing the increase of rents except with the sanction of the Courts, otherwise the right of occupancy will prove nugatory.

Occupancy right: Position of Jewish agricultural tenants.—In the case of Jewish tenants conditions are much better than in that of the Arabs. The Jewish tenant of the Keren-Kayemeth (Jewish National Fund) has not yet got any document authorising his holding or specifying its conditions, but it is certain that he will ultimately be furnished with a lease, of which it is intended that the term will be 49 years renewable. There is no question of uncertainty of tenure in this case.

The P.I.C.A. either sells land to the occupant, payment being made by instalments over a long term of years, or provides him with a long-term lease. In fact, the Jewish settlement is in the interest of the occupant of the soil, while the Arab enjoys no such advantage. There is thus no necessity for legislation for conferring the occupancy right on the Jewish tenant. At the same time, legislation providing for the creation of such occupancy right generally would not in any way interfere either with the policy of the Jewish landlord or with the amenities of the Jewish tenant. It is true that the creation of occupancy right will effect a very radical change in the position of the Arab tenant vis-à-vis his landlord. It will also reduce the market value of land occupied by tenants. It is, however, the only measure likely to arrest the present tendency to divorce the fellahin from the soil.

Register of tenants.—The creation of occupancy right will entail not only the preparation of a register of existing tenants but also the necessary machinery for keeping that register up to date. It is in any case desirable that such information should be available, as it will enable the Government to watch the movement of the agricultural population from the soil to the village or the town. It will provide information as to the course of rents, and so will facilitate periodical revision of any tax on land which may be imposed. It is an essential of any efficient policy of agricultural development. It is desirable that this register of tenants should be prepared by the Settlement staff in the case of settlements now in progress, and I advise that this should be done.

Palestine: Survey.—At the present time a survey of Palestine is in progress, which will afford information, of which the want has always been felt seriously with regard to the areas of the country.

Land Settlement.—The main objects of the Settlement are two: the first is to obtain an exact record of the rights of all proprietors of agricultural land, the second, to provide a basis on which a reasonable system of land taxation can be founded, in order that the antiquated systems of Tithe and of Werko may be abolished.

Land registration fees.—As to the first of the above objects it may be said that the settlement results will prove of strictly temporary utility if the existing fees on registration of transfers and dispositions of land remain in force. One of the chief reasons for the avoidance of registration of title in the past has been the expense which that registration entailed on the applicant. In Appendix 6 the rates of fee for registration of various kinds are detailed. It will be seen that they are in fact very onerous.

Land registers.—It is highly desirable that, once the record of rights prepared by the settlement officers is complete, its maintenance as an accurate record shall be easy. Otherwise the record will very rapidly again become inaccurate. For this reason, the fees to be charged on the registration of changes in the record should be so light that they will not prove to be a serious burden on the person to whom a property has been transferred.

Maintenance of record of occupancy right.—It has been suggested above that the village records should include a record of tenants as well as one of the proprietors. If this proposal is accepted, it will be necessary to have a machinery to keep the tenants' register up to date. The same agency might deal with the register of owners. Responsibility for application for amendment of the register should not be removed from the shoulders of the proprietor or the tenant, but the official who is charged with the maintenance of the records will be in a position to bring to notice those cases in which that responsibility is not in fact discharged. If a penalty were to attach to failure in this matter of application for amendment of the register, and at the same time there existed an official in a position to know the facts, there should be little difficulty in keeping the registers accurately up to date. An accurate record of this kind will be of great value, not only to the authorities but, and perhaps even more importantly so, to the proprietors and to the tenants of the village.

CHAPTER V.

Jewish Settlement on the Land.

Agencies of Jewish Settlement.—Areas, being Jewish property either of the various colonisation agencies or of private individuals, are shown on map No. 6.*

The two chief agencies of Jewish settlement on the land are the Palestine Jewish Colonisation Association, commonly known as the P.I.C.A., and the Colonisation Department of the Zionist Organisation, which is financed by the Keren Hayesod. The former buys land and instals settlers; the latter is purely a settlement agency, the land being purchased by the Palestine Land Development Company for the Jewish National Fund, which places it as required at the disposal of the Keren Hayesod. Before being handed over for settlement, the land is improved by the Jewish National Fund (Keren Kayemeth).

In addition to these two major agencies of settlement, there are a large number of land or settlement companies which either dispose of land in small lots to would-be settlers, or prepare and plant the land and sell it, either when planted, or when mature and bearing, to immigrants.

Private agencies : The Benei-Benjamin.—There is also a number of private agencies which prepare land for settlement, as for instance the Benei-Benjamin. This is a society of young Jews, having members both in Palestine and abroad. It has borrowed money and has purchased a tract of 9,000 dunams of land, which it is preparing and planting, for settlement of other members of the Society who hope in time to come to Palestine. It is interesting to observe the difference in policy between a society of this kind and an ordinary commercial society, such as Palestine Plantations, Limited, which has acquired a large area and is developing it as orange plantations for sale to immigrant Jews. The former

---
* See Note on page 3.

society has its plantations in the village of Nataniya, in the Maritime Plain. It charges its members £85 per dunam for developed orange groves at the end of the fifth year, when the trees are coming into bearing. The trees are all grafted. Tel Mond is the colony where the plantations of Palestine Plantations, Ltd., are situated. It was ascertained from the Company's local manager that for similar groves of the same age the price is £110 per dunam.

Amount of land held by Jewish organizations.—From information received from the Jewish agency in Palestine and from the Palestine Land Development Co., Ltd. (a purchasing agency not only for the Jewish National Fund but for many of the public and private companies), it appears that in June, 1930, Jewish land in Palestine amounted to 1,250,000 dunams. The Statistical Abstract of 1929 gave an area of 1,200,000 dunams. Though this fact is not stated in the Statistical Abstract or in the Memorandum submitted by the Jewish Agency, it has been ascertained that the dunams referred to are not metric dunams, but Turkish dunams.

In addition to this land so held, the various Jewish agencies hold options over a further area of between 80,000 and 85,000 metric dunams.

(1) The P.I.C.A. Settlements.

Of the various Jewish settlement agencies the largest and most important is the P.I.C.A., whose colonies number 34. This association commenced work in 1882, under the designation of the Jewish Colonisation Association (I.C.A.), and its operations since that date have been supported by generous expenditure on the part of Baron Edmond de Rothschild. The P.I.C.A. now owns 454,840 metric dunams of land. To the activities of this organisation are due the foundation of the well-known colonies of Petach Tikvah and Rehovoth, which have recently developed with rapid strides. The former was in origin a colony of 28 families settled on 2,000 dunams of land. It has grown into a country town of some 10,000 inhabitants and comprises 25,000 dunams of land, of which considerable areas are owned by private individuals. Rehovoth is also extending rapidly. At the start 20 families were settled on 10,600 dunams; the population of the village is now estimated at 2,800 and the area attached to the colony is 22,600 dunams, also owned in large part by private individuals. This colony was famous for its almond plantations, and still exports large quantities of almonds through its Co-operative Society of Almond Growers. The almond industry is now overshadowed in all this region by the orange, and the area under orange groves is increasing with great rapidity.

Richon-le-Zion, with its famous cellars, and Zichron-Jacob are other well-known P.I.C.A. colonies.

The Kabbara concession.—The P.I.C.A. has two important projects in course of completion, both in the Maritime Plain. In

1921 the Association obtained a concession for the manufacture of salt at Athlit, for the drainage of the Kabbara swamp and for the development of the Caesarea sand-dunes. The first of these projects has been transferred to a company which is producing salt in considerable quantities. The drainage of the Kabbara swamp and the irrigation canals which will cover this area are now approaching completion. The total extent of land included in the Kabbara concession was 5,170 dunams, and in addition the P.I.C.A. already owned 2,300 dunams adjoining. The whole area has been reclaimed and rendered cultivable. At the time of my visit a large part of the area was carrying rich crops of linseed. The drainage work has proved particularly difficult, owing to the existence of springs in the bed of the swamp for whose drainage subsidiary arrangements are necessary. At one place 126 of these springs were discovered in three and a half dunams of land, less than an acre. The drainage of all these springs has added much to the cost of reclamation, and £92,000 has already been spent on the work.

Pardessana.—The second project is the development of the Pardessana colony, south of the Kabbara swamp, and lying among the undulating sandy hillocks of the Maritime Plain which are so favourable to the growth of the orange. The preparation of the land for that colony, which will provide holdings for 450 families, besides 1,000 families of workmen, has almost been completed. Wells have been and are being sunk, electric current has already been provided, both for power and light, and the town site has been laid out. The individual lots have been marked on the map, and in the case of the few colonists who have already arrived, also on the ground. The work reflects the greatest credit on those responsible for it, and, given the possibility of creating a sufficient market for the largely-increasing supply of Jaffa oranges, the future of this colony is most promising.

A feature of Pardessana is the provision of small lots for families of the labouring class. An area of 5 dunams, with cow-house and poultry-house, is attached to each of the workmen's dwellings, which are composed of two rooms and a kitchen.

Benjamina.—Similar provision is made for the labouring class, in this case Jews from Georgia, in the colony of Benjamina, lying south of Pardessana. In that colony a perfume factory has been started successfully, and both the colonists and the labourers have been encouraged to reserve a small area for jasmine, and have been instructed in the method of cultivation and in that of plucking the flower. The produce of the factory is stated to be of good quality, and to sell for high prices in France or in England. The actual profits to the grower are not large, as cultivation and plucking absorb much labour and occupy much time. The industry is, however, well suited for allotment holdings such as those with which the labourers are provided.

41

Colonies in Galilee.—Apart from its colonies in the Maritime Plain the P.I.C.A. has established a number of settlements in Upper and Lower Galilee. These are chiefly of the old-fashioned kind, with somewhat extensive holdings, and grow principally cereals and other country crops. In some of the colonies the settlers are acquiring cross-bred cattle of a superior type, which provide an income from dairy produce. In most of these colonies Arab labour is employed.

Bitania.—One of the P.I.C.A. settlements, named Bitania, in the Upper Jordan Valley, deserves special mention. It contains an experimental area in which fruit of various kinds, and the more valuable vegetables—tomatoes, cucumbers, egg-plant—are being cultivated. It has been found that the land of this colony, which lies to the north of the Jordan Valley and not far from the Lake of Tiberias, is specially suitable for the cultivation of grape-fruit and bananas. The grape-fruit of Bitania is first-class in quality, almost seedless, with the minimum of pulp, of fair size and thin-skinned. Its flavour is excellent. It has been ascertained by experiment that the fruit can be stored and kept in good condition at least until the month of June. These results of the experimental cultivation of the grape-fruit are most important, for the soil is unsuited to the orange and the grape-fruit provides an even more valuable crop.

Relations of P.I.C.A. Colonists with Arabs.—The relations of the old P.I.C.A. colonists with their Arab neighbours and with their Arab workmen were excellent—a mutual advantage to both communities. Had the P.I.C.A. policy of friendship and conciliation with the Arab been permitted to continue, there is no doubt that in the neighbourhood of their colonies none of that bitterness which is now so prevalent need have arisen.

(*ii*) THE ZIONIST SETTLEMENTS.

The Jewish National Fund.—The Jewish National Fund holds approximately 270,000 metric dunams. According to a statement submitted by the Jewish Agency and reproduced as Appendix 7 to this Report, there are 20 co-operative groups, 16 smallholders' settlements, 5 girls' groups, 4 Yemenite settlements 2 agricultural settlement stations and 2 experimental stations. In addition, there are 9 settlements described as " supported ". On the other hand, the statement submitted by the Jewish National Fund (Keren-Kayemeth) records the following :—

" The types of settlement on the land are as follows :—

    18 smallholders' settlements ;
    27 co-operative group settlements ;
     7 Yemenite settlements ;
      Agricultural experimental station and its branches."

42

Zionist settlements.—The settlements of the Zionist organisation have not been in existence for as long a time as those of the P.I.C.A., and they work on different principles. The outstanding principle is " self-labour ", which implies that no settler shall have more land than the area he is able to cultivate by the unaided labour of himself and his family. In the case of the co-operative group, the area is determined by the amount which the group is able to cultivate without assistance. Notwithstanding the fact that the settlers receive a certain agricultural training as " chalutzim " (i.e., pioneers) before arrival in Palestine, they are not by early training agriculturists. They are drawn from all walks of life. There is no lack of ardour or enthusiasm, and there can be no doubt that in time the settlements will be able to support the cultivators, especially in those districts where plantation is possible. Meanwhile, there are few if any, of the settlements which are truly self-supporting, and there appear to be none in which any payment has been made in respect of the outlay by the Jewish National Fund or the Keren-Hayesod.

Expenditure by Keren-Kayemeth and Keren-Hayesod.—The amounts spent by these two agencies have been formidable, and it is quite impossible that they will ever be repaid in full. In the former case no question of repayment arises, as the land is not to be sold to the settlers. Yet it is certain that no adequate interest in the form of rent could be paid by the settlers on the outlay of the Fund on their holdings. In the case of the Keren-Hayesod also the outlay has been lavish, and the whole of the colonies are so over-capitalised that it will prove essential both to write off a considerable amount of the outlay and to fix the rate of interest on the balance at an uneconomic level if the outlay is to be liquidated. The Jewish National Fund and the Keren-Hayesod have very kindly submitted consolidated statements of their expenditure, which are printed as Appendices 8 and 9 to this Report. In the former, excluding the items " Urban Land ", " Urban Buildings ", and " Lands ", the sum of £1,545,659 appears to have been spent on agricultural colonisation. In the latter, the items " Urban Colonisation ", " National Organisations ", " Investments ", and " Jewish National Fund " do not appear to be expenditure on colonisation in the country. The balance is £3,345,531. Adding these two sums together, the total cost of agricultural colonisation by the Zionist Organisation appears to have been £4,891,190.* The number of persons actually settled for this sum is shown in Appendix 10—a statement submitted by the Jewish agency.

Population of settlements.—The total population of the Zionist settlements in 1930 (included therein being the " supported settle-

---

* The whole of this sum has not been expended on families actually settled. It includes an amount spent on land still in reserve.

ments ") consisted of 4,408 adults, and 2,364 children under 15 years of age. The cost of colonisation of a family has thus been very large.

Area of Zionist settlements.—In Appendix 11 is reproduced a statement submitted by the Jewish Agency as to areas held. This shows that included in the settlements belonging to the Zionist Organisation are 129,466 dunams of land, in addition to 14,758 dunams belonging to settlements described as " supported ". These latter are settlements belonging to other agencies for whose continuance the assistance of the Zionist Organisation is required. Of the 129,466 dunams actually the property of the Zionist Organisation, and included in the settlements, 15,137 dunams are leased to others, 11,958 dunams are shown as fallow, and 7,390 are " idle, fit for cultivation ", i.e., in all 34,485 dunams, or 26.6 per cent. of the total of the cultivable area of these settlements was for one reason or another not cultivated during the last year by the settlers themselves.

Reserve area.—As has been recorded, the total area of land held by the Jewish National Fund is 270,000 metric dunams. From the statement in Appendix 11 it appears that, excluding the settlements called " supported " only 114,329 dunams were cultivated. This implies that of the land held by the Fund over 155,500 dunams are in reserve. The Zionist Organisation has been engaged in colonisation work since before the War, though only since the War has development been rapid. It has now a reserve of land sufficient for a programme for a number of years. This is satisfactory, in that it will enable a general programme of development to be worked out for the country without interference with the work of Zionist settlement.

Emek colonies and contagious abortion.—A large number of the Zionist colonies are in the Emek. They tend more and more to be based on dairy produce, poultry, and fruit. The price of milk is now falling. The Zionist colonies have large herds of fine cows, many of them being pure-bred Holsteins, or the Holstein-Damascus and the Holstein-Gaulan cross. They are heavy milkers. It is unfortunate that with the cows has also been imported Bang's bacillus, and that contagious abortion is present in the large majority of the stall-fed dairy herds. The matter has been taken in hand by the Department of Agriculture, and it is hoped in time to eradicate the disease. Meanwhile, its appearance cannot but affect the estimates of the cost of settlement and throw back the date at which the dairy settlements will definitely become self-supporting.

Experts' opinion as to completion of establishment.—On page 40 of their Report the Experts wrote as follows :—

> " . . . . that no expenditure for planting new colonies should be made unless the development of existing colonies has been completed, or the money required for their full development has been provided. The amount required for this will absorb the probable normal income of

the Colonisation Department for several years to come. Delay in providing settlers with needed equipment and improvements is now causing serious losses and disappointments. It is lowering the efficiency of the settlers, it is the cause of large deficits, even in the older colonies, and is placing on the Zionist Organisation, rather than on the settlers, the responsibility for making the colonies self-sustaining . . . ."

These remarks are still applicable. The colonisation settlements in the Emek, which were examined by those Experts, are still not fully equipped. Indeed, it is stated that the sum of £300,000 is necessary for expenditure during the next two years if these colonies are to be a success.

On July 2nd, 1930, an article appeared in the English supplement of the Jewish Labour paper, "*Davar*," the organ of the General Federation of Jewish Labour, and published by that Federation. The article is entitled " At the Bottom of the List." Referring to an article in the Hebrew issue of the paper on the consolidation of the Zionist colonies, the writer says :—

" A detailed plan adopted in 1927 by the Zionist Colonisation Department placed the investments still needed to make all settlements self-supporting at £499,029. It was resolved to complete the process within two years . . . . and it was with this understanding that the above sum was fixed. The Labour Movement submitted to the necessity of letting consolidation take precedence over all other activities . . . . The plan was sound, but what of its fulfilment? The two years have passed, the third year is nearing its close, and the goal is yet to be reached. In 1927-28 a sum of £136,000 was expended; in 1928-29 another £78,000, and 1929-30 yet another £130,000. This makes a total of £344,000, which, being subtracted from the original total, leaves an arithmetical balance of £155,000 still outstanding. But the economic balance is much greater. In the development of a farm there is a tremendous difference between obtaining the budget in cash so that it can be invested productively at once, and having to wait for windfalls, meanwhile living from hand to mouth. The present position is that instead of £155,000, not less than £300,000 will in all probability be needed to complete the equipment, and again on the understanding that the balance will be forthcoming during the remainder of the present year and the following one . . . . Now that the time has come for the preliminary drafting of the Agency budget for the next Jewish year those responsible should know that the patience of the Emek settlers is finally exhausted, and that they insist upon means being found to complete the equipment of their farms during the present year . . . . "

Self-supporting Zionist settlements.—In the Memorandum submitted by the Jewish Agency, at page 24, the following is written :

" Those settlements which have received their full equipment from the Keren-Hayesod are now self-supporting. The other settlements that have not yet received their full settlement loan are most of them by now very near to the stage of being ' self-supporting.' In this connection we mean by the term ' self-supporting ' that the ordinary farm expenditure and living expenditure, including renovation, but not including depreciation, nor repayment of settlement loan, nor rent (which is not yet payable), are covered by the ordinary farm income. In this sense the following settlements in the valley of Esdraelon are already self-supporting, viz., Nahalal, Ginegar, Balfouria, Kfar Yeheskiel."

45

The Consolidation Budget.—By the courtesy of Dr. Ruppin, statements were submitted bringing up to date the information contained in Table I printed on page 72 of the Experts' Report. This table gives, among other information, the amount of the " Consolidation Budget," that is, the amount still necessary to complete the settlement of each colony. From the statements it appears that for Nahalal (which is described in the Memorandum as " self-supporting ") a sum of £10,000 is still required, for Ginegar the sum is £23,000, for Balfouria, £3,500.

Kfar Yeheskiel: Cost of Settlement.—Only in the case of Kfar Yeheskiel can the colony be said to be self-supporting, and in the modified sense of that word used in the Memorandum. This colony contained 59 families in 1930. In the statement on p. 72 of the Experts' Report, the cost of the land for this colony and its amelioration was shown at $342,090, say £70,389. In the statement now submitted the cost of the equipment is shown as £63,935 in addition. The total expenditure of settling 59 families is, therefore, £134,329, an average of £2,277 per family.

Keren-Hayesod : Budget.—In view of the continuing necessity for expenditure on existing colonies it is remarkable to find that in the year 1928-1929 the budget of the Keren-Hayesod for agricultural colonisation fell from £167,090 of the previous year, to £93,123, while at the same time the expenditure on urban colonisation rose from £4,747 to £91,949.

Further, there is at present a plan in preparation with the object of placing one thousand families of labourers on the land. The following is an extract from the Report of the Palestine Jewish Agency, published in the " Palestine Weekly " of July 4th, 1930 :—

" . . . . It is also a matter of common knowledge that at the last meeting of the Administrative Committee of the Jewish Agency, which took place in London, it was resolved to settle one thousand families of workers, by means of extra budgetary funds, in the vicinity of the big plantation colonies. The plan is still in the preparatory stage . . . ."

Influence of Federation of Labour.—A second criticism of the Experts was directed to the submission of the colonisation authorities to the influence of the General Federation of Jewish Labour, and the tendency to use the Zionist colonies as a method of forwarding the Federation policy of social reform. This tendency is still strongly in evidence, and will be discussed later.

Kvutzoth Colonies.—A third criticism is directed against the Kvutza, the communal colonies. In those colonies land is held in common, and the community lives in one or more large communal houses, one, or sometimes two, rooms being allowed to each couple. For the children there is a separate children's house, where they are cared for by nurses specially detailed to this duty.

The work of the settlement for the next day is distributed each evening among its members by the community in meeting after the evening meal, and it is understood that each member takes his or her turn at all the domestic or agricultural duties of the group. The employment of paid labour is against the principles which govern such communities. At the time of writing, however, parties of boys belonging to the junior branch of the Federation of Labour have been deputed to some of the Kvutzoth colonies in the Emek to assist in harvesting the grapes. It was explained by one of the officials of the labour executive that, on the one hand, the employment of labour for this purpose would be too expensive for the means of the colony and that, on the other hand, the outing was in the nature of a holiday for the children and that it had the additional effect of stimulating interest in agricultural pursuits. This Kvutzoth system is still in full vigour and new colonies of this type for the labourers are being constructed to-day.

Smallholding colonies.—These differ, of course, from the smallholding colonies, in which each family has its separate dwelling (in almost all cases surrounded by a garden) and its separate agricultural lot. In these, family life is preserved. In some there is an aversion to the employment of paid labour, and much work is done in common, as, for instance, the threshing of the grain at harvest. Many of the smallholders' colonies are highly attractive in appearance and show signs of progress. This is specially the case in the Maritime Plain, where the orange has proved a great source of wealth, but there are also attractive colonies of this kind in the Plain of Esdraelon, where farming is of the mixed type, the main branches being dairy, and vegetable and fruit cultivation. Even in the smallholders' colonies there is a keen communal feeling, and during the inspection of one of these a complaint was made that one of its members, who had failed financially and left the village, had sold his agricultural outfit to a stranger, without consultation with the village Council. The members of the colony expressed no objection to the new-comer, who was in every way satisfactory. Objection was rather to the manner of his coming among them.

Emek and Upper Jordan Valley Colonies: Nahalal.—Among the Zionist settlements probably the most successful and the most attractive are some of those in the Emek and in the Upper Jordan Valley. Nahalal is the outstanding instance of a progressive colony of smallholders. Founded ten years ago, with 80 families, it now has 75 agricultural and 35 non-agricultural families. The colony has been well laid out. It is not yet completely equipped and housing will require a considerable outlay, but progress is substantial. The colony commenced as a grain-growing colony, but has since changed over to more intensive methods, specially to dairy farming and poultry keeping. All the grain produced is used as fodder for birds and animals, and no grain is now sold. In 1922 the colony had 38 cows. It now has about 500 and the income from the sale of animals this year has been £1,500. The colonists also own over 30,000 fowls.

47

The average holding is 100 dunams. At present it is not more than is sufficient to maintain a family, but it is anticipated that water can be pumped for irrigation and that when this is done there will be room for a few further settlers.

"*Regulating Societies*".—One feature of the colony is what are described as "regulating Societies", which afford help to colonists who suffer from sickness or from poverty. The members arrange among themselves to cultivate the land or tend the animals of a sick member, charging him with the cost. If it is found that the colonist cannot pay, the debt is carried forward to the following year. Some bad debts are made, but the Societies put aside a sum every year to meet such losses.

It was reported that some of the colonists are putting money into their farms. This argues an income in excess of that necessary for the maintenance of the family. The colonists have not yet begun to repay any of the money due to the Keren-Hayesod for installation, nor is rent being paid to the Keren-Kayemeth.

Kfar Yeheskiel.—Another successful colony in the Plain of Esdraelon is Kfar Yeheskiel. Here the average lot is 85 dunams, but six of the 40 cultivating families have additional land in a neighbouring village. In this colony also the basis is dairying. The colonists own 300 cows and live by selling the milk and the young stock. In addition many fowls are kept and 20,000 eggs are sold on the average each month. Some of the colonists are specialising in fruit and it has been found by experiment that the grape-fruit will flourish. The colonists estimate that the net income in cash is £60 per family. Repayment to the Keren-Hayesod and payment of rent have not yet commenced. The total number of families in this village is 60, of whom 20 are engaged in trade or in work other than agriculture.

Dagania A.—Of another type is the Kvutzoth colony Dagania A in the Upper Jordan Valley. This colony was founded 20 years ago. The area was stated by residents on the spot to be 7,000 dunams, of which 800 are irrigated by pumps worked by electric power. There are 255 residents, of whom 116 are children. The industries of the village are dairying and fruit, and the gross produce was said to be £20,000 per annum. Bananas are the staple fruit of the colony and do well. This colony is certainly prospering, but here also no payments are being made in respect of debt or of rent.

Kiryath Anavim.—A colony which is looked upon by the Zionist Organisation as a great success is the hill colony Kiryath Anavim, a few miles distant from Jerusalem. It is a dairying and fruit colony, with a small area under cultivation. The fodder for 40 Dutch cows comes up by lorry from colonies near to Jaffa, and the settlers stated that its cost was met by the income from the manure of the cowhouses. The milk is sold in Jerusalem. The adult population of the village is 70. Enquiry was made on this point, but it was not explained how this large number of colonists was occupied with work on a dairy farm with 40 cows and on a small area of fruit. The colony was described as paying its way, and a profit of £164 was stated to have been made in 1929. It appeared, however, from further enquiry that the sum of £1,080 was earned as wages of labour in Jerusalem and elsewhere, that £400 is still required for consolidation, that the outlay of the Keren-Hayesod on establishment of the colony was £23,015, that the accumulated deficit is £5,115, and that nothing has been paid towards the debt, or for rent. This settlement cannot seriously be characterised as a financial success.

Jewish rural population.—It is somewhat difficult to ascertain how many Jews have been settled on the land. The Report[*] of the Commission on the Disturbances, at page 8, records the Jewish rural population as 35,000, distributed over 135 settlements. On the other hand, the Vaad-Leumi, in a Memorandum submitted to the Mandates Commission of the League of Nations, says that the rural Jewish population is 46,000. The exact numbers will not be known until the census of next year, but there can be little doubt that the figure contained in the Memorandum of the Vaad-Leumi is exaggerated, as the total of the detailed statements for each settlement submitted in the course of this enquiry by the Jewish Agency with their Memorandum is 38,777. This figure, again, may not be exactly accurate, but it is as near the truth as can be ascertained at the present time. It is estimated by the Vaad-Leumi that there were 10,000 Jews in Jewish colonies in 1919 and that since June, 1921, and up to the end of 1929, 89,926 Jews immigrated into Palestine. If the figure of the Jewish Agency's Memorandum be accepted, the increase of population in the colonies since 1921 is certainly not greater than 28,777, that is to say, that of immigrant Jews less than 1 out of 3 is settled on the land. The immigration movement is in major part a movement of immigration to the towns.

Zionist Settlements not self-supporting.—Of the agricultural settlements it may be said that none of the Zionist settlements are self-supporting in the sense that they would be able to maintain themselves without further assistance and pay back to the Keren-Hayesod a reasonable amount towards satisfaction of their debts, and to the Keren-Kayemeth an economic rent. It is indeed admitted that no such consummation is anticipated. Many Zionist settlements would cease to exist if further support were not forthcoming. The P.I.C.A. colonies include in their number several old colonies which are radically established, and which will unquestionably flourish in the future. Even of the P.I.C.A. colonies, however, there are a number, including some of the older

---

[*] Cmd. 3530.

colonies, which still require support and in some cases reorganisation. I understand that this reorganisation is in progress.

Excessive cost of Zionist settlement.—The system adopted by the Colonisation Department of the Zionist Organisation is immensely costly; it demands very little from the settler himself. Indeed however hard a settler may work, and however desirous he may be to pay back sums that the Fund expended on him, by no possibility can he arrive at that result. The debt which he owes cannot be repaid by any effort on his part.

Jewish settlement in Russia.—It is interesting to compare the principles and cost of Jewish settlement on the land in Russia with the corresponding cost and principles which obtain in Palestine. Jewish colonisation is proceeding on a large scale in Southern Russia, under the auspices of the Joint Distribution Committee, known in its colonisation activity as " Agro-Joint." Conditions are of course different, as the Russian Government supplies the necessary land free of charge. Apart from the land, it is costing £150—£200 to settle a family on the land in Russia. This includes preparing the land (tractor operations and well-sinking) though in a number of cases the digging of the wells is done by the settlers themselves. Of the total expenditure on settlement 82.25 per cent is described as "returnable expenditure." The balance represents expenditure on what is called "agricultural extension" and on administration. The latter item amounts to the remarkably reasonable percentage of 6.64 per cent. of the total expenditure. It is recorded in a report for 1926 that the new settlers of the 1923-24 season were already paying their debts.*

In a report on the work in Russia by J. Billikopf and Dr. Maurice B. Hexter, written in 1926, the following occurs :—

> "It is to be noted that nothing is donated outright to the settler except technical instructions and medical-assistance; other than technical and medical aid all else is charged to a settler's account, of which the colonist has current information."

Settlement of refugees in Greece.—Similarly, in the case of the Greek refugee settlement, all the money spent on settlement by the Refugee Settlement Commission was repayable. It has recently been arranged that the actual overhead expenses of administration shall not be repaid by the agricultural refugees, nor the cost of construction of certain major works of public utility, as for instance an irrigation canal and arterial roads, but that, as a general rule, all other expenditure on the settlement of the individual family, including the price of the land, shall be recovered. Repayment is actually in progress. The cost of settlement of the agricultural refugees in Greece amounted on

---

* Report by Joseph A. Rosen, Director of the Agro-Joint, submitted to the Chicago Conference of the United Jewish Campaign, October, 1926.

the average to less than £80 per family, but this sum did not include the price of the land, and about half the houses were provided by the Government, being houses evacuated by exchanged Turks and Bulgarians. These houses, however, required radical repairs.

Expenditure on settlement and effect of non-repayment.—It is undesirable, from the point of view of ordinary morality, that colonists should be allowed to benefit by the large expenditure which has been made for their settlement and yet to escape payment of the amounts spent upon them. Nothing could be worse than that the Jewish immigrants should feel that they have the right to be established in Palestine at the expense of others. There is a danger that this view will prevail and that settlers will look upon what is described as the " inventory," this is, provision for their settlement, as a right. If a strong, healthy and self-respecting peasantry is desired in the Jewish colonies in Palestine, it should be made quite clear to the settlers that they are under the obligation to repay the outlay which has been made on their behalf.

(iii) THE EFFECT OF THE JEWISH SETTLEMENT ON THE ARAB.

P.I.C.A.'s relations with the Arab.—In discussing the question of the effect of Jewish Settlement on the Arab it is essential to differentiate between the P.I.C.A. colonisation and that of the Zionist Organisation.

In so far as the past policy of the P.I.C.A. is concerned, there can be no doubt that the Arab has profited largely by the installation of the colonies. Relations between the colonists and their Arab neighbours were excellent. In many cases, when land was bought by the P.I.C.A. for settlement, they combined with the development of the land for their own settlers similar development for the Arabs who previously occupied the land. All the cases which are now quoted by the Jewish authorities to establish the advantageous effect of Jewish colonisation on the Arabs of the neighbourhood, and which have been brought to notice forcibly and frequently during the course of this enquiry, are cases relating to colonies established by the P.I.C.A., before the Keren-Hayesod came into existence. In fact, the policy of the P.I.C.A. was one of great friendship for the Arab. Not only did they develop the Arab lands simultaneously with their own, when founding their colonies, but they employed the Arab to tend their plantations, cultivate their fields, to pluck their grapes and their oranges. As a general rule the P.I.C.A. colonisation was of unquestionable benefit to the Arabs of the vicinity.

It is also very noticeable, in travelling through the P.I.C.A. villages, to see the friendliness of the relations which exist between

Jew and Arab. It is quite a common sight to see an Arab sitting in the verandah of a Jewish house. The position is entirely different in the Zionist colonies.

Zionist colonisation: the Arab.—In the Memorandum submitted by the Jewish agency attempts were made to establish that the purchase of the villages in the Esdraelon valley and their settlement by the Jews had not had the effect of causing the previous tenants to join the landless class. A list of the ejected tenants was submitted as an annex to the Memorandum, giving the subsequent employment of each one of these tenants in so far as they could be traced. The annex dealt with 688 tenants. The following is an extract from the Memorandum :—

> " . . . . Very few traced belong to the landless class; 437 are continuing farming—58 as harraths; 89 are shepherds—they were all shepherds before the evacuation, farming being with them a merely subsidiary occupation; 4 are craftsmen, 14 are merchants; 50 are urban labourers; 4 are vegetable vendors; 10 are camel drivers; 2 are milkmen; 37 died; 41 whereabouts unknown. In addition, out of the 688 not less than 154 have become property owners—that is, they now possess a house and lot of their own."

In explanation of the above statement it must be pointed out that a " harrath " is a farm servant; he is not a tenant farmer. The real result of this enquiry is to establish that of 688 Arab families which cultivated in the villages in the Vale of Esdraelon which were purchased and occupied by the Jews, only 379 are now cultivating the land. Three hundred and nine of these families have joined the landless classes. In the cases described as " died " it is not the family that is extinguished, but the head of the family who has died. Presumably, the descendants are still alive and earning their bread in some other walk of life than agriculture. It is also to be recorded that the number, 688, does not by any means include all the families who were displaced. According to the records of the Area Officers at Nazareth and Haifa, the number of " farmers " displaced from those villages was 1,270, nearly double the number accounted for in the Memorandum. In addition to farmers, there are, of course, many other residents who, though not in occupation, have interests in the land. With reference to these the District Commissioner, Northern District, writes :—

> " . . . . It appears quite clear that the persons who claimed, or at any rate who received compensations, by no means included all those who had interests in land, who according to the census figures amounted to 4,900. The census figures are usually taken as being about 20 per cent. below the truth, owing to the objections to a census which was connected with military service . . . ."

Government responsibility towards Arab cultivators.—The Jewish authorities have nothing with which to reproach themselves in the matter of the Sursock lands. They paid high prices for the land, and in addition they paid to certain of the occupants of those lands a considerable amount of money which they were not legally bound to pay. It was not their business, but the business of the Government to see to it that the position of the Arabs was not adversely affected by the transaction. In Article 6 of the Mandate it is the duty of the Administration of Palestine to ensure that the rights *and position* of the Arabs are not prejudiced by Jewish immigration. It is doubtful whether, in the matter of the Sursock lands, this Article of the Mandate received sufficient consideration.

P.L.D.Co.'s attitude towards Arab cultivators.—The question of the treatment of Arab cultivators on the lands purchased by Jewish agencies for development and settlement is already one of importance, and will become increasingly important as further purchases are made. It is a question which intimately concerns the good government of the country, and one to which the Administration of Palestine will doubtless direct its attention. The importance of the question was brought forcibly to notice by Mr. Hankin, an agent of the Palestine Land Development Company. In a letter dated 14th July, 1930, he writes:—

" . . . . Had we desired to disregard the interests of such workers of the land as are dependent, directly or indirectly, upon lands of the landlords, we could have acquired large and unlimited areas, but in the course of our conversation I have pointed out to you that this has not been our policy and that, when acquiring lands, it is our ardent wish not to prejudice or do harm to the interests of anybody. We feel it our duty to settle the workers and enable them to continue their agricultural occupation, either in the same place or elsewhere. But we have the possibility of acquiring 100,000 dunams without having to make any settlement for the tenants, since the acquisition of such an area will not cause harm to anybody and will not oust anybody from his lands; only after this area has been acquired we shall have to see to a proper settlement for the tenants . . . ."

The above is a translation from a Hebrew letter sent subsequent to an interview, of which the note records that Mr. Hankin said: " . . . . it is possible still to make arrangements for settling Arabs off 100,000 dunams which we may purchase . . . . but not after that. Then it will be necessary to make arrangements for the Arabs, as for the Jews, on the land purchased. They will have to be colonised, as the Jews, but it will be cheaper. For the Arab worker, £150; for the fellah, £300; for the Jewish worker, £300; for the Jewish cultivator, £600 to £700 . . . ."

At a later stage of this report the question of the sufficiency of land for Arab cultivators will be examined. It is sufficient at this stage to record the fact that Mr. Hankin, who has probably a more intimate knowledge than any other Jewish representative of the facts regarding agricultural land, is of the opinion that the balance of new land available for settlement at the moment is 100,000 dunams at the outside.

The effect of the Jewish colonisation in Palestine on the existing population is very intimately affected by the conditions on which the various Jewish bodies hold, sell and lease their land.

53

The Constitution of the Jewish Agency: Land Holding and Employment Clauses.—The Constitution of the Jewish Agency for Palestine was signed at Zürich on 14th August, 1929. Article 3 (*d*) and (*e*) read as follows :—

> " (*d*) Land is to be acquired as Jewish property and subject to the provisions of Article 10 of this Agreement, the title to the lands acquired is to be taken in the name of the Jewish National Fund, to the end that the same shall be held as the inalienable property of the Jewish people.
>
> " (*e*) The Agency shall promote agricultural colonisation based on Jewish labour, and in all works or undertakings carried out or furthered by the Agency, it shall be deemed to be a matter of principle that Jewish labour shall be employed . . . ."

Keren-Kayemeth draft lease: Employment of Jewish labour only.—I have been favoured with copies of the draft of the lease which it is proposed to execute in respect of all holdings granted by the Keren-Kayemeth (Jewish National Fund). The following is Article 23 of this lease :—

> " . . . . The lessee undertakes to execute all works connected with the cultivation of the holding only with Jewish labour. Failure to comply with this duty by the employment of non-Jewish labour shall render the lessee liable to the payment of a compensation of ten Palestinian pounds for each default. The fact of the employment of non-Jewish labour shall constitute adequate proof as to the damages and the amount thereof, and the right of the Fund to be paid the compensation referred to, and it shall not be necessary to serve on the lessee any notarial or other notice. Where the lessee has contravened the provisions of this Article three times the Fund may apply the right of restitution of the holding, without paying any compensation whatever."

The lease also provides that the holding shall never be held by any but a Jew. If the holder, being a Jew, dies, leaving as his heir a non-Jew, the Fund shall obtain the right of restitution. Prior to the enforcement of the right of restitution, the Fund must give the heir three months' notice, within which period the heir shall transfer his rights to a Jew, otherwise the Fund may enforce the right of restitution and the heir may not oppose such enforcement.

Keren-Hayesod Agreements: Employment of labour.—In the agreement for the repayment of advances made by the Keren-Hayesod (Palestine Foundation Fund) to settlers in the colonies in the Maritime Plain the following provisions are included :—

> " *Article 7.*—The settler hereby undertakes that he will during the continuance of any of the said advances, reside upon the said agricultural holding and do all his farm work by himself or with the aid of his family, and that, if and whenever he may be obliged to hire help, he will hire Jewish workmen only."

In the similar agreement for the Emek colonies there is a provision as follows :—

> " *Article 11.*—The settler undertakes to work the said holding personally, or with the aid of his family, and not to hire any outside labour except Jewish labourers."

54

Zionist policy in regard to Arabs in their colonies.—The above-quoted provisions sufficiently illustrate the Zionist policy with regard to the Arabs in their colonies. Attempts are constantly being made to establish the advantage which Jewish settlement has brought to the Arab. The most lofty sentiments are ventilated at public meetings and in Zionist propaganda. At the time of the Zionist Congress in 1921 a resolution was passed which " solemnly declared the desire of the Jewish people to live with the Arab people in relations of friendship and mutual respect, and, together with the Arab people, to develop the homeland common to both into a prosperous community which would ensure the growth of the peoples." This resolution is frequently quoted in proof of the excellent sentiments which Zionism cherishes towards the people of Palestine. The provisions quoted above, which are included in legal documents binding on every settler in a Zionist colony, are not compatible with the sentiments publicly expressed.

The same remark applies to the following extract from the Memorandum submitted by the General Federation of Jewish Labour to the " Palestine Commission of Enquiry " (i.e., the Commission on the Palestine disturbances of August, 1929) :—

> " The Jewish Labour Movement considers the Arab population as an integral element in this country. It is not to be thought of that Jewish settlers should displace this population, nor establish themselves at its expense. This would not only be impossible both from the political and economic standpoint, but it would run counter to the moral conception lying at the root of the Zionist movement. Jewish immigrants who come to this country to live by their own labour regard the Arab working man as their compatriot and fellow worker, whose needs are their needs and whose future is their future."

The effect of the Zionist colonisation policy on the Arab.—Actually the result of the purchase of land in Palestine by the Jewish National Fund has been that land has been extra-territorialised. It ceases to be land from which the Arab can gain any advantage either now or at any time in the future. Not only can he never hope to lease or to cultivate it, but, by the stringent provisions of the lease of the Jewish National Fund, he is deprived for ever from employment on that land. Nor can anyone help him by purchasing the land and restoring it to common use. The land is in mort-main and inalienable. It is for this reason that Arabs discount the professions of friendship and good will on the part of the Zionists in view of the policy which the Zionist Organisation deliberately adopted.

Reasons for the exclusion of the Arab.—Attempts were made to ascertain the reasons for these drastic provisions directed to exclude every Arab from the land purchased. The Executive of the General Federation of Jewish Labour were perfectly frank on the subject. They pointed out that the Jewish colonies were founded and established by Jewish capital, and that the subscriptions of which this capital is composed were given with the intention that Jews should emigrate to Palestine and be settled there—that these subscriptions would never have been given had it been thought that they would be employed to support Arab labourers—that it was the business of the Zionist Organisation to cause immigration into Palestine of as many Jews as possible, and that, if Arabs were employed, posts would thus be filled up for which Jews might have immigrated—that the position of agricultural labourer in the colonies, when occupied by a Jew, serves as a training for the immigrant and prepares him to take over a holding himself at a later date—and, finally, that if these posts were left open to the ordinary competition of the labour market, the standard of life of the Jewish labourer would be liable to fall to the lower standard of the Arab.

Policy contrary to Article 6 of Mandate.—All these arguments are thoroughly logical, and have a basis in fact. They are, however, irrelevant, in view of the provisions of Article 6 of the Mandate. The principle of the persistent and deliberate boycott of Arab labour in the Zionist colonies is not only contrary to the provisions of that article of the Mandate, but it is in addition a constant and increasing source of danger to the country. At the moment this policy is confined to the Zionist colonies, but the General Federation of Jewish Labour is using every effort to ensure that it shall be extended to the colonies of the P.I.C.A., and this with some considerable success. Great pressure is being brought to bear on the old P.I.C.A. colonies in the Maritime Plain and its neighbourhood—pressure which in one instance at least has compelled police intervention. As a symptom of that pressure may be cited the construction of a labour Kvutzoth (communal colony) on the outskirts of the P.I.C.A. village of Ness-ziona. It is certain that the employers of that village will not be able to resist the arguments of the General Federation, reinforced by the appeals of the vigorous labour colony at its gates.

That this replacement of Arab labour by Jewish labour is a definite policy of the Zionist Organisation is also evident from the following quotation, taken from " A Guide to Jewish Palestine " published by the Head Office of the Keren-Kayemeth Leisrael—The Jewish National Fund—and the Keren-Hayesod, at Jerusalem in 1930 :—

" . . . . up to the end of the war the old plantation settlements employed practically only Arab workers. The transfer of Jewish labourers into the old villages has been a source of constant care of the Zionist Executive, which latterly succeeded in placing approximately 6,500 workers in these centres, chiefly in the form of Havuroth, i.e., closely organised groups, which contract with farmers for specific pieces of work, and are themselves settled on small farms. Under this category come also the Yemenite settlements near the plantation villages . . . . "

It will be a matter of great regret if the friendly spirit which characterised the relations between the Jewish employer in the

P.I.C.A. villages and his Arab employees, to which reference has already been made, were to disappear. Unless there is some change of spirit in the policy of the Zionist Organisation it seems inevitable that the General Federation of Jewish Labour, which dominates that policy, will succeed in extending its principles to all the Jewish colonies in Palestine.

The present position, precluding any employment of Arabs in the Zionist colonies, is undesirable, from the point of view both of justice and of the good government of the country. As long as these provisions exist in the Constitution of the Zionist Organisation, in the lease of the Keren-Kayemeth and in the agreement of the Keren-Hayesod it cannot be regarded as desirable that large areas of land should be transferred to the Jewish National Fund. It is impossible to view with equanimity the extension of an enclave in Palestine from which all Arabs are excluded. The Arab population already regards the transfer of lands to Zionist hands with dismay and alarm. These cannot be dismissed as baseless in the light of the Zionist policy which is described above.

(iv) GOVERNMENT LANDS.

The question of the Government lands.

The Jewish Agency, and the Jewish community in general, are insistent in pressing their claim to all lands in the ownership of the Government. A list of these lands, and of other lands to which Government lays claim, or to which it has laid claim in the past are entered in Appendix No. 12 and their position is shown on Map No. 1.*

Huleh and Beisan.

The lands fall into various categories. The question of Huleh and of the Beisan lands is discussed at length in another portion of this report. In both of these cases the position is a " fait accompli ". If the Government wishes to obtain proprietary possession of the former Government lands in the Huleh Basin, it will either have to await the problematical chance of the denunciation of the concession, or to purchase the rights of the concessionnaire. In the case of the Beisan Chiftlik lands, the Government can only regain possession by purchase, or by expropriation on payment of compensation. These were the two most important and valuable areas of Government property, and are still those to which the eyes of the Jewish organisations are turned with longing and with invincible expectation.

Chiftlik Estates.

Of the areas still remaining, there is a class of property, which the Government has leased to the Arabs on the spot. The Government claims ownership. These Arabs have been in actual possession for very many years, and in certain cases claim that they

---

* *See* Note on page 3.

have rights, and have made application to be treated in the same manner as the tenants with whom the Ghor Mudawwara agreement was made in 1921. The following is the list of properties of this kind, with their areas :—

(1) Mansourah ... ... area 2,500 dunams
(2) Kokab ... ... area 3,750 do.
(3) Zalafieh ... ... area 2,700 do.
(4) Tel-el-Dahab ... ... area 2,400 do.
(5) Deir Ghazaleh ... ... area 2,700 do.
(6) Mazra'a el Hamra ... ... area 11,300 do.
(7) Akrabenieh ... ... area 960 do.
(8) El Farush ... ... area 1,656 do.
(9) Sajad ... ... area 7,000 do.
(10) Hamadieh ... ... area 500 do.
(11) Zeita ... ... area 5,350 do.
(12) Jaladiyeh ... ... area 4,143 do.
(13) Kofakha ... ... area 9,200 do.
(14) Muharraka ... ... area 4,580 do.
(15) Rafa ... ... area 90,000 do.

The Government share in the village of *Kokab* is 3-24th in an undivided village. If this share were to be transferred the other sharers would have the right of pre-emption.

A part of the *Rafa* lands was offered to the Jews, but for financial reasons was refused. The same is the case with *Tel Arad*. Part was offered to the Jews for settlement by ex-service men, but attempts to find water were not successful and the offer was not accepted.

In the general development of agricultural Palestine which will be recommended as the only solution of the present difficulties, the whole of these properties will doubtless be examined in detail and will fall into the appropriate place in the scheme which must be prepared. It is obvious that unless development is undertaken as a preliminary to closer settlement, the Arabs who are now existing on these properties can neither have their holdings reduced, nor can be expelled in order to make room for Jewish settlers.

Jazzair, which extends to about 418 dunams, is leased to an Arab tenant of long standing for 20 years.

Hassaniyeh, for which demands have been made, lies in the Safad sub-district. The claim of the villagers to this property has been recognised and it is no longer State Domain.

Dahnuneh and Mubarakeh, also in the Safad sub-district, have been settled with a Jewish Co-operative Society on a 50 years' lease. Their area is small.

Tob-Alti, at Acre, is largely occupied by the Agricultural Station, and by sites reserved for the Central Prison and for the Men's Elementary Training College. The balance consists of building sites, many of which have already been sold under a scheme initiated by the Ottoman Government.

The property of *Subeih*, in the Nazareth sub-district, was of the same class as the group of villages on which the Arab tenants are allowed to remain on payment of 10 per cent. of the gross produce as rent, which have been detailed above. The total area is 9,000 dunams. Of this, 2,000 dunams have been taken for the Jewish Agricultural School to be founded from the Kadoorie Bequest. The Government has agreed to sell the remaining portion of the village to the Arabs who are settled thereon and have been for at least the past century. There are reported to be 140 families, of whom 70 are actual cultivators and the rest graziers or workmen. Parts of the boundaries of the village lands are in dispute and the case is before the court.

The Government property in *Rakayik* has been leased to a Jew.

The *Acre Sands*, 12,225 dunams, have been reserved for exchange and lease to the Haifa Bay Development Company (now the Bayside Land Corporation)—a Jewish concern. When the Haifa Port is developed these lands are likely to become exceedingly valuable.

The *Kishon Lands* consist largely, if not entirely, of wadi beds drained by the Government, the work being done as a relief work for the Jewish unemployed in 1926-27. These lands are only 450 dunams in extent and should assuredly be reserved by the Government, in view of the keen demand for land in that neighbourhood, both for Government and other buildings on the completion of the Haifa Harbour works. The Jewish community already holds a large area of land in Haifa itself and in the immediate neighbourhood.

The *Rushmia* property, 3,385 dunams, occupies a large area on the Carmel ridge, and is in the immediate neighbourhood of Haifa. An application for a lease to the Jewish National Fund is under consideration. In view of the outlook for Haifa, this again will be a property of rapidly increasing value. It is fair that the enhanced value which results from the Government's expenditure at Haifa should redound to the financial advantage of the Government. This property is not an agricultural property in the ordinary sense. It will rapidly become a suburban property. The wiser course would seem to be to split up the property into blocks and dispose of these on long lease to individuals. If this land is leased to the Jewish National Fund, the result will be that no Arab can ever hope either to occupy a portion of the land or possibly to be employed thereon as a labourer or workman.

Athlit, *Kabbara* and *Caesarea* have already been granted to the P.I.C.A. under a concession. *Cherkaz* and *Hudeidoun* are occupied by the same organization. The two latter are small areas.

The *Toubas lands*, in the Nablus sub-district, are 41,700 dunams in extent and are occupied by Arab cultivators who have never acknowledged the Government claim to proprietary right. The Arabs have never paid rent and do not do so at present. It is reported to be very questionable whether the claim of the Government has any basis.

Bassat el Yaraki is a swamp. The total area is 2,500 dunams. The right to cut reeds in the swamp is sold annually. There are claims to grazing rights by certain Arab stock-breeders. It is stated that the swamp is not capable of economic drainage.

Basset el Mulabbis is already leased to the Jewish colony of Petach Tikvah.

There is litigation in progress on the subject of the *Jaffa sand-dunes*, which cover an area of 35,000 dunams. These are, of course, largely uncultivable. An area of 21,000 dunams is earmarked for lease to the Jewish colony of Rishon-le-Zion, subject to the result of the action in court.

The *Ahata* property, 15,000 dunams, lies on the road from Jerusalem to Jericho, in the ravines of the Judaean Hills. The ownership is disputed. The whole area is uncultivated and the major portion uncultivable.

There is a large area of land in the *Jericho Chiftlik* and *Es Suwaideh*, *Gharabeh* and *Jahayyer* lying between the Dead Sea and Jericho. Apart from the area irrigated from the Ain Sultan, there is only a small area of this land at present cultivable, and considerable development will be necessary to render any portion of it fit for cultivation. Irrigation is essential.

Of this area, 11,000 dunams were offered to Jewish organizations, but were refused as unsuitable.

Ain Feshka, on the Western shore of the Dead Sea, is uncultivable. The land is highly saline.

Near *Gaza* there are 6,000 dunams of sand-dunes, included in the list of Government properties. There is at the moment an action in Court on the question of ownership. These sand-dunes are in the main uncultivable and the tract is the site of the New Gaza.

The above deals in detail with all the Government properties to which the Jews have laid claim. Had different action been taken in the case of the Huleh Basin and the Beisan Lands, doubtless some portion of the demand could have been met. It is clear, however, that of the land which remains with the Government at the present time the area is exceedingly small, with the exception of tracts which, until developed, are required in their entirety for the maintenance of the Arabs already in occupation. It cannot be argued that Arabs should be dispossessed in order that the land should be made available for Jewish settlement. That would amount to a distinct breach of the provisions of Article 6 of the Mandate.

There will be an addition to the area of Government lands, and possibly a material addition, as the settlement proceeds and areas of Mewat are determined. Meanwhile the general idea that the Government has command of large areas which it could, but will not make over for Jewish settlement is far removed from the facts. This myth is based on a tradition of disappointment because of the action of the Government of Palestine in regard to the concession of Government lands in the Huleh Basin, and to the settlement of the area covered by the Ghor Mudawwara Agreement with the Arabs in possession of that area.

CHAPTER VI.

The Position of the Fellah.

Available information.—The present enquiry has fortunately occurred at a time when the question of the economic position of the fellah has formed the subject of two serious investigations. The first of these has been made by a Commission appointed by the Administration which, after a detailed enquiry into the position in 104 representative villages, submitted its report to the Government on July 3rd, 1930. The results of the second are recorded in a volume by Dr. Wilkansky, head of the Zionist Agricultural Experimental Station of Tel-Aviv. This volume is not yet published in English, but the proof sheets have been made available by the courtesy of Dr. Wilkansky for the purposes of this enquiry.

Area of cultivable land occupied by the Fellah.—The question of the cultivable area of Palestine has been examined in another part of this report, and the estimate of the Director of Surveys has been accepted as the most reliable available estimate. He puts the cultivable area of the whole of Palestine, including Beersheba, at 8,044,000 dunams. For the purposes of the present enquiry the Beersheba tract—as to whose area little is in fact known, and which depends on an erratic and insufficient rainfall—is omitted, and consideration directed to the cultivated areas in the Hill country and the Five Plains which have already been described. The total cultivable area of these two regions is 6,544,000 dunams. Of these at least 900,000 dunams are already in the possession of the Jews.* There are thus 5,644,000 dunams available for the Arabs at the present time.† This figure differs materially from the figure quoted by the Commission on the Disturbances on p. 113 of its Report, and used in the arguments on pp. 120 et seq.

---

* The total Jewish holdings are reported at 1,250,000 Turkish, *i.e.*, 1,149,000 metric dunams. Allowing 20 per cent. for uncultivable land, the remainder will exceed 900,000 dunams.

† There are some areas held by German colonists and certain ecclesiastical authorities, but they are comparatively so small that they need not be taken into account in this calculation.

61

The " Lot viable ".—On pp. 120 and 121 of their Report that Commission writes as follows :—

" .... Now, the area of land required to support the average family must vary with the fertility of the soil. From evidence given before us it would appear that where the land is used for the purpose of growing cereals the area which will provide a living for an Arab family varies from 100-150 dunams. No other figures were put forward from the Arab side, but Dr. Ruppin informed us that the average area of a Jewish colonist in the old wheat-growing colonies in Lower Galilee is 250 dunams, in the Zionist settlement in the Plain of Esdraelon with dairy-farming it is 100 dunams, and in the Coastal Plain, where orange growing is the principal occupation, it is 10-20 dunams.

" From the figures given by the experts who were appointed by the Joint Palestine Survey Commission and who visited Palestine in 1928, it would seem that the average Jewish holding of land in the Zionist colonies is to-day 130 dunams. These gentlemen found that few of the Jewish colonists were able to make a satisfactory living on their present holding. The experts were of opinion that in many districts the area of the average holding should be increased."

The joint Palestine Survey Commission, at p. 67 of their report, write the following :—

" Palestine experience shows that a dry farm should have from 40 to 80 acres, whether in the Coastal Plain or in the Emek, and that 60 acres is a safer limit than 40."

That is to say that in their opinion, the absolute minimum for a farm in either of those two areas is 160 dunams and that 240 dunams is a safer minimum than 160. It will be remembered that the Emek is looked upon as one of the most fertile regions of the country.

The " Lot viable ", the holding necessary to support its occupants in a reasonable standard of life, varies of course with the class of land of which the holding consists. Not only is there a wide difference between the unirrigated holding necessary for this purpose and the similar irrigated holding. Among dry holdings some are much more productive than others. For this reason it is impossible to fix any holding which might be taken as the standard holding in irrigated and unirrigated tracts respectively. Although it is true that no such standard holding can be taken, it is well to arrive at an approximate average holding for lands of various kinds. Many such averages have been suggested, and have been treated as to a certain extent authoritative.

The question of appropriate holdings in the various zones and for different types of farming have been discussed at length in a " Key for the Settlement of Various Zones in Palestine ", being the reports of the Preparatory Commissions appointed by the Zionist Organisation to consider the question of the preparation of the land for the settlement of Jewish immigrants. The Key was, it is understood, written by Dr. Wilkansky. On p. 6 the unit area of the ameliorated colonies on non-irrigated heavy soil is fixed at 200 to 250 dunams, though a few may be as small as 160 dunams. On pp. 16 to 20 is discussed the unit of an improved farm of fixed system. The basis of the farm is dairying, and it is assumed that the settler is supplied with six cows. For such a farm the unit required is 130 dunams. It is added : " With land not so well improved it will be necessary to add 10-20 dunams according to the fertility. In certain districts, therefore, the unit area will have to be increased to 140-150 dunams ".

Again, on p. 37, there is an estimate of the area required for a farm in the stage of transition, that is to say, when it is being improved for the reception of the settlers. At that stage one settler's family is put on to a double farm. When it is improved he retains one half and a second family is installed on the other half. The total area of the farm is 280 to 300 dunams, the size of the individual farm, again a dairy farm, being from 140 to 150 dunams. For a heavy soil farm, entirely irrigated and to support 8 cows, the area is estimated at p. 42 of the Key to be 25 dunams. Finally, at page 44, an estimate is given of a typical farm in a dry grain section, with 10 dunams of irrigated land, and the area required is found to be 80 dunams. Here again the basis is dairying, with four cows. In all the cases dealt with in the Key, the lot is so calculated as to be workable by the members of the family without any outside assistance. In all cases also the basic industry is dairying and the farm is planned for the feeding of cows. The anticipated yield of milk is in each case considerably higher than the milk yield of the common country cow.

An interesting piece of evidence on the subject of the " lot viable " is contained in the negotiations between the Administration and Mr. Ben Zvi of the General Federation of Jewish Labour, on the subject of a grant of land at Tel-Arad for Jewish ex-service men. An area of 200 dunams per settler was demanded. It was pointed out by the High Commissioner that in other cases 70 dunams had been granted to settlers. Mr. Ben Zvi maintained that this was where there were plantations and that the P.I.C.A. allowed 250 dunams for each family. Later he stated that 200 dunams was the minimum that would suffice for a family and this basis was accepted.

Saleem eff Farah was of the opinion that 150 dunams of unirrigated land is the minimum which will support the family of the fellah in a reasonable standard of comfort.

In the Memorandum on " Land and Agricultural Development ", submitted by the Jewish Agency, the question of the lot viable in various areas is dealt with. In the Emek it is calculated at 100 to 150 dunams. Where water is available, the area can be reduced at the ratio of one dunam of irrigated soil to four or five dunams of dry soil. In the " Key " to which reference has been made above, Dr. Wilkansky considered one dunam of irrigated soil as equivalent to three dunams of unirrigated soil. In the Maritime Plain irrigated areas suitable for oranges can be settled on the basis of one family to 15 dunams, if only partly suitable for oranges one family to 22 dunams.

Dealing with the Huleh area the Memorandum of the Jewish Agency considers that 25 dunams of irrigated heavy soil or 22 dunams of irrigated light soil should be sufficient for a holding.

Mr. Hankin, on the other hand, considered 40 dunams, of which half irrigated, as the correct holding. The experts of the Jewish Agency are of the opinion that 25 dunams are sufficient in the case of the Beisan and Semakh lands if irrigated, and recommend 86 dunams of unirrigated and 14 of irrigated in that area. On the slopes and the heights to the north of the Haifa Semakh railway line they consider 150 dunams necessary. For the Lower Jordan valley a standard holding of 21 dunams is suggested. This suggestion is made tentatively and admittedly without close detailed knowledge.

The most surprising suggestion on this question of the "lot viable" is contained in an Appendix to the Jewish Agency Memorandum, supplied by Dr. Joseph Weiz. He deals with the Hill country and alleges that the area that can be cultivated is 5,137,495 dunams. This compares with the estimate of the Director of Surveys of 2,450,000 dunams. The basic lot should, he suggests, consist of 30 dunams, 10 dunams containing olive and fig trees, eight containing fruit-trees, seven containing grape-vines, and five occupied by the farmyard and vegetable patch. By arranging in this manner he concludes that there would be room for a further 74,000 families in the Hills. It is difficult to take the proposal as a serious contribution to the study of this important subject. That Dr. Weiz has his doubts may be concluded from the last sentence of his note :—

> "Even if a further reserve of 50 per cent. is made, it would follow that there would be room for the additional settlement of 35,000 families in the Hill country during the next thirty years."

The report of the Committee on the Economic Condition of Agriculturists records the opinion, at page 32 of the report, that :—

> "To provide the minimum cost of living for a family, a holding of 75 dunams seems to be necessary for an owner-cultivator while a tenant requires 130 dunams."

This opinion was arrived at on a consideration of the gross return from the holding at the prices of the years 1924 to 1928. As has been shown elsewhere, present-day prices are but 50 per cent. of those adopted by the Committee in arriving at its deductions.

A detailed investigation was made into the conditions in the village of Beer Zeit, in the Hill country, for the purpose of this enquiry. Of the cultivation 27.4 per cent. consisted of olive groves 8.2 per cent. of figs and other fruit-trees, 17.8 of vines and 46.6 of cereals. It was found that there were 180 families in the village, that the "lot viable" was 112 dunams, and that the village could only provide holdings of that area for 65 families. There were therefore 115 families in excess of the number which the village could actually support. The total debt of the village amounts to £7,000, an average of about £39 per family. The sources of maintenance beside cultivation were remittances from persons who had emigrated to America from the village, daily labour in the village and elsewhere, and additional borrowing from the moneylenders. And Beer Zeit is regarded as a village above the average of Hill villages in prosperity.

Conclusion.—It is clear that in unirrigated land the " lot viable " is not less than 130 dunams, unless command of considerable capital enables the tenant to maintain a dairy herd of foreign or cross-bred animals, in which case in the richer tracts, the holding may possibly, but questionably, be reduced to 100 dunams. Where irrigation is available and where dairying is possible, the holding may be reduced to 40 dunams of which half irrigable. Where plantations are established the " lot viable ", at present prices of Jaffa oranges and bananas, may be placed at 15 to 20 dunams.

Economic position of the fellah.—Evidence from every possible source tends to support the conclusion that the Arab fellah cultivator is in a desperate position. He has no capital for his farm. He is, on the contrary, heavily in debt. His rent is rising, he has to pay very heavy taxes, and the rate of interest on his loans is incredibly high. On the other hand, he is intelligent and hardworking, and pitifully anxious to improve his standard of cultivation and his standard of life. And very little has been done for him in the past.

Distribution of available area.—It has been shown that there are about 61,408 fellah families who cultivate some 5,644,000 dunams of land. This gives an average holding of 91.9 dunams per family. It is true, as pointed out in the memorandum of the Jewish Agency on the Report of the Commission on the Disturbances, that there are a number of Arabs who cultivate orange groves and vegetables. Their number, however, is not material to the argument and may be set off against the reduction in the area due to the German villages and to a certain area of agricultural land held by some of the churches.

The enquiry of the Commission on the Economic Condition of Agriculturists in 104 villages resulted in a very different estimate. In the cases of 16,633 families it was found that the average holding was 75.00 dunams per family. It was also established that of 23,573 families resident in those villages only 5,477 farmers live entirely from agriculture. Of these 3,873 hold over 240 dunams and 1,604 from 120-240 dunams. Not a single farmer who held less than 120 dunams was able to live on the produce of his farm without outside employment, and of 3,261 holding from 120-240 dunams 1,657 found it necessary to procure employment in addition to their farming, in order to maintain themselves and their families. From this it is quite clear that 120 dunams is not a lot sufficient to support a fellah family with cereal cultivation. This bears out the opinion of the Experts quoted by the Commission on the Disturbances on p. 121 of their Report, to the effect that the area required for a holding varies from 160 dunams per family in good soil suitable for dairy farming, to 320 dunams in the less productive soil of the cereal-growing districts. In fact the average existing fellah holding is insufficient to maintain anything like a decent standard of life.

The requirements and standard of life of the Fellah.—The life of the fellah is one of great struggle and privation. The Director of Education, in the course of a note, makes the following remarks :—

"The economic state of the agricultural population is desperate. Hardly any Arab village exists which is not in debt. The fellahin are so over-taxed that they find great difficulty in paying the tithe. Moreover, after an excellent harvest, they are unable to sell their corn or barley or oil. In 15 villages recently visited by the writer in Galilee, the same desperate state of affairs was evident. Money is so scarce in some places that the people purchase the necessities of life by barter, and they cannot pay the tithe without further borrowing. This means increasing their already overwhelming debt to the moneylender . . . . 'We have been struggling in deep water for several years, and very soon the water will close over our heads' was the statement made in one village, which may be taken as typical of the state of mind in every village . . . .

"If the state of the Arab fellah is to be improved, and it is evidently one of the most important problems which face the Administration in Palestine, his children must be given an education which will help them to avoid falling into the situation in which the present generation finds itself to-day."

Dr. Wilkansky writes as follows :—

" . . . . The diet of the fellah is poor and monotonous. His staple food is 'pittah,' [cake of unleavened bread] which he bakes every day. A few pittahs, with onions or radishes form his morning and midday meals. A cooked meal, called by him 'tabiach,' is only prepared for him in the evening. It consists of the herb—'hubza'—flavoured with onions and pepper. When tomatoes are in season he eats tomato salad flavoured with pepper. Pepper and oil are his two condiments. Most of his requirements are provided by his own fields, and he buys but little outside . . . . The fellah uses very little meat. For entertaining visitors he will kill a sick sheep, or some sick fowls. They also have meat when an ox or a camel falls ill beyond recovery. They then kill the animal and treat the members of the village with a portion of the flesh. Sometimes with the money which the woman obtains in the market from the sale of fowls, cheese and eggs, she purchases a pair of trotters, a head or so forth, from which she prepares a special treat on returning home."

The Fellah's capital.—The fellah may or may not own his land but he has no free working capital. The amount invested in his farm is detailed by Dr. Wilkansky as follows :—

	£
Oxen, or a camel	15 to 20
1 ass	3 to 4
1 plough	0.40
1 threshing board	0.60
2 wooden picks	0.15
1 iron pick	0.20
7 sacks for straw	0.60
1 scythe (?sickle)	0.10
1 yoke or pole	0.60
Ropes for binding	0.30
2 sieves	0.25
Total	£21.20 to £27.20

In addition he may have 20 sheep worth £1 each, a cow worth £6-£10, a goat worth £0.80 to £1, and 30 fowls £3 to £4, making a grand total of £51 to £62.20.

The fellah's plough.—It is a common impression that the fellah's cultivation is entirely inadequate, and a good deal of ridicule has been and is poured upon the nail-plough which he uses. In the stony country of the Hills no other plough would be able to do the work at all. With regard to the use of that plough, Dr. Wilkansky writes :—

> " . . . . The Arab plough is like the ancient Hebrew plough . . . . Its distinguishing characteristic is that it cuts the surface soil and does not turn it up. It performs, very slowly, it is true, but very thoroughly, all the functions for which a combination of modern machines is required —a plough, a roller and a harrow. Its great virtues are that it does not bring up clods, that it does not press or crush the moist earth, but flits as it were over the ground with its coulter which resembles a duck's foot in its base, and that it penetrates the ground with its point, which is sharp and long like the head of a spear. It produces the requisite loose and broken crust by itself, without the aid of other implements. . . . . But the ploughing of the fellah is above reproach. His field, prepared for sowing, is never inferior to that prepared by the most perfect implements, and sometimes it even surpasses all others. The defect lies only in the slowness, which calls for modification in order to adapt the working process to the rate of speed in our time."

The fellah as a cultivator.—The fellah is neither lazy nor unintelligent. He is a competent and capable agriculturist, and there is little doubt that were he to be given the chance of learning better methods, and the capital, which is a necessary preliminary to their employment, he would rapidly improve his position. Meanwhile, however, the income which he can procure from his inadequate farm is insufficient to maintain him in a decent standard of comfort and leaves no margin whatever for improvements.

The method on which the average cereal farm of the fellah is worked is that the holding is divided into two areas. In one of the areas he sows his winter crops, while the other lies fallow. In this fallow portion, in the spring, the summer crop is sown; in the former portion, after reaping the winter crops in May and June, the land lies fallow until the following spring, when the summer crops are sown. In the latter portion, after the reaping of the summer crop, the winter crop is at once sown. Thus in each portion two crops, one summer and one winter, are taken in two years.

The return from the fellah's farm.—The return from a farm of 120 dunams is very small. The gross income is estimated at £40, of which £10 is payable as tithe, leaving £30 for the family expenses of the year. (Mr. Smilansky's pamphlet : " The Jewish Colonisation and the Fellah "). Dr. Wilkansky has made a detailed estimate of the income and expenditure of an ordinary fellah on a holding of 80-100 dunams in his work on " The Fellah's Farm," to which reference has already been made. This estimate

67

and estimates contained in the report of the Committee on the Economic Condition of Agriculturists are included in Appendix 18.

In connection with Dr. Wilkansky's estimate it is to be remarked that nothing is shown as payable for rent, also, that income is shown from milk, but nothing on the expenditure for the feeding of the cow. The balance available for personal expenditure of the whole household for a year is 18s. This sum has to meet all luxury expenditure, including expenditure on the purchase of meat and this for five or six persons.

Deductions from the figures supplied by 104 *villages.*—In the enquiry conducted by the Committee on the Economic Condition of Agriculturists, returns were made showing the gross income declared as received from all sources in the 104 villages in question. This declaration was revised by the Committee on the basis of average prices of the previous four years taken in 1928 for the purpose of commutation of the Tithe. In the Committee's estimate also the total produce reported by the villages was revised to agree with the average yields per dunam used for the commutation of the Tithe. The returns thus calculated given in that Report are appended to this Report in Appendix 13. Prices have fallen very materially since the commutation of the Tithe in 1928, and a calculation has been made of the gross income of the 104 villages, applying the prices prevailing in May, 1930. The sum reached is £306,043, as compared with the declared return of £301,999, and the Committee's calculation of £483,600. The yield accepted by the Committee has been taken as the actual yield for the purposes of the new calculation. That on which the declaration was based is considerably smaller. (For yields, *see* Appendix 24.)

On the figures adopted by the Committee the gross average yield of 100 dunams of field crops only amounts to £51. On the revised figures now calculated it is £32.

The above figures refer only to the income from the field crops. From fruit trees, stock, dairy produce, poultry and other village sources, and from transport and labour outside the village there was a declared income of £242,882. This figure was examined in detail by the Committee. They have raised it to £429,070. They have, however, continued to take the prices on which the Commuted Tithe was based rather than existing prices. For instance, they estimate the value of olive-oil at £53 a ton, while the present price is but £33 a ton. Making an adjustment on this account a figure of £388,373 may be accepted as the income from other sources than crops. Thus the following result is reached:—

	£
Declaration made by the villages as total income	544,881
Income as calculated by the Committee	912,670
Income as now calculated	694,416

The gross income per family on the above totals works out at £P.23.050, £P.38.350, and £P.29.20 respectively. Out of this amount has to be met (a) expenses of production, estimated by the Committee at £P.22; (b) Taxes, calculated at £P.5; (c) The maintenance of the fellah and his family. The household expenditure is shown by Dr. Wilkansky to be £P.49.50. In none of the cases, therefore, does the total income cover the essential expenses of the cultivator.

The fellah's debts.—In addition to these facts it must be borne in mind that the average holding of 104 villages is not 100 dunams, but 75 dunams, and that the average debt per family amounts to £P.27, on which the rate of interest of 30 per cent. is usual, that is to say, that for interest alone the family must pay £P.8 per annum. The rate of 30 per cent. is regarded as quite reasonable, and is indeed exceeded in many cases. It is a usual practice for the moneylender or the merchant to make an advance on terms known as "ashara-hamastash," which means that a sum of £P.10 advanced at the time of sowing is repaid by a sum of £P.15 at the time of harvest. Another common arrangement is interest at the rate of 1s. in the pound per month.

Legal rate of interest.—In regard to this question of interest, it is true that the legal rate of interest is 9 per cent. per annum. This law is a dead letter. There are many obvious methods of evasion, and even were there no such methods, no fellah would dare to defend himself by means of this law, as he would unquestionably close to himself the door of the moneylender for ever. Without the moneylender he cannot live.

Financial situation of the Fellah.—As to the financial situation of the Arab farmer the Committee on the Economic Condition of Agriculturists write :—

> " . . . . Up till the middle of 1929, the net income of the average agricultural family has been between £25 and £30, and the family has contrived to live on this income. It is clear, however, that there must have been many families less favourably situated, who have been obliged either to lower their standard of living or to fall into debt . . . many farmers now owe sums that are quite beyond their capacity to pay . . . ."

At another place they write :—

> " . . . . We think that it may safely be assumed that, with very rare exceptions, every village can provide its own subsistence even if the standard of living may fall slightly below the figure we have estimated. The farmer is often—perhaps habitually—short of ready cash, but there is no evidence that he or his family are ever without sufficient food for their subsistence . . . ."

It should be remarked that between the middle of 1929, to which period the Committee refer in discussing the net income of any agricultural family, and the month of July, 1930, the price of agricultural produce fell heavily. In the graph appended to this report (No. 1) it is seen that the price of wheat fell in the twelve. months in question from £11 to £6 per ton, that of barley from £5 to £3, and that of durrah from £8 to £4. The net income of the family cannot therefore now be regarded as £P.24 or £P.30. It has reached vanishing point. The calculation of the Committee showing that the net return of 100 dunams to the owner-cultivator is £P.35.200 and to the tenant £P.20, has been revised on the basis of the prices of July 1930. The calculation is contained in Appendix 15 to this report. The result shows a net return of £P.11.800 mils in the case of the owner-cultivator and £P.3.600 mils to the tenant.

From this the interest on debt—on the average not less than £8 per family—clothes for the whole family, and all other living expenses, must be met. It is no exaggeration to state that the fellah population as a class is hopelessly bankrupt.

Commutation of the Tithe and the result of the fall in prices — The position of the Arab cultivator has always been one of extreme poverty, but there are at the present time certain circumstances which render it more desperate than has been the case in the past. In the year 1928, steps were taken to commute the Tithe. This payment was based on the average yields and prices of the four preceding years. Since that time there has been a progressive fall of prices of agricultural produce. (Vide Appendix 14.) During the present year the fall has become more rapid and more pronounced. As a result, the Arab cultivator has now to sell, not one-tenth, but one-fifth of his crop in order to pay the Tithe in cash. Indeed, in many cases the amount is more than one-fifth for the prices for commutation of the Tithe were based not on prices of the village but on those of the market town, and the two rates vary largely. In addition, the price of sale is lower than the price of purchase, and the price of forced sale is still lower. At the time of this enquiry actual prices of sale were in certain cases extraordinary. Villages found it exceedingly difficult to sell at all, and there was an established case reported in which barley was sold at Gaza at £P.2 a ton, when the quoted market price was £P.3.100, itself a price exceedingly low.

Diminution of the size of holdings.—There is also a progressive diminution in the areas of the holdings; in every village visited there were complaints on this score. Portions of the holdings have been sold either to pay off debts or to pay the Government taxes or to obtain the wherewithal to keep the family alive.

The population of the villages is increasing faster than in Turkish times, owing in large measure to the cessation of conscription. There is consequently increasing competition for land, and division of holdings among the increased number of members of the family.

Rise in rents.—Rents are rising; those who wish to rent land find it difficult to obtain it, and offer rents which frequently cannot be paid and yet leave a surplus for the maintenance of the family in a standard of reasonable comfort. Cases were reported in which fellahin who desired to obtain land offered 50 per cent. of the produce, the landlord paying the Tithe. The Committee reports that the commonest rent is 30 per cent. of the produce, the tenant paying the Tithe, or 40 per cent., the Tithe falling on the landlord. Money rents are now beginning to appear in some parts of the country, as was to be expected as a consequence of the commutation of the Tithe. These rents vary from about 50 mils to 250 mils the dunam. The most common is 100-150 mils (i.e., 2s. to 3s.). Above it has been reported that the gross income from 100 dunams of field crops is £32 at present prices. At 3s. a dunam the rent would be £15 for 100 dunams, that is, equal to about 47 per cent. of the gross income. One case reported has reference to land owned, but not yet settled, by Jews, of which Arab tenants in an adjoining village rent 5,600 dunams. Up to the year 1926-27 the cultivators paid 20 per cent. of the produce in kind. Since then, the lease has been put up to public auction and in 1927-28 produced £260, in 1928-29 £400, and in 1929-30 £525. It is not suggested that the rent is even now excessive, but the rise of more than 100 per cent. in the past three years demonstrates the amount of competition that exists for land.

Warrants and imprisonment for debt.—A further symptom of the economic position of the Arab cultivator is found in the number of cases in which it is necessary to issue warrants for debt. Attempts were made to collect information on this point, but it has been found difficult to concentrate figures. The Supreme Court gave information with respect to warrants issued for debt in all districts during the first two months of the present year, except in the district of Jaffa, for which the figures were not available, and the actual imprisonment figures for Haifa, which were not reported. The statement is therefore not complete, but even so it shows that in the two months in the area included in the return 2,677 warrants were issued for debt and 599 persons imprisoned.

A report on this point was received from the Director of Agriculture in respect of the Haifa district for the past year. From this it appears that in the Magistrates' Court at Haifa alone and for the Sub-district of Haifa, with a population estimated at 67,800, there were heard 8,701 proceedings for debt, issued 4,872 orders for execution and filed 2,756 applications for imprisonment for debt. Assuming that the average family consists of 5 persons, the total number of families in the Sub-district was 13,560. The execution proceedings taken were thus in number equal to 64.2 per cent. of the number of families of the Sub-district. According to the census of 1922 the Jewish population represented less than 20 per cent. of the population of this Sub-district.

Taxes on agriculture.—The taxes paid by agriculturists are :—
    (1) The Tithe.
    (2) The Werko.
    (3) The Animal Tax.

71

In addition the agriculturist pays indirect taxes upon imported goods which he purchases, and fees on registration when land is transferred.

Tithe.—1. The Commuted Tithe has now replaced the tithe, except in the case of a small number of Bedu tribal areas in the Beersheba Sub-district, where the Tithe at the rate of 10 per cent. of the produce of the land is still collected in money. As has been noted above, the commutation of the Tithe was carried through in 1928. In Appendix 14 of this report the market prices of the chief crops during the four years of which the prices formed the basis of commutation, the rate adopted for conversion and the market rate of July, 1930, are shown.

House and Land Tax.—2. The Werko is the house and land tax, authorised by the Ottoman Law of 5th August, 1886. It is assessed on capital value, and at various rates which are shown in Appendix 16. The rate on lands subject to Tithe, and on ordinary farm buildings is 4 per mille. An addition to this tax aggregating 41 per cent. on buildings and 56 per cent. on lands was levied from time to time by Ottoman Decree, and is still collected, except in the case of buildings and lands re-assessed since 1919.

The Animal Tax.—3. The Animal Tax is imposed per capita once annually at the following rates :—

Sheep and goats	48 mils.
Camels and buffaloes	120 mils.
Pigs	90 mils.

Camels and buffaloes used solely for ploughing are exempt from the tax. Double taxes are charged on all animals not declared by the owners at the time of enumeration.

Recovery of taxes.—The following note was prepared by the District Officer of Jaffa on the question of the taxation of the fellah.

" .... The information given .... at Lydda, that sometimes a man's whole crop is attached for taxes is correct. The further statement, however, that he is prevented from selling a part of it in order to redeem the rest needs qualification .... The crop of the villager is the only thing that a revenue officer can find if he wants to attach for taxes. This crop can be got hold of only before threshing. ... The only way to do this is to place a guard during the time that threshing is going on. This guard fully gives the impression that no crop may be disposed of before the tax is paid. He is, of course, kept at the expense of the defaulters, and his wages are an additional burden. Rather than pay these wages the defaulters often incur debt in order to pay off the tax and get rid of the guard. The impression therefore remains that attachment could not be removed until the whole tax is paid. In fact the villager finds a great deal of difficulty in threshing, and then selling just a part of his crop while attachment is going on at his expense. To deal with a small crop in bits is not easy, nor is the disposal of it in small quantities easy. It means a special journey to town, where he may have to spend a day or two before he can sell and get his money . . . . In many cases, the only way out of it has been to incur debt . . . . In conclusion, I feel it is my duty to mention a frank opinion in regard to the collection of taxes in the villages . . . . I believe that at least 50 per cent. of the rural population, on account of their very small incomes, which do not exceed £30 per annum per family of six persons, ought to be relieved from all taxation. To such persons the price of crops is immaterial, as they have practically nothing surplus to sell. . . . . The villagers . . . . have in these cases paid, by allowing themselves to suffer privations or by incurring debt . . . . I am . . . . thoroughly convinced that if these villagers were to refuse payment and say ' we are sorry, but we would pay if we only could ', we should find ourselves totally unable to collect the taxes by legal methods. This is a point which deserves the serious consideration of Government . . . . I submit therefore that it is essential that a minimum be exempt from taxes with as little delay as possible. The amount which these villagers pay is not great, but in proportion to their income it is excessive."

The above has been quoted at some length, as it is typical of the complaints and proposals made in every quarter. The holding of the fellah is so small, and his out-turn so exiguous that the agricultural tax falls on him with special force. And this is aggravated by the present fall in prices. Everywhere this year the small cultivator has had to borrow in order to pay his taxes, when he has paid them. In very many cases he has found it impossible to pay them at all. The arrears of agricultural taxes are very heavy. In Appendix 17 a statement of these arrears is shown. It gives a total of £238,000.

Taxation: Remedial measures —Of the seriousness of this question of agricultural taxation evidence is afforded in the Report of the Committee on the Economic Condition of Agriculturists. The Committee found that the Tithe and Animal Tax together amounted to 19 per cent. of the net return from the use of land. The net return was reached by deducting from the assumed gross return the cost of production and the rent. But in arriving at the figure of net return they used prices of the Tithe commutation which are admittedly double those of the market to-day. The incidence of taxation would therefore be much higher if to-day's prices were applied. In fact, the Tithe, in place of being 10 per cent. of gross income, as it was at the time of commutation, is to-day actually 20 per cent. of the gross income.

Government action to relieve the burden of taxation.—The whole question of taxation is at present engaging the attention of the Palestine Government. At the moment the burden is not adjusted to the various classes of the community in accordance with their ability to pay. It is intended to replace the Tithe and the Werko by a land tax fixed in accordance with the quality of the land. The settlement is being carried out with this intention. Until it is possible to impose such a tax, the Tithe should be entirely remitted, if feasible. If it is found financially impossible to grant this measure of relief, as a temporary measure it might be possible to vary the Tithe in accordance with the variation of the market prices of agricultural produce. As at the present time these prices stand at about half of the prices at the time the Tithe was commuted, the relief so afforded would amount to about 50 per cent.

THE BEDUIN POPULATION.

One of the problems of land administration in Palestine lies in the indefinite rights of the Beduin population. The problem was discussed by Mr. Snell in his Note of Reservations at pp. 177 and 178 of the Report of the Commission on the Disturbances. His examination does not lead to any specific recommendation and it is indeed exceedingly difficult to arrive at any definite conclusion on the subject of the treatment of the Beduin.

Of these nomads there were estimated to be 103,331 belonging to five main Tribes and 75 sub-Tribes at the time of the census of 1922, but it is generally agreed that this figure is inaccurate. The majority of these Beduin wander over the country in the Beersheba area and the region south and east of it, but they are found in considerable numbers in the Jordan valley and in smaller numbers in the four other plains. Their rights have never been determined. They claim rights of cultivation and grazing, of an indefinite character and over indefinite areas. Mr. Snell recorded that they have established a traditional right to graze their cattle on the fellah's land after the harvest. In the region which they regard as their own, they divide the country among their various tribes, and in the tract recognised as the sphere of a tribe, the Sheikhs or the Tribal Elders divide the individual plots among the families of the tribe.

The position is unsatisfactory. If, for instance, artesian water were discovered in the Beersheba area, there is little doubt that claims would immediately be urged, by the tribes of the Beersheba tract, to the land commanded by that water.

The Beduin are an attractive and a picturesque element in the life of the country, but they are an anachronism wherever close development is possible and is desired. At the same time their existence cannot be overlooked. In any solution of the Palestine problem, they are an element which must be recognised. Also in any plans of development it will be necessary carefully to consider, and scrupulously to record and deal with their rights

Complaints are made by these people in respect of the Jewish settlement both in the Vale of Esdraelon and in the Maritime Plain. A deputation of the Sheikhs of the Beersheba Sub-district stated that they had been in the habit of taking their stock up to the North of Palestine during the summer months when there is no grazing in the South, and that it had been their invariable custom to graze their flocks and herds on the stubbles after the harvest had been carried. This allegation is generally characterized as baseless, but in the report of the Department of Health for the year 1929, it is recorded that Beduin Tribes from the Beersheba District were " heavily infected " with malaria, " during their migrations up the Jordan Valley." It is also known that they bring their flocks of camels up to the tract north of Jericho during the calving season. It is also true that a few years ago when there was serious drought in the South of Palestine, very large numbers of animals belonging to the Beduin were transported to the North of Palestine, where they were allowed to graze.

At the time of inspection of the Wadi Hawareth lands a large number of Beduin tents were found in that area. It was stated that their migration to this region is a new departure and is connected with the attempt to defeat the efforts of the Jews to colonize that tract. This information comes from Jewish sources. From Arab sources it was alleged that the migration was annual, in connection with the summer grazing.

Their rights in the Jordan Valley will require careful enquiry before any scheme of development and settlement is undertaken in that area. If rights are established, and the tract over which they extend is necessary to the scheme, the Beduin must be compensated for the loss of those rights. The future of the Beduin is a question bristling with difficulties and by no means free from anxiety. It must be faced and a definite policy adopted. Otherwise there is always the danger that an outbreak may occur over some trivial and casual circumstance. It is impossible to anchor these people in houses or in villages. It may be that the only possible policy will be to create for them a reserve, which will be apart and excluded from the area designated for development.

CHAPTER VII.

Agricultural Development.

A. Existing Agencies.

Jewish Agencies for agricultural development.

The Experimental Station.—One of the important and progressive branches of Jewish activity in Palestine is the scientific development of agriculture. The Experimental Station of Tel-Aviv, with its extension farms in various settlements in the country, is not only engaged in research work of the highest value to Palestinian agriculture in general, but it is also the centre of agricultural instruction for the Jewish settlements. The Institution was founded in 1922, and since that year some £85,500 has been spent on its equipment and maintenance. It is staffed by 40 scientists, has three laboratory divisions, (Plant Pathology,. Entomology, Agricultural Chemistry) and seven field divisions (Agronomy, Plant breeding and Variety testing, Horticulture, Horticultural breeding, Farm Management and Rural Economics, Dairy husbandry and the Extension Division).

The Extension Division.—The Extension Division is of great importance for practical agriculturists. It not only maintains demonstration fields, but also nine district instructors under a chief of division. The services of these instructors are available for any of the settlers who desire to refer to them. In the division of dairy husbandry the Institution is carrying out experiments in conjunction with the Empire Marketing Board on the questions of the uniformation of the herd, of the substitution of other feeding stuffs for milk in the rearing of calves and of the proper feeding rations for cows and calves.

The Hebrew University.—In addition to the Agricultural Experimental Station of Tel-Aviv with its extension farms, agricultural work of a scientific character is also done by qualified research chemists and analysts at the Hebrew University of Jerusalem.

Department of Agriculture of the Palestine Government.

The third agency for Agricultural Development is the Department of Agriculture of the Palestine Government. This Department has done outstanding work in two practical directions—in locust campaigns and in veterinary service, which has succeeded in stamping out the cattle plague. In both of these directions the work has been of untold value to the country. The Department has a very limited budget, and a criticism may be allowed that it has not the money requisite for practical demonstration work, work which is of particular importance in a country where agricultural practice is eminently backward.

The Agricultural Department is a composite Department, comprising the following services :—Agriculture, Forestry, Veterinary, Horticultural, Entomological, Irrigation, Fisheries, Stock-breeding, Analytical, Sericultural, Meteorological. It also controls the Kadoorie agricultural schools, which were founded with funds left for the purpose by a generous and wealthy Jew.

Expenditure.—The expenditure of the Department was £76,713 in 1929, and the estimate for 1930 was £77,054.

Relations with Jewish agencies for agricultural development.—There is a danger that the Government services will overlap the services supported by Jewish agencies and the Hebrew University.

This danger was early recognised by the Director of Agriculture, who wrote in 1921 :—

" . . . . The need for elasticity was pointed by a comprehensive programme of agricultural research drafted by the Zionist Commission early in 1920. This undertaking promised to limit our financial responsibility if correlation of effort could be secured. It was consequently agreed at a Conference held in June 1920 that certain clearly defined branches of investigation should be left to the Commission's technical advisers . . . . It was nevertheless decided that as Zionist co-operation was assured at no distant date, certain emergency services should be created to meet existing needs, irrespective of final plans for an organisation entailing considerable capital expenditure and a permanent staff."

Insufficiency of Budget Allotments.—At the moment, the Government services are hampered for want of money, and some of them are so poorly equipped with funds that it seems questionable whether their continuance is desirable. In the case of the Fisheries Service, for instance, and the Sericultural Service the major portion of the funds are spent in salaries. The former service costs £1,589 in personal emoluments, and the balance of expenditure is £300 for the maintenance of a launch and £400 for investigations. The grant-in-aid for sericulture is £450, of which £300 is the salary of the expert. Similarly, in the stock-breeding service, salaries account for £3,651, while other expenditure amounts to £2,060, namely :—

	£
Forage	360
Stock-breeding service	1,100
Purchase of stock	600

Budget.—In the estimates for 1930 the total budget for agriculture and forests is £77,054. Of this the total of personal emoluments is £45,009, leaving £32,045 for other expenditure.

Development activities.—From the point of view of the agriculturists, the chief activities of the Agricultural Department, apart from the locust campaign and the eradication of the cattle plague, which have already been mentioned, consist in the maintenance of the Agricultural Experimental Stations at Acre and Beisan, and the Horticultural Experimental Stations at Jerusalem and Jericho. The Beisan station is not fully utilised, owing to stringency in the budget. The Acre Station is an excellently organised institution and is reported to be visited by many interested cultivators. The Horticultural Stations both at Jerusalem and Jericho serve useful purposes, but in the case of the latter financial resources do not permit of full development. The Department maintains a staff of peripatetic instructors. It also issues many leaflets.

The stock-breeding service.—Its stock-breeding service provides pure-bred South Devon bulls for crossing purposes, and has now several bulls of the first cross. Some of these are very popular animals with the fellah cultivators. At the Acre station a number of pure-bred Arab stallions were imported from England in the hope of improving the local breed of horses. An outbreak of dourine put a stop to these operations. It is questionable whether the decision to import expensive stallions was sound. Where funds are so restricted the interests which should be preferred are those of the most needy, in the case of Palestine the ordinary fellah cultivator, not the larger man, who can keep horses of the pure-bred Arab type.

Poultry husbandry.—One of the most highly successful branches of development throughout Palestine is in poultry husbandry. In all the Jewish villages large flocks of high-grade poultry are kept, chiefly White Leghorns and Rhode Island Reds. The poultry farm attached to the Acre Station of the Department of Agriculture is an outstanding instance of success. It is reported that this farm pays its way and affords a profit to the Department. It is of very great value to the villagers of the neighbourhood. Settings of eggs are sold at a reasonable figure, and each year hundreds of cockerels are distributed. The favourite birds are the White Leghorn and the White Sussex, both of which are easily acclimatised. It may appear that the introduction of an improved breed of poultry is a small matter. In the case of the fellah, however, every piastre is of moment, and the effect of this measure is of real importance.

The importance of the demonstration plot.—There are certain directions in which the Department of Agriculture can be of very special use to the ordinary cultivators. The most important service that can be rendered is education by means of the demonstration plot, where the advantages of improved agricultural methods are brought home to him. It appears that a system of demonstration plots was at one time initiated by the Department, but that it was not successful. The reasons of failure should be considered, for plots of this kind have proved exceedingly useful elsewhere. In a country of small-holdings they are indeed the chief means of bringing the results of improved practice to the notice of the small cultivator. It is a mistake to believe that knowledge filters down in such countries from the estate of the large proprietor. The contrary is the case. The diffusion of practical knowledge of agriculture among small men can best come through demonstration on holdings of the character which they themselves cultivate.

Scientific services.—The scientific side of agriculture is, of course, of immense importance. In Palestine, fortunately, it should be possible to obtain all that is required on that side by the use of existing institutions, and so to avoid duplication. There are competent chemists at the Experimental Station at Tel-Aviv and at the Hebrew University of Jerusalem who are capable of any scientific enquiry that may be necessary for the country. It cannot be questioned that if the Government were prepared to offer to pay for work done or to furnish a grant-in-aid, these institutions would readily undertake any work that the Government may require. Palestine is such a small country that it is particularly inadvisable that institutions of a scientific character should overlap. Especially is this the case where money is not plentiful. The whole question deserves serious consideration, with a view to using the available funds to the best advantage, if necessary by reducing the number of services to those which do not duplicate services obtainable elsewhere, and by abolishing services for which adequate funds cannot be provided.

The distribution of trees.—The Department of Agriculture has ceased to sell young trees from its nurseries to the cultivators. The reason given is that it is undesirable to compete with private enterprise. Private nurseries are almost entirely Jewish, though there is one well-known German nursery. The decision of the Department in this matter was criticised on many occasions, and the interference in private enterprise is in fact very small, as the fellahin would neither be willing, nor in most cases be able, to pay the price asked by the nurseries for trees. The importance of trees from the national, as well as from the individual point of view is so great that it is desirable to encourage planting by every possible means. So far from refusing the sale of seedlings in order to prevent competition with private enterprise the Department would be well advised to sell these seedlings at a nominal price or even to give them away, if by so doing the area under trees could be increased.

The Forest service.—At present the Forest service it attached to the Department of Agriculture. This seems to be a mistake. It is undesirable to burden the Department of Agriculture with matters other than agriculture proper specially in view of the importance of agricultural development at the present time and the necessity of its extension. The Forest service is developing rapidly. There are now 704,000 dunams of forest reserve, and newly afforested areas are showing good promise.

Jewish plantations.—The great possibilities of afforestation have been established by Jewish activities in this direction. There is a small Jewish village called Motza, close to Jerusalem, where a farmer of the name of Broza has planted an orchard, on what seemed to be sterile and barren rock. The trees and the vines have flourished, and what was a wilderness without vegetation of any kind is now a fine orchard producing a large income for its proprietor. The result is the more praiseworthy in that the planter received no assistance from any Jewish or other sources, but created the property by his own exertions. Another instance of development on the same lines is the orchard planted by the Zionist Organisation at Dilb (Kiryath Anavin). The land on which that orchard has been planted was similar to that of Motza. The trees were not irrigated but they have succeeded wonderfully. A similar instance is to be found in the Jewish suburb of Beth-Hakarem, close to Jerusalem, where a hillside which appeared to be hopelessly bare and arid is now covered with gardens containing trees of every kind. Everywhere the Jews are planting, and have planted trees, and there is no one of their colonies where this branch of agricultural activity is not in evidence.

B. EDUCATION.

The Jewish schools.—The first essential to any scheme of agricultural development in Palestine lies in primary education. The Jewish population is magnificently provided with educational facilities and nearly 100 per cent. of Jewish children attend Jewish schools. These are maintained by the Jewish authorities with the aid of a small grant from the Government, and it is a matter of common complaint in Jewish circles that this grant is limited to £20,000. It is based on the proportion of Jews to Arabs in the population of the country. The total expenditure on schools maintained by or affiliated with the Department of Education of the Palestine Zionist Executive for the year 1928-29 was £162,500. 227 schools were maintained, with 19,449 pupils.

The State schools.—The education of the Arabs provides a very different picture. In the year 1928-29, the number of elementary schools was 308, of which 259 were in the villages. Of the schools in the towns 29 were girls' schools and in the villages 8. The total number of schools had decreased by four during the year. The number of pupils in the schools was 25,219. Of these 12,539, including 573 girls, attended village schools. The rural Arab population, excluding tribal populations, at mid 1930, was 478,390. It is impossible to determine with accuracy the numbers of children of school-going age which are included in that figure. At the last census of the whole population, 37.1 per cent. were under 15 years of age. It is therefore safe to assume that at least 20 per cent. of the Arab population of the villages consists of children of school age. This would give over 95,000. Of these, as noted above, only 12,539 are taught, or 13.2 per cent.

The reason for this small number does not lie in any reluctance of the Arab to send his children to school. On the contrary, in every village complaints are made on the score of the inadequacy of educational facilities. Everywhere a demand for instruction is found, and that not only on behalf of the boys, but on behalf of the girls also. Far more applications for admission to existing schools are made than can possibly be accepted.

The Budget.—No agricultural development is possible among the Arabs until steps are taken to remedy the present state of affairs. The educational budget for the year 1929 was £144,119, more than £18,000 below the budget of the Jewish organisation for the same year for the same purpose. Of this sum £139,789 were spent, and there was a saving of £4,330—a most unfortunate economy. It is clear that an expenditure very much more important than £140,000 is necessary if the Arabs are to be given a fair chance to improve their standard of life.

The necessity.—The following is extracted from a note furnished by the Director of Education :—

> ". . . . With a rapidly increasing population, and a growing desire for more education, expansion in size and in the number of schools is not only desirable, but, in the interests of the people, absolutely necessary. The demand, however, has not been met, and the Arab population, not unnaturally, feel resentment against Government, the revenue of which is largely contributed by them, for not giving them what they desire, above all else, whereas the Jewish Agency, with the help of other organisations, has been able to provide almost universal education for Jewish children. The Arabs see in every Jewish colony a well-equipped school with a trained teacher, providing accommodation for every child of school age. They realise that without education they are precluded from social and economic progress . . . . Every year a larger number of boys and girls are refused admission to urban schools owing to lack of accommodation. In the rural schools, which at present are mainly confined to boys, more classes are needed and at least 250 villages, each containing a population of 300 or more, are not yet provided with any school. The demand for female education in towns is little less insistent than that for boys, and is increasing in the rural districts."

Its importance to agricultural development.—Until facilities for ordinary primary education are more general than is the case at present the fellahin will not be in a position to benefit generally by any special agricultural education that may be afforded. On the subject of agricultural education the Director of Agriculture has submitted a note, from which the following is extracted :—

> ". . . . Obstacles to progress in the agricultural education of the Arab cultivator are, in order of importance, insc/ency, illiteracy, and absence of instructors of local origin with the necessary qualifications . . . ."

> "The futility of urging on a bankrupt industry improved practice involving considerable capital outlay is at last being generally admitted. It is to be reported in an authoritative statement within the next few days that from a gross average income of £25 per annum the typical fellah is required to support a family of six, and contribute £8 as interest . . . . on unproductive loans . . . . Any hope for marked development of agricultural practice lies with the rising generation now being educated in recently established village schools."

> "The agricultural school at Tulkarem . . . . represents the first institution of its character in Palestine available to the Arabic speaking population . . . . It is recognised, however, that the impression which could be ensured by the education of some 40 residential students would be quite inadequate to the demands of the situation. It is consequently proposed to afford all village schoolmasters in rotation a special course of 12 months' duration at the school, for the purpose of ensuring an agricultural bias to primary education in the villages."

Agricultural schools.—The school to which Colonel Sawer refers in the above extract owes its existence to a bequest by a wealthy Jew. This is a useful commencement, but it should be pointed out that the Arab agricultural population forms more than nine-tenths of the rural population of Palestine, and that this is the only school on which they must depend for their agricultural education. The Jews already have an agricultural school at Mikveh-Israel with accommodation for 160 students. They also have a school provided by the Kadoorie bequest and they have several agricultural training schools' for girls, and a children's village where orphan children are taught agriculture. If the Arab population is to have opportunities of agricultural development on the same scale as the Jew, a score of large agricultural schools would have to be provided.

The village school and agriculture.—The Department of Education has already introduced a system intended to encourage more modern methods in agriculture. It has attached to many of the village schools agricultural plots where practical work is done. It also teaches sericulture, fruit-farming, and bee-keeping. At the present time this movement is hampered by the ignorance of the village teacher in agricultural matters and the whole of this branch of village education is dependent on a single supervisor, himself only partly trained.

Need for additional expenditure.—It is clear that the Government of Palestine must face very considerably increased expenditure on education, both primary and agricultural. As to the former, a plan should be worked out for expansion over a term of years. If the educational budget, at present standing at £150,000, could be increased by £15,000 a year for the next ten years, at the close of that period important progress would have been made towards the solution of the problem of primary education.

It seems desirable that the grant-in-aid to Jewish education should be increased proportionately with the increase in the general education budget of the State. Assuming that the Jewish children of school age bear the same proportion to the total population as is the case with the Arabs, the grant-in-aid from the present year should be increased by £1,500 per annum for the next ten years if a total annual increase of £15,000 in the Educational Budget proves feasible.

Technical education in agriculture.—For technical education in agriculture also a plan should be prepared to cover the next ten years. Its first object should be to provide accomodation for a largely increased number of students at Tulkarem. There is no reason why that school should not provide education for 120 to 150 boys. The present grant-in-aid is £1,000 a year. It would be necessary to increase the grant by at least £1,500 for the increased number of students. But the plan should not be confined to an increase in the accommodation at Tulkarem. It will prove essential to institute similar schools elsewhere, though probably not on the same elaborate scale. The matter is one for very careful examination by the Government.

Agricultural certificated school-masters.—Meanwhile it should be made a condition of employment of schoolmasters in the rural schools that they should be in possession of a certificate from the Tulkarem school, or from some other recognised agricultural school, that they have attended a course in practical agriculture for at

82

least six months. One year seems to be an unnecessarily long period for that purpose. It would be an advantage if arrangements could be made for training of these teachers at one of the Jewish schools as well as at Tulkarem, for it would be regrettable that the water-tight system should be observed even in agricultural instruction.

In the case of existing schoolmasters, the Educational Department will have to make the best arrangements possible to release them in batches for this training.

Collaboration between Departments of Agriculture and Education.—It is of course essential that the Department of Agriculture and the Department of Education should collaborate closely in order to ensure the success of the arrangements proposed for agricultural education in rural primary schools. There should be no difficulty in such collaboration. The curriculum of the rural school, in so far as it includes agricultural instruction, should be worked out by the two Departments in consultation as also the curriculum for the six months' training period of the village schoolmaster.

C. IRRIGATION.

The existing waste of water.—A most important condition of agricultural development is water for irrigation. On Map No. 5* will be found indicated the more important sources of water supply at present known to exist in the country. As a general rule irrigation water is wasted. This is very obvious in the irrigated areas of the Jordan Valley, the Beisan area, the Wadi-Fara'a and the Jericho area. In each of these areas it is probable that scientific management of the irrigation would save enough water to double the irrigable area from the existing supply.

The Aujha Concession.—It is regrettable that one of the chief sources of irrigation in the country, the Aujha River, has been included in a concession. This concession, originally given with the object of the production of electric power, and subsequently as a purely irrigation concession when it was discovered that the current was not required for power, has as yet not been employed for irrigation on a modern scale. A comparatively small portion of water is pumped by riverain proprietors for the irrigation of their orange groves, but the great mass of the water flows into the sea. A further drawback to the exercise of the Aujha concession by the concessionaires is found in the fact that if its water were to be used generally for irrigation of the plantations of the Maritime Plain, the existing demand for electric power to pump irrigation water from wells in the plantations would be liable to diminution or possibly to cessation. The concession for this power was in the same hands as that for the

---
* See Note on page 3.

Jordan River, but in 1929 the Palestine Electric Corporation promoted a separate irrigation Company to take over its irrigation rights in the Aujha Concession. This transfer was approved by the Government on condition that an irrigation scheme should be submitted to the Government within a year and that the work must be done on the scheme within a period of two years of its approval, a condition which was accepted by the Company.

In the latter portion of 1929, the Company submitted an irrigation scheme for the lands of Petach Tikvah. This scheme was sent for the examination of the Government technical advisers. It is believed that no report on the scheme has yet been rendered in consequence of the occupation of those advisers on the locust campaign. The irrigation scheme has not yet been commenced.

The irrigation of the Aujha basin is a work of great importance and it is desirable that it should be pushed on, in so far as it lies in the hands of the Administration to forward it. The original concession was given in the year 1922. Eight years have passed and so far nothing has been done. It is desirable that the scheme put forward by the concessionaires last year should be examined and reported upon as soon as that is possible. The sooner irrigation is available for the plain the better.

Nebi Rubin.—In the Maritime Plain there is an area claimed as Waqf known as Nebi Rubin, which is now being drained, and arrangements made for the irrigation by the Supreme Moslem Council. The area capable of irrigation is some 5,000 dunams. The plan for this work of drainage and irrigation is stated to have been prepared by an engineer of the Rockefeller Foundation. The work is being carried out satisfactorily. This will provide a useful area for the Arab tenants of the Waqf.

The Acre Plain.—The Acre Plain is said to be entirely irrigable, either from the Kurdani Spring (marked No. 2 on Map No. 5 attached to this Report) or from subterranean water at a reasonable depth. A large portion of this Plain is in the hands of Jewish organisations. As yet the practice of irrigation in this area is not general.

The Huleh Area.—The Huleh area is all irrigable. The property might be a very valuable one and it is regrettable that the area owned by the Government therein has passed almost in its entirety out of the hands of the Government into the hands of a concessionaire, Selim Bey Salam of Beyrouth. The concession was originally made by the Turkish Government before the War, but was renewed by the Government of Palestine. The concessionaire at one time desired to get rid of the concession and has been on various occasions in treaty with the Zionist Organisation and subsequently with the Walbrook Trust. The negotiations came to nothing in both cases, and the concession still exists. The concessionaire is about to commence operations with the object of draining a portion of the marsh by deepening the bed of the Jordan and so lowering the water level of the surface of the lake.

In Huleh, the extent of a holding necessary to support an agricultural family would not be greater than 40 dunams, of which half irrigated. There will thus be a large reserve of land in that area, when it is properly developed. The question of the drainage of the Lake was considered by Mr. Henriques and was reported upon in the volume of Reports of the Experts at p. 400. His estimate is that to drain the Lake by blasting out the gorge through which the Jordan river flows after leaving the Lake, would cost over £1,000,000, to include deep ploughing of the reclaimed area, drainage as might be necessary, and arrangements for irrigation.

If the concession falls in, as is possible, it seems essential that the Government should retain the proprietary right in the area, for development purposes. The estimate of Mr. Henriques is that of an expert, but was not founded on the preparation of any detailed plans. If the Huleh area should revert to the Government, a technical study should be made in order to ascertain the actual cost of the suggested drainage.

The Beisan Area.—Another area that has unfortunately passed from the ownership of the Government consists of the lands of Beisan, Semakh and Ghor-ul-Fara'a, which are the subject of the agreement concluded in November, 1921, and known as the Ghor Mudawwara Agreement. It was probably politically desirable that the lands covered by this Agreement should be settled with the Arab tenants who had undoubtedly enjoyed the use of the tract in the time of the Ottoman Government. At the same time the result of the Agreement, and specially of the modification of the Agreement made in September, 1928, published in the Official Gazette of 16th September of that year have taken from the Government the control of a large area of fertile land, eminently suitable to development and for which there is ample water available for irrigation.

The Beisan Agreement.—By the original Agreement property was created in favour of the existing cultivators in respect of the lands cultivated by them (Art. 1). Article 5 provided for such areas of Metruké land as might be " necessary for the requirements of the village ". A minimum holding of 150 dunams per family was fixed by Article 8. In Article 9 provision was made for the constitution of tribal areas, as also for the transfer of areas to families which have not hitherto cultivated, if the tribe to which they belong has generally lived and cultivated on the West side of Jordan. Grazing areas for tribes were permitted to the extent determined by the Department of Agriculture. In Article 16 is laid down that there should be no disposition of the land " except by way of mortgage to the Government or of succession . . . . until the whole transfer

85.

price (badal tatweeb) has been paid ". This last was a very wise provision.

The revision of the Agreement carried through in 1928 modified this last condition. The following is the relevant extract from the statement of policy embodying the changes in the Agreement :—

"8. Government are prepared under certain conditions to waive the requirement that the whole transfer price must be paid before the transferee has freedom to dispose of his surplus land.

"The two principal conditions which attach to this modification of Clause 16 are:

"(1) that the surplus land be transferred to persons approved by Government and having as their object the promotion of close settlement and the intensive cultivation of the land; and

"(2) that in every case shall the transferee retain such extent of land in the area to which the Ghor Mudawwara Agreement of 1921 applies or elsewhere as will in the opinion of the Government suffice for the maintenance of himself and his family."

At the time of the original agreement clearly no grant of surplus land " to any individual was contemplated.

The whole of the Beisan lands have been distributed, and large areas have already been sold. Further large areas are in the market. The grant of the lands has led to land speculation on a considerable scale. The custom is that the vendor transfers to the vendee the liability for the price of the land still owing to the Government and in addition takes from him a sum varying from three to four pounds a dunam for land in the Jordan Valley. These proceedings invalidate the argument which was used to support the original agreement. It was made in order to provide the Arabs with a holding sufficient to maintain a decent standard of life, not to provide them with areas of land with which to speculate.

As to the irrigation of Beisan it is stated that there is ample water to irrigate all the cultivable area if the water were properly used. At present it is used exceedingly uneconomically. Under the powers which the Government propose to take under the Draft Irrigation Ordinance now under consideration, it will be possible so to regulate the use of the water that it will serve a much larger area than is the case at present.

There were complaints from the Arabs that the sources of the water supply had passed into Jewish hands and that there was consequent difficulty in obtaining the water necessary for irrigation. It is true that certain of the sources of irrigation water in this area lie in lands now held by the Jews. If the Draft Irrigation Ordinance finally becomes law, all difficulty on that score can be regulated.

The Jordan Valley.—In Chapter I, reference is made to areas in the Jordan Valley. A comparison of the views of Dr. Strahorn, expressed in the Report of the Experts at pp. 203 to 206, with the views expressed by the members of the Committee who examined the Lower Jordan Valley this year for the purposes of the present enquiry, shows that there is room for wide difference of opinion. The Irrigation Officer and the Government Geologist are convinced of the possibility of cultivation of considerable areas in that valley if water proves available. The Committee of which they were members reported the possibility of the irrigation of 100,000 dunams in addition to that already irrigated, with the water already available, if that water is economically used. It is well within the bounds of possibility, both that arrangements could be made which will provide a larger supply of water than that at present in sight, and that a larger area of land may prove to be cultivable than is at present recognised and included in the cultivable area.

Other possibilities.—The remarks recorded above have reference only to certain of the known sources of irrigation. It is urgently necessary that attempts should be made to discover further sources. Both in the course of the settlement of the refugees in Greece, and more recently in Cyprus, steps were taken to determine the subterranean supply. In both countries these enquiries are believed to have resulted in success. In Macedonia, in Thrace, and in Old Greece, an artesian supply was discovered which has resulted in the sinking of hundreds of wells which give a copious yield of water. It is well possible that serious attempts might result in a similar discovery in Palestine. As has already been remarked, the discovery of an artesian supply of water in the Beersheba region would revolutionise the possibilities of colonisation in Palestine. It is worth while to devote a considerable sum to a hydrographic survey of Palestine in the hope of locating the water-table both of spring water and of artesian water, if the latter exists. A study of all existing sources of irrigation should also be undertaken, and plans prepared for scientific and economic use of the water in question.

The Draft Irrigation Ordinance.—In Appendix 19 will be found a resumé of the Draft Irrigation Ordinance. Legislation to empower the Government to regulate the use of water for irrigation should be enacted as rapidly as possible. It is a question for the Government whether the powers contained in the Draft Ordinance for control over the sinking of wells is necessary. There was at one time a fear that the multiplication of wells in the Maritime Plain had caused a fall in the water-table in that area. The matter was examined by an expert Committee which came to the conclusion that the fear was not well founded. The water-table had fallen in a certain region, but there remained an ample supply at the deeper level.

Constitution of a separate service.—By an unusual arrangement the Irrigation Service is also placed under the control of the Department of Agriculture. This arrangement is not satisfactory.

87

In fact, it has resulted in the Irrigation Officer being employed, and necessarily employed, on urgent duties not connected with irrigation. For instance, during a considerable part of the present year he was engaged on a locust campaign. This was doubtless a work of great urgency, but while he was thus employed his regular work as Irrigation Officer was in abeyance. That work is of the first importance in view of the backward state of irrigation in Palestine. It is desirable that the Irrigation Service should be detached from the Department of Agriculture and constituted a separate service.

D. CO-OPERATION.

The Jewish movement. Information available.—A notable feature in connection with Jewish immigration and settlement is the rapid growth of co-operation. The fact may be due to the influence of the countries whence the immigrants have come, for the movement is powerful both in Poland and in Russia, the countries of origin of 66 per cent. of the Jewish settlers. The movement is confined to the Jews. There is no Arab Co-operative Society at work in Palestine.

There are 249 co-operative societies registered, but of them only 173 are known to be working. The live societies are classified as follows :—

Agricultural societies	39
Credit societies	52
Industrial producers	27
Land purchase and building	34
Kvotzoth	14
Miscellaneous	7

Data have been collected for 134 of these societies as at the end of May, 1930, and have been submitted by Mr. Harry Viteles, the General Manager of the Central Bank of Co-operative Institutions in Palestine.

These 134 Jewish co-operatives had at that date 33,436 members, and share capital, reserves and other owned capital amounting to £334,827. In addition to this sum, they have in members' deposits and savings £711,445. At the same time the total indebtedness to banks and other creditors was £294,411. In fact, the co-operative societies work, to a large extent, on the money provided by their members, a position highly satisfactory.

Rates of interest on deposits and loans.—High rates of interest are paid both on deposits and on loans from Banks, and the Societies charge their members 10 to 13 per cent. on the loans and advances made to them. This rate of interest is not only high in itself, but is an indication of the still higher rates which are charged by the moneylender. If the general rate of interest charged elsewhere for accommodation of the kind furnished by the Societies were not excessive, and it is known to be excessive, it would clearly not be to the advantage of the small man in the town and in the village to resort to a co-operative which demands 10 to 13 per cent. The fact is also an indication of the uselessness of the legal limit of 9 per cent.

On this question of the rate of interest Mr. Viteles remarks in his note :—

> "This interest is out of proportion to the earning capacity of the population—particularly of the farmers—served by the co-operatives."

Activities of Co-operative Societies.—The Agricultural societies are of many types and serve every purpose of the settler. Through them he makes his purchases and sells his products, through them he insures his cattle, through them again he receives advances on his crops. Of these societies there are some which are of outstanding merit. The "Pardess" Co-operative Society of Orange Growers shipped during the last season over 470,000 cases of oranges belonging to its members, about 40 per cent. of the total orange crop of Jewish growers. It has just opened a co-operative packing house with a capacity of 60,000 cases, equipped with the latest grading and packing machinery. This society also interests itself in the development of existing markets and the discovery of new avenues of disposal. Of the wine produced in Palestine, 90 per cent. is manufactured and sold by a co-operative society of wine-growers. "Hamashbir" is a society established and managed by the Jewish Federation of Labour. It serves as a Co-operative Wholesale Society and the central organ of the four consumers' (distributive) societies already in existence. More of the latter type are contemplated in rural localities. The co-operative marketing of milk and dairy products, eggs and poultry and vegetables, formerly constituting a branch of the activities of "Hamashbir," have been taken over by three autonomous co-operatives functioning in Jerusalem, Tel-Aviv and Haifa respectively, under the name "Thnuva." The produce sold by these three bodies during the year ending 30th September exceeded in value the sum of £96,000, and is rapidly increasing. Another co-operative connected with the Labour Federation is "Yakhin," which undertakes the preparation, planting and maintenance of agricultural holdings, particularly of citrus groves. This work is done both for residents in the country and for prospective settlers. The society commenced in the middle of 1928, and had completed work of a value of £49,000 before the close of 1929. The contracts on hand on 31st May, 1930, were for £32,000.

Jewish Co-operative Movement: Co-operative Industrial Producers' Societies.—The Labour Federation has organised a special Department to promote and to supervise Co-operative Industrial Producers' Societies. At the end of 1928 there were 50 such societies with a total of 326 members, an average of less than 7 per society. At the end of May, 1930, there were 41 with a membership of 507, more than 12 per society. In addition to the members, these societies employed 235 hired workers and apprentices. The most remarkable of the societies of this type are the transport societies, in which the members transfer to the society the property in their motor vehicles and are credited with the capital value as their share capital. It is said that these societies command most of the internal traction of the city of Jerusalem and town of Tel-Aviv and a large proportion of the commercial transport between the two places.

Land-purchasing Societies.—A considerable number of the more important co-operative societies are those which have been organised for the purchase of land both in rural and in urban areas. In the case of the former type of transaction, the land is frequently bought and developed for members not yet resident in Palestine, but who hope to immigrate later. The total present value of the land, improvements, buildings, etc., the property of members of these societies, is reported to be nearly one and a-half million pounds.

Jewish Co-operative Movement: Membership of Societies.—It is clear that the co-operative movement has not only been successfully launched among the Jewish population, but has already become a highly important economic factor in its daily life. On the whole the societies are extremely well-managed. Some of the Credit Societies appear to be too large for efficient control by the members themselves. There is one with over 3,000 members, there are eight with membership in excess of 1,000. In other cases there is a tendency in the opposite direction, and new members are not welcomed. But there can be no doubt that the co-operative societies are doing magnificent work and are a valuable asset both to the villages and to the residents in the towns.

Necessity for extension to Arab population.—As has been pointed out, the whole of the co-operative organisation in Palestine is Jewish. It is very much to be regretted that no efforts have as yet been made to popularise the co-operative idea among the Arab population. The need is desperately urgent. The fellah population is so tightly bound in debt that no credit whatever is available to enable that development of agriculture which is so essential for progress.

The view is commonly expressed that the Arab will not co-operate. It is said that one attempt was made to form a co-operative society of the tobacco growers, but that the society failed owing to the disloyalty of its members. The great probability is that the cause of failure might be found either in ignorance of the principles of co-operation or in the constitution of the society. The Arab is ignorant, but he is at the same time highly intelligent and hard-working. That he can learn is evident from an inspection of the

Arab villages in proximity to the German and to the older Jewish (P.I.C.A.) colonies. That he is ready for practical co-operation is patent from instances which have been observed recently. One case was noticed in a village close to the German colony of Wilhelma. There three fellahin desired to have the use of a tractor and tackle for deep ploughing. No one of the three could afford the expenses of transport. The three joined together, hired the outfit, had all three holdings ploughed and shared the expense. In another village, near Ramleh, a case was observed in which five cultivators pooled their teams in order that power might be available for deep ploughing. Those cases, though perhaps of little intrinsic importance, indicate that the co-operative sense is not absent in the Arab cultivator.

There is nothing but co-operation that will save him from his present depression. He cannot hope ever to escape from the burden of debt unless cheaper credit is made available. Only by co-operation can that object be obtained. It is well that Mr. C. F. Strickland is making an enquiry into the methods by which co-operation may be made available for the fellahin of Palestine.

Treatment of existing debts.—One of the most difficult of questions in approaching the problem of the foundation of Arab Co-operative Societies, is the policy to be followed in respect of existing debts. As has been noted, these are everywhere exceedingly heavy, and the prospect of agricultural development of the Arab holdings, a development which will be dependent on the facility for obtaining working capital at a reasonable price, is at the moment rendered impossible. The Arab is crippled by debt. His chance of advance is hampered by debt. How is he to be released from his burden as a preliminary to improving his chances of advance?

Mr. Strickland, who was in Palestine at the time of this enquiry, and was himself examining the possibilities of co-operation among the Arab population, favoured me with a note on the clearance of old debts by co-operative societies. His considered opinion is hostile to a policy of loans at a low rate of interest in order to enable the peasant to pay off existing debts at high rates of interest. In the course of his memorandum he writes :—

" . . . . My own experience during twenty years of co-operation has been everywhere the same. An indebted and usually illiterate peasant has not the strength of character to refrain from further borrowing from money-lenders, if he is suddenly released from debt. He borrows again and all the good work is undone. After trying several methods I found the best way in a rural Society of Credit to be the limitation of loans in the earlier years to such amounts as would meet the agricultural and ordinary needs of the members without attempting to repay the old debt. At the end of three years, if it was found that the members had broken off all connection with their old source of credit, a list of the debts of each member was drawn up, and a special loan for the repayment of the total amount made to a number of selected persons, but not to all the members at the same moment. Thus by clearing a

91

few members in each year by a special loan the Society was kept in a constant state of struggle, which, however unpleasant, is extremely beneficial to the co-operative character of the persons concerned."

He adds that the Jewish Credit Societies apply the same policy of refusal at once to clear the debts of a new member.

At a later stage of the memorandum, Mr. Strickland writes:

" . . . . I do not consider that peasants who have become accustomed to a condition of permanent indebtedness can be taught to help themselves, except by an unpleasant and somewhat long course of discipline. Therefore they must for two or three years prove their loyalty to their Society by dealing in small sums. This process forms their character and makes them such men as can be trusted with large sums. They must also have the courage to defy the moneylender and boldly invite him to go to court. When he does so the Society can help them, but a total payment of their debt at an early date is too strong a medicine for them to digest, while a partial payment of a moneylender's debt is a mere waste of money. When crediting it he charges the full rate of interest, but when coming to a final settlement he will agree to a lower, rate."

It is exceedingly satisfactory that this question of credit for the fellah is at the moment the subject of enquiry by an expert in co-operation, and that there is justification for the hope that the best steps possible will be taken to improve the prospects of this important class of agriculturists in financing their agricultural operations. Nothing is more important from the point of view of the agricultural development of the country.

Desirability of joint action between Jews and Arabs.—In view of the great desirability of a rapprochement between the Arab and the Jewish population of Palestine, it would be of advantage if the Jewish co-operative societies were to encourage Arab membership. In the case of " Pardess," for example, it would be to the advantage of the Jewish orange growers themselves to enlist the Arab growers in their Society. The price of oranges abroad is said to be based on the price of the cases of least merit. The higher the quality of the inferior product, the better for those who ship oranges of good quality, well-graded and well packed. If " Pardess " were to lay itself out to serve the Arab groves as well as the Jewish, it would obtain its reward in a general rise in the standard of the cases shipped from Palestine. And this is only one of the directions in which enlistment of Arab cultivators would actually strengthen the co-operatives of the Jews. In addition, naturally, the political difference would tend to become less acute than is at present the case. The more the Jew can identify himself with the economic interests of the Arab, the better for the general peace of the country. Nothing is more fatal for the peace of Palestine than emphasis on the difference rather than on the common interests of these two constituents of the population.

CHAPTER VIII.

Agricultural Produce.

(a) CITRUS CULTIVATION.

Origin of orange cultivation.—The cultivation of the orange, introduced by the Arabs before the commencement of Jewish settlement, has developed to a very great extent in consequence of that settlement. There is no doubt that the pitch of perfection to which the technique of plantation and cultivation of the orange and grapefruit have been brought in Palestine is due to the scientific methods of the Jewish agriculturist.

Area available.—In the Reports of the Experts at page 199 *et seq* there is an interesting statement of the opinion of Dr. Strahorn as to the areas in which citrus cultivation is in his opinion possible. His deduction on this subject is to be found on Page 201 and is recorded in the following words :—" . . . It is felt that the absolute area of irrigated plantations in Palestine will not exceed 300,000 dunams." This is a very important pronouncement by an expert of world-wide reputation. This question is discussed in the Memorandum submitted during the course of the present enquiry. The experts of the Jewish Agency do not agree with the opinion thus expressed by Dr. Strahorn; on the contrary, they consider that there are 595,000 dunams in the Maritime Plain which are irrigable and of the light soil usually found suitable for orange cultivation. Including the irrigable area of the Beersheba series of soils, which they take as 503,347, and deducting an assumed area for " nasaz," they conclude that an area of 500,000 dunams of the Maritime Plain is suitable for citrus cultivation. " Nasaz " is thus described by Dr. Strahorn :

> " The term ' nasaz ' indicates a sub-soil structure where, due to some peculiarity, the horizon is but very slowly pervious to moisture, and the structure is sufficiently dense to cause most roots of plants to turn and follow a horizontal direction. In boring the soil-auger encounters a definite resistance where the ' nasaz ' horizon is penetrated. Mechanical analyses seldom show a texture heavier than a sticky loam or a sandy loam, and fine sandy loam textures seem quite prevalent . . . . As a rule, ' nasaz ' is non-calcareous . . . ."

It is, of course, impossible to determine the " nasaz " area by inspection of the surface soil. That area will only be determined when a soil survey, which includes an examination of the sub-soil, is completed.

All that can safely be said on the subject of the irrigable light soil fit for orange cultivation in the Maritime Plain is that there appears to be an area of at least 200,000 dunams still available and undeveloped, and that this area would provide for 10,000 holdings, if the price of oranges in the European market does not fall materially. In addition there is an area, estimated by the experts of the Jewish Agency at 300,000 dunams, which may prove on examination to be suitable for citrus. Should this anticipation prove correct, and the largely increased area not result in a fall in the price of oranges, this area would provide for another 15,000 families.

Area under citrus cultivation.—Details of the areas now under orange cultivation and of export and prices are given in Appendix 20. It is generally assumed that this fruit may be successfully cultivated in the whole of the soil suitable to its growth. A limiting factor may prove to be that of water for irrigation, in certain regions. Hitherto water has been found at reasonable depth, ranging from 9 metres to 53 metres (Report of the Experts, p. 26). In general tube wells are used, with filters, and the pumps are worked either with oil engines or by electric power obtained from the Palestine Electric Corporation. Last year there were symptoms which seemed to indicate that the water-table was receding in depth. There were also complaints that salt water had penetrated into certain of the wells. An enquiry was held into the matter, and it was found that in the region where orange cultivation had been longest in vogue, there had in fact been a fall of about 4 metres in the level of the springs, but that the supply at this lower depth was ample. It was also considered that the fall was possibly due to temporary conditions, following as it did two years of rainfall below the average. As to the salt, this was found in two wells only. No explanation of the phenomenon could be suggested, as these two wells were in close proximity to other wells in which the water was sweet.

Future of the orange trade.—It is unsafe to prophesy on the subject of the future of the orange trade. Opinions among experts in Palestine vary. On the whole they are optimistic. The chief orange growers feel little doubt that a crop of ten or twelve million cases will be absorbed by the European market. They realise that the possibility of that absorption will depend in large measure on the method in which the oranges are marketed. At the present time this leaves much to be desired. The Jewish growers are taking steps to ensure by co-operation that the standard of the fruit despatched from their groves is uniform and that grading and packing are satisfactory. It is regrettable that the Arab growers are not yet convinced of the necessity of the adoption of similar measures.

The question of the future of the orange trade is one of very great importance for the development of agricultural Palestine. In the main, it is the development of this particular culture which will justify the belief that the country can support a much larger population than it contains at present. If the market can absorb, within the next ten or twelve years, some 30 million cases of oranges, where to-day it is absorbing less than 3 million, the 200,000 dunams, which is the minimum area still awaiting development in the Maritime Plain, will support a population of at least ten thousand families of orange growers, with the ancillary population connected with the business, on an area which to-day is supporting probably less than 2,000 families. Should the suitable area prove to be larger than 200,000 dunams, as is reported by the experts recently employed by the Jewish Agency, and whose opinions differ from that of Dr. Strahorn, the additional population supportable will be increased *pro tanto*.

On the other hand, if development goes on at the present pace, and the market proves unable to digest the enormous increase in supply, not only will disaster overtake the new families who may be settled in the Maritime Plain in the future, but the large population now settled in that region will share in the disaster. It is the path of wisdom to proceed with the policy of orange plantation without undue precipitancy and to await the result of the work of the past four years before embarking on a more ambitious scheme of the same kind.

(b) THE GRAPE FRUIT.

Of orange groves now planted, one-tenth of the area is habitually put under grape-fruit. For this the market is satisfactory, and is expanding. The Palestinian grape-fruit is of very fine quality, and there is in this direction every probability of a large and increasing trade.

An additional advantage in the cultivation of the grape-fruit lies in the fact that it flourishes in soils much too heavy to permit of successful cultivation of the orange, and there is room in the Jordan Valley for considerable extension of the area under this crop. The drawback to the grape-fruit is its quality as eminently a luxury fruit. This is even more the case than with the Jaffa orange. The grape-fruit requires preparation before it can be eaten. It also requires sugar. The Jaffa orange is easily eaten, without preparation and also without sugar. It cannot therefore be expected that the area ultimately planted with grape-fruit will ever compare with the area under oranges, but, nevertheless, it will in the end be sufficiently considerable to warrant a place in a development programme.

(c) THE BANANA.

Area under cultivation.

Careful enquiry has established that the area under the banana in Palestine in 1930 amounts to 2,368 dunams. The fruit can be grown in the whole of the Jordan Valley where the soil is fertile. It is also grown in a few areas outside the Jordan Valley, but with more difficulty.

Cost of production and yield.

The cost of production is £37 a dunam up to the bearing stage and thereafter £18 per annum for maintenance. At 15 mils a kilo, with a yield of 2,000 kilos from a dunam in full bearing, the gross annual income is £30. This year the price is very low, and the growers have found difficulty in disposing of their fruit.

Marketing possibilities.

The Palestine banana is a fruit of excellent quality in consumption, though its appearance leaves much to be desired. The whole question of cultivation and marketing was discussed at length by Mr. George M. Odlum, in a report to the Palestine Economic Corporation in 1927. This has been published, by the courtesy of the Corporation, as a leaflet of the Department of Agriculture in Palestine (No. 11). The general result at which Mr. Odlum arrives does not encourage the hope that the possibility of creating a market in the banana will afford scope for widespread extension of cultivation. He sees "considerable possibilities for a banana industry of moderate dimensions in Palestine." The difficulty is largely one of marketing. The Palestine fruit could not compete with the Canary and West Indian bananas in Western Europe. It is bound to be restricted to local markets and the undeveloped markets of Eastern Europe. The possibility of expansion in these latter markets should however be explored, and meanwhile the methods of packing and transporting the fruit improved. It is a matter of great regret that the nematode (Egyptian eelworm) (from which Mr. Odlum recorded that Palestine was free), has now appeared and is found spread generally among the banana groves of the country.

(d) MELONS.

Exports to Egypt and Syria.

There is a very large trade in water-melons with Egypt and a smaller, but still considerable, trade with Syria. The former, in 1929, amounted to 49,000 tons, the latter in 1928 to 6,800. In both directions the trade has been affected by fiscal measures. In Egypt an import duty of 500 milliemes per ton was imposed last year. In Syria the town of Damascus has imposed an octroi duty on melons, which is of course of a general nature, affecting Syrian as well as Palestinian melons, but which at the same time tends to reduce the amount exported from Palestine.

Adverse effect on export of imposts in Egypt and Syria.

Complaint on the score of these imposts was general, and it was suggested that the Syrian case should be taken up with the French Government and that in the Egyptian case the Palestine

Government should retaliate by penalizing imports from that country. Petitions on the subject were submitted to the Palestine Government. The District Commissioner of Haifa, in reporting on the Egyptian question, gave figures which establish that the cost of transport of a ten-ton truck, including transport to the railway, cost of loading, demurrage fee, unloading and commission, and customs dues, totalled £P25.005. The average wholesale prices in Egypt range from £20 to £25 per ten-ton truck, and there is consequently little or no profit to the producer in Palestine. He was of the opinion that the new tariff will seriously affect the trade in melons.

The matter is one for negotiation with the Egyptian Government. The balance of trade is so seriously adverse to Palestine that every possible effort should be made to encourage its exports. Of these the melon holds quite an important place.

The Syrian question is more difficult. No preference is being accorded to Syrian melons. Doubtless the Damascus Municipality requires the additional income which the octroi on melons will afford. It does not seem possible to suggest that Palestine melons should have a preference over the local product in the Damascus market, and probably no steps can usefully be taken in the matter.

(e) ALMONDS.

Production and Export figures.

Appendix 21 gives the figures of production and of export from three sources. It is unsatisfactory that they differ so widely, and a remarkable fact indicated by those figures is that over a period of seven years the total export of almonds has been far in excess of the total production. No explanation of this fact can be offered, unless it can be attributed to under-estimation of the crop for purposes of assessment of tithe.

Area under Almond cultivation.

The most recent enquiry into the area under almonds was made in the early months of 1927. It indicated a total area under this tree of 27,776 dunams, of which 21,175 were in Jewish colonies. The tree is easy to cultivate and flourishes on land which is unsuitable for plantation of any other kind. It gives a return per dunam six times that of cereal crops. It is therefore a useful culture for the development of poor soil.

Replacement of Almonds by Oranges.

The area under almonds has been affected by the popularity of the orange. Even before the enquiry in 1927 a considerable area of almond groves had been uprooted in order to make room for oranges, and in certain cases for grapes. In the report of the Department of Agriculture for 1925 it was already recorded that:

> "Licences have been issued in considerable number for the felling of almond trees affected with gummosis, or borer . . . . Almonds are giving way to apricots and figs which, in improved varieties and properly dried, command ready local sales at very favourable prices . . . ."

Since that time the cultivation of the orange has advanced with great rapidity, and wherever the land is suitable there is a tendency for the orange to replace the almond.

Pests.

In the heavier soils the borer has done very serious damage, but in the poorer soils the almond groves are frequently unaffected by this pest. The same is the case with gummosis.

Markets.

In 1929 a consignment of almonds was forwarded to England and handled by the Empire Marketing Board. The report was not very encouraging, but in the issues of the " Grocer & Oil Trade Review " of 11th August and 15th September of that year Jordan almonds were quoted at the highest price in the London market. On the former date the best Jordans sold for more than the best Valencias.

The chief markets are in Egypt and Damascus, in both of which centres large quantities are imported.

There is no doubt that at recent prices almond cultivation has been a paying proposition, and in view of the suitability of the tree to the poorer soils, it will doubtless take its place in any general scheme of agricultural development for Palestine.

(f) GRAPES.

Exports of Wine.

Table grapes and grapes for wine are both cultivated in considerable areas in Palestine. But both in the case of wine manufactured in the country and in the case of grapes for the table, the export trade has suffered a severe and continued set-back during the past seven years. In 1922 over 2,700,000 litres of wine were exported of a declared value of £58,821. In 1927 the corresponding figures are, quantity slightly in excess of 900,000 litres, value £21,686.

Exports of Table Grapes.

In 1922, 1,334 tons of table grapes were exported. In 1928 the figure had fallen to 246 tons.

Competition in the markets.

In the case both of wine and of table grapes the most active market is Egypt. During the years 1922 to 1927 the export to Egypt fell from 1,175,000 litres to 564,000. The reason did not lie in a general reduction of imports of wine to Egypt; on the contrary that import shows a large increase. Wines of the Palestinian type are manufactured also in Cyprus and in Greece, and it is the increase of the export from these two sources which has replaced the loss in imports from Palestine. To quote from an article in the Bulletin of the Palestine Economic Society, of October, 1928, written by Mr. Harry Viteles : —

> "Palestine is losing the wine markets in Egypt, Syria, and the United Kingdom, primarily because it appears to be unable to compete with the other wine-producing countries . . . ."

Still more evident is the successful competition of Cyprus and Greece (with Crete) in the matter of table grapes. Since 1922 the import of table grapes from Cyprus to Egypt has increased from 261 tons to 1,338 tons in 1927; that from Greece and Crete from 3,141 tons to 5,068 tons.

Trial consignments to London.

A trial consignment of table grapes was on two occasions sent to London and was dealt with on each occasion by the Empire Marketing Board. The reports were not very favourable, but they indicated that given better methods of harvesting the fruit, most of which arrived in a condition over-ripe, there was a prospect of a market for certain of the varieties submitted, specially the Salti.

Complaints against Excise Duty and Licence Fees.

In the course of this enquiry a representation was made by the Co-operative Society of Vine-Growers of Richon-le-Zion and Zichron-Jacob Cellars on the subject of the very heavy recent increases in the licence fees for manufacture and in the Excise duty on intoxicating liquors. From this representation the following is extracted :—

> "Licence Fees: As a matter of fact, up to 1925 we have paid £P.5 per annum. By successive additions the Licence Fees have been increased to the amount of £P.2,250 for the current year; £P.1,600 for the manufacture of wine and £P.650 for the manufacture of alcohol and other spirits.
>
> "We do pay Licence Fees for manufacture of alcohol that are 15 times as big as the Licence Fees existing now in England, and with regard to Licence for manufacture of wine, we don't know any country where such Licence Fee should exist, meanwhile we are paying a little less than one mil per litre, making £P.1,600.
>
> "Should the Government continue to impose the Licence Fees to the actual level, it would practically mean taking from the viticulturist £P.0.250 per kantar of grapes for the licence only.

"It is indirectly a tax imposed on the viticulturists, and since the average crop of a dunam is two kantars of raisins, this tax will be to £P.0.500 per dunam. The question is if the viticulturist should pay so heavy a tax in addition to the other land taxes as Osher and Werko, and if a land product should be so heavily taxed . . . ."

It is true that the cultivator of grapes pays the tithe and the Werko as stated, and that the increase in the Licence Fees does in effect impose an additional tax on him, as it is impossible for the manufacturer to increase the price of his product to the consumer. This is a question which deserves careful reconsideration in view of the depressed condition of all agricultural industry at the present time.

A similar complaint was made by the Salesian Fathers in respect of the manufacture of wine at their Farm School at Beit Jemal.

The Excise Duty was first imposed by the Intoxicating Liquor Ordinance of 1927, and amounted to 3 mils per litre of wine not exceeding 15° of alcohol, and six mils per litre exceeding 15° but not exceeding 25°. These duties were doubled with effect from 1st April, 1930.

(g) TOBACCO.

Extent of the Tobacco Trade.

There is no reason why this country should not produce large amounts of high-class tobacco. At the present time, the amount produced is of poor quality and until 1929 has been insufficient to meet the demand for home consumption. The following statement shows for the past three years the amount produced, the amount consumed locally, and the amount imported:—

	1927.	1928.	1929.
	kgs.	kgs.	kgs.
Crop—			
Tobacco	495,000	334,600	1,057,300
Tombac	52,000	7,400	10,700
Disposal of Crop—			
Tobacco to factories	446,000	615,000	476,000
Exported	197,000	15,000	22,000
Imported—			
Tobacco	125,000	123,000	124,000
Tombac	74,000	70,000	100,000
Output of Local Factories—			
Cigarettes	401,815	493,720	531,887
Tobacco	23,844	16,167	20,108
Tombac	87,714	83,919	100,127
Snuff	64	57	1,210
Total output	513,437	593,863	653,332

Local Leaf.

Attempts have been made by the cigarette manufacturers to induce the cultivators to produce in this country the amount of tobacco of a higher class which is necessary for the manufacture of cigarettes of better quality. These attempts have not been successful. The local cultivator prefers a tobacco which gives a large yield. The seed of the better grade of plant is smaller and lighter than that of the coarser tobacco, and for this reason alone is unacceptable. In addition, the cultivator cannot realise that a smaller crop of the finer leaf is more valuable than a heavier crop of the coarser kinds.

Necessity for instruction in improvement of methods.

This prejudice might perhaps be overcome, but there is an additional difficulty in that the finer tobacco requires manipulation of a special kind, with which the Palestinian cultivator is not familiar. He does not know how to prepare his tobacco for the market, nor does he know the method of packing. Both of these difficulties are easily overcome. It is a question of education, and an expert from Cyprus or Greece could readily teach the cultivator. The Arab cultivator is intelligent, and, if taught, would find no difficulty in learning the methods of those countries.

One of the tobacco manufacturing firms advanced £20,000 to the tobacco growers in the course of last year. The result was entirely satisfactory, and the money has been repaid practically in full.

Complaints in regard to the Tobacco Ordinance.

There were complaints of two different kinds against the administration of the Tobacco Ordinance. On the part of the cigarette merchants it is alleged that smuggling is rife, especially after the disturbances of August last, and it was urged that much more severe measures are required on the part of the authorities in order to combat that evil. On the other side there were frequent complaints on the part of the fellahin that the Tobacco Ordinance is not only harsh in its terms, but is, in addition, administered in a cruel manner.

Minimum Area of Two Dunams.

There are certain provisions of the Ordinance which are special subjects of complaint. It is, for instance, argued that there is no good reason why the minimum area of cultivation should be two dunams. On the face of it the complaint is well founded. The reason for the provision is given in the following extract from a letter of the Director of Customs, Excise and Trade :—

" . . . . It is desirable that tobacco shall only be grown on a commercial scale and if it is assumed that 50 kilograms is the average crop of a dunam two dunams produce 100 kilograms or five bales of 20 kilograms each .... If you refer to Section 10 of the Tobacco Ordinance you will find that no quantity of less than 20 kilograms of unmanufactured tobacco may be sold at any one time by a grower to a dealer or manufacturer, and it was found that people who grow small areas in most cases were planting for their own consumption or illegal sale and small areas are very difficult to control. I have taken the liberal view of the two dunams so that if a fellah has two pieces of land within sight of each other but not actually touching, I count them as one for the purposes of the Law even if the total of each is less than two dunams. The interests of the tobacco manufacturers are those of the Department in this matter and they are always consulted when any change is made in the Ordinance.

"A committee of representatives of the Departments of Agriculture and Customs and of Tobacco Growers and Manufacturers was held in 1926. This Committee recommended that the minimum area planted by any one grower should not be less than half a dunam, but later it was considered desirable to increase the area to two dunams ...."

The reason why the minimum was fixed at two dunams was doubtless to check the consumption of unexcised tobacco. In fact, however, it precludes the poorer man from cultivating a crop which gives a high return. It is desirable that the minimum area should be fixed at a lower figure than two dunams. Half a dunam appears a sufficiently high minimum.

Prohibition of use of home grown Tobacco.

Another provision which is subject to bitter criticism is that which renders it a criminal offence for the cultivator to smoke his own home-grown tobacco. It is rightly pointed out that compulsion to purchase excised tobacco raises the price to the cultivator by about 60 per cent. On the other hand it is clear that if the cultivator were to be allowed to smoke his own tobacco, a door would be opened for illicit consumption which might have serious results on the excise revenue.

The following table gives the number of offences against the Ordinance during the past two years and the action taken in respect of them :—

Year.	Number of Seizures.	Number of Offences.	Number of Offences Compounded.
1928	5,952	5,010	2,176
1929	5,984	4,551	1,962

All cases of infringement of the Tobacco Ordinance are dealt with by the Director of Customs himself, and he is personally responsible for compounding such of these offences as seem to be suitable for this action. There is no doubt that the Ordinance is properly administered.

(h) Olives.

Grade of oil.

There is a large production of olive oil in the country. As a rule the oil is of inferior quality, containing a high percentage of acid. This is due to the primitive nature of the machinery of extraction, to the absence of cleanliness in connexion with the process, and to the antiquated receptacles in which the oil is stored. A reform in methods is a necessary preliminary to a pure and sweet oil.

Methods of culture.

Cultural practice is also as a rule ignorant and primitive. The olives are removed from the trees by beating the branches with sticks. Partly as a result of this practice the crop of the following year is affected so much, that the olive is looked upon in this country as a tree that yields well one year and very poorly the next. A further drawback to successful culture is the ignorance of the fellahin on the subject of pruning the tree. It may be said with truth that in large areas pruning is actuated not by any desire to improve the tree or the crop, but by the necessity to obtain firewood.

Instruction in improved methods.

These are all directions in which instruction would have good results and this could best be afforded by demonstration. The same absence of knowledge of pruning was remarked in the case of many of the Greek refugees, and it was necessary to employ travelling instructors to teach the peasants how to treat their olive trees. There is no reason why such a method should not be adopted in Palestine. The financial results of the system in Greece fully justified the expense.

Extension of area under cultivation.

There are wide spaces in the hill country where the olive would grow and where it would give a better return, even at the present low prices, than is obtained from cereal crops. It would be of advantage to the country if these areas were put under olives rather than cultivated each year with cereals. It was suggested that in cases where cereal land in the hill country is put down to trees, the tithe should be excused on that land until the trees are in bearing. This seems a fair suggestion, not only in the case of olive groves but also where fruit trees are planted, and not only in the hills but in the plains also.

103

(i) Sesame.

Imports and Exports.

Everywhere a demand was made that the import duty on sesame, which had been removed in 1925 in order to help the Jewish Oil Factory " Shemen " should be re-imposed, and the Palestine Government has agreed to the re-imposition. The sesame position is curious. In the year 1929 while 3,539 tons were exported at an average price of £P.20.436 mils per ton, 3,470 tons were imported at a price of £P.23.278 mils per ton. The imported sesame comes chiefly from China and is generally said to be an inferior seed to the Palestinian seed.

Value as a summer crop.

The cultivation of sesame has a value apart altogether from its crop. It is a summer crop, and requires a great deal of careful weeding and cultivation. It is followed by the winter cereal crop, and the land is in a good condition to receive the seed when the sesame has been pulled. Sesame is therefore a crop to encourage, apart from its commercial value.

Cultivation.

The Jewish colonies grow no sesame, as it is a crop demanding labour both of women and of children at time of harvest. The crop is not reaped; each individual stalk is pulled by hand, labour of a kind which the Jewish population does not favour, in part perhaps because there are not yet many children of an age to help in the harvest. The value of the yield at present prices would not support the expense of hired labour. The fellah carries through the harvest with the help of his family.

(j) Barley.

Export trade.

Before the War considerable quantities of Palestinian barley were exported to the United Kingdom for malting purposes. In one year, 1908, the export from Gaza was 38,000 tons. In 1913 it amounted 18,400 tons. Since the war this trade has not revived; the maximum amount exported to the United Kingdom in any one year having been 1,600 tons.

Possible reasons for reduction of overseas trade.

One of the principal reasons for the failure of the trade to revive appears to be that prohibition in America has released large quantities of Californian barley, which now finds its way to the United Kingdom. There are, however, other reasons. The rainfall of the Gaza area is very erratic, and a crop cannot be depended on each year. Probably the merchant prefers to deal where he is certain regularly to find the amount he desires. The Gaza barley contains a good deal of extraneous matter. A proposal was made to purchase a cleansing plant on behalf of the Government, as it is understood has been done in the Sudan, and to demand that all exported grain should be cleaned previous to export. This scheme fell through for financial reasons.

It is also suggested that the United Kingdom demand for malting barley has fallen and that the reduced demand is met to a larger extent than formely by supplies produced locally. Also that the time of shipment from Gaza, i.e., the end of June, is too late for the market. Further, the freight from Gaza to the United Kingdom amounts to 4s. 6d. a ton, which compares with 3s. 3d. from Canadian ports, and 3s. 6d. from New Orleans. From New York it is said to be 1s. 9d.

Proposals for revival of the trade.

There seem to be a number of reasons which explain the failure of the barley trade with Great Britain. For its revival, if that revival is possible, there are three necessary preliminaries. First, there must be co-operation between the growers and the merchants in Palestine. Next, grading and cleaning are essential. The outlay on the necessary machinery is considerable and it is probable that Government assistance is a condition of its purchase. Finally, a reduction is required in the freight charges from Palestine to the United Kingdom. The last is probably the most difficult of the three conditions.

(k) MINOR AGRICULTURAL PRODUCTS.

The Silkworm.

The Department of Agriculture employs an expert in the breeding of the silkworm. The budget allotment is so small that the activities of the Section are crippled. This is the more unfortunate in that there is a group of Arabs who are familiar with the culture of silk, and there is a definite demand in other quarters for instruction, for provision of mulberry trees and for assistance to breed silkworms. This is a demand which should be met, if at all possible. Nothing of any importance is possible with the exiguous sums provided in the past, and it is of little use to pay an expert £300 a year in order to stimulate a demand, unless the creation of the demand is to be followed by some more positive action.

Present position of Silkworm Culture.

The culture of the silkworm is suitable to the conditions of smallholders both in the Jewish settlements and in the Arab villages in many parts of the country, and this is a useful line of development of a minor type; where the family income is small and every additional piastre makes a difference. Of the reality of the demand there is no doubt. The Arabs of Nablus, to whom reference is made above, were willing to provide £100 towards the creation of a small factory if the Government would lend a further £100 to help them. A second application received from the same town in the month of May this year, stated that 4,000 men were out of work in the town and that, if a loan were given to the applicant, he would start a factory which would provide employment for at least a few of them. In some of the Jewish villages in the Emek the work has already been begun on a small scale.

In general it may be said that the outlook for this small industry is not unfavourable. Its practice is being taught in some of the Government village schools. An effort might well be made to extend its usefulness.

Bees.

The production of honey is another activity for the smallholder. This industry is gradually extending, both among the Jews and among the Arabs, though the number of hives kept by the Jews is probably the larger. Export of honey first commenced in 1925 when 9 tons were despatched; in 1926 the amount exported was only 5 tons which sold for £325. The export rose to 11 tons in 1927, 17 tons in 1928 and 24 tons in 1929. The value of the honey exported in 1929 was £P.1,625 f.o.b.

Prevalence of Foul-brood.

Foul-brood first broke out in Palestine in 1924, when 400 hives were destroyed. Since that time there have been minor outbreaks from time to time, until last year, when there were two serious outbreaks in Jewish settlements, costing the settlers hundreds of hives. It is said that if taken at once, this disease is easily controlled.

Expansion of the industry.

Palestine honey is said to be as good as any in the world. With the extension of the orange groves the production of orange-flower honey has very largely increased; the same is true of eucalyptus honey. Wild thyme is becoming less plentiful, as the land on which it flourished is being broken up, but Palestine has a wealth of wild flowers and there is practically no limit to the possible extension of bee-keeping. It is an occupation in which the fellah rapidly becomes expert, and which is popular among the Jewish settlers. The Government employs an expert, Mr. Lipshitz, who is also in charge of the Acre Poultry Farm. If the industry increases at a rapid rate, as it promises to do, it will be necessary to strengthen the personnel of the Department which deals with it.

(l) Dairy and Stock Breeding.

Contagious abortion.

In many of the Jewish colonies the basis of settlement is the dairy. A large number of bulls and cows were imported from Holland, and, as has been recorded in another chapter, an epidemic of contagious abortion has broken out. The Chief Veterinary Officer states that there are records of the existence of this disease in 60 per cent. of the dairy herds, but that it is probable that all cases have not been reported and that about 80 per cent. are in fact infected. The farms have been planned on the assumption that each cow will provide 2,500 litres of milk for sale, after the necessary deduction for consumption by the family, and for feeding of the calves. The price of milk has been estimated at 13 to 15 mils. The success of the farm naturally depends on the accuracy of these two assumptions. They have been vitiated by the epidemic of contagious abortion, which reduces the yield of the dairy affected for obvious reasons, and by the fall in the price of milk, which was selling in the Emek at the time of this enquiry at 10 mils net the litre.

Stall-feeding of dairy stock.

Stall-feeding of stock and sale of dairy produce is probably the most efficient way of using land in the larger area of the non-irrigable, or semi-irrigable, tracts. In the agricultural development of the country as a whole, the method must take its place. But it must at the same time not be forgotten that the local market for dairy produce is very strictly limited, and that unless some method of disposal of the products is adopted, differing from the ordinary sale in the market, prices will fall so that the area taken as a unit will prove to be insufficient to support a decent standard of life. It is therefore essential to explore the possibility of creating a canning industry for dairy products, and of manufacturing cheese for export. In both of these directions keen competition will be experienced, but unless the efforts made are crowned with success, the dairy cannot be regarded as the basis of settlement except in an area comparatively small, and the size of the holding will have to be enlarged.

CHAPTER IX.

Palestinian Industry.

Census of Industries : Summaries.—In the year 1928 the Department of Customs, Excise and Trade undertook a census of the Industries of Palestine. This census indicates that, at that time, there were 3,505 factories, establishments and workshops, employing in all 17,955 persons of whom 10,186 were wage-earners, the balance of 7,769 including owners, clerks, technicians and, apparently, contract labour. Graph No. 2 appended shows the distribution of persons employed by groups, age, sex and occupation.

The average number of persons employed was 5.1 per establishment. This is an indication of the very small scale of the industry which is carried on in Palestine.

In the year 1927 the total expenditure of these establishments, including raw materials, salaries and wages, and fuel amounted to £2,975,401—an average of £849 per establishment. (Vide Graph No. 3.) They produced in all, industrial articles valued at a total sum of £3,886,149, or £1,109 on the average for each establishment. The total capital invested was £3,514,886, averaging just over £1,000 per establishment. Graph No. 4, appended, shows the racial distribution of the number of undertakings established, pre-war and post-war, and the capital invested.

Food, Drink, Tobacco.—The most important group was that dealing with Food, Drink and Tobacco. In this group there were 473 establishments, with a capital of £1,319,912, with an expenditure of £1,664,083 and production valued at £2,036,272. The group included flour milling, distillation of intoxicating liquors, bakeries, tobacco and cigarette manufacture.

Chemicals and allied trades.—The next group in importance is that of Chemicals and Allied trades, including olive oil presses, soap-making, etc. It employed a total capital of £638,313. The expenditure of the year 1927 was £506,409 and the production was worth £649,523.

Cement, Brick, Stone and Clay trades.—The group, containing the Cement, Brick, Stone and Clay trades, includes one of the largest and most important individual factories in the country, the " Nesher " Cement Works. In the group are 148 establishments. The total capital invested was £517,106, the expenditure £155,903, and the value of the out-turn £209,994.

Census of Jewish industry.—The Jewish Agency has supplied a Memorandum on Jewish industry based on a census carried out in the month of March, 1930. It covered 2,274 urban enterprises, which gave work to 9,362 persons, had an annual wage bill of £476,452 and used raw materials to a value of £904,881. They produced finished articles to a value of £1,635,462 and estimated their invested capital at £998,904. Thus the average number of workers per establishment is 4.11, who are paid on the average about £51 per annum. The raw materials used average £398 per establishment per annum. Per establishment the finished articles averaged £718 for the year, and the average invested capital was about £435.

In the case of these purely Jewish industries also the average establishment is very small indeed.

The Memorandum divides the industries into three classes. In the first class there are 1,725 enterprises, in each of which less than five persons are employed. In the second class, employing from five to nine, there are 418 establishments. The third class comprising 131 establishments are those which provide occupation for 10 and over.

Of these Jewish enterprises, the most active period of foundation was that covering the years 1920 to 1924. That period saw the foundation of 50 of these larger enterprises, which now employ 1,515 persons and have a capital of £291,930. The following period, 1925 to 1929, was responsible for the creation of 56 enterprises, but they employ at the present time only 1,204 persons and have a capital of £188,489.

Principal industrial undertakings.—Certain of the industrial concerns are deserving of special mention.

Of all the industries of Palestine at the present time, the two potentially most important are the concessions granted to Mr. Rutenberg for the production of electric power from the Jordan, now being worked by the Palestine Electric Corporation, Ltd., a company registered in London, and to Messrs. Novomejsky and Major Tulloch for the exploitation of the salts of the Dead Sea. This concession is now being operated by Palestine Potash, Ltd., also a company registered in London.

The harnessing of the Yarmuk and of the Jordan for the purpose of the first concession is now complete, and it will be no long time before electric current is available all over the North of Palestine, both for power and for light. Meanwhile all that is required is provided from the Company's Power Houses in Tel-Aviv, Haifa and elsewhere.

Palestine Potash, Ltd., is also approaching the stage at which manufacture will begin. The waters of the Dead Sea are already being pumped up into the sand pans in which they will be evaporated by the sun and from which the concentrated liquor (carnallite) will be conveyed to the factory.

" *Nesher* " *cement works.*—A large individual enterprise is the " Nesher " cement works at Haifa. These works are the property of the Portland Cement Company " Nesher," Ltd., registered in London with an authorised capital of £300,000, of which £250,000 is paid up. The Company has issued £50,000 of first mortgage debentures.

The factory produces first-class cement. It employs at the present time 390 wage-earners, of whom 250 are Jews, 10 Jewesses and 130 Arabs.

The Company commenced business in 1925. At that time the import duty on cement was 200 mils (4s.) per ton. In 1926 the total sales were 41,610 tons, of which 2,045 tons were exported.

109

In 1927 the total sales rose to 45,888 tons, of which 9,012 tons were exported. In November of that year the duty was raised to 600 mils (12s.) per metric ton.

In 1928 total sales were 59,165 tons, of which 11,332 tons were exported. In December, 1928, the protective duty was again raised, from 600 to 850 mils (12s. to 16s. 6d.) per metric ton.

In 1929, the total sales rose to 68,661 tons, of which 7,699 tons were exports.

In the sixth annual report for the year 1928 the Company's profit was shown as £19,271, and a dividend of 6 per cent. tax free was declared.

The Company's cement is sold in Palestine at £P.2.700 mils (54s.) per ton. Last year, 1929, cement was exported to Syria, Cyprus and Egypt, but the major portion went to Syria, where it was sold at an average price of 45s. a ton—9s. a ton cheaper than the Palestine price, notwithstanding the cost of transport to Syria. The Manager of the Company explained that building activity in Palestine is irregular, and that, in order to meet any sudden demand, it is necessary to maintain production at a higher rate than that justified by the average local demand. For this reason there is a necessity to dispose of the excess product so manufactured even at a price that is not remunerative.

"*Nesher*" *cement: Effect of protective tariff.*—It is clear that the Company would have made a loss in place of a profit had the whole production been sold locally at the Syrian price. Also that the industry could not be maintained were it not for the protective tariff. The sole good reason in favour of the tariff is that it enables the Company to employ 260 Jews and Jewesses and 130 Arabs who might otherwise have been without employment. This argument is not convincing to the purchaser in Palestine, who ultimately has to pay the protective duty in the price of his cement. Specially is the argument unconvincing to him when the profit created by the protective tariff for which Palestine is paying passes into the pockets of an English Company registered in London. The expediency of increasing the protective tariff from 12s. to 16s. 6d. a ton in view of the profits gained under the lower rate of tariff is also frequently canvassed, and with reason.

Eastern Oil Industries, Ltd.—The " Shemen " Works, of the Eastern Oil Industries, Ltd., a Company registered in London, were founded in 1929 by Messrs. Paenson and Wilbush. The Company was known as the Palestine Oil Industry " Shemen," Ltd., and it subsequently transferred the business to the present proprietors. The works are situated at Haifa. The factory manufactures olive, sesame and other oils from Palestinian products, and also coconut oil from imported copra. It makes toilet and washing soaps, cooking fats, boiled linseed, oil-paints, perfumes and sweets (such as " Halwa "); from the residue, cattle cake is pressed.

The following statement shows the output, the sales and the maximum number of workers employed during three years 1927, 1928, 1929 and the present year up to 1st May :—

Year.	Output in Tons.	Sales in Tons.	Value.	Maximum Number of Workers.
			£	
1927	2,742	2,308	96,700	122
1928	3,959	3,298	130,700	228
1929	7,706	6,462	168,700	258
1930 to 1st May	—	1,143	33,000	110

No manufacturing appears to have been done during the first four months of the present year. In all probability this is due to the present position in the oil-stuffs industry. Over-production of oil is universal in Palestine, and the price of all oil has fallen very heavily in consequence.

The labour employed is entirely Jewish.

Soap.—Nablus is the great centre of the olive-oil soap factories, and the export of this soap is by far the most important of industrial exports from Palestine. The soap is manufactured in very primitive fashion, and maintains its market, chiefly in Egypt, owing to its well-founded reputation for the employment of the purest ingredients. Animal fats of every kind are avoided, a fact which renders the soap pure in the eyes of the devout Moslem. The total value of the production of the Nablus factories is estimated at £240,000 per annum. The proprietors of the factories and all the workmen, who number about 200, are Arab.

Tobacco: Messrs. Karaman, Dick and Salti.—The factory employing the most labour is the tobacco factory of Messrs. Karaman, Dick and Salti at Haifa. The labour force, which is almost entirely Arab, numbers over 500. The factory manufactures cigarettes for the local market, and does a large increasing business. A second tobacco factory, that of Messrs. Maspero Frères, Ltd., belongs to a company registered in London, and also does an increasing business. Its personnel, which is chiefly Jewish, exceeds 100.

Grands Moulins de Palestine.—Haifa is also the seat of the Grands Moulins de Palestine. These Flour Mills were originally founded by Baron Edmond de Rothschild, and it is understood that he still takes an interest in the venture. They commenced working in 1923, and the value of the annual outturn has varied between £90,000 and £145,000. They cater almost entirely for the home market, but occasionally export flour to Syria. The same company operates also a factory for the production of " matzot," the unleavened Passover cakes. The annual output of this subsidiary factory is from 330 to 440 tons. Of the production about one-half is consumed in Palestine and the other half exported.

The two factories together employ slightly over 100 men and women, all of them Jews.

Complaints are made that no protection is offered to this industry. It is said that the competition of imported flour is such that the mills only produce to half their full capacity. It is pointed out that the import of foreign flour is actually greater than the amount of flour milled in the country. The manager of the mills expressed the hope that the import duty on flour might be increased and that on wheat reduced, as this would enable the local mills to grind flour from foreign wheat for the local market. He pointed out that the local wheat does not lend itself to the production of a white flour, such as is required to make white bread. All the local wheats are of the macaroni variety, and produce what he described as a " thick " flour, yellowish in colour. He also complained of the high cost of transport by the Palestine Railways. He stated that business was decreasing on account of competition, in meeting which the mills were at a disadvantage owing to the facts cited.

The wine industry.—Wine is manufactured in the German Colonies, by the Salesian Fathers at Beit Jamal, and on a small scale in a number of ecclesiastical institutions. But the most important cellars are those attached to certain of the P.I.C.A. villages. The famous cellars of Richon-le-Zion and of Zichron Jacob were erected by Baron Edmond de Rothschild at his own expense, and he has leased them since 1906 at a nominal rental to the Co-operative Society of the Vinegrowers of the Cellars of Richon-le-Zion and Zichron Jacob, Ltd. The cellars at Rehovoth and the distillery at Gedera are the property of the Co-operative Society. During the last season the society has produced :—

    1,650,000 litres of dry wine.
    1,035,000 litres of sweet wine.
       56,000 litres of grape juice.
     137,000 litres of spirit distilled from grapes and raisins.
      70,000 litres of araki manufactured from alcohol or molasses.

The above has a total value of £80,000. Of this total production wine to the value of about £35,000 is exported.

The Co-operative Society complains of the high rates of Licence fees and Excise Duty, to which reference has been made earlier in this report. It also complains, as do other industries, of the high rate of railway freights on the Palestine Railways. In a note submitted for purposes of this enquiry the society writes as follows :—

> " Generally the business was improving up to the period of the disturbances in August last. The hard economical conditions nearly everywhere in Europe and the Orient, the fall in quotations of wine abroad, the doubled taxes and fees in Palestine, the troubles and disturbances

in that country, the last order of the Palestine Government to restrict the immigration and very deep disappointment provoked amongst the Jewish Communities abroad, have necessarily affected the trade unfavourably in the home market and abroad."

Other industries.—The smaller and newer industries, as a general rule prefer Tel-Aviv to Haifa. These have in most cases been established by immigrants who have arrived in Palestine since 1920. A large number of them seem to provide employment for women rather than for men.

Printing.—One of the industries which is growing rapidly and which shows signs of extension is that of printing. It is reported in the Memorandum submitted by the Jewish Agency that in Jewish establishments alone 1,030 persons are employed. At the time of the census of industries, the total number employed was 992, of whom 18.4 per cent. were Arabs. Assuming the same percentage of Arabs to be employed to-day and making the consequent addition to the Jewish return, the total number employed in 1930 would be 1,230, an increase of over 24 per cent. in the three years. That this industry should prosper is natural. It is engaged largely in the printing and publication of Hebrew books, for which there is an increasing world demand.

Smaller industries.—Of other smaller industries the more interesting are those for the manufacture of artificial teeth, of fancy leather goods, of textiles and fruit products.

As to the factory of artificial teeth, the Memorandum of the Jewish Agency contains the following :—

"No one writing on the industrial possibilities of Palestine could by any logical course of reasoning arrive at the apparently fantastic conclusion that Palestine is a country particularly suited to the manufacture of artificial teeth.

"But a Jew who had immigrated to the United States some forty or fifty years ago had become a most successful manufacturer of artificial teeth, and on coming to Palestine he found that he could manufacture them in Palestine successfully as well. They are now being made in Tel-Aviv in a nice modern factory which gives work to over 50 workers and they are being exported, mainly to England . . . ."

Fancy Leather industry.—The leather bag industry, which is showing distinct signs of progress, was introduced by some Polish Jews, who had technical knowledge of the leather industry. The "Zetge" Company now makes leather hand-bags in Tel-Aviv and exports them to Egypt and elsewhere. The Company started in 1926 with one workman. It now employs 65 persons altogether. The Company made a request that leather should be considered as a raw material and should be admitted free of import duty. There is a protective duty of 15 per cent. *ad valorem* on Ready Fancy leather goods, and the import duty on expensive light leather has been reduced by 50 per cent. These measures appear to have assisted the industry considerably, and its very success tends to show that conditions of competition are not so severe as materially to affect the Company.

113

Textile industry.—Of textile factories, according to the Census of Jewish industries, there are 40, of which 12 employ more than 10 persons apiece. Among these there is one which is producing stockings on a considerable scale. The exports of Stockings and Hose have increased from a value of £430 in 1925 to £17,532 in 1928 and £18,919 in 1929. Of this sum the major part is due to the " Lodzia " Stocking Factory. Its history is interesting, and is thus described in the Memorandum of the Jewish Agency :—

> " . . . . Some time ago some people came from Poland and started manufacturing these articles. They had some small experience of the business but not sufficient, and the factory proved a failure in their hands. It was taken over by another Jewish immigrant who all his life (in Russia) had been doing this particular business; he also had sufficient means and he made the factory into success."

The stocking produced is a very cheap article and evidently supplies a considerable demand both locally and in adjoining countries.

Fruit-juice and fruit products.—An industry which, as yet of small proportions, may ultimately prove of great importance to Palestine is that of fruit-juice and fruit products. The " Assis " Company manufactures fruit-juice of excellent quality from oranges. There is a considerable quantity of oranges which for various reasons are not fit for export though perfectly sound fruit. With the increasing production of the orange the number of these unexportable oranges will increase rapidly, and the " Assis " Company is one of the agencies for profitable disposal of this fruit. It is desirable that efforts should be made to popularise the products of this and of similar concerns, in the interests of the orange-growers. The produce of this factory much resembles that of a well-known Australian factory.

The Development of Industry.

Industrial enterprises before the War and subsequent increase.— Of existing industrial establishments 1,236, with a total capital in excess of one million pounds were in existence before the War. Since the War therefore the number of establishments had increased up to the date of the Industrial Census by 2,269 or 183 per cent. and the capital by two and a half million pounds, or 250 per cent. This is a very material increase and it is almost entirely due to the importation of Jewish capital and the immigration of a Jewish population.

Industry in the past.—Views of very differing nature are expressed in different quarters both in regard to the expansion of industry in Palestine in the past and as to its prospects in the future.

The remarkable feature of the past is the rapid increase of the small industry and the comparatively stationary position of the large. It is clear that the " Nesher " Cement Factory is dependent on protection not only for its profits, but for its existence. It could not compete with imported cement, were the protective tariff withdrawn. The withdrawal of the duty on imported oilseeds appeared to be a necessity to the success of the "Shemen" oil factory. The Cellars of Richon-Le-Zion and Zichron-Jacob owe their very existence, not to economic action, but to the liberality and interest of Baron Edmond de Rothschild. The industry continues to prosper by reason of the protective duties on imported wines and spirits. The textile trade benefits by the import of its raw materials free of duty and by a 12 per cent. *ad valorem* tax on similar goods imported into the country. In fact, large industry in Palestine appears to depend on manipulation of the tariff. The rest of the population is taxed in order that the proprietors of these industrial concerns may be in a position to pay the wages of their labourers and to make a profit for themselves.

Small industries.—The number of very small industries is most surprising. In the Memorandum submitted by the Jewish Agency it is stated that in the Colonies and Villages there are over 400 enterprises in which 700 persons are engaged; i.e., on the average less than two persons per enterprise. It is difficult to imagine such an establishment as being more than an instance of home industry.

Number of persons employed.—The figures of the Industrial Census of 1928 are very illuminating on this point of the small workshop. In 31.4 per cent. of the establishments no paid labour at all was employed, in 20.1 per cent. one wage-earner, in 26.2 per cent. two or three, in 13.3 per cent. four or five. That is to say, that of the whole of the industrial establishments in Palestine at that time 91 per cent. employed five wage-earners or less. At the other end of the scale twelve establishments, or 0.3 per cent. of the whole, employed over 100 wage-earners, fifteen, or 0.4 per cent., employed between 50 and 100. The number of establishments employing over 50 wage-earners was therefore twenty-seven in the whole of Palestine, and they formed 0.7 per cent. of the total of industrial concerns.

Future development of industry: Jewish.—The question of the future development of industry in Palestine is discussed at considerable length in the Memorandum of the Jewish Agency to which reference has been already made. The Memorandum considers that "from the point of view of Industry the whole talk of the absorptive capacity of the country is out of place and should be disposed of once and for all." The aim of Jewish industry is not "to cater for the wants of 600,000 Arabs, three-quarters of whom are poor peasants . . . . it is to the Jewish Community itself and to Export that Jewish industry looks in the first place. It is quite incorrect to believe that Jewish Immigration is dependent on a market being already available; it is before all things Jewish immigration that creates the home market and conquers the foreign market . . . . What really defines the possibilities of future Jewish Industry in Palestine is a factor which has not yet received sufficient attention and which indeed is not yet to its full extent known even to the Jews themselves : *it is the human factor.*

115

" The fundamental question *is not*
Where are we going to take the power?
nor
What raw materials are available?
not even—although it is an important question,
What are the best markets?

" The fundamental question is: Are there Jews, and how many of them are there, who are prepared to immigrate into Palestine if sufficiently encouraged, or at least not discouraged, and who will bring with them sufficient capital and adequate business experience, but preferably a sufficient knowledge of a particular industry in order to set up industries which may, each in its own line, compete with similar industries; and are there other Jews who are prepared to immigrate into Palestine to supply the skilled and unskilled labour required?

" If such Jews do not exist at all or are not available in any large numbers then the present investigation with respect to the possibility of an industrial immigration as distinct from an agricultural immigration becomes obviously purposeless. The problem will then have been solved by its non-existence. It is the contention of the Zionists that such Jews do exist and that they are available in large numbers, that they clamour for admittance and that in settling in Palestine they will not drive (? away) the Arab population that it holds at present."

Possibilities of an extension of industry.—The Memorandum goes on to point out certain promising directions in which there is scope for an extension of industry. It mentions the Clothing industry as a specifically Jewish industry all over the world, it suggests that there is no reason why Palestine should not rival Egypt as a centre of the Tobacco industry, it points out that the Jews of Poland play an important part in the Textile industry. It goes on to say that there are prospects in Preserved Fruit and Vegetables, it refers to the success of the Printing industry, it anticipates great development of the Chemical industry as the result of the Dead Sea concession.

It then dwells upon the importance of the Tourist industry with all the subsidiary occupations accessory thereto. Finally, after pointing out the opportunities and the demands in the Building industry, the Memorandum closes by relying on the success of the past as an indication of the possibilities of the future, and insisting that such part of Jewish immigration as is meant to be absorbed by industry should not be limited by any imaginary absorptive power of the country.

" . . . . The absorptive capacity of the country, from the point of view of industry, is dependent only on the willingness and ability of Jewish capitalists to start industries which they may understand and the products of which they can market, and of Jewish labour to come in and work."

Future of Palestinian industry.—It is a difficult thing to forecast the future of industry in a country, and not easier in the case of

Palestine than in that of others. In fact it is more difficult, as the future development will not depend, as is ordinarily the case, on the economic capacity of the country, but on a stimulus which may be called artificial, without misuse of that word.

The Director of the Department of Customs, Excise and Trade wrote as follows on this subject:—

" .... It is doubtful whether some of the larger concerns .... would be able to stand without outside help; but there are certainly several small factories which are making a profit and show every prospect of success and a striking example of this is the Artificial Tooth Factory ....

" It would appear that for a factory to have any real chance of ultimate success it must look to the markets of Egypt and Syria to take the larger proportion of its manufactures, and not to the Palestine market; it is therefore those factories which are manufacturing articles likely to find a ready sale in those countries which would seem to have the most prospect of success and to be worthy of Government assistance in the way of exemptions for raw material.

" It cannot be said that there are any prospects of the heavy industries enumerated above requiring any fresh labour, but certain additional labour might be required as some of the smaller factories progress. Probably at least 50 per cent. of such additional labour would be female ....

" A recent examination of the exports of manufactures from Palestine does not show that rapid expansion which is desired, even allowing for the set-back owing to the disturbances in August, 1929. On the other hand, there is progress, although slow, and although many of the weaker concerns must fail, there are reasonable hopes of progress for certain industries in Palestine—but not on anything like the scale that was at one time anticipated. In fact it would seem probable that it will be a matter of many years before Palestine is likely to be able to claim to be an industrial as well as an agricultural country."

Immigration as a solution of industrial problems.—There is in certain quarters an optimism with regard to the industrial possibilities of Palestine which is founded chiefly on hope, partly on conviction. It has been quite seriously argued that the difficulty of disposal of an excess of dairy produce could be solved by the arrival of immigrants in sufficient numbers. A similar argument has been used with regard to housing. The more immigrants arrive, the more employment there will be for those whose occupation it is to build houses. From such a point of view, it is true that the introduction of capital and labour and the erection of textile mills on a large scale in Haifa and Tel-Aviv would bring prosperity to the country until the capital was expended. But it is the duty of the Government to look further than the immediate present. There seems no reason why a Textile industry on the grand scale should be a success in Palestine, with labour paid at the rates fixed by the General Federation of Jewish Labour, while the mills of Japan and of Bombay, equipped with the most modern machinery, and employing the cheapest of labour, are unable to find sufficient markets for their goods. From the point of view of those whose ardent desire it is to import Jews from Poland and Russia and the Yemen into Palestine in large numbers, and whose object is gained when the immigrant has arrived in Palestine, it may be sufficient that temporary employment is assured. But the Government is responsible not only for the present, while the imported capital is supporting the new population, but for the future, when spending of the imported capital will be at an end and the immigrant will have to live on employment, which will then be dependent on the success of the mill in competition with the mills of the world.

Progress of industry.—An examination of the figures of exports due to the existing industries does not support the view that the industry of Palestine is making very rapid progress. Mr. Goldwater has written for the Palestine Corporation Ltd. a most interesting and important general report on Palestine for the year 1929. At the end of that review he gives the figures of export of the principle products of industry, for the years since 1925. The totals of those figures for the past three years are the following:—

	£
1927	426,983
1928	426,160
1929	482,826

In the first two of the three years, soap, an ancient indigenous industry, accounted for more than half the exports.

Industries likely to succeed.—There are industries for which there is every hope of success in Palestine. There is no reason, as is pointed out in the Memorandum, why the Tobacco industry should not become increasingly important. It is exceedingly desirable that a Canning industry should prove a success if the Dairy industry and the Fruit industry are to expand in the future. Every effort should be made to extend the market for and the production of fruit-juice. The Printing industry will doubtless develop naturally into an important branch of the industry of Palestine. If the Dead Sea concession proves to be a successful venture, it is impossible to forecast the magnitude to which the Chemical industry arising therefrom may expand. The Tourist industry (if it can legitimately be so designated) will doubtless continue to grow and to afford employment for a greater number of persons each year All of these are perfectly natural developments.

Danger of unemployment.—It would be a bad, and might prove a fatal policy, to attract large capital in order to start doubtful industries in Palestine, with the object of justifying an increase in the number of immigrants. The Memorandum spends much effort in an attempt to establish that the year of " so-called " crisis in 1926 was not in fact a year of crisis at all. It is a question, somewhat academic, of the meaning to be attached to the wor-

" crisis ". In that year the provision of relief works for the Jewish immigrants who could not otherwise obtain a living was actually necessary. Whether or not that should be designated a crisis is immaterial. It was an episode of which no Government would willingly contemplate the recurrence. The importation of large numbers of immigrants to be employed on new industries of extensive character whose economic success is quite problematical, might well cause a crisis compared with which the " so-called " crisis of 1926 would indeed seem unimportant.

Concentration on industries showing vitality.—The correct principle governing the problem is to concentrate on those industries which already show signs of vitality and success, and to attempt to create those, such as are detailed in the Memorandum and above in this report, whose effect will be to increase the exports of manufactured goods and to employ as raw material Palestinian products of which it is impossible otherwise to dispose.

Arab industries.—There exist certain indigenous Arab industries besides that of soap, to which reference has been made earlier. There is a Tanning industry, there is a Pottery industry, there is a Weaving industry and a Carpet-making industry. All of these are on a very small scale. In any attempt to develop the country, the claims of Arab industry should not be overlooked. There is in existence a Society of a semi-charitable nature which is designed to encourage and stimulate the indigenous industries. It will find its place in any general scheme of development.

Mineral deposits.—The mineral resources of Palestine have been examined by the Government Geologist, who has published an interesting report.* There is no doubt that phosphatic rock exists in very large quantities, both in Palestine and in Trans-Jordania, and that some of it is of good marketable quality. Transport is an outstanding difficulty. Bitumen has also been found, and there are oil-shales in certain tracts. Recently an important deposit of sulphur is said to have been discovered in the Gaza area, and a syndicate formed to work it. Copper is believed to exist in the Akabah peninsula.

Though nothing very definite has so far been done, the chances of mineral development of the country exist, and this possibility should not be overlooked.

---

* " The Mineral Resources of Palestine and Trans-Jordania," by G. S. Blake, Jerusalem, 1930.

CHAPTER X.

Immigration.

The figures of Immigration since 1st November, 1922, are included in Appendix 22, and of Emigration in Appendix 23.

Early history.—For the purposes of this report it is unnecessary to discuss the early history of immigration into Palestine. The original Immigration Ordinance came into force in 1920, under which the Zionist Organization were authorized to introduce into the country 16,500 immigrants per annum, on condition that they accepted responsibility for their maintenance for one year. This system was not found to be a success, and in May, 1921, immigration was suspended until revised conditions could be imposed.

Pronouncement of 3rd June, 1921.—Those conditions were announced in a public pronouncement by the High Commissioner on 3rd June of that year.

The following categories of immigrants were permitted in accordance with the pronouncement:—

(a) Travellers who did not intend to remain in Palestine for more than three months,

(b) Persons of independent means who intended to reside permanently in Palestine,

(c) Members of professions who intended to follow their calling,

(d) Wives, children and other dependents of persons resident in Palestine,

(e) Persons with definite prospects of employment with specified employers,

(f) Persons of religious occupation, who could show that they had means of maintenance in Palestine,

(g) Returning residents.

It was found by experience that these regulations were not altogether satisfactory; and in September, 1924, a series of new orders were issued under the form of Regulations under the Immigration Ordinance.

Immigration Ordinance, 1925.—In the year 1925 the existing Ordinance was repealed and replaced by the Immigration Ordinance of that year, which, as amended in 1928, is still in force. Regulations under the Ordinance were issued in September, 1925. These again have been supplemented by Regulations dated 1st July, 1926, and amended by Regulations of 1st December, 1927. This Ordinance and these regulations are the legal authority which govern immigration into Palestine to-day.

120

Categories of immigrants.—Immigrants into Palestine fall into one of the following nine categories :—

A.—(i) Persons in possession of £1,000 and upwards, and their families.

A.—(ii) Professional men in possession of £500 and upwards.

A.—(iii) Skilled artisans in possession of £250 and upwards.

A.—(iv) Persons enjoying an assured income of £4 per month.

B.—(i) Orphans destined for institutions in Palestine.

B.—(ii) Men and women of religious occupation, whose maintenance is assured, and their families.

B.—(iii) Students, whose maintenance is assured.

C.—Working men and women and their families.

D.—Dependent relatives of residents in Palestine, who are in a position to maintain them.

Class C is intended to include all who seek or accept employment, with the exception of those admitted under A (ii) or (iii). It is also the intention not to admit in Class A (iv), B (ii) or (iii) and D, any persons who will seek employment or go into trade.

It has been found by experience that the regulations are not entirely effective in this respect. Immigrants of Classes D and A (iv) are found to engage in trade. Formerly immigrants under Class D sought employment in many cases and still do so. Those under B (iii) also occasionally do so.

Unrecorded immigration.—In addition to the persons of the categories provided for those who desire to settle in Palestine, a large number of persons, amounting to some thousands each year, secure admission to the country in the guise of travellers. Only a minority come under notice and, of these, those qualified are registered as immigrants under their respective categories. Those of the working class and under 35 years of age are counted against the Labour Immigration Schedule. The rest are refused permission to remain in Palestine, but it is exceedingly difficult to secure their departure, and a large number remain in the country. In addition a number of persons, not inappreciable, secure admission by evading such controls as exist on the frontiers.

No effective control of immigration into Palestine is possible unless steps are taken to deal with these two classes of irregular entrants.

Procedure in regard to the issue of Immigration Certificates.—With reference to the Labour Schedule on which the number of immigrants under Class C is based, the Commission on the Palestine Disturbances wrote on pp. 104 and 105 of their report :—

" . . . . We were informed by the Chief Immigration Officer that in the allocation to individuals of the certificates which are supplied in blank to the General Federation of Jewish Labour, it is the practice of that body to have regard to the political creed of the several possible immigrants rather than to their particular qualifications for admission to Palestine. It is clearly the duty of the responsible Jewish authorities to select for admission to Palestine those of the prospective immigrants who are best qualified on personal grounds to assist in the establishment of a Jewish National Home in that country; that political creed should be a deciding factor in the choice between applicants is open to the strongest exception."

This statement of the Commission has been disputed by the Zionist Agency, who refer to Mr. Snell's Reservations at p. 175, where he describes the actual procedure. From enquiries made from the Executive of the Jewish Agency it appears that the regular practice is that described by Mr. Snell.

The Influence of the General Federation of Jewish Labour over immigrants and immigration.—There is nevertheless a very close connection between the General Federation of Jewish Labour and the immigrant, even before he leaves the country whence he comes.

In each of the countries whence immigrants come, there exists an organization for preliminary training in agricultural practice. Close to Warsaw, for example, there is a large farm on which the Chalutzim, the Pioneers, obtain agricultural training and instruction. In Galicia they become paid agricultural labourers. Similar arrangements exist in Germany and in France. To each of these centres of training, the General Federation of Jewish Labour has deputed instructors. At the time of writing twenty of these teachers, almost all of whom are so deputed, are employed. These men, though representatives of the General Federation, receive from that Federation only the cost of their journey. Their expenses in the country in which they work are met either by their own earnings or by funds provided by some Zionist Organization.

The actual choice of the individual immigrant is, it is true, made by the Committee to which reference is made by Mr. Snell in his note of Reservations. It is at the same time clear that all the immigrants who come in on the Labour Schedule are trained by teachers deputed by the General Federation before they are so chosen. The large majority become members of the Federation immediately on arrival. The official in charge of the Hostel in which immigrants reside on their arrival at Jaffa is himself a member of the Executive of the General Federation of Jewish Labour, and as the Jewish Agency point out in a Memorandum on immigration which they have submitted in connection with this enquiry, the Immigration Department of the Jewish Agency provides for the registration of all arriving immigrants as members of the Kupat-Cholim (the Sick Fund of the General Federation of Jewish Labour).

It is therefore somewhat disingenuous to suggest that the General Federation of Jewish Labour is unconnected with the choice of the individual immigrant. In the great majority of cases the immigrant would have no chance of a permit, unless he were *persona grata* to the Labour authorities.

The following is an extract from the Memorandum submitted to the " Palestine Commission of Enquiry " (i.e., the Commission on the Disturbances of August, 1929) by the General Federation of Jewish Labour. After describing its many and important activities in Palestine, it says :—

> " . . . . The Federation exercises a decisive influence upon Zionist youth in the Diaspora, anxious to bring about the fulfilment of the Zionist ideal by their own labour. Practically all over Europe there exist ' Hehaluz ' (the Pioneer) organizations training Jewish boys and girls in agriculture and industry for the purpose of taking a direct part in the upbuilding of Palestine. These organizations, which supply the bulk of the human material for the Zionist work in Palestine that is based on manual labour, are organically linked with the Histadruth (i.e. the General Federation) which controls their educational work. An immigrant Halutz automatically becomes a member of the Histadruth upon his arrival in Palestine. . . . "

A further quotation bearing on this point is the following, extracted from a communication from Agudath Israel, the body of orthodox Jews :—

> " . . . . We do not think that there is any ground for the anxiety expressed in the Report of the Shaw Commission regarding the alleged party influence on the distribution of certificates, but the attitude towards immigrants of the religious class has been very unsatisfactory up to the present. In Poland, the chief source of Palestine Jewish immigration where orthodox Jewry, i.e. Agudath-Israel, holds a very important position, young men of this class were refused immigration certificates, in spite of the fact that such religious people have a still greater longing for Palestine owing to the holiness of the land and to the respective religious bidding . . . . "

From the above it is evident that though the detailed facts alleged before the Commission may not have been exact, the statement made did in essence convey a general description of the position, which is not by any means far from accurate.

Preparation of Labour Immigration Schedules.—The preparation of the Labour Immigration Schedules is governed by Regulation 8 made under the Immigration Ordinance. Twice in each year the Jewish Agency presents a memorandum giving the number of men and women immigrants whom they consider will be needed for new employment during the period under review, and exposing the reasons in detail. This memorandum is considered by the Chief Immigration Officer in the light of information received also from other sources, as, for instance, the Director of Public Works, the General Manager of the Palestine Railways, the principal employers of labour, the General Federation of Jewish Labour. Information which has come to officers of the Immigration section in the course of their regular work and investigations is also taken into consideration.

The information available from all sources is then tabulated in the following form :—

A. Jewish Unemployed.
B. Jews whose employment will cease during the half year.
C. Total.
D. Additional Jewish labour required by larger employers and public bodies.
E. Estimated requirements of small employers.
F. Reserve.
G. Total.

Assuming that G exceeds C, the difference is recommended to the High Commissioner as the figure for the Schedule and this recommendation is considered by him in Executive Council.

The Reserve to which reference is made is a number of 300 placed at the disposal of the Chief Immigration Officer to meet special cases which may occur during the six months, as for instance applications for particular skilled men wanted by an employer for his work, the need having arisen after the preparation of the Schedule. This reserve is authorised by Regulation 9 (1).

Procedure adopted after schedule approved by High Commissioner.—A schedule having been approved by the High Commissioner, the necessary number of immigration certificates is prepared. Of these the required number is reserved for private employers in Palestine whose applications have been approved and whose candidates are qualified for the Schedule. Certificates are also reserved for working men and women within the ages laid down, who are found during the Schedule period to be in Palestine without permission. The remainder of the certificates less the " Reserve " (F. above) are placed at the disposal of the Jewish Agency, which is expected therefrom to provide to all Jewish young men and women (excepting wives) of the working class on whose behalf application is made by relatives for immigration certificates during the half year.

Authorization of Visas.—The Jewish Agency is asked to indicate where the respective visas will be claimed and in reply a list is sent in the following form :—

	Men.	Women.
Warsaw (say)	500	300
Berlin	200	100
	etc., etc.	

The original certificates are then sent in blank to the Agency for distribution to its representatives in the towns concerned, duplicates being despatched to the British Passport or consular officers in the same towns.

Instructions are conveyed to Passport or Consular Officers intimating that visas may be granted to persons who fulfil the conditions laid down, and who are nominated by the Jewish Agency representative, and that those who are married may obtain visas at the same time for their wives and minor children. Visas should in no circumstances be granted to men and women to whom there is known political or medical objection, or objection on account of character.

Failure of the system.—The system described above fails to work well in certain particulars. In many cases persons have been admitted who, if the facts had all been known, should not have received visas. A large number of these cases have been examined. A considerable number concern Yemenite Jews who immigrate from Aden. The following cases all concern immigration certificates which have been used during the last three months, and were issued by the representatives of the Jewish Agency at Aden : —

(i) A man aged 30 with a wife aged 20 and a son aged 12. This would imply that the son was born when his mother was eight years old.

(ii) A man aged 28 with a wife aged 18 and their son aged 12. In this case the mother must have been six years old when the son was born.

(iii) A man aged 23 with a wife aged 10 and their daughter aged 5.

(iv) A man aged 35 with a wife aged 24 and their daughter aged 15.

(v) A man aged 35 with his wife aged 25 and their daughter aged 16.

(vi) A man aged 35 with his wife aged 26 and their son aged 15.

(vii) A man aged 30 with a wife aged 22 and a son aged 12.

The Immigration Officer writes with reference to cases such as these :—

" . . . . It would appear that the practice is growing up in Aden—it is not unknown elsewhere—of attaching wives and families to persons entitled to immigration certificates so that by this means the passport control of this Government may be evaded . . . ."

The following is the copy of a letter dated 14th April, 1930, from an immigrant who has been in the country some years :—

" . . . . My wife arrived in Palestine on 26th November, 1925, together with (A.B.) as the latter's wife. She was unable to arrive as my wife because I, myself, entered as a traveller and was not yet in possession of a permission to remain in the country. Since my wife strongly wished to join me and meanwhile the wife of (A.B.) became ill (he was in possession of a permission to enter Palestine on her behalf) my wife and our son . . . . arrived on his passport.

" (A.B.) left the country approximately in May, 1926, for Canada via Jaffa—Paris. I am unaware of the exact date of his departure.

Respectfully,
Y.Z.

NOTE.—I cannot recollect whether the first name of Mr. (B) was (A) or (C)."

The above illustrates two typical cases of irregularity. The writer had entered as a Traveller and remained without permission. The wife was introduced on an immigration certificate by fraud.

Weakness of, and responsibility under the present system.—The second case and the cases of the Yemenites discussed earlier indicate a weakness in the present system. The authority responsible for the issue of the certificates is the local representative of the Jewish Agency. He is also responsible for seeing that the person who actually travels, is the person for whom the certificate was issued. It is true that the Yemenite cases should have been detected by the officer who dealt with the visa. The facts were not concealed. They were actually stated on the passport. But the primary responsibility rests with the local agent of the Jewish Agency.

Selection of immigrants abroad.—In the Memorandum of the Jewish Agency on Immigration, the subject of the selection of the emigrants abroad and of the care with which they are chosen and assisted till their arrival at their destination is described in full. The following is a quotation from that Memorandum :—

" . . . . The selection of the immigrants for Palestine is the first and paramount responsibility of the Palestine Offices abroad, which represent all the Zionist circles interested in the up-building of Palestine. These Offices act on the periodical instructions of the Immigration Department of the Jewish Agency, which in turn are given after consultation with the Immigration Board."

It is clear therefore that the Jewish Agency accepts the fullest responsibility for these cases of irregularity. That fact, however, does not render it any the easier to rectify matters, when the immigrant has arrived in Palestine.

Government control abroad.—It is difficult for the Passport Officer or for the Consular Officer to examine all these cases minutely. At the same time it is most important that they should be so examined, both in order to prevent persons being admitted to Palestine who have no right to enter, and to protect the country from characters who may be undesirable. The Immigration Department used to have its own representative at Warsaw to deal with immigration from that centre. The post was abolished for reasons of economy. It is desirable that the post should be reconstituted. It is also desirable that there should be officers representing the Immigration Department in all the centres whence immigration is on a large scale. Only thus will it be possible to ensure both against irregularities in connection with the certificates and against the immigration of undesirables.

Travellers remaining in Palestine.—The case of the traveller who enters with permission to remain for a limited time and then stays on without sanction to do so, is exceedingly common. It is calculated that the numbers of such cases were 2,400 in the year ending June 30th, 1928, 3,400 in the following year and 2,000 in that ending on June 30th, 1930, that is to say, that in the last three years 7,800 persons stayed in Palestine without permission.

Evasion of the frontier control.—Another serious feature of immigration is the number of persons who evade the frontier control and enter Palestine without formality of any kind. It is exceedingly difficult to maintain any effective control of the various frontiers of Palestine. At the present time such control as exists is carried out at police posts on the roads. The immigrant who wishes to evade the control naturally leaves the road before reaching the frontier and takes to the footpaths over the Hills.

Mr. Dowbiggin, who recently enquired into the police of Palestine, remarked on the fact that this duty of controlling immigrants is not a duty which the police should be called upon to perform. It is eminently a duty for the Immigration Department, and it is understood that the Palestine Government is about to replace the Police who are employed on this duty by officials of that Department.

Discouragement of illicit entry.—As to the treatment of such immigrants when they are discovered, it should be the rule that they are at once returned to the country whence they came. The rule may possibly work harshly in individual cases, but unless it is understood that detection is invariably followed by expulsion the practice will not cease. It is probable that it will cease entirely as soon as it is discovered that the rule is actually in force.

The case of the " pseudo-traveller " who comes in with permission for a limited time and continues in Palestine after the term of his permission has expired is more difficult. Each case requires consideration on its merits. Where the case is flagrant, recourse should certainly be had to expulsion. In cases of no special flagrancy, and where there is no objection to the individual, it is probably sufficient to maintain the present practice, under which he is counted against the Labour Schedule, though this method does a certain injustice to the Jewish immigrant outside the country whose place is taken by the traveller concerned.

Immigration and the General Federation of Jewish Labour.—In order to understand the connection between the question of immigration and the labour movement in Palestine it is necessary to have some idea of the activities and policy of the General Federation of Jewish Labour. This powerful Federation is in reality far more than a federation of labour in the ordinary sense. In the Memorandum which the Federation submitted to the Commission on the Disturbances it describes itself and its own activities as follows :—

> " The General Federation of Jewish Labour (Histadruth Haovdim Haivrim Haklalit) is the largest organised body within the Jewish population of Palestine. It numbers 27,000 members, men and women, and encompasses the whole range of the organised activities of the Jewish working class in town and country. It embraces all the Trade

127

Unions and all the different types of workers' co-operatives—in colonisation, production, consumption, contracting and credit. Workers' co-operative settlements on the land affiliated with the Histadruth cover practically the whole field of the agricultural colonisation carried out by the Zionist Organisation during the last twenty-five years. Out of the total number of 123 Jewish agricultural communities, settlements of this type number 46. The Federation conducts educational work among adult and adolescent workers and workers' children for which purpose it has built up a net-work of schools, libraries and reading-rooms in all labour centres. It issues a daily paper and an agricultural journal and publishes books and pamphlets on social, educational and scientific subjects. It carries on a medical and sanitary service through the Workers' Sick Fund, which maintains hospitals, clinics, dispensaries, convalescent homes, and scores of physicians and nurses. The Federation represents a widespread social organism, its members and their families accounting for over a quarter of the Jewish population . . . . The Labour Federation constitutes an important factor within the world Zionist movement. At the last Zionist Congress more than a quarter of the total number of delegates represented such Zionist circles, both in Palestine and abroad, as are indentified with the Federation. . . ."

Settlement of cases in which members are concerned.—This Federation refuses to allow its members to have recourse to the Courts of the land in cases of dispute with another member. It has its own Courts of first and second instance and its Labour High Court to which appeals from the subordinate tribunals lie.

Jewish labour as the key-stone of the Jewish National Home.— It looks upon Jewish Labour (which it most effectively represents) as the key-stone of the Jewish National Home. By permission the following is quoted from a letter of Dr. Arlosoroff, one of the members of the Executive of the Federation. Referring to that view, he says :—

" . . . . (a) The up-building of the National Home means not only the return of a homeless and drifting race to the soil; but, at the same time, the return of a people which for centuries have been cut off from the sources of productive work to a life of labour and toil, the life of a self-supporting community.

" (b) Without the manifold kinds of manual work which naturally form part of a people's everyday life being undertaken by Jews, the National Home in Palestine could never attain to that degree of self-reliance and coherence without which it cannot have any meaning whatever in modern Jewish life.

" (c) The National Home—which is not the profit-hunting enterprise of a Chartered Company—must not be built upon the foundation of cheap native labour exploited by immigrant capitalism.

" (d) Jewish enterprise in Palestine is the result of a conscious effort on the part of various Jewish groups and individuals to co-operate for the purpose of the National Home; it is based on the influx of Jewish capital—public and private—and should therefore provide the natural centre of absorption for Jewish labour.

" (e) The young Jewish immigrants, most of whom are coming to this country with the intention of settling on the land, need a training ground for their future independent career as farmers or planters; employment at Jewish plantations or farms during a number of years provides the necessary training."

The above note puts shortly the argument for the admission of Jewish labour in the interest of building up the Jewish National Home, though there may already be other labour in the country competent to do the tasks available. In another letter the Executive Committee of the General Federation wrote :—

> " . . . . When, therefore, immigration is restricted by administrative measures, not only is the inalienable Jewish right of return to Palestine assailed but an obstacle is also placed in the way of the country's general progress. At this point our meaning must not be misunderstood. We are not basing our claims to unrestricted immigration on the benefits which the Jewish influx confers upon the other elements of the population. We believe ourselves to be fully entitled to serve the interests of the Jewish masses and to let this consideration determine our line of action . . . . This is our stand in principle, but it is our privilege to point to the fact that in practice our immigration and settlement, far from ousting other elements, has actually spelt more plentiful employment and a higher standard of life for the rest of the population . . . . The checks to Jewish immigration are bound to hamper the country's progress and can therefore bring no good to any part of its population . . . . Our basic right recognised by the Mandate, is to bring in without hindrance as many Jews as Palestine can be made to absorb by its natural possibilities and by our own constructive efforts. We are, therefore, opposed to any restriction of immigration which is not based on the prospects of employment, but upon such political or economic reasoning as fall outside the scope of Jewish efforts. It follows that the control of immigration must be left in the hands of the Jewish Agency, this being the only responsible body that is both under an obligation and in a position to strike a balance between the needs of immigration and the constructive efforts of the Jewish people."

The General Federation of Jewish Labour has adopted a policy which implies the introduction into Palestine of a new social order, based on communal settlements and the principle of self-labour. Where self-labour is impossible, it insists on the employment of Jewish labour exclusively, by all Jewish employers. It has been sufficiently powerful to impose the policy on the Zionist Organisation, to the extent that, as it points out in the memorandum from which a quotation has been given above, 46 of the Zionist colonies are based on the principle of communal settlement. This principle was condemned both by the Experts in their report and by the Joint Palestine Survey Commission, but that fact has had small effect either on the Labour Federation itself or on the Zionist Organisation, for communal labour colonies are still being constructed.

The question of the power, the principles and the activities of the Federation were discussed by Dr. Elwood Mead and his Associates, and at pp. 51 to 53 of the Experts' Report they wrote as follows :—

> " The activities of organised labour and its conception of the extent to which it should participate in the founding and organisation of settlements and in the selection of settlers was candidly set forth at a conference between the Commission and five representatives of the

129

Agricultural Workers' Association and four members of the General Federation of Jewish Labour. At this conference the Commission asked these representatives to explain their relation to rural colonisation and what the Federation or its subsidiary branch, the Agricultural Workers' Union, sought to accomplish. The principal reply was made by Mr. Shertok, who is a labour official, and an editor of a Palestine labour paper. He is a man of ability, sincerity and great influence in the organisation. A part of his statement is incorporated:—

" ' In respect to the agricultural wage-earning workers it (The Jewish Federation of Labour) acts as a Trade Union Executive, negotiates conditions of employment, etc., but in respect to the settlements it is not a trade union at all, but is more or less an economic authority, that is, it is responsible on behalf of all these people towards the Zionist Executive, the Keren Hayesod, etc., for the plan of settlement, the yearly budget, and also it is responsible for the human composition of these settlements. The Union as such has the say as to who is going to settle and how these groups are going to combine. The Union is the authority for all these settlements.'

" In further explanation of the colonising activities of the General Federation of Labour and of the Agricultural Workers' Union, Mr. Shertok said:—

" ' We must try and bring in people and press for more employment and make all sorts of arrangements that will facilitate penetration of a Jewish working class element in these colonies. When we come to the Zionist Executive with a claim for new settlement and are told that it is impossible at the moment we do not always rest content with such an answer. We know the land, and so we can come forward with proposals, we make suggestions, we tell them that we are going to help them, and we also give suggestions, sometimes, as to obtaining financial means.'

" In response to the Commission's statement that settlers were suffering great hardships and money was being wasted by founding settlements faster than the funds at the control of the Executive warranted, Mr. Shertok replied:—

" ' Your contention may be valid only on one assumption, it is that the Zionist Organisation, however small its means may be, has an assured influx of money, which is not the case. This is the most decisive factor. You say it is better to go slowly but surely, and then it will go quicker in the end, but the thing is that the Zionist Organisation gets its money from Jews abroad. Jews are giving money for Palestine for a variety of psychological reasons. They are making great financial sacrifices; and the most important factor is the work that is being done in Palestine. Perhaps it will be true to say that not Keren Hayesod made the Emek, but the Emek made the Keren Hayesod. The fact that land was bought and people rushed to that land, made great sacrifices, contented themselves with very little, gave an impetus to Zionists abroad to give money, and to Jews at large, because they saw what things were being done in Palestine.'

" The Commission feels strongly that this belief that it is necessary to establish new colonies, regardless of ability to equip them properly, in order to secure money from abroad is a delusion. It is confident that the interest in a national home does not have to be sustained by wasting money or squandering the time and efforts of settlers as is now being done. Furthermore, the financial situation which is being created will discredit the Zionist movement unless promptly changed.

> The financial and economic statements that have been secured ought to be carefully studied by those interested in this matter.
>
> " It is the view of the Commission that activity of a particular group or party is undesirable; that the influence of the Jewish Federation of Labor is giving these colonies a character not in harmony with the ideals and aspirations of the Jewish race. It is believed that the opportunity to live in the open country ought to be available to the Jewish people regardless of their views on social or economic questions. To place one party so largely in control is a discrimination against many who would be valuable additions to the rural life of Palestine.
>
> " The Commission has been unable to escape the conclusion that the rate at which colonies have been founded, the selection of settlers for those colonies, and the organization and equipment of the Colonization Department have been largely influenced, if not controlled, by the General Federation of Jewish Labor. We are therefore of the opinion, as already stated in our major conclusion No. 4, ' that the Department of Agricultural Colonization should be reorganized and placed in charge of officials committed to the primary aim of creating a self-sustaining agriculture, rather than of establishing a new social and economic order.'
>
> " The Commission has no opposition to labor. On the contrary, its members believe in organised labor, but it has the same opposition to labor control and colonization in Palestine that it would have to control by bankers, lawyers or any particular party or economic group . . . ."

In Sir John Campbell's " Report on the Jewish Settlements ", published in the same volume, he wrote at p. 436.

> " . . . . Effective practical control has in a large measure passed out of the hands of the Palestine Executive into the hands of a political organization. The Labour Federation has, in practice, controlled the situation. From the initial selection of the immigrants, down through finance and technical departments to the choice of the men to be settled, the place where they are to be settled, the resources to be placed at their disposal, the plan to be followed in establishing them, the apportionment of funds as between different classes of settlers, the Labour Federation has governed the situation. In other words, the body which is technically and ostensibly responsible for the work has not in practice effectively controlled that work; power has been, more or less completely divorced from responsibility."

These extracts from the reports of the Experts describe the position as it is to-day with remarkable accuracy. The General Federation of Jewish Labour continues to carry out, at the expense of the generosity of World Jewry a social and economic experiment of great interest, but of questionable value. The Jewish Agency either approves of this experiment or is impotent to suppress it.

The sources of immigration.—Of the Jewish immigrants over 70 per cent. come from Poland, Russia and Roumania. Of recent years there has also been a large influx of Yemenite Jews.

In a supplement to the Memorandum of the Jewish Agency submitted for the purposes of this enquiry, the reasons for the extent of the immigration from these four countries is explained. With reference to Poland it is said :—

> " . . . . This situation was aggravated by the fact that there simultaneously arose amongst the Poles themselves a movement to enter that field of activity which was previously controlled by the Jews. This

economic penetration was accompanied by a national economic struggle, in which State and people worked together to eject the Jews from their former economic positions, making considerable use of the co-operative movement for this purpose. All these factors combined to bring ruin upon the Jews of Poland, rendering immigration on a large scale imperative. It is particularly for the Jewish youth of Poland, which aspires to go over to manual labour and productive pursuits, that Palestine affords the essential solution."

In regard to Russia it records :—

" . . . . The Jewish religion also has been singled out for malicious and savage persecution. Thus for the Jews of Russia the appalling economic conditions to which they have been reduced, and the political and religious persecution to which they are continuously exposed, make emigration the only possible alternative to economic extinction on the one hand and racial and moral degeneration on the other . . . ."

As to Roumania it is recorded :—

" With the post-war annexations by Roumania of Bessarabia, Bukovina, and Transylvania, the Jewish population rose from 960,000 souls, whose economic condition is aggravated by the fact that a considerable proportion of them—those of Bessarabia—have been cut off from their former economic hinterland in Russia. Political depression and periodical anti-Semitic excesses are further factors in the Palestine movement among the Jews of this country, where Zionism has been strong since the founding of the first Jewish Colonies in Palestine and the inception of modern Zionism . . . ."

In regard to the Yemen it is written in the supplement :—

" . . . . The Jewish community dates back to pre-Islamic times and estimates as to its numbers vary from forty to sixty thousand souls. These Jews are deprived of all civil rights, while there is in force a monstrous decree that all orphans who are minors become wards of the Imam, and must adopt Islam, a decree which in recent years has been enforced more rigorously than previously. The Jews of the Yemen are for the most part skilled workers in handicrafts or agriculturists, while being bred to life in the Orient they very readily assimilate Palestinian conditions. The journey from the Yemen to the coast of Aden takes twenty days; and is fraught by perils of brigandage and murder, yet by this terrible route some 2,000 Yemenite Jews have entered Palestine since the War. Of these no less than 600 entered during the past year, their departure from the Yemen being largely stimulated by fear of the decree as to the forcible conversion of orphan children . . . ."

The above is a very frank explanation of the reasons which have actuated the movement from these four countries to Palestine. By the Zionist Palestine is regarded as the haven of refuge for the distressed Jew, and the National Home is being peopled to a great extent for the time being, by those who escape from countries where distress is most pronounced.

Immigration and Unemployment.—It is widely believed and commonly alleged among the Arabs that unemployment among them is due to Jewish immigration and the competition of Jewish labour. In so far as Jewish labour is employed on works which are being carried out solely with imported Jewish capital, there is no basis for the belief. It is however impossible to ascertain whether labour has been imported in excess of what is necessary for these purposes. Indeed from the fact of the increased employment of Jewish Labour on other enterprises, as for instance in the Public Works Department, on the railways, in building enterprises such as Hotel, Y.M.C.A. buildings and other edifices not paid for by purely Jewish capital, it might be argued that more Jewish labourers have been imported than are necessary for purely Jewish requirements, and that, to this extent, the Arab labour market has been adversely affected by Jewish immigration. On the other hand, there is no doubt that the development which has followed on Jewish immigration during the last nine years, has provided additional openings for Arab labour. The expansion of the orange trade alone requires the services of a large number of Arab porters and boatmen at the ports. The same may be said of the large imports of machinery and material in connection with the Jordan Concession, with the Dead Sea Concession, and with the construction and working of the " Nesher " Cement Company. All of these have provided a certain amount of work for Arabs, chiefly on the heavier and more menial tasks. In many directions Jewish development has meant more work for the Arabs, and it is a fair conclusion that the competition of imported Jewish labour is equalized by those increased opportunities.

Figures in regard to the numbers of unemployed.—No statistics of unemployment, except those provided monthly by the Immigration Department, exist, and these are admittedly unreliable. The reported figures for the current year are as follows :—

Month.	Jews.	Arabs.	Total.
1930—			
January	850	2,000	2,850
February	800	2,400	3,200
March	600	2,300	2,900
April	1,000	2,400	3,400
May	650	2,200	2.850
June	1,300	2,600	3,900

The information on which the monthly unemployment figures are based is obtained, under existing arrangements, by officers of the Immigration Department in Jerusalem, Jaffa and Haifa, and by Police Officers elsewhere. Enquiries into changes in wage-rates and into conditions of labour are made by the same officers. Other Departments may be and are from time to time consulted, and readily communicate any available information, but in their case also the machinery necessary to an effective enquiry does not exist. The staff of the section of the Immigration Department responsible for collecting labour information was reduced to a minimum in 1929 for reasons of economy, and since that time the work in connection

with immigration proper, including, as it does, reference to Londc
and to the Commandant of Police in every case of a visa for Pale
tine, in favour of a resident in Russia, has resulted in superficial ar
hurried preparation of the estimates of Arab unemployment. It
reported that information collected by the Police is even less sati
factory. The duty is one for which the Police officers have no trai
ing, no time and no aptitude. Enquiries necessary for the prepar
tion of unemployment returns are in no sense a police function.
fact, in this instance they are called upon to perform a duty wi
which they should never have been charged.

For the Jewish authorities, with their extensive system of Labo
Exchanges and the Statistical Department of the Labour Feder
tion, it is an easy matter to provide information on the subject
Jewish unemployment which may be regarded as accurate a:
exact. In the case of Arab unemployment, no adequate machine
exists which would enable an opinion, even approximately accurat
to be formed at any given moment.

Arab unemployment.—At the same time there can be no dou
that there is at the present time serious unemployment amoı
Arab craftsmen and among Arab labourers. For this u
employment there are several causes. Motor transport, largely
the hands of the Jews, is driving the camel and the donkey off t:
roads, and with them the Arab camel-driver and the Arab donke
man. The motor car, again largely owned and driven by Jews,
displacing the horse-drawn vehicle and its Arab driver. The i
creased use of cement, reinforced concrete and silicate brick, ɛ
manufactured by Jews, is replacing dressed stone for construction
purposes, and so displacing a large number of stone-dressers aɪ
stonemasons, nearly all of whom are Arabs. The Arab quarrymɛ
are also being displaced.

But probably the most serious cause of additional unemployme
is the cessation of conscription for the army, prevalent under tl
Turkish Government. The young men now remain in the village
Formerly they were despatched to the Yemen or to Anatolia, aɪ
many, indeed the majority, of them, failed to return.

In Jewish circles the story of Arab unemployment is regarded ;
a myth. There are also individual members of the British Color
at Jerusalem who do not consider it serious.

It is difficult to form an opinion, impossible to dogmatise, on tl
subject of Arab unemployment, but careful consideration of availab
information on the subject supports the belief that suc
unemployment not only exists but is serious and widespread. Tl
estimate submitted by the Supreme Moslem Council, tha
altogether from 30,000 to 35,000 Arabs are unemployed, may b
discarded. The figures were described as "fairly reliable." N
explanation was offered as to the authority by whom they wer
supplied. There is, however, ample other evidence. A not
by Miss Margaret Nixon, Government Welfare Worker, recorc

that from her personal knowledge there is very serious unemployment among Arabs of the artisan class in Jerusalem. She suggests that the reason lies in the refusal of Jewish employers to engage Arab labourers in view of the riots of last August. Enquiry was made from a British Police Officer who had made a personal investigation into the question at Haifa. He reports that in that town alone 2,050 Arabs are unemployed, including 200 carpenters and 300 stonemasons. From Trans-Jordan it was ascertained that a report that further recruits were required for the Frontier Force resulted in " well over " 4,000 men, mainly from Palestine and Northern Trans-Jordan, besieging the Headquarters of the Force in hope of employment. In Ramleh there were 120 applicants for the post of scavenger overseer on a salary of £2.750 mils (£2 15s.) a month.

The Director of the Public Works Department was consulted on the question and stated that there was no difficulty whatever in obtaining all the labour required for his Department. The programme of that Department for the future is important and includes 12 or 13 buildings which will cost from £140,000 to £150,000. In his opinion, even if Jewish immigration were to cease altogether, there would be no difficulty in obtaining the personnel necessary to complete these undertakings.

The Resident Engineer of the Haifa Harbour Works wrote on this subject :—

> " . . . . There is no question but what there is a very great deal of unemployment in the Arab section of the population, and I have little doubt that, so far as the Harbour Works are concerned, labour requirements could be met two or three times over. Just as an illustration, about a fortnight ago we engaged some 40 additional men to work at the Quarries near Athlit. The news that more men had been started quickly spread, and on one morning last week I myself saw a huge crowd of Arabs seeking work, and they must have numbered some 400 or 500 men . . . ."

Many of the Area and District Officers were consulted. They expressed an unanimous opinion that Arab unemployment is serious and general.

In the face of this information from independent sources it is impossible to avoid the conclusion that unemployment among the Arabs is a serious feature of the economic life of Palestine at the present time. Much information was also volunteered as to the trend of Arab wages, from which it would appear that unemployment, as is natural with unorganised labour, is affecting the standard of life. The information obtained indicates that in the case of skilled artisans, carpenters and stone-dressers the fall in wage rates amounts to 50 per cent. A competent artisan can still earn 15 to 20 piastres (3s. to 4s. per day). A fellah workman is content to accept 8 to 10 piastres (1s. 8d. to 2s.). The Deputy District Commissioner of Jerusalem stated that this year (1930) tenders for municipal contracts were at half the rates demanded in 1929, the decrease being due to the fall in Arab wages. The tales told by Arab workmen themselves were impressive. Several of them were men who had enjoyed a certain measure of ease and prosperity in the past, but whose conditions had deteriorated during recent years. There were master-masons who used to employ a number of subordinates, yet now are not only not in a position to employ any assistants, but are themselves destitute, owing to the inability to find work. There were carpenters who produced excellent certificates and are in the same plight. There were labourers who are willing to accept any wage if only they could obtain work. All of them ascribed their misfortunes, probably quite erroneously, to Jewish competition.

Further immigration and its effect on Arab unemployment.—It is thus evident that Arabs are unemployed in at least considerable numbers, and that the fact is resulting in a distinct reduction of the standard of life among the Arab labouring class. As has been pointed out, the policy of the Jewish Labour Federation is successful in impeding the employment of Arabs both in Jewish colonies and in Jewish enterprises of every kind. There is therefore no relief to be anticipated from an extension of Jewish enterprise unless some departure from existing practice is effected.

Recent increase in Jewish unemployment.—There is also evidence of increasing unemployment among the Jews at the present time. The return of unemployment for the month of June showed that 1,300 Jews are out of work as compared with 650 in the previous month. The Labour paper, "Davar," published by the General Federation of Jewish Labour, wrote on 8th July :—

> " . . . . Conditions of employment during the last weeks have grown worse . . . . Hundreds of cheap labour are employed in seasonal work . . . . And the Jewish labourer goes idle . . . . The help from our central organisations is required in order to avoid undesired developments, especially at the present time."

Next day it wrote :—

> " . . . . The present situation requires the mobilisation of all public forces to meet the danger. Many of the employers in the colonies have recently forgotten all shame when dealing with the question of Jewish employment."

The Chief Immigration Officer writes on this question, after a visit to the large village of Petach Tikvah :—

> " . . . . The presence of men and women without work could not be concealed. The representative of the local trade union admitted about 200 unemployed but assured us that this was merely a temporary matter . . . . The local police estimated unemployment at between 300 and 350, a figure that is probably correct . . . ."

The reason for the unemployment probably lies in the fall in the price of oranges, which renders it difficult for the growers to pay the higher rate of wages for Jewish pluckers, and so they employ Arab or Yemenite labour.

136

Duty of Government in regard to immigration.—A serious question thus arises in connection with the immigration of Jewish labour, and with the labour schedule which regulates that immigration. There appears to be no question as to the policy which should be adopted by the Palestine Government in this matter. It is the duty of the Government to look upon the country as one unit. The solution of the question facing the Government, in determining the number of Jewish labourers to be admitted, must depend, not on the amount of Jewish unemployment in reference to anticipated employment in the half-year for which the schedule is framed, but on unemployment generally in Palestine. It is wrong that a Jew from Poland, Lithuania, or the Yemen, should be admitted to fill an existing vacancy, while in Palestine there are already workmen capable of filling that vacancy, who are unable to find employment. This policy will be unacceptable to the Jewish authorities.

Employment of Arabs in Jewish concerns.—One of the Executive of the Jewish Labour Federation put the case quite clearly. He said, " We would not initiate the work if we were compelled to employ Arab labour. The Zionist object in development is to employ Jews. Unless Jews can be employed we fail in our object." The principle underlying this statement is logical and comprehensible. The Jews do not spend their capital in the development of Palestine in order that Arab unemployment should be overcome. Nevertheless, by the Government, Palestine must be treated as an entity and there must be no discrimination between the races which it contains. If there is unemployment, whether Jewish or Arab, it is clearly the duty of the Government to prevent immigration if such immigration will intensify that unemployment or prevent its cure.

" *Derived Demand.*"—There is one special case to which the principles enunciated above will not apply. It has been pointed out that Jewish capital will not be brought into Palestine in order to employ Arab labour. It will come in with the definite object of the employment of Jewish labour and not otherwise. The principle of " derived demand " would justify the immigration of Jewish labour even when there are Arab unemployed in the country if the newly-imported Jewish labour is assured of work of a permanent nature, through the introduction of Jewish capital to provide the work on which that labour is to be employed. It is clearly of no advantage to the unemployed Arab that Jewish capital should be prevented from entering the country, and he is in no worse position by the importation of Jewish labour to do work in Palestine for which the funds are available by the simultaneous importation of Jewish capital. In fact, he is better off, as the expenditure of that capital on wages to Jewish workmen will cause, ultimately, a demand for the services of a portion of the Arab unemployed. It is in this way that the principle of " derived demand " works in his case.

The Government, however, must be well assured that the employment for which the Jewish labour is imported is permanent in its nature, that this labour will not be employed for a time and then thrown on to the labour market. This would only aggravate the unemployment position in the country.

It would be justifiable that the Government should demand from the Jewish Organisations that a security fund should be initiated, to assure against Jewish unemployment in all such cases. If a substantial sum were deposited with the Government as a guarantee, to provide for the maintenance of over-imported labour, in case of unemployment, it would be a much easier task for the Government to deal with the Labour Schedule. Negotiations on this subject might be undertaken between the Palestine Government and the Jewish Agency for Palestine.

Unemployment statistics and Government Employment Exchanges.—The principle that the preparation of the Labour Schedule shall depend on the total unemployment in Palestine demands that the existence of that unemployment shall be accurately determined. As has been shown above, no machinery exists at the present time which permits of an accurate estimate of Arab unemployment. Such machinery must be devised. In the towns this result could be obtained by the creation of Government Employment Exchanges, with which the existing Jewish exchanges might be amalgamated. Arrangements to facilitate the employment of the unemployed is the function of a Government rather than that of one section of the population. The existence of Employment Exchanges would permit of a comparatively accurate estimation of the number of Palestinian unemployed, whether Arab, Jew or other, at any moment.

In the villages, the question is of great difficulty. Registration of unemployment might be entrusted to the Area and District Officers, who could obtain the information through the Mukhtars (Headmen) of the villages. The question of machinery is one for the Palestine Government, but whatever machinery may be employed it should be such as will afford to the Government at any time, or at such stated intervals as may be laid down, accurate information as to the total number of unemployed, classified according to their occupations. Only when such reliable information is available will it be possible to prepare the immigration schedule on a rational basis.

Seasonal and occasional labour.—There are two obvious dangers against which provision must be made in the execution of any measures dealing with the registration of unemployment. The first lies in the large amount of casual and temporary unemployment of the agricultural labourer and indeed of the small Arab cultivator. Of this class many individuals flock to the towns in order to earn something in addition to what is yielded by the land. The agricultural labourer is paid entirely in kind, while, in the case of the small cultivator, unless he can eke out his income during the agricultural off-season, he is frequently unable to obtain the cash necessary to pay his taxes or his moneylender, and for the year's purchases which are essential for his household. There can be no valid reason for refusal to register as unemployed temporary labourers of this kind, if they are in fact in the labour market, and in fact unemployed. The regulations of the employment exchanges should, however, be so framed as to ensure that the names of persons of this class seeking employment should be removed when seasonal activity causes them to return from the towns to the villages.

Importation of other than Jewish labour.—Further, it is clear that if unemployment is a valid reason for preventing Jewish immigration, it is also a reason for preventing importation of labour of other nationalities. At the time of writing, even with marked unemployment among Arabs, Egyptian labour is being employed in certain individual cases, and its ingress has been the subject of adverse comment in the Press.

Prevention of illicit immigration.—Finally, in closing the front door, steps should be taken to ensure that the backdoor should not be kept open for would-be immigrants into Palestine. The Chief Immigration Officer has brought to notice that illicit immigration through Syria and across the northern frontier of Palestine is material. This question has already been discussed. It may be a difficult matter to ensure against this illicit immigration, but steps to this end must be taken if the suggested policy is adopted, as also to prevent unemployment lists being swollen by immigrants from Trans-Jordania.

Arab unemployment as a political pawn.—The question of unemployment and immigration has been treated solely from the economic standpoint. It has immediate political repercussions with which this enquiry is not concerned, but which must receive consideration from His Majesty's Government in arriving at a decision. Two of these repercussions will require particular attention :

First, Arab unemployment is liable to be used as a political pawn. Arab politicians are sufficiently astute to realise at once what may appear an easy method of blocking that immigration to which they are radically averse, and attempts may and probably will be made to swell the list of Arab unemployed with names which should not be there, or perhaps to ensure the registration of an unemployed man in the books of more than one exchange. It should not prove difficult to defeat this manoeuvre.

Article 6 of the Mandate and its effect on immigration.—Second, there is the repercussion on the policy of the Jewish National Home. It is evident that any interference with freedom of immigration is a limitation to the admission of Jews who desire to take part in the local constitution of that Home. Article 6 of the Mandate, however, directs that the rights and position of other sections of the population shall not be prejudiced by Jewish immigration. Clearly, in cases in which immigration of Jews results in preventing the

Arab population obtaining the work necessary for its maintenance, it is the duty of the Mandatory Power, under the Mandate, to reduce, or, if necessary, to suspend, such immigration, until immigration will not affect adversely the opportunities of the Arab for employment.

Elsewhere in this report the exclusion of Arab labour from the land purchased by the Jewish National Fund has been discussed, and it is pointed out that this exclusion is liable to confirm a belief that it is the intention of the Jewish authorities to displace the Arab population from Palestine by progressive stages. This belief, which, however unfounded it may be, is unfortunately very widely held, will be confirmed when it is realised that the immigration of Jewish labour is permitted while the Arab cannot earn his daily bread. On general grounds, therefore, as well as in order to carry out the terms of Article 6 of the Mandate, it is necessary that the existence of Arab unemployment should be taken into consideration when determining the number of Jews to be admitted at the time of preparation of the Labour Schedule.

Suspension of the Labour Schedule.—A question which has developed marked political importance is that of the suspension of immigration under the Labour Schedule which was ordered by His Majesty's Government at the end of the month of May of the present year. That Schedule was prepared in the ordinary way and sanctioned by the High Commissioner. Its suspension caused the greatest excitement, which has even now not altogether subsided. At the time there is no doubt that the recommendations of the Chief Immigration Officer, and the decision of the High Commissioner were justified by the prospects of work in Palestine. Since that time conditions have changed and there are at the moment signs of an economic crisis in Palestine. Prices have fallen suddenly and heavily. As has been shown in this Chapter, unemployment is widespread and is increasing. The immediate outlook for industry is bad. Economically it would be unwise to allow into the country a large number of additional workmen for whom work must be found, when there is at the moment difficulty in finding work even for Jewish workmen.

To leave the economic argument for a moment, it is said that there is an important psychological aspect of the question which escapes the notice of an enquiry purely economic. The suspension of labour immigration, it is alleged, has created the impression that the British Government is, if not hostile at least apathetic in the matter of the National Home and that this attitude finds its expression in the suspension in question. As a result of the impression so created, the flow of capital to Palestine and of subscriptions for the settlement work in that country have both been affected. The capitalist doubts the security of his capital. The benevolent questions the utility of his subscription if the National Home is in the end to prove a phantom.

Those who use these arguments, and they are universally used among the Jewish community, suggest that there is in fact no danger in re-opening immigration. On the contrary they are of the opinion that the cancellation of the order of suspension would at once restore confidence, stimulate the flow of money to Palestine, and so prevent the very economic difficulty which is anticipated.

There is weight to be attached to these opinions and those arguments. They are held and used by those who have the most acute knowledge of Jewish psychology. Yet from the purely economic standpoint, it has to be said that to cancel the suspension would be to take a risk, not justified by the economic position of the moment. It is not the province of this report to suggest whether it would or would not prove justifiable from the political standpoint.

Preparation of the Labour Schedule: Proposed change in method.—It is probable that a slight change in the method of preparation of the Labour Schedule would tend to increase the amicable relations between the Jewish authorities in Palestine and the Immigration Department. There is no reason why the Schedule should not be prepared by the representatives of the Jewish Agency and of the Immigration Department working together. If thought desirable some commercial authorities outside the Agency and the Government might be called into council as, for example, the Manager of Barclay's (Overseas) Bank at Jerusalem and the Manager of the Anglo-Palestine Company, each of whom is in intimate touch with the economic position in Palestine.

If the representatives of the Agency and the Department were in full agreement the agreed schedule would be submitted for the orders of the High Commissioner, who would doubtless accept it as it stood. If on the other hand there were disagreement on any of the items of the Schedule, the items on which agreement had been reached might be submitted under the signature of both parties, and separate schedules submitted in respect of items on which there was disagreement. The High Commissioner would then pass such orders as he thought fit.

Formation of a Department of Immigration, Labour and Travel.—At the present time the Immigration work is done by a section of the Police Department. The work is very voluminous and important and it is unsuitable that it should be connected in any way, even nominally, with the Police. The amount of work and the size of the staff both justify the creation of a Department of Immigration, specially as the Immigration staff deal also with Travel and with Labour. In view of the additional work which will fall upon this staff in consequence of the necessity to create a service for the registration of unemployment, it is exceedingly desirable that the Immigration Service should be detached from the Police Department and constituted a Department of Immigration, Labour and Travel.

141

CHAPTER XI.

Conclusion.

In this Report the subjects of Land Settlement, Development and Immigration have been examined in that order as it is evident that the question of Immigration depends on the action taken in respect of the first two. It now remains to make a resumé of the facts which have been established in the course of this enquiry.

LAND.

Land available for settlement. (Chapter II.)

It has emerged quite definitely that there is at the present time and with the present methods of Arab cultivation no margin of land available for agricultural settlement by new immigrants, with the exception of such undeveloped land as the various Jewish Agencies hold in reserve.

Government Lands. (Chapter I. Section (iii).)

The most important of lands, the property of the Government at the time the Mandate was given, were the Beisan area and the Huleh Basin. Of these the Beisan area was settled, in accordance with the terms of the Mudawwara Agreement of 1921, with the Arabs already in occupation or who had claims to possession. The Huleh Basin was subject to a concession already granted by the Ottoman Government which was confirmed by the Palestine Government. Of other considerable areas the Kabbara Swamp, the Caesarea Sand-dunes and a portion of the lands of Athlit, an area in the neighbourhood of 39,000 dunams, were ceded to the P.I.C.A. It is an error to imagine that the Government is in possession of large areas of vacant lands which could be made available for Jewish settlement. In fact free areas are negligible in extent. The Government claims considerable areas which are occupied and cultivated by Arabs. Even were the title of the Government admitted, and it is in many cases disputed, it would not be feasible to make those areas available for settlement in view of the impossibility of finding other lands on which to place the Arab cultivators.

The provision of a margin depends on material progress in the development of the land already included in holdings. It has been shown that the area of cultivable land in Palestine (excluding the Beersheba region) is 6,544,000 dunams, considerably less than has hitherto been estimated. It has also been shown that, while an area of at least 130 dunams is required to maintain a fellah family in a decent standard of life in the unirrigated tracts, the whole of the cultivable land not already in the hands of the Jews would not afford an average lot in excess of 90 dunams, were it divided among the existing Arab cultivators. (*Chapter III.*) For an average holding of 130 dunams, about eight million dunams of cultivable land would be required. It also appears that of the 86,980 rural Arab families in the villages, 29.4 per cent. are landless. It is not known how many of these are families who previously cultivated and have since lost their land. This is a matter which should be ascertained in the course of the Census which is to take place next year.

Present agricultural policy.—The condition of the Arab fellah is little if at all superior to what it was under the Turkish régime. No definite policy of agricultural development of the country held by the Arabs has been adopted. The sole agencies which have pursued such a consistent policy have been the Jewish Colonisation Departments, public and private. With this exception agricultural progress of any kind has been haphazard and of small extent or value.

Jewish and Arab advantages and disadvantages. (*Chapter V.*)— The Jewish settlers have had every advantage that capital, science and organization could give them. To these and to the energy of the settlers themselves their remarkable progress is due.

(*Chapter VI.*)—The Arab has had none of these advantages and has received practically no help to improve his cultivation or his standard of life. The Arab population has increased with great rapidity and the land available for its sustenance has meanwhile decreased by about a million metric dunams which have passed into the hands of the Jews.

Compensation of Beduin for loss of grazing rights. (*Chapter VI.*)—The problem of the Beduin requires careful investigation, in order that their rights may be ascertained. Where those rights conflict with the requirements of the State for agricultural development, the Beduin should be compensated, if those rights are annulled.

Alterations of terms under which Jewish National Fund purchases and leases land. (*Chapter V. Section (iii).*)—Reference has been made to the terms on which the Jewish National Fund purchases and leases its land. It is there recorded that those terms are objectionable and should be radically altered.

Government's duty under the Mandate.—It is the duty of the Administration, under the Mandate, to ensure that the position of the Arabs is not prejudiced by Jewish immigration. It is also its duty under the Mandate to encourage the close settlement of the Jews on the land, subject always to the former condition. It is only possible to reconcile these apparently conflicting duties by an active policy of agricultural development, having as its object close settlement on the land and intensive cultivation by both *Arabs and Jews*. To this end drastic action is necessary.

143

Agricultural Development Scheme. (Chapter VII.)—A methodical scheme of agricultural development should be thought out and undertaken, which will ensure the use of the land of the country to better purpose than has been the case hitherto. This development should have two distinct aims :—

Improvement of the Fellah's methods. (Chapter VII.)—In the first place, to improve the method of cultivation of the Arab fellah in the dry tracts, and also to extend irrigation wherever that is possible, so that the fellah will be able to gain a reasonable livelihood from a smaller area of land than that which has been essential hitherto.

Re-arrangement of holdings.—In the second place so to re-arrange holdings of land, that there will be a margin for further settlement in accordance with the terms of Article 6 of the Mandate.

Development of irrigation.—If such development is undertaken in accordance with a definite plan and the cultivable land of the Plains of Palestine improved, as in many places it can be improved, by the provision of water for irrigation, there will unquestionably be sufficient land both for Arabs and for additional Jewish settlement. The results desired will not be obtained except by years of work.

Jewish reserves of land.—It is for this reason peculiarly fortunate that the Jewish organizations are in possession of a large reserve of land not yet settled or developed. Their operations can continue without a break while the general scheme of development is being worked out and brought into operation.

Control of disposition of land.—Until the scheme is worked out the control of all disposition of land must of necessity rest with the authority in charge of the development. Transfers should only be permitted in so far as they do not interfere with that scheme.

Powers for Government purchase of land.—In order that any scheme of development should be a success, the authority controlling the development must be able to obtain the land which it is intended to develop. It may be possible that arrangements to this end can be concluded amicably between the Government and the owner of land required. In such cases naturally the Government would buy the land. It should also have the power to purchase at a valuation all land for sale in the market. On the other hand in any case in which the Government refuses to sanction a sale of land, the would-be vendor should have the right to demand that the Government take over that land at a valuation.

It may be however that the Government will not be able to acquire the land it needs by private arrangement or by purchase at a valuation. In such a case it already has the power to act under the Expropriation of Land Ordinance No. 28 of 1926, and to acquire the land at a valuation, as being required for a public purpose.

Development Commission.—The development of the land could best be ensured by the appointment of a Development Commission, invested with the necessary powers.

It is desirable that there should be a Chairman of British nationality, one Arab Commissioner and one Jewish Commissioner.

Responsibilities of the Development Commission.—The Commission would not only undertake the development of the land but would also be responsible for its colonisation, both by Arab and by Jew. Until the survey is finished and the census is taken next year, it is impossible to say what the actual area available for cultivation may be and the number of Arab families whom it may be necessary to displace.

Available areas in the plains.—The Jewish Agency has made a calculation which indicates that there is room for 54,900 additional families in three of the five plains, namely, the Maritime Plain, the Huleh Plain, and the Jordan Valley, including Beisan. This is the result of a careful and detailed examination of the cultivable area and of the possibilities of development. It is true that the figures adopted in this calculation differ from those of the Director of Surveys in certain areas, and it would not be possible to accept the estimate as strictly accurate. It is at the same time certain that a large number of additional families can be provided with improved holdings in these areas.

It is impossible to give anything like a reliable estimate of the number of families who could be accommodated in Palestine, if the whole country were adequately developed. The development of 100,000 dunams in certain areas of the Maritime Plain might perhaps provide sufficient land for the settlement of 5,000 to 6,500 families. Accommodation would probably be thus provided in such an area for the families already on the spot, together with 2,000 families of Arabs from the congested areas in the Hills and 2,000 families of Jewish settlers. A similar area in Beisan would accommodate possibly only one-half or two-thirds of the number of new families. Everything depends on water for irrigation and markets for the produce. But there can be no doubt that systematic and methodical development over a series of years will change the whole aspect of agricultural Palestine, and admit of a largely increased population.

Co-ordination of Development Schemes.—Any scheme of development should provide for the settlement *both of Jews and of Arabs* on the developed area, and should take into consideration the plans of colonisation of the Jewish agencies, in order that development by those agencies and by the Commission might be co-ordinated. It might well prove possible to combine two schemes of development in certain areas with mutual advantage and with considerable economy.

145

Cost of settling a family.—It is assumed that the average expenditure on settling one Arab family will be about £60. This does not provide for anything luxurious in the way of settlement. The Arab builds his own house. It costs him £10 per room. If he builds a house of two rooms, £40 will remain, which will be sufficient to provide him with a good cow, an iron plough and a harrow. The family will already have cattle and implements and it will not be necessary to provide maintenance. Though the standard of life of Arab and Jew differ materially, no difference could be made either in the size of holding allotted or in the amount granted for settlement. If the Jew desires a more liberal settlement, and he will desire it, clearly he must obtain its cost elsewhere than from the Development Commission.

Distribution of developed land.—The distribution of the developed land should be made to Jews whose names are borne on lists supplied to the Commission by the Jewish Agency, and to Arabs named by the District Commissioners. The claim of would-be settlers of both sections of the population should be considered simultaneously, and the Commission must have the final decision on the claims.

Co-operation between Jewish agencies and the Development Commission.—The scheme proposed depends for its success on loyal co-operation of the Jewish Colonisation Agencies with the Development Commission. The Commission should be in constant touch with those agencies, and their schemes of development, though intended for Jewish settlement alone, must be so framed as to fall in with the scheme for the development of the country as a whole. This is the only way in which the provisions of Article 6 of the Mandate can be observed and close settlement of Jews on the land encouraged while the position of the other sections of the population is not prejudiced. There will doubtless be difficulties at the commencement in co-ordinating Jewish plans with those of the Commission, but with goodwill on either side and a realization of the common object those difficulties should be capable of resolution.

Artificial inflation of land values.—It is also only by co-operation that artificial inflation of the price of the land will be prevented. At the present time, the price of land in Palestine has risen to an exaggerated height, owing to the determination of the various Jewish purchasing agencies to buy, at all hazards and at any price, land which comes into the market, and the fact that the owner knows that if he only holds, he can get his price. As the price of the land, or an adequate percentage on that price in the form of rent must be collected from the population to be settled, the scheme will fail if the land is bought at an unreasonable price, such as the present price. It is thus an essential condition of success that the land should be bought at a reasonable price. This is only possible either by agreement between the Government and the Jewish purchasing agencies, or by Government control over dispositions of land. The object desired might be attained by a " gentleman's agreement " between the Jewish Agency and the Commission. Control, however, would be essential in any case in order to prevent the incursion of third parties desirous of speculating in land.

Ascertainment of the number of landless Arabs.—The forthcoming census should be used in order to ascertain the number of Arabs who have become landless. It would also be well if the number of fellahin who have not a holding on which they are able to maintain a reasonable standard of life could be ascertained through the Area and District Officers. These two classes are dealt with by Mr. Snell in his Note of Reservations to the report of the Commission on the Disturbances. He says on page 177—" . . . . The Arab, on the other hand, should be secured in the possession of sufficient land to provide him with a decent standard of life . . . . " and on p. 181, " . . . . If there are still Arabs who are landless through the failure of the Palestine Government to apply administratively the provisions of the Land Laws in force in that country, steps should be taken by the Government to settle them on the land at the public expense. . . . . "

Migration: Its difficulties.—The task of a Development Commission will not be easy. It will involve, among other problems, that of migration. Evidently it will not be possible to increase the size of a fellah's holding in the Hills, except by arrangement which will involve the transfer of some other fellah from the Hills elsewhere and the use of the latter's holding to increase that of the former in the attempt to create a " lot viable."

> " The process of migration involves many difficulties . . . . of which not the least is the understandable objections of the occupiers in the neighbourhood of the new holding to immigrants being given land to which they consider they and their families have a prior claim. Much tact and foresight are necessary in planning migration schemes and inducing holders to migrate to a part of the country where the local associations . . . . would be strange to them . . . . Though migration formed a definite part of the policy of the late Congested Districts Board in dealing with their Estates . . . . the inherent difficulties . . . . prevented a development of the policy on a very extensive scale . . . . The now almost universal scope of land purchase in Saorstat Eireann makes it possible to effect more extensive schemes of migration."

The above is a quotation from the Report of the Irish Land Commissioners for the year ending 31st March, 1929. There is no doubt that similar difficulties will be encountered in any policy of development which entails migration as a consequence. In the case of the fellah, however, the conditions under which he lives are so unbearable that the difficulty of migration is not likely to be presented to the same degree. He is always migrating, even at the present time. He goes to any spot where he thinks he can find work. Many have left the country altogether. Emigration of a similar nature is understood to be common both in Syria and in 'Iraq.

Relations with the Department of Agriculture.—The relations between a Development Commission and the existing Department of Agriculture will require determination and definition. There is danger both of jealousy and of overlapping. Both of these dangers are evitable. The object of the two agencies is identical, namely, the improvement of the condition of the smallholder. If the relations between the Commission and the High Commissioner are close and cordial, as must be the case if the scheme is to have full success, those between the Commission and the Department should not fail to be satisfactory.

Spheres of action of the Development Commission and Department of Agriculture.—The broad principle of division between the two agencies is the following :—It is the duty of the Development Commission to improve the land for the cultivator; to introduce irrigation if possible, to regulate the size of the holding so that it shall be appropriate, and to arrange for its occupation either by migration of Arabs already in the country, or by the settlement of Jews who have immigrated under the auspices of the Jewish organizations. It is the duty of the Department of Agriculture to look after the technical side of the cultivator's life, to provide him with education and, if possible, training, to render him more capable than he is at present to use the improved land to the best advantage when it is made available for him by the Development Commission.

There will be border-line cases. For instance, it is conceivable that the Development Commission may establish nurseries to provide trees for the improved land. The Department of Agriculture may also have nurseries to provide trees for the cultivators generally. But by the application of ordinary common-sense, there should in practice be no difficulty in arranging the spheres of action of the two authorities.

Hydrographic Survey.—It has been recommended that the Government should institute a hydrographic survey of Palestine. This is essential to satisfactory development of the country and to methodical development of irrigation. Meanwhile one of the first tasks of a Development Commission will be the examination of the available water resources, in order that development may commence where there is the most immediate likelihood of success. They will require the services of the irrigation engineer of the Government for this purpose.

Urgency of Irrigation Legislation (Chapter VII).—The contemplated legislation to regulate irrigation and to render it more efficient should be passed as soon as possible. The control of all irrigable water should remain with the Government, and all surplus

148

water above that on which rights have been or may be established should be its property. It is regrettable that the Government has in one case parted with the irrigation rights in an important source to a concessionaire, and steps should be taken to ensure that in that case satisfactory arrangements are made for a supply of water for irrigation at an early date.

Formation of an Irrigation Department.—It is not desirable that the irrigation services should be a branch of the Agricultural Department and subject to the Director of that Department. They should be constituted a separate service with a Department dealing only with irrigation.

Occupancy Right.—The question of the creation of occupancy right of the agricultural tenant is discussed. No measure short of such right will suffice to secure the tenant against ejectment or the imposition of an excessive rental. The bestowal of the right will, it is true, reduce the market value of the property on which the tenant is settled, but it is essential that his tenure should be rendered more secure than it is at the present time. Legislation should be introduced as soon as is possible to confer on the tenant in Palestine that right, which exists all over India. This legislation should also secure the tenant against increases in his rent except under the orders or with the sanction of a Court. A register of all tenancies should be compiled in the course of the settlement now in progress.

Partition of Mesha'a (Chapter IV).—The tenure in common known as mesha'a which prevails in nearly half of the Arab villages of Palestine has been described and discussed, and it has been recorded that this system is a great obstacle to any agricultural development of the country. It is essential that steps should be taken to partition the mesha'a villages as expeditiously as possible.

Acceleration of land settlement (Chapter IV).—It has been pointed out that the maintenance of the record of rights which is now being prepared, and of a register of tenancies, is a necessary condition of good administration of the agricultural tracts. The work of the settlement, which is extremely complicated, is proceeding very slowly, and should be accelerated, if that is possible. If the delay is due to the expense of the settlement, and the inadequacy of the Settlement Budget, that Budget should be increased. The work is so important to the Government for its general purposes, and so essential to activities of a Development Commission, that no avoidable delay should be tolerated.

Abolition of imprisonment for debt (Chapter VI.)—Imprisonment for debt is an anachronism and should be abolished.

Redistribution and reduction of taxation (Chapter VI).—Agricultural taxation is excessive in Palestine at the present time. The Tithe is based on prices of produce which have fallen by about 50 per cent. since the Tithe was commuted. Until arrangements can be made so to redistribute the burden of taxation that it will fall more fairly in accordance with the financial ability of the taxpayer, the Tithe should, if possible, be suspended. If that is not possible, it should vary with the average market price of produce.

Registration fees—Reduction of fees.—The fees at present charged for the registration of dispositions of land, especially those on sale, mortgage and succession, are so high as to prevent the registration of changes in title consequent thereon. It is desirable, in the interests of the maintenance of an accurate record of rights, that these fees should be reduced.

AGRICULTURE.

Co-ordination of Agricultural Scientific Services (Chapter VII, Section A).—It is urgently necessary that steps should be taken to prevent overlapping between the scientific establishments of the Government, of the Jewish Agency and of the Hebrew University. It is preferable, and would be more economical, that the Government, rather than duplicate such services, should grant a subvention or should make payments for services rendered.

Increase of Department of Agriculture's Budget (Chapter VII).—It is a question whether the Agricultural Department should maintain certain minor Services, as, for instance, the Fisheries Service and the Sericultural Service, with its present limited Budget. The existing Budget is insufficient for the work which the Agricultural Department should perform. It should be increased.

Demonstration plots (Chapter VII).—Of all the agencies of an agricultural department in a country of small-holders none is more valuable than the Demonstration Plot. It is also one of the most economical methods of bringing practical and practicable improvements to the notice of the peasant cultivator. It is suggested that this method might well be adopted by the Agricultural Department in Palestine.

Distribution of trees (Chapter VII).—Another valuable agency for improvement of the holding of the peasant is the distribution of trees either at cost price or below it.

Separation of the Forest Service (Chapter VII).—The Forest Service is not one which should be attached to the Agricultural Department. It should be constituted as an independent service.

EDUCATION.

Increase of Budget of Department of Education.—The educational budget is by far too small for the requirements of the country, and it is recommended that it should be increased.

150

Agricultural course for Schoolmasters (Chapter VII).—Agricultural development is dependent on the spread of elementary education. It is desirable that all village schoolmasters should be given a six months' course at an agricultural school, and that the curriculum of the village school should include elementary instruction in agriculture. Each village school should have a small plot of land which will serve as a school garden and demonstration plot. There should be close co-operation between the Departments of Education and of Agriculture.

CO-OPERATION.

Encouragement of co-operation between Arab and Jew in Orange Industry. (Chapter VII, Section D.)—The Jewish Communities are very well served by a series of efficient Co-operative Societies. It would be to the general advantage of the country if these societies or such of them as are suitable for the purpose, could be made available to Arab members. It would be of special value if the orange grading and packing Society " Pardess " could enlist Arab orange-growers into its membership.

Constitution of Co-operative Credit Societies.—The constitution of Co-operative Credit Societies among the fellahin is an essential preliminary to their advancement. The whole question is being examined at the present time, by Mr. Strickland, on behalf of the Palestine Government.

AGRICULTURAL DEVELOPMENT.

Government acquisition of the Huleh Concession. (Chapters 1 and VII, Section C.)—If the Huleh Concession falls in; the land should be retained by the Government for development purposes. This area is one of the most fertile in the whole of Palestine and provision could be made for a large number of families on a comparatively small developed area.

Limitation of orange cultivation. (Chapter VIII, Section (a).)—The area under the orange is increasing with very great rapidity. It appears doubtful whether the market will be able to digest the amount of fruit which will be produced at the end of the next five years, when all groves now planted will be in bearing. Generally there is an optimistic spirit among the growers, but it would seem to be the path of wisdom to await the result of the recent rapid extension before further increasing the area.

Development of other fruit crops. (Chapter VIII, Sections (b), (c), (e), (f).)—Attempts should be made to encourage the cultivation of other fruits and valuable crops, rather than to depend entirely on one crop. The grape fruit offers good prospects. The Palestine fruit is excellent and it grows in soil which is too heavy for the orange. The prospects for the banana do not appear bright, but attempts should be made to develop the markets in Eastern Europe.

151

Import duty on melons in Egypt. (*Chapter VIII, Section (d).*) —The Egyptian Government has placed an import duty on Palestinian melons which is likely to restrict the trade. The Damascus Municipality has imposed an octroi duty on the same fruit.

Improvement of grades of tobacco. (*Chapter VIII, Section (g).*) —Efforts should be made to foster the cultivation of a better grade of tobacco, experts in manipulation and in packing being employed to teach the cultivators. There is every prospect that high quality tobacco could be grown in Palestine. It is probably advisable that, at least for the present, the cultivation of tobacco should be restricted to the northern part of the country, where the better qualities of leaf can be grown.

Amendment of minimum area of tobacco. (*Chapter VIII.*)— There is no good reason for the present rule, which prevents the cultivation of tobacco on an area of less than two dunams. It would be sufficient if the area were restricted to a minimum of half a dunam. The interest of the cultivators should be considered, as well as that of the manufacturer, in framing legislation governing the cultivation of tobacco.

Improvement of quality of olive oil and pruning of trees. (*Chapter VIII, Section (h).*)—Steps should be taken to teach the cultivator the method of producing olive oil of better quality than that now manufactured by the small grower. It would also be an advantage that instructors in pruning olive trees should be employed to tour the country and to teach the peasants the correct method of pruning their trees.

Steps to revive the barley export trade. (*Chapter VIII, Section (j).*)—The question of the export trade in barley deserves consideration. That trade, which was of a certain importance before the war, has not revived since the Armistice. The reason for its failure to revive should be examined, and the purchase of a cleaning plant again be considered.

Encouragement of sericulture and production of honey. (*Chapter VIII, Section (k).*)—If serious efforts are contemplated to this end it is necessary to make a more adequate provision in the budget on their account than is done at present.

Possibility of a canning industry for dairy produce. (*Chapter VIII, Section (l).*)—The market for dairy products is circumscribed and it will soon be impossible locally to dispose of the dairy products of the country. Prices are already falling. It is necessary that an attempt should be made to cultivate the foreign market for dairy produce. The possibility of a canning industry for dairy products, and of the manufacture of cheese for export should be examined.

Palestinian industry. (*Chapter IX.*)—The larger manufacturing industries are dependent on the protection afforded by the import tariff. It is questionable whether in certain cases the protective tariff is justified by the results. In the case of the cement industry, the tariff appears to have been raised unnecessarily.

Reduction of excise on wines. (*Chapters VIII, Section (f), and IX.*)—The wine-industry is very heavily taxed in licence fees and Excise duty, which are passed on to the grape growers. These already pay the ordinary agricultural taxes, tithe and werko. In view of the present agricultural depression it would be advantageous, if possible, to reduce these taxes.

The smaller manufacturing industries are succeeding in many cases. This type of industry seems specially suited to the country.

Position of industries. (*Chapter IX.*)—There is not any reason to believe that Palestine offers special attractions to large industrial concerns. The industries likely to succeed are those that are based on local products or, being based on imported products, show special vitality. It would be a speculation dangerous to the economic future of the country, if an attempt were made to start a textile industry in Palestine on a large scale.

Encouragement of Arab industries. (*Chapter IX.*)—Indigenous Arab industries exist and should be encouraged.

Preparation of Labour Immigration Schedules. (*Chapter X.*)—It is recommended that in the future the Labour Immigration Schedules should be prepared by the representatives of the Jewish Agency and of the Immigration Department in consultation, with the help of non-official persons acquainted with the economic position of Palestine, as, for instance, leading bankers.

Immigration officer at towns abroad. (*Chapter X.*)—It is suggested that a representative of the Immigration Department should be stationed at each of the towns whence immigration to Palestine is most common.

Expulsion of illicit immigrants. (*Chapter X.*)—Proposals are made, that in the case of illicit entry into Palestine, the entrant should invariably be returned to the country whence he came, and that in the case of " pseudo-travellers " unless there are reasons to the contrary, the same procedure should follow detection.

Registration of Unemployment and Labour Exchanges. (*Chapter X.*)—The whole question of Arab unemployment should form the subject of study and steps should be taken to create a machinery for the registration of Arab unemployment. Government Employment Exchanges should be created, without which determination of the number of Arab unemployed is not possible.

If there are Arab workmen unemployed it is not right that Jewish workmen from foreign countries should be imported to fill existing vacant posts.

Constitution of a separate Department of Immigration, Travel and Labour.—The Immigration Office, which is now a section of the Police Department, should be constituted a separate Department.

Part of expenditure of Development Commission recoverable.— Both the expenditure necessary for the purchase of land in connection with a Development Commission, and the expenditure of the Commission itself are largely in the nature of outlay which will in time be repaid. This outlay is in fact reproductive expenditure. Of the advances for development, 85 per cent. to 90 per cent. should prove recoverable.

Intensive development of rural Palestine essential.—In closing this Report I desire to record my opinion that the observance of the Articles of the Mandate, and specially of Article 6 of the Mandate, presents extraordinary difficulty. The sole way in which the Mandate can be carried out is by the intensive development of rural Palestine. It will not be sufficient to develop a small portion. The unique condition of success is the development of the whole, which, as has been said before, is a task requiring not only years of work, but also material expenditure. There exists no easy method of carrying out the provisions of the Mandate. Development is the only way. Without development, there is not room for a single additional settler, if the standard of life of the fellahin is to remain at its present level. With development that standard could be raised so that it would permit reasonable conditions of livelihood to that backward class of the community and a margin of land could at the same time be provided for additional colonisation.

The introduction of settlers possible if development carried out.— It is my personal belief, founded on the enquiries which I have made and on my inspections, that with thorough development of the country there will be room, not only for all the present agricultural population on a higher standard of life than it at present enjoys, but for not less than 20,000 families of settlers from outside.

Necessity of joint endeavour.—Any scheme for development presents serious difficulties. Unless such a scheme is accepted by both Jew and Arab it may very well fail. Of both it will require the support if it is to have the desired result, namely, the advancement of a neglected but historic country in the path of modern efficiency, by the joint endeavour of the two great sections of its population, with the assistance of the Mandatory Power.

INDEX OF APPENDICES, MAPS, AND GRAPHS.

Appendices.

No.	Description.	Report Ch.	Page.	Authority.
1.	The Jordan Valley—Areas, etc. ...	I	19	—
2.	The Rural Population of Palestine	III	24	—
3.	Areas of Palestine—Figures	II	22	Director of Surveys.
4.	Population year by year ...	III	24	Director of Health.
5.	Births, Deaths and Infantile Mortality Ratios, 1923–29.	III	25	,, ,,
6.	Land Registration Fees ...	IV	37	Director of Lands.
7.	Zionist Settlements—Numbers, etc.	V(ii)	41	Jewish Agency.
8.	Investments of the Jewish National Fund, 1914 and 1920–29.	V(ii)	42	,, ,,
9.	Allocation of Keren Hayesod Funds, 1921–29 ...	V(ii)	42	,, ,,
10.	Zionist Settlements—Population 1930 ...	V(ii)	42	,, ,,
11.	,, ,, Distribution of Area	V(ii)	43	,, ,,
12.	Government Lands	V(iv)	56	Director of Lands.
13.	Gross Income from 104 Villages ...	VI	67	Report: "The Economic Condition of Agriculturists," 1930.
14.	Redemption Prices of Crops 1924–27 and prices July, 1930.	VI	69	District Commissioners.
15.	Return from 100 dunams ...	VI	69	Report: "The Economic Condition of Agriculturists," 1930.
16.	House and Land Tax—Rates ...	VI	71	Treasurer.
17.	Statement of Arrears of Tithe and House and Land Tax.	VI	72	District Commissioners.
18.	Income and Expenditure of a Fellah ...	VI	66	"The Fellah's Farm," by Dr. Wilkansky.
18. cntd.	Do. do. ...	VI	67	Report: "The Economic Condition of Agriculturists," 1930.
19.	Resumé of Proposed Irrigation Ordinance ...	VII	86	Director of Agriculture.
20.	Oranges—Area of Groves and Cost of Production	VIII	93	—
21.	Almonds—Production and Export ...	VIII	96	—
22.	Statement of Immigration since 1922 ...	X	119	Chief Immigration Officer.
23.	Statement of Emigration since 1922 ...	X	119	Do.
24.	Average Crop Yields ...	VI	67	—

155

Maps.

No.	Description.		Report. Ch. Page.	Authority.
1.	‡Tours / Government Lands } Palestine 1/250,000	...	{ Covering letter / IV(iv)56 }	Director of Lands.*
2.	‡Divisions for purposes of Areas, etc.: Sketch Map 1/750,000.		I 13	Director of Surveys.
3.	†Lake Huleh Area: Photograph of Plan ...	...	I 18	—
4.	‡Palestine: Soils ...	...	Covering letter II 24	By courtesy of Geographical Review, N. York, and Dr. Strahorn.
5.	‡Rainfall Zones / Certain Water Sources } Sketch Map, 1/750,000.		{ VII(c)82 / I 20 }	Director of Agriculture*
6.	‡Lands in Jewish Ownership: Administrative Districts and Sub-Districts ...	Palestine 1/250,000	V 38	{ Jewish Agency. / Director of Surveys. }

Graphs.

1.	Market Prices of Crops	...	...	...	VI 68	Director of Agriculture.
2.	†Distribution of Industrial Labour	...	...	IX 107	Director of Customs, Excise and Trade.
3.	†Principal Industrial Expenditure...	...	...	IX 107	Do.
4.	†Racial Distribution of Industry ...	...	...	IX 107	Do.

---

* Prepared by Director of Surveys.   † Not reproduced.
‡ To be published later. *See* Note on page 3.

[For maps 1, 2, 5, and 6 see Maps 8-11 in the Map Box]

156

APPENDIX 1.

The Jordan Valley.

The Experts did not make any detailed examination of the Jordan Valley, except for the soil survey made there by Dr. Strahorn, and even that survey did not cover the whole valley. In the memorandum submitted by Dr. Ruppin on behalf of the Jewish Agency various figures are quoted as supplied by their experts.

On page 48 of the Memorandum of the Jewish Agency it is said that the area of the Beisan and Semakh lands is 370,970 dunums. On page 49 of the same Memorandum it is stated that the experts of the Jewish Agency estimate the irrigable area of Beisan Chiftlik at 113,000 dunums and the non-irrigable area at 94,500 dunums, a total of 207,500 dunums. On the same page there appears the following:—

> "The area [? the Beisan area] also contains some 108,500 dunums stretching towards the northern hills and consisting of deep clay soils which, as far as irrigable, are suitable for forage crops and vegetables, but not for citrus culture. Of these, about 14,000 dunums can be irrigated with the existing water-supply."

Much time has been spent in attempting to reconcile the details of the Memorandum with the Government figures with regard to these areas of the upper Jordan Valley. No hesitation, however, need be felt in adopting the Government figures for the Semakh and the Beisan areas as these were surveyed for the purpose of distribution, and the figure of 388,517 metric dunums given by the Government are therefore exact for the whole of the lands covered by the Ghor Mudawwara land Agreement.

For the lower Jordan Valley there were practically no figures of cultivable area before the commencement of this enquiry. For the Joint Palestine Survey Commission Dr. Strahorn made a soil survey of a considerable area of this tract. In his report to the Commission there is published opposite to page 204 a map showing the results of the survey. It appears that Dr. Strahorn considered 49,800 Turkish dunums, equalling 45,800 metric dunums, to be irrigable. In other very large areas he found the soil to be so alkaline that cultivation in his opinion was impossible.

APPENDIX 2.

The Rural Population of Palestine.

The increase of the population of Palestine is even more marked in the towns than in the rural areas. The three chief towns are Jerusalem, Haifa and Jaffa with Tel-Aviv. For Jerusalem the figures of population in 1922 and 1926 respectively were 62,578 and 74,000. In Haifa for the same two years 24,634 and 33,773. Jaffa, with Tel-Aviv, increased from 47,709 to 73,000 in the same space of four years. The total population of the three towns thus increased from 134,921 to 180,773, an increase of 33.98 per cent. in four years. The preponderance of Jewish residents in the towns as compared with the Jewish population in the rural districts is very marked. In May, 1928, the Palestine Zionist Executive made a census of the Jewish population, which the Department of Health of the Palestine Government regards as fairly accurate. This census gave the total Jewish population at 149,000, of whom 118,500 were town residents and 30,500 inhabitants of

157

agricultural settlements, i.e., that of the Jews in Palestine on that date 79.6 per cent. lived in the towns and only 20.4 were settlers in the country. Of the latter a considerable proportion are not cultivators, but labourers, or employed on other occupations in the settlements.

In order to arrive at the rate of increase for the non-Jewish population between the years 1922 and 1930 it is necessary to deduct from the total for the former years, as well as the latter, the Jewish population and the Bedu population in 1922. If the total of the Bedu and Jewish populations in 1922 are deducted from the total population of that year, the balance is 570,057. The corresponding figure for 1930 reached in the same manner 680,591. This shows that the non-Jewish population (apart from the Bedu population) has increased by 110,534 during the eight years. In view of these figures the argument employed by the Commission on page 123 of the Report on the Disturbances in 1929 receives additional force, for it is clear that the figure there suggested of an ultimate increase of the population of 300,000 within the next 30 years by natural increase is likely largely to be exceeded.

According to calculations of the Department of Health, if natural increase and other factors continue as at present, the total population will be doubled in 28.4 years.

The figure of 30,500—the Jewish inhabitants of the agricultural settlements in 1927—is analysed on page 88 of the Statistical Abstract for Palestine, 1929, published by the Keren-Hayesod. This analysis shows that 49.7 of the population resident in the settlements is actually engaged in agriculture. The accuracy of this estimate is supported by the statement on page 8 of the Report of the Department of Agriculture of the Government dated 16th March, 1922, where it is stated that for every 49 colonists engaged in actual cultivation in the Jewish settlements there are 51 persons engaged in other occupations. It was pointed out in the Blue Book of the Palestine Government for 1928 that there was an under-estimation of the population of Palestine for that year by about 20,000-25,000, owing to unrecorded immigration. This immigration consists in part of Arabs who enter from adjoining countries, in part of Jews who come into the country in various ways without the ordinary formalities of regular immigration. In June, 1930, the National Council (Waad Leumi) of the Jews of Palestine submitted to the League of Nations a Memorandum in which this question was discussed, and it was claimed that the Jewish rural population might be taken as 42,500 on the basis of official figures, but as 46,000 if allowance were made for unrecorded immigration (page 16). If the latter figure were accepted there would be about 23,000 Jews, including children, actually engaged in agriculture. The following is the relevant quotation from the Memorandum of the Waad Leumi:—

" According to the Government estimate the number of Jews in Palestine on 1st July, 1929, was 154,330, and at the beginning of 1929 153,000. Accordingly, the number of Jews in the colonies was about 39,000. Since that date, the Jewish population has increased by about 7,000 (3,500 by natural increase and the rest by surplus immigration) . . . Thus the population of the Jewish colonies increased in 1929 by at least 3,500, and their number at present is therefore 42,500. It must be borne in mind that this calculation is based on the official estimate which, as Government themselves admit, is somewhat understated. According to the estimate of the Zionist Executive, the number of Jews in Palestine is by 14,000 greater than the official Government estimate, and had the figures arrived at by the Zionist Executive served as the basis of our calculations, the Jewish population in the colonies would have figured at 46,000."

The arguments employed in the above extract depend upon many assumptions which it is impossible to verify. It is preferable to arrive at the number of the Jewish settlers in the colonies in another way. The figure of 35,000 taken as the figure of the Jewish population in 1929 on page 86 of the Statistical Abstract amounts to 22.6 per cent. of the total Jewish population at that time. For mid-1930 the Director of Health reports the Jewish population as 162,069. (*Vide* his letter dated 14th July, 1930). Applying to this last figure a percentage of 22.6, a total of 36,627 is obtained as the Jewish agricultural population of that date. Assuming that 50 per cent. of this population settled is actually engaged in agricultural occupations, the number of Jewish immigrants in fact settled as members of cooperative groups or as smallholders, or members of small-holding families is slightly in excess of 18,300. Assuming also that the figure of 162,069 given by the Director of Health as the total Jewish population is correct, the percentage of those engaged in agriculture is about 11.3 of that population. Of the total population of the settlements more than one-quarter resides in Petach-Tikvah and Rehovoth.

Arab Rural Population.

On page 120 of their Report, the Commission on the Disturbances accept the number of 460,000 as that of the Arab rural population of Palestine, excluding the Beduins, and consider that there are 92,000 Arab families dependent on the soil for their subsistence. These figures were based on information submitted by the Director of Lands and supplied to him by the Director of Agriculture. It is not clear how he arrived at them.

These figures are examined and criticised in the Memorandum of the Jewish Agency on the Report of the Commission on pages 107 *et seq*. With regard to the figure 460,000, the Memorandum points out that even on the assumption that this figure is correct, it is unreasonable to assume that the whole 92,000 families are cultivators of the soil. This criticism is just.

It is also difficult to support the figure of 460,000 published by the Commission. The estimate of the Director of Health of the population as at mid-1930 gives the following result:—

(1) Urban population	340,962
(2) Rural population	501,698
(3) Tribal population	103,331
	945,991

The tribal population is the estimate accepted in 1922 at the time of the census. No attempt has been made to bring this estimate of the tribal population up to date. It represents nomad tribes not only in the Beersheba area but also elsewhere.

The natural increase of the Arab population since the census of 1922 has been estimated at 26 per thousand per annum. The population in the Beersheba area in 1922 was 75,254. Adding the natural increase of 26 per thousand per annum, the population at this time—mid-1930—is 90,012. The total rural population consists of items (2) and (3) of the estimate made by the Director of Health, i.e., 605,029. In order to arrive at the Arab rural population it is necessary to deduct from this total the Jewish rural population, and, as the Beersheba area is being left out of account for the present, in estimating the area of land available for settlement, to deduct also the population of that area. The Jewish population of the settlements has been shown to be 36,627. The total of the two items is 126,639. Deducting these, the rural Arab population in the Hills and the Five Plains will be 478,390.

APPENDIX 3.

Statement showing composition of Areas in KM2 or thousands of metric dunums.

	Total Area.	Sand dunes.	Marsh.	Forest.	Water.	Unclassified land undefined.	Barren land.	Cult. land.	Percentage of total area cultivable.	Percentage of total area surveyed.
Coastal Plain	3,218	344	19	—	—	192	—	2,663	82·8	88
Acre Plain	550	28	15	100	—	28	—	379	68·9	30
Plain of Esdraelon	400	—	—	—	—	28	—	372	93·0	71
Huleh Plain	191	—	38	—	17	10	—	126	66·0	0
Plain of the Jordan	1,065	—	**	**	170	341	—	554	52·0	75
Inhabited Hills	6,124*	—	—	—	—	3,674	—	2,450	40·0	0
Unhabited Hill Wilderness	2,738	—	—	—	488	—	2,250	—	0·0	0
Beersheba Area	3,200††	—	—	—	—	1,700§§	—	1,500	46·8	0
Southern Desert	8,672	—	—	—	—	—	8,672	—	—	0
Totals	26,158	372	72	100	675	5,973	10,922	8,044	—	—

** Classed as uncultivable—no figures available.
* Total length of all strips photographed shown by blue lines on Map No. 2 364 KM2.
  Total area photographed 697 KM2.
†† Total area of drainage basin referred to by Government Geologist in his 1928 Report—pp. 44, 45.
§§ Very rough estimate obtained from War Office 1/4 M. Map.

APPENDIX 4.

Estimated Population—Palestine.

	Moslems.	Jews.	Christians.	Other Religions.	Totals.
Census, 23rd October, 1922	486,177	83,790	71,464	7,617	649,048
Excess of Births over Deaths 1-11-22 to 30-6-23.	6,723	1,265	892	160	9,040
Excess of Immigration over Emigration 1-11-22 to 30-6-23.	−69	4,450	−456	—	3,925
Estimated Population on 30-6-23	492,831	89,505	71,900	7,777	662,013
Excess of Births over Deaths to 30-6-24.	12,912	2,291	1,740	278	17,221
Excess of Immigration over Emigration to 30-6-24.	−783	2,873	−107	28	2,011
Estimated Population on 30-6-24	504,960	94,669	73,533	8,083	681,245
Excess of Births over Deaths to 30-6-25.	11,374	2,302	1,495	191	15,362
Excess of Immigration over Emigration to 30-6-25.	−440	23,588	−247	—	22,901
Estimated Population on 30-6-25	515,894	120,559	74,781	8,274	719,508
Excess of Births over Deaths to 30-6-26.	14,926	2,830	1,524	235	19,515
Excess of Immigration over Emigration to 30-6-26.	−407	24,009	−729	—	22,873
Estimated Population on 30-6-26	530,413	147,398	75,576	8,509	761,896
Excess of Births over Deaths to 30-6-27.	15,377	3,489	1,595	109	20,570
Excess of Emigration over Immigration to 30-6-27.	−565	−3,200	−332	—	−4,097
Estimated Population on 30-6-27	545,225	147,687	76,839	8,618	778,369
Excess of Births over Deaths 30-6-28	13,112	3,244	1,538	232	18,126
Excess of Emigration over Immigration to 30-6-28.	−688	−1,377	86	—	−1,979
Estimated Population on 30-6-28	557,649	149,554	78,463	8,850	794,516
Excess of Births over Deaths to 30-6-29.	15,040	3,469	1,646	216	20,371
Excess of Immigration over Emigration to 30-6-29.	−246	1,307	116	—	1,177
Estimated Population on 30-6-29	572,443	154,330	80,225	9,066	816,064
Estimated Population on 30-6-30	692,195	162,069	82,506	9,221	945,991

APPENDIX 5.

Schedule showing the Birth, Death, and Infantile Mortality Ratios per 1,000 of the sub-divisions of the population for period 1923 to 1929 inclusive.

		Moslems.	Jews.	Christians.	Other Religions.	Whole Country.
1923	Births	51·02	36·60	35·68	53·10	47·43
	Deaths	29·26	14·63	15·78	16·07	25·67
	Infantile Mortality.	199·30	125·76	134·80	77·48	184·76
1924	Births	55·5	38·3	40·4	39·0	51·3
	Deaths	29·9	12·6	16·8	19·3	25·0
	Infantile Mortality.	199·0	105·7	151·9	146·0	184·8
1925	Births	54·7	33·2	37·2	59·3	49·3
	Deaths	31·2	15·1	18·8	32·5	27·2
	Infantile Mortality.	200·5	131·3	162·4	124·2	188·6
1926	Births	60·2	36·0	40·0	55·0	53·4
	Deaths	28·6	12·1	17·9	34·9	24·3
	Infantile Mortality.	172·5	108·1	158·0	170·9	163·0
1927	Births	56·1	35·1	38·9	50·3	50·3
	Deaths	33·0	13·4	20·1	28·1	29·0
	Infantile Mortality.	216·7	115·3	187·2	156·6	200·5
1928	Births	60·9	35·4	40·4	45·6	53·9
	Deaths	35·1	12·1	18·9	21·0	28·0
	Infantile Mortality.	203·5	95·8	157·9	121·2	186·3
1929	Births	57·74	34·06	37·84	43·67	51·15
	Deaths	31·67	11·79	17·93	26·69	26·50
	Infantile Mortality.	204·91	89·78	155·79	166·66	187·47

APPENDIX 6.

Land Registration Fees under the transfer of Land Ordinance 1920-21.

	Scale of Fees. Per Cent.
1. Sale.	
On the purchase price mentioned in the deed of sale, if the Registrar considers that it represents the market value of the property or the rights transferred	3
If the Registrar thinks that the price mentioned does not represent the market value of the property, or the rights transferred, the value shall be assessed by the Director of Lands.	
Provided that such fees shall in no case be less than 500 mils.	
2. Exchange.	
On one-half of the aggregate market value of the properties exchanged	3
Provided that such fee shall in no case be less than 500 mils.	
3. Gifts.	
(a) On the market value of the property, if the gift is to a descendant or ascendant or wife or husband	2
(b) On the market value of the property, if the gift is to any other person	3
Provided that such fee shall in no case be less than 500 mils.	
4. Lease.	
(a) On the rent for one year, when the lease is for a term of more than 3 years and less than 10 years	5
(b) On the rent for one year, where the lease is for a term of 10 years and over	10
Provided that such fee shall in no case be less than 250 mils.	
The municipal Registration fee of $\frac{1}{4}$ per cent. of the amount of the rent shall be payable in addition on leases of property within a municipal area.	
5. Mortgage.	
On the amount of loan	1
Provided that such fee shall in no case be less than 250 mils.	
6. Further Charge.	
On the increased amount secured	1
Provided that such fee shall in no case be less than 250 mils.	
7. Transfer of Mortgage.	
On the amount of the secured loan transferred	$\frac{1}{2}$
Provided that such fee shall in no case be less than 250 mils.	

8. Sale of Mortgaged Properties at the Request of Mortgagees.

	Scale of Fees. Per Cent.
(a) On the purchase price realised on sale by auction—Registration Fee	3
(b) On the purchase price realised on sale by auction—Execution fees	2½
(c) On the purchase price realised on sale by auction—Auctioneer's fee	1

9. Succession.

(a) On the value, as registered in the Land Registers or Werko Registers, of the interest transferred by way of succession to each descendant or ascendant or husband or wife 1½

(b) On the value, as registered in the Land Registers or Werko Registers of the interest transferred by way of succession to each brother or sister or any one of their descendants 3

(c) On the value, as registered in the Land Registers or Werko Registers of the interest transferred by way of succession to any heir other than those mentioned in (a) and (b) 5

Provided that such fee shall in no case be less than 50 mils in respect of the interest transferred to any one heir.

10. Bequest.

(a) On the market value of the property transferred by way of bequest if the legatees are not legal heirs of the testator 10

(b) If the legatees are legal heirs of the testator, the fees payable are as set out in section 9.

Provided that such fee shall in no case be less than 250 mils.

11. Partition.

On the market value of the property the subject of the partition ..... ¼

12. Issue of Certificate of Registration when property does not appear on the Register.

On the market value of the property in respect of which a certificate is applied for, provided that the applicant shall have proved his title to the property before a competent Court or Government Department, and that the Director of Lands, to whom each case should be referred, approves of the issue of the certificate. This provision includes registration of land to which a title by prescription is established 5

13. Fees on Transfer of Waqf Land.

Fees payable on the constitution of land as Waqf of the market value of the land up to the value of £P. 200 ..... 2½
On the value of the land in excess of £P. 200 ..... ½

The fees payable on the transfer of Waqf land shall be the same as those specified in this schedule.

One half of the fees levied in respect of the constitution of Waqf, or the transfer of Waqf, shall be paid to the Waqf Administration and one half to the Treasury where the Waqf is a Moslem Waqf.

164

14. *Search.*

	Mils.
For every property in respect of which search is made	50

15. *Extracts from the Registers and Documents.*

For every one hundred words, or a fraction of same, on making a copy of a document or extract from any of the registers	40
For every one hundred words, or a fraction of the same, on certifying any copy to be a true copy	20

In addition to the fees payable for preparing the copy the search fee of 50 mils shall be payable in respect of every property included in the copy supplied.

16. *Printed Forms.*

For forms for each transaction	50
For each certificate of registration	10

17. *Correction of the Register.*

For every property in respect of which correction is required, provided that the applicant shall have first obtained the necessary authority for the correction from a competent Court or Government Department, and that the Director of Lands, to whom each case of this kind shall be referred, approves of the correction being entered in the Register	250

If the correction is of a clerical error on the part of the Registry Staff, it can be made free of charge on the order of the Registrar.

18. *Survey.*

The fee for a survey for which application is made by the owner of the land, or for checking the plan of a licensed surveyor deposited by the owner of the land, in connection with the registration of a transaction in land prior or subsequent to the Land Settlement, or on supply of a certified copy of registration plan, shall be paid at the rate of 125 mils for each hour or part of an hour that each surveyor or draughtsman is employed upon the work.

19. *Inshaat (Accretion).*

For the registration of any buildings or tree:	
(a) Of a value less than £P. 50	60
(b) Of a value of £P. 50 to £P. 100	110
(c) For each further amount of £P. 100 or part thereof.........	50
(d) Of a value exceeding £P. 1,000	£P. 1.060m.

Under the Land Settlement Ordinance 1928.
Fees payable on Land Settlement.

The fees payable under Land Settlement on the registration of a right in the Register are:—

(1) A registration fee of $2\frac{1}{2}$ per cent. of the value of the land;

(2) A partition fee of $\frac{1}{4}$ per cent. of the value of the land.

165

The Settlement Officer decides in what cases a fee may be paid in instalments and the number and period of instalments.

Where application is made for partition of a parcel owned in undivided shares, within a prescribed period, no fee is charged on account of the partition.

Where any right to land registered in existing Registers is recorded without modification, no fee is charged and, when there is a modification only, the Settlement Officer may waive any fee in whole or in part.

Under the Correction of Land Registers Ordinance 1926.
Fees payable on transfer from unofficial Land Books.

1. The fee payable on an application for the registration of an interest recorded in an unofficial land book prior to the 1st of October, 1920, shall be LP.1. No fee shall be payable on the registration of such an interest.

2. The fee payable on an application for the registration of an interest recorded in an unofficial land book subsequent to the 1st of October, 1920, shall be LP.1. This fee shall be refunded to the applicant if the interest claimed is subsequently registered.

3. The fee payable on the registration of an interest recorded in an unofficial land book subsequent to the 1st of October, 1920, shall be as follows:—

(1) If the interest registered is that of ownership and the land is registered in the official registers and the applicant has acquired such interest by:—

(a) *Purchase.*—3 per cent. on the market value of the land acquired at the date of acquisition provided that the fee shall not be less than 500 mils.

(b) *Exchange.*—3 per cent. on the one half of the aggregate market value of the lands exchanged at the date of exchange, provided that the fee shall not be less than 500 mils.

(c) *Gift.*—(i) 2 per cent. on the market value of the land at the date of the gift if the applicant is a descendant or ascendant, or wife or husband of the donor.

(ii) 3 per cent. on the market value of the land at the date of the gift if the applicant is not a descendant or ascendant or wife or husband of the donor, provided that in either case the fee shall not be less than 500 mils.

(d) *Succession.*—(i) $1\frac{1}{2}$ per cent. on the market value of the land at the date of acquisition if the applicant is a descendant or ascendant or wife or husband of the deceased.

(ii) 3 per cent. on the market value of the land at the date of the acquisition if the applicant is a brother or sister of the deceased, or a descendant of a brother or sister of the deceased.

(iii) 5 per cent of the market value of the land at the date of acquisition if the applicant is not one of the heirs of the deceased described in (i) or (ii) above:

Provided that in any case the fee shall not be less than 250 mils.

(e) *Bequest.*—(i) 10 per cent. on the market value of the land bequeathed at the date of the death of the testator if the applicant is not a legal heir of the testator.

(ii) $1\frac{1}{2}$ per cent. on the market value of the land bequeathed at the date of the death of the testator if the applicant is descendant or ascendant or wife or husband of the deceased.

(iii) 3 per cent. on the market value of the land bequeathed at the date of the death of the testator if the applicant is a brother or sister of the deceased or a descendant of a brother or sister of the deceased.

166

(iv) 5 per cent. on the market value of the land bequeathed at the date of the death of the testator if the applicant is an heir of the testator but not one of the heirs of the testator described in (ii) and (iii) above.

Provided that in any case the fee shall be not less than 250 mils.

(f) *Partition.*—½ per cent. on the market value of the land acquired by partition at the date of the partition.

(g) *Prescription.*—5 per cent. on the market value of the land, together with all improvements thereon, at the date of the entry in the unofficial land book.

(2) If the interest registered is that of ownership and the land is not registered in the official registers 5 per cent. on the market value of the land (together with all improvements thereon) at the date of registration.

(3) If the interest registered is a leasehold interest:—

(i) 5 per cent. on the rent for one year if the lease is granted for a term of more than three years but of less than 10 years.

(ii) 10 per cent. on the rent for one year if the lease is granted for a term of 10 years or more than 10 years.

Provided that in either case the fee shall be not less than 250 mils.

(4) If the interest registered is that of a mortgage:—

(i) If the applicant is the original mortgagee, 1 per cent. on the amount of the lease and on any sum advanced by way of further charge.

(ii) If the applicant is a transferee of a mortgage ½ per cent. on the amount of the loan transferred.

Provided that in either case the fee shall not be less than 250 mils.

4. If an applicant is registered under the Ordinance as the owner of the land on which he has erected improvements after the date of the entry in the unofficial land book on which his application was based and he desires to register such improvements, the fees payable on the registration of the improvements shall be the inshaat fees prescribed by the Law for the issue of Kushans for Mulk of 28th Rajab 1291 A.H.

APPENDIX 7.

1930 Census of Agricultural Settlements of the Jewish Agency—Population, Area and Investments (Summary).

TABLE No. 8 (SUMMARY OF TABLE 7) vide NOTE TO TABLE No. 7.

	No. of settlements.	Area operated by farmers in dunums 1929.				No. of families in settlement plan.	No. of families or couples in Colony 1930.	Population June, 1930.			Investment Z.O. up to 30.9.1930.		Deficit up to 30.9.1929.	Consolidation Budget for 1930 and 1931.
		Gross Area.	Cultivable	Cultivated 1929.	Irrigated 1929			Adults.	Children.	Total.	For land and its amelioration.	Keren Hayesod for equipment.		
1	2	5	6	7	8	9	10	11	12	13	14	15	16	17
1. Co-operative Groups.	20	62,935	53,057	49,246	2,905	616	711	1,592	548	2,140		L.P. 354,900	L.P. 86,185	L.P. 129,200
2. Smallholders' Settlements	16	62,579	60,245	57,264	981	615	615	1,589	1,055	2,644	Information not yet available.	367,684	—	116,300
3. Settlements supported.	9	14,758	13,659	12,961	1,922	207	178	534	273	807		54,516	—	13,350
4. Girls' Groups	5	813	699	663	125	—	73	166	—	166		20,629	—	—
5. Yemenite Settlements.	4	1,155	990	776	67	—	—	493	462	955		5,442	—	—
6. Various	2	1,984	1,540	1,088	66	—	12	34	6	40		10,378	—	—
7. Experimental Station.	2						Not yet enumerated.							
Total	58	144,224	130,190	122,003	6,066	1,438	1,555	4,408	2,344	6,752		863,541	86,185	—

NOTES—
1. *Vide* Notes to Table No. 7.
2. The Settlements of Hulda, Kefar Uriya, Ber Tuvlya destroyed during the riots were not enumerated.
3. The population of Moshav Beth Hanan (circa 200) and Kevuza Kerkur (circa 50) are not included.

APPENDIX 8.

Investments of the Jewish National Fund in LP.

POSITION AT END OF EACH YEAR.

	1914	1920	1921	1922	1923	1924	1925	1926	1927	1928	1929
Rural land	23,704	37,623	148,053	254,522	328,363	410,915	559,319	668,445	831,687	950,420	1,154,629
Reclamation	2,769	7,504	20,916	37,327	56,691	59,656	62,756	68,484	75,683	84,239	92,224
Urban land	912	912	17,852	34,392	65,455	69,474	83,766	103,421	112,853	119,127	132,493
Farm buildings	25,124	29,218	33,810	35,782	39,284	40,628	40,395	40,122	39,143	39,673	40,653
Water installation	3,382	4,093	4,529	6,792	20,535	34,403	40,592	46,452	57,564	74,364	84,545
Urban buildings	12,881	10,790	10,848	11,051	9,002	8,684	8,011	8,171	10,144	10,400	19,972
Plantations and afforestation	23,230	69,283	86,085	96,753	102,851	108,320	112,920	117,350	121,869	127,331	137,574
Loans	36,218	33,679	37,233	30,092	23,748	23,216	23,399	21,048	10,400	9,793	9,105
Agricultural loans	11,392	15,906	18,968	19,882	20,029	23,736	28,821	28,826	29,010	29,046	23,901
Pipes	—	—	—	—	—	—	—	10,905	18,372	15,879	12,133
Total	144,642	209,008	378,294	527,193	665,958	779,032	959,979	1,113,224	1,306,730	1,460,272	1,707,229

Source: "Statistical Abstract, 1930" (page 113) issued by the Keren Hayesod.

APPENDIX 9.

Keren Hayesod: Allocation of Funds in Palestine.

TABLE No. 104.

	1921—Apr.–Sept.	1921—1922	1922—1923	1923—1924	1924—1925	1925—1926	1926—1927	1927—1928	1928—1929	Total 8¼ years.	Percentage.
	L.P.	L.P.	L.P.	L.P.	L.P.	L.P.	L.P.	L.P.	L.P.	L.P.	L.P.
1. Agricultural Colonisation	50,000	124,627	93,682	130,111	137,275	226,221	156,899	167,090	93,123	1,179,027	31·2
2. Education	36,586	116,041	75,100	75,425	88,581	88,192	99,972	66,215	78,909	725,111	19·2
3. Public Works	7,330	52,363	23,381	43,810	32,303	80,657	175,963	73,496	23,862	513,168	13·5
4. Immigration	17,000	70,542	52,600	37,990	52,316	69,627	33,378	10,903	11,211	355,496	9·4
5. Health	3,000	59,463	36,101	28,178	36,438	46,273	39,876	6,000	8,153	263,482	6·9
6. Urban Colonisation	465	1,577	2,962	9,279	8,727	18,919	17,668	4,746	91,949	156,292	4·1
7. National Organisations	9,000	21,606	13,256	11,369	18,802	17,622	18,845	13,851	9,869	134,240	3·5
8. Investments	43,153	6,670	44,497	32,904	18,706	7,409	42,350	13,608	89,178	120,128	3·1
9. Religious Institutions	6,800	9,705	10,367	15,146	11,105	11,106	10,448	3,500	2,000	80,177	2·1
10. Jewish National Fund	—	2,000	17,591	5,312	1,776	148	5,934	—	—	32,761	0·9
11. Administration (P.Z.F.)	3,000	25,281	24,455	20,254	22,627	22,095	28,565	18,032	17,601	182,811	4·8
12. Miscellaneous	—	—	—	—	1,000	3,430	5,550	11,310	24,960	46,259	1·3
Total	176,334	489,875	394,082	409,738	429,656	591,700	635,458	389,660	272,457	3,788,952	100

(8) Year ending 30th September.
(11) Deducted due to transfer to Urban Colonisation a/c (6).

APPENDIX 10.

1930 Census of Agricultural Settlements of the Jewish Agency Population Summary (compiled from Table No. 6).

TABLE No. 5.

Type of Settlements.	No. of Farms or Couples.	No. of members in co-operative groups.	Members of Settlements.						Other Residents.					Grand Total.
			Working Population.		Children under 15 years.	Relatives.	Total.	Single.	Families.					
			Male.	Female.					No. of families.	No. of persons.		Total.		
										Adults.	Children.			
1	2	3	4	5	6	7	8	9	10	11	12	13		14
Co-operative Groups	711	1,418	812	606	542	52	2,012	106	9	16	6	128		2,140
Smallholders' Settlements(1)	615	—	765	679	998	36	2,478	7	42	102	57	166		2,644
Settlements supported	178	—	250	216	242	16	724	1	21	51	31	83		807
Girls' Training Farms	73	143	—	143	—	—	143	23	—	—	—	23		166
Yemenite Quarters(3)	—	—	—	—	—	—	—	1	205	492	462	955		955
Various(2)	12	23	13	10	6	—	29	11	—	—	—	11		40
Experimental Stations	—	—	—	—	—	—	Not yet enumerated.							
Total	1,589	1,584	1,840	1,654	1,788	104	5,386	149	277	661	556	1,366		6,752

(1) Does not include Beth Hanan (not yet enumerated) (circa 150—200 persons).
(2) Does not include Kerkur group (not yet enumerated) (circa 50 persons).
(3) Yemenite settlers possess small areas and were not considered as farmers, the same applies to other persons having small plots.

APPENDIX 11.

1930 Census of Agricultural Settlements of the Jewish Agency.

DISTRIBUTION OF AREA IN DUNUMS: SUMMARY (COMPILED FROM TABLE NO. 2).

TABLE NO. 1.

	Total Area.			Distribution of Area.									
					Cultivated.								
	Permanent	Leased.	Total.	Fruit trees.	Forest.	Prepared for plantation.	Crops.	Fallow land.	Total.	Under buildings and yards.	Idle fit for cultivation.	Idle unfit for cultivation.	Unspecified.	Total.
Co-operative Groups	57,757	5,178	62,935	2,752	1,465	438	34,759	9,832	49,246	2,040	3,811	2,424	5,414	62,935
Smallholders' settlements	53,062	9,517	62,579	2,720	1,304	693	50,521	2,026	57,264	1,203	2,882	508	722	62,579
Settlements supported	9,218	5,540	14,758	2,230	173	189	9,794	575	12,961	525	698	11	563	14,758
Girls' Training Farms	813	—	813	87	43	6	532	—	668	31	31	13	70	813
Yemenite Quarters	1,113	42	1,155	74	—	—	702	—	776	151	214	8	6	1,155
Other settlements	1,584	400	1,984	60	8	—	920	100	1,088	45	452	309	—	1,984
Experimental stations							Not yet enumerated.							
Total	123,547	20,677	144,224	7,923	2,993	1,326	97,228	12,533	122,003	3,995	8,088	3,363	6,775	144,224

APPENDIX 12.

Government Lands.

Serial.	Name of Property.	Sub-District.	Dunums.	Remarks.
1	Lake Huleh Lands	Safad	52,000	
2	Jazzair	Safad	418	
3	Hassaniyeh	Safad	8,200	
4	Dahnuneh and Mubarakeh	Safad	780	
5	Mansourah	Safad	2,500	
6	Kharab and Awameed	Tiberias	360	Antiquity Site. Uncultivated.
7	Samakh	Tiberias	20,416	
8	Delhamieh	Tiberias	12,049	Lands handed over to Arab Cultivators in 1925 in pursuance of judgment.
9	Subeih	Nazareth	9,548	
10	Kokab	Nazareth	30,000	3/24 shares only. Area over-estimated.
11	Tob Alti	Acre	2,500	
12	Rakayak	Acre	1,600	
13	Acre Sand Dunes	Acre	12,225	
14	Kishon Lands	Haifa	450	
15	Rushmia	Haifa	3,385	
16	Athlit	Haifa	1,500	
17	Kabbara	Haifa	8,665	
18	Caesarea	Haifa	31,440	
19	El Bourj-Tantura	Haifa	145	
20	Cherkaz	Haifa	95	
21	Hudeidoun	Haifa	600	Under litigation.
22	Zalafieh	Jenin	2,700	
23	Tel el Dahab	Jenin	2,400	
24	Deir Ghazaleh	Jenin	2,700	
25	Beisan Jiftlik	Beisan	302,000	
26	Toubas Lands	Nablus	41,700	
27	Akrabanieh	Nablus	960	
28	Mazra'a el Hamra	Nablus	11,300	
29	El Farush	Nablus	1,656	
30	Basset el Yaraki	Nablus	2,500	
31	Ghor el Fara'a	Nablus	75,000	
32	Basset el Mulabbis	Jaffa	2,418	
33	Jaffa Sand Dunes	Jaffa	35,000	
34	Sajad	Ramleh	7,000	
35	Hamadieh	Ramleh	500	
36	Anata	Jerusalem	15,000	
37	Jiftlik Land	Jericho	75,000	
38	Ain Feshka	Jericho	1,300	
39	Es Suwaideh	Jericho	17,000	
40	Gharabeh	Jericho	108	
41	Jabayer	Jericho	20,000	
42	Zeita	Hebron	5,350	

Serial.	Name of Property.	Sub-District.	Dunums.	Remarks.
43	Tel Arad	Hebron	37,000	
44	Jaladieh	Gaza	4,143	
45	Kofakha	Gaza	9,200	
46	Moharraka	Gaza	4,580	
47	Rafa	Gaza	90,000	
48	Gaza Sand Dunes	Gaza	6,000	

N.B.—The serial numbers refer to those shown on Map No. 1.

Areas shown are as registered but are only approximately correct as they have not been surveyed.

APPENDIX 13.

Extract from Report dated 3rd July, 1930, of the Committee on "The Economic Condition of Agriculturists."

REVISED GROSS INCOME FROM ALL SOURCES OF 104 VILLAGES.

	Lp.	Lp.
Cultivation :—		
Field Crops	—	483,600
Fruit Trees :—		
Olive	107,846	—
Other	112,066	219,912
Total income from Cultivation	—	703,512
Stock, Dairy Produce, Poultry, etc.	—	95,720
Total Agriculture	—	799,232
Other Village Sources	—	14,112
Transport and Labour outside the Village	—	99,326
Total income from all sources	—	912,670

PRODUCTIVITY PER DUNUM ON COMMUTED TITHE FIGURES.

Crop.	Area.	Gross Produce.	Average Yield per dunum.
	Dunums.	Tons.	Kilos.
Wheat	352,425	24,673	70
Barley	144,085	8,525	59
Qatani	92,148	4,725	51
Dura	216,720	8,036	37
Simsim	113,257	989	9
Other Crops	19,375	1,234	64
Melons	10,746	1,509,168 (number).	140 (number).

174

COMMUTED TITHE FIGURES OF PRODUCE IN KIND AND VALUE.

Crop.	Total Produce.	Value.	Average Price per ton.
	Tons.	Lp.	Lp. Mils.
Winter Crops :—			
Wheat	24,673	279,638	11.333
Barley	8,525	62,587	7.342
Qatani	4,725	41,526	8.789
Other	—	6,242	—
	—	389,993	—
Summer Crops :—			
Dura	8,036	61,477	7.650
Simsim	989	23,008	23.264
Other	—	6,241	—
Melons (number)	1,509,168	2,881	—
	—	93,607	—
	—	483,600	—

APPENDIX 14.

Statement showing in respect of Six Crops the Redemption prices on which the Tithe was commuted and present market prices. (Compiled from figures supplied by District Commissioners).

Commodity.	District.	Tithe Redemption Prices per kilo.					Market price July 1930.	Fall from the average Redemption Price.
		1924	1925	1926	1927	Average		
		mils	mils	mils	mils	mils	mils	per cent.
Wheat	Northern	11	13·5	11	10·2	11·4	5·9	48
	Southern	10	15	11	10	11·5	5·7	50
	Jerusalem	10	15	11	10	11·5	6	48
Barley	Northern	8·1	8·2	6·4	6·5	7·3	3·2	56
	Southern	7·5	10	6	6·5	7·5	2·4	68
	Jerusalem	7·5	10	6	7	7·6	2·5	67
Qatani	Northern	9·8	10·6	8·7	8·1	9·3	4·5	52
	Southern	8	13	8	7·5	9·1	3·3	64
	Jerusalem	8	12	8	7·5	8·9	2·5	72
Sesame	Northern	24·7	26·5	24·6	23·9	24·9	13·3	46
	Southern	23	27	25	23	24·5	15·1	38
	Jerusalem	24	28	25	23	25	20	20
Dura	Northern	8·5	7·6	6	6·5	7·1	3·4	52
	Southern	9	9	6	6	7·5	2·8	62
	Jerusalem	9	9	6	7	7·8	3	61
Olive oil	Northern	53·7	53·5	54·6	58·1	54·9	30·5	44
	Jerusalem	53	55	52	57	54·2	30	44

175

APPENDIX 15.

Revised Calculation showing Return to the Owner Cultivator and to the Tenant based on average Market Prices July, 1930.

From 100 dunums of which 76 dunums cereals, 18 dunums fruit trees and fallow, and 6 dunums uncultivated.

GROSS INCOME.

Field Crops— Lp. Mils.
```
  Wheat   37% = 28 dunums @ 70 kilos = 1,960 kilos @  5·9 mils  11.564
  Barley  15% = 11    ,,   @ 59  ,,  =   649   ,,  @  2·7  ,,    1.752
  Qatani  10% =  8    ,,   @ 51  ,,  =   408   ,,  @  3·4  ,,    1.387
  Dura    23% = 18    ,,   @ 37  ,,  =   666   ,,  @  3·1  ,,    2.064
  Sesame  12% =  9    ,,   @  9  ,,  =    81   ,,  @ 16·1  ,,    1.304
  Other    3% =  2    ,,   3·3% of value of other crops           540
                                                                ──────
                                                                18.611
                                                        say     18.600
```

Fruit Trees—
```
  Olive  ...  ...  ...  ...  ...  ...  ...  6.000
  Other  ...  ...  ...  ...  ...  ...  ...  9.000
                                            ─────
                                                   15.000
                                                   ──────
          Total from cultivation   ...  ...  33.600
Stock, Dairy Produce, Poultry, etc.  ...  ...  ...   7.000
                                                   ──────
          Total  ...  ...  ...  ...  ...     40.600
Cost of production  ...  ...  ...  ...  22.000
Taxes—
  Tithe       ...  ...  4·5
  Werko       ...  ...  1·8
  Animal Tax  ...      5              6.800
                                             ──────
                                             28.800
                                             ──────
          Net return to owner-cultivator ... ... 11.800
Rent at 30% of income from cultivation, viz., Lp. 10 less Lp. 1·8
  Werko paid by landlord  ...  ...  ...  ...  ...   8.200
                                                  ────────
Net return to tenant  ...  ...  ...  ...  ... Lp. mils 3.600
```

Note.—The average market prices of crops were taken from the returns of District Commissioners, otherwise the figures used above are those arrived at by the Committee on " The Economic Condition of Agriculturists " or based thereon.

APPENDIX 16.

House and Land Tax.

The House and Land Tax is assessed on the capital value and is levied at the following rates:—

Per *Mille.*

(1) *Property not Built Upon:*—
  (a) Lands, fields, vineyards, gardens, subject to tithe, or to the equivalent of tithe (Badal-ushur), or changed into land of the muquataa category 4
  (b) Land destined for building purposes 4
  (c) Lands not paying tithe, nor paying the equivalent of tithe, nor changed into muquataa land 10

(2) *Property Built Upon*:—
- (a) Farm buildings ... 4
- (b) Farm buildings hired and occupied by tenants not exceeding 200,000 mils capital value ... 5
- (c) Farm buildings hired or occupied by tenant not exceeding 200,000 mils capital value ... 8
- (d) Farm buildings within the area of a town or village ... 5
- (e) Wakf buildings (mussaqafat waqfieh) ... 4
- (f) Houses inhabited by the proprietors, the value of which is below 200,000 mils ... 5
- (g) Houses inhabited by the proprietors, the value of which is over 200,000 mils ... 8
- (h) Buildings leased or rented by their owners ... 10

Additions to this tax aggregating 41 per cent. on buildings and 56 per cent. on lands were made from time to time under Ottoman Decrees. These additions are still collected, except in the case of buildings and lands re-assessed since 1919. Immovable property registered in the names of corporate bodies is subject to an additional tax varying from 1/2 to 1 per mille of its assessed value.

APPENDIX 17.

Statement of Arrears of Tithes and House and Land Tax.

Supplied by District Commissioners, June, 1930.

Sub-District.	Tithes.		House and Land Tax.		Remarks.
	Assessment for one year.	Arrears.	Assessment for one year.	Arrears.	
	Lp. mils.	Lp. mils.	Lp. mils.	Lp. mils.	
orthern District.					N.B.—The figures for Beersheba Sub-District are not included.
Baisan	7,000.837	3,190.926	2,331.344	2,183.847	
Safad	12,407.029	5,272.409	6,156.995	4,071.246	
Tiberias	6,429.505	9,611.823	1,929.685	2,882.979	
Nazareth	11,188.000	11,502.876	6,342.000	9,702.298	
Acre	8,685.060	12,160.000	2,441.893	4,756.000	
Jenin	21,695.925	2,721.755	7,565.754	1,488.827	
Tulkeram	18,479.151	1,452.940	5,642.371	2,578.170	Of the total Assessment about 85 per cent. is non-Jewish, and 15 per cent. Jewish, and of the arrears about 75 per cent. are non-Jewish and 25 per cent. are Jewish.
Nablus	18,543.242	4,442.893	12,218.075	3,177.451	
Haifa	21,460.257	27,750.045	39,229.232	29,505.340	
nuthern District.					
Jaffa	24,641.336	5,368.405	53,009.608	36,918.159	
Ramleh	8,602.699	8,604.726	10,423.194	6,860.202	
Gaza	28,676.000	4,557.590	14,245.000	3,328.177	
Hebron	17,484.000	35.974	8,088.000	1,686.479	
rusalem Division.					
Jerusalem, Bethlehem and Jericho	11,063.045	7,599.975	14,227.285	19,049.044	
Ramallah	9,493.575	1,205.308	9,074.018	4,286.072	
	225,849.661	105,477.645	192,924.454	132,474.291	

APPENDIX 18.

Extract from "The Fellah's Farm" by Dr. Wilkansky.

Income and Expenditure of an ordinary Fellah.

(Area 80-100 dunums, number of souls 6-9.)

1. EXPENDITURE:

   (a) *Expenses*:

	£E.	
Food for 2 oxen, 2 kantars sesame cake or beans	7.00	
Seeds	6.50	
Communal charges	1.60	
Various, repairs, etc.	0.30	
Osher and Verko (tithe and land tax)	4.50	
		19.90

   (b) *Household expenditure*:

4 kantars of wheat at £E 4	16.00	
3 kantars durra at £E 2.50	7.50	
600 litres of milk at Pt. 1.5	9.00	
400 eggs	2.00	
Olive oil, 7 jars	5.00	
Clothing	4.00	
Vegetables, rice, lamp-oil, sugar, etc.	6.00	
		49.50

   Total expenditure . £E69.40

2. INCOME:

30 dunums wheat at 50 kg.	20.00
10 dunums barley at 60	6.00
10 dunums karsena	6.00
30 dunums durra	6.50
10 dunums sesame	3.00
800 litres milk	12.00
1,000 eggs	5.00
Outside labour	12.00

   Total Income ... £E70.50

Extracts from the report of the Committee on the "Economic Condition of Agriculturists," dated 3rd July, 1930.

Cost of Production of 100 dunums Field Crops—   LP. Mils.

Annual share of cost of plough animals	2.000
Implements	1.000
Forage for plough animals	7.000
Seed	6.500
Hired labour	3.500
Transport to village	2.000
Total	**LP. 22.000 mils.**

Cost of Living of a family of six—

Wheat and durra	10.000
Olives and olive oil	3.000
Other village produce	4.000
Other necessaries not of village origin	3.000
Clothing	5.000
Communal expenditure	1.000
Total	**LP. 26.000 mils.**

Average net return from 100 dunums of all kinds of land.

Gross Income—

Field crops	39.000

Fruit Trees—

Olive	9.000
Other	9.000
Total for cultivation	57.000
Stock, dairy produce, poultry, etc.	7.000
Total	**64.000 mils.**
Cost of Production ... LP. 22.000	

Taxes—

Tithe	4.500	
Werko (House and Land Tax)	1.800	
Animal Tax	500	
		28.800

Net return to owner-cultivator	35.200
Rent at 30% of income from cultivation, viz., LP. 17, less LP. 1.8 Werko paid to landlord	15.200
Net return to tenant	LP. 20.000 mils.

N.B.—The above does not represent a true net profit, since no account has been taken of the labour of the farmer and his family. The cost of producing olives and stock is ignored and also the cost of feeding and watering animals.

179

APPENDIX 19.

Résumé of Proposed Irrigation Ordinance.

1. A central Board, partly or wholly official, is to be appointed. This Board has the power, subject to the terms of this Ordinance, *inter alia*, to control water and to construct water works.

2. All untapped underground water and all waste water is the property of the Government and all other surplus water is to be deemed to be the property of Government.

3. An area may be declared an Irrigation Area and such area is to be controlled by Commissioners, who will prepare a schedule or rights of water, provision being made for the due protection of the interests of persons claiming rights to water. The holder of a water right may not claim more water than is necessary for economic irrigation or reasonable use of machinery.

The final schedule of rights is to be filed at the office of the Registrar of Lands, and from that date no separate transfer of a water right will be permitted without the consent of the Board, and no claim not recorded in the schedule will be admitted.

4. Subject to these admitted water rights, the Board may dispose of the surplus water at its discretion. The appropriation of a supply of such surplus water to any particular piece of land will be completed by registration in the Land Registry. The Board has the power, during times of shortage, to reduce the water supplies at its discretion.

5. The Board will prepare a specification of the land affected by the water works. This specification will be prepared in accordance with the terms of the Ordinance, and will be conclusive evidence of the facts set out therein.

6. Water rates or charges will be fixed or varied by the High Commissioner, and will be a prior charge. (The manner of levying and collection has not yet been fixed.)

7. The High Commissioner has the power to acquire land for water works or for accommodation works.

8. The Ordinance provides penalties for the theft of water and for contraventions of the terms of the Ordinance, but provides for the free taking of water, other than from water works, for domestic use and for the watering of animals.

9. *Wells.*—Wells may not be dug without notifying the Board. The Board may require information during the operations, regarding strata and flow, or may send an inspector to obtain this information.

10. The Board may declare a " Well Registration Area ". A Well Register will be kept containing a schedule of every well used for the purpose of irrigation, with full details of depth, discharge, machinery, etc. The onus of notification rests with the owner or occupier of the land, but the fact that a person is registered as the owner of the well is not to be deemed as evidence that he is the owner thereof.

11. All wells within the area are to be open to inspection and the inspector may demand all reasonable information.

In a registered area no new wells may be sunk (? or existing wells enlarged or deepened) unless a formal declaration, with plans, has been submitted to the Board, who may, within one month, prohibit the work, such prohibition being subject to appeal.

180

APPENDIX 20.

Orange Cultivation.

Of the total area of some 300,000 dunums of land suitable for orange growing, altogether only about 100,000 dunums are under cultivation. Estimates of the total area actually planted up to the end of 1929 vary from 90,000 to 120,000 dunums. Of these, 35,000 are bearing, of which 11,250 dunums belong to Jews, the balance, 23,750, belong to Arabs. Of new groves not bearing fruit the Arabs are estimated to have 25,000 dunums. Of similar groves, the Jews planted 17,860 dunums before the end of 1928 and 14,800 in 1929. In addition, they will have planted 14,200 in 1930. By the end of the present year the Jews will thus have a total area under oranges of 58,110 dunums, and the Arabs 48,750 dunums, making a grand total of 106,860 dunums, plus the area planted by the Arabs in 1930 which is not yet ascertained. The land under oranges will thus have increased by more than 200 per cent. in the last four years.

Of the newly-planted orange groves large areas have been planted on behalf of Jews who are as yet not resident in Palestine. It is estimated that these areas amount in all to 18,785 dunums. The areas have been developed both by plantation companies and by settlers already in the Jewish colonies. The following table shows the export of oranges from Palestine during the years 1926-27 to 1929-30:—

Country of destination.	1926—1927.		1927—1928.		1928—1929.		1929—1930.	
	No. of cases.	Percentage of total.	No. of cases.	Percentage of total.	No. of cases.	Percentage of total.	No. of cases.	Percentage of total.
United Kingdom	1,904,240	94	1,729,219	86·7	1,258,795	79·9	1,870,000	69·3
Continent..	110,825	5·5	262,052	13·1	317,348	20	596,000	22·1
Other countries	9,656	0·5	4,924	0·1	4,401	0·1	230,000	8·6
Total ...	2,024,721	100	1,996,195	100	1,580,544	100	2,696,000	100

During the last season there was already difficulty in disposing of the fruit sent to the United Kingdom, and growers in Palestine suffered considerable loss. These were made good to a certain extent by the satisfactory prices realised on consignments in the Continent of Europe, but it is already clear that the prices for oranges on the tree in the season which is about to commence will be lower by nearly 20 per cent. than the corresponding prices of last year, while it is not expected that the Continental market will provide the same satisfactory prices as was the case.

Cost of Production of Oranges.—The estimates of cost of a case of oranges delivered in the United Kingdom vary considerably. Mr. Harry Viteles (" The Status of the Orange Industry in Palestine in April, 1930 ", p. 19), says:—

"In Palestine, the cost of a box of oranges is about 5s. to 6s. on board the boat; 1s. 6d. to 2s. the cost of transportation to the United Kingdom, and 1s. 6d. to 2s. represent selling costs, making a total of 8s. to 10s."

181

Dr. Clark Powell says:—

"The average delivered cost of a case of Palestine oranges is about Pt. 57, or 11s. 6d., roughly speaking, Pt. 60, or 12s.". (Government of Palestine Agricultural Leaflets No. 9. "The Citrus Industry in Palestine", p. 33).

One of the most successful of the Jewish orange growers in Palestine has submitted a memorandum in which he estimates the cost as follows:—

Cost of production	2s. 0d. to	2s. 6d.	per box.
Picking, packing and delivery f.o.b. steamer from	3s. 6d. to	4s. 0d.	,,
Freight to United Kingdom	1s. 10½d. ...	1s. 10½d.	,,
U.K. charges and commission from	1s. 9d. to	2s. 0d.	,,
Total	9s. 1½d. to	10s. 4½d.	per box.

The prices in Great Britain were, during 1928-29, on an average 14s. 7d., and in 1929-30 about 12s. per box. The prices now ruling in Palestine for oranges on the tree are 5s. a box, compared with 6s. to 7s. last year. It is thus clear that the United Kingdom prices of 1930-31 are not likely to exceed those of 1929-30.

The Fruit Export Commission, which sat in 1927 in order to enquire into the conditions of the Orange Industry, examined the price-structure of oranges sold in the United Kingdom. It found that the net return to the grower where the sale price in the United Kingdom was 14s. a case amounted to Pt. 10.36, that is, slightly less than 2s. 1d. A price of 12s. a case would, on this estimate, give practically no profit (vide p. 28 of the Report of the Commission).

The chief competitor with Palestine in the orange market in the United Kingdom and in the European market is Spain. It is admitted that oranges from that country can be placed on the market at a price which compares favourably with that of the Jaffa orange. The average import of oranges to the United Kingdom in the five years 1924-1928 was about 12,250,000 cases. In 1929 the figure increased to 14,833,600 cases, which perhaps explains the difficulty experienced in disposing of the increased Palestinian crop. The Spanish orange was responsible for 67 per cent. of the imports of last year. It is, of course, true that there is a wide difference between the two oranges. The Jaffa orange might be described as a luxury orange, and the Spanish orange as the ordinary popular orange of the country. It is believed that the Jaffa orange compares very favourably with the Spanish orange in quality.

In 1935, when the groves planted in the 1930 season will all be in bearing, the number of cases available for export from Palestine is expected to be 10,000,000 to 12,000,000 compared with the figures of 2,700,000 exported in 1929-30. If and when development of the whole of the available land in the Maritime Plain is complete, the number of cases for export will rise to 30,000,000 or thereabouts. Should development continue at the present rate, the whole area will be planted in the course of the next ten years. It is difficult to believe that the consumption of oranges in Europe will increase with sufficient rapidity to provide a satisfactory market for this enormous increase by the year 1940.

APPENDIX 21.

Almonds.

Year.	Production in tons.		Exports in tons.	
	Blue Book figures.	Figures of expert's report, page 327.	Blue Book figures.	Department of Agriculture figures.*
1922	463	478	513	466
1923	471	509	687	627
1924	516	517	1,060	964
1925	589	568	1,033	939
1926	302	648	534	448
1927	411	—	683	—
1928	298	—	767	—
Total	3,050	—	5,277	—

* In leaflet No. IV/18, the Department of Customs being quoted as the authority.

APPENDIX 22.

Immigration into Palestine.

Statement of Persons Registered as Immigrants since 1st November, 1922.

Period	Jews							Non-Jews							By Religion			Grand Total
	Working class immigration			Dependants on residents of Palestine	Various			Working class immigration			Dependants on residents of Palestine	Various			Jews	Christians	Moslems	
	Persons of capital or assured income, including families	Working men and women	Dependants of workers		Persons of religious occupation, including families	Students, Orphans. Distributed under other categories	Persons exempted from the provisions of the Immigration Ordinance	Persons of capital or assured income, including families	Working men and women	Dependants of workers		Persons of religious occupation, including families	Students, Orphans. Distributed under other categories	Persons exempted from the provisions of the Immigration Ordinance				
1.11.22–31.12.22	264	381	297	465	9	106	—	36	236	31	54	85	99	—	1,416	41	13	1,470
1923	967	2,033	2,338	2,048	35	45	—	139	270	41	133	114	129	—	7,421	402	168	7,991
1924	5,281	3,181	2,162	2,194	38	69	—	139	326	53	133	104	99	—	12,856	510	187	13,553
1925	11,794	10,723	5,438	5,717	129	81	—	98	303	83	158	94	80	—	33,801	741	99	34,641
1926	1,613	6,630	2,472	2,108	62	17	—	60	289	89	152	200	13	—	13,081	611	218	13,910
1927	393	1,063	248	943	21	—	—	85	345	67	115	177	—	202	2,713	758	124	3,595
1928	709	535	173	625	7	—	—	114	403	90	135	247	—	246	2,178	710	198	3,086
1929	715	2,640	945	854	11	—	3	16	111	35	181	73	—	—	5,249	1,117	200	6,566
1.1.30–30.4.30	116	1,607	518	301	9	—	—				46			448	2,568	480	60	3,108
Total	21,912	28,793	14,501	15,345	321	318	3	687	2,285	489	1,103	1,151	420	448	81,283	5,370	1,267	87,920
		43,384			642				2,774			2,019			92.5	6.1	1.4	100

APPENDIX 23.

Emigrants from Palestine.

Statement of persons recorded as leaving permanently since 1st November, 1922.

Period.	By Religion.				By Class.							By categories under which the Returning Immigrants entered Palestine.		
	Jews.	Christians.	Moslems.	Total.	Jews.		Non-Jews.		Total.			Persons of Capital or assured income.	Working men and women.	Dependants on residents of Palestine and other categories.
					Res.	R. Imm.	Res.	R. Imm.	Res.	R. Imm.		Including families.		
1/11/22–31/12/22	244	108	102	454	58	186	168	42	226	228				
1923	3,466	713	768	4,947	940	2,526	1,225	256	2,165	2,782				
1/7/24–31/12/24	507	353	251	1,111	212	295	557	47	769	342				
1925	2,151	1,201	748	4,100	666	1,485	1,753	196	2,410	1,681				
1926	7,365	1,505*	559	9,429	413	6,952	1,281	783	1,694	7,735				
1927	5,071	813	1,094	6,978	640	4,431	1,634	273	2,274	4,704		24%	66%	10%
1928	2,168	547	407	3,122	605	1,563	909	145	1,414	1,708		20%	66%	14%
1929	1,746	792	297	2,835	701	1,045	890	199	1,591	1,244		17%	50%	33%
1/1/30–30/4/30	739	166	161	1,066	311	423	268	59	579	487				
TOTAL	23,457	6,198	4,387	34,042	4,546	18,911	9,555	2,000	13,131	20,911				
					23,457		10,585		34,042					
PERCENTAGE	69	18	13	100										

Res. = Resident in Palestine before the establishment of the present Government in July, 1920.
R. Imm. = Settlers in Palestine subsequent to June, 1920.
* Including 279 Armenian orphans.

APPENDIX 24.

Average Crop Yields in Kilos per dunum (1,000 m2).

Commodity.	Report on Economic Conditions 1930.*					Department of Agriculture Report 1922	1. Elazari Volkani (Dr. Wilkansky).			"The Fellahs Farm."		Arab Experimental farm.	England.	All India 1914–27.
	Declared 104 villages.	Commuted Tithe.	Selected Evidence.	Official Estimated.	Bait Jamal.†		"Transition from Primitive to Modern Agriculture."			Arab Tenants 1914–1922	Selected Arab Tenants 1914–1922			
							Average.	California.						
Wheat	48	70	57	67	86	80	60	150		53·136	69·889	77	210	79–93
Barley	63	59	54	74	129	108	80	250		78·515	101·210	—	180	—
Qatani	35	51	58	61	70	—	—	—		—	—	35	—	—
Dura	44	37	54	65	74	90	40	—		23·730	45·842	47	—	—
Sesame	10	9	25	39	—	30	15	—		23·257	33·159	27	—	—

* It is observed in the "Report of the Committee on the Condition of Agriculturists and the Fiscal Measures of Government in relation hereto" dated 13th July, 1930, that the winter crop accounts for 63 per cent. of the area cultivated and 81 per cent. of the total value of crops—page 11 *et seq.*
† In view of the scientific methods employed at the Salesian Agricultural School of Bait Jamal it is natural that their figures should be high.

7.03

THIS DOCUMENT IS THE PROPERTY OF HIS BRITANNIC MAJESTY'S GOVERNMENT.

Refugee Settlement Commission,
Athens, August 18, 1930.

(Personal and Confidential.)

My dear Lord Passfield,

WITH my letter of the 22nd inst. I have forwarded to you my report on the enquiry into Land Settlement, Development and Immigration in Palestine. That report suffers from the fact that it was prepared with great speed and under great stress of work, and that I had no time to polish it in any way. It comes to you exactly as originally drafted.

2. There is a good deal on the Palestine question, which it is desirable that you should know, but which, for obvious reasons, it was undesirable to include in a report of which the publication might be demanded, or might seem to you desirable. For this reason, I propose to mention in this letter a number of points which have either been omitted from the report, or have been mentioned but not developed.

3. In the first place, I do not think that the Palestine Government or, indeed, the Mandatory Power can escape the criticism which is freely made, that there has been failure to carry out the terms of the Mandate. The fact that those terms are exceedingly difficult of observance does not excuse neglect of their express provisions.

Under Article 2 of the Mandate the Mandatory is responsible, *inter alia*, for the establishment of such economic conditions as will secure the establishment of the Jewish National Home.

Under Article 6 the Administration of Palestine is bound to ensure the rights and position of other sections of the population against prejudice, and at the same time to facilitate Jewish immigration, and to encourage the close settlement of Jews on the land.

Under Article 11 the Administration is bound to introduce a land system appropriate to the needs of the country, having regard, among other things, to the desirability of promoting the close settlement and intensive cultivation of the land.

4. The Administration has not in fact succeeded in accomplishing any of these things. It has stood aside and allowed the Jews to purchase large areas of land and to settle them on conditions which, as shown in the Report, have constituted a serious infringement of the position of the Arabs whom they displace. It has not assisted the Jews actively in the matter of immigration. On the contrary (probably with unconscious wisdom), it has done much to impede immigration. It has taken no serious steps towards the development of the country and the combination of land purchase by the Jews, with failure to develop the land held by the fellah, has produced a serious state of affairs among the fellahin.

5. The attitude of the Administration has resembled that of a spectator—perhaps an interested spectator—of a social experiment carried on before his eyes, but in which he does not feel that he has a duty to take an active part. Now and then when trouble developed the Government has been compelled to take a hand, but once the trouble over, the *status quo* was resumed.

6. It is a curious but unfortunate fact that all British officials tend to become pro-Arab, or, perhaps more accurately, anti-Jew, though it would be quite untrue to suggest that the failure to carry out the Mandate is due to that point. Personally I can quite well understand this trait. The helplessness of the fellah appeals to the British official with whom he comes in touch. The offensive self-assertion of the Jewish immigrant is, on the other hand, repellent. And this self-assertion is a common characteristic of the Chalutzim—the Jewish "Pioneer."

If the official is a Jew, his sympathies are naturally all the other way, and the Jews are the most clannish of people. For this reason I think it is unfortunate that Bentwich holds the position of Attorney-General. He is a nice fellow and a very able man, but he is in a false position. No one outside the Jewish circle can trust him to act without Jewish bias.

7. Palestine, at the moment, is a land with two main sections of the population. On the one hand, the Arab, in a large majority, chiefly an agricultural population, primitive in cultural practice, intelligent enough and most desirous to learn, but ignorant and devoid of the capital which is necessary to agricultural

development. On the other hand, we have the Jew, intelligent, educated, forceful, with every advantage of ample capital and expert advice, and who, whatever his leaders may say for public consumption, is entirely unmoved by any consideration of what suffering may be inflicted on the Arab by the Jewish determination to create a Jewish State in Palestine. That is the true object of the settler. It is, of course, not ventilated generally, but conversation with the men, and still more so with the women, makes it quite clear. The women all believe that the correct policy for the Government lies in the transfer of the Arab population to Trans-Jordania in order to make room for an influx of Jews.

8. When Jewish settlement first began in the eighties of last century, it connoted no political ambition, and the Rothschild colonies lived in peace and amity with their Arab neighbours, and were, in fact, of great assistance to them, providing them with regular employment, and assisting them to develop the Arab lands in proximity to the new Jewish Settlements. The same practice prevailed in the case of the German Colonies. Even to-day, though things are changing rapidly, and under Zionist pressure the P.I.C.A. colonies are being compelled gradually to part with their Arab workmen, the friendly spirit animating the Arab towards the old settlers in the P.I.C.A. colonies is in marked contrast to their keen hostility to the settlers introduced by the Zionist organization. Had the method of the P.I.C.A. continued, no political question would have arisen, and the Jews could have effected a peaceful penetration of Palestine without any opposition on the part of the Arab population.

9. The Zionists were provided with very large funds, and proceeded to purchase extensive properties, mainly from non-resident landlords. No effective steps were taken by the Government to protect the interests, not only of the peasant cultivator, but also of the other residents of the areas purchased. Attempts were, indeed, made by legislative means, but without success, to secure that the tenants of these lands at least received some land in lieu of compensation for disturbance. The Jews were not illiberal in this matter—they did more than was strictly required of them by the law. In the event, however, the money compensation which they gave was rapidly spent, and in a large number of cases there can be no doubt that those who in the past had been cultivators of the land have been compelled to join the ranks of casual labour. The position of the rest of the population of a purchased village was even worse. They received no compensation of any kind. The village which had afforded them a home and a livelihood disappeared and was replaced by a Zionist settlement, which either, in accordance with its principles, employed no labour whatever, or, equally on principle, when employing labour, employed Jewish labour only. In addition to the labourers of the village there was a class of graziers, who, by custom, were permitted as of right to use the waste lands of the village, and, after harvest, the cultivated lands, for the use of their flocks and herds. These men also were left to make such arrangements as they could, and have found it exceedingly difficult to make any satisfactory arrangements at all.

10. This process has gone on until the Jews themselves realize that the problem of the landless Arab is becoming serious. I was informed by Mr. Hankin, the buyer of the Palestine Land Development Company, which purchases land not only for the Zionists, but also for a considerable number of private persons and land companies, that after he has purchased another 100,000 dunams of land, it will be impossible to acquire any more without making arrangements on the purchased property for the Arabs who had hitherto found their livelihood there. My enquiry suggests that the view expressed by Mr. Hankin does not go far enough. It has revealed without any doubt that even now the fellahin have not got enough land to enable them, with their present method of cultivation, to obtain sufficient to provide a decent standard of life. It is essential that every available dunam of land should now be retained, to provide holdings for those who, having lost their land, desire to cultivate, and to increase the size of the existing holdings where the fellahin have not got sufficient land for their needs. This should be done until arrangements can be made for the development of the land, for an agricultural education of the fellah, and for some form of agricultural credit on reasonable terms.

11. A further fact established by the enquiry is the appalling state of debt in which the fellah finds himself. This is in part due to our system of law. In the Turkish Courts much latitude was left to the Judge to apply equity in his decisions. He was not bound by statute in the way in which a Judge under our régime is bound.

and I have no doubt that in many cases in which it was found that the debt was greater than the fellah could pay equity was considered to demand that a decree for a less amount would meet the justice of the case.

12. In our Courts all this is changed. The Wadi Hawareth case is a good instance. In that area there are a large number of persons who have no rights which they can establish in the Courts, but who have exercised certain privileges for many years and who cannot find any similar area for the exercise of those privileges elsewhere. They are to be ejected in favour of Jewish purchasers. According to law, it is right that they should be so ejected, but I doubt whether any Turkish Court would have carried out an ejection of the kind.

In that same area the Beduin of the Beersheba area (many miles away) allege that they were accustomed to graze their animals in the summer when the Beersheba area affords no grazing. There is no proof which our Courts would accept that they have the right to this grazing. It is difficult to establish the existence of a custom *ab antiquo.* I do not know that they have made any claim in the Courts. It is extremely improbable that they would. They are wild and semi-civilized people. But when they find that the land has been taken and enclosed by the Jews, and that the grazing grounds of their cattle and their camels have been transformed into orange groves, into which they are not allowed to trespass, they will conceive hatred not only for the Jew—this they already entertain—but also for the Government, whom they will hold responsible for what they will consider a grave injustice.

13. In the matter of debt, it is true that our law limits the interest to 9 per cent. The intention was to prevent unconscionable burdens of interest accumulating against the debtor. In fact, the provision is quite useless. In the first place, the bond is never for the actual sum advanced, but for a larger sum, which discounts the possibility of a reduction of the interest by the Court. In the second place, even were the interest included at a higher than the legal rate, it would be impossible for the debtor to defend himself in Court on this ground, as, if he did so, it would be quite certain that he would never again receive financial accommodation, either from the money-lender in question or from any other. The ordinary system is what is known in Arabic as "Ashara bil hamastash," *i.e.*, "ten-fifteen." The debtor receives a sum of £10 and signs a bond for £15, payable at harvest. The rate of interest works out at about 75 per cent. per annum.

14. But not only is the fellah class in debt. The effendi is in debt also, and it is in satisfaction of debt that many estates are sold up. This would be an advantage if the result of the sale were the break up of the large estates. That is not the result. There are no purchasers in Palestine at the present time except the Jews and, to a minor extent, the religious orders, especially those of Italy. So the large estate passes to the Jewish National Fund, and becomes "the inalienable property of the Jewish people." It will be used for the settlement of Jews on conditions which render it impossible that any but a Jew can ever hold the land in future, *or can ever be employed on it as a labourer.* This is, from every point of view, a most serious happening. It is undesirable from the economic point of view, for unemployment among the Arabs is already a serious problem. The political aspect of the matter is even more serious, for it confirms the Arab in the belief commonly held that Jewish policy is designed deliberately to oust the Arab from the land of Palestine. And it is impossible to affirm that this belief is unfounded. The policy of the Zionists indicates that their ultimate intention, by means of steady and consistent land purchase and settlement with the provisions noted, is to buy the country, and to buy it under conditions which will render it impossible for any Arab to earn his daily bread in the territory which they have acquired. It is a policy of the inevitability of gradualness of the most sinister kind.

15. There are a number of serious questions raised in the report which I need not re-examine in this letter. The question of tenant right will require orders. That of indebtedness will, I suppose, be dealt with on Strickland's report. It is for this reason that I have not gone into the question of an Agricultural Bank. The most important question with which I have dealt is that of the provision of facilities for the development of the land. In this matter the Administration is to blame. The Department of Agriculture has doubtless done what it could, but the results are very small. There has been a lack of realization both there and in the general policy of the Administration of the very serious nature of the problem. The Department has done very fine work in locust campaigns and in veterinary

operations in connection with cattle plague and foot and mouth disease. But much expenditure has been misdirected, as, for instance, the importation of pure-bred Arab stallions from England*—a luxury for the well-to-do and of no value whatever for the ordinary cultivator, on whose behalf every available penny should have been spent. The Departmental expenses are very high, and seem to me to be out of proportion with the amount spent on practical work. The latter is the great necessity if the general cultural standards of the country are to be improved. There was also much criticism on the subject of the salary of the Superintendent of the Acre Station. General McNeill holds that position. He was, I understand, appointed by Lord Plumer. He is not in any sense an agriculturalist, though a very attractive man personally. He knows a horse, and when it was intended to breed pure-bred Arabs, he may have been not unsuitable. The stallions, however, have been infected with dourine. The horse-breeding operations have come to an end, and the important person for the bulls and cows is the stockman. There was, therefore, a certain justification for the criticism. There is no work in the station to justify an appointment of £1,000 a year.

16. In my report I suggest the creation of a Development Commission, with the object that the land of Palestine may be rendered capable of holding a larger population than it does at present. *There is no other way of carrying out Article 6 of the Mandate.* Either the existing area must be rendered capable of supporting more cultivators, or the admission of Jews to settle on the land must be prevented. And more cultivators can obtain subsistence from the soil of Palestine only if that land can produce more sustenance, that is to say, if the land is developed. You will see from the Report that there is not, in fact, room in Palestine for the existing agricultural population. It is my opinion that, with efficient development, there will be room, not only for the existing population, but for one considerably larger. In the Report I have ventured the personal opinion that the additional number for whom room can be found will be **not less than 20,000 families.** It might well be 40,000.

There are three points which I consider essential to successful development by the Commission. The first is that when a tract is taken up for development, the Commission should make up its mind from the start, from what area it is going to draw the excess Arab cultivators for settlement on the land of that tract when developed. The second, that in each tract developed a certain number of Jews should be settled simultaneously with the Arabs. The third, that the Commission should not sell the land, either to Jew or Arab, but should let it on long lease. The reason for this last is obvious. The scheme contemplates expropriation of land, which in the nature of things can only be Arab land. If this is sold to Jews, the unanswerable accusation will be made that the Government, after forcing down the price of land by its policy of control, has taken Arab land by expropriation, and has sold it at this reduced price to the Jew. In view of Article 6 of the Mandate, we must be careful to avoid any justification of an accusation of the kind. It will be sufficiently difficult to meet the accusation that the land has been expropriated at a low price in order that it may be used for settling the Jew as a tenant. An ancillary advantage from the policy of leasing rather than of sale will be found in the cessation of Jewish mortmain, which I regard as an intolerable system. The terms of the lease will be Government, not Jewish, terms. The Jew will be a tenant of the Government rather than the proprietor of an inalienable portion of Palestine. It is noticeable that the Mandate contains no provision whatever, contemplating *purchase* of land by Jews.

17. It is proposed that the Development Commission should consist of a British Chairman, who should be its executive and administrative officer, a Jewish and an Arab member—all three appointed by the League—the Commission to be subordinate to the Secretary of State. I do not know whether any political difficulty is likely to arise from such a constitution. It appears to me to have the advantage of directing attack from the High Commissioner to a body, nominated by the League, and at the same time to remove any suspicion that the Commission is simply an instrument of His Majesty's Government.

18. The scheme will cost money, and that to His Majesty's Government. The actual loss of money will be small, as most of the expenditure will be repayable. It will all be reproductive. This expenditure cannot be avoided. The Palestine Budget cannot bear it. And it is right that the expense should fall on the British people.

* From the Wentworth stud.

5

for it was their Government which accepted this remarkable Mandate. This was not done by the Palestinian people. The last thing which they desired was the establishment of a Jewish National Home in Palestine. Unless Great Britain is prepared to surrender the Mandate (and I understand that the Dutch are willing to accept it), she will be compelled to undertake the expense of development. These are the two alternatives, and there is no avenue of escape.

19. The relations between the Palestine Government and the Jewish Agency are not of the character contemplated by the Mandate. In practice, these relations amount to the submission by the Jewish Agency of such information as may be from time to time requested by the Government, and of visits by the Chairman of the Executive of the Jewish Agency to the High Commissioner, either when sent for in cases of difficulty between Jew and Arab, or, and this is the more frequent, when there is matter which the Jewish Agency deems to be matter for complaint. Then the Chairman requests an interview with the High Commissioner in order to voice the Jewish "demands." As a general rule, the Government does not consult with the Jewish Agency as to their operations, or make suggestions to them on the advisability or otherwise of their course of action. The High Commissioner does not send for Kisch and say to him "What are you doing about this, or why are you doing that?" There is no live interest in the detail of the activity which is going on under the auspices of the Jewish Agency.

For instance, at the moment a communal colony for workers is being constructed just outside the P.I.C.A. village of Ness Ziona. This is being done as a method of enforcing the policy of the General Federation of Jewish Labour, to exclude the Arab workmen from Jewish villages, and the workers' colony is, in fact, a threat and a menace. This was a case which should have been known to the Government, and in which the Government should have called on the Jewish Agency to explain what it was doing. It is probable that in time there will be trouble about labour in Ness Ziona. The price of oranges is falling, and shortly it will not be possible to employ Jewish labour at the rates fixed by the General Federation and at the same time to export oranges. Yet the labourers who are being planted on the borders of Ness Ziona will demand employment, and will take steps to see that Arabs are not employed for the picking and packing of the fruit. This was eminently a case in which consultation between the Government and the Jewish Agency was desirable before the construction of the labour colony commenced, and the relations should be such that schemes for the construction of a new colony should be discussed as a natural thing.

20. It is true that it is exceedingly difficult to initiate relations of the kind discussed in the last paragraph. Colonel Kisch is Chairman of the Executive of the Jewish Agency in Palestine. He is not a man who inspires confidence, and, personally, I do not feel that I could trust him. I know that Chancellor finds that he cannot trust him. I also know that the non-Zionist group, of whom Felix Warburg is a representative, does not trust him either. It is a very difficult matter to have intimate and satisfactory relations with a man in whom you have no confidence.

21. There are extensive changes in prospect in the circles of the Jewish Agency. The American group, represented outstandingly by Felix Warburg and Brandeis, do not at all approve of the way in which matters have hitherto been run in Palestine. Hexter is their representative on the Agency, and is a most competent man. He is gradually acquiring authority on the Executive. As he represents the mass of the American money, he wields powerful force. It is desirable that both the C.O. and the High Commissioner should maintain the closest touch with this group. The High Commissioner can do that by close relations with the Jewish Agency, even before the revolution occurs, which I foresee in the comparatively near future.

22. In regard to Jewish Immigration, there is one important point, only lightly touched upon in the report. A large portion of the Jewish population depends for its livelihood on the continuance of charitable subscriptions. In the report it is recorded that to settle on the land 4,408 adults and their children has cost the Zionists £4,891,000; and these people are not yet self-supporting. They still depend on the Zionist funds. In addition there is a very large number of people in the towns who, in fact, depend on the money that comes in from outside. If that flow of money were for any reason to cease, the Government will be faced with an acute economic crisis. Thousands of Jews will require relief and maintenance. It is

highly possible that, if my report is published and the true facts become known, subscriptions will fall off materially.

In the report it is suggested that, in certain cases, security should be demanded as a condition of allowing immigration of labour which might subsequently be left unemployed. That is a principle which is capable of wider application—indeed, application to the whole system of Jewish immigration. It would be justifiable to demand, as a condition of the continuance of immigration that the Jewish authorities should deposit with the Government a large sum, say, £500,000, in order to ensure against a possible cessation of funds, and a consequent expense on relief of the Jewish population by the Palestine Government. The existing economic basis of Palestine Jewry is exceedingly precarious. The Jews themselves say, as I have noted in the report, that the income from subscriptions depends on the continuance of immigration. That of itself demonstrates the precarious nature of the present position.

23. Politically, the difficulty between Jew and Arab is largely due to the Grand Mufti. He is a man of small attainments, and, had he not been appointed Grand Mufti by Sir Herbert Samuel, nothing would ever have been heard of him. Before I left Jerusalem I had a long interview with him, in which I attempted to induce him to come to agreement with the Jews on the subject of the Wailing Wall. I acted, of course, purely in a private capacity. The impression which he made on me was that of a man who had no conception of the method in which such a subject should be handled. He has a petty mind, and his whole attention is directed to manœuvres which will fortify his personal position. I understand that there is an intention to remove him. The sooner that is done the better for Palestine.

The Mufti's power is based on his command of the purse. In the Report I have pointed out that an income of £30,000 from tithes of waqf properties is collected by the Government and handed over to the Muslim Council. There is at present no audit of the expenditure of this money, and little doubt that the Mufti is using it for his own ends. Chancellor is contemplating legislation to provide for an annual audit. That will be excellent.

The Turkish Government has abolished waqf altogether. Such a radical measure would be impossible for us, but, if the waqf income were properly administered, it is possible that a material sum might be made available for education of the Arabs. This would be an appropriate application of waqf funds.

24. I visited Trans-Jordania. It is a fine country with room for a large population. Parts of it are very fertile.

At the present time the Jew is not welcomed; indeed, not allowed in Trans-Jordania. If settlement were forced upon the Trans-Jordan Government, it would be essential to take extraordinary and expensive steps for the defence of the colonists. The settlement of Jews in Trans-Jordania is, indeed, altogether out of the question.

It was frequently suggested that Arabs should be removed from Palestine to Trans-Jordania in order to make room for Jews. This is a matter of policy on which I am not called upon to report. In my personal opinion such a policy would be most unjust, and could not fail to lead to grave political reactions.

25. If the pipe-line from Iraq were to come to Haifa, the result would be the provision of livelihood for a large number of persons, and would be of great assistance in settling the immigration problem. The construction of a railway to Iraq, which has been mooted, would also react favourably. There is a general opinion that the initiation of a motor service through Amman to Rutba Wells and so on to Baghdad would be of great value to Palestine. To me it seems that the effect of such a service would be small.

26. The treatment of the Palestine Government by His Majesty's Government in financial matters was the subject of frequent criticism. From the loan the Palestine Government paid a lump sum of £1,000,000 for the railway and a further sum of £219,145 for the Jaffa–Jerusalem line. For the latter it also paid £287,793 from revenue. The return of the railways to the Palestine Government is negligible.

From revenue the Palestine Government has paid £813,893 in respect of its share in the Ottoman Debt. Also, from revenue it has paid to His Majesty's Government £206,451 on account of the deficit incurred during the Military Administration. This does not seem a fair charge. It was, in truth, a military expense, and should have been debited to the War expenditure.

7

The finances of Palestine have been extraordinarily well managed by Davis, otherwise these payments could never have been made. It is now clear that the Government will have to face material additional expenditure on Police, on Education, on Health and on Agriculture. The Palestine Budget cannot stand this additional expenditure. It is due to the Jewish influx, the consequent need for increased forces for security, and the urgency of the measures of development. It would be just that His Majesty's Government should come to the assistance of the Administration by a grant-in-aid. What its amount should be will depend on the increase in the estimates of expenditure of the Palestine Government, and I can offer no useful opinion.

27. When we meet, I shall have the opportunity of speaking to you on the general question of the Administration of Palestine. It is a subject entirely outside my terms of reference, but is of great importance and gives rise to certain obvious criticisms in several directions. Here it is sufficient to say that the powers of the district and area officers, specially of the latter, should be considerably enlarged. They will be the officers mainly concerned with the work of the Development Commission. They are the only officers, with the exception of some of the medical staff, the settlement officers, and some of the officers of the Lands Department, who are in constant touch, or should be in constant touch, with the villages. They should be the eyes and hands of the Administration. At the moment their statutory position is obscure and their powers much restricted.

28. The Zionist position is altogether anomalous. In Palestine the policy is dictated by the General Federation of Jewish Labour. Hitherto the Jewish Agency in Palestine has not been able to resist the influence of the Federation. The immigration of Jews comes in far the greatest measure from Poland, from Russia and from the Yemen. The governing principles of immigration appear to be two: that the immigrant should come from one of the countries where the Jews are oppressed, and that he should support the peculiar doctrines of the General Federation of Labour. Palestine is at the moment, from the Jewish point of view, serving two purposes. It is a place of relief for distressed Jews, and it is the scene of a social experiment of the Communist type on a very large scale. The religious element enters into the matter scarcely at all. Of the people being settled in the communal colonies, there are very few, if any, who are religious people. They are ardently nationalist. And this communistic experiment is being carried out at the expense of the rich Jew of America, who probably disapproves of the organization of labour and to whom anything in the nature of Communistic experiment is anathema maranatha. The American Jews have no knowledge of the position. It is never published or ventilated. Hexter has asked me to give him a note on the activities of the General Federation of Labour in order that he may show it to Warburg. You will be able to advise me whether I should do that or not, once the report and the shouting are over. The experiment is not proving a financial success. It is costing an enormous amount of money, and the settlements, which have been founded at great expense, are in few cases only self-supporting in the sense that they are no longer demanding subventions from the Zionist funds. In the majority of cases they demand that support. In no case are they as yet repaying anything. One of the indications of the importance of the General Federation is found in the fact that in the communal colonies the colonists have demanded that this Federation shall be made a party to the lease of the National Fund and to the bond of the Keren Hayesod.

29. I am writing a separate letter in reply to yours of the 15th August. With the present letter I enclose a copy of the Conclusions Chapter of the Report, as originally drafted. You will see great changes in the Chapter, as it will come to you with the balance of the report. I had drafted this letter before yours of the 15th arrived, and have replaced the last page. This will explain to you what might otherwise have seemed a discrepancy in the dates of these two letters.

I apologize for the length of this communication.

With kind regards,
Yours sincerely,
J. HOPE SIMPSON.

7.04

HIGH COMMISSIONER FOR PALESTINE,
JERUSALEM.

Confidential.

January, 1931.

Reference No. CF/481/31.

Sir,

Enclosure.

I have the honour to refer to Lord Passfield's despatch No. 487 of the 26th June, 1931, on the subject of the Development Scheme, and to forward herewith for your information, the Report which the Director of Development has submitted in accordance with the instructions contained in paragraph 5 (iv) of that despatch.

2. It is assumed in the paragraph of the despatch quoted above, that this Report will contain practical proposals, some at least of which will have been drawn up in consultation with the Director's Jewish and Arab Advisers. On this assumption it was laid down that before the High Commissioner's recommendations were submitted to Government, the observations of the Jewish Agency and the Arab Executive should be invited. I have not followed this course, partly because I do not feel that the proposals contained in the Report are such that any appreciable benefit will be derived from subjecting them to the criticism of either the Jewish Agency or the Arab Executive, and also because the Report contains passages which, in

my /

The Right Hon. Sir Philip Cunliffe-Lister, M.P., G.B.E., etc., etc.,
His Majesty's Principal Secretary of State
for the Colonies.

- 2 -

my judgment, will be resented by the Jewish Agency and will render it more difficult to persuade them to cooperate in the Scheme. I propose, therefore, unless I receive instructions from you to the contrary, that the Report in its present form shall remain a confidential document.

3. The greater part of Mr. French's Report consists of a discussion of what he describes as the five essential prerequisites which have to be decided upon before any large schemes of development can be considered in detail. I am substantially in agreement with Mr. French's views as set out under these five headings, which for convenience of reference I quote below :-

   1. Acceleration of Survey and of Settlement Operations.

   2. Acceleration of Partition of Village lands held in common (Masha').

   3. Establishment of a Land Administration Agency.

   4. Government control of lands in the areas coming under Development.

   5. Government control of water in similar areas.

I may mention here, however, that I do not agree with the view expressed in paragraph 60 of the Report regarding the proposed legislation for the restriction of land transfers. Mr. French holds that the proposed Ordinance must apply to the whole country and that any areas to which it is not to be applicable must be specially exempted. I agree that this would be the preferable course. But I realise that it may not be practicable to enact legislation which would be so entirely

entirely unacceptable to the Jews. I believe that sufficient control to achieve a useful amount of land development can be obtained by passing an Ordinance which would give the High Commissioner power to control dispositions of land in defined areas, these areas being specified in the original Ordinance or by subsequent proclamation, as and when the Director of Development is prepared to begin active operations within them.

Since Mr. French is clearly of opinion that he can proceed with no scheme of land development, until some such legislation is authorised I trust that the enactment of legislation on these lines will be authorised in the near future.

4. I shall in due course address you on various other subjects which are dealt with in Mr. French's Report, in particular on the Sections which deal with the Beisan area and the Huleh area. I have already addressed you, in my despatch No. 114 of the 21st December, on the proposal that a hydrographic survey should be carried out within the next twelve months.

5. It is clear to me – and indeed the fact is recognised in Mr. French's Report – that the complete fulfilment of Mr. French's five prerequisites will take many years to attain, and that if nothing is to be done by way of development and settlement in the meanwhile there can be no hope of any alleviation of those problems and difficulties which in their nature require that an early solution should be devised.

I have therefore impressed it upon Mr. French that I expect him to apply his energies to the working

out /

- 4 -

out of immediate palliatives as well as to the maturing of large scale and necessarily slow measures of development. I had hoped that he might be able in this Report to give me information as to land (State or other) which might be made available at a fairly early date for settlement thereon of dispossessed Arabs. I had also hoped that he might by now be in a position to inform me of any areas to which an Ordinance dealing with control of disposition of land might be made immediately applicable. I had recognised, however, that it might not be possible for him to give me this information simultaneously with the Report, which was due on the 31st of December, and I therefore asked him on the 7th of December to give me the required information by the 15th or, at the latest, by the end of January.

I hope, therefore, to be in a position to address you within the next month on one aspect of the matter which to my mind is of great importance, namely the immediate execution of some part, even though it be small, of the projected schemes for the development of Palestine and for the promotion of contentment amongst the inhabitants.

I have the honour to be,

Sir,

Your most obedient, humble

servant,

Arthur Wauchope

HIGH COMMISSIONER FOR PALESTINE.

FIRST REPORT

ON

AGRICULTURAL DEVELOPMENT AND LAND SETTLEMENT

IN PALESTINE

by

LEWIS FRENCH, C.I.E., O.B.E.

DIRECTOR OF DEVELOPMENT

Jerusalem.   23rd December, 1931.

I N D E X

Part I

	pages
General Remarks	1 to 19
Acceleration of survey and settlement operations	20 to 24
Acceleration of partitions of undivided lands (Mesha'a)	25 to 32
Establishment of a Land Administration Agency	33 to 44
Government control of lands	45 to 60
Government control of water supplies	61 to 70
Recommendations for legislation	71 to 74

Part II

The Beisan area	75 to 81
The Huleh area	82 to 88
Other areas	89 to 91
Miscellaneous	92 to 94

Appendices

I   Dispatch No.487 dated 26.6.31 from Secretary of State to High Commissioner for Palestine

II   List of State Domains

III A)   History of the Beisan Area
III B)   The Beisan Agreement
III C)   Statement of Policy

IV A)   History of the Huleh Concession
IV B)   The Huleh Concession

V   Map of Palestine

GENERAL REMARKS.

1. In Dispatch No. 487+ dated the 26th June, 1931, from the Secretary of State for the Colonies to the High Commissioner for Palestine dealing with the agricultural development and land settlement of the country, reference was made to the papers in which His Majesty's Government have explained their policy in regard to these matters. The intention was also stated of finding the funds required for the active pursuit of this policy by means of a loan which Parliament would be asked to authorise His Majesty's Government to guarantee. Before, however, the Bill for the guarantee of the development loan could be settled, a Report or Interim Report was to be awaited from the Director of Development whom it had been decided to appoint for the purpose of carrying out the policy of His Majesty's Government.

Objects of H.M.G.'s policy.

2. The major objects of this policy which the Director of Development has been instructed by the terms of the Dispatch to consider may be summarized as:

+ vide Appendix I.

-2-

(i) the re-settlement of landless Arabs of the category specified in the Dispatch:

(ii) the ascertainment of what State and other lands are or properly can be made available for close settlement by Jews under reference to the obligation imposed upon the Mandatory by Article 6 of the Mandate:

(iii) the improvement and intensive ievelopment of land in the hills in order to secure to the fellahin a better standard of living without, save in exceptional cases, having recourse to transfer.

The displaced Arabs.

3. The Arabs whom I have compendiously named "landless" were defined in the Dispatch as those "who can be shown to have "been displaced from the lands which they "occupied in consequence of the lands falling "into Jewish hands, and who have not obtained "other holdings on which they can establish "themselves or other equally satisfactory "occupation".

A /

A register was to be prepared of those who can be shown to come within this definition: and to assist in its preparation a legal assessor was to be appointed whose duty it was to be to scrutinize claims and advise the Director as to the sufficiency of evidence in each case before the claims were admitted.

Scope of development enquiry

4. The scope of the enquiry necessitated by the second of the objects named above was to include the whole land resources of Palestine; the area of cultivable land, the possibilities of irrigation and the absorptive capacity of the country in relation to immigration being all elements pertinent to the issue to be elucidated.

The Director's investigation, it was further enjoined, should include

(i) the feasibility and advisability of providing credits for Arab cultivators and Jewish settlers, and if so, the best methods of achieving this purpose: and

(ii) proposals for draining, irrigating and otherwise reclaiming land not at present cultivated or cultivated only to a limited extent.

The Director/

The Director was to estimate as closely as possible the cost of re-settling landless Arabs and of carrying out the other/objects specified above; and he was to intimate the order of preference in which schemes should be taken up. Towards the cost of the necessary preliminary surveys and experiments His Majesty's Government announced their intention of authorising the High Commissioner to incur expenditure not exceeding £.50,000.

Finally, the Director was asked to submit his Report or such Interim Report as could be completed, not later than 31st December, 1931.

Development staff

5. Such were the instructions which I brought to Jerusalem when, accompanied by the Deputy Director, Mr. G.C. Kitching, O.B.E., late of the Iraq Service, I took up the appointment of Director of Development on the 20th August. This assumption of office was somewhat earlier than originally intended; but it was obviously desirable that I should have the benefit of the advise of the High Commissioner, Sir John Chancellor, before he left Palestine early in September.

Shortly after my arrival, the services of the Irrigation Officer, Mr. J. Dawson Shepherd, O.B.E., were transferred from the Agricultural to the Development Department.

The Dispatch/

Director's Jewish & Arab Advisers	6. The Dispatch, in defining the status of the Director, announced that it was under contemplation to give him the assistance in an advisory capacity of two members, one each nominated by the Jewish Agency and Arab Executive respectively. It had also been decided that an officer should be appointed from the British Treasury to take up his residence in Palestine in order to be in a position to advise the Director readily in financial questions connected with expenditure from the Development loan when it, or part of it, should be floated.
Appointment of Legal Assessor	7. Circumstances have so fallen out that at the time of writing the solitary member of the proposed staff who has actually taken up his appointment is the Legal Assessor, Mr. A.H. Webb, K.C., lately President of the District Court, Nablus, and this event occurred as late as the 23rd November.
Advisers not yet appointed	With the appointment of Arab and Jewish Advisers no progress has been made. Before I reached the country the Arab Executive had made it plain that they would have nothing to do with the Development Scheme. They declined to enter into any

discussions/

- 6 -

discussions on the subject unless Government assented to their condition that such a scheme should not be based on the principles embodied in the letter addressed by the Prime Minister to Dr. Weizman, then President of the Jewish Agency.

The Jews, on their part, have taken no positive steps to make an appointment of their representative. [One ground for their inaction has been explained to me by one of their most prominent representatives as the belief that if one party appoints while the other refrains, the abstinent will gain because the Director will feel constrained to support his cause against the other's. The reason given at least conveys a veiled compliment to British officials; but] in many respects the failure of both parties to afford me assistance in a very difficult task is regrettable.

In regard to the Financial Adviser, it was felt that until expenditure from funds provided by a sanctioned loan began, his presence in Palestine would be superfluous.

8./

it is omitted

Registration of landless Arabs

8. As indicated above, the first work of the Director is concerned with the landless Arabs. At the time of writing this Report no actual registration has been begun, because scrutiny by the Legal Assessor has necessarily not proceeded far enough. The Jews, who have in many cases paid displaced cultivators generous pecuniary compensation, have consistently contended that there are practically no Arabs - or at the most very few - who can legitimately be brought within the purview of the definition of landless Arabs given above. Whatever the facts may turn out to be, I am absolved, since the claims are now under scrutiny, from making any comments which are not merely explanatory of the initial procedure I decided to adopt.

From experience of somewhat similar work in India, I thought it inadvisable to request Government to issue public proclamations inviting applications, since such notifications are apt to lead to idle claims. It has been estimated that the Jewish Organisations hold over one million dunams of land - not all of which, however, have been acquired since the War. It was obvious that, whether this extensive area has been bought from large

Arab/

- 8 -

Arab proprietors or from small land-holders, the acquisitions for permanent settlement by immigrants could not have been effected without considerable displacement of existing cultivators. Accordingly, the District authorities were instructed to ascertain in what villages displacement of Arab cultivators had occurred and to see that if claims were made, some *prima facie* evidence was forthcoming which satisfies the conditions prescribed in paragraph 3 above.

The result is that up to the time of writing some 3,700 claims (out of 4500 or more preferred) have been forwarded to my office for scrutiny and decision. The collection of this mass of material has been accomplished with the minimum of friction. Apprehensions were from time to time expressed of the political results of these preliminary enquiries: and vague accusations of pressure on one side, and of intimidation on the other, were advanced. But, although I have offered to have any definite charge specially investigated, I have so far received none; and even at this stage I should like to pay a tribute to all the District authorities who have rendered such willing and tactful assistance in a by no means easy task.

9./

Methods of procedure

9. It is possible - I will not risk a charge of prejudice by saying it is certain - that a proportion of the claims put forward will be found to be baseless: but impartiality demands the investigation, without encouragement or discouragement, of all possible claims even though much of the labour involved prove fruitless. I have only to add that the process of converting Arab cultivators into landless Arabs does not necessarily cease with the receipt of claims already put in.

When it is to be remembered that the Jews are anxious to have an opportunity of expressing their views in each and every case, it will be understood that proceedings are likely to be protracted beyond the period fixed by sanguine expectations in some quarters that this difficult, intricate and important investigation would be solved within a few short weeks.

Scheme for landless Arabs not yet possible

10. What the total requirements in land for the proved landless Arabs will be, and what the total cost of resettling them will work out at, it is quite impossible at this stage to estimate. There will be no need, of course, to await final decisions about all the claims of landless Arabs before commencing the resettlement of some at least of those whose

claims/

claims have been definitely approved. A beginning may be made with such lands as can be purchased by private negotiations and at reasonable cost from funds provided out of the £.50,000 advanced for this and other purposes. Annual leases may be given in the first instance, if advisable, to those selected and be followed up in due course with permanent leases to them as Government tenants, after special legislation such as I have recommended below in paragraph 68 shall have been enacted. Other legislative action is also called for, if acquisition of private lands is not to be hampered by the speculation which will inevitably follow the knowledge that Government is in the market for such property.

Financial conditions 11. Since my arrival in Palestine, financial and economic conditions in Great Britain have materially altered; and it has now become problematical when the proposed Development loan, or part of it, will be floated: but it is not too early to discuss certain considerations in regard to the utilization of

such/

– 11 –

such funds as may eventually become available.

Provision of land for landless Arabs

12. If the class of landless Arabs has to be provided for by Government on any scale, it is obvious that land on which they are to be settled must be forthcoming: and the general question at once arises where the land can be obtained for them, as well as for immigrant Jews.

Government domains

13. The subject of Government-owned lands was reviewed in some detail at pages 56 – 60 of the Hope Simpson Report and the current belief that Government has command of large areas which it could transfer to colonists was rightly dismissed as an illusion, although the opinion was expressed that as settlement operations proceed, an addition – possibly a material one – would be made to these Government lands.

One of the earliest steps I took was to obtain the Commissioner of Lands' consent, readily accorded, to an alteration in his scheduled programme of settlement operations which would allow of the early settlement of State Domains, with a view to discovering whether any unoccupied lands would be available for allotment to new settlers.

14./

-12-

Present occupation of all State domains

14. It might be thought from a glance at Appendix II that the very extensive areas therein enumerated would yield some results in the desired direction. It is, however, to be remembered that not only has no cadastral survey of these areas ever been undertaken, but there are no village records-of-rights whatsoever; and, ⌈while there are grounds for surmising that since the Occupation many valuable rights in Government lands have been squandered⌉ I incline to the belief that little or no land of any cultural worth in any State Domain is now likely to be discovered which is not already subject to hereditary or analogous tenancy rights.

[margin note: Now omitted]

In the very short time during which "advanced" settlement operations have been in progress in two Government estates, confirmation of this presumption has been received. It is reported that both are cultivated by tenants who have been in undisturbed occupation for 35 to 50 years, and not unfairly regard themselves as having prescriptive rights. They are, in fact, hereditary or occupancy tenants who could only be expropriated, if necessary, on equitable terms.

What/

What is true of those two estates will be found to be true, I venture to predict, of all other Government Domains. In their case, as in that of any privately-owned land, if land is required for colonists, Arab or Jew, it must be bought with cash or its equivalent from existing owners.

Questions of cost and conditions of settlement
15. This conclusion leads up to the general questions, what will it cost to settle a new colonist on land which Government may think fit to acquire ? and what should be the terms and conditions granted to him ?

The former question can only be answered after determination of the appropriate "lot viable", or minimum holding from which a farmer can gain a reasonable livelihood.

Close Settlement
16. The declared policy of Government aims at closer settlement of the existing and future population of Palestine. Close settlement means higher farming: that is, the abandonment of the production of food crops of low monetary value in favour of the more remunerative cultivation of fruits such as citrus and bananas; dairy farming; stock-raising; and poultry and egg production.

A priori, the aims are admirable: but

idealism/

idealism must not blind us to the very grave risks that hover round this policy.

The theory is, roughly, that in making such small allotments as 7½ acres (30 dunams), each farmer will be able to devote a third of this area or less to citrus, bananas and vegetables, etc., while the remainder of his allotment will be devoted to food and fodder crops. It has yet to be proved, however, that citrus fruits can be grown as successfully in such areas (for example) as Beisan and the Huleh as in the Maritime Plains: and rapid though the spread of the local banana-eating habit appears to be, and rich though the gains are at present, the vast expansion of orange groves in the Maritime Plains and the scramble to grow bananas where possible raises apprehension in thoughtful minds as to the future.

There have already been failures in banana-growing in the Beisan tract owing to unsuitability of soil or water: and such oranges as I have come across in the Upper Huleh Basin have a medicinal rather than a gustatory value.

17./

Markets   17. The question of markets, as an essential concomitant or consequence of large development schemes, is one that cannot, of course, be burked: but in the present state of the world no definite decisions or policy in this matter can be foreshadowed. The problem, however, is a serious one. The virtual exclusion from Egypt, by imposition of high duties, of melons grown in Palestine has ruined that industry quite recently. Another blow is threatened by a similar raising of the tariff against Nablus soap, the manufacture of which for the Egyptian market is another important industry. If this export trade, too, is extinguished, olives will not be needed for their fats and oils: and the detrimental effects on olive production by the fellahin requires no emphasis.

If every farmer settled for high or intensive farming is to depend for his livelihood on growing the same products as his neighbour and exports are precarious or nil, the prospects are not very rosy. [Enthusiasts and idealists will for their own reasons prefer to ignore this side of the picture: the practical administrator has to bear it in mind.]

Now settled

18./

The minimum farm	18. To revert to the "lot viable".

A great deal of discussion has been devoted to this question which need not be repeated here. For the purposes of this First Report, I propose to take, provisionally, an average farm unit for irrigated land of 30 dunams and for unirrigated land of 130 dunams, with the reservation that these figures are liable to variation later in the light of further knowledge and practical experience. In my opinion, a study of local conditions alone can really determine what is an appropriate minimum for any particular allotment.

Accepting the figures at page 145 of the Hope Simpson Report of settling a family in a house and stocking a farm at £.60, I would note that to this figure must be added the capital cost of the land and, in the case of artificially irrigated land, the expenditure on a share in a cooperative well and engine-pump installation, alignment of water courses and the planting up with citrus or other fruit of, say, eight dunams out of thirty.

Cost per unit farm	19. In the case of the Arab settler, I

had hoped the figures would not work out to more than £.500 per unit farm, whether of irrigated land (30 dunams) or unirrigated land (130 dunams): but closer calculations

indicate/

indicate that possibly not less than £.350 to £.400 will be the initial cost, provided prices remain at their present level. In the case of a Jew colonist assisted by one of the Jewish Organisations who would build his house and stock his farm, the cost may be taken as £.60 per family less.

In areas such as Beisan and Huleh, where flow irrigation would be general, the cost of the Arab settler and Jew colonist might, on similar hypotheses, be assumed to be respectively £.270 and £.210 per family for developed land. Such development would include drainage and reclamation of land, development of springs, canalisation and construction of roads and bridges, all by Government agency.

Terms of settlement.
20. From the views repeatedly expressed to me, it is evident that exaggerated notions of free gifts of all and everything in a Development Scheme have been entertained. I have not hesitated to deprecate such extravagances. The plans I have myself had in mind for recommendation are grounded on the fact that the funds are to be provided from a loan: and that any scheme advocated must show that it will be ultimately reproductive. If there are any returns to be obtained, Government which bears the resposibilities must receive them.

All/

-18-

All outlay to be incurred must be repaid by the settler on the basis of reasonable instalments. These repayments must be strictly insisted on: and be a prior charge on a settler's income.

Such a scheme has not only a political, but also a sociological aim: that of giving both a landless Arab and a Jew colonist a fresh start in life.

Co-ordination of development schemes.
21. This outline of methods advocated for settlement of both Arabs and Jews does not preclude the co-ordination of development to which Sir John Hope Simpson refers at pages 144 and 145 of his Report. The Jewish Agencies have still reserves of land which they will want to colonize on lines similar to those hitherto followed: but in fresh schemes of settlement of immigrant colonists by Government the Jewish Agencies will necessarily be consulted, just as the Arab Executive will be, if they are willing to take up the responsibility.

Pre-requisites of new schemes of settlement
22. Before, however, any such large schemes can be considered in detail there are certain essential pre-requisites on which Government must give its decisions. These are five in number :-

(1)/

(1) Acceleration of survey and of settlement operations:

(2) Acceleration of partition of village lands held in common (mesha'a):

(3) Establishment of a land administration agency:

(4) Government control of lands in the areas coming under development:

(5) Government control of water in similar areas.

When these decisions are given, detailed schemes can gradually be evolved: but the time required to carry them through must be reckoned in years not in months.

A discussion of each of these prerequisites follows.

(1) **ACCELERATION OF SURVEY AND
SETTLEMENT OPERATIONS**

Progress of Survey

23. Survey is the basis of settlement operations now being conducted in certain villages by the Commissioner of Lands. The preliminary or basic process of triangulation over the whole country, which represents the framework, is expected to conclude in 1937. Survey directly for "settlement" comprises the

(i) formation of fiscal blocks, or parcels of land, with the ultimate object of revised taxation:

(ii) formation of registration blocks, with the ultimate object of registration of ownership: and

(iii) survey of the areas of individual fields, i.e., cadastral survey.

The fiscal block survey is expected to be completed by the end of 1935. The rest of the survey is scheduled to end in 1942 - eleven years ahead.

24./

Question of accelerating Survey. Its cost.

24. The question of speeding up this programme has been carefully considered. The Director of Surveys estimates that with his present supervisory staff it is not possible by any means to curtail the period by more than three years. The acceleration would result in a total increased expenditure of £.12,000 spread over eight years, the "peak" period being the four years 1936-1939 when the full efficiency of the aditional establishment required would be attained. It is the time taken to reach this efficiency that costs the extra money.

On the other side, it is not to be forgotten that while the survey has hitherto been costing seven pence (30 mils) per dunam, the survey fee charged recoups five pence (20 mils) of this sum: and as efficiency of staff is increased with greater experience, the cost to Government will be lower.

The improved progress of operations is illustrated by the following figures. Last year 384 registration blocks were surveyed: this year, with the same staff, 650 have been completed. The latter figure represents 230,000 dunams: next year, the out-turn should be more than 50 per cent greater.

25./

Relation of Survey to settlement operations.	25.	For settlement purposes, survey operations must always keep several months ahead of settlement: and the corresponding expedition of settlement operations referred to below seems to postulate greater acceleration of survey than increased efficiency alone will provide.
Private Surveyors as recruits probably not possible.	26.	The feasibility of employing as additional recruits some of the private licensed surveyors in the country has not been lost sight of. If the more competent members of this profession could be employed on Government work at no excess cost and with satisfactory results, this reinforcement would, on occasions, prove useful. There remains, however, the difficulty of supervision and check by the Government Department: for work cannot be given the official *imprimatur* unless the Director has satisfied himself of its reliability.
Acceleration of settlement operations.	27.	Decisions have recently been reached which will allow of settlement operations also proceeding more speedily. So far, in three years of active work, only some 30 villages out of over 1,000 have been finished: though the pace in this Department also is improving. The elimination

of/

of superfluous investigations into undisputed claims of ownership, and changes in the system of assessing fees - reforms which have long been recommended by the Commissioner of Lands - will, it is hoped, be achieved before long: and, in addition, an alteration in the form of certificate of ownership registered will make proceedings more expeditious. Unless, then, accelerated survey operations can continue to keep ahead of settlement proceedings a deadlock will be reached.

In considering the scheduled programme of survey, the contingency has to be considered that indeterminate demands will be made by the Development Department. If Government has to acquire land for landless Arabs or Jewish colonists, that land, unless already settled, must be surveyed before any contract can be completed; but it must also be subjected to some sort of "settlement" to allow of a clear field on which to plant newcomers: and the equilibrium between the two departments remains *pro tanto* undisturbed.

28./

Future relation of survey to settlement operations at present obscure

28. The position, then, is that merely by adherence to the schedule drawn up, survey is proceeding more rapidly as efficiency increases: on the other hand, settlement operations will also move more actively by reason of the innovations described above. It is not at present possible to determine which Department will make the longer strides forward. Therefore, highly important though the acceleration of the long-drawn-out survey and settlement work is, I suggest that in view of prevailing financial conditions it will be wiser to defer consideration of expediting further the survey programme until we have a clearer insight into the future than speculation at present affords.

(2) ACCELERATION OF PARTITION OF
UNDIVIDED LANDS (MESHA'A)

What mesha'a denotes and connotes

29. The system of mesha'a or unpartitioned land held in customary joint ownership is described at page 51 of the Hope Simpson Report, where it is shown that the survival of this archaic system of land tenure had been the subject of investigation by a Government Commission as long ago as 1923, with no practical results. The continued existence of this joint ownership in land is, next to the want of cadastral survey, the greatest stumbling block to agricultural development of the countryside. It is difficult for the English reader of to-day to realise the evils of the system. If he can imagine an English village where every farmer each year is compelled to pass on his lands and buildings to a neighbour for cultivation and occupation, and receive some other neighbour's farm in exchange, he will get some inkling of what obstacles to progress can exist to agricultural development in Palestine.

A wealthy Arab landowner, who is a co-partner with kinsmen of an extensive estate, recently described his position to me succinctly:-

I am/

"I am supposed to be a rich man: in reality
"I own very little. I cannot plant a tree on
"my lands: next year they will have passed to
"another's cultivation: I cannot fertilize my
"fields; another shareholder will get the
"benefit next year, and why should I spend a
"pound per bag of manure for another person's
"advantage ? I cannot build a stable for my
"horse or my cattle; it will belong to another
"n ext year. "

Some aspects of the custom

30. One remarkable feature of this Arab system of customary joint ownership of land is that in theory the Ottoman Land Code (still the basis of land administration) categorically forbids it: another feature is the numerous forms that it assumes. Of these forms two examples only will be cited.

Strictly, females are entitled to share in the common inheritance: in practice, they are usually induced, for obvious reasons founded on marriage customs, to waive their rights.

One peculiar form of title is based on the present alone and is purely communistic. Every male - from the new-born babe to the old man on the brink of the grave - alive in the village on the day of partition is entitled to a share in the common heritage. Thus, the

amount/

amount of the share of each co-partner is constantly changing: and sales of land or permanent partition are alike impossible.

Methods of partition. 31. The expensiveness of official partitions and the, generally, unsatisfactory results of unofficial partitions are alluded to by Sir John Hope Simpson, who has made the pregnant remark which I fully endorse that "one of the "essential pre-conditions of development "is that the land shall be partitioned." At present, the only really practical means of partition are two: one by the villagers themselves in agreement, the other through settlement operations which are planned to last over many years.

Disintegration of this primitive land system. 32. The system, which is recognised on all hands as an evil, is gradually though very slowly breaking down, as is proved by the most recent figures available. These show that whereas in 1923 unpartitioned villages formed 56 per cent of the total, in 1930 only 46 per cent were so returned. If my latest figures are correct, the present proportion, owing partly to the compulsory partitions of settlement, is rather less than 40 per cent.

This/

−28−

This residue will, of course, present the most stubborn cases to be handled.

The only criticism I have heard directed against the break-up of unpartitioned lands is that it is calculated to lead to multiplication of land transactions. This result is inevitable.

Beneficial results of partition.   33.   I have been much impressed during various tours by the rapid development by owners, Arab and Jew, of their lands in villages where partitions and settlement of rights have been concluded. Side by side may be seen the waste lands of estates which have not yet had the benefits of those operations, and the newly-planted citrus groves of the more favoured villages. In two small tracts of the Maritime Plain out of 250,000 dunams covered by settlement operations, one-sixth of the whole area has already been devoted to citrus plantations by Arab and Jew cultivators. One-half of this total is attributed by the Settlement Officer directly to his official labours, while in the case of the other moiety progress has been helped by security of title and credit facilities, thanks to "settlement".

34./

Past schemes for accelerating partitions.	34. Since the Commission of 1923, many fresh proposals have been put forward for accelerating the desired disintegration: but always with little effect. The new scheme for expediting settlement operations will have favourable reactions on partition; but much more is wanted.

"Unofficial" partitions in advance of settlement have been advocated and tried. Where an especially interested Area Officer has used persuasion or given counsel, a good deal has been achieved. Some weeks ago in company of the Area and District officers, Nablus, I myself participated in negotiations between the peasant proprietors of an undivided village for the unofficial partition of their mesha'a. Difficulties were smoothed away and an agreement reached in my presence. Recently, the Area Officer has reported completion of the partition on the ground. The credit of this division rests very largely with the officers mentioned, whose personal interest and good offices have facilitated the task.

Still, partition work involves a great deal of tedium and places a strain on the patience which every busy officer is not able to bear with equanimity.

35./

―30―

The real remedy.

35. The remedy is, I think, to accept the suggestion revived at page 33 of the Hope Simpson Report for the appointment of a small special staff of selected Palestinian officials for the work of partition in advance of settlement. If the work is to be done thus, theory no doubt counsels the precise official methods used in settlement operations: because its accomplishment is tantamount to the previous performance of work which must otherwise be done subsequently in settlement.

But there is a tendency to dwell too much on the imperfections of practice which falls short of the best, and too little on the (very natural) Oriental prejudice against innovations, which does at times lead to absurd results.

Both Sir John Hope Simpson and Mr. Strickland (in his Report on Agricultural Cooperation) refer to the case of the landowner whose land (partitioned without any official guidance) measured over 3½ miles long and averaged 14 feet in breadth. I have no doubt in practice the tillage results were not as bad as indicated on paper: for I have myself seen excessively long strips of land lying side by side which belonged to

separate/

separate members of the same family and when cultivated, as they were, as a plough unit constituted a respectably-shaped field.

Even in North India, where the peasantry have been accustomed to partitions and cadastral survey for decades, anomalies of this nature are not unknown. In a brochure on Cooperation published in the Punjab, Mr. Strickland, demonstrating that it has been possible to correct undesirable partitions after settlement by means of village cooperative societies, writes:-

"One zamindar (fellah) had his land in
"284 different places: it is now altogether
"in one place. Another man had only 1½
"acres but never cultivated them because
"his holding was not worth sowing in tiny
"and remote patches: he now for the first
"time finds himself a zamindar. It is even
"found at the conclusion of a village re-
"distribution that surplus land is left over,
"and can be sold for the common good, since
"innumerable field-boundaries are removed
"when bigger fields are treated. "

36./

-32-

Partitions in advance of settlement to be encouraged in every way.

36. Almost any partition, however officially bad, is better than no partition at all: and cases have come to my knowledge where villagers have been persuaded to plan reasonably good partitions; but refused eventually to carry them out on their lands when pressed to abide by too precise official instructions.

When the traditional usages of centuries are being broken down, the transition from one set of conditions to a new set needs to be very tenderly handled; and even if in the end some of the work has to be done over again, lenienoy and sympathy in applying a minimum of rules are not wasted.

Legislation required for advanced partitions.

37. For the appointment of special officers, as advocated above, only very simple legislation appears to be required. Under clause 51 of the Settlement Ordinance of 1928 the High Commissioner is empowered at any time to direct a Settlement Officer to carry out the partition of any land held in undivided ownership if such partition is deemed to be in the public interest. That power relates only to areas included in settlement operations. An Ordinance conferring similar powers outside the settlement areas could easily be enacted, making the agents not the Settlement Officer but other officers, whether district or specially appointed.

(3)./

(5) ESTABLISHMENT OF A LAND ADMINISTRATION AGENCY

Existing land administration authorities.

38. In chapter IV of the Hope Simpson Report will be found an account of land tenures in Palestine. The chief controlling authority is the Commissioner of Lands who has charge of settlement proceedings. The Survey Department which performs so large a part of these operations; and the Lands Department which is, in effect, the department established by the Ottoman Government for the purpose of compiling and maintaining a record of all estates and transactions in immovable property, are closely connected with the Commissioner.

Complexity of land laws.

39. Nothing is simple in Palestine: and nothing is more complex than the land laws, based as they are on the vague and primitive Ottoman system; but complicated by a series of intricate Ordinances enacted under British administration with a view to supplementing deficiencies in the Turkish Code.

It is not necessary in this Report to discuss in detail these land laws; nor am I qualified by my brief experience to

analyse/

analyse the very great difficulties which have beset Government in its attempts to administer these laws in a not altogether unsophisticated community.

[marginal note: to be omitted]

History of existing land administration.

40. I abstract from an unpublished Report the following historical retrospect:-

In 1858 the Ottoman Government established a Department of Land Registries for the purpose of compiling and maintaining a record of all estates and transactions in immovable property. The record was primarily personal and not territorial. In the absence of a cadastral survey no attempt was or could be made to mark on the ground the area of land to which each transaction related. Moreover, though registration was by law compulsory, it was not in fact enforced and much land remained unregistered and was held in virtue of privately and primitively drawn contracts.

During the campaign in Palestine many of the registers were removed by the Turkish military authorities and the registries were closed till October, 1920, when the Land Registries Department was established, which took over all the functions of the Ottoman department. The present Department of Lands

dates/

dates from 1922, when the Department of Land Registries and the Land Department and Land Commission, which were created in 1920 for the purpose of controlling State Domains and advising the Government on matters of land policy, were amalgamated.

Existing land administration. Land Registries.
41. The duties of Land Registry are to record all transactions in immovable property.

The Registrar is responsible for seeing that the parties to a disposition have a good title, and all title deeds are examined; and all documents evidencing transactions are prepared in thirteen district Land Registry offices. The registration of a transaction, or of an entry in an unofficial register, does not give the person in whose name the land is registered any title to the land. It is merely evidence which may be rebutted of ownership.

Objects of the scheme of settlement operations.
42. Thus, the Land Registers of the Turks were very incomplete and only a fraction of the actual transactions were registered. In 1928 began a "settlement" under a special Ordinance of all claims and the registration of titles thereto. This comprises a cadastral survey in each village being settled, partitions of land held in common

and/

and a full investigation of all claims to
ownership of land and finally a registration
of title which it was hoped to make indefeasible.

The defects of the scheme. 43. The scheme described suffers from several defects. The proposals drawn up for post-settlement registration will not suffice to ensure the due maintenance of the registers. There is a long-standing and intelligible prejudice, dating from the Turkish *regime*, against registration of title where it can possibly be avoided. Fellahin will not resort to district offices willingly in order to register their titles. It is only when some transaction compels them that they have recourse to the land registries.

The alternative is to bring the registration agency to their doors, and make all registrations of ownership and tenancy simple and easy, by the appointment to a village, or group of villages, of a resident official corresponding to the Indian village registrar.

Further, the scheme has no place for the economic aspects of agricultural life; it ignores the existence of the tenantry (who are estimated to comprise 50 per cent of the cultivators), and concerns itself solely with a proprietary body.

Lastly/

Lastly, and consequentially, it makes no provision for a subordinate agency through which the land may be duly administered by Government. It assumes that, Palestine being a small country, this administration can be attempted in future, as hitherto, from headquarters in Jerusalem rather than through the natural channels of the District Commissioners and their subordinates. In the past, the results have been unsatisfactory: and a continuance of the system of centralization can only produce similar consequences.

Inadequacy of existing land administration agency. The Mukhtar's incapacity.

44. In effect, the only local agency between the land and headquarters is the village representative known as the mukhtar, assisted more or less by a body of elders. If you go into a Palestine village (except in the case of some Jewish colonies), you will find no one on the spot to whom you can appeal for reasonably accurate local information. The mukhtar is probably quite illiterate and can only answer enquiries with the vaguest replies. His village not having been cadastrally surveyed, he is ignorant of areas based on measurements. He will describe fields by some such vague term as a "fedan", which may be anything from 50 to 250 dunams according to the local method of reckoning

the year's

the year's work of the plough animals: or he may reply by letting you know how many pounds of seed are required to sow his dunams, all of which conveys more to himself than to his interlocutor. The mukhtar employs any chance literate person there may be in his village to assist him with his papers. Local village records of transaction in lands, or of crops, or of rights and changes therein do not exist. Nor are there any registers to show the relation of tenants to their landlords. A few assessment papers detailing the taxes assessed on, or the individual assessees of, the village are the only official papers the mukhtar can produce.

Benefits of survey and settlement

45. Every man in the village knows (or thinks he knows) his own rights - approximately: and this qualification explains, at any rate in Arab villages, many of the internal disputes and feuds which might be avoided if accurate data were at hand.

There is no doubt that the survey and settlement proceedings are one of the most powerful temporary incentives to development that can be devised: because they enable a landowner, large or small, to know for the first time exactly what his rights in the land are vis-à-vis other landowners.

45./

Tenant's rights not covered by settlement. Other deficiencies in land administration.	46. But, as the enactment of various Ordinances proves, tenants have rights which should be protected: and if, as has been advocated by Sir John Hope Simpson, and as I advocate in this Report, occupancy rights for tenants (which in fact exist in State Domains, at any rate) are to be recognised by law, "not only the preparation "of a register of existing tenants but also the "necessary machinery for keeping that register "up to date" must be devised. If there is to be a sound and equitable system of land taxation, full information as to the prevailing rents paid by tenants from time to time must be easily available, as well as knowledge of the cash value of these rents paid in kind. The present collapse of world prices, and the consequent breakdown of the system of commuted tithes, both bear witness to these clamant needs. At present, the administration is not in a position to furnish evidence of any value in those respects: nor has it any statistics worth the name which will demonstrate the advance or retrogression of any particular tract.

47./

Machinery required: its uses.

47. Conviction as to the necessity of some sort of official rural machinery will be strengthened by a perusal of pages 90 and 91 of the Minutes of the Twentieth Session of the Permanent Mandates Commission. It was not found possible to reply to a series of very pertinent questions put by the Vice-Chairman: and it is not possible even now to answer them. The required statistics could all have been easily furnished by an agency of village registrars such as that sketched out below.

Similarly, in recurrent questions such as the extent of "unemployment" in Palestine, this agency would be effectively employed in ascertaining from time to time true statistics of the lack of occupation, seasonal and permanent, in all areas with which it is constituted to deal.

The Administration Report of 1930 (at page 98) specifically refers to the difficulty experienced at present in the collection of reliable statistics of unemployment.

Attempt by Dept. of Agriculture to provide more statistical information.

48. The Department of Agriculture deserves credit for its recognition that agricultural progress must depend largely on knowledge derived from statistics: and its institution of village note books providing for their collection is a praiseworthy innovation. But the attempt is really beyond the Department's strength: and

when/

-41-

when a body of village registrars has been organized, the latter will be able to take over and widen the scope of the work which is now being essayed with a tiny staff of technical Agricultural Assistants.

Mr. Strickland, in paragraph 57 of his Report on Agricultural Cooperation in Palestine, has also pointed out the advantages for his scheme to be derived from the appointment of village registrars.

Appointment of village registrars advised. 49. It will be observed that I have not adopted the word village "accountant", because that term connotes a connection of this official with finance or revenue. That is not his primary concern. In North India he assists the headmen of the villages by drawing up the statement of State dues: but he is not involved in the collection of land revenue or land taxes, which remains the duty of the headman or mukhtar.

The attempts to make this latter miserably-remunerated official responsible for all sorts of duties which he is quite incapable of performing have culminated lately in manifestations by these village mukhtars in several parts of the country of their extreme disinclination to continuance in office. The situation will be relieved by the proposed institution of village registrars.

50./

Duties of such officials	50. The chief duties of a village registrar should be:-

(i) The maintenance of a record of crops grown at each harvest;

(ii) The maintenance of the record-of-rights in land and water, both of tenants and of owners, by the punctual record of all mutations of such rights occurring in the villages of his circle; and

(iii) The maintenance of accurately prepared statistical returns incorporating the information derived from the harvest inspections, registers of mutations, and standing records-of-rights.

Land administration duties wrongly imposed on Department of Agriculture rather than District Officers.	51. These village registrars will in due time require a supervisory intermediary between them and their District Officer, who at present tends to be divorced from all concern

with what should constitute one of the most important of his duties - those connected with land administration. These duties include a variety of interests quite wrongly at present entrusted to Agricultural Assistants who are inferior in status and capacity to the District Officers, and should rather be engaged in the experimental and technical work of the Agricultural Department for which they have been recruited, and in the performance of which they are impeded owing to their diversion to extraneous work.

52./

The training of village registrars.	52.	Village registrars of the type indicated are made, not born; and before a staff, however small, is employed, it will have to be trained: and in the absence of any ready-made material the trainers themselves will need education. In the most favourable circumstances, a considerable time must elapse before the scheme can be put into operation even in the villages where settlement proceedings have been completed, and where the benefits accruing therefrom and the great expense incurred thereon will be wasted, if some sort of action to maintain and improve records is not shortly taken.
Estimated cost of proposed agency.	53.	The cost of such a staff of village registrars cannot be foretold with any accuracy until survey and partition have further advanced: but as a provisional estimate the initial expenditure may be put at £.500 per annum, rising in the course of a number of years to the completed establishment (for the 1039 villages of the country) of from £.15,000 to £.20,000 per annum. The expenditure will be well worth while, if the agency is maintained with efficiency.

54./

Deputation of District Officer advocated.

54. In my view a capable Palestinian District Officer should be deputed for some months to North India to study the land revenue administration and organization there with a view to the adaptation of an analogous system to the needs of this country.

Revenue administration not dealt with.

55. I refrain in this Report from entering on the sphere of the revenue administration, which seems to me also to need re-organization.

(4) GOVERNMENT CONTROL OF LANDS.

Problems to be considered.

56. For the purposes of this section of the Report I divide the problems under consideration into four heads:-

(i) Re-settlement of landless Arabs:

(ii) Close settlement of immigrant Jews:

(iii) Relief of the congestion among the hill fellahin: and

(iv) Prevention, as far as possible, of the creation of fresh landless Arabs.

The two first-named subjects have in some aspects to be considered together: the same is true of the third and fourth.

How to re-settle landless Arabs.

57. (i) The method of re-settling landless Arabs, once their claims have passed scrutiny, may seem a simple one to those who are misled by memories of pioneer colonists on vast virgin lands. For example, in the Punjab canal colonies, millions of acres of such waste lands were available, inhabited only by nomad tribes similar to the Beduin. Yet even under these conditions colonisation work lasted for years and proved to be of a very complex and special nature. The puzzle, if less comprehensive, is far more intricate in a country where virtually every cultivable dunam ($\frac{1}{4}$ acre) is already subject to proprietary or tenancy rights.

Every /

Every suitable dunam will have to be expropriated in some way or another. There is no escape from this difficulty.

Even if the actual occupier of any land required be a willing seller, there arises the question whether the land is subject to the custom of joint ownership in one of its numerous forms (mosha'a): and whether a body of co-partners, some of whom may be resident, temporarily or permanently, in distant countries, is willing to sell: and at what prices.

Difficulties described
58. The question of suitability is one for the most careful reflection. It is not the quality of the selected land and its adaptability for cultivation that will be the issue here: rather, it is whether the selected settler or settlers can be put down among the strangers who cultivate the surrounding lands. If the numbers of landless Arabs turn out to be considerable, it will be necessary to acquire, with circumspection, the estates or portions of estates of many individual proprietors willing to sell, or in possession of, surplus lands.

You cannot introduce a clan of Beduin among fellahin: for example, it would be futile to expect these tribesmen to settle down on a plot/

-47-

plot of land I know to be purchasable (at a price) near Jerusalem. Terrorism or boycott or both would at once become features of the countryside. Of settlement in anything but name there would be none. Police and other factors of administration also come into play.

Even if the difficulties of location are surmounted, the area which is to be peopled with landless Arabs, however large or small, must, as I have said above, be surveyed, subjected to some form of settlement of existing rights, and cut up into allotments. Comparatively easy though this sounds, it means that special survey parties have to be detached from their scheduled programme to the dislocation of other equally important, if not equally urgent, work. It takes many months to train additional parties: and the limits of supervision by the available officers cannot be overlooked. Almost all these obstacles are to be encountered whether small or large areas are being dealt with: they can only be smoothed away by patient application.

Restriction on land transfers. Proposed legislation.

59. Some restriction on free transfers of land must, in any case, be imposed, if Government is to make its purchases at a fair market value and not be subjected to the exactions of land speculators. To encompass this aim a Transfer of Land Ordinance is required which empowers Government to prevent land speculation against itself by Arab individuals and Jewish Corporations.

60./

–48–

Scope of proposed legislation. 60. In my opinion, the only effective way such Ordinance can be used is to apply it to the whole country with power to the High Commissioner to exempt therefrom such districts as do not come within the ambit of any Development Scheme.

The alternative plan is to empower Government to apply the Ordinance, district by district, as appears at the time needed – a procedure that invites protests and embitterment.

The former method is in the country's interests without discrimination of race.

Jewish methods of colonisation. 61. (ii) In the past, as the Hope Simpson Report at pages 50 et seq. points out, Jewish settlement in Palestine has been effected by the Palestine Jewish Colonization Association and the Zionist Organization.

In the former class of colony the land was bought by the Corporation and has been, or is being in the fullness of time, transferred outright to the colonists as their own property; in the latter case, the colonists remain, virtually, occupancy or permanent tenants of land which by the constitution of the Jewish Agency for Palestine has become "extra-territorialized".

It is further shown that this latter method of colonizing is in its effects not only contrary to the provisions of Article 6 of the Mandate, but it is in addition a constant and increasing source of danger to the country.

62./

-49-

The State's part in colonization schemes.

62. In considering the factors which are calculated to assist the moral and material development of Palestine, the position of the State in regard to the settler must be carefully determined. In my opinion, the State which undertakes the provision of the land on which the settler, Arab or Jew, is to be placed should retain its control of the land, and not allow any third party to be interposed between itself and the beneficiary.

In undeveloped countries the State has in modern conditions found it necessary, itself, to take a hand in and order colonization or settlement operations on any considerable scale; and this interference is even more necessary in a partially-developed country where conflicting interests have to be reckoned with. It has been pithily said "that a large scale of colonization cannot be conducted "independently of a Government, that it is Government "enterprise by nature and can only be completed if the Government by legislative and administrative action "supports the colonization".

63./

—50—

Settlers should be Government tenants. 63. Any settler of Government-owned land should remain a Government tenant, with occupancy rights: or, in other words, the tenant should not be liable to eviction except for certain specified defaults to his landlord, and he should have no power of permanent transfer or alienation of his land.

Arab and Jew are, under the terms of the Mandate, to be placed on terms of equality without discrimination: and my proposal applies alike to both races. The acceptance ~~of this proposal~~ in the case of State owned lands [illegible] of inalienability of land, which has been adopted by the Jewish ~~Agency~~ National [Fund] in its settlement of its own tenants, will obviate any possibility of any Arab or Jew settler under Government auspices becoming "landless".

[Margin note: *The proposal applies to both races alike.*]

State acquisition of lands necessary to settlement. 64. To obtain land for closer settlement by Arab and Jew, as I have said, land must be acquired. There are certain comparatively large tracts - the Huleh Basin, the Beisan tract, the Jordan Valley, and the Beersheba district - where possibilities exist. If these or any of these tracts (or any other tracts) are to be developed for close settlement, it is an indispensable condition that Government should take over control both of

the land/

-51-

the land and water in these areas, expropriate them where necessary and re-settle them by redistribution of the land and water to the best possible advantage of all, and with the least possible disturbance of existing owners who may be prepared to settle down again to more intensive cultivation than the present chaotic conditions permit. The only alternative that I can see is to allow each and all to buy and sell at will, with the inevitable result that there will be re-created once more - and then too late - the problem of the landless Arab with which we are attempting at present to grapple.

The process of displacing Arabs in the Beisan Area.

65. In the Beisan area, for example, symptoms of this process may already be detected. Purchases have been made, or options taken on, areas of a considerable proportion of certain villages, where the transferees have fulfilled the conditions of the Agreement of 1921. The next step will certainly be acquisition of the essential water rights; resulting in, not the extrusion of the present owners from their lands, but the silent reduction of these lands to unirrigated, which in the Beisan tract practically means uncultivable areas and, finally, starvation of the cultivators.

A similar sequence of events is to be feared in the Jericho State domain (vide para.108).

66./

- 52 -

The State's methods of settlement.

66. Among objections to my proposal for Government control of land is one grounded on expense. But Government will not, I assume, place tenants on the land that it has developed by construction of roads, efficient canals, etc., and allow a state of affairs in which the colonist is placed on his farm at heavy cost and forgets all about the capital expended on his settlement and the interest due on that capital. Government under my scheme will recoup its expenditure on land and development by selling the permanent occupancy rights (less valuable than proprietary rights) to the new settler on reasonable instalments, thus training him to shoulder his responsibilities as a worthy member of the community.

If he be a displaced Arab, Government will replace him, as a son of the soil, on the land of his country and provide him with a house, farm and stock at a cost over all of, say £.10 to £.12 per dunam. In the case of the Jewish immigrant, it will suffice to sell him the developed land on equal terms, and leave the Jewish organisations to help the settlers, as they now do, with all the requisites of home and farm.

The only/

The only differentiation here will be that Government will surely recover in due course all its expenditure from the Arab settler: while from the Jewish colonist it will recover only the cost of the developed land, leaving the Jewish bodies to recover their share.

Development schemes necessarily lengthy. 67. The expenditure of public funds will be gradual, lasting over a number of years. To demarcate and partition the 388,000 dunams (97,000 acres) of the Beisan area has taken 10 years; and a prominent Jew agricultural scientist showed some sense of possibilities, if an extreme pessimism, when he recently opined that a development policy worth the name would cover three decades.

Special legislation needed. 68. To enable this colonization or re-settlement of lands in an extensive tract to be successfully carried through, a special Ordinance apart from the contemplated Transfer of Land Ordinance will be needed. Such special Ordinance would cover expropriation and re-settlement of lands already settled and would be administered in close relation to, and co-ordination with, the powers obtained under the proposed Irrigation Ordinance referred to in the following section of this Report.

69./

-54-

Relief of congestion of Arabs in hills & prevention of creating more landless Arabs.

69. (iii) and (iv). There are two serious economic dangers which threaten Arab peasant proprietors in Palestine: the reduction in the size of holdings below a self-supporting minimum; and the unrestricted transfer of land by sale or mortgage to Jews or to Arab capitalists, leading to "displacement". The former of these perils has been accentuated by the substitution of the British for the Ottoman administration. Under the Turks, conscription of the young manhood of the country is estimated to have deprived the effective population annually of some 10,000 to 20,000 youths, the majority of whom never returned to their homes. The required statistics are not yet available from the recent census: but enquiries show that in many Arab villages the computation of an average of five persons per family living on the "lot viable" is now far exceeded.

The hills: displacement of Arab peasants by Jews and by Arab effendis.

70. In the hill tracts, there are two directions in which unrestricted transfers of land are proceeding. In some parts, it means the advance of the Jews, without such noticeable progress in development as in the Coastal Plains, but with similar results in reinforcing the class of landless Arabs. In

other/

other parts, it is the absorption, gradual but inevitable, of the Arab peasant proprietor by the Arab effendi or capitalist landlord. [Both dangers must be regarded with grave apprehension.] *[margin: But fact and to be faced]* Some form of protection for the small owner appears vital, in order to ensure that the concentration of numerous small holdings into the hands of large proprietors does not lead to the same evil as is anticipated from excessive expropriation by the Jews. In one sub-district in the hilly tracts, it is reported that in a decade no less than 30 per cent of the land has passed from Arab peasants to Arab capitalists.

Security of tenure needed for Arab peasants 71. The first essential to the improvement and intensive development of land in the hills in order to secure to the fellahin a better standard of living is security of tenure for his land, as a safeguard against those economic evils which the [Mandate policy has brought upon him by the] undue rise in the values of land [and the foreign rivalry to which he is subjected.] If the process of dispossession continues, in another three or four decades the Arab peasant proprietor will become almost extinct. [It is perhaps not irrelevant to speculate at long range as to whether the Arab effendi will eventually sell his lands at a profit to the Jews, and leave Arab cultivators *[illegible handwritten continuation]*

-56-

or tenants to become the serfs of the Jews, (if they care to employ them on the land), or merely hewers of wood and drawers of water in the towns. If this consummation is desirable, an hypothesis which the existing (comparatively small) scheme to relieve landless Arab refutes, then restrictive legislation need not be any further considered. But if it is not under any conditions right to allow the Arab peasantry to be entirely dispossessed of their lands, some form of legislation to restrict the power of alienation is essential; and I hold that no threats or suasion should divert Government from action on these lines.

The question has assumed its gravity because of the influx of Jews. The great ideals which have inspired the well-wishers of the Jewish movement have resulted in the provision of immense resources against which no peasantry in the world could unaided stand up. It is only since these immense donations or subscriptions of foreign money were made available in Palestine that the prices of land have risen to their present high - most would say uneconomic - level, and free transfers of land have, in consequence, so vastly increased.

72./

-57-

The Maritime Plains: restriction of transfers to Jews also necessary.

72. In the Maritime Plains, where the penetration of the Jews is most marked, some restriction of free transfers of land from Arab to Jew is also highly desirable. It is in these plains, where water is readily obtainable and the soil is especially suitable, that the capital and energy devoted to the extension of citrus cultivation, primarily by the Jews and secondarily by the Arabs, is most conspicuous. [I think no unprejudiced mind can deny that the acquisition by the Jews of surplus undeveloped Arab lands has been of immense economic benefit to the country at large; and if the possible wants of posterity are not to be weighed, I see no other reason why the process should not be allowed to continue, provided it does not go too far. Here lies the crux.]

[Margin note: In passing it might be of interest to record an estimate that 30% to 40% of the citrus groves are in the hands of the Jews, which the balance is with the Arabs. Although the average production of the former is at present the higher, the Arabs are rapidly learning from experience.]

[Margin note: Nas omitted]

The policy of the Arab leaders.

73. References are made from time to time in the Arabic press to the part played by some members of the Supreme Moslem Council or Arab Executive in sales by Arabs to Jews; from which it is not unfair to infer that in some leading Arab quarters such disposals of surplus lands are viewed with no disfavour. But the chief [danger ~~risk~~]—an ever present one—is that the progress of the Jews, supported or impelled by the ~~large financial~~ *comparatively large process backed by plentiful financial resources*, which

[Margin note: [ ] omitted]

/

~~financial resources of wealthy corporations, which~~ weight the scale so heavily against the independent small Arab proprietor, will mean the entire and permanent displacement of the latter from the soil.

The need of a restrictive Ordinance.

74. The dangers I have depicted seem to me further to emphasize the need of a Transfer of Land Ordinance in some form or other.

75./

- 59 -

Advantages of restrictions on land transfers illustrated.

75. I may conclude this part of the Report [with a personal reference.

Of those who have been intimately associated with the Palestine Administration I am fortunate enough to have had the unique experience of having passed my official life in a Province of India where a parallel condition of things existed when I entered Government service. The peasantry — preponderantly Mohammedan and of the same virile type as the Arabs — were being devoured by Hindu moneylenders. In 1900 the Punjab Land Alienation Act was placed on the Statute Book.] All the gloomy predictions usually associated with restrictive measures of this nature have been falsified. The value of land has increased; and the corrosion eating into the heart of the peasantry stayed. There is no living land administrator of the Punjab with experience of the pre-existing conditions who would dream of advocating a return to the bad old days.

[handwritten marginal note: by remarking that in the Indian Province in which I served a Land Alienation Act for the protection of the peasant proprietor was successfully placed on the Statute Book in 1900.]

76./

–60–

A Land Transfer Ordinance to allow reasonable transfers of land to Jews.

76. The enactment of a restrictive Transfer of Land Ordinance "does not imply a prohibition of acquisition of additional land by Jews": but it does contemplate a control of land disposition and transfers while a scheme of settlement lasting over a period of years is to be undertaken. Given clear instructions as to the manner in which His Majesty's Government wish that control to be worked by the Development authority, for the benefit of Arab and Jew alike, I see no reason why the protection of the one race and the legitimate aspirations of the other should not be achieved under the operation of the Ordinance.

(6) GOVERNMENT CONTROL OF WATER SUPPLIES

A hydrographic survey to be undertaken.

77. The subject of irrigation is dealt with in detail at pages 82 - 87 and page 147 of the Hope Simpson Report, where emphasis was laid on the necessity of instituting a hydrographic survey of Palestine, and it was pointed out that one of the first tasks of a Development authority would be the examination of the available water resources of the country in order that development may commence where there is most likelihood of success. Immediately on my entry on my duties, Government transferred to the Development Department the services of the Irrigation Officer and the study of water problems was actively pursued. I have recently been able to submit to Government my proposals for the early initiation of this hydrographic survey which will co-ordinate and complete the various disconnected studies of available water supplies which have been pursued in the last few years.

The proposals, which have involved the appointment of an Irrigation Inspector, contemplate completing the investigation within about one year, at a cost of about £.8,000.

Importance to Palestine of water problem.

78. It is noteworthy that until comparatively recent times the vast importance and the nature of the water problem has not been fully appreciated by the Administration. For example, even in the Beisan Agreement (vide Appendix III B.) there is not a single reference to any of the local water supplies on which the whole cultivation possible in this arid tract practically depends. I believe the subject was scarcely mentioned or considered at the time the Agreement was made.

In 1929 the late Director of Agriculture and Forests brought the subject prominently to the notice of Government and, as the result of the report of an Irrigation Committee, the proposed Ordinance was drawn up.

Intricacy of the problem described.

79. The whole matter is one of extreme intricacy and complexity of which some illustrations are needed to make the situation more intelligible to the reader, particularly if he has not studied local conditions. Water may be derived from (a) surface supplies: (b) underground supplies.

(a) Surface/

(a) Surface supplies, or flow irrigation, where little or no human effort is needed to supplement nature's gift, is more commonly devoted to extensive than intensive cultivation. The distribution of such water is universally based on period not volume. The period allowed depends on the size of the stream and the number of cultivators. The application of the law of inheritance has often reduced a share to a 15 minutes supply, to be utilized at intervals of six weeks. Sub-division is reducing "turns" still further. So long as communal cultivation of undivided land subsists, the system is a practicable one: it is only when partition of land occurs that the holder of a very small periodical "turn" suffers. In irrigated areas there is frequently as much traffic in water as in land; and when the latter is sold, it is common to include a definite, but not necessarily coincident, period or fraction of the water with it: e.g. a cultivator will sell half his whole area but only one-quarter of his water rights. Thus small areas may have excessive water supplies, and *vice versa*. The affluent purchaser of a large area with small supply, immediately sets about increasing his water supply — even from a distance, — thus possibly entailing the transfer of water from one main spring on to the distributary

of/

of another spring. The complications are innumerable. Water may be leased for a crop, a season, a year or period of years. It may be pawned; and it may be sold in periods, or fractions of periods for one rotation, etc. etc. When distribution from a copious spring is by means of several distributaries under such conditions, and some of the supply is intended for intensive and some for extensive cultivation, the weaker man usually goes to the wall.

Intensive cultivation generally benefits large owner most under existing legislation

80. Intensive cultivation is spreading and the fellah (an extensive cultivator) is being steadily squeezed out; because intensive cultivation calls for a reduction in the extent of area ploughed, unless additional supplies of water are made available; and the ownership of water in the free-flow areas is tending to pass into the hands of the capitalist who usually ~~by the common Oriental methods~~ gets more than his fair share of water.

Waste of water universal

81. On all sides waste of water is apparent, whatever the status of the owner or user. If such owner or user has a right to all the water in the stream for a certain time and cannot use it he will, to safeguard his rights, rather let the surplus run to waste than allow another to absorb the precious supply

82./

Ottoman water law outlined.

82. In addition to springs, there are rivers or streams which I need not specify here in detail. I may, however, take the opportunity of explaining in skeleton outline some of the main principles of Ottoman or Islamic water law, because I believe that the influence of these principles has spread through many countries of the world.

Water is common to all; and private ownership exists only when water is collected and reduced to possession. The water of a public river, i.e. one not flowing in a channel which is the private property of a body of individuals, is "common to all". Everyone may take the benefit of large sheets of water: and irrigate his lands from public rivers. The proviso imposed by law on any newcomer is that his operations do not damage any other user. The question of control of these streams by Government is obviously a most important one.

Troubles of well-owners.

83. (b) Of well-irrigation little need be said. Its extension where water is known to exist is restricted by lack of capital. All through the Coastal and Acre Plains water of varying quantities and qualities and at varying depths can be found. The real

trouble/

-66-

trouble is that in various parts of these plains saline water is occasionally struck at different depths in close proximity to sweet water. Particularly towards the south, a well-owner having found his first supply of sweet water insufficient, deepens his well and occasionally strikes strata holding saline water. Whether still deeper boring will result in the tapping again of sweet water has not been satisfactorily proved.

Control of well-sinking

84. At page 86 of the Hope Simpson Report the question is raised whether powers for control over the sinking of wells in any Ordinance is necessary. It is stated that at one time a fear existed lest "the multiplication of wells in the "Maritime Plain had caused a fall in the "water-table in that area. The matter was "examined by an expert Committee which came "to the conclusion that the fear was not well "founded. The water-table had fallen in a "certain region, but there remained an ample "supply at the deeper level."

85./

-67-

Facts as to water-table in Maritime Plains.

85. There appears to have been some misapprehension of the facts.

During the years 1925 - 1929 the water-table did fall in the Plains, owing, it is believed, to the lack of rainfall during those years. But in 1929 the level of the water in certain areas, apparently as the result of a better rainfall, began to rise again; from which it may be argued that the extension of citrus cultivation was not the essential cause of the reduced level. I cannot find that any expert Committee ever investigated the matter. The Irrigation Officer and another expert, with an intimate knowledge of the Coastal Plains, have informed me that the question has never really been thoroughly examined; and for this reason and in view of the great extension of plantations during the last year or two, it is essential that Government should have power to control the underground supplies in any intensively-cultivated tract and establish observation stations for the purpose.

Californian experiences.

86. A recent visitor to a part of California with conditions of climate similar to those of Palestine has described to me how large areas of land in the former country, which were once devoted to the production of various kinds of fruit, such as/

-68-

such as citrus and grapes, and to orchards, have been steadily thrown out of cultivation owing to the fall in the water-table having rendered all fruit-growing unprofitable. It is vital in the case of Palestine that no such disaster should overtake the citrus groves of the Maritime Plains where at present they are being extended without any regard to their possible ultimate effects on subterranean water supplies.

The rights of the State in water. Water Law in British Columbia as a parallel.

87. It has been shown above that according to Ottoman law water belongs to all, or in other words is vested in the State or Commonwealth; but that law, conforming to an almost universal concept that everyone has the right to waste water as he likes, did not advance further to the comparatively modern doctrine that the State has also rights in the use of water.

I have before me as I write the Water Act of the Province of British Columbia - a province well endowed with surface irrigational supplies. It prescribes that "the property in and right to "the use of all water at any time in any stream "in the Province is for all purposes vested in the "Crown in the right of the Province etc."

88./

-69-

State should re-assert rights in water and waste water.

88. It is in my opinion essential for any scheme of development that the State should in the interests of the community assert (or rather re-assert) its rights to the ownership of all water, and also to the use of all water which is running to waste because it is in the private possession of no user who has any concern for it. In a country where water is scarce, inefficient methods of its distribution and its uneconomical use in cultivation are public sins which have been too long overlooked and call for early remedy.

Illustration of connection of Haifa water problem with agricultural development

89. The inter-connection of current water problems with the prospect of agricultural development is illustrated by the position of the town of Haifa. The Haifa Harbour Works on which so large a sum of money is being expended are now tending towards completion: and the future of Haifa as a port is affording much material for speculation. But, so far, no permanent provision has been made whatever for an assured water supply and an efficient drainage scheme. The water at Haifa is very scanty and its quality so indifferent that ships calling at the port have to lighter their water across the bay from Acre: and the locomotives and machinery employed on the

harbour/

-70-

harbour construction works have almost
monthly to renew parts which with less
saline water would last years. The
provision of sweet water for a large port
is indispensable; and the only solution
of this very urgent problem at present
advanced is to bring water some distance
from the Kabri springs which already supply
Acre The diversion of the whole water of
these springs to urban domestic supplies will
affect the agricultural development of the
countryside unless additional supplies of
water can be tapped in the neighbourhood.
This is one of the questions that will need
careful investigation and research.

(6) RECOMMENDATIONS FOR LEGISLATION

Summary of Recommendations for legislation.

90. Recommendations contained in sections (1) - (5) of this Report are summarized as follows:

(1) The question of acceleration of survey and settlement operations beyond that already contemplated should be deferred until the situation is clearer. Meanwhile, the approved amendments of the existing Settlement Ordinances should be effected without delay. (Paragraph 28).

(2) The partition of undivided village lands outside the settlement areas should be expedited by the appointment of special officers, one for each district; assistance being rendered by the existing administration. Legislation, of as simple and broad a nature as possible, should at once be enacted to achieve the object. (Paragraphs 35 & 37).

(3) With a view to the establishment of a land administration agency, a Palestinian District Officer should be deputed to Northern India to study the system known there as the "land revenue administration". On his return the required agency should be established. (Paragraph 54)

(4)/

-72-

(4) Legislation should be passed with a view to

    (a) the constitution of a class of occupancy tenants: (paragraph 63)

    (b) the control of transfers of land under the Transfer of Land Ordinance: (paragraphs 59, 60, 71, 72, 74 and 75)

    (c) the constitution of a class of State occupancy tenants in tracts to be expropriated and re-settled by Government: (paragraph 63)

    (d) the due State control and administration of such tracts: (paragraphs 68, 94, 106)

(5) The re-assertion of the rights of the State to the ownership of all water and to the use of all waste water. (Paragraphs 88, 94, 106)

Simplification of legislation   91. In concluding this part of my Report I venture to trespass, it may be, beyond the limits of my task; because the question I touch on is a serious one and concerns closely the development of this country in all spheres of life. If legislation for the promotion of development schemes is to be enacted, I would plead most

                                            earnestly/

earnestly that it should be framed on the broadest and simplest lines possible, all minor details being left to rules and regulations which can, if necessary, be first submitted to public criticism.

In the Province of India in which I served, a law covering, *inter alia*, the fields of land settlement and land revenue (or taxation) stood unamended for forty years. It consisted of some thirty clauses, and held good over a Province containing more than twenty times the villages and population of Palestine. Rules and regulations under that Act were amended or changed frequently, as experience dictated: but the principles of the Act were untouched. In this country (where, of course, experience has to be gained) very detailed Ordinances and Amending Ordinances, (which comprise over 100 clauses) have already been issued dealing with the sole field of settlement operations: and further amendments are under consideration. The result is that settlement legislation, even after three and a half years, is becoming too intricate for the comprehension of the plain man.

The/

-74-

The multiplicity of existing Ordinances, Amending Ordinances and Special Ordinances embracing all aspects of the Administration cannot, perhaps, be simplified now, except at the cost of years of labour: but I submit that the Secretary of State, the Palestine Government and the people of the country would be saved much travail and confusion if future legislation, in general, be directed to the embodiment of main principles only in all new laws, leaving the rest to rules and regulations duly gazetted under the Ordinances.

PART II

SOME SPECIAL MATTERS

Special areas. 92. Instructions have been conveyed to me that the problems of the Beisan tract and the Huleh Basin should receive my special and early consideration.

I now turn to these two questions.

I. – THE BEISAN AREA

The future of the area. 93. The modern history of Beisan – the Beth-Shan of the last chapter of the First Book of Samuel – is set forth in some detail in Appendix III A.

~~Upon this fertile tract the Jews have quite~~ naturally cast longing eyes, and ~~been insistent~~ that Government should ~~take~~ such action as will enable them ~~to~~ acquire easily areas of land in ~~Beisan which they can cultivate intensively.~~

As that history shows, the situation is extremely complex. Reduced to simple language the problem is, How is it possible to deal with this tract, the permanent settlement of which with the original cultivators has only just been brought to completion; but which is clearly susceptible of development on more intensive lines ? Development is proceeding as I have stated in paragraph 65 above: but wide spaces of demarcated and partitioned land are

lying/

lying untilled, awaiting intensive development by the extension to them of water supplies which in default of unified control are being wasted and will continue to be wasted until such control is applied.

Possible course of action in regard to the area. State control recommended.

94. There are four courses from which a choice can be made:

(1) To leave matters in their present state. This would be tantamount to perpetuating chaos and nullify the declared policy of His Majesty's Government to further intensive settlement.

(2) To relax the terms of payment of the transfer price and allow newcomers to buy land more freely than has hitherto been permitted; in fact, permit this class to spread themselves, as and when they can over all the estates in which they can find a footing.

The result would, of course, be a rapid creation of another landless Arab problem with possibly more serious political results, because of the propinquity of the tract to Trans-Jordan and the Hauran.

(3) For Government to take control of the water and its distribution; but to allow newcomers to reap the advantages of penetrating the lands at will.

This /

-77-

This would not obviate the recurrence of the landless Arab question. For, inevitably, as is noted in paragraph 65 above, the new settlers would secure a predominant hold over available water supplies and thus force out of possession the existing cultivators.

(4) For Government to take unified control of land and water, and create an entirely new settlement of land and water for the benefit of the existing settlers and orderly development by introduction of new settlers.

This last is the only method by which an adequate use of this fertile area can be secured, with justice done to all its cultivators, actual and potential.

The complications of the situation in the Beisan Area. 95. A reference to the section of this Report which deals with the subject of water control will give some clue to the irrigational complexities of a tract where there are some 27 named springs or streams of varying qualities of water. The question of control of the land presents difficulties almost as great. Use of land and water is at present as unsystematic and chaotic as can be conceived. Areas of well-cultivated land are interspersed with areas thickly overgrown with weed and jungle shrubs: and water channels

wander/

-78-

wander about apparently with no object and no system. Yet they are all subject to well-known rights. If economical use is to be made of this water, and equitable distribution secured, it will be imperative to group all intensive cultivation and all extensive cultivation (that may remain) separately. Nor are the difficulties of land and water the only problems. The primitive habits of a large part of the transferees, their intense suspiciousness and unresponsiveness to civilizing methods are political considerations which have all to be taken into account; and even when at length the cultivators shall have been re-settled, they will need careful control and supervision for years. And, in addition, the whole tract will require much closer and more vigilant administration than has been found necessary in the past. Many years must elapse before the work can be completed. The possibilities of re-settlement and colonization were very carefully investigated by the Irrigation Officer last year, under the instructions of the High Commissioner, Sir John Chancellor.
Mr. Shepherd, who examined the whole tract in the light of his great experience in Egypt, and made the most detailed calculations, came to the conclusion that, in theory at any rate, close settlement of about 3,500 families in an irrigable

area/

area of 105,000 dunams was possible.

The expenditure at a conservative estimate for the whole scheme was put at over a half million pounds. Given a thriving community he believed the value of the land would multiply perhaps fivefold.

The state of the existing Arab population

96. It is certain that, speaking generally, the present holders if left to themselves can never develop this fertile tract. They have neither the education nor the resources.

Some two years ago the Director of Lands reported that in no case had a transferee, even under the modified terms of the 1921 Agreement, been able from his own resources to discharge his financial obligations. The local authorities were of opinion that while the terms of the Agreement were not unduly severe, the indebtedness of the transferees prevented them from paying up the capital sums due. If a prize were offered to the cultivator who had done best, it would fall to one who still required 22 years to pay off the capital sum, quite apart from any interest. For villages to clear off the original capital sums due for the land, without interest, periods ranging from 45 to 143 years will be required. It is added that the "transferees are fully aware of "their obligations under the Agreement and that "the land will revert to Government at the end

of the/

-80-

"of the 15 years, if the total amount due is "not paid, and are merely trusting that Government "will, in due course, solve the problem for them".

Perhaps, it is not unfair to these fatalistic cultivators to hazard the opinion that they are shrewd enough to believe that Government would not eject them from their lands and leave them stranded, any more than the Turks did. Probably, they anticipate, at the worst, confiscation of their proprietary rights - and a return to the <u>status quo ante</u>.

The potentialities under State control of the area.	97.	If solution (4) be adopted, the legislation mentioned in paragraph 90 will be required. I have already

sketched roughly in paragraph 66 the methods of settlement and re-settlement that might be adopted. The latest estimates of families actually resident on the irrigated lands is about 950. If there is room for 3,500 families in all as suggested in paragraph 95, the number of new families that can be introduced on about 110,000 dunams (not 105,000) of irrigable land will be approximately 2,500. These figures are, of course, only estimates.

What/

—81—

What the total cost would be must depend on the numbers of Arabs and Jews settled, and the principles adopted for settlement.

Political effects. 98. Finally, the political repercussions among the Arabs of any disturbance of the status quo cannot fail to be considerable; particularly, as long as the ultimate benefits of any scheme devised are not fully understood by the fellahin and Beduin. This factor in the situation must, in any case, be faced, unless things are to be left to drift on in their present unsatisfactory condition.

II.

-82-

II. - THE HULEH AREA AND CONCESSION

The Huleh Plain
c unit.   99.   References to the Huleh Basin will be found at pages 18 and 83 of the Hope Simpson Report; and any repetition by me is superfluous. Appendices IV A and B should be consulted.

Taking the whole Huleh plain as integral, it may be stated emphatically that no scheme of development which does not embrace the entire basin can be of any real use. I have explored the whole area, personally, and arrived at the following conclusions. In no other part of Palestine has nature provided such a super-abundance of water: and in no other tract has nature endowed the soil with such fertile qualities. The existing agriculture is primitive and thriftless. Except in a few patches intensive cultivation is practically unknown. Of the 165,000 (more or less) dunams at which the total area is estimated, 65,000 dunams are said to belong to absentee/Syrian landlords: and about 45,000 to fellahin or Bedu families: the residue is comprised within the Concession which is the key to the situation.

100./

-83-

Reasons for water-logging 100. Owing to geological conformations, the waters poured into the lake and marshes by the affluents cannot be discharged quickly enough by the outlet channel into the Jordan bed: and the only relief possible is the deepening of this basalt-bedded channel by sub-aqueous blasting operations along a stretch of water of, approximately, 2½ miles. Once the water can be got away, drainage will automatically effect some reclamation of the marshes - how much it is impossible to say because no one knows to what extent they are fed from hidden springs.

Recent survey results 101. The Concession area, the history of which is given in Appendix IV A, has only recently been scientifically surveyed for the first time. The result is that the real areas are now available. Marsh accounts for 30,450 dunams; lake for 13,800 dunams and cultivated land for 11,165 dunams. That is to say, that out of the total area in the Huleh plain, 55,415 dunams have under the Turkish concession, - the validity of which has been upheld by all legal authorities, - been made over to concessionaires, the members of one family most of whom are resident on the banks of the lake where they watch vigilantly over their own interests.

102./

-84-

Attitude of local population to concession. 102. It is, perhaps, unnecessary to add that the existence of this concession is a source of resentment not only to would-be Jewish colonists, but much more to the fellahin who live in and around the area. The complaints of the alleged oppressive measures taken by the concessionaires to defend their supposed rights are incessant, and almost, if not quite, universal.

[margin note: felt by the local population as conflict with their interests or supposed interests. ... omitted]

Methods of dealing with the concession. 103. There are four possible means of dealing with this concession.

First, to leave the concessionaires to fulfil their obligations at their own good will, in which case, at the best, some portion of the marshes will be reclaimed and the lake will be left shrunken but otherwise uncontrolled. Further, the more reclamation and drainage of the concession will not effect the development of the upper area of the Basin outside the concession area. It will still remain subject to the effects of over-irrigation and the consequent malaria that has had such pestilential effects on the local population, now reduced to some 4,200, inclusive of Jewish settlements.

Secondly, Government can wait until the concession falls in owing to default on the part of the concessionaires. It has always been contended that they have never been anxious

[margin note: it is possible that the Concessionaires may eventually find the performance of the conditions beyond their strength. In such an]

an event, it is to be presumed that they would either forgo the concession, or Govt would exercise its rights of resumption of the [?], as is provided for in the agreement.

~~anxious to fulfil their obligations and carry out the objects for which the concession was ostensibly granted: and that during the several years in which the concession has been actually or potentially in their possession their endeavours have been directed only to gaining time. However this may be, the fact remains that until now no work of any real value in draining the marsh lands has been accomplished: and several years must elapse before Government can hope to take action on proved default.~~

The third course, is to buy out the concessionaires if they would accept a reasonable sum. Hitherto, their demands have been considered exorbitant.

Lastly, there is the method of compulsory expropriation in the interests of the community at large.

Necessity of appointing a Boundary Commission. 104. The official survey of the concession area which has only just been completed has disclosed the fact that there are numerous boundary disputes between the concessionaires and the neighbouring fellahin. These disputes are variously attributed to the vagueness and unreliability of the old Turkish maps and to the steady subsequent encroachments by the concessionaires on their neighbours' property or rights.

It is/

-85-

It is quite certain that a Boundary Commission is the only method by which these disputes can be settled: and I trust that as soon as it is practically possible, such commission will be appointed. In this connection, it is to be remembered that, owing to the state of the ground in winter and spring, no useful purpose would be served by constituting such a commission before next July when free locomotion in the tract will again become possible.

Possibilities of reclamation considered. 105. Whether, if the marshes of Huleh are drained, they will become available, generally, for cultivation remains to be seen. Small areas on the outside of the marshes have been, and are still being, reclaimed by fellahin cultivators: but the experience of draining the Kabara swamps on the Coastal Plain at enormous and uneconomic cost is not encouraging. It is a not unreasonable inference in the case of Huleh, that the presence in a land flowing with water of these undrained marshes argues the existence therein of numerous underground springs which are likely to prove as intractable as those in the Kabara swamps.

106./

Necessity of
State control
of the Huleh Area. 106.
I have said above that the whole Huleh Basin should be treated as a unit from a development point of view. To ensure such development it will be necessary to bring under the control of Government both the whole land and water. It is reported that the Syrian absentee landlords in some cases refuse to pay their taxes, because they find cultivation of their lands unremunerative. Their tenants in this rich area are so poor, and cultivate so poorly, as to be unable to spare anything for their landlords. Malaria decimates the population, or so enfeebles it, as to completely nullify nature's rich gifts. The only way in which development, agricultural and hygienic, can proceed is for Government to reduce to order the irrigation from the numerous rivers and springs by canalization, and at the same time take over the necessary lands of those who own broad acres in order that it may carry out its declared policy of closer settlement.

What the cost would be of re-settling the whole Huleh plain - inside and outside the concession - in farms of 30 to 40 dunams (on a general average with possible exceptions); of providing duly canalized irrigation and drainage and, at the same time, stamping out

the/

-88-

the dreaded malaria, cannot at present be estimated. Intricate and difficult though the problem be, I cannot but think the estimate of one million pounds made by Jewish experts to be exaggerated, though to express any decided opinion without further detailed research would be hazardous. [I ~~certainly think that~~ settled as Government tenants, a leavening of Jewish colonists in this tract would tend to an acceleration of the desired development after the marshes have been drained.]

Possible political effects of Jewish settlements. 107. [It must be added that any proposal to settle ~~Jews~~ in this tract, surrounded as it is on all sides by ~~indigenous~~ tribes, may raise a political problem which it ~~is~~ not for me to discuss in this Report.]

I certainly believe that, settled as Government tenants, a leaving of Jewish colonists on this tract would tend to an acceleration of the desired development after the marshes have been drained.

III./

III. - OTHER AREAS

Other areas described   108.   Besides the Beisan and Huleh tracts, there are the Jordan Valley and Beersheba plains which demand attention. In the former there is undoubtedly a large area - estimated at 100,000 dunams - capable of cultivation if water can be brought to it. If a high-level canal taking out of the Jordan be practicable (I think it may be found so) at a reasonable expenditure (a more dubious condition), it will not be an easy undertaking to be completed in a few months. The project would be one that will take years to carry out, involving, as it does, preliminary and complete surveys by a skilled irrigation-engineering staff and, inevitably, costly operations. I can frame no estimate for such a work, which may well be postponed until progress has been made with other schemes.

        In the Jericho Jiftlik (or State Domain) in the lower Jordan Valley, there is an area of 3,000 or 4,000 dunams which depend for their irrigation on a famous Jericho spring. Approximately, 1,000 dunams are cultivated as gardens, oranges, bananas and other fruit and vegetables growing profusely in the sub-tropical climate to be found 1,200 feet below the sea level.

The rest/

-90-

The rest of the cultivated lands are occupied by Beduin: and the cultivation is of the indifferent, expansive type usual among such tribesmen. Without irrigation, the lands are uncultivable. The use of the water by the garden owners is admittedly wasteful and they, on their part, have agreed to control on reasonable conditions. But, so far, it has not been found possible to persuade the suspicious tribesmen to abandon their extensive for intensive cultivation, despite close personal efforts directed to this end by the Irrigation Officer. A success here would be a great object lesson for other tribesmen: and hopes are still entertained.

The waterless stretch of fertile lands in the Beersheba sub-district cannot be colonized without artificial irrigation owing to the scanty and precarious rainfall. To what rights this tract actually is subject is not known. It has not been surveyed and there are no records of rights worth the name. The first attempt to ascertain whether deep boring will produce the water supplies necessary for irrigation is actually under way. The success or failure of this attempt will not be known for some months. Until we have learned the upshot, we shall not be justified in risking

further/

further costly experiments of the same nature. In short, even if good fortune attend this experiment, years must elapse before we should be in a position to place settlers on the land.

The future of the Auja Concession is still under consideration by the Secretary of State: and I am not yet in a position to make any definite report about the irrigation of the Auja Plain.

No order of preference for schemes yet advised.

109. The main object of the proposals made in this First Report being to obtain orders on the principles which should, in my opinion, be adopted before schemes of development can be more fully considered, I have not thought it useful at this stage to attempt advice as to the order of preference in which such schemes should be carried out.

IV. - MISCELLANEOUS

COOPERATIVE CREDIT

Appointment of a Registrar a necessary preliminary.

110. As a consequence of the investigation and Report made by Mr. C.F. Strickland, C.I.E., last year, the Palestine Government had, before I took up my duties, requested the Secretary of State to arrange for the appointment of a Registrar of Cooperative Banks. In making such appointment a dilemma had to be faced: either a trained officer had to be invited from outside who would know nothing of Arab and Jewish agricultural methods and physchology, or else an officer must be appointed from the Palestine administration who was not conversant with the principles and technique of the subject of cooperative credit. It has finally been decided to act on the latter alternative: but it cannot be anticipated that the officer appointed will need less than six months experience of various systems in force abroad before he is adequately equipped for his duties.

I am not myself qualified, from such experience as I have had in the past in India, to act as an expert adviser on this highly technical subject, and therefore feel that it

would/

would be useless for me to advise precisely in this First Report on the feasibility and advisability of providing credits for Arab cultivators and Jewish settlers. It has been represented to me that, in the case of the former, individualism is too strong to warrant any hope of success in organizing in their villages a system of cooperative credit: Mr. Strickland thinks otherwise: and I am optimistic enough to agree with him. The establishment of cooperative credit rural societies has been tried in many quarters of the world and has always proved successful, I believe, when effectively organized.

As regards the Jewish settlers, I have no doubts.

For the best means of attaining the desired ends, I must await the advice of a trained expert before reporting my own detailed opinions.

Miscellaneous 111. The subject of leases of Government lands: the establishment of another Agricultural Experimental Station at Gaza: the distribution of trees for planting in the hills, and the extension of terracing in the hills are other matters which have been actively dealt with during the four months that I have been in the country.

Much/

-94-

Much of that period has been taken up with duties not strictly germane to any scheme of development. But so far am I from complaining of this extra labour, that I wish to express my appreciation of the opportunities afforded of gaining a valuable insight into the administration of the country which could only have been otherwise acquired after much longer experience, and then with difficulty.

Concluding remarks.   112. It only remains to add a tribute of my gratitude to Their Excellencies Sir John Chancellor and Sir Arthur Wauchope, and Mr. M.A. Young, Officer recently administering the Government, and to all other officers of the Palestine Administration for the kind and unsparing assistance that they have consistently rendered; and to Mr. Kitching the Deputy Director, Mr. Shepherd the Irrigation Officer, and the members of my small office staff for all their energetic labours in the Development Department.

APPENDIX I

The following is the text of Palestine Despatch No.487, of the 26th of June, 1931, from His Majesty's Principal Secretary of State for the Colonies to the High Commissioner for Palestine, on the subject of the initial steps to be taken to give effect to the policy of His Majesty's Government in regard to Agricultural Development and Land Settlement in Palestine

Sir,

As you are aware, I have recently had under consideration the initial steps to be taken to give effect to the policy of His Majesty's Government in regard to agricultural development and land settlement in Palestine.

2. The need of a more methodical agricultural development was made apparent by Sir John Hope Simpson's Report on Immigration, Land Settlement and Development in Palestine (Cmd.3686). The Statement of Policy (Cmd.3692) issued simultaneously with that Report, gave (in paragraphs 21 to 25), a brief outline of the policy to be adopted by His Majesty's Government in this matter, and the policy was further explained in paragraphs 9 to 13 of the Prime Minister's letter to Dr. Weizmann, dated 13th February, 1931. It is the intention that the lands required for this purpose should be found by means of a loan which Parliament will be asked to authorise His Majesty's Government to guarantee.

3/

3. I have already been in correspondence with you in regard to the initial steps to be taken for carrying out the policy of His Majesty's Government in regard to agricultural development and land settlement. As a result of this correspondence, the outline of a scheme was drawn up, in consultation with yourself, which was communicated to the representatives both of the Jewish Agency and the Arab Executive for such comments as they might desire to offer.

4. I have since had the opportunity of discussing the question orally with you during your recent visit to England. After full consideration of your views, and of the comments received from the quarters mentioned above, I have approved the revised proposals set out in the following paragraphs.

5. (i) His Majesty's Government will take steps for the appointment at an early date of a Director of Development and a nucleus of staff. The Director will be subordinate to the High Commissioner but will be independent of existing Government Departments in Palestine, though in carrying out the work of development he will be in liaison with them.

(ii) The Jewish Agency and the Arab Executive will be invited to nominate one member each to assist the Director in an advisory capacity.

(iii)/

(iii) The Director of Development will proceed to carry out the following preliminary work:

(a) He will prepare a register of such Arabs as can be shown to have been displaced from the lands which they occupied in consequence of the lands falling into Jewish hands, and who have not obtained other holdings on which they can establish themselves or other equally satisfactory occupation. The Director in preparing the register will have the assistance of a legal assessor, whose duty it will be to scrutinise claims and advise the Director as to the sufficiency of evidence in each case before the claims are admitted.

(b) After the preliminary work of registration, the Director will draw up a scheme of resettlement of registered displaced Arab families with as close an estimate as possible of the cost. When the scheme has been approved by the High Commissioner the resettlement will be carried out as quickly as possible.

(c) Further, the Director will investigate the methods to be adopted to give effect, within the limits of the funds available, to the intention of His Majesty's Government as to the policy of Land Settlement as outlined in paragraphs 10 and 11 of the Prime Minister's

letter/

letter to Dr. Weizman in the following terms:-

" In framing a policy of Land Settlement, it is essential that His Majesty's Government should take into consideration every circumstance that is relevant to the main purposes of the Mandate.

The area of cultivable land, the possibilities of irrigation, the absorptive capacity of the country in relation to immigration are all elements pertinent to the issue to be elucidated, and the neglect of any one of them would be prejudicial to the formulation of a just and stable policy.

" It is the intention of His Majesty's Government to institute an enquiry as soon as possible to ascertain, <u>inter alia</u>, what State and other lands are, or properly can be made, available for close settlement by Jews under reference to the obligation imposed upon the Mandatory by Article 6 of the Mandate. This enquiry will be comprehensive in its scope, and will include the whole land resources of Palestine. In the conduct of the enquiry provision will be made for all interests, whether Jewish or Arab, making such representations as it may be desired to put forward.

" The question of the congestion amongst the fellahin in the hill districts of Palestine is receiving the careful consideration of His Majesty's Government. It is contemplated that measures will be devised for the improvement and intensive development of the land, and for bringing into cultivation areas which hitherto may have remained uncultivated, and thereby securing to the fellahin a better standard of living, without, save in exceptional cases, having recourse to transfer. "

(d) Such investigation will also include the following :-

(1) The feasibility and advisability of providing credits for Arab cultivators and Jewish settlers, and if so, the best method of achieving this purpose.

(2) Proposals for draining, irrigating and otherwise reclaiming land not at present cultivated or cultivated only to a limited extent.

(o) It is the intention of His Majesty's Government to authorise the High Commissioner to incur expenditure not exceeding £.50,000 in the foregoing investigation including all necessary surveys and experiments, such expenditure being met in the first instance from Palestine funds.

(f)/

(f) The Director will make in reference to each of the above enumerated matters in (c) and (d) estimates as close as the circumstances will allow of the cost of the works proposed, and give an intimation of their order of preference.

(iv) The Director will submit his Report or such Interim Report as can be completed, not later than 31st December, 1931. The High Commissioner will take the Report into consideration and will, before submitting recommendations to His Majesty's Government, invite the observations of the Jewish Agency and the Arab Executive upon the practical proposals of the scheme and will afford them an opportunity of making representations regarding such proposals as have not already received the concurrence of the Jewish and Arab Advisers.

(v) The Report or Interim Report as abovementioned will be transmitted by the High Commissioner along with any representations of the Jewish Agency or the Arab Executive thereon to His Majesty's Government who will decide whether effect should be given to the Report and its recommendations, or to which of them and in what manner.

(vi) The Bill for the guarantee of the development loan will not be settled until the Report or Interim Report as abovementioned of the Director of Development is received and considered along with the representations, if any, to be made as provided for.

6. I am taking the necessary steps for the selection at an early date of an officer for the post of Director of Development and will address you further upon the subject as soon as I am in a position to do so.

> I have the honour to be,
> Sir,
> Your most obedient,
> humble servant,
> (Sgd.) PASSFIELD

High Commissioner
Lieutenant-Colonel
    Sir J. R. Chancellor, G.C.M.G.,
        G.C.V.O., D.S.O.
        etc., etc., etc.

APPENDIX II.

STATE DOMAINS

List corrected up to December, 1931

Serial No.	Name of Estate	Sub-District	Reputed area in dunams	Remarks
1.	Lake Huleh Lands	Safad	55,415 (actual)	Subject to the Ottoman Concession.
2.	Samakh	Tiberias		Transferred under Beisan Agreement, 1921.
3.	Beisan Jiftlik	Beisan	381,771 (actual)	
4.	Ghor el Fara'a	Nablus		
5.	Dahnuneh and Mubarakeh	Safad	780	Leased to Jewish Agricultural Cooperative Society for 50 years from 1.10.1921
6.	Rakayak	Acre	1,600	Leased to a Jew for 99 years from 18.1.23.
7.	Rushmia	Haifa	3,385	Leased annually to Jewish National Fund.
8.	Athlit	Haifa	1,500	Disputed. Concession to Palestine Jewish Colonization Association.
9.	Kabbara	Haifa	8,655	Concession to P.I.C.A.
10.	Cherkaz	Haifa	95	Leased to P.I.C.A. for 50 years from 1.10.26.
11.	Caesarea	Haifa	31,440	Concession to P.I.C.A. but under litigation.
12.	Basset el Mulabbis	Jaffa	2,418	Leased to Jewish Colony of Petah Tiqva for 50 years from 11.11.21
13.	Jaffa Sand Dunes	Jaffa	35,000	Under litigation. 21,000 dunams granted to Jewish Colony of Rishon-le-Zion. Partly uncultivable.
14.	Jazzair	Safad	418	Leased to Arabs for 20 years from 23.12.26.
15.	Mansourah	Safad	2,500	Occupied by Arabs who pay 10% rental tithe.
16.	Subeih	Nazareth	9,548	ditto : but part taken for Agricultural School.
17.	Kaukab	Nazareth	30,000	$\tfrac{1}{2}$ shares (only) which are occupied by Arabs who pay 10% rental tithe. Area overestimated and boundaries disputed by neighbouring village.

-2-

Serial No.	Name of Estate	Sub-District	Reputed area in dunams	Remarks
18.	Kishon Lands	Haifa	450	Under drainage: small isolated plots.
19.	Hedeidoun	Haifa	600	Under litigation.
20.	Zarafieh	Jenin	2,700	Occupied by Arabs who pay 10% rental tithe.
21.	Tel el Dahab	Jenin	2,400	ditto
22.	Deir Ghazaleh	Jenin	2,700	ditto
23.	Akrabanieh	Nablus	960	ditto
24.	Mazra'a el Hamra	Nablus	11,300	ditto
25.	El Farush	Nablus	1,656	ditto
26.	Sajad	Ramle	7,000	ditto
27.	Hamadieh	Ramle	500	ditto
28.	Jericho Jiftlik	Jericho	75,000	A small portion as above. Rest uncultivable.
29.	Ain Feshka	Jericho	1,300)	Uncultivable
30.	Es Suwaideh	Jericho	17,000)	
31.	Gharabeh	Jericho	108	Leased
32.	Jahayyer	Jericho	20,000	Small area leased. Rest uncultivable.
33.	Zeita	Hebron	5,350	Occupied by Arab cultivators.
34.	Tel Arad	Hebron	37,000	ditto - waterless.
35.	Jaladieh	Gaza	4,143	Occupied by Arab cultivators who pay 10% rental tithe.
36.	Kofakha	Gaza	9,200	ditto
37.	Moharraka	Gaza	4,580	ditto
38.	Rafa	Gaza	90,000	ditto - but 70,000 uncultivable sand dunes.

39./

-3-

Serial No.	Name of Estate	Sub-District	Reputed area in dunams.	Remarks
39.	Anata	Jerusalem	15,000	In dispute. Uncultivated: mostly uncultivable.
40.	Kharab and Awameed	Tiberias	360	Antiquity site. Small part leased to Tiberias Municipality.
41.	Tob Alti	Acre	2,500	Government Stud Farm, etc.
42.	Acre Sand Dunes	Acre	12,225	Uncultivable. Part to be leased to Iraq Petroleum Company.
43.	El Bourj Tantura	Haifa	145	Antiquity site.
44.	Basset el Yaraki	Nablus	2,500	Swamp. Leased annually by public auction.
45.	Gaza Sand Dunes	Gaza	6,000	Site of new Gaza. Part under litigation: mainly uncultivable.
46.	Khirbet el Tabaka and	Nablus	600 ⎫	Occupied by Arab cultivators. Title in dispute: Government claim considered dubious.
47.	Toubas Lands	Nablus	41,700 ⎭	

APPENDIX III A

HISTORY OF THE BEISAN AREA

The tract as it was described.

1. A description of the Beisan area, as it was in 1921, has been kindly furnished me by one of the officers then in charge. Part of the tract was inhabited by fellahin who lived in mud hovels, suffered severely from the prevalent malaria and were of too low intelligence to be receptive of any suggestions for improvement of their housing, water supply or education. Large areas of their lands were uncultivated and covered with weeds. There were no trees, no vegetables. The fellahin, if not themselves cattle thieves, were always ready to harbour these and other criminals. The individual plots of cultivation, such as it was, changed hands annually. There was little public security: and the fellahin's lot was an alternation of pillage and blackmail by their neighbours, the Beduin.

The same.

2. These latter occupied the other part of the sub-district in similar conditions; except that cultivation by these nomads was even more scanty. In the spring the countryside was a mass of wild flowers: at other times of the year a waste of weeds and thorn bushes. Only the roughest of tracks existed: and these became impassable in winter. The Beduin, wild and lawless by nature, were constantly at foud

with/

-2-

with their neighbours on both sides of the Jordan: and raids and highway robberies formed their staple industry: while such cultivation as the Beduin were capable of filled in the intervals of more exciting occupation.

Desertion by original cultivators of the area.

3. In general, it may be said that the tenants who were cultivating the Beisan area in 1920-1921 were the original owners or descendants of the original owners+ of these lands. For various reasons, due to absence of public security, raids by marauding tribes and exactions of corrupt tax collectors and other Turkish Government officials, accompanied by poor harvests and inequitable assessment of tithes, the owners became unable to pay the arrears of the crop and land taxes which had accumulated against them.

Ottoman Enquiry.

4. In the year 1870 the Ottoman authorities appointed a Commission to investigate and report on the lands of Beisan which had been abandoned in consequence of the state of affairs indicated above. Two years later

directions /

+ The word "owner" describes here the holder of the most common, if somewhat restricted, form of property under Turkish land law.

directions were given that the whole of the lands comprised within the Beisan "Jiftlik" or State Domain (with the exception of those of two Arab tribes) should be put up for sale by public auction.

The desertion of their lands by reason of the calamities enumerated above, and consequent failure to cultivate over periods ranging from 20 to 30 years, constituted under Turkish law a default of which the Turkish Government, though itself mainly the cause of the default, took advantage. At the time the Commission reported, one part of the land was stated to be still uncultivated, while other parts had only recently been re-cultivated by the original tenants who had been induced to return to their lands, with the supplement of a few later comers from neighbouring villages. None of these cultivators had themselves occupied their lands sufficiently long to establish a prescriptive right under the Turkish law by occupation for 10 or more years.

Sale of lands: purchase by the Sultan.

5. Accordingly, the lands were auctioned; and certain villages - of exceptional quality as might have been expected - fell to Sultan Abdul Hamid: others were registered in his name on instructions received direct from Constantinople.

At a/

At a later date the Sultan also purchased the lands of the two excepted Arab tribes mentioned above - one of the areas being now included in Trans-Jordan. On the deposition of the Sultan in 1908, the lands were transferred to the Public Treasury - and so remained until the British occupation.

Following the common practice, the original owners had been retained on the land as State tenants. They, no doubt, still regarded themselves as _de jure_ owners, - the only practical difference in their status being that they were compelled to pay a rental tithe of 10% of their produce in addition to the ordinary tithes. They were treated by the officials as tenants holding perpetual leases: or in other parlance, as "occupancy tenants".

1921 Commission of Enquiry

6. In 1921 the High Commissioner appointed a Commission to report upon State Domains and advise about their development. Considerations of law possibly, considerations of equity and policy certainly, forbade the Government in such a wild and unsettled locality to terminate the leases of these tenants. No one had any title to the Beisan area other than these original cultivators: and it was felt that their confirmation in the occupancy of these lands would go far towards re-assuring the Arabs that they had no reason to doubt Government's

impartiality/

impartiality. Substantial tracts of the area were under the cultivation of Bedu Arabs: and there was at the time a real danger that if these semi-nomads were deprived of, or were allowed to dispose of, their lands, Government would be faced with a serious increase of crime. Beduin are notoriously not adaptable as farmers: and if they were tempted subsequently by dazzling offers of high prices, made by land speculators on their own behalf or that of powerful outside bodies, to dispose of their rights in their lands, the certainty was that the purchase money received would not be employed in buying other lands, both by reason of the Bedu nature and because their presence in the middle of other tribes would not be tolerated.

Recommendations of Commission

7. The Commission in due course recommended that the tenants of Government Jiftlik Areas should be secured in their tenancies by long term leases: but when the High Commissioner had this suggestion conveyed to the cultivators, the latter refused the offer. They appeared to be labouring under the well-established belief, current in Turkish times, that if their names were recorded in the Government registers, they would _eo ipso_ become liable to military and other service. It was, in any

case/

-6-

case, of no use to have their individual names recorded or their identity disclosed except as owners. They, moreover, declined utterly to admit the legality of the ex-Sultan's act of despoliation.

The allotment of the area to cultivators.

8. Following on a visit to the area by the High Commissioner, against whom a hostile demonstration was organized, Government decided to proceed with the allotment of cultivated areas to the tenants in occupation, with a minimum of 150 dunams (about 36 acres) per family. No sort of census was available, and no reliable records of the actual area, which had never been officially surveyed and was variously estimated to comprise from 700,000 to 350,000 dunams, including the Trans-Jordan portion of the Jiftlik. Computation of numbers and areas was therefore largely guess-work. It seems to have been thought at the time, - not unnaturally, - that allocation on the above lines would leave a considerable surplus area for occupation by other interests. Government then entered into the Agreement which was signed on the 19th November, 1921.+

9./

+ Appendix III B.

–7–

Methods of allotment. 9. Severe criticism has been directed at the methods adopted in deciding on the size of allotments to the original owners who were cultivating as Government tenants. I have, therefore, ascertained the facts, as officially reported.

Particulars were collected by the Commission in the village areas at meetings of the villagers. The data obtained were the names of claimants; numbers in family; number of years during which land had been held and cultivated (Article 7 of the Agreement); and areas or shares claimed. These areas were, of course, given by the number of *fedans* (vide paragraph 44 of this Report), which had been assigned to each cultivator during the annual village distribution of lands (vide Section 2 of this Report). The claims so preferred were verified as far as possible by independent enquiry and by comparison with the (incomplete) tithe records. With such primitive statistics furnished by interested or partizan cultivators, who were entirely ignorant of measured areas, no accurate schedule of rights could possibly be made.

10./

Results of allotment.

10. The upshot was that those who had cultivated land exceeding 150 dunams each were allotted the areas to which enquiries showed them to be entitled; and those whose area was shown to be less than 150 dunams, or who by virtue of the numbers in their family were entitled under the Agreement to over 150 dunams, had their allotments made up to the amounts due. Where the poorer transferees, however, appeared unable to cultivate 150 dunams, they were assigned smaller appropriate areas, often at their own request because they did not wish to commit themselves to the purchase of the above minimum.

Nature of Agreement between Government and Tenants.

11. The nature of the Agreement (set forth in Appendix III B) is best described in the words used in the Indenture:-

" Now this is to witness that this Agreement "has been made between the Government of Palestine "and the cultivators of the land as a _permanent_ "_settlement_ of their respective rights. "

The wording of this phrase (the italics are mine) is quite clear and unmistakable. The Agreement is not one which can be cancelled without a breach of faith and law, whatever _post factum_ criticism may be levelled at its terms. It will be noticed from a perusal of the Agreement (attached) that the words "vendor", "purchaser", or "purchase price" do not appear. The cultivators refused

absolutely/

absolutely to admit that the arrangement come to represented the sale and purchase of areas. Their contention that they had <u>ab antiquo</u> rights to the land was thus, at least tacitly, admitted by Government.

Effects of the Agreement.
12. In entering on this Agreement, Government realized that these "tenants" – whether personal absentees or working cultivators is here immaterial, seeing their rights were as stated above – would not be able to develop their lands easily or rapidly. They were not backed by wealthy Corporations and they were compelled to rely in their struggle with nature on their own impoverished resources, unassisted by any outside help, technical or financial. The sequel indicates that in the fixation of the transfer price these considerations were not given full enough weight, and that the expectations of the agricultural wealth to be produced from the large tracts of unirrigated land were too optimistic.

Modification of terms.
13. The financial terms imposed on these cultivators proved too onerous: and in 1928 Government issued a "Statement of Policy" + the effect of which was to extend the period of payment of the "transferee price" to a maximum of 30 years and to permit the transferee to dispose of a portion of his holding provided that

(a)/

+ Appendix III C.

-10-

    (a) he is unable to cultivate adequately the holding to its full extent;

    (b) he will retain sufficient land for the maintenance of himself and his family; and

    (c) he will transfer the part of the land to persons approved by Government who have as their object to promote the intensive cultivation of the land.

The Demarcation Commission 14. To carry out the terms of the Agreement of 1921 it became necessary to appoint a Demarcation Commission, which took up its work in that year and has this year - after a decade - practically completed its laborious task. The lands actually allotted are as follows:-

    Cultivable and irrigable   - 111,720 dunams
    Cultivable but unirrigable - 123,334 dunams
    Unallotted waste (roads,etc.) - 146,717 dunams
                      Total   381,771 dunams

It is anticipated that in winding up the work within the next month or two some 3,000 more dunams may be obtainable from the waste for allotment to unsatisfied transferees.

15./

Present state of development in the tract

15. To complete the picture, it is necessary to add a few words as to the present state of the whole area. Assertions have been made that the state of cultivation in the tract is deplorable; and that the tribal lands are merely grazed over by a few wandering goatherds. The officer who presided over the Commission for 5½ years reported in 1928, when relinquishing charge of his office, that the population of these tribal areas was then about 2,000 persons: and considering the short time that had elapsed since parcellation of the lands, the development in a few of the villages had been remarkable. He regarded as the most important benefit conferred by the Agreement, the parcellation of fields among the various owners of lands previously owned in common. Where such partition had been longest in existence, improvement in cultivation was most noticeable. From the political point of view, the transferees were satisfied that the Government had confirmed them in what they deemed the rights of ownership of the lands. The discontent arising from the fear that they would be deprived of their occupation, which was rife in 1921, and which led to the turbulent scenes already referred to, had disappeared with the removal of the cause.

APPENDIX III B.

AGREEMENT BETWEEN THE GOVERNMENT OF PALESTINE
AND THE CULTIVATORS OF THE GHOR LANDS

dated 19th November, 1921

WHEREAS the lands described in the Schedule hereto were formerly registered in the name of Abdul Hamid II, Sultan of Turkey, and were treated by the Turkish Constitutional Government established in 1908 as State Lands (Mudawara) and leased to cultivators, subject to the payment of an annual rent amounting to 10 per cent. on the gross income in addition to the Tithes; and

Whereas the Government of Palestine has continued to collect the rental in addition to other taxes payable on Mudawara lands; and

Whereas the present cultivators have jointly appointed Wadie Eff. Bustany as their agent to deal with the Government of Palestine, and the High Commissioner for Palestine has appointed Major Albert Abramson, Chairman of the Land Commission, to enter into this Agreement on behalf of the Government of Palestine.

Now/

Now this is to witness that this Agreement has been made between the Government of Palestine and the cultivators of the land as a permanent settlement of their respective rights.

1. Subject to the conditions herein, the present cultivators of the Mudawara lands mentioned in the Schedule hereto shall become owners of Miri land, and the lands cultivated by them shall be transferred to them in the Land Register of the Government.

2. Subject to the provisions of Article 16 of this Agreement, the Title Deed (Kushan Tabu) to be given to the transferees shall be as valid as any Kushan held by owners of other Miri land; and it shall contain a clause that in case an adverse claim is made out to any land granted by the title deed (Kushan), the Government shall refund to the transferee the Transfer Price (Badal Tatweeb) paid by him for such land or such portion of the price as has been paid by him, together with such interest and damages as may be determined by the Court.

3./

3.-(1) A Land Registry Office shall be established at Beisan as long as required for the purpose of issuing title deeds to the transferees.

(2) No registration fee shall be payable for the issue of a Kushan except the sum of P.T.1 for the title deed. The Werko assessed on the Transfer Price and any other taxes due on Miri land shall be payable by the transferees as from the beginning of the financial year following the date of this Agreement.

4. Any arrears of tithes or rental due from a person entitled to a transfer shall be paid to the Government prior to the first instalment of the transfer price; until such payment is made the provisions of this Agreement shall not apply to him.

5. Areas of Metroukeh land necessary for the requirements of the villages shall be demarcated by the Commission to be appointed. Such areas shall comprise the land for public institutions and public use, such as mosques, schools, hospitals, public gardens for which

no/

no transfer price shall be charged. The title deed for Metroukeh areas shall be issued in the name of the village concerned.

6. No transfer price shall be paid in respect of the land on which houses and other buildings erected by the transferees are situate.

7.—(1) Each head of a family who has purchased or acquired by succession, or has exercised for ten years or more successively, cultivation rights shall be entitled to a transfer of the lands so held, and to have registered in his name as Miri property the whole of the area on which he has cultivated summer and winter crops during the last years whatever such area might be.

(2) Each adult married person at the date of this Agreement is recognised as the head of a separate family for the purposes of this Agreement, and a woman who is the head of a family shall have the same right as the male head of a family.

8./

8.-(1) A family which is found to have cultivated less than one hundred and fifty dunums shall be entitled to the transfer of an area which with the land that they have cultivated shall total in all one hundred and fifty dunums. If the family consists of more than five individuals, thirty additional dunums shall be transferred for each additional member.

(2) The area shall be allotted in localities as near as possible to the areas cultivated by the transferees or to the village where they live.

9.-(1) Where the transferees are members of a tribe, the lands transferred to all the members under this Agreement shall constitute one tribal area. The title deed (Kushan) for the tribal area shall contain a list of the heads of the families jointly owning the area. Nothing in this Article shall be construed to prevent the individual head of a family from obtaining a separate title deed for his holding in the event of the chiefs of the tribe consenting that such individual title deed shall be issued.

(2) The chief of the tribe shall be entrusted by the Government with the just allotment of the areas to individuals and with the collection and payment of taxes and tithes to the Government and of the instalments of the transfer price (Badal Tatweeb) due from the members of the tribe for the area pertaining to them; provided, however, that this shall not derogate from the liability of the individual for such payments in the event of the Chief failing to make payment.

(3) In addition to the provisions of Articles 7 and 8 of this Agreement, any family of those tribes generally living and cultivating on the west side of the Jordan which has not hitherto cultivated any area shall be entitled to the transfer of an area not exceeding one hundred and fifty dunums to be included in the above-mentioned tribal area.

10. An additional area for such tribes as live principally on their flocks and herds, to be known as the tribal grazing area, the extent of which shall be determined by the Department of Agriculture

after/

– 7 –

after the signing of this Agreement, shall be leased to the tribe on an annual rent so long as the tribe uses it fully for grazing purposes; provided that the Government may diminish the area in proportion as a tribe decreases its use for such purposes. The annual rental of such area per dunum shall be ascertained by dividing the total fees to be paid, according to the scale following, for animals belonging to the tribe at the date of the lease by the total number of dunums assigned for grazing to the tribe.

    For each goat or sheep .. 5 Milliemes per dunum
    For each horse, donkey, mule or cow .. .. .. 25 " " "
    For each camel .. .. .. 50 " " "

Where the inhabitants of a village live principally by their flocks and herds, they shall be entitled to a grazing area on the same terms as a tribe.

11. The District Commissioner shall deal according to equity with any exceptional cases of hardship to which the provisions of this Agreement do not strictly apply.

12./

12.—(1) The Transfer Price to be paid to the Government shall be 150 Egyptian Piastres per dunum of irrigable land, and P.T.125 per dunum of non-irrigable land payable with the tithes, in accordance with an undertaking to be signed by each transferee, in fifteen equal annual instalments within fifteen years of the date of the signature of this Agreement.

(2) No interest shall be charged on such amount for the first five years, but interest at the rate of six-and-a-half per cent. per annum shall be payable after the end of the fifth year on the instalments payable during the last ten years.

(3) Each transferee shall sign an undertaking to pay the transfer price (Badal Tatweeb), and shall not be entitled to the benefit of this Agreement until the undertaking is signed.

(4) If the transferee fails to pay any instalment due, the Government shall have the right to recover ten per cent. on the gross yield of the land for the period in which the payment is in arrear, together with any interest due on the outstanding instalment; and the amount recovered shall be credited to him on account of the transfer price.

The/

The transferee shall have the right to pay at any time any sum beyond the annual instalment.

13. If the transfer price (Badal Tatweeb) is not fully paid by the end of the fifteenth year, the transferee shall be deemed to have forfeited his right to his title deed and to have been a tenant of the Government. He shall pay to the Government a rental at the rate of ten per cent. on the gross yield of the area cultivated during the fifteen years, less the total of the instalments of the transfer price which he shall have paid; and he shall forfeit any interest prescribed in Article 12 which he may have paid on any instalment. He shall, however, retain his rights to any buildings erected or trees planted by him on the land, subject to the power of the Government to purchase the same from him at a fair compensation to be determined by arbitration.

14.-(1) The demarcation of the areas to be transferred and of the areas to be leased as grazing areas shall be carried out by a Commission composed of a representative of the Lands Department, a representative of the District Commissioner, and two representatives

elected/

elected by the transferees; it being understood that the latter shall not be entitled to any payment or allowances from the Government.

(2) The Commission shall have the powers of an Arbitration Tribunal for the purpose of carrying out this Agreement, and for settlement of any dispute which may arise in connection with the allotment of areas; provided that their award shall be subject to reference to the Courts in the same way as the award of any Arbitration Tribunal. In case of disagreement, the members of the Commission shall appoint a fifth person on the Tribunal for that particular case.

15. This Agreement shall be recognised by all the Courts in Palestine in the same way as a valid decree of the Government.

16. As from the date of this Agreement, all persons entitled under its provisions as transferees shall be deemed to be owners of Miri lands, and subject to the Laws relating to such lands, and free to exercise all the rights and privileges relative to the owners

of/

-11-

of Miri land, such as the planting of trees and the erection of buildings on the land transferred to them; provided that no disposition, except by way of mortgage to the Government or of succession, shall be made until the whole transfer price (Badal Tatweeb) has been paid.

17. The agent of the transferees may register a true copy of this Agreement with any Notary Public attached to any Court in Palestine.

The attached Arabic translation shall be treated as an official translation.

- - - - - - -

-12-

S C H E D U L E

Lands of Ashirat el Sugr;
Lands of Ashirat el Ghezawich on the West
  of the River Jordan;
Lands of Ashirat el Boshatweh on the West
  of the River Jordan;
Lands of Boisan Town;
Lands of Soreen Village;
Lands of Samakh;
Lands of Kefr Misr Village;
Lands of Tireh Village;
Lands of Denna Village;
Lands of Kefra Village;
Lands of Kawkab el Hawa Village;
Lands of Mutilleh Village;
Lands of Jobbool Village;
Lands of Yubla Village;
Lands of el Beereh Village;
Lands of el Murassa's Village;
Lands of Samrieh Village;
Lands of Farwaneh Village;
Lands of el Shrafieh Village;
Lands of Tel el Shak Village;
Lands of Jisr el Majamie Village;
Lands of Ghor el Faran

APPENDIX III C.

GHOR MUDAWWARAH AGREEMENT, 1921.

STATEMENT OF POLICY
(Published in Official Gazette of 16.9.38)

1. This Agreement signed in November, 1921, relates to a part of the Jiftlik estate in Palestine which lies in the Sub-Districts of Beisan, Tiberias and Nablus.

2. The principal object of the Agreement was to secure permanent settlement on the estate of those persons who were cultivators of the lands.

3. Under that Agreement a Commission was set up to examine the claims of all those who professed to be the "present cultivators" with whom the Government concluded the Agreement. Those whose claims were admitted became transferees under the Agreement and received holdings the size and character of which were determined in accordance with the terms of the Agreement.

4. Clause 12 of the Agreement is as follows:
" The Transfer Price (Badal Tatweeb) to be paid to the Government shall be 150 Egyptian Piastres per dunum of irrigable land and 125 Egyptian Piastres per dunum of non-irrigable

land/

land payable with the tithes in accordance with an undertaking to be signed by each transferee in 15 equal annual instalments within 15 years of the date of the signature of this Agreement.

" No interest shall be charged on such amount for the first five years, but interest at the rate of $6\frac{1}{2}$ per cent per annum shall be payable after the end of the fifth year on the instalments payable during the last ten years.

" Each transferee shall sign an undertaking to pay the transfer price (Badal Tatweeb) and shall not be entitled to the benefit of this Agreement until the undertaking is signed.

" If the transferee fails to pay any instalment due, the Government shall have the right to recover 10 per cent on the gross yield of the land for the period in which the payment is in arrear together with any interest due on the outstanding instalment; and the amount recovered shall be credited to him on account of the Transfer Price (Badal Tatweeb).

" The transferee shall have the right to pay at any time any sum beyond the annual instalment. "

5. It has been represented to Government that the period of 15 years is too short a time in which to redeem holdings especially when for climatic and other reasons cultivation

has/

has not led to an adequate return to the transferees

6. Government are prepared in appropriate circumstances and under certain conditions to modify in individual cases the terms of Clause 12 in the direction of extending the period within which the transfer price must be paid in full. The extended period will be from 25 to 30 years; and there will be a contingent condition that if a transferee defaults for two consecutive years in the payment of the reduced annual instalments of the purchase price, the shorter period of repayment prescribed by the original agreement will be re-applied.

7. It has also been represented to Government that in certain cases the transferees have not been able adequately to cultivate their holdings to the full extent. Under Clause 16 of the Agreement such transferees have been unable to make dispositions of their land except by way of mortgage to the Government or of succession until the whole transfer price has been paid.

8. Government are prepared under certain conditions to waive the requirement that the whole transfer price must be paid before the

transferee/

transferee has freedom to dispose of his surplus land.

The two principal conditions which attach to this modification of Clause 16 are:

(1) That the surplus land be transferred to persons approved by Government and having as their object the promotion of close settlement and the intensive cultivation of the land; and

(2) That in every case shall the transferee retain such extent of land in the area to which the Ghor Mudawwarah Agreement of 1921 applies or elsewhere as will in the opinion of Government suffice for the maintenance of himself and his family.

9. Detailed conditions on the modification proposed will be determined principally on individual applications. Such applications should be addressed to the Director of the Department of Lands, Jerusalem; and the Director will transmit these applications to the Government in the usual manner.

APPENDIX IV A

HISTORY OF THE HULEH CONCESSION

Nature of Concession and its terms.

1. What is known as the Huleh Concession was originally granted by the Ottoman Government in June 1914 to two Beirut merchants named Mohammed Omar Beyhum and Michael Sursock "for the drainage of Lake Huleh and the adjacent marshes". The lake and swamps comprised the State domain or Jiftlik: and it is noticeable that in the text of the Agreement the word "lake" nowhere occurs.

The conditions on which the concessionaires received the concession will be found set forth in full in Appendix IV B.

Action taken by concessionaires.

2. They duly received charge of the area, with instructions to commence operations; but did nothing: and in October 1915 they received permission for a postponement. Whether this permission was intended to cover all work is not clear: but no drainage work was carried out, although it appears from statements made to me by the concessionaires that the German engineers who were engaged in the requisite survey work were not, for personal reasons, at all anxious to expedite completion of their task as long as the war lasted.

3./

Transfer of concession to a company during the war	3. In March 1918 the Turkish Ministry certified that the concession had been taken over by a duly constituted corporation known as the Syreo-Ottoman Agricultural Company. In the latter part of the same year, the area of the concession, owing to the circumstances of the occupation of the northern part of Palestine, fell partly in the territory occupied by the British, and partly in that administered by the French. The concessionaires, as Syrians of Beirut, paid the rent demanded by the Syrian authorities for the years 1918 and 1919. In 1920 and 1921, however, they defaulted. During this time they were not in occupation of that part of the area which had been included in Palestine; and it was only in 1920 that application was made to the Palestine Administration for the recognition of the concession.
Negotiations with Secretary of State. Validity of concession accepted.	4. The position in regard to Ottoman concessions in Palestine during the military administration was that only those were recognised which were in actual operation prior to the Occupation. Accordingly, the Administration questioned the validity of the Huleh concession on various grounds. Negotiations took place; and finally the question was referred for the decision of the Secretary of State. In the opinion of the

Palestine/

Palestine Government there were grounds for accepting the validity of the concession: but there were also reasons which suggested the advisability of making modifications in the Agreement before it was confirmed. The Secretary of State, while upholding the validity of the Agreement, obtained the consent of the concessionaires to a revision of the terms suitable to the now economic conditions: and in 1924 it was arranged that a fresh concession should be substituted for the original Agreement.

Proposed new contract. 5. This arrangement provided that in consideration of the surrender of the old concession within one year, and the constitution within the same period of a new Company, having an authorised capital of £.250,000 and a subscribed capital of at least £.50,000, a fresh concession schedule should be granted.

Failure of concessionaires to execute. Their new claim. 6. This agreement the concessionaires on various grounds failed to implement; and in 1927 they claimed a further period of grace in order to enable them to negotiate with an English financial group. The Secretary of State agreed to this extension of time only on condition, inter alia, that the Ottoman Concession should be absolutely surrendered.

The/

The concessionaires, failing to obtain the help of their English supporters, finally fell back on the old Ottoman concession, and offered to sell to the Palestine Government their concessionary rights - an offer which was declined. They then claimed from Government the revenue of the Huleh area which had been collected from the time of the Occupation, with deduction of the rental fixed in the Ottoman Agreement. They based their claim on the fact that they had been in possession from July 1914: but that in October 1917 they had been deprived of the rents and profits of the lands, although they had actually paid rental to Government until September 1919.

Compensation paid to concessionaires for temporary dispossession.

7. The Palestine Government again referred the case to the Secretary of State, maintaining that the rights of the concessionaires in Palestine under the Ottoman concession did not become effective until the agreement made by the concessionaires with the Crown Agents in 1924 was finally determined by the former. They were not in possession in 1918 when the British forces occupied the Huleh area: and, therefore, they were not entitled to the benefit of the concession during the period prior to its recognition nor, consequentially, to the benefit

of it/

of it during the subsequent period when the Agreement of February 1924 was subsisting and the Ottoman concession was suspended. These contentions were not accepted by the Secretary of State; and arbitration on the dispute by a President of a Palestine District Court was accepted, with the result that in March 1930 Government paid the concessionaires compensation to the extent of £.3,585.

Meantime, in accordance with the arrangement made in December 1928 the concessionaires entered into possession of the lands on the 1st January 1929.

Plans of concessionaire for reclamation not yet approved.

8. Plans of the reclamation schemes proposed were submitted to Government by the concessionaires on the 19th June 1929: but up to the time of writing no such schemes have been definitely approved owing to failure on the part of the two parties to agree on the matter. A preliminary but integral portion of the drainage scheme, which involves the deepening of the Jordan channel below its outlet from Lake Huleh, is the reconstruction of the Benât Yakûb bridge across the Jordan. So far, no such reconstruction has taken place owing to disputes as to the plans submitted. A notarial notice, however, was served on the concessionaires by Government on the 17th January 1931, requiring them to begin the necessary works

within/

within six months of the approval of the plans and to complete them within six years.

Inaction of concessionaires. 9. The Inspection Commission, which is provided for under Article 22 of the Turkish concession, was appointed in the spring of this year: but, as no work of any importance has yet been carried out, it has not entered actively on its duties.

Failures of concessionaires to transfer their concession. 10. As noted by Sir John Hope Simpson at page 83 of his Report, unsuccessful attempts have been made by the concessionaires at times to sell their rights in the concession to outside parties.

The Rutenberg Jordan concession is subject to the pre-existing Hulch concession.

APPENDIX IV B.

GOVERNMENT OF PALESTINE

NOTICE

The following translation of the original Turkish Concession for the Drainage of Lake Huleh and the adjacent Marshes, is published for information.

S. MOODY
Acting Chief Secretary

6th November, 1931.

(Q/2a/31)

CONCESSION FOR THE DRAINAGE OF LAKE HULEH AND THE ADJACENT MARSHES

AGREEMENT
Concluded between

JAVID BEY, Minister of Finance, acting on behalf of the Imperial Ottoman Government, on the one part, and MUHAMMAD OMAR BEYHUM and MICHEL SURSOCK, merchants, of Beirut, on the other.

ARTICLE 1. A concession is granted to MUHAMMAD OMAR BEYHUM and MICHEL SURSOCK, by the Imperial Ottoman Government, for the drainage and reclamation of the Huleh marshes, consisting of Government land, and situated within the Kazas of Safad and Merj 'Ayun attached to the Beirut Villayet, in order that the marsh land aforesaid may be rendered fit for cultivation. The concession is granted subject to the following conditions, which have been agreed to by the Concessionaires.

ARTICLE 2. The Huleh marshes shall be handed over to the Concessionaires within a period of forty days as from the date upon which copies of this agreement are exchanged by the parties, in accordance with the contents of the map preserved in the Office of the Land Department, Beirut.

The Concessionaires shall, within one year as from the period above mentioned, draw up the necessary schemes of work and submit them to the Imperial Ministry of Public Works. The aforesaid schemes shall be examined within a period of three months as from the date at which they are submitted. Should they be approved, they will be adopted as they stand. In the contrary case, they will be adopted after the necessary modifications and corrections have been made. In the event of the formalities connected with the adoption of the schemes of work not being completed within a period of three months, such schemes shall be considered to have been adopted.

ARTICLE 3. The Concessionaires undertake to commence operations within a period of six months as from the date upon which the schemes of work drawn up by them are approved by the Imperial Ministry of Public Works, and to complete the work of reclamation within a period of six years. In the event of circumstances arising which amount to *force majeure*, however, of which timely notice shall be given in writing to the local authorities and the Imperial Ministries of Finance and Public Works, an additional period will be allowed within which to complete such reclamation, corresponding to the period during which operations have been interrupted owing to such circumstances. The work of reclamation shall be carried out on scientific lines, and in accordance with the approved schemes.

ARTICLE 4. Detailed maps and statements required in connection with the reclamation operations shall be drawn up by the Concessionaires and submitted to the Imperial Ministry of Public Works for examination, as follows: —

(1) A detailed topographical map shall be drawn up, to a scale of $\frac{1}{10,000}$ showing the position of the marshes and water channels. This map shall show at proper distances, all elevations and contour lines, together with figures, and shall contain all signs usual in topography. It shall also show the lower and upper levels of the marshes and the areas which are surrounded by water during flood time, whether ordinary or extraordinary, and the boundaries of areas which are under water either permanently or temporarily. In addition, a general map of the same nature shall be drawn up to the scale of $\frac{1}{100,000}$. Ten copies each of the detailed map and of the general map shall be sent to the Ministry of Public Works. All registers and records likely to prove the accuracy of the detailed map and that it reproduces the actual position of the land, and all figures and records showing in what manner the reclamation operations are being carried out, may at any time be examined by technical officials to be appointed by the Ministry of Public Works. All level indicators to be set up on the land whether made of stone, or of wrought iron, or consisting of wooden pegs and used for the preparation of the map or thereafter for putting the schemes of work into execution on the land, or for determining the site for technical operations, shall be affixed in a solid manner. In order that the position of such indicators may easily be identified in the future, and in order that new ones may be erected in the event of any being lost, a list thereof, together with a map, shall be drawn up.

(2) The places into which the water coming from the marshes to be reclaimed, and from elevated regions in the neighbourhood thereof, and from mountains and hills, is to be conducted by channels to be constructed for such purpose, shall be shown on the maps, and the volume thereof calculated. A record shall be kept by means of special instruments showing the amount of rainfall, the degree of heat, humidity, and evaporation of the air during the various seasons over the whole concession area. The results shall be sent regularly each year to the Imperial Ministry of Public Works.

(3) The Concessionaires shall show in red, on a copy of both the detailed and general maps, the operations they propose to carry out. After approval or modification, such operations shall be entered on the other copies. Plans of the water courses shall be drawn up longitudinally and submitted, to the scale of $\frac{1}{10,000}$ in length and $\frac{1}{50}$ in height. Plans of the technical operations and of the water courses showing cross sections shall be drawn up as may be necessary to a scale of $\frac{1}{200}$ or $\frac{1}{50}$. The places where the trial operations are

carried out with a view to determining the foundations of the technical operations, and the results thereof, shall also be shown on these maps.

(4) The area of the marshes to be reclaimed and the area of any land lying within the boundaries thereof which is owned by a private owner shall be shown on a map to the scale of $\frac{1}{1000}$. The Concessionaires shall submit a memorandum together with the map and plans which shall contain detailed technical explanations of any scheme or work adopted or arrangements made.

The necessary hydrographic calculations shall be furnished in order that the cross sections of the water channels may be determined. Figures shall also be furnished showing resistance in order that the distances separating the various technical undertakings may be established.

ARTICLE 5. All work, the execution of which is deemed necessary, such as the opening of canals and construction of bunds with a view to the reclamation and improvement of land within the concession area, the boundaries of which are to be defined, and which are either permanently or temporarily under water; the cleansing of existing water courses; and the filling up of any particular area; shall be shown on the plans.

ARTICLE 6. The Concessionaires, in order to ensure the carrying out and successful termination of the work of reclamation, shall have the right of demanding the alteration, destruction, or removal of the canals, dams or intakes which belong to private persons and are situated on the land to be reclaimed, on condition that they compensate the owners thereof. Any obstacles found in the said water courses, such as the pillars of old bridges, stakes, or debris, may be removed.

ARTICLE 7. The Concessionaires are bound to maintain at their own expense any roads and paths, whether great or small, which are crossed by new canals or water courses. Should it be found necessary to change the direction of any of such roads or paths adjoining the area where work is being carried on, the gradient of such alterations, wherever they occur, should not exceed the maximum gradient already existing elsewhere. The breadth of the bridges to be built over canals and creeks may vary between three and ten metres. The actual width of such bridges and the type of construction, shall be determined by the Government. The Imperial Government shall have the right of constructing bridges and roads over canals, water courses and creeks of such a breadth as to ensure the easy flow of water therein.

ARTICLE 8. Building material shall be of the best quality and all work shall be carried out on scientific lines.

ARTICLE 9: Should any farmers or land owners, who have hitherto benefitted by the waters of the Huleh marshes, suffer any loss in consequence of the reclamation operations, the Concessionaires are responsible for ensuring their supply of water as formerly. Should this be impossible, the Concessionaires shall indemnify them for any loss which may result. Similarly, should

— 4 —

any land which is now protected from being submerged be flooded, in whole or in part, by reason of the reclamation operations, the Concessionaires shall drain such land at their own expense and compensate such persons for any loss or damage they may suffer.

ARTICLE 10. Should the Concessionaires and the land owners fail to come to an agreement regarding the expropriation of lands, buildings, etc., in the possession of private persons, the expropriation of which is essential, in the public interest, to the carrying out of the reclamation operations, action shall be taken in accordance with the Law of Expropriation. Should it be necessary to occupy any land temporarily while operations are being carried on, such land may be used for the time being, provided that the owners shall be compensated by the Concessionaires, through the Imperial Government. If unoccupied Government land happens to fall within the areas required for the operations, and any work dependent thereon, such land shall be given free of charge to the Concessionaires. Should any part of such land be required for temporary use during the course of the operations, such land may be utilised free of charge.

Maps prepared with a view to expropriation and occupation of land shall be to a scale of $\frac{1}{1000}$. In cases, however, where this scale proves to be insufficient, the Concessionaires may have maps drawn up to a larger scale, as may be necessary.

ARTICLE 11. Any modification which may be made during the course of the operations to schemes of work already approved, and similarly, any schemes drawn up with regard to new and additional works, the execution of which is considered to be necessary, shall be submitted for approval to the Ministry of Public Works, in accordance with the provisions of Article 2 hereof.

ARTICLE 12. Upon the Concessionaires stating that they have completed the undertaking, a report shall be drawn up by a technical Commission appointed by the Imperial Ministries of Finance and Public Works, containing the results of an examination made by them and thereupon a provisional acceptance shall be granted. After the expiration of a period of two years from the date of the provisional acceptance, a further examination of the undertaking shall be carried out by a technical Commission. If it appears that the work has been carried out in accordance with the terms of this Agreement and with due observance of technical principles, and that the Concessionaires have fulfilled all the undertakings contained in this Agreement, final acceptance shall be granted. Travelling and any other expenses properly incurred by the Commission shall be borne by the Concessionaires.

ARTICLE 13. With a view to ensuring the due performance of their undertakings, the Concessionaires shall, within one month from the date of the confirmation of this Agreement, deposit at the Ottoman Bank, a guarantee to the amount of one thousand Turkish pounds either in cash or in Turkish Treasury Bonds at market value. If bonds are deposited and depreciate in value, the Bank undertakes to make good any loss. This guarantee shall be refunded after the provisional acceptance has been granted. If within the said month, the Concessionaires fail to deposit the necessary guarantee, they shall lose all rights under the concession, there being no need for any legal steps to be taken, nor any protests served.

ARTICLE 14. The Concessionaires shall, within a period of twelve months as from the date of the exchange of copies of this Agreement, form an Ottoman Limited Liability Company in accordance with the relevant Regulations. The shares shall bear the name of their holders, who must be Ottoman subjects, born of Ottoman parents and grandparents. The Articles of Association must be confirmed by the Ministry of Commerce and Agriculture in the usual way, and the concession shall be transferred to the Company, failing which, the Concession shall be rescinded, without taking any legal steps in the matter.

ARTICLE 15. The Imperial Government reserves the right of setting up such trenches and fortifications as may be deemed necessary within the concession area, and the Concessionaires shall have no right of claiming damages in respect thereof.

ARTICLE 16. Upon the completion of the undertaking and after final acceptance has been given, a Committee of six shall be set up with a view to ensuring the permanent working of the undertaking. Three members shall be elected by the Ottoman Limited Company on behalf of the Concessionaires, and all land owners concerned. The other three shall be appointed by the Government. The duty of this body shall be to supervise the proper working of the improvements made, in order that each person concerned may be guaranteed the enjoyment of his portion of the property and the proportional benefit accruing thereto. The members elected by the land owners must be agreed to and confirmed in their posts by the Government. All Regulations regarding general procedure, moneys to be collected, and the expenditure thereof shall be submitted to the Imperial Government for approval.

ARTICLE 17. Apart from the tithe payable to the Treasury in respect to land situated within the marshes and now under cultivation, the Concessionaires shall pay annually into the Imperial Treasury a sum equivalent to the whole of what is due in respect to such land, calculated on the average of the preceding five years. These sums shall be paid until such time as a title deed has been delivered in respect to the land, after reclamation, conferring the ownership thereof upon the Concessionaires.

ARTICLE 18. As soon as the reclamation and cultivation of the land has been commenced, the Concessionaires shall pay to the Government a total sum of LT. 20,000, this being at the rate of LT. 2 per dunam in reference to an area of approximately 10,000 dunams reclaimed by the cultivators, whereupon a title deed shall be issued to the Concessionaires conferring the ownership of the land upon them. The Concessionaires shall then sell the land to the former cultivators concerned, upon payment of reasonable instalments, after adding the approximate expenses occasioned by the reclamation of the ten thousand dunams in question, together with the legal rate of interest.

ARTICLE 19. After the marshes have been reclaimed, the land shall be surveyed and registered at the Land Registry in the name of the Company, on behalf of the Concessionaires, at the rate of two Turkish pounds per dunam. The price shall be paid to the Government without interest, and in equal instalments, within a period of fifteen years as from the termination of the period of six years allowed for reclamation. The fixed instalments shall be payable in the month of November of each year. Should payment not be effected by that date, the land shall be attached and legal action taken according. The Concessionaires or the Company on their behalf, shall pay a rent in respect to the produce obtained from the parts reclaimed during the period of six years allowed for reclamation, equal to the rent payable in the case of similar land.

ARTICLE 20. The hotel and the inn and the shops belonging to the Treasury and situated in the neighbourhood of Jisr-Banat Ya'qub shall be sold to the Concessionaires at prices to be estimated in the ordinary way. These buildings shall be delivered immediately, together with the land, to the Concessionaires. Upon the expiration of the period allowed for reclamation, the ownership of the buildings, together with the land, shall be conferred upon the Concessionaires, the value thereof being paid forthwith to the Treasury. The Concessionaires, shall pay the rent due each year in respect to the period intervening between the date of this Agreement and the date of the transfer of ownership, on the basis of the rent at present payable.

ARTICLE 21. The dues payable in respect of *halfa*, papyrus, and fishing obtained from the marshes and the lake have been put up to auction by the Imperial Government on behalf of the Treasury for a period of five years as from the year 1329, and the amount produced in shells for a period of three years. In the event of the Concessionaires being unable to come to any understanding with the persons to whom the collection of the dues has been auctioned, the matter shall be settled by arbitrators to be appointed by the parties. Should this be impossible, the question shall be settled by a second arbitrator to be elected by the Administrative Council.

ARTICLE 22. Special commissioners shall carry out an inspection of the work and all other operations and undertakings relating to this Concession until the date of final acceptance, in order to ascertain whether such work is being properly done. A monthly inspection fee of LT. 15 shall be payable by the Company on behalf of the Concessionaires as from the date of delivery of the land until provisional acceptance is granted.

ARTICLE 23. The Concessionaires, or the Company on their behalf, shall be subject to all present and future laws and regulations of the State. All technical officials, workmen, and other employees who may be required for these operations, shall be Ottoman subjects, with the exception of a chief engineer, who may be a foreigner.

ARTICLE 24. Antiquities and the like which may be discovered during the operations, shall be dealt with according to the special regulations relating thereto.

ARTICLE 25. If during the operations the Government shall deem it necessary to instal technical officers or gendarmes, the buildings necessary for their accommodation shall be set up by the Concessionaires.

ARTICLE 26. As from the date of the exchange of copies of this Agreement until final acceptance, the Company, on behalf of the Concessionaires, shall establish its registered office at Beirut, or shall have in that town a duly authorised representative empowered to serve and receive service of

— 7 —

uments, to institute and to defend actions and to perform all acts necessary in connection with a power of attorney, failing which, service on the Municipality shall be considered to be service on the Company on behalf of the Concessionaires.

ARTICLE 27. Any dispute arising between the Imperial Government and the Concessionaires regarding the application of the terms of this Agreement, shall be settled by the Imperial Council of State. Any other actions between the Concessionaires and private individuals shall be settled in the Ottoman Courts concerned.

ARTICLE 28. Should it become necessary to pull down the Banat-Ya'qub Bridge, the Company, on behalf of the Concessionaires, shall put up another, the site, design and type of which shall be approved by the Ministry of Public Works.

ARTICLE 29. If the Company, on behalf of the Concessionaires, fails to prepare the plans according to the terms of this Agreement and within the period fixed therein, or in the event of its failing to complete the operations specified in the approved scheme of work without any justification such as *force majeure*, or in the event of failure to fulfil its obligations after being granted a reasonable period in which to do so and after due notification by the Ministries of Finance and Public Works, the guarantee shall be confiscated and the concession cancelled.

In the event of the concession being rescinded, the whole undertaking, including building machinery and implements shall be valued and put up for public auction, after the Concessionaires have been heard, with a view to ensuring the continuation and completion of the undertaking and all the commitments of the Concessionaires.

Neither the Company nor any person considered unsuitable or who has failed to pay the guarantee referred to in this Agreement may bid at the auction. The person acquiring the undertaking by virtue of this auction will be subject to the terms of this Agreement, and all rights and liabilities of the Concessionaires will be transferred to him. After deducting expenses occasioned by the auction as well as all other expenses, the amount realized will be payable to the Concessionaires.

Should no bid be made at the auction a second auction shall be held after the expiration of three months without estimating the value of the undertaking.

Should no bids be made at this second auction, the Concessionaires shall lose all their rights in the undertaking, which shall be transferred to the Ministry of Finance free of all cost and any charges whatsoever, together with all tools, implements and equipment. Should the Concessionaires desire to bid at the auction they should deposit a fresh guarantee of twice the amount of the guarantee which has been attached.

This contract has been drawn up in two copies and signed and exchanged in Constantinople, dated June, 1330.

7.05

PALESTINE

COMMITMENTS IN CONNECTION WITH LAND SETTLEMENT AND DEVELOPMENT.

5

Reference	Commitments	Remarks
	I. Settlement of Arabs.	
(1) 1930 Statement of Policy - Cmd 3692, para.15	"Even were the title of the Government to these areas" (i.e. areas claimed as Government land) "admitted, and it is in many cases disputed, it would not be possible to make these areas available for Jewish settlement in view of their actual occupation by Arab cultivators and of the importance of making available additional land on which to place the Arab cultivators who are now landless."	
(2) Prime Minister's letter M.E.No.39, para.9.	"The landless Arabs to whom it was intended to refer in the passage quoted" (see above) "were such Arabs as can be shown to have been displaced from the lands which they occupied in consequence of the lands passing into Jewish hands, and who have not obtained other holdings on which they can establish themselves or other equally satisfactory occupation. The number of such displaced Arabs must be a matter for careful enquiry. It is to landless Arabs within this category that His Majesty's Government feel themselves under an obligation to facilitate their settlement upon the land."	
(3) Prime Minister's letter, para.15.	"That principle" (i.e. the principle of 'absorptive capacity') "is vital to any scheme of development. The primary purpose of which must be the settlement both of Jews and of displaced Arabs upon the land."	
(4) Dr Shiels' speech in House of Commons on 17th November, 1930. Hansard 5th series, vol.245, columns 95 and 96.	"The scheme" (i.e. the development scheme) "is intended in the first place to provide for those landless Arabs who can be shown to have been dispossessed as a result of land passing into Jewish hands, and any balance will be available for both Jewish and Arab settlement."	

Reference	Commitments	Remarks
(5) Secretary of State's despatch No. 487 of 26th June, 1931.	"5(3) The Director of Development will prepare a register of such Arabs as can be shown to have been displaced. He will draw up a scheme of resettlement of registered displaced Arab families, with an estimate of cost. When the scheme has been approved by the High Commissioner, the resettlement will be carried out as quickly as possible."	Director of Development has been appointed: Register of displaced Arabs is in course of preparation. Director's Supplementary Report contains proposals for settlement within next 18 months of between 100 and 200 displaced Arabs at a cost of £400 per family, and contemplates further resettlements as opportunity offers on irrigated lands at a cost of £800 per family.
(6) Sir A. Wauchope's statement to Arab Executive (with authority of Secretary of State) on 27th January, 1932. No. 18 on 97049/32.	"The object which H.M.G. had in view was to take early action, if financial circumstances permit, to put into operation a scheme of development, limited in its scope, providing first for the resettlement of Arabs who had been displaced, etc., and second for some assistance to Jewish settlement in Palestine."	

II Settlement of Jews.

(1) Palestine Mandate, Article 6.	"The Administration of Palestine, while ensuring that the rights and position of other sections of the population are not prejudiced, shall facilitate Jewish immigration under suitable conditions, and shall encourage, in cooperation with the Jewish Agency,..... close settlement by Jews on the land, including state lands and waste lands not required for public purposes."	

Reference	Commitments	Remarks
(2) 1930 Statement of Policy – Cmd 3692, para.21.	"It is the duty of the Administration under the Mandate to ensure that the position of the 'other sections of the population' is not prejudiced by Jewish immigration. <u>Also it is its duty under the Mandate to encourage close settlement of Jews on the land, subject always to the former condition.</u>"	
(3) do. para.23.	"Only by the adoption of such a policy" (i.e. methodical agricultural development) "will additional Jewish agricultural settlement be possible..... It is for this reason fortunate that the Jewish organisations are in possession of a large reserve of land....."	
(4) Prime Minister's letter M.E.No.39 para.10.	"It is the intention of H.M.G. to institute an enquiry as soon as possible to ascertain <u>inter alia</u> what state and other lands are or properly can be made available for close settlement by Jews, under reference to the obligation imposed upon the Mandatory by Article 6 of the Mandate. This enquiry will be comprehensive in its scope and will include the whole land resources of Palestine. In the conduct of the enquiry provision will be made for all interests, whether Jewish or Arab, making such representations as it may be desired to put forward." (N.B. The minutes of meetings between Jewish representatives and the Cabinet Committee, when the terms of the Prime Minister's letter were under consideration, show that it was agreed on both sides that the special purpose of this enquiry was to ascertain whether land for Jewish settlement could be made available in the Huleh and Beisan areas.)	The Reports of the Director of Development show that he has already examined this question and that, pending further investigation beginning with a hydrographic survey, it is not possible to make any definite statement with regard to the possibilities of Huleh or Beisan for Jewish or Arab settlement. Appended to the Reports is a long list of state lands which have been examined by the Director, and which for various reasons offer no possibilities.
(5) Prime Minister's letter, para.15.	See under I(5) above.	

Reference	Commitments	Remarks
(6) Secretary of State's despatch No.487 of 26th June, 1931, para.2(c)(iii)(2).	"Enquiry into land resources to ascertain what state or other lands can be made available for close settlement by Jews." - see under 2( ) above.	
(7) Sir A. Wauchope's statement to Jewish Agency (with authority of Secretary of State) on 27th January, 1932.	See under 1(6) above.	The Reports of the Director of Development contain no proposal for direct assistance of Jewish settlement. The possibilities of Huleh and Beisan (see above) cannot be ascertained for some time, and even if these areas were found suitable it would be uneconomic to promote new settlements there until the possibilities of the coastal plain (which calls for no costly irrigation works) have been exhausted. Furthermore, there is a danger in bringing in new settlers until the market prospects for citrus fruits are more certain.

III Agricultural Development.

Reference	Commitments	Remarks
(1) Palestine Mandate, Article 11.	"The Administration shall introduce a land system appropriate to the needs of the country, having regard, among other things, to the desirability of promoting the close settlement and intensive cultivation of the land."	

Reference	Commitments	Remarks
(2) 1930 Statement of Policy - Cmd.3692, paras 22 and 23.	"H.M.G. are satisfied that in order to attain these objects" (i.e. close settlement of Jews on land without prejudice to other sections of the population) "a more methodical agricultural development is called for, with the object of ensuring a better use of the land..... The result desired will not be obtained except by years of work..... (Jewish) operations can continue without break while more general steps of development, in the benefits of which Jews and Arabs can both share, are being worked out."	
(3) Prime Minister's letter M.E.No.39 para.9.	"The recognition of this obligation" (i.e. the obligation to resettle displaced Arabs) "in no way detracts from the larger purposes of development which H.M.G. regards as the most effectual means of furthering the establishment of a national home for the Jews.	
(4) Prime Minister's letter, para.11.	"The question of the congestion amongst the fellahin in the hill districts..... is receiving the careful consideration of H.M.G. It is contemplated that measures will be devised for the improvement and intensive development of the land and for bringing into cultivation areas which hitherto may have remained uncultivated, and thereby securing to the fellahin a better standard of living without, save in exceptional cases, having recourse to transfer."	This is dealt with in Mr French's Reports.
(5) Prime Minister's letter, para.13.	"H.M.G. feel bound to point out that they alone of the Governments which have been responsible for the administration of Palestine since the acceptance of the Mandate have declared their definite intention to initiate an active policy of development, which, it is believed, will result in substantial and lasting benefit to both Jews and Arabs."	

Reference	Commitments	Remarks
(6) Dr Shiels in House of Commons on 17th November, 1930, Hansard 5th Series, para. 245.	"His Majesty's Government have come to the conclusion that to achieve the object in view, it is necessary to provide for an expenditure not exceeding £2,500,000, a large part of which would be devoted to works of a productive character..... namely, irrigation, drainage and other schemes designed to increase the general productivity of the country, and which it is estimated would provide for the settlement on the land of approximately 10,000 families. In view of the present financial situation in Palestine, the only way in which a sum of this magnitude can be provided is by means of a loan under the guarantee of H.M.G. During the first years of the development scheme it will be necessary to provide from British votes such annual amounts as may be required to meet the interest and Sinking Fund charges upon the loan."	
(7) Secretary of State's despatch No. 487 of 26th June, 1931.	Duties of Director of Development. "This investigation would also cover the question of credits for Arab cultivators and Jewish settlers, and proposals for draining, irrigating, or otherwise reclaiming land at present wholly or partially uncultivated."	Mr French's Reports urge the early encouragement of cooperative credit societies amongst Arab cultivators. As regards long term credits for Jewish settlers, Mr French and Mr Skevington are unable to approve the Jewish proposal for an Agricultural Bank, while prepared to consider the question of facilitating such credits on a business basis at some future date for the purpose of enabling settlers

Reference	Commitments	Remarks
		settlers to improve the productivity of their holdings, they think that existing facilities in this respect are adequate.
	IV Allocation of Development Funds.	
(1) Dr Shiels' speech in House of Commons on 17th November, 1930.	Guaranteed loan of £2,500,000 - see under III(6) above. "The scheme is intended in the first place to provide for those landless Arabs who can be shown to have been dispossessed as a result of land passing into Jewish hands, and any balance will be available for both Jewish and Arab settlement.	
(2) Permanent Mandates Commission, June, 1931.	In June 1931 the Permanent Mandates Commission was informed of the proposal to raise a development loan of £2,500,000.	
(3) Secretary of State's despatch No.487 of 26th June, 1931.	"It is the intention that the funds required for this purpose" (i.e. the development policy outlined in paragraphs 21-25 of Cmd 3692 and in paragraphs 9 to 13 of the Prime Minister's letter) "should be found by means of a loan which Parliament will be asked to authorise H.M.G. to guarantee. The Director will draw up a scheme of resettlement of registered displaced Arab families with as close an estimate as possible of the cost. When the scheme has been approved by the High Commissioner, the resettlement will be carried out as quickly as possible. Further, the Director will investigate the methods to be adopted to give effect, <u>within the limits of the funds available</u> to the intention of H.M.G. as to the policy of land settlement as outlined in paragraphs 10 and 11 of the Prime Minister's letter."	
	"It	

Reference	Commitments	Remarks
	"It is the intention of H.M.G. to authorise the High Commissioner to incur expenditure not exceeding £50,000 in the foregoing investigation, including all necessary surveys and experiments, such expenditure being met in the first instance from Palestine funds."	Provision of £50,000 sanctioned and devoted towards the cost of development.
(4) Sir A.Wauchope's statement to Arab Executive and Jewish Agency on 27th January, 1932 (encl. in No.18 in 97049/32 Pt 2.)	"While it was not possible for him at this stage to say anything definite about the provision of funds for development purposes, he could tell them that the object which H.M.G. had in view was to take early action, if financial circumstances permit, to put into operation a scheme of development, limited in its scope, providing first for the resettlement of Arabs.. ... and second for some assistance to Jewish settlement in Palestine."	
(5) Sir A.Wauchope's statement to Dr Arlosoroff on 27th January, 1932.	"He"(the High Commissioner)"did not interpret the intention to be that the whole Arab share should be expended first, and then the Jewish share, but of course freedom of action must be allowed." "His Excellency said that the direct deduction from the instructions he had received was that, if a loan was sanctioned, then a portion, though what portion he did not know, of the funds would be devoted to the benefit of Jewish settlement." "His Excellency said he imagined that the first duty of the Development Commission would be to resettle a number of displaced Arabs; but that did not mean that a portion of the funds should not be spent simultaneously on objects that would be for the benefit of Jewish interests."	Mr French's Reports recommend immediate expenditure of possibly £60,000 on settling 150 families of displaced Arabs within the next 18 months, and the gradual settlement of other Arabs, between 1,000 and 2,000 in all, on irrigated lands, as may be possible in future, at a cost of £800 per family. Mr French also recommends a Government contribution of £32,000 to the Jewish Agricultural Research Station; £8,000 on a hydrographic survey

Reference	Commitments	Remarks
		survey which will in the first place enable the possibilities of Huleh and Beisan to be determined; recurrent reaching a maximum of £20,000 a year on the appointment of village Registrars; £7,500, spread over 3 years, on the appointment of special staff for the partition of mesha'a lands, and an unstated sum on experiments in animal feeding and breeding; also £12,000, spread over 8 years, on additional survey staff, if this is found to be necessary in connection with land settlement.

V Land Legislation.

(1) Statement of Policy 1930 - Cmd 3692., paras 23 and 24.	"During this period" (i.e. while the development scheme is being worked out) "the control of all disposition of land must of necessity rest with the authority in charge of the development. Transfers of land will be permitted only in so far as they do not interfere with the plans of that authority. Having regard to the responsibilities of the Mandatory Power, it is clear that this authority must be the Palestine Administration."	
	"Consideration must also be given to the protection of tenants by some form of occupancy right, or by other means, to secure them against ejectment or the imposition of excessive rental."	

Reference	Commitments	Remarks
(2) Prime Minister's letter, February 1931, paras 12. and 13.	"In giving effect to the policy of land settlement as contemplated in Article 11 of the Mandate, it is necessary, if disorganisation is to be avoided and if the policy is to have a chance to succeed, that there should exist some centralised control of transactions relating to the acquisition and transference of land during such interim period as may reasonably be necessary to place the Development Scheme upon a sure foundation. The power contemplated is regulative and not prohibitory, although it does involve a power to prevent transactions which are inconsistent with the tenour of the scheme. But the exercise of the power will be limited and in no respect arbitrary. In every case it will be conditioned by considerations as to how best to give effect to the purposes of the Mandate. Any control contemplated will be fenced with due safeguards to secure as little interference as possible with the free transfer of land. The centralised control will take effect as from such date only as the authority charged with the duty of carrying out the policy of land development shall begin to operate. The High Commissioner will, pending the establishment of such centralised control, have full powers to take all steps necessary to protect the tenancy and occupancy rights, including the rights of squatters, throughout Palestine." "Further, the Statement of Policy of H.M.G. did not imply a prohibition of acquisition of additional land by Jews. It contains no such prohibition, nor is any such intended. What it does contemplate is such temporary control of land disposition and transfers as may be necessary not to impair the harmony and effectiveness of the scheme of land settlement to be undertaken."	

Reference	Commitments	Remarks
(3) Statement of British Accredited Representative to Permanent Mandates Commission - Cmd 3552 May 1930.	"Legislation is to be introduced with the object of controlling the disposition of agricultural lands in such a manner as to prevent the disposition of the indigenous agricultural population. These temporary measures will be superseded in any case by such permanent enactments as may be decided upon when future policy is determined in the light of Sir J.Hope Simpson's Report."	
(4) Dr Shiels' reply to Colonel Howard-Bury, 2nd June, 1931.	"In accordance with the last sentence of paragraph 12 of the Prime Minister's letter to Dr Weizmann of 13th February, an Ordinance was promulgated on Friday last to protect tenancy and occupancy rights (Protection of Cultivators Amendment Ordinance 1931), including the rights of squatters throughout Palestine. As stated in the preceding part of that paragraph, the centralised control of land transactions will take effect as from such date only as the authority charged with the duty of carrying out the policy of land settlement shall begin to operate."	Mr French recommends the enactment of two land Ordinances (a) the Homesteads Protection Ordinance, and (b) the Occupancy Tenants Ordinance, both directed towards keeping the Arab cultivator on his land. The former Ordinance involves general control of transfers of agricultural land, and the second apparently replaces the Protection of Cultivators Ordinance. The question whether the proposed Ordinances could be enacted without infringeing any of the commitments given to the Jews is discussed on 97072/32.
(5) Sir A.Wauchope's statement to Dr Arlosoroff on 27th January 1932, in 97049/32, Pt.2.	"His Excellency said he could not give a guarantee that the proposed land Ordinance restricting purchase and lease of land over the whole country would be abandoned, because H.M.G. had not given such a guarantee. But he could say that he had no intention at present of asking for permission to enact such an Ordinance, as he saw no necessity for it in connection with the work at present on hand. Nor did he think such an Ordinance to be necessary for Mr French in his present task of finding immediate remedies to deal with the present situation. "His Excellency said that Government could not bind itself for	

7.06

19th January, 1932.

My dear Wauchope,

I told you in my last letter of my plan to submit to the Cabinet a memorandum on all the big outstanding questions of Palestine policy. We have done a good deal of work on this memorandum, and I am now in a position to send you, for your criticism, the first two Parts. I propose to divide the memorandum into three Parts; Part I - The proposed Legislative Council; Part II - Immigration; Part III - Land settlement and cognate problems. I propose that, in the covering memorandum, I should summarise as shortly as I can the various commitments which successive Governments have made and the action taken up to date, and set out the policy under each head which I think we ought to follow and which I shall ask the Cabinet to endorse. I shall attach appendices, which will be much longer and fuller documents, elaborating the covering memorandum.

Parts I and II of the covering memorandum and their appendices are now ready and I send them herewith. Part III is much more complicated. Nor can it be finally drafted until we have French's special report and your recommendations. We are, however, working on a rough skeleton of this, in which the commitments and facts up to the present will be set out, and also the general line of policy which we propose hereunder/within.

  I think on all the questions you and I are in substantial agreement, but of course I want you to criticise absolutely frankly and to make any alternative suggestions.

  I have answered your telegram about the preparation of an immediate settlement scheme as well as I can. You will appreciate that I cannot give you a final answer until I have discussed the position with the Chancellor and with the Cabinet. I cannot usefully embark on such discussions until

until I am able to put up a concrete scheme and an estimate of the cost, and this is impossible until I have the general outline of your scheme. I think, therefore, that clearly you must go ahead with the preparation of the scheme, but you must make it clear that in present financial circumstances you cannot guarantee when a scheme requiring a British Loan (and particularly if it be a guaranteed loan) could be undertaken.

Your telegram also raises the question of whether the settlement scheme should include some provision for Jews or be confined to displaced Arabs. Here again, I think I shall be bound to put this proposition to the Cabinet as part of the policy questions which I shall submit in the memorandum. At the same time I think that in fact there is an implicit commitment (to put it no higher) that the development scheme will include some provision for Jews. Moreover, whether this is so or not, I believe it would be politically impossible from your point of view to confine the scheme exclusively to displaced Arabs. I know this is your own view, and in the circumstances I felt justified in answering your question by
saying

saying I agreed that the scheme ought to contain some provision for Jews.

There is one point of detail which I have not raised as an issue in the memorandum, on which I should like your advice, namely, the conditions attaching to the reduction of the independent means limit from £1,000 to £500. As I understood it, the limit is now fixed at £500, subject to the approval of the Immigration Officer in any particular case. Is this qualification really worth maintaining? Its maintenance obviously detracts from the face value of the concession. I should have thought that its practical value was small, and that it was a very difficult and invidious task for the Officer to discriminate between one entrant and another, and to say that a man who would be admitted if he had £1,000 was such a waster that you would exclude him if he only had £500. Nor, as I understand it, if means be the test, could you say that a £500 man was to be excluded because you don't think he would have a chance of carrying on his particular trade while you would have to admit him if he had £1,000. You would really there be applying not an independent means test but an absorptive capacity test.

I appreciate what you say that the Arabs would have liked it better if my message to the Jews had contained something about the other side of the Mandate. The message which I gave was very anodyne in its character, and if I had added to it something about the Arabs, it would have discounted its value to the Jewish Agency to a minus quantity. I really don't think that anyone could construe the message into an undue preference.

Yours very sincerely,

(SD) P. CUNLIFFE-LISTER

CABINET.

PALESTINE.

Memorandum by the Secretary of State for the Colonies.

There are certain questions of policy affecting Palestine on which I consider it essential to have a decision by the Government. These are -

(1) The setting up of a Legislative Council;
(2) Jewish immigration;
(3) Development and Land Legislation.

In this memorandum these three questions are dealt with so as to indicate briefly in regard to each the position as to existing commitments and action already taken; followed by a discussion of action now to be taken and the conclusions which I recommend for adoption.

More detailed information on all three subjects is given in the Appendix.

(1) Legislative Council.

(i) Commitments.

His Majesty's Government are committed to taking some action for the establishment of a Legislative Council by Article 2 of the Mandate, the statements of policy published in 1922 and in October, 1930, and by a statement by the accredited representative at the 20th Session of the Permanent Mandates Commission at Geneva.

(ii) Action already taken.

Provision was made in 1922 by Orders in Council for the Constitution of a Legislative Council with an unofficial majority, which would be

on

on an elective basis. An Arab boycott of the elections led to the substitution of an Advisory Council of officials. Fresh proposals for a Legislative Council were submitted by the High Commissioner in 1929. Consideration of these proposals was deferred in consequence of the disturbances of that year but revised proposals were put forward by Sir John Chancellor in August, 1931, on which the new High Commissioner, Sir Arthur Wauchope, has been invited to express his views.

(iii) <u>Action now to be taken.</u>

On the one hand it may be argued, as Sir John Chancellor did, that it is impossible to continue to resist the pressure of the Arabs for a measure of self-government; further, that a Legislative Council might help to reconcile the conflicting interests of the Jews and Arabs. On the other hand it must be noted that the Arabs have never ~~accepted the Mandate~~ and that there is little hope of their now accepting anything short of complete self-government which would be incompatible with ~~the~~ our Mandatory obligations ~~of His Majesty's Government~~. Further, the Jews remain opposed to a Legislative Council in which they would be in a minority as against the Arabs. Also in present circumstances it seems likely that a Legislative Council would accentuate rather than diminish friction between the Jews and the Arabs.

If ~~His Majesty's Government~~ we were entirely free to decide, the balance of considerations would,

I think, be clearly in favour of taking no steps at present for the establishment of a Legislative Council. In view, however, of our commitments I am afraid that we cannot remain entirely passive.

But it would be impolitic to seek to impose a form of Constitution for which there was no general demand and which both Arabs and Jews for different reasons at present regard as objectionable.

I suggest, therefore, that the first step should be to endeavour to arrange for a Conference in Palestine between the Palestine Administration and representatives of the Jewish and non-Jewish communities - or if such a Conference should prove impracticable, for separate discussions between the Palestine Administration and the various interested parties.

If His Majesty's Government had not committed themselves publicly in 1922 to an unofficial majority, it would, I think, have been preferable to insist at the outset on an official majority. As things stand, however, this is not practicable, and it would seem best not to put forward any specific proposals as a basis for discussion but merely to submit the question: What should be the composition of the unofficial element on the Legislative Council and how the unofficial members should be appointed. As regards the powers of the Council it should be laid down as fundamental that they must be such as to enable His Majesty's Government to discharge their Mandatory obligations. This would entail placing

powers

powers of veto and certification in the hands of the High Commissioner in the event of the Conference leading to agreed recommendations for the setting up of a Council with an unofficial majority.

Should the efforts of His Majesty's Government to bring about such discussions prove fruitless or should the discussions lead to no generally accepted conclusions, His Majesty's Government should be regarded as having done all that can reasonably be expected for the discharge of their commitments.

Even if it should not be found possible to establish a Legislative Council as a result of such discussions, it may be that proposals could be formulated for the advisory co-operation of the two communities, with the Palestine Administration, through the medium of Consultative Committees on specified subjects somewhat on the lines of the General Agricultural Council set up in 1930, in addition to officials, comprises representatives of the Arab, Jewish and German farming communities, the Salesian Fathers who conduct an agricultural school near Jerusalem, the Hebrew University, the Palestine Jewish Colonisation Association, and the Executive of the Jewish Agency.

(2) Jewish Immigration.

(i) Commitments.

His Majesty's Government ~~are committed~~
(a) Under the Mandate, to facilitate Jewish immigration under suitable conditions while ensuring that the rights and position of other sections of the population are not prejudiced,
(b) By the 1922 Statement of Policy, to ensure that the volume of immigration does not exceed the economic capacity of the country to absorb new arrivals, ~~and~~ (c) Under the 1930 White Paper, as interpreted by the Prime Minister's letter to Dr. Weizmann, to maintain the absorptive capacity principle, Government control of immigration, and the proper application of the Immigration Regulations. ~~Also, if in consequence of the~~ Jewish policy of exclusive employment of Jewish labour on undertakings carried out or furthered ~~by the Jewish Agency~~, Arab labour is displaced or existing unemployment becomes aggravated, that is a factor to which His Majesty's Government are bound to have regard.

Finally, the desirability is admitted of closer co-operation and consultation between the Jewish authorities and the Palestine Government, especially in regard to the preparation of the Labour Schedule, i.e., the half-yearly schedule by which the immigration of wage-earners is mainly regulated.

(ii) Action already taken.

Powers have been taken by Ordinance, with detailed

detailed regulations thereunder, to enable the Government to exercise proper control of immigration, with special provisions with regard to the Labour Schedule.

Amendments of the Ordinance and Regulations have recently been made to improve generally the machinery for regulating immigration.

In the summer of 1931, the late High Commissioner, Sir John Chancellor, reported various steps he had taken to improve the machinery for co-operation between the Government and the Jewish Agency in the preparation of Labour Schedules. Further improvements in the machinery for determining the Labour Schedules, ~~with special reference to questions of unemployment~~, must, it is considered, wait until the financial position will allow of the extra expenditure ~~which would be~~ involved.

(iii) <u>Action now to be taken.</u>

The Jewish Agency formally accepted the absorptive capacity principle in 1922. But they have remained dissatisfied with its interpretation and application by the Palestine Government. Various attempts have been made by the Jewish Agency to secure relaxation of the existing Regulations, especially as regards wage-earners. Successive ~~Secretaries of State~~, however, have maintained the principle of absorptive capacity and have refrained from interfering with the discretion of the High Commissioner as regards the number of wage-earning immigrants to be admitted
under

under any Labour Schedule. The only exception to this policy was when in May 1930 the issue of certificates under the Labour Schedule was suspended pending the receipt and consideration of the report of Sir John Hope Simpson.

In urging relaxation or a less restrictive interpretation of existing Regulations, the Jews have argued that the sanction of a larger Labour Schedule would encourage the inflow of subscriptions for the Jewish National Home, and that this would allow of additional schemes of work, which would provide for, and so justify, the extra number of immigrants who would have been permitted to enter the country. This argument, which has recently been urged with some insistence, has not so far been accepted. On the other hand, the Arabs, who are in any case opposed to or suspicious of anything designed to increase the number of Jews in Palestine, continue to complain that Jewish immigration is allowed in excess of the absorptive capacity of the country. They attribute the existing Arab unemployment largely to the immigration policy of the Government and call for a complete prohibition of further Jewish immigration.

It appears to me that to yield to pressure from either side would be both impolitic and inconsistent with the commitments and declared policy of His Majesty's Government. Also, to take out of the hands of the High Commissioner the determination of matters of fact, such as the absorptive capacity at any given time, would be impracticable, and ~~even if practicable, it would~~

be

unsound ~~to do so~~. In my opinion, the only
policy which can consistently be adopted is to
maintain strictly the principle of absorptive
capacity;   to leave the final determination of
facts relevant to its application entirely in
the hands of the High Commissioner ~~and his officials~~
to encourage, as far as possible, co-operation
between the Palestine Executive of the Jewish
Agency and the Palestine Government in regard to
Jewish immigration, and to continue, so far as the
means of Palestine permit, the improvement in the
machinery for determining factors necessary for
the proper application of the principle of
absorptive capacity.

APPENDIX.

(1) **LEGISLATIVE COUNCIL.**

I. COMMITMENTS.

1. Article 2 of the Mandate provides, inter alia, that the "Mandatory shall be responsible for placing the country under such political, administrative and economic conditions as will secure ...... the development of self-governing institutions ......".

2. The following appears in the 1922 Statement of Policy (page 20 of Cmd.1700):-

"Nevertheless, it is the intention of His Majesty's Government to foster the establishment of a full measure of self-government in Palestine ..... The first step was taken when, on the institution of a civil administration, the nominated Advisory Council, which now exists, was established .... it is now proposed to take a second step by the establishment of a Legislative Council ....".

3. The following passages are taken from the 1930 Statement of Policy (page 4, Cmd.3692):-

"They (His Majesty's Government) have decided that the time has arrived for a further step in the direction of the grant to the people of Palestine of a measure of self-government compatible with the terms of the Mandate. His Majesty's Government accordingly intend to set up a Legislative Council generally on the lines indicated in the Statement of British Policy in Palestine issued by Mr. Churchill in June, 1922, ...".

"...... they

"...... they (His Majesty's Government) consider it in the interests of the population of the country as a whole that the further step now proposed should no longer be deferred".

4. The Permanent Mandates Commission was informed at its Twentieth Session of the intention to set up a Legislative Council. The Permanent Mandates Commission in one of their special observations welcomed the statement.

II. ACTION ALREADY TAKEN.

1. In October, 1920, there was set up in Palestine an Advisory Council composed in equal parts of Official and nominated Unofficial Members. Of the 10 Unofficial Members, 4 were Moslems, 3 were Christians and 3 were Jews.

2. The attempt to set up by Order-in-Council a Legislative Council in 1923 failed owing to the refusal of the Arab population as a whole to participate in the elections for the Council.

3. Two further opportunities were given to representative Arab leaders in Palestine to co-operate with the Administration in the government of the country, first, by the reconstitution of a nominated Advisory Council, but with membership conforming to that proposed for the Legislative Council, and, secondly, by a proposal for the formation of an Arab Agency.

4. Neither of these opportunities was accepted, and, accordingly, in December, 1923, an Advisory Council was set up consisting only of Official Members. This position

position still continues; the only change being that the Advisory Council has been enlarged by the addition of more Official Members as the Administration developed.

5. With the object of enabling the people of Palestine to obtain practical experience of administrative methods and the business of government and to learn discrimination in the selection of their representatives, Lord Plumer, who was High Commissioner for Palestine from 1925 to 1928, introduced a wider measure of local self-government than had previously obtained under the British regime by the establishment of Municipal and Town Councils.

6. Sir John Chancellor considered the question on his assumption of the office of High Commissioner. He consulted representatives of various local interests and put forward certain proposals in June, 1929. Discussion of the question was, however, suspended in consequence of the disturbances in August, 1929.

7. In June, 1931, the Secretary of State asked the Acting High Commissioner to consider the whole question in the light of the policy laid down and to submit proposals as to the best means of giving practical effect to that policy. The Secretary of State pointed out that it was clear that, having regard to the language used in the 1930 Statement of Policy, the question could not be allowed to remain indefinitely in abeyance.

8. Sir John Chancellor submitted his revised
proposals

proposals in August, 1931. They provide for a
Council generally on the lines laid down in the
Legislative Council Order-in-Council, 1922, but with
an official membership of 16 (excluding the High
Commissioner) and an unofficial membership of 18,
of whom 5 were to be nominated and 13 elected. Of
the 5 nominated members not more than 3 were to be
Arabs and not more than 2 Jews. The apportionment
of the unofficial seats to the various sections of
the population was to be deferred until the census
report had been received, when the allotment of
seats as between the religious communities would be
made in accordance with the figures of the present
population. Consideration of Sir John Chancellor's
revised proposals has been deferred pending an
expression of the views of the new High Commissioner.

III. CONSIDERATIONS AFFECTING ACTION NOW TO BE TAKEN.

1. Sir John Chancellor, in putting forward his
proposals in 1929, expressed the view that it would be
difficult to resist much longer the demand for some
form of legislative body, more particularly since the
demands of the Arab community had become more
insistent since the establishment of representative
government in the politically less advanced
territory of Trans-Jordan.

2. The High Commissioner believed that the Arabs
were then more favourably disposed to co-operation
than they were in 1923. He considered that, in view
of the undertakings given and the offers made, it was
impossible indefinitely to maintain the present
position, and that unless some steps were taken
before long, there was reason to think that political
agitation against the Government might assume an
objectionable

objectionable and even a dangerous character.

3. The Commission of Enquiry into the Disturbances of 1929 expressed the view that the Arab people of Palestine were united in their demand for a measure of self-government. The Commission stated that it was their belief that a feeling of resentment among the Arabs of Palestine consequent upon their disappointment at continued failure to obtain any measure of self-government was greatly aggravating the difficulties of the local administration (page 162 of Cmd.3530).

4. The Financial Commission which visited Palestine in 1931 referred in its Report to the desirability of the Government taking every opportunity of associating with itself representatives of the public, and pointed out that a Legislative Council, if and when established, would furnish the most effective machinery for this purpose. (Page 8 of Middle East No.43).

5. The Arab leaders have never formally recognised the Mandate. The indications are that whatever prospects there were in 1929-1930 of the Arabs co-operating in a form of self-government compatible with the terms of the Mandate, their attitude towards the Mandatory and the Administration has undoubtedly undergone a considerable change since the issue of the Prime Minister's letter to Dr. Weizmann in February, 1931, (Middle East No.39). Their present attitude, so far as can be gathered, is one of non-co-operation with the Administration unless and until the Mandate is revoked.

6. The Jewish attitude is and always has been
one

one of opposition to any proposal to establish a Legislative Council, while the Jewish people are in a minority. It is true that the Zionist Organisation accepted the 1922 Statement of Policy with its proposal to set up a Legislative Council. They would no doubt argue that their acceptance must now be regarded as having been withdrawn in view of subsequent events, particularly the refusal of the Arabs to co-operate in the establishment of a Legislative Council in 1923. Moreover, it is understood that they would take the view that a Legislative Council would, in present circumstances, accentuate rather than diminish the friction between themselves and the Arabs.

7. The position appears to be that on the one hand the Arabs regard a form of self-government compatible with the terms of the Mandate as unacceptable, and would refuse to co-operate, while on the other hand the Jews are definitely opposed to any proposal for a Legislative Council at the moment.

8. The Jews and the Arabs are the two main communities in Palestine, and it would therefore be a case of forcing upon the community a measure for which there was no general demand, and to which in some quarters at any rate there was considerable objection.

(2) JEWISH IMMIGRATION.

I. COMMITMENTS.

1. Article 6 of the Mandate privides, inter alia, that the Administration of Palestine, while ensuring that the rights and position of other sections of the population are not prejudiced, shall facilitate Jewish immigration under suitable conditions.

2. The following passages occur in the 1922 Statement of Policy (see pages 19 and 20 of Cmd 1700).

"This (Jewish) immigration cannot be so great in volume as to exceed whatever may be the economic capacity of the country at the time to absorb new arrivals. It is essential to ensure that the immigrants should not be a burden upon the people of Palestine as a whole, and that they should not deprive any section of the present population of their employment".

"It is necessary also to ensure that persons who are politically undesirable are excluded from Palestine ...."

"It is intended that a special committee should be established in Palestine, consisting entirely of members of the new Legislative Council elected by the people, to confer with the Administration upon matters relating to the regulation of immigration".

3. The following passages occur in the 1930 Statement of Policy (pages 20 to 22 of Cmd.3692).

"In view of its responsibilities under the Mandate, it is essential that the Palestine Government, as the agent of the Mandatory Power, should

should be the deciding authority in all matters of policy relating to immigration, especially having regard to its close relation to unemployment and land development policy".

"Clearly if immigration of Jews results in preventing the Arab population from obtaining the work necessary for its maintenance, or if Jewish unemployment unfavourably affects the general labour position, it is the duty of the Mandatory Power under the Mandate to reduce, or, if necessary to suspend such immigration until the unemployed portion of other sections is in a position to obtain work".

"It is clearly desirable to establish closer co-operation and consultation between the Jewish authorities and the Government, and the closer and more cordial co-operation becomes, the easier it should be to arrive at an agreed (labour) schedule based upon a thorough understanding on both sides of the economic needs of the country".

4. The following passages appear in the Prime Minister's letter to Dr Weizmann (pages 6 and 7 of Middle East No.39):

"But the intention of His Majesty's Government appears to have been represented as being that "no further immigration of Jews is to be permitted so long as it might prevent any Arab from obtaining employment". His Majesty's Government never proposed to pursue such a policy. They were concerned to state that, in the regulation of Jewish immigration, the following principles should apply, viz., that "it is essential to ensure that the immigrants should

should not be a burden upon the people of Palestine as a whole, and that they should not deprive any section of the present population of their employment" (White Paper, 1922)".

"That principle (the absorptive capacity principle) is vital to any scheme of development, the primary purpose of which must be the settlement both of Jews and of displaced Arabs upon the land. It is for that reason that His Majesty's Government have insisted, and are compelled to insist, that Government control of immigration must be maintained and that immigration regulations must be properly applied. The considerations relevant to the limits of absorptive capacity are purely economic considerations".

"In determining the extent to which Immigration at any time may be permitted, it is necessary also to have regard to the declared policy of the Jewish Agency to the effect that in "all the works or undertakings carried out or furthered by the Agency it shall be deemed to be a matter of principle that Jewish labour shall be employed". His Majesty's Government do not in any way challenge the right of the Agency to formulate or approve and endorse such a policy. The principle of preferential and, indeed, exclusive employment of Jewish labour by Jewish organisations is a principle which the Jewish Agency are entitled to affirm. But it must be pointed out that if in consequence of this policy Arab labour is displaced or existing unemployment becomes aggravated, that is a factor in the

situation

situation to which the Mandatory is bound to have regard".

II. ACTION ALREADY TAKEN.

The control of immigration is vested in the High Commissioner by means of an Immigration Ordinance and Regulations.

Broadly speaking the immigrants fall into two divisions, namely,

(a) those possessing capital up to a minimum amount; and

(b) those without capital, but with definite prospect of employment.

The conditions governing the admission of immigrants under (a) are laid down in the Ordinance and Regulations. These conditions have been varied from time to time, and it has recently been decided to reduce the minimum capital required /in the case of ~~one of the categories of~~ immigrants

The admission of immigrants under (b) is regulated in the case of wage earner by half-yearly "labour schedules" drawn up by the Palestine Government after consultation with the Jewish Agency, and reflecting the actual state of the labour market from time to time.

In and about the year 1925 immigrants were allowed to enter the country in numbers that were far too large. A temporary economic boom, under which this excessive immigration took place, was speedily followed by a slump. The situation was at its worst about the middle of 1927, when Jewish immigration was to all intents and purposes - brought to a standstill.

No labour schedules were issued during the year September 1927 - September 1928. The situation was subsequently restored to a great extent, though there is still a Jewish unemployment problem in Palestine.

In May, 1931, the Secretary of State asked for the High Commissioner's views on the various questions concerning immigration referred to in the 1930 Statement of Policy and the Prime Minister's letter to Dr. Weizmann. In July Sir John Chancellor reported the action which he was taking for improving the machinery in the desired directions. This comprised (1) an amending Ordinance and regulations which have now been framed to improve generally the machinery for regulating immigration; and (2) arrangements to promote co-operation between the Palestine Government and the Palestine Executive of the Jewish Agency in the preparation of the labour schedule. Estimates of the number of labour immigration certificates for the coming half year are now prepared separately by the Chief Immigration Officer and the Jewish Agency. After the Agency's estimate has been examined by the Chief Immigration Officer, joint discussions take place with a view to reaching agreement, and opportunity is afforded for further discussion, if necessary, with the Chief Secretary or the High Commissioner before the schedule is settled in Executive Council.

Pending the setting up of more elaborate machinery, when the financial position permits, efforts are

are being made through the officers of the District Administration to arrive at more accurate figures of unemployment for use in determining the half-yearly labour schedule.

III. CONSIDERATIONS AFFECTING FUTURE ACTION.

1. The Jewish Agency is concerned to secure increased Jewish immigration into Palestine, and representations have been made on more than one occasion with a view to the relaxation of the conditions governing the admission of immigrants. The Agency has also endeavoured to induce the Secretary of State to intervene in the matter of the number of immigrants to be admitted under the half-yearly labour schedules. The Jewish Agency, although they formally accepted in 1922 the principle of absorptive capacity, have urged that the administration of the Immigration regulations should be delegated to them, including the determination of the number of persons to be admitted. Failing that, they have recently argued that in framing the labour schedule "absorptive capacity" should be determined not only by the actual number of openings for wage earners for which at a given date it can be shewn that there is a reasonable prospect, but also by the anticipated influx of new capital which would, it is claimed, be stimulated by a more generous allotment of labour certificates.

It has not so far been found possible to accept the contentions of the Jewish Agency.

2.

2. The Arabs are strongly opposed to Jewish immigration, and they complain that Jewish immigration has been allowed to flow freely since 1920, regardless of the economic capacity of the country to absorb the immigrants.

3. Having regard to the general principle governing the volume of Jewish immigration, namely, that of the absorptive capacity of the country, the final decision on all matters effecting immigration must necessarily rest with the High Commissioner, who, with the assistance of his advisers, is in the best position to judge the capacity of the country to absorb immigrants and to reach an impartial conclusion. If and when a Legislative Council is set up, it will be necessary to consider whether a special committee should be established, consisting of members of the Legislative Council, to confer with the Administration upon matters relating to regulation of immigration.

(3) DEVELOPMENT AND LAND LEGISLATION.

I. Commitments.

1. Article 2 of the Mandate provides, inter alia, that the Mandatory shall be responsible for placing the country under such political, administrative and economic conditions as will secure the establishment of the Jewish National Home.

2. Article 6 of the Mandate provides, inter alia, that the Administration of Palestine, while ensuring that the rights and position of other sections of the population are not prejudiced, shall encourage, in co-operation with the Jewish Agency, close settlement by Jews on the land, including State lands and waste lands not required for public purposes.

3. Article 11 of the Mandate states ". . . . . . . It (the Administration) shall introduce a land system appropriate to the needs of the country, having regard, among other things, to the desirability of promoting the close settlement and intensive cultivation of the land.

4. In the 1922 Statement of Policy (page 19 of Cmd.1700), it was stated that "when it is asked what is meant by the development of the Jewish National Home in Palestine, it may be answered that it is not the imposition of Jewish nationality upon the inhabitants of Palestine as a whole, but the further development of the existing Jewish communities, with the assistance of Jews in other

parts

parts of the world, in order that it may become a centre in which the Jewish people as a whole may take, on grounds of religion and race, an interest and a pride."

5. The 1930 Statement of Policy (Cmd. 3692) set out certain conclusions which had emerged and certain facts which had been established as the result of Sir John Hope Simpson's enquiry into land, immigration and development. Included among these was the following:-

"...... It is, however, an error to imagine that the Palestine Government is in possession of large areas of vacant land which could be made available for Jewish settlement. The extent of unoccupied areas of Government land is negligible. The Government claims considerable areas which are, in fact, occupied and cultivated by Arabs. Even were the title of the Government to these areas admitted, and it is in many cases disputed, it would not be possible to make these areas available for Jewish settlement, in view of their actual occupation by Arab cultivators and of the importance of making available additional land on which to place the Arab cultivators who are now landless."

6. The 1930 Statement of Policy also contains the following passage.

"21. As indicated in the immediately preceding paragraph, it is the duty of the Administration under the Mandate to ensure that the

the position of the "other sections of the population" is not prejudiced by Jewish immigration. Also, it is its duty under the Mandate to encourage close settlement of the Jews on the land, subject always to the former condition.

22. As a result of recent investigations, His Majesty's Government are satisfied that, in order to attain these objects, a more methodical agricultural development is called for with the object of ensuring a better use of the land.

23. Only by the adoption of such a policy will additional Jewish agricultural settlement be possible consistently with the conditions laid down in Article 6 of the Mandate. The result desired will not be obtained except by years of work. It is for this reason fortunate that the Jewish organizations are in possession of a large reserve of land not yet settled or developed. Their operations can continue without break, while more general steps of development, in the benefits of which Jews and Arabs can both share, are being worked out. During this period, however, the control of all disposition of land must of necessity rest with the authority in charge of the development. Transfers of land will be permitted only in so far as they do not interfere with the plans of that authority. Having regard to the
responsibilities

responsibilities of the Mandatory Power, it is clear that this authority must be the Palestine Administration."

7. The following passages occur in the Prime Minister's letter to Dr. Weizmann (Middle East No. 39).

".(9).. It is desirable to make it clear that the landless Arabs, to whom it was intended to refer in the passage quoted, (i.e., the passage quoted above in paragraph 5), were such Arabs as can be shown to have been displaced from the lands which they occupied in consequence of the lands passing into Jewish hands, and who have not obtained other holdings on which they can establish themselves or other equally satisfactory occupation. The number of such displaced Arabs must be a matter for careful enquiry. It is to landless Arabs within this category that His Majesty's Government feel themselves under an obligation to facilitate their settlement upon the land. The recognition of this obligation in no way detracts from the larger purposes of development, which His Majesty's Government regards as the most effectual means of furthering the establishment of a National Home for the Jews.

"(10) In framing a policy of land settlement, it is essential that His Majesty's Government should take into consideration every circumstance that is relevant to the main

main purposes of the Mandate. The area of cultivable land, the possibilities of irrigation the absorptive capacity of the country in relation to immigration are all elements pertinent to the issues to be elucidated, and the neglect of any one of them would be prejudicial to the formulation of a just and stable policy.

It is the intention of His Majesty's Government to institute an enquiry as soon as possible to ascertain, inter alia, what State and other lands are, or properly can be made, available for close settlement by Jews under reference to the obligation imposed upon the Mandatory by article 6 of the Mandate. This enquiry will be comprehensive in its scope, and will include the whole land resources of Palestine. In the conduct of the enquiry provision will be made for all interests, whether Jewish or Arab, making such representations as it may be desired to put forward.

"(11) The question of the congestion amongst the fellahin in the hill districts of Palestine is receiving the careful consideration of His Majesty's Government. It is contemplated that measures will be devised for the improvement and intensive development of the land, and for bringing into cultivation areas which hitherto may have remained uncultivated, and thereby securing to the fellahin a better standard of living, without

save

save in exceptional cases, having recourse to transfer.

"(12). In giving effect to the policy of land settlement, as contemplated in Article 11 of the Mandate, it is necessary, if disorganization is to be avoided, and if the policy is to have a chance to succeed, that there should exist some centralised control of transactions relating to the acquisition and transfer of land during such interim period as may reasonably be necessary to place the development scheme upon a sure foundation. The power contemplated is regulative and not prohibitory, although it does involve a power to prevent transactions which are inconsistent with the tenor of the scheme. But the exercise of the power will be limited and in no respect arbitrary. In every case it will be conditioned by considerations as to how best to give effect to the purposes of the Mandate. Any control contemplated will be fenced with due safeguards to secure as little interference as possible with the free transfer of land. The centralised control will take effect as from such date only as the authority charged with the duty of carrying out the policy of land development shall begin to operate. The High Commissioner will, pending the establishment of such centralised control, have full powers to take all steps necessary to protect the tenancy and occupancy rights, including the

the rights of squatters, throughout Palestine.

"(13). Further, the statement of policy of His Majesty's Government did not imply a prohibition of acquisition of additional land by Jews. It contains no such prohibition, nor is any such intended. What it does contemplate is such temporary control of land disposition and transfers as may be necessary, not to impair the harmony and effectiveness of the scheme of land settlement to be undertaken. His Majesty's Government feel bound to point out that they alone of the Governments which have been responsible for the administration of Palestine since the acceptance of the Mandate have declared their definite intention to initiate an active policy of development which it is believed will result in substantial and lasting benefit to both Jews and Arabs.

"(15). .... the proper application of the absorptive capacity principle. That principle is vital to any scheme of development, the primary purpose of which must be the settlement both of Jews and of displaced Arabs upon the land."

8. It was announced in the House of Commons in November 1930 that it was the intention to raise a loan, under the guarantee of His Majesty's Government, of £2,500,000 for financing a development scheme. It was stated that a Bill was

was to be introduced "after Christmas" for this purpose.

9. The Permanent Mandates Commission was informed in June 1931 of the proposal to raise a development loan of £2,500,000. In their report to the Council of the League the Permanent Mandates Commission "noted that the preparation of a systematic plan of agricultural development was to be entrusted to a special commissioner. Lastly the Commission welcomed the recognition by the accredited representative of the fact that the improvement of relations between the Arabs and Jews depended on a just settlement founded on a detailed study of a series of questions of an economic nature, for which the Mandatory Power was asking the assistance of the population.

II.

II. **Action already taken.**

1. **Legislation enacted.**

In May 1931 an Ordinance was enacted, providing for the protection of tenancy and occupancy rights pending the establishment of centralised control as contemplated in the last sentence of paragraph 12 of the Prime Minister's letter to Dr. Weizmann. This Ordinance is a temporary enactment which will expire in May 1932, unless expressly renewed.

2. **Development Scheme.**

A. **Summary of Secretary of State's despatch of 26th June 1931.**

The following is a summary of a despatch to the High Commissioner setting out the initial steps to be taken to give effect to the policy of His Majesty's Government in regard to agricultural development and land settlement. This despatch has been published in the official report of the proceedings of the House of Commons.

(a) Appointment of staff.

A Director of Development with a nucleus of staff to be appointed. The Jewish Agency and the Arab Executive would be invited to nominate one member each as advisers to the Director, who would also have the assistance of a legal Assessor.

(b) The expenditure of £50,000 authorised (to be borne by Palestine funds in the first instance) to defray the cost of investigations in connection with the development scheme, including all necessary surveys and experiments.

(c)

(c) Preliminary work to be undertaken by the Director.
  (i) The preparation, with the assistance of the Legal Assessor, of a register of such Arabs as can be shown to have been displaced from the lands which they occupied in consequence of the lands falling into Jewish hands, and as have not obtained other holdings on which they can establish themselves or other equally satisfactory occupation.
  (ii) Preparation of a scheme for the re-settlement of such Arabs, with as close an estimate as possible of the cost. "When the scheme has been approved by the High Commissioner, the re-settlement will be carried out as quickly as possible". (The sentence quoted has been understood to mean that the High Commissioner, after the Secretary of State has given approval, should begin such preliminary work in connection with re-settlement of Arabs as is possible within the limit of £50,000 referred to at (b), without necessarily waiting for approval of the general scheme of development referred to later).
  (iii) Investigation of methods to be adopted to give effect, within the limit of the funds which would be made available, to the policy of land settlement, as indicated in paras.10-11 of the Prime Minister's letter.

Briefly

Briefly this involves:

(1) Taking into consideration the area of cultivable land and all other factors and possibilities relevant to the problem and to the main purposes of the mandate.

(2) A comprehensive enquiry into land resources, to ascertain, inter alia, what State or other lands are, or properly can be made available for close settlement by Jews under reference to the obligation imposed upon the Mandatory by Article 6 of the Mandate. This enquiry will be comprehensive in its scope and it would include the whole land resources of Palestine. In the conduct of the enquiry provision will be made for all interests, whether Jewish or Arab, making such representations as it may be desired to put forward.

(3) Consideration of the question of relieving the congestion of fellahin in the hill districts without, save in exceptional cases, having recourse to transfer.

This investigation would also cover the question of credits for Arab cultivators and Jewish settlers, and proposals for draining, irrigating or otherwise reclaiming land, at present wholly or partially uncultivated.

(iv) The Director to prepare estimates of the cost of work recommended as a result of investigation with order of preference, and to submit, by the 31st December 1931, a report or interim report which would, after the observations of the Jewish Agency

Agency and the Arab Executive have been invited, be submitted by the High Commissioner who would submit his recommendations to the Secretary of State with any representations received from the Jewish Agency or the Arab Executive.

His Majesty's Government would then take a decision as to what development work should be undertaken.

(v) The bill for guaranteeing the development loan would not be settled pending consideration by His Majesty's Government of the report or interim report of the Director, with any representations forwarded therewith by the High Commissioner.

B. <u>Action taken in consequence of despatch summarized under A.</u>

(a) The Director, Deputy Director and Legal Assessor have been appointed.

Neither the Arab nor the Jewish Adviser has been appointed. After the publication of the Prime Minister's letter, the Arab Executive passed a resolution declaring that they were not prepared to co-operate in the development scheme and did not therefore propose to appoint an adviser.

The reason for their refusal would appear to be that to co-operate would imply acquiescence in the Mandate and in the White Paper of October 1930, as interpreted by the Prime Minister's letter to Dr. Weizmann, to which the Executive are so far irreconcilable.

The

irreconcilable.

The Jewish Agency have not, so far, accepted the invitation to appoint an adviser. Their reasons are understood to be as follows:-

They have taken exception to the legislation for the control of land transactions which, as explained in the succeeding section of this memorandum, was contemplated by His Majesty's Government, and they represented that it would not be possible for them to co-operate in any activities connected with the development scheme until satisfied that any legislative or administrative action contemplated would not prejudice essential Jewish interests. Also, in view of the uncertainty as to the extent to which the Government's intentions with regard to the development scheme will be carried out, in the changed financial circumstances, they wished to be satisfied that there is a prospect of substantial advantage to Jewish interests in any scheme that may be contemplated. Since at this stage the Director is concentrating upon the register of displaced Arabs, the Agency feel they would be placed in an invidious position if they appointed their adviser, whose functions at present could only be to criticise the claims of Arabs to be put on the register.

(b) The Director and his nucleus of staff, with the assistance of the Legal Assessor, are engaged on investigating the claims of Arab families to be placed on the register of
displaced

displaced Arabs. It is also understood that the Director is investigating tentatively possible schemes for resettling such Arabs as are eventually registered. Little progress has been made as regards the latter investigation, for the reason explained in paragraph 3 below.

(c) Investigation in connection with general development policy.

Little or no progress under this head is at present possible. In the first place, the register of displaced Arabs and work connected therewith is understood to be fully occupying the Director's time.

In the second place, the change in the financial position has raised doubts as to whether it will be possible for His Majesty's Government, having regard to their general financial policy, to guarantee the flotation of a development loan of £2,500,000 in the near future. This is one of the questions which await decision by His Majesty's Government.

3. <u>Legislation to control land transactions.</u>

Centralised control of land transactions was stated by the Prime Minister in the letter already quoted under "Commitments" to be necessary in giving effect to the policy of land settlement, such control to take effect only when the development authority began to operate. The Director of Development

Development began his preliminary work in August 1931, but so far it has not been found practicable to enact the desired legislation.

To make clear the reasons for the delay it is necessary to rehearse briefly the past history of the proposal.

His Majesty's Government, as early as May 1930, announced their intention, in the Statement with regard to British policy (Cmd. 3582, paragraph 5), to introduce legislation with the object of controlling the disposition of agricultural land in such a manner as to prevent the dispossession of the indigenous agricultural population. This was referred to as a temporary measure to be superseded in any case by such permanent enactment as might be decided upon when future policy was determined in the light of Sir John Hope Simpson's Report. Subsequently, however, His Majesty's Government decided that it would be politically undesirable to introduce such temporary legislation.

Sir John Hope Simpson's Report recommended legislation for the control of land transactions which in general and guarded terms were endorsed by the October 1930 White Paper, Cmd. 6952 (paragraph 23). The object, however, of the legislation recommended by Sir John Hope Simpson and accepted in the October 1930 White Paper was not to prevent dispossession of the agricultural population in general but to prevent transfers of land from interfering with the plans of the
development

development authority.

   Sir John Hope Simpson's Report envisaged development on a very large scale at the cost of several millions of pounds, which if carried out would, it was hoped, enable further development of Jewish land colonization without prejudicing the existing Arab agricultural population.

   The restriction of the Development Scheme by the decision of His Majesty's Government in connection with their Statement of Policy in October 1930 to limit expenditure to £2,500,000 and the restriction of the proposed legislation for control of land transactions to prevention of interference with the plans of the development authority have thus left the general problem of the dispossession of the agricultural population practically untouched. On the issue of the Prime Minister's letter to Dr. Weizmann steps were taken to prepare draft legislation for centralized control of land transactions in connection with the proposed Development Scheme in order that such legislation should be ready for enactment as soon as the Director of Development took up his duties. It was considered necessary that the legislation should be drafted so as to give very wide and general powers to the Palestine Government. Copies of the draft legislation were communicated to the Arab Executive and to the Jewish Agency for comments. The main criticism of the Arab Executive was that the proposed

           legislation

legislation did not go far enough, and that it should prohibit all sales of land by Arabs to Jews. The Jewish Agency on the other hand took the line that the legislation was drafted in such wide terms as to be contrary to the intentions of His Majesty's Government as indicated in the letter from the Prime Minister to Dr. Weizmann. The Agency urged that any such legislation should be much more limited in scope and should not take effect until the whole Development Scheme has been approved by His Majesty's Government after consultation with the Agency, and the Director is ready to begin actual development work, i.e., that it shall be postponed until a scheme is approved and funds are available. The Agency deny the need for legislation to be applied even to selected areas and suggest that the position, so far as it relates to any preliminary investigations which the Director of Development may wish to undertake, could be adequately safeguarded by administrative measures taken by him in consultation with the Palestine Executive of the Agency.

The Director of Development on the other hand does not agree that this is practicable. He has been pressing that this legislation should be enacted before he takes any active steps to investigate the possibility of making land cultivable which at present is either not cultivable or only cultivable under uneconomic conditions. He gives as his reason that such

investigation

investigation would involve experimental well-sinking. If well-sinking operations prove successful, and there was no controlling legislation in force, the Administration would run the risk of the Jews reaping the immediate profits by taking options on the land in the neighbourhood of successful experiments, and of the Administration having to buy the land back from them later at enhanced prices, and probably in the face of protests from the Jewish Agency, since all land acquired by the Jewish National Fund becomes, under the constitution of the Agency, the inalienable property of the Jewish people.

In view of the difficulties which have been raised by the Jewish Agency, the Director of Development has suggested that as regards legislation matters should be left in suspense without any kind of promise to the Jewish Agency that modifications of the proposed legislation will be entertained, and that in the meantime the enquiry with a view to establishing a register of displaced Arabs should proceed. The Acting High Commissioner, while agreeing generally with the Director's views, has expressed the hope that it may yet be found possible to enact the proposed land legislation without delay and without substantial modifications.

In view of the political objections to taking action which may lead to a violent controversy with the Jews, and of the practical difficulties indicated by the Palestine Government,

no

no decision has yet been taken with regard to the enactment in any form of legislation for the control of land transactions.

4. **Enquiry as to land resources.**

The Prime Minister's letter to Dr. Weizmann announced the intention of His Majesty's Government to institute an enquiry into the whole land resources of Palestine in connection with their policy of land settlement. This enquiry is referred to in the Secretary of State's despatch summarised in Section II 2 A.C.iii above, but no decision has yet been taken as to the precise method of undertaking the enquiry or as to how soon it should be begun.

III.

III. CONSIDERATIONS AFFECTING FUTURE ACTION.

(1). Legislation already enacted.

The Ordinance passed in May 1931, providing for the protection of tenancy and occupancy rights, was designed to prevent an increase in the number of "displaced" Arabs to be resettled pending the establishment of centralised control of land transactions contemplated in connection with the Development Scheme. This legislation is due to expire in May 1932, and the question whether it should be further extended must depend upon the scope and nature of any legislation for centralised control which, in the meantime, may have been enacted. It seems unlikely, having regard to the complicated and controversial nature of the problem, that by May 1932 circumstances will be such as to justify His Majesty's Government in permitting this protective legislation to lapse. Unless, therefore, in the meantime, legislation for centralised control is enacted, which includes the equivalent protection for tenancy and occupancy rights in general, it is for consideration whether the existing temporary Ordinance should not be continued for at least another year.

(2). Development Scheme.

1. There are three possible courses to be considered:-

(a) To proceed with the preparation of the Development Scheme, including the resettlement of "displaced" Arabs, to the full extent
contemplated

contemplated when the Secretary of State's despatch of the 26th June 1931 was written, involving the guarantee by His Majesty's Government of a loan of £2,500,000.

(b) Having regard to the general financial position, to abandon the scheme altogether, or at any rate, postpone it indefinitely.

(c) To devise a modified scheme for which a smaller total sum than £2,500,000 would suffice.

The general argument in favour of the adoption of either course (a) or course (c) rests upon the precise nature of the commitments of His Majesty's Government, especially in regard to the resettlement of "displaced" Arabs.

On the other hand, the general argument in favour of course (b) is the difficulty of the present financial situation.

Since the issue of the White Paper of October 1930 and of the Prime Minister's letter of February 1931, the financial situation has deteriorated so much that it might be argued that His Majesty's Government would be justified, despite the extensive undertakings which they have given, in reconsidering any commitments involving substantial expenditure, especially if such commitments implied a contingent liability upon the United Kingdom taxpayer. But, even if it is assumed that some modification of the commitments of His Majesty's Government will be necessary in the changed financial position, it may be held that, in view of the probable effect of such a

change

change of policy upon Arab opinion whose confidence in His Majesty's Government has already been impaired by the course of events following upon the publication of the White Paper of October, 1930, it is politically undesirable to abandon completely the commitments which His Majesty's Government have undertaken. It may, therefore, be thought that the balance of considerations is in favour of adopting a middle course, that is to say, to devise a modified scheme for which a smaller total sum than £2,500,000 would suffice.

2. On the assumption that such a middle course would be adopted, three alternatives present themselves:-

(i) To limit such a scheme to the resettlement of "displaced" Arabs.

(ii) To devise a "miniature scheme", which would make provision both for Jews and for Arabs, including the resettlement of "displaced" Arabs.

(iii) To devise a lesser "miniature scheme", which would be limited on the Arab side to the resettlement of "displaced" Arabs and would make some provision for Jewish settlement.

3. The view which has hitherto been taken at the Colonial Office is that the resettlement of "displaced" Arabs is a primary obligation, in view of the terms of Article 6 of the Mandate. This Article while enjoining upon the Administration of Palestine the duty of facilitating Jewish immigration under suitable conditions and encouraging close settlement by Jews on the land,

makes

makes it clear that in so doing the Administration must ensure that the rights and position of other sections of the population are not prejudiced. It was because it was held, as the result of investigation by Sir John Hope-Simpson, that the rights and position of the "displaced" Arabs had in fact been prejudiced, that His Majesty's Government decided that steps must be taken with a view to their resettlement on the land.

4. On the Jewish side it is claimed that from the beginning of the negotiations which led up to the issue of the Secretary of State's despatch of 26th June, 1931, there has been an implied understanding that Arab resettlement is not a prior charge upon the Development Loan but merely part of one single process of general development. It may, therefore, be assumed that so far from being willing to co-operate, the Jewish Agency will offer strong protests and resistance if His Majesty's Government should decide that, since for financial reasons it is not possible to carry out the full development scheme, the only thing that it is possible to do is provide just enough money to resettle displaced Arabs. In short, if Jewish co-operation is to be expected, they must be given a substantial share in the benefits of any funds expended on development, including in this term resettlement of displaced Arabs.

5. Two points arise out of the Jewish view:
(a) the question of "parity":
(b) the need for Arab resettlement.

(a).

(a) Jewish claim to "parity".

The Secretary of State's despatch of the 26th of June, 1931, was written as a result of negotiations between the Jewish Agency and a Departmental Committee presided over by the Lord Advocate for Scotland. In a letter dated 5th June, 1931, commenting on a memorandum giving the substance of the proposed despatch, which was communicated to the Agency by the Lord Advocate, Dr. Weizmann, while appreciating that His Majesty's Government had gone a considerable distance towards meeting Jewish criticisms, reverted to certain suggestions which had been put by the Agency before the Committee as to the allocation of the Loan funds. These were briefly:-

(1) £1,000,000 for the resettlement of "displaced Arabs" and for credits to existing Arab cultivators;

(2) £1,000,000 for credits to Jewish settlers;

(3) £500,000 for reclamation and other works of benefit to the country as a whole.

Dr. Weizmann went on to refer to the view of His Majesty's Government "that no allocation of the Loan is possible until the Development Authority has had an opportunity of studying on the spot the number of 'displaced Arabs' and possible schemes for resettling them, as well as all the other ways that can be adopted for developing the country for the benefit of both Jews and Arabs".

Arabs". While adhering to his view as to the best form of development scheme, Dr. Weizmann went on to say that the Agency were prepared to accept the view of His Majesty's Government as to the difficulty of deciding now upon the programme of work and the allocation of funds. He went on, however, to say that underlying the previous proposals of the Agency there was a fundamental idea "that the benefits of the development scheme should go to the Jews and Arabs on a basis of equality".

Writing to Dr. Weizmann on the 3rd July, the Lord Advocate stated the position as follows:-

"1. As regards the question of parity, it is not considered practicable to decide in advance whether anything in the nature of specific allocation of the Fund can be contemplated, or the principle upon which any such allocation could be based.

2. The settlement of the displaced Arabs should begin as soon as reasonably practicable, but, of course, any resettlement will have to keep in view any larger scheme of development that may ultimately be decided upon."

It will thus be seen that the principle of parity has never been accepted by His Majesty's Government, though it has not been definitely ruled out; the implication being that until, among other things, it was known how much the resettlement of displaced Arabs would cost, it was not possible to determine any general allocation. It may

may be noted that the principle of parity was emphatically re-affirmed by the Jews in a resolution passed at the Seventeenth Zionist Congress in Basle (June 30th to July 15th, 1931), in which it was argued that the initial steps which were being taken in regard to Arab resettlement were contrary to the statement in the Prime Minister's letter that "the primary purpose (of any scheme of development) must be the settlement both of Jews and of displaced Arabs upon the land".

The fact that the Arab population is so much in excess of the Jewish population may be regarded as one argument against the acceptance of parity as a principle. It is also clear that the heavier the cost of resettling displaced Arabs may prove to be, the more difficult it will be to proceed on lines of parity. This difficulty will obviously be increased if it is decided that there must be a substantial reduction below the original sum of £2,500,000 contemplated as the total amount to be made available.

(b) Arab resettlement.

The Jews recognise it as politically desirable to remove the Arab grievance by undertaking some resettlement scheme. The Jews, however, do not admit that the grievance is a substantial one, nor do they admit that His Majesty's Government are under any <u>obligation</u>, moral or otherwise, to resettle any Arab families.

As to the Arab view, it is doubtful how far the Arab Executive represents the attitude of the

the fellahin, who, of course, are the people mainly concerned in any development scheme. In so far, however, as the Arab Executive expresses Arab public opinion, it may be said that the present attitude of the Arabs is one of non-co-operation with the Government both as regards the development scheme and other matters. Their attitude has been embodied in resolutions which indicate that the development scheme was rejected in its present form because it was framed on the basis of the Mandate, the Balfour Declaration, the Secretary of State's despatch and the Prime Minister's letter, which the Arabs repudiated. There are indications that the interpretation placed by Arab opinion upon the Prime Minister's letter has had a good deal to do with their present attitude, since they regard it as evidence that His Majesty's Government are more concerned with Jewish interests than with the safeguarding of the rights and position of the Arabs.

6. Provided that it is possible to make the necessary funds available, it would appear that considerations of equity demand at least the prosecution of a scheme for the resettlement of displaced Arabs. In view, however, of the definite attitude of the Jewish Agency, supported by the resolutions of the Zionist Congress, considerations of policy would seem to call for something more, viz: the adoption of a "miniature scheme" of development, which should comprise provision for either (i) Jews and Arabs, including the resettlement of displaced Arabs, or (ii) on a lesser scale,

scale, Jews and only displaced Arabs requiring resettlement.

7. Considerations of finance, however, are clearly of first importance in present circumstances, and unless it is decided to rule out any development scheme whatever, it would appear essential before attempting to reach conclusions as to a "miniature scheme" to obtain information as to the cost of (a) the resettlement of displaced Arabs and (b) the sum of money required for any "miniature" development scheme which would be economically feasible, i.e., a scheme which would allow of an adequate return to Government for the money expended. As regards (a), it will be necessary to await a report from the Director of development; and as regards (b), it will be necessary to consult the High Commissioner after a decision has been reached as to the general scope of any such "miniature" scheme, i.e., on the Arab side whether it should or should not be confined to the resettlement of displaced Arabs, and on the Jewish side what proportion, having regard to their claim to parity, should be allotted to work of direct benefit to Jewish interests.

(3) <u>Legislation to control land transactions.</u>

There are two separate matters:-

(a) Restrictive land legislation independent of any development scheme.

(b) Similar legislation in connection with a development scheme.

(a) <u>Restrictive land legislation independent of any development scheme.</u>

The Commission of Enquiry into the disturbances of 1929 drew attention to the existence of a land problem, and recommended that an enquiry should be undertaken. As a result of this recommendation Sir John Hope Simpson was sent to Palestine to enquire into immigration, land settlement and development. One of Sir John Hope Simpson's conclusions was that with the present methods of Arab cultivation no margin of land is available at the present time for agricultural settlement by new immigrants, with the exception of such undeveloped land as the various Jewish Organisations held in reserve. As already explained under Section II (3) (Legislation to control land transactions), Sir John Hope Simpson's Report envisaged development on a far larger scale than the £2,500,000 which His Majesty's Government decided was the maximum commitment which they could undertake to guarantee. It was on the assumption that such development would take place that the control of land transactions which Sir John Hope Simpson regarded as necessary was directly related to the operations of the Development Scheme which

he

he envisaged. It is clear therefore, that since the Development Scheme to be undertaken is in any case to be on a much smaller scale than contemplated in that Report, the question has to be faced whether on the assumption that Sir John Hope Simpson's conclusions as to the margin of land available are justified by the facts, it may not be necessary to introduce restrictive legislation of general scope, quite independently of any Development Scheme, in order to prevent a serious situation from arising.

The Jews, however, have questioned Sir John Hope Simpson's conclusions with regard to the land available for settlement, and they are definitely opposed to the introduction of any general restrictive land legislation.

Owing to the doubts cast by the Jews on Sir John Hope Simpson's conclusions, and the terms of the Prime Minister's letter to Dr. Weizman, which foreshadows a further enquiry, the facts must be regarded as still uncertain. It must, however, be recognised that sooner or later His Majesty's Government will have to come to a decision as to whether, having regard to their mandatory obligations and the interests of the non-Jewish communities of Palestine, they can continue to permit the unrestricted acquisition of land for the Jewish National Home. The flow of immigration is already restricted by the economic capacity of the country to absorb new immigrants, but no similar limitation exists as regards the acquisition of land by the Jews. To attempt to impose any limitation may lead, as is shown by the events of the winter of 1930, to a world-wide outcry from the Jews, intensive propaganda

propaganda and various forms of direct or indirect pressure upon His Majesty's Ministers. On the other hand, to allow the present situation to develop uncontrolled may lead to serious Arab disaffection, possibly amounting to armed rebellion, with the risk of reactions in other Moslem countries both neighbouring and further afield.

For the moment, however, it would appear that no final conclusions can be reached on this subject pending the result of the comprehensive enquiry into land resources referred to in Section II (2) (A) (c) (iii) (2); it being clearly desirable that in view of the highly controversial nature of Sir John Hope Simpson's conclusions, steps should be taken to verify them on the spot by an enquiry the results of which may be accepted by His Majesty's Government with confidence.

(b) <u>Restrictive land legislation in connection with a development scheme.</u>

The view of the Palestine Government is that wide powers of general application must be conferred upon the High Commissioner for the control of all land transactions if any development scheme is to proceed on satisfactory lines. Otherwise it will be open to speculators to buy or obtain options upon land required for development purposes, and the Palestine Administration will have no choice but to buy back such land, probably at an uneconomic price: if such land has been acquired by the Jewish National Fund, there would be

difficulty

difficulty in buying it back, as it would become the inalienable property of the Jewish people.

Another point made by the Palestine Administration is that restrictive legislation is essential before the Director takes any steps to investigate the possibility of making intensively cultivable (e.g. by sinking wells) land at present either not cultivable or only cultivable under uneconomic conditions; otherwise he anticipates land speculations and a rise in price of land. If this view is accepted, it means that the Director is for the present debarred from taking any active steps, except perhaps in a few special cases, to ascertain the possibility of providing land, even for the resettlement of displaced Arabs, unless recourse is had to purchase of land in Jewish ownership.

The Arab view with regard to land legislation is, briefly, that all acquisitions of land by Jews should be prohibited absolutely. Failing such an absolute abolition they profess to have no confidence in any discretionary powers given to the Palestine Administration.

The Jews on the other hand object to any attempt to safeguard the Development Scheme by legislation extending to the whole country. They further object to the enactment of any legislation for centralised control pending the final approval of a definite development scheme, and suggest that in the interim the position can be adequately safeguarded

safeguarded by administrative measures taken in consultation with their local Executive in Palestine. The Director does not agree that this is practicable.

An alternative suggestion put forward by the Jewish Agency is that the powers possessed by Government under the Expropriation of Land Ordinance are themselves sufficient to safeguard the Development Scheme. The Palestine Administration have not accepted this view. It is, however, for consideration whether its possibilities should not be further explored in consultation with the High Commissioner. But there may be a political difficulty in relying upon such a procedure owing to the fact, as already pointed out, that any land acquired for the Jewish National Home becomes under the constitution of the Jewish Agency, "the inalienable property of the Jewish people". <u>Primâ facie</u> this merely restrains the Agency from themselves disposing of the freehold of land so acquired. It is not improbable, however, that the expropriation by Government of land which has become the inalienable property of the Jewish people would arouse intense resentment which would be fostered by the Revisionists, and would prove a source of embarrassment to His Majesty's Government and hamper the smooth working of the Development Scheme.

(4)

(4) ENQUIRY INTO LAND RESOURCES

The scope of this enquiry is indicated in Section II (2) (A) (c) (iii) (2). As already stated in Section III (3), an attempt was made by Sir John Hope-Simpson to estimate the land resources of Palestine, and he arrived at the unwelcome conclusion that, unless more land could be made available by development, there was no margin not in Jewish hands which could at present be made available for close settlement by Jews. His conclusions have been called in question by the Jews as being based on a hurried and incomplete investigation and on erroneous inferences drawn therefrom. Particular emphasis has been laid by the Jews upon State and waste lands being placed at the disposal of the Agency, as contemplated by Article 6 of the Mandate, and in this connection the Agency has repeatedly referred to the possibility of land being placed at their disposal in two areas, viz., Huleh and Beisan. Sir John Hope Simpson's conclusions as to the availability of State and waste lands were, generally speaking, negative. As regards the two areas, on which special emphasis has been laid by the Jews, the difficulty about the Huleh area is that it is at present covered by a concession held by concessionaires domiciled in Syria, which is an inheritance of the Palestine Government from the Turkish régime. The
Concessionaires

concessionaires have not yet developed the area, but so far they have done nothing which would enable the Government to cancel their concession. Efforts are being made to ensure strict observance with a view to its cancellation as soon as it is legally possible to do so, if development does not take place.

As regards the Beisan area, the difficulty is that under an agreement made in the time of Sir Herbert Samuel the existing Arab cultivators of the soil were enabled to acquire holdings covering the greater part of this area on easy terms. The Jewish case is that, whatever may be the merits of the original agreement, the way in which it has been carried out has been unsatisfactory, in that the cultivators have been allowed to acquire more land than they were individually capable of cultivating, with the result that if the Jewish Agency wishes to acquire land in that area they have to do so by purchase on uneconomic terms. The exact position at the moment is not altogether clear.

Both these areas should be included within the scope of the proposed Land Enquiry. It would appear to be extremely important that this enquiry should be taken in hand in the near future in order to dispose, so far as it is possible to do so, of the controversy as to matters of fact, which has arisen since the publication of the Hope-Simpson Report.

Report. The injunction of Article 6 of the Mandate that the Palestine Administration, "while ensuring that the rights and position of other sections of the population are not prejudiced, shall....encourage ...... close settlement by Jews on the land, including State lands and waste lands not required for public purposes" cannot be complied with in a way which can be satisfactorily defended either against Jewish or Arab criticism or against criticism by the Permanent Mandates Commission, unless it can be shown that an investigation has been made which has been both comprehensive, scientific and impartial.

As to the method of carrying out the enquiry, there are various possibilities, viz., that it should be undertaken by (1) the Government of Palestine alone, (2) an independent investigator alone, (3) either (a) the Government of Palestine, with Jewish and Arab cooperation, or (b) an independent investigator, with Jewish and Arab cooperation. The aim must clearly be that the results are such as can be regarded as authoritative and will be generally accepted. From this point of view, it may be thought that neither the Jews nor the Arabs would be likely to accept the conclusions of the Government of Palestine alone, as both parties regard the Government with suspicion.

If an independent investigator is to undertake the task, the question arises by whom he should be selected. In order to remove any suspicion of
partiality,

partiality, it is for consideration whether the Council of the League of Nations might be invited to nominate a neutral, or neutral might be appointed by His Majesty's Government with the approval of the Council of the League. There might, however, be considerable difficulties in obtaining on acceptable terms the services of a suitably qualified neutral investigator. It does not follow that his impartiality would be above suspicion, and on general grounds it may be thought undesirable to invite the intervention of the League in what should be regarded as purely an administrative matter within the sphere of responsibility of the Mandatory. If this view is accepted, there is the further consideration that an independent investigator, whether or not a British subject, and however appointed, would be unfamiliar with the complicated problems relating to land in Palestine, and would be largely dependent upon the asistance of local officials if his investigations were to be completed within any reasonable time. It would seem, therefore, that the most practicable method of investigation would be for it to be carried out by the Palestine Government with suitable arrangements for associating Arab and Jewish representatives with the officials charged with the enquiry.

The Secretary of State's despatch of the 26th June 1931, while not prescribing any precise procedure,

procedure, implied that the Director of Development would play a part in this investigation. It would appear, however, that it could most appropriately be carried out, not by the Director and his staff, as such but by a small Committee of local officials of whom the Director of Development should be one. The exact constitution of the Committee and the method whereby Arab and Jewish representatives should be associated with it are questions upon which it would be desirable to obtain the High Commissioner's considered views. It may, however, be remarked that if Arab and Jewish representatives are made members of the Committee, it is highly probable that there would be both Jewish and Arab minority reports.

The expenses of the enquiry would have to be defrayed from the sum of £50,000 already referred to under Section II,(2) (A) (b).

GOVERNMENT HOUSE,
JERUSALEM.

5th March, 1932.

Dear Sir Philip,

    Many thanks for your letter of the 16th, and the account of the conversations with Brodetsky and Goldsmid, and with Sir Robert Cohen. It is helpful to me to have accounts of such conversations. I am glad you liked D'Avigdor Goldsmid: I have known him slightly for some years, and I had one or two meetings with him last autumn, and agree with you that he is both sound and willing to be helpful. I will deal with the question of Cooperative Societies and one or two other points later officially.

    As you know I am in general agreement with your proposed Memorandum for the Cabinet. Before arranging a Conference with representative Palestinians to deal with the question of a Legislative Council, I considered it advisable to have some very private talks in Government House with various "leaders of opinion" as to the possible formation of a Legislative Council. I will write officially later the results of these conversations.

Sir Philip Cunliffe-Lister, G.B.E., M.P.,
       etc., etc.

**GOVERNMENT HOUSE,
JERUSALEM.**

-2-

Roughly speaking, the Arabs are in favour of the proposal, though I doubt if Haj Amin will welcome any form acceptable to Government. The Jews do not want any such Council, and Arlosoroff tells me he thinks 95 per cent. of the Jews would refuse it at the direction of their official organisations. These private conversations must be conducted slowly:

(1) to preserve secrecy;
(2) to enable me to use such influence as I possess to persuade leaders to moderate their demands for complete self-government to a reasonable form which Government could accept.

Before arranging a Conference with the leading Palestinians, I hope it may be possible to give me an answer to the question I put to Sir Samuel Wilson as to whether the Colonial Office had a definite policy in the event of the Arab leaders accepting the proposal of a Legislative Council and the Jews definitely refusing it. Should the Arabs prove to be united in favouring the formation of a Legislative Council the Arabs will not consider we have fulfilled our pledges if we decide to give up the proposal of a Legislative Council on account of Jewish opposition.

GOVERNMENT HOUSE,
JERUSALEM.

-3-

On the other hand, if we form a Legislative Council against the declared wishes of the Jewish Organisations they will probably say they will no longer co-operate with the Government. That is a threat which both Arab and Jew leaders use to me fairly frequently: the Arabs because we have during the past years unduly favoured the Jews; the Jews because we have unduly favoured the Arabs. As neither party know exactly what they mean by this threat, it has not hitherto greatly perturbed me. But there is no doubt in my mind that if we form a Legislative Council without the Jews they will exert all pressure possible to make us give way.

Equally if we desist, the Arabs will exert all pressure possible to make us continue. Both sides, by entirely different methods, can exercise very great pressure.

The bitterness between the pro-Mufti Party and the Nationalist Party increases. I do not think either side intend to make trouble either now or at the time of Nebi Musa; but the rivalry between the two parties is so great that there might well be a clash leading to local disturbances. I need hardly say I am doing my best to moderate the extremists of both sides, and the Press is now more restrained than 10 days ago.

GOVERNMENT HOUSE,
JERUSALEM.

-4-

Mr. French is finding difficulties very great in regard to the acquisition of land suitable for settlement of landless Arabs. He now tells me that he does not expect that his second report will be ready until some time in April.

Dr. Arlosoroff is very anxious that I should show him a copy of Mr. French's first report. Though I have great trust in Dr. Arlosoroff's discretion I do not think it right to show him this copy before I show it to the Arab Executive, but I do suggest that it would be advisable to show the first report as soon as you think it advisable, and mid-April is some time ahead. However, the demand to see it is not very insistent.

I have no intention of taking up the question of settling either Jews or Arabs in Transjordania at present. But it is only right for me to tell you that there is even now a certain activity going on in this direction. I informed you that Lord Reading had raised the question with the Amir and, under certain conditions, I do not think the Amir would oppose such a settlement. Dr. Arlosoroff told me some time ago that four Amirs, who own large tracks of land in Trans-Jordan, had separately approached him last year on the subject of the settlement of Jews on their estates and that

GOVERNMENT HOUSE,
JERUSALEM.

-5-

the Zionist Organisation had sent an agent to examine the possibilities of Jewish settlement in Trans-Jordan.

This information from Dr. Arlosoroff should be treated as confidential although he did not tell me it was for my private information.

My visits through the country make me realise what many District Officers have told me as to the extreme poverty of the fellaheen especially this year. I find many of the poorer fellaheen are obliged to purchase flour, many others lost half their flocks through starvation. Every village I have visited is deeply indebted to the money lender and a feeling of general hopelessness prevails in each community.

It is inevitable under these circumstances that the fellaheen are ready to believe in anyone who tells them that the Government is to blame for their unhappy situation. Well does Haj Amin know the Arabic proverb that the Sultan's worst enemy is the empty belly of the Fellah. The plea that Government has done little for the fellaheen during the past ten years is widely held. That the interests of the Fellah have been considered and that he has from time to time received help, is true. But the fact remains that his

**GOVERNMENT HOUSE,
JERUSALEM.**

-6-

position is economically deplorable. I hope to have some constructive proposals to put forward after I have been longer in the country. The chief difficulty, of course, is finding money.

It is hard to help anyone in this time of economic difficulties, but in this connection I may say that the cutting down of expenditure, both ordinary and extraordinary, might perhaps be considered as regards Palestine not only from the purely economic view but also as to its political results, due to the contraction of employment and lessening of resources in various parts of the country.

I have had several requests to urge you to consider the question of Preferences for Palestine. I have replied that I know from the very start you have worked ceaselessly to help Palestine and the matter could not be in better hands.

I would add that, in order to give suitable Palestinians a wider share in the administration of their country, I have decided to appoint non-official members to sit as members of the Road and Railway Boards and of the Standing Committee for Commerce and Industry. This is in agreement with the policy outlined on page 3 of the Cabinet Memorandum,

**GOVERNMENT HOUSE,
JERUSALEM.**

-7-

and mentioned in my letter to you of the 13th February.

I am sending, under official cover, a note of a discussion I had recently with Cox, Peake and others on Trans-Jordan matters.

I am very grateful to you for your Private and Personal telegram regarding the £.500 limit for immigrants. I agree with the Director of Immigration that it would not be advisable to go further in the present economic conditions. I have referred to this in my official telegram Confidential No. 54.

Yours very sincerely,
Arthur Wauchope

7.07

SUPPLEMENTARY REPORT

ON

AGRICULTURAL DEVELOPMENT AND LAND SETTLEMENT

IN PALESTINE

by

LEWIS FRENCH, C.I.E., C.B.E.

DIRECTOR OF DEVELOPMENT.

Jerusalem.   20th April, 1932.

I N D E X.

	Pages.
Corrigenda to First Report.	1
Preliminary Remarks.	2

Part I.
The Re-Settlement of Landless Arabs.	3 – 26

Part II.
The Facilitation of Jewish Colonisation.	27 – 40

Part III.
Proposals for Preventive Measures.	41 – 57

Part IV.
Promotive Measures.	58 – 82

Part V.
Concluding Remarks.	83 – 89

Appendices.

S.R. I.   State Domains.

S.R. II. Transfer of Land Ordinance: 1920-1921.

S.R. III. Draft Homestead Protection Ordinance.

S.R. IV. Draft Occupancy Tenants Ordinance.

S.R. V.   Citrus Experimental Station and Citrus Demonstration Station.

CORRIGENDA TO FIRST REPORT OF 23.12.31.

Page 13, line 7: For the last word "owners" read "occupiers".

Page 17, paragraph 19, 1st and 2nd paras: and page 52, paragraph 66:

These figures, in the case of dry-farmed areas, must be deemed to be superseded by the revised calculations embodied in paragraph 28 of the Supplementary Report.

The figures for citrus-growing on co-operative lines will be found in paragraph 36 of the Supplementary Report.

The estimates for the Beisan and Huleh areas will need revision in the light of the further knowledge already acquired and of the reports of preliminary irrigation surveys, when undertaken.

Page 28, line 12: For "waste lands" read "unirrigated fallows".

Page 52, line 23: For "the developed land" after "sell him" read "the occupancy rights of the developed land".

SUPPLEMENTARY REPORT ON AGRICULTURAL DEVELOPMENT AND LAND SETTLEMENT IN PALESTINE.

------oOo------

Preliminary.

The contents of the First Report.

1. The First Report on Agricultural Development and Land Settlement in Palestine was submitted to the Palestine Government on the 23rd December, 1931. It dealt, in the main, with certain pre-requisites to a broad scheme of development, and also set forth in detail the modern history, and the existing situation in the Beisan and Huleh areas.

The contents of the present Report.

2. The present or Supplementary Report, which should be read with the First Report, discusses the measures which in the light of further and closer knowledge of the country appear to me possible for -

(i) the re-settlement of landless Arabs, both in the near and later future:

(ii) the facilitation of further Jewish colonisation:

(iii) the prevention of certain obstacles to, and

(iv) the promotion of certain aids to, the prosperous development of Palestine as a whole.

References to the First Report.

3. This report is, it will be seen, prefaced by some references to, and revision of, certain passages in the First Report which needed correction.

The Financial Adviser.

4. On the 11th February, 1932, the services of Mr. F. Skevington, M.B.E., of the British Treasury, were placed at my disposal, to advise from the financial aspect on specific proposals for settlement and development which I might consider for inclusion in my Supplementary Report.

I./

I.

THE RE-SETTLEMENT OF LANDLESS ARABS.

The landless Arab problem.

5. In paragraph 10 of the First Report, I remarked that, at that stage, it was impossible to estimate what the total requirements in land for the proved landless Arabs would be and what the total cost of re-settling them would amount to. The position three months later in these respects is much the same.

Procedure for investigating claims.

6. The procedure being adopted in verifying claims by Arabs, who have been displaced from the lands which they occupied in consequence of the lands falling into Jewish hands, and who have not obtained other holdings on which they have established themselves or other equally satisfactory occupation, is as follows:

Each claim is carefully examined by the Legal Adviser who gives his opinion as to its *prima facie* merits. Where the claim appears to be invalid it is submitted to me and, if I concur, rejected. Where *prima facie* the claim appears sustainable, papers dealing with it are sent to the Jewish Agency who are asked to submit their views. Where they object to the validity of the claim, the Legal Assessor proceeds to the locality concerned and makes further investigation on the spot, then submitting the case with his opinion for my final orders.

With the best will in the world, the investigation of claims *prima facie* sustainable must be a slow and tedious process. The previous habitat of the claimant must be referred to, and papers official and unofficial - often quite obscure and incomplete - must be examined

before/

before any definite opinion can be formed as to the tenability of any particular claim.

The numbers of claims.

7. Up to the 1st April, 1367 claims had been examined by the Legal Assessor and sent to the Jewish Agency for further scrutiny. Of this total 310 had been returned with comments. Seventy-two claims have been finally, and 80 provisionally, accepted by me. Six hundred and forty-eight have been rejected.

The accepted claims all emanate from the landless Arabs of the well-known Wadi Hawareth case for whom land has to be found during the course of the next 18 months.

It is, as I have indicated, impossible to forecast what numbers will eventually have to be provided for out of the 3,700 claims preferred. Jewish estimates recently made to me range from 200 to 1,200. I am not prepared myself to attempt at present any more precise conjecture than one which puts the figures between 1000 and 2000.

The problem of resettlement: the meaning of "surplus" lands.

8. My description of the existing difficulties which have to be faced in the re-settlement of landless Arabs must be prefaced by a few remarks of a general nature.

When we talk of the sale of "surplus" lands by Arab proprietors to the Jews for the purposes of development, it is, I think, necessary to grasp clearly what is really meant by the word "surplus".

In large or not fully exploited countries of the "New World", where lands are spacious and population relatively scarce, surplus lands are those lying uncultivated and unpeopled, which can by pioneer

colonisation/

colonisation be brought for the first time within history under the plough and developed for settlement. From confusion of thought and imperfect acquaintance of the facts, the word "surplus" is in this country frequently used in a similar sense.

No surplus lands really available.

9. Leaving aside a few insignificant areas in the hills, temporarily abandoned because the owners have lost their cattle or other simple resources and are too much indebted to be able to replace them, in reality there are at the present time no cultivable lands at all which are surplus, in the sense that they are not already subject to cultivation or occupancy by owners or tenants. If there were available areas of such land, there would either be no problem of landless Arabs to solve or no difficulty in solving it: for the Arabs who were displaced from their lands by Jews would already have transferred themselves there in the search for the only means of livelihood familiar to them, or they could easily have been re-settled thereon by the Government. Admittedly, no such transference has taken place on any appreciable scale. I have personally visited numerous villages where offers of land have been made or reported to me. Enquiries made on the spot as to the amount of suitable land really available for further settlement have resulted (as appears from paragraph 25 below) in the discovery of potential areas that reach a comparatively small aggregate.

The meaning of "surplus" lands in Palestine.

10. Another meaning must therefore be assigned to the phrase "surplus lands", when used in regard to

Palestine/

Palestine, namely, those lands which are at present devoted to extensive or cereal farming; and which in the opinion of colonising experts can be devoted to more intensive and more profitable farming and so carry a denser population.

Concrete example of "surplus" lands.

11. To take a concrete example:

An Arab landowner may hold in the Coastal belt an area of, say, 500 dunams, where at present the traditional dry-farming is carried on by, say, five families of tenants. On the theory that this area is peculiarly adaptable to citrus growing, and so capable of yielding at present prices an annual nett profit of, say, £10 to £12 per dunam after allowing for interest and amortisation of capital expenditure on development, as against a maximum return of 10/- (500 mils) per dunam under dry-farming, the would-be purchasers point to this land as an instance where a proprietor possesses "surplus" lands which can be developed by closer settlement.

Results of developing "surplus" lands.

12. But those "surplus" lands are already fully cultivated by tenants of long standing, each of whom holds an average of 100 dunams: and if the hypothetical landowner is to part with his property in order that this area may be carved up into as many as 25 plots of the low average of 20 dunams each, the purchasers must either turn the existing five cultivators off the 500 dunams with cash compensation for the disturbance, or else arrange that the compensation should take the form of, say 20 dunams

of/

of _developed_ land for each cultivator so that he may pursue his agricultural avocation. If the former method of compensation be adopted, the ignorant cultivator will almost certainly devote the money to expenditure of an unreproductive nature and subsequently become a "landless Arab": if the latter method be pursued, the result, by simple arithmetic, means that of the 500 dunams, about one-fifth must be reserved for, and be developed for, the existing tenants: while only the balance of four-fifths - i.e. 400 dunams - is made available for closer settlement by newcomers.

Some of the changes involved.

13. I have stressed the words _developed_ lands above, because if a cultivator is deprived of a large part of his "lot viable", rendering the remainder uneconomical for dry-farming, and is called on to devote this residue to intensive farming such as a citrus orchard, which takes five or six years in all to come into bearing, his land must be made irrigable from a well-bore and stocked with young trees: and he must be provided with some means to live and to keep his orchard in good order during the waiting years, however shortened by future scientific research these years may come to be.

The transitional period is not an easy one for the tenant. He is called on to change entirely his traditional methods of extensive farming for the restrictions of intensive cultivation: and at the same time, while waiting for his small grove to reach maturity, to seek his livelihood by casual labour on other lands or some other kind of manual labour, eked out by the produce of a vegetable patch which has been

reserved/

- 8 -

reserved from his young orchard.

If land be acquired in this way for the re-settlement of landless Arabs, Government will be obliged to bear the cost of providing the existing cultivators also with developed holdings, including, during the waiting period, maintenance charges and possibly subsistence allowances (if the means of livelihood cannot be obtained entirely by casual labour in the neighbourhood). Plainly this will add substantially to the cost of resettling landless Arabs, although the additional outlay, or some of it, may be ultimately recoverable in the form of rent.

How such changes can be effected.

14. If Palestine had been generously endowed with water supplies, the problem of closer settlement would not be as intricate as it is: but with the paucity of visible or surface water supplies, the process of general development by denser settlement can be successfully achieved only by means of well-matured and carefully-planned schemes, if it is not to cause hardship to the existing rural population - the very evil that we are seeking to remedy. Some such action as is indicated in paragraph 94(4) of the First Report will be needed.

The possibilities of early re-settlement of landless Arabs. No land available in State Domains.

15. In paragraph 10 of the same Report the question of early settlement of some landless Arabs is mentioned; and I now address myself to the possibilities of immediate action.

Detailed investigation of the State Domains proves conclusively that, as foreshadowed in paragraph 14 of the First Report, there are no lands at all

therein/

- 9 -

therein available in existing conditions, either for resettlement or colonisation. A study of Appendix S.R.1 will disclose that all domains are either conceded for special purposes to Jewish bodies or already fully leased to Jewish or Arab cultivators. In some cases of the last named, the cultivators have actually had to supplement their livelihood from occupation of State lands with leases of other lands from surrounding villages. The sole method by which room can possibly be found for more cultivators is the introduction of artificial irrigation by the sinking of wells or bores: and few domains appear, on examination, to offer real scope for this form of development which would, in any case, take a long time to mature and be inordinately costly, if it were proved to be feasible at all.

The answer then of the careful enquiry made into the question what State lands are or can, in existing conditions, be made available for (i) resettlement of landless Arabs, or (ii) new Jewish colonisation, must be re-stated as, None at all: if the $B_e$isan and Huleh areas which are discussed in paragraphs 93-107 of the First $R_e$port and paragraphs 41-43 of this $R_e$port are excluded.

The availability of other lands for landless Arabs. 16. There remains the question what other lands can without waiting be made available for the two purposes indicated.

I deal first with the more urgent of the two problems - the resettlement of the landless Arabs. It is the more urgent because it is the first practical work to which, under the instructions received, the

Director/

- 10 -

Director of Development is enjoined to bend his energies: and also because the Jewish Organisations have, undisputedly, reserves of land, which cannot be less, and may be more, than 40,000 dunams, still awaiting development by colonisation.

Privately owned land acquirable only by purchase. Essential conditions of acquisition.

17. The one method of acquiring land for re-settlement is by purchase from existing owners, vide paragraph 57 of the First Report. If land is to be purchased in dry-farming areas - and, as indicated in later paragraphs of this Report, it is only in such areas that re-settlement can be effected within a comparatively short time - it should satisfy certain essential conditions:-

 (a) be of cultural value;

 (b) yield a good title;

 (c) be purchasable at a reasonable price;

 (d) be within reasonable distance of drinking water;

 (e) be so situate as to be reasonably congenial to the new settlers;

 (f) be clear of tenants, or be capable of being so cleared satisfactorily;

 (g) be land for the acquisition of which the Jews are not already proved to be under contract.

To find land which complies with these fundamental requisites in a country such as Palestine, with its large stretches of uncultivable soil and congested population, is a task of the greatest difficulty. I will briefly describe some of the perplexities which surround the problem under consideration.

(a) Cereal lands only possible for early resettlement

18. (a) The only lands which allow of early settlement are cereal lands, producing, at the best, fair wheat and barley as winter crops; and millet, sesame, etc.,

- 11 -

as summer crops. These lands must be situate in an area with sufficient rainfall.

(b) Clear title required.

19. (b) Before Government can buy, it must be assured that the owner has a clear title to sell: and in the case of villages where the joint owners, present or absentee, have made their own partitions of mesha'a land without the assistance or authority of the Courts, the intricacies to be unravelled are abundant. It is common for one owner to have his fields scattered about in dozens of localities in the same village. He, himself, whether he cultivates through tenants or labourers, is often totally unable to identify his own property, being entirely dependent on the Mukhtar and fellahin for such recognition. There is no guarantee that when it comes to a sale, some other owner may not raise a claim to a particular plot of land, seeing that the partition or alleged partition, is covered by no official or legal authority. Moreover, as no cadastral survey operations will have been carried out in the village concerned, verification by official survey will be required as to the actual areas of the plots being offered for sale.

(c) Price to be reasonable.

20. (c) What is a reasonable price for the land, depends, of course, on the market. There can be little or no doubt that, except perhaps in the tracts adapted to special cultures such as citrus, land in Palestine is not intrinsically worth the prices which have recently been paid, and are now being asked, for it. But there is a severe land hunger, due to special reasons, with considerable buying by Arab capitalists, partly speculative and partly for investment. Both causes combine to render

the/

the demand greater than the supply: and it is not possible to control market prices of land, which seem to me on the whole to be rising steadily. And the advance is not likely to be checked, in view of recent alterations in the law regarding imprisonment for debt which are said to be turning the attention of moneylenders more and more to the acquisition of landed property.

(d) Propinquity to drinking water requisite.

21. (d) Most dwellers in Palestine are familiar with the subject of shortage of water supplies; but the straits to which residents of villages entirely dependent for their water supplies on catchment in cisterns of the year's rainfall are reduced, are not always fully appreciated. It is impossible successfully to put bodies of colonists down on lands such as those in the Beersheba area, where in winter only a few muddy rain-fed pools or cisterns afford a scanty supply which completely dries up in summer, without alternative drinking resources within many miles.

(e) Surroundings and security of rainfall.

22. (e) Reference to this subject of "congeniality" will be found in paragraph 58 of the First Report. I have traversed this year, in company with the Financial Adviser, the plains of Beersheba which up to the beginning of March, at any rate, were wearing a richer cloth of cultivation than they have been decked with since 1919. We have, therefore, seen them under as favourable an aspect as this dry-farming area, cultivated by semi-nomadic Beduin, can wear. And yet we feel assured that even if the non-existent drinking water were available, the conditions are such as the

ordinary/

ordinary _fellahin_ could not tolerate. In the dry tracts of this area more than one good harvest in five years cannot be counted on. In the other years, the yield may be poor: or it may be nil. The semi-nomadic Beduin cultivators, if their crops fail, will go far afield to seek some scanty pasture for their flocks: _fellahin_ if placed in such areas could save themselves from starvation only by deserting their holdings or seeking subsistence in the form of relief from Government until Nature again showed herself bounteous.

It was freely stated at the end of last year that claimants as landless Arabs were being deterred by their landlords and others from preferring claims by rumours deliberately spread that Government intended to resettle them in the more desolate parts of the Beersheba sub-district. Whether the story was true or not, it illustrated popular fears and aversions. Unless, therefore, artesian supplies of water can be derived from such deep bores as that which is now being experimentally sunk between Beersheba and Gaza, negotiations for the acquisition by Government of lands in this tract are vain. Similarly, in the direction of Beisan, it would be imprudent to try to acquire areas where the rainfall is so precarious as to make failures much more probable than successes.

(f) Land must be unoccupied by tenants.

23. (f) The purchase of land for re-settlement of landless Arabs necessitates, of course, that the land should be free of tenants. This is a crucial matter. Obviously, it is no use buying land which is fully cultivated or occupied by existing tenants. Their displacement would merely create one set of landless

Arabs/

– 14 –

Arabs in substitution for another. I have investigated numerous offers of sale of lands by comparatively large landlords: but in only about half a dozen instances have the lands which I have inspected been offered as "clear of tenants"; and in some, at least, of these cases the representation of the state of affairs is doubtfully correct. I may quote a concrete instance of an offer which seemed worth pursuing. The indebted owner was prepared to give a clear title to his land, provided he had 18 months' notice. He asserted that all his tenants were also owners of other lands. This statement was found to be contrary to the facts. The owner then averred that most of his tenants had come from villages already sold to the Jews. Investigation disproved the allegation. Shifting his ground he, then, threatened that if Government did not buy, he would be constrained to sell his land to a Jewish organisation and thus render his tenants "landless", though he had previously maintained they were owners of land of their own.

The effendi landowner frequently cultivates by means of labourers – *harrathin* – and when asked what will become of these if he sells, his answer is usually somewhat callous:– "They can go elsewhere or on the roads to work".

It is true that some of these labourers or farm servants are "casual" or "nomadic", changing their masters year by year; but in many cases they are scarcely to be distinguished from old-established tenants, except in the terms of their agreements. There is often not much difference in effect between

the/

the tenant who himself supplies the seed, cattle and labour, reserving 4/5ths of the produce as his share, and the <u>harath</u> who, working year after year for the same master, takes from him seed and the use of the plough-animals, receiving as his guerdon 1/5th of the produce.

If he is evicted from the purchased land and cannot find employment on public works (the programme of which during the next few years may have to be materially contracted), he must join the ranks of the unemployed, or the landless Arabs. It is necessary, therefore, to investigate very carefully how far lands can be bought by Government for the re-settlement of landless Arabs without displacing existing tenants who have only barely sufficient land to cultivate.

(g) Land must not be under contract of sale to Jews.

24. (g) This condition, I presume, needs no explanation: it is only mentioned because it would, in some cases, circumscribe my action and restrict severely possibilities of acquisition.

Results of personal investigations.

25. So far, my tours and inspections have disclosed only some 15,000 dunams of cereal or dry-farming land which, provided they fulfil all the other conditions, may possibly be suitable for purchase. The proviso is all-important.

It will be understood that I am dealing only with immediate necessities: i.e. with the case where a beginning should be made in order that the landless Arabs may be able to recognise that the policy laid down in their behalf is being put into effect.

Only effective methods of re-settlement.

26. If the re-settlement of all those who fall legitimately within the category of landless Arabs is

to be/

– 16 –

to be carried out successfully, then the only prudent and effective methods for the great majority of this class would seem to be similar to those which have been adopted by the Jewish organisations. Mass colonisation has seldom proved effective; and then only under the most favourable conditions, which do not exist in Palestine.

It will be necessary, then, to expropriate estates or parts of estates suitable for growing citrus fruits; develop these over a period of years and then in due course introduce settlers, or during this period introduce the settlers and, while the orange orchards are maturing, find other work for them. If the 20 or 30 dunam holding is to produce some other special culture such as grape-fruit or bananas, the period of waiting can be shortened. There seem good grounds for believing that grape-fruit (which matures appreciably earlier than the orange, and can be grown in heavy soil) is an established success. The case is different with the banana, as this year's unfortunate experience proves. The culture is in its infancy, and it is still rather doubtful if the experiment will eventually be a success. The frosts which occurred in December even in the Coastal plains and as low down as Beisan, have damaged some of the banana plantations and not only destroyed masses of fruit on the trees, but, possibly, a proportion of the trees themselves. I may refer in this connection to the concluding sentences of paragraph 16 of the First Report.

Numbers of Arabs who can be resettled during the next 18 months.

27. Taking all factors into consideration, I do not think that within the next 12-18 months it will be

possible/

-17-

possible to resettle, or begin the resettlement of, more than 100 to 200 landless Arabs, as an initial proceeding. I am quite sure it will not be wise to attempt more than this.

The costs of resettlement.
28. As to costs of resettlement, I assumed in paragraphs 18 and 19 of the First Report for general purposes an economic holding of 30 dunams of irrigated and 130 dunams of unirrigated land, subject to certain qualifications. In view, however, of the extreme pressure on the land, the high costs involved, and the fact that the fellahin have on the average smaller areas than those specified, I think that we shall be constrained to reduce the figures to smaller dimensions, despite the economic risks involved.

It was originally calculated that the maximum cost of re-settlement on a dry-farming area might be put at £400 per unit Arab family. Apart from the cost of land there will be, as explained in paragraph 18 of the First Report, certain unavoidable expenditure involved in putting a family on its holding. It must not be overlooked that there is in fact a close season in the agricultural year. From some time in April, when sowings for the summer crops cease, until about October, when preparation for the winter crops begins, from a purely agricultural point of view, there is no advantage in placing a new settler in possession of his holding. All that is required is to get him to build his house and collect his implements and cattle. A long period during which he will be maintained by Government is to be avoided. Again, it must be remembered that the

- 18 -

landless Arab is, virtually, an agricultural labourer; and Government cannot legitimately be expected to provide him in his fresh start in life with more than the simplest necessities. A simple hut; implements; plough animals; seed (perhaps obtainable from the Government farms); forage for the animals for 6 months and subsistence allowance for the family for 8 months or so should all come within a budget of LP. 110-120, as now estimated. In the circumstances already described, I do not think it possible to contemplate a system of cooperative dry-farming by primitive Arabs. The attempt to improve their system of dry-farming on such lines would certainly end in failure.

The need for provision of equipment and some maintenance for a resettled Arab.

29. At page 145 of the Hope Simpson Report it is suggested that the resettled family will already have cattle and implements, and that the provision of maintenance will be unnecessary. I am afraid that I must reluctantly differ here. If the displaced Arab has still his cattle and implements and sufficient resources for maintenance, it would seem that he will have obtained satisfactory occupation and needs no resettlement.

The provision of satisfactory plough cattle will need careful consideration. The Jewish organisations, I am told, use special agents at times who go as far afield as the Hauran in Syria in search of suitable plough animals. It will be advisable to secure a Government mortgage on all the chattels or animals obtained at the cost of the State: and to make some provision for contingencies such as mortality of cattle, which is high in Palestine.

30.

- 19 -

Re-settlement on dry-farming lines possible only for limited number of cases.

30. The re-settlement of landless Arabs under extensive or dry-farming conditions has, so far, been discussed mainly with a view to immediate or early possibilities. If, in the course of further investigations, additional areas of land suitable for such re-settlement are discovered, they will not be overlooked: but I am convinced that the greater part of these Arabs will have to be replaced on the land under conditions of intensive cultivation, and that means, at present, citrus-growing.

The distinction between fellahin and Beduin cultivators.

31. We have two distinct types of landless Arabs to deal with: (a) the industrious _fellahin_ or agriculturists who will easily adapt themselves to new conditions; and (b) the _Beduin_ (so-called) who are semi-nomads with all the agricultural defects which that description connotes. These semi-nomads are neither by habit nor inclination intensive cultivators: but that in process of time men of this type can be gradually - very gradually - converted from pastoralists to agriculturists has been demonstrated, not only in Palestine, but also in other countries. Quite apart from other considerations, it must be recognised that there is an urgent need for an evolution of the habits of these semi-nomads into practices more consonant with the modern requirements of a country suffering from severe pressure on its available land resources owing to the rapid increase of population.

The distinction drawn between the two classes of landless Arabs must be observed in any scheme of re-settlement: because, for one important reason (_inter alia_), the progress of the one section should not be hampered by too close association with the other section which presents far more difficult obstacles to overcome.

32./

General re-settlement must be under intensive farming conditions on co-operative basis.

32. Re-settlement under conditions of intensive cultivation must, at the outset, partake largely of the nature of experiment, and it will be liable to modification in the light of experience gained. It will be educative; and consequently demand infinite patience and firmness: for even in the case of <u>fellah</u> settlers there will assuredly be a proportion found to be averse from, or incapable of, changing their former habits. It is futile to imagine that landless Arabs, whether <u>fellahin</u> or <u>Beduin</u>, can be settled on an area, however fully developed, and then left to their own devices.

Much reflection leads to the conclusion that the only prospect of really successful re-settlement must follow cooperative lines. There must, in the initial stages at least, be a system by which cultivators, under Government supervision and tutelage, will co-operate for the development of their holdings. In this matter, we have before our eyes the experience and methods of the Jewish organisations. In propounding a scheme for the re-settlement of landless Arabs under conditions of intensive cultivation, I wish to make it clear that where the particulars now given differ from those incorporated in Part I of the First Report, the former should be taken to supersede <u>pro tanto</u> the earlier preliminary conclusions.

A model scheme propounded. The 1,000 dunam colony.

33. As a model scheme, an area of 1,000 dunams in the Coastal Plain is taken, capable of settling 50 families, each with a holding of 20 dunams. The land must conform to the pre-requisites named in paragraph 17 above: in addition it must, before purchase, have been surveyed in order to ensure that the area is what it purports to be. The sinking of well-bores (possibly after a preliminary test) and provision of irrigation

apparatus/

apparatus, will have to be arranged for: and the area will be parcellated into the required holdings. The settlers will be placed on the colony area at the beginning of the work, being housed in temporary shelters of their own tents. They will, themselves, carry out all the unskilled labour required for building, cultivating and irrigation.

The lay-out of the "farm" unit.

34. Each holding will be laid out in 10 dunams of citrus orchard; while of the other 10 dunams, half will be devoted to irrigated field cultivation and half to dry or rain-farming. While the orchard is maturing, some subsistence allowance will have to be provided for each cultivator. In the first year, this will be met by the wages paid by the settlement authority for labour. Thereafter, such provision will be made for each family as is deemed to be sufficient, after taking into account any wages that they may be able to earn by casual labour in the neighbourhood as well as the produce yielded by the 10 dunams not devoted to citrus-growing.

The area of 1,000 dunams, with its complement of plough-animals, implements etc., will be treated in its initial stages, and until cooperation among the settlers is assured, as one farm under the charge of a manager and foremen instructors. When the citrus grove is established, and the unit holdings are in being, the animals and implements will continue to be allocated as required, under the supervision and direction of the manager.

As regard housing, the most economical and satisfactory arrangement will probably be the construction in one range of the required number of two-roomed houses.

It is/

- 22 -

It is assumed that ample water will be found at depths of 10 to 20 metres (say 35 to 70 feet).

In normal circumstances, and with no undue setbacks, it is calculated that the settlement can be made self-supporting in the sixth year after the commencement of the scheme.

Expropriation of land required for "farms".

35. To obtain the lands required for re-settlements of the nature described above, as well as for those in the dry-farming areas, it will probably be necessary to obtain powers of expropriation. This question has been referred to in paragraph 90(b) of the First Report.

Costs of such a scheme.

36. The cost of such a scheme must obviously depend, among other things, on the number of existing tenants that will have to be re-settled on the 1,000 dunam area. Assuming that each existing tenant on the 1,000 dunams is cultivating by extensive methods 100 dunams, there will be 10 such re-settlements; and 200 dunams will have to be set aside for that purpose. Thus only 40 registered landless Arabs can be settled on the 1000 dunam area in addition to the 10 existing tenants. The only practical difference between the batch of 40 and the batch of 10 will, probably, be that the latter will already have house accommodation in the village and some other resources. Their animals, etc., will have to be taken into the common stock or pool. The cost of settling each unit of 50 families must also depend on the price at which land can be bought, and the depth at which water is actually found. It is estimated, roughly, at £600 to £700 per family unit, allowing simple interest at 5% per annum on the out-lay during the period of six years before the holding can be self-supporting. If, however, the

estimated/

estimated total cost is divided only by the number (40) of registered landless Arab families re-settled, it works out at £800 for each such Arab family unit.

The progress of re-settlement a slow one.

37. It will be obvious from the above outline that re-settlement on the lines now proposed must be a matter of years. It will be imprudent to attempt at the start more than one such colony. As experience is gained and mistakes are rectified, costs per unit should be capable of reduction, provided there is no serious advance in the price of land.

The tenure of the re-settled Arabs.

38. The tenure of all these landless Arabs and existing tenants on re-settlement should be that of Occupancy Tenants as provided in Appendix S.R.IV.

Proposed economic survey of the Coastal Plains.

39. It will be realised that the underlying assumption of the foregoing remarks is that the citrus area is the only one on which, in the present state of agricultural development in Palestine, dense colonisation can take place without undertaking any of the major schemes connected with Beisan, Huleh and the Jordan Valley, to which reference is made in Section II of this Report. I propose, if this conclusion be accepted, to undertake in the autumn a village-to-village economic survey of the maritime tracts in order to ascertain what areas in the various villages which have not passed into the hands of the Jews or been touched by the settlement operations of the Settlement staff, are really capable of such closer settlement. This enquiry will be directed to obtaining reliable data of the existing owners, the areas held by them and occupied by tenants: the classes of soil and the possibility of water supplies. As soon as this survey is complete, we shall know what lands are really available for citrus growing or closer settlement: i.e, what lands can be made available for re-settlement of landless Arabs and further

-24-

colonization of the Jews. The survey can be done by the Development staff with the assistance, perhaps of a selected District Officer and of such of the Survey establishment as can be made available by the Survey Department. Before personal inspections are made by myself or my staff, the District Commissioners will be invited to furnish me with any preliminary data required in addition to those which the Commissioner of Lands has already kindly supplied or will be able to supply when occasion arises. In this way time will be saved: and very trifling extra expense will be involved.

Other considerations calling for gradual stages in re-settlement. The citrus industry.

40. There are other considerations than those outlined above which enjoin the need of deliberation in re-settling landless Arabs.

The rapidity of the growth of the citrus industry in recent years points to the certainty of marketing problems in the near future (See Section IV(b) of this Report): and it would, I submit, clearly be imprudent to proceed otherwise than slowly and cautiously with the re-settlement of landless Arabs on citrus lands before it is known whether and how these problems can be solved, particularly as the cost of such re-settlement is very heavy.

The proposals to re-settle the Beisan tract in relation to cereal farming.

41. In section IV(f) below I have recommended, <u>inter alia</u>, an Irrigation survey of the Beisan tract which is dealt with in Part II of the First Report, in order to determine to what extent it would be practicable, and at what cost, to irrigate a larger area than at present with the available water supplies, and so make possible closer settlement in the tract, provided arrangements satisfactory to the existing cultivators can be made for their re-settlement on smaller holdings

under/

- 25 -

under intensive cultivation. I have also drawn attention in paragraphs 50-51 to the dangers of attempting close settlement on very small areas unless and until it is clear that crops can profitably be grown for export under such conditions. It will be a matter for consideration, when the irrigation survey has been completed, whether it would be desirable to arrange for the re-settlement of both landless Arabs and Jewish immigrants in the tract on the basis of irrigated cereal farming, if the outlay is not too costly.

Cereal farming compared with more intensive settlement.

42. I believe that an irrigated area of 40 to 50 dunams devoted to cereals etc. would suffice for the support of an Arab or a Jewish family. This is 2 to 2½ times the area which would support a family with a holding of 20 dunams, 10 of which are under irrigation for citrus growing and 10 for vegetables, etc; but citrus trees require, perhaps, about three times as much water as cereals, and bananas many times as much. An irrigated cereal holding of 40 to 50 dunams would, therefore, require little, if any, more water than a much smaller holding devoted to more profitable crops. It is often overlooked that with given supplies of water which cannot be increased, intensive cultivation, with its demand for more water, connotes the irrigation of much smaller areas than extensive cultivation does. Accordingly, it may possibly be found that by careful, scientific distribution the water supplies surplus to the requirements of the existing cultivators could be made available for as many, or almost as many, additional holdings under cereals as under more profitable crops.

It is, however, highly improbable that the expenditure required would yield an adequate return, and the

question/

question of markets or outlets for the produce would remain.

Tracts other than the Buisan Area.

43. As regards the Huleh Basin, the Jordan Valley and other tracts, remarks will be found also in Section II and Section IV (f) Hydrographic and Irrigation Surveys of this Report. Otherwise, I have nothing to add to the remarks recorded in Sections ii and iii of Part II of my First Report.

II.
THE FACILITATION OF JEWISH COLONISATION.

The question of facilities for fresh Jewish Colonization.

44. What can be done to facilitate close settlement by the Jews in accordance with the policy of His Majesty's Government ?

The only areas of any consequence which are potentially suitable for closer settlement, i.e. where water is known to be available, are (a) parts of the Coastal Plain, (b) Beisan, (c) Huleh, and (d) a portion of the Jordan Valley. The Beersheba district would become an additional area if the boring investigations now in progress disclose the presence of artesian supplies of water in sufficient quantity.

Progress in the Coastal Plains.

45. The Coastal Plain is being actively developed for citrus fruit growing: and in my opinion the rate of progress is, and will probably continue to be, fully as rapid as the circumstances warrant, having regard to the considerably increased output of oranges and grape-fruit already in prospect; the likelihood that prices will fall when that larger output has to be marketed; and the time which must inevitably elapse before development of the industry due to research and experiment and other means designed to reduce costs can become fully effective.

Danger of a collapse in the citrus industry.

46. The paths of modern agricultural history are strewn with the disasters that have, all the world over, attended too rapid or too extensive production of commodities which has ended in glutting foreign markets and ruining

over-sanguine/

-28-

over-sanguine producers. The dangers to
Palestine of a similar collapse in the citrus
industry must be foreseen and guarded against
with all the greater vigilance, inasmuch as
there is no evidence that if the bottom falls
out of the citrus-growing industry, it can
be replaced by any other reasonably profitable
product of agriculture.

The position in regard to other tracts.

47. It has been shown in paragraph 67 of
the First Report that the other areas specified above, if technically capable of irrigation,
and if then capable of producing economic crops,
would (subject to other factors) allow of the
re-settlement of landless Arabs and colonization by immigrant Jews - by gradual development
over a series of years; thus affording relief
from the pressure on the western tracts of
Palestine.

Need for caution in developing intensive cultivation.

48. Even if there are no insuperable technical difficulties in providing irrigation for
these areas, or any of them, there would remain the crucial questions whether profitable
markets can be found for the crops to be grown
on the irrigated lands, and whether Government
would be likely to obtain an adequate return
on its outlay. To encourage any considerable
number of persons to settle on lands made
available by Government at great expense, on
which there is no reasonable prospect of
raising payable crops, is calculated to cause
hardship to the settlers, to bring discredit

on/

-29-

on Government, and to place on the Palestine tax-payers a financial burden which they can ill afford to bear.

Citrus the only major export of Palestine.

49. All the areas in question are remote from local markets, and in any case the settlers would have to rely primarily on foreign markets for the disposal of their produce. Oranges and grape-fruit are the only products of intensive farming in Palestine which can at present be profitably exported in any quantities: and even if conditions in these other areas were found to be suitable under irrigation for citrus fruit growing, there would be no justification for incurring considerable expense in opening up new areas, so long as it remains in doubt whether foreign markets will be able to absorb all the fruit that is being, and is capable of being, produced in the coastal plain where water is readily obtainable.

At present opening up of new areas not likely to prove economic.

50. The subject of marketing is referred to again in Part IV (b). It may be that in time it will be found possible to raise new products for export, or so to reduce the production and marketing costs of produce already being grown as to permit of its export at a profit; but I am forced to the conclusion that even if funds could be made available for opening up any of these areas, their exploitation would not be an economic proposition at the present stage of agricultural development in Palestine.

Prospects of success in re-organization of Beisan etc. areas at present dubious.

51. The demand for an early re-organization of the existing settlement of the Beisan and Hulch areas, and the new colonization of the

only/

-30-

only waste areas in the country, namely those in the Jordan Valley, - three projects which attract the deep and continuous interest of the Jews - is intelligible enough from one standpoint: but the demand is founded on highly optimistic expectations which have already been criticised in the First Report (*vide* paragraphs 16 and 17). It is assumed, with a perhaps pardonable blindness to probabilities, that whatever the nature of the climate, the famous Jaffa orange and Palestine grape-fruit can be successfully cultivated to an indefinite degree: and that the extension of its cultivation, anywhere and everywhere, will be followed automatically by the emergence of foreign markets capable of absorbing unlimited supplies of these fruits. To my mind this concept errs, to use a homely phrase, in putting the cart before the horse.

I have, however, proposed in Section IV (f) of this Report that, as part of the hydrographic survey recommended in paragraph 77 of the First Report, preliminary surveys of all these areas should be undertaken now by an expert Irrigation Engineer and suitable staff, in order that there may be no unnecessary delays if and when the time for economic development is ripe.

Reorganization of Beisan and Huleh must be by Government agency.

52. In Part II of the First Report - paragraphs 94 *et seq* - I have given reasons for thinking that any re-organization of the Beisan area must be carried out directly by Government, if justice is to be done to the transferees with whom a permanent

settlement/

-31-

settlement has been made.

The position of the Huleh area concession is set forth also in the same Part of that Report (paragraphs 99-107).

Immediate aid to Jewish colonization. Views of the Jewish Agency.

53.   As to immediate aid to the Jewish Organizations in the work of direct colonization, it has to be remembered that these bodies have, admittedly, in their possession reserves of land, aggregating over 40,000 dunams, which have yet to be effectively colonized.

It is the expressed view of the Jewish authorities that assistance for the consolidation or amelioration of colonies already founded, or in the process of establishment, would not be an appropriate method of applying development funds. The Jewish Agency consider that development funds, if at all applied to direct colonization, should be applied in establishing new settlements. So far as Jewish settlements are concerned, I agree myself with this opinion. The intrusion of Government into the internal economy of colonies existing or in process of establishment would be undesirable from every aspect.

The proposals of the Jewish Agency for an Agricultural Bank.

54.   In accordance with their views, the Jewish Agency have submitted to me proposals for the establishment, with Government financial support, of a Jewish Agricultural and Settlement Bank. This scheme provides that the long-term credits which would become available under it should be used to facilitate new colonization rather than for the consolidation of existing settlements. The colonization of the reserve lands which the

Jewish/

-32-

Jewish National Fund and other colonization agencies hold at present would, it is believed, involve an expenditure exceeding the funds that would be provided by this Bank if established on the lines proposed.

The scheme explained.

55. The scheme as placed before me in tentative outline is as follows :-

(a) A Bank would be established with power to issue debentures to a total amount not exceeding a specified multiple of the issued share capital. The ratio 4 : 1 was tentatively suggested. If this ratio were adopted, an issued capital of £P. 200,000 would make possible the issue of debentures to a total of £P. 800,000, making the total funds at the disposal of the Bank £P. 1,000,000.

(b) The share capital would be provided by Jewish bodies, largely, if not entirely, by transferring to the Bank existing mortgages held by the shareholding institutions. If a large Development loan were raised by the Palestine Government, the Government would take up the debentures out of the proceeds of the loan: otherwise, the debentures would be issued to the public, with a Government guarantee of the payment of the interest and the repayment of the principal over a period of years.

(c) The debentures would be issued in convenient instalments, as required; and before each issue the requisite amount of share capital would be called up. There would not be a minimum amount of share capital to be subscribed before the issue of any debentures.

(d) The function of the Bank would be to provide long term credit (say, from six to twenty years) for Jewish agriculture, by granting

loans/

-33-

loans up to 60% of the value of the farm. The loans would be made strictly on a commercial basis, with adequate security and foreclosure in proper circumstances, but a reasonable latitude would be allowed to settlers temporarily in default through causes beyond their control, e.g. failure of crops through drought or pests.

(e) The management of the Bank would be placed in the hands of representatives of the Jewish community, but the Government would have one or more representatives on the Board. The Board would be required to conduct its business in conformity with principles and rules laid down by agreement with Government. The Government representatives would not be expected to take an active part in the day to day work of management, but they would be given adequate powers to enable them to satisfy themselves that the principles and rules laid down were being adhered to, and to check any departures therefrom.

(f) The establishment of the Bank would enable the Jewish Agency or other Jewish colonizing agencies to obtain additional funds for new colonisation; and this, in the case of the Jewish Agency, would be achieved in the following manner -

The Agency have invested considerable sums in providing buildings and other equipment for Jewish colonies.

The amounts invested are repayable, with interest, by the settlers over a period of years. The assets provided in this way remain the property of the Agency until the settler has completed

his/

-34-

his repayment instalments. The assets are, however, divided into categories, and when the settler has repaid a specified amount, one category of assets is transferred to his ownership; when a further specified amount has been repaid, a further category is transferred: and so on.

The Agency would be prepared to arrange for the transfer of all their assets to the settler, in order that he might be in a position to obtain a loan from the Bank on the security of them. This would be on the understanding that the settler would hand over to the Agency, in part repayment of his debt, the proceeds of the loan, less any portion that might, by arrangement between the settler and the Agency, be retained by the settler for further necessary equipment or desirable improvements.

The Bank would have a first charge on the assets: and the Agency a second charge. The Agency would accordingly have more difficulty in recovering the balance of their advances, but would be prepared to face this if they could thereby obtain funds for new colonization.

(g) The Bank's funds could be used also to provide new colonization directly: for example, persons or groups of persons might be encouraged to establish new holdings in the faith that, after substantial progress had been made, loans for completion would be obtainable from the Bank.

(h) The Bank would not be able to obtain an income sufficient to cover its outgoings (debenture interest, administration expenses and losses by bad debts) unless it charged interest on its loans at a higher rate than agriculture in Palestine
could/

could bear. The Jewish Agency estimate that their settlers in mixed farming areas, established at an average cost of about £P. 700,+ cannot afford to pay more than £P. 20 per annum in interest and repayment of principal, representing about 3% on the outlay. If, therefore, a settler were to borrow £P. 300 from the Bank, he could not afford to pay more than 7% per annum on it, to cover both interest and repayment of principal; and then the Jewish Agency would not ordinarily be able to collect any interest or repayment instalments in respect of the balance of their advances to the settler. This would not, however, apply to the orange growers, who are in a position to pay more because their nett returns are greater. The representatives of the Agency expressed the opinion that the Government, as an aid to development, should consider the advisability of providing special facilities (which would mean a heavy subsidy) to enable the Bank and any other Government agricultural credit institution, whether for Jews or Arabs, to charge a rate of interest that agriculture could bear.

The scheme of the Bank criticised.

56. Such is the scheme put forward by the Jewish Agency. It is in my opinion open to weighty objections, and I cannot see my way to recommend it for acceptance.

There can be no doubt that agriculture in Palestine could not stand the high rate of interest which such a Bank would have to charge in order to cover all its outgoings, including losses by bad debts.

For/

+ Apart from the cost of the land, which belongs to the Jewish National Fund, and for which a rent will be payable to the Fund.

-36-

For instance, the Central Bank of Cooperative Institutions in Palestine makes intermediate and long term loans at 8% interest. The loans are made to cooperative societies, the members of which are collectively responsible for the payment of the interest and the repayment of the principal; and, before any loan is granted, a careful investigation is made by the Bank of the circumstances of the prospective borrower member, not only as to the adequacy of the security he has to offer, but also as to the likelihood of his having an income sufficient to enable him to meet the interest and repayment without difficulty. The business is, therefore, selective, and the risk of losses is thus reduced to a minimum. Moreover, the Central Bank has the special advantage of obtaining its loan funds at the low interest rate of 4%. Nevertheless interest has to be charged to borrowers at the rate of 8%.

Further defects in the scheme.

57. The business of the proposed Bank could not be selective. The chief object of the Bank, would appear to be to grant loans to established settlers in existing Jewish Agency colonies, the proceeds in whole or part being handed over by the settlers (in part repayment of their debts) to the Agency for the purpose of financing new colonization. Except to a limited extent, in cases where he would be allowed to retain a portion of the loan to finance the completion of his equipment or desirable improvements, the settler would have nothing to gain by obtaining a loan from the Bank. He would in fact substantially worsen his position. If he is in a mixed farming area, as the great majority of the settlers are, instead of

paying/

paying about £P. 20 per annum, as at present, in interest and repayment of pricipal in respect of his loan of £P. 700 from the Jewish Agency, he would have to pay that amount to the Bank (assuming the Bank did not charge more than 7% per annum in all for interest and repayment instalments) on account of the Bank's loan of £P. 500, and he would also be indebted to the Jewish Agency for the balance (£P.400) of the original £P. 700 loan. He would not, therefore, be a willing borrower from the Bank: and he could not be expected in the circumstances to entertain any lofty notions regarding his interest and repayment obligations. Poor seasons, which recur in Palestine with distressing frequency, would be likely to be made the excuse for failure to meet liabilities: and the political difficulties which would be experienced if attempts were made to foreclose on a wholesale scale in Jewish colonies need no emphasis.

Further, the land in all Jewish Agency colonies is owned by the Jewish National Fund, and is let to the settlers on long leases, with certain restrictive conditions, notably that the land must never be occupied by a non-Jew. The Bank could not, therefore, take a mortgage on the land or on any immovable property of the borrower: it could take a charge only on the leasehold interest, and in cases of foreclosure it would have to find — and this might prove difficult — other suitable Jews who would be prepared to assume all the obligations of the lease

and/

-38-

and of the Jewish Agency and Bank loans.

Improbability of the Bank's prosperity.

58. All things considered, it would, I fear, be over-sanguine to expect that with this class of business the Bank would have any surplus, after meeting administrative expenses and losses, for the payment of interest on its debentures. In the case of the Central Bank of Cooperative Institutions, with its selective business, the margin between the rates of interest paid by the Bank and charged to the borrower, available for expenses and losses, is 4%. If the proposed Bank could not charge more than 7%, to include interest and repayment instalment, and if the repayment were spread in all cases over as long a period as 25 years, only about 5% would represent interest. Accordingly, even if the debentures could be raised at the low rate of 5% interest, which is unlikely, the Bank would have no margin for expenses and losses.

Presumably, it would not be possible in the case of loans to new settlers, for the purpose of enabling them to complete their equipment, to charge more than 7% for interest and repayment instalment together. If so, in these cases also there would be no margin between the interest rates paid by the Bank and charged to borrowers. And the business would obviously be less selective than that of the Central Bank, as there would be no satisfactory evidence of the settler's ability to farm his holding efficiently and to meet his loan obligations.

59/

-39-

Improbability of Government obtaining a return on its outlay.

59. I am, therefore, forced to the conclusion that if Government were to raise a loan and use it to take up debentures in such a Bank, it would get no return on its outlay, and the interest and amortisation charges of the loan would be a direct burden on the taxpayers of the country. For a loan of £P. 1,000,000 raised at 5% interest, and repayable by a 1% sinking fund over a period of 40 years, the Palestine taxpayers would have to provide 40 annual payments of £P. 60,000, or £P. 2,400,000 in all. The position would be similar if Government were to guarantee the interest and repayment of a public issue of debentures, or to provide a subsidy on the scale which would be required.

Palestine is predominantly agricultural, and to impose extra taxation on agriculturists, generally, in order to provide uneconomic credit facilities for a limited number would be manifestly unfair. The extra taxation would, moreover, deplete the resources of taxpayers and make it more difficult for Government to impose taxes for necessary administrative and legitimate development services.

The only justification for Government's provision of long term credits.

60. The only purpose for which in my opinion Government might be justified in providing long-term credit for Jewish agriculture is improvement of holdings whereby a larger nett return could be obtained from the land. If it were considered desirable to provide such credit, the most satisfactory arrangement would be for Government

to/

to place funds at the disposal of a commercial bank at such a rate of interest as would enable that institution to undertake the full financial responsibility of granting the credits, on the lines of the arrangement which exists between the Palestine Economic Corporation, Inc., of New York and the Central Bank of Cooperative Institutions in Palestine Ltd. The credits would then be granted with proper discrimination, and the cost to Government would be limited to the excess, if any, of the interest paid by Government on the money borrowed for re-lending to the Bank over the interest charged to the Bank. I do not feel satisfied that there is sufficient justification at this stage for Government supplementing the funds already available for this purpose from other sources. The position may be different later, when marketing difficulties and other obstacles to the profitable export of payable crops have been removed.

III.

PROPOSALS FOR PREVENTIVE MEASURES.

(a) GENERAL.

Mistakes have caused unnecessary displacement from land of Arabs.

61. The decision of Government to re-settle on the land Arabs who have been dispossessed of the holdings which they were cultivating before the Jews superseded them is a recognition of, and a move to retrieve, the mistake which permitted the displacements to occur as they did. It needs no argument to prove that a repetition of the error can only lead to a recurrence of the present situation.

The prevention of future mistakes.

62. As I have demonstrated in Section I of this Report, re-settlement will be a very costly operation on which Government is not likely to obtain an economic return for its outlay. This heavy expenditure, and the burden which it will impose on the taxpayers of Palestine, can, I submit, be justified only by a simultaneous attempt to prevent a re-creation of the problem.

If it be intended - and on this point I have no information - that Government, in pursuance of the policy declared, should re-settle any Arabs who become dispossessed of their holdings in the future owing to their lands falling into Jewish hands, the solution of this problem will, as time goes on, be rendered more and more arduous by reason of the high rate of increase in the Arab population (which, on the figures disclosed by the recent census, cannot be less than 13,000 per annum), and

the/

-42-

the steady shrinkage in the areas of land available for Arab cultivation. The re-settlement would, as in the case of most of the qualified Arabs whose claims have already been admitted, need to be effected on irrigated lands: and at present this means on citrus lands. It will be seen from paragraph 36 of this Report that the outlay required for the re-settlement on citrus lands of one dispossessed Arab family is estimated at about £. 800. That is to say, for every 1,000 dunams of land purchased in the future which would involve the displacement of, say, 10 existing Arab cultivators, Government would have to incur an outlay of about £.8,000 on re-settlement.

If evidence were needed as to the agrarian unrest caused by the past policy of *laissez faire*, and the consequent difficulties now confronting the Administration, it is furnished by the various land disputes which are constantly cropping up and leading to breaches of the peace between Arabs and Jews, with threats of more serious trouble. It is necessary to avoid any undue emphasis of these phenomena, which are often the inevitable sequels to the absence of a properly-organized system of land administration: but the following picture of events illustrates the need of some such limited control of land transfers or dispositions, as I have referred to in paragraphs 71-74 of my First Report.

A picture of the defects of the existing system of land transfers.

63. An Arab of the effendi class acquires at auction or by other means under the Ottoman administration, proprietary rights in a large tract

in/

-43-

in return for a comparatively trivial outlay: and is content to collect such rents as he can from some occupiers. Others, being illiterate and cut off from common sources of information, do not recognise the existence of an alleged owner who himself is certainly quite unable to identify the boundaries of his own supposed property. These limits are described in his title deeds only in such vague terms as are possible in an unsurveyed area with few distinctive topographical features, and so may be today, practically unidentifiable.

A Jewish organisation buys this land from the owner, and, as entitled under the law, proceeds to take possession for development of its property. That proceeding involves eviction of a number of men who have possibly heard of the late owner merely as a neighbouring effendi, and who have grazed a more or less indeterminate local area for generations without paying the alleged owner any rent. The eviction displaces them from land of which, to all intents and purposes, they are and have been for generations hereditary occupiers - as Settlement Officers have recently held cultivating tenants in Government domains *de facto* and *de jure* to be (vide paragraph 77 below). Monetary compensation is no solace for such men as these who can find no other pied-à-terre: and who can recognize no reason for the change of circumstances which deprives them of the only form of livelihood known to them. And the offers by organizations to provide money for the purchase

of/

-44-

of land elsewhere for the re-settlement of evicted tenants represent simply the familiar device of transferring a nuisance from oneself to one's neighbour.

The need for protecting the rights of all.

64. It is, of course, impossible to make the world stand still, or to stay the march of progress, but the inequity of the present system which suffers such changes as I have depicted, will not, I imagine, be disputed. If the extensive and ill-defined rights of the literate and powerful are on the one side maintained, care should be taken that similarly extensive and ill-defined rights of the poor and uneducated on the other side are not over-ridden. Provided that a *via media* doing justice to both parties can be found, it ought to be adopted as a solution. Some provision should be made whereby the occupiers of the land described above can, at least, be left in undisputed possession of a minimum area of land sufficient to allow of their continuing to earn their living; and of their learning in due course from progressive neighbours how to develop that minimum to the best advantage. Such a policy can be put into operation if such limited restriction is imposed on the free alienation of land as is compatible with the attainment of the object in view.

The need for preventive measures in future.

65. Given the physical limitations of a poorly-endowed country such as Palestine; and given the declared policy of His Majesty's Government as

regards/

-45-

regards further Jewish colonization, the present embarrassments in which Government finds itself must make it evident, I submit, that there is something radically wrong in the methods hitherto pursued in attempting to carry out this policy; and that for the future the truth that prevention is better than cure should be held up as the guiding principle, particularly when the preventive measures advocated involve no departure from the stated intentions of His Majesty's Government: inflict no hardship on any existing colonist or immigrant: and are calculated to prevent further embitterment between the two great races. Adherence to the past policy of *laissez faire* demonstrably has entailed in the past, and must inevitably entail in the future, what is felt to be harshness and injustice towards part of the indigenous population.

Another aspect of the present rural situation. Indebtedness of the Arab peasantry.

66. In the above remarks I have presented the picture from one angle. There is another from which it must be viewed.

In the course of tours among Arab villages in the company of the Financial Adviser with a view to the inspection of possibly purchasable lands, I have come into close contact with, and studied the economic position of the *fellahin* and rural *effendis*, who are almost without exception oppressed by the burden of debts. We have also seen and heard some of the other side - their money-lending creditors. Numerous offers of sales of land have been made to me by debtors with a view to clearance of these debts: and it

has/

-46-

has been worth while to consider closely their origin; and whether any practicable means are possible of easing the load, so as to allow of the landowners developing at least some of their lands.

Reasons given for this indebtedness. Existing system of taxation unpopular.

67. The subject of debt has been dealt with at length in Mr. Strickland's Report on the possibility of introducing a system of agricultural cooperation in Palestine, 1930. The reasons usually given for indebtedness by the fellahin are -

(1) Government taxation:
(2) high expenditure during, and in the years immediately succeeding, the war.
(3) low prices for crops: and
(4) natural calamities.

The subject of Government taxation is one that has been recently exciting universal interest: and it would seem that among the fellahin the proposal to substitute a single, for the existing dual form of tax or land revenue is generally approved. But there is no doubt that if the reforms stop short here, existing widespread discontent will not be removed. While the present incidence of taxation on extensively-cultivated land is, with certain exceptions, admittedly too high, the keenest resentment is voiced at the inequity of a system by which taxation falls on the landowners or occupiers, however small, and entirely passes over the money-lending and professional classes who derive such a large proportion of their income from the peasant classes. The demand for an income tax on the commercial and professional classes in some form is insistent among

-47-

the rural population: and is one from which it is impossible to withhold sympathy. The burden of the reiterated complaints is that while the cultivator of, say, 50 to 100 dunams of cereal land, yielding a bare livelihood, is mulcted in taxation and very little in the way of providing rural amenities is done for him by Government, the moneylender, who draws his income or amasses a fortune largely from the vital necessities of the peasantry, escapes almost scot free. Except for comparatively trifling payments under the Urban Property Tax Ordinance he enjoys all the facilities of schools, good roads etc. furnished cheaply or gratis in the towns in which he lives.

Indebtedness of the peasantry not mainly due to taxation.

68.   But taxation is, in reality, not the heaviest load borne by the peasant. His indebtedness from other causes far outweighs this burden: and it is very difficult to devise any effective means of escape for him.

As elsewhere, the course of events in Palestine during the years after the war, when prices ruled high, has been the undoing of the fellah. After the war, animals and implements were needed to replenish the denuded farm: and were bought at high prices. Expenditure of a less reproductive character was incurred: and then, when natural calamities occurred and prices collapsed, the peasant found himself saddled with debts which were not correspondingly scaled down by his creditor, but were maintained at their inflated figure, with interest continuously growing. Government is

called/

-48-

called on to adjust its demands to the altered state of affairs: the moneylender is not.

The indispensability of the local moneylender.

69. How all-absorbing this indispensable village institution - the moneylender - is, is illustrated by two items of information gleaned in the course of my enquiries.

In one Area Officer's charge extending over three sub-districts there are 14 Government tax collectors: one moneylender alone in one of those sub-districts was said to employ 26 mounted debt collectors. This case is not unique: and Government is obviously at a disadvantage in the contest to recover its dues.

Again, in a village where large sums of money are regularly disbursed by a party excavating an ancient site, practically the whole of the payments go straight into the pockets of the creditors of the village without benefitting the villagers at all.

The need for reducing the peasant's facilities in obtaining cash credits.

70. Pending the institution on a wide scale of village cooperative credit societies on the lines advocated by Mr. Strickland in his Report, I can discern no practical method of ameliorating this very serious situation except by severe contraction of the cultivator's credit. The Arab, like other peasants, is notoriously improvident: and the more he has to pledge, the greater his opportunities for borrowing money for non-productive and non-essential purposes.

The larger the landowner, the more, no doubt he is indebted: but it is the small cultivator

whose/

-49-

whose protection is called for: and one of the surest ways of contracting his credit is to make some portion of his land secure from possibility of alienation, except under specified conditions.

Preventive measures
Concrete proposals for legislation.

71. For the protection then of the Arab small cultivator against complete expropriation or eviction, which may lead to his joining the class of landless Arabs, I have attached to this Report, as a basis for consideration and discussion, two draft Ordinances - (i) the Homestead Protection Ordinance and (ii) the Occupancy Tenants Ordinance vide Appendices S.R. III and IV. These measures aim at affording early practical, and, in my judgment, indispensably necessary, remedies for the alleviation of the situation.

(1) The Homestead Protection Ordinance.

72. The Homestead Protection Ordinance.

The Five Feddan Law of Egypt is not strictly comparable to the first of the two Ordinances now proposed. In that Law the principle was laid down of exemption from seizure for debt of agricultural holdings of small farmers. The Egyptian peasant was left free to sell or otherwise dispose of his land voluntarily; because it was believed that his love of the soil was so strongly rooted in his nature that he would not proceed to this extreme.

Pressure of circumstances on the Palestinian Arab has been too strong to enable such a belief to be cherished in his case. It is recommended, therefore, that a minimum or "homestead" area of

a/

-50-

a cultivator should be made inalienable, unless the vendor of such shall satisfy the District Commissioner that he has a "lot viable" elsewhere or has obtained permanent occupation off the land. Varying minimum areas would be prescribed for the various zones into which the country would for the purposes of the Ordinance be divided e.g. in the coastal zone the minimum, being an irrigated area, would be comparatively low: in the hills or dry-farming areas the minimum area must be much higher.

Objection may be raised that the constitution under the proposed Ordinance of numerous legally inalienable minimum parcels of land in the midst of alienable "surplus" areas would cause an insuperable difficulty in the acquisition of the latter. Experience in the past shows that this is not the case. For instance, if there were a scheme by an organization to buy a village for development, it would be possible in the future, as in the past, for voluntary arrangements to be made whereby homestead areas could all be reserved in one compact block of land, separate from the areas passing under the control of the purchasers. The question of landless Arabs would never have arisen, and will not arise again, if the protection contemplated by the draft Ordinance and the draft Occupancy Tenants Ordinance referred to below had been, or be now, given.

73./

-51-

The principles of inalienability and protection not novel.

73. The principle of inalienability of land is, of course, not a novel one. It exists in Palestine in the cases of the Waqfs and the Keren Kayameth lands; in the old English system of entail; and also in India.

The principle of protection of a part of a cultivator's holding in Palestine was affirmed when, in 1928, Government issued its "Statement of Policy" in regard to the Beisan cultivators, permitting them under certain conditions to dispose of a part of their holdings provided that they retain sufficient land for the maintenance of themselves and their families.

Some details of the draft "Homestead" Protection Ordinance discussed.

74. Among other points which require consideration are the following:-

The definition of "cultivator" in Article 2 of the Ordinance includes an occupancy tenant on the assumption that an Occupancy Tenants Ordinance will be enacted simultaneously with a Homestead Protection Ordinance. It is possible that the homestead area of an occupancy tenant may differ in extent from that of an owner.

The Articles (3, 4 and 7) dealing with the "homestead area" do not impose anything in the nature of a general restriction upon dispositions of land: they merely require previous consent, which would be given as a matter of course in any case not involving permanent alienation or mortgage of the "homestead area". The particulars prescribed by Article 4 (1) will enable the District Commissioner to decide whether the proposed transaction is one which can stand or not. For example, a man wishes to sell or mortgage 20 dunams/

-52-

dunams which is the "homestead area" in the zone where this property is situated. If the transaction is registered without any previous enquiry, it may turn out that this was all the land that he possessed, and therefore alienation should have been in one of the prescribed forms. But if he produces to the District Commissioner title deeds for other land owned by him, the transaction will stand. In other words, enquiry before completion of the transaction is contemplated instead of a subsequent action to upset it.

Again, if the mortgagor owns more than a bare "homestead area", the power of mortgaging the excess area and the form of mortgage remain unaffected: but the "homestead area" cannot be sold. It can only be mortgaged under Article 8.

The form of mortgage provided under Article 8 (3) is one that leaves the cultivator in possession of his land, the lender being paid off by instalments in the form of rent. Although the amount of rent must be limited, in order to avoid its representing usurious interest on the original loan, the amount and the period of tenancy should be adequate. Whatever these might ultimately be determined to be, the limits would tend to restrict easy rural credit - a desirable consummation.

In Article 14 an attempt to deal with the difficult subject of mortgage by means of conditional sale is made. The question of dates

in/

OCCUPANCY TENANTS ORDINANCE.

Previous attempts to protect tenants.

75. In paragraph 24 of the Statement of Policy made by His Majesty's Government in October, 1930, it is laid down that "consideration must "also be given to the protection of tenants by "some form of occupancy right, or by other means, "to secure them against ejectment or the imposi-"tion of excessive rental".

I have reproduced in Appendix S.R. II the Transfer of Land Ordinances 1920/1921 which, to quote the words used on page 115 of the Report of the Commission on the Palestine Disturbances of August, 1929, "were designed to avoid the " danger which appears now to be imminent, namely, " that large numbers of Arab tenants and cultivators " for whom no alternative land is available would " be deprived of their holdings". Explanations are given in the same Report of the reasons for the failure of those Ordinances to effect their designed object: and a further discussion of the subject will be found at pages 34 - 38 of the Hope Simpson Report.

Omissions in past or existing legislation.

76. As pointed out by the Commission, the Protection of Cultivators Ordinance, 1929, did not afford the necessary safeguards for tenants who may be driven into indebtedness. It did nothing to secure to those dispossessed "a sufficient "area for the maintenance of their families". This unsatisfactory Ordinance was indeed

strengthened/

strengthened in some directions last year, and additional amendments are now under consideration.

Recent decision by Settlement Officers purporting to create occupancy rights.

77. A new element has been introduced into the situation by recent decisions of Settlement Officers in certain state domains which lay down that lands therein cultivated by tenants of long standing are "subject to hereditary and "assignable rights of occupancy and tenancy "..........against payment of rental tithe to the "Government of Palestine". These decisions are now under appeal by Government in the Civil Court, as hitherto occupancy rights are believed not to have existed under Ottoman, i.e. current, land law.

A draft occupancy Tenants Ordinance.

78. In conformity with the promise of His Majesty's Government quoted above, it is sought by a draft Occupancy Tenants Ordinance (which, I would repeat, is put forward as a basis for consideration and discussion) to grant protection against eviction to tenants who, if not so safe-guarded, must, in a very large number of cases, become landless Arabs, such as have now to be re-settled at great expense to the State.

Many difficulties in framing a scheme.

79. That the fulfilment of any scheme to give " protection of tenants by some form of occupancy right" bristles with difficulties cannot be gain-said: but I have presumed that it is intended to face the issues, and some assistance in framing the draft Ordinance has been obtained from the Irish Land Act 1881. In Ireland, as still in

Palestine/

-55-

Palestine, the normal form of lease was an annual tenancy without written contract.

The question of date for enactment.

80. One of the great difficulties in all cases of this nature centres round the date when an Ordinance of the kind contemplated shall come into operation. Unless a suitable date is selected, attempts are made as soon as the proposals become known to anticipate and frustrate their effects. Accordingly, I suggest as appropriate the date on which the Protection of Cultivators' Amendment Ordinance came into operation, namely the 29th May, 1931.

Some explanations of the provisions of the draft Ordinance.

81. It is not necessary, I conceive, to state at length in this Report the reasons which have led to the inclusion in the draft Ordinance of all its provisions: but I conclude this Section of the Report by adding some explanations of certain salient features.

In Article 3 there is a provision whereby a tenant, who was on the date named above cultivating a holding, acquires a right of occupancy therein; even though that holding has been left vacant since, or has been let to a subsequent tenant; as has in fact occurred in numerous cases in order to prevent the acquisition of rights under the Protection of Cultivators Ordinances, 1929-31. In the latter case, the occupancy tenant would have to apply to the Court for possession: and the Court would give him possession upon such date as is equitable, regard being had to the rights of the person who has become tenant since the 29th May, 1931.

It is/

It is to be remembered that in the normal course of affairs, probably, the great majority of tenants cultivate in the same villages year after year, and are to all intents and purposes hereditary cultivators.

In Article 5 there is a provision for fixed rents in ordinary circumstances. This follows the normal custom of the country.

In Article 6 there is a provision for fixity of tenure. An occupancy tenant can be evicted only for breach of the contract of tenancy. There is, however, an important proviso in sub-clause 1 (f) of that Article. It has been felt that where an owner has purchased his property before the Ordinance comes into force, not with speculative or merely acquisitive aims, but with the genuine intention of development or colonization etc; and has made temporary lettings of the land pending the commencement of active development or colonization, the land should not be subject to occupancy rights.

In sub-clause (ii) of the same Article there is a provision against attempts to defeat the Ordinance by collusive evictions.

In Article 7 there is a provision for sale of occupancy rights subject to the restrictions imposed in the Homestead Protection Ordinance.

In Article 11, there is a provision that where the immediate landlord of an occupancy tenant is a middleman, the determination of the

latter's/

-57-

latter's interests will not affect the tenancy except in so far as the occupancy tenant will become tenant to the superior landlord.

In Article 12 there is a provision that the sale of the landlord's interest in execution proceedings will not affect the tenancy rights.

In Article 14 there is a provision whereby the acquisition of tenancy rights is excluded in cases where the landlord and tenant have entered into an agreement such as colonizing bodies make with tenants.

In Article 15 there is a provision for the resumption of a holding from an occupancy tenant with the permission of the District Commissioner for purposes of development or colonization etc. upon proper provision being made for the future maintenance of the tenant.

I have limited the draft to main principles without the elaboration of details which a completed Ordinance would necessarily require.

IV.

PROMOTIVE MEASURES.

(a) <u>Citrus Experimental and Demonstration Stations</u>.

Citrus Stations for experiment and demonstration.

82. I turn now to a scheme for the promotion of the all-important citrus industry, which in Palestine is still in its youth. The proposals that I recommend are for a Government subvention towards the maintenance of an efficient Citrus Experimental Station and the establishment by Government of a Citrus Demonstration Station in connection therewith.

The citrus industry in Palestine, which has expanded so remarkably in the last few years, will certainly continue its progress so long as suitable land is available. The high prices at which the Jaffa orange has been sold hitherto puts the fruit in the "luxury" category. When recently-planted groves come into bearing, and the supply of oranges is thereby considerably increased, the appeal will have to be made by means of lower prices to the less affluent public. The greater the output, as more and more groves come into bearing, the keener will be the competition in world markets, and the more pronounced the tendency towards further depression of prices. Another aspect is that the extension of the area under cultivation will increase the risks and dangers of the pests peculiar to citrus.

Necessity for research and experiment in citrus industry.

83.- To enable the industry to dispose of its produce profitably at falling prices, research and experiment in all branches of the industry (cultural, packing, transport and marketing) must be actively and continuously pursued; and, inasmuch as the great majority of the growers are smallholders, steps must be taken to demonstrate

the results/

results of the experiments and to encourage their wide application.

The work already done by Jewish bodies.

84. Much good research and experimental work has already been done by the Jews, but much more remains to be done. Other citrus countries have been working at their problems for years, and those of Palestine are largely special problems arising out of local conditions for which the results of research in other countries form little guide.

Government's stake in the citrus industry.

85. Government has a lively interest in the success of the industry, and any funds which it may have to provide in order to ensure adequate research, experiment and demonstration will be amply rewarded in the form of increased taxable capacity. It is, indeed, under contemplation to enhance substantially the taxation on the products of new citrus groves; and it seems to me incumbent on Government to assist with all its power an industry on which it depends, and will continue to depend, so largely for its revenues.

Alternative courses open for establishment of required Citrus Stations.

86. Agriculturists of small means are notoriously reluctant to provide funds for research, and Governments commonly have to lead the way. Fortunately, in Palestine, the Jewish organisations are keenly interested in the success of the citrus industry and have already shown appreciation of the importance of, and willingness to provide funds for, research. The work of their scientific staff appears to have been done efficiently; and certainly at a very low cost.

If Arab growers are at present unable to provide funds for Experimental and Demonstration Stations,

maintained/

—60—

maintained, jointly, by the Jewish and Arab sections of the industry, the only other courses open to Government are (i) to cooperate with and subsidise the Jewish Agency, or (ii) to set up its own stations.

Proposal for Government cooperation with the Jewish bodies explained.

87. The former course would certainly be much cheaper for Government, and it may be assumed that the work would be done not less efficiently. On these grounds, I would recommend in principle the plan of cooperation and subsidy. The scheme advocated may be briefly described thus:-

The Jewish Experimental Station.

88. The Jewish Agency holds 120 dunams of citrus land at Rehoboth and 500 dunams of undeveloped citrus land, hardby, at Ness-Ziona. The land at Rehoboth is occupied, or will be occupied, by the nurseries and laboratories (in course of construction) of the Agency's Experimental Station, which will in due course be transferred, with the staff, from its present temporary station at Tel-Aviv.

To the existing five scientific divisions, some of which deal with general, as well as citrus, research, it is proposed to add a sixth General Citricultural Research Division for the field experiments of which part of the Ness-Ziona land will be used. At the outset, 100 dunams only will be set aside for this purpose: leaving the remainder for future extension of field experiments, which will be required as fresh problems open up. In addition to this Experimental Station, a separate Demonstration Station - a Government institution - is needed for the purpose of demonstrating and encouraging the adoption by growers of the best methods now practised and of future improvements established by the research done, and experiments made, at the Ness-Ziona Experimental Station.

89./

-61-

Establishment of a Government Demonstration Station.

89. Careful consideration of the matter in all its bearings has led me to the conclusion that the Government Demonstration Station should be established on a main road and in the vicinity of Jaffa: so that its accessibility to growers would encourage their resort thereto. It would be necessary to purchase for this purpose 200 dunams in all; on 100 of which would be given demonstrations of the best cultural methods now pursued. A small packing house would illustrate modes of picking and packing fruit for export. As the work of the Experimental Station proceeds, the results of new research and experiments would be demonstrated on the remaining 100 dunams of the Demonstration Station, where variety tests would also be made.

Distribution of costs of scheme between Government and Jewish bodies.

90. Particulars of the estimated expenditure on the Experimental and Demonstration Stations up to the end of the fifth year are set forth in Appendix S.R.V, and it is suggested that Government should agree to contribute half the nett expenditure (i.e. after crediting receipts from sales of fruit produced) on both Stations, excluding the capital expenditure already incurred or being incurred by the Jewish Agency on the Experimental Station and the value of any additional Jewish Agency lands at Rehoboth which may be appropriated for field experiments.

This would involve total contributions by Government over a period of five years of about LP 28,365; and by the Jewish Agency of a similar amount, in addition to the excluded capital expenditure (amounting to LP 10,700) and the additional lands referred to above.

It will be seen from the Appendix S.R. V that the expenditure to be borne in equal shares by Government and the Jewish Agency would be much greater in the first

-62-

year than in any of the succeeding four years. It might be necessary for Government, as a provisional arrangement, to spread its contributions unevenly over the five years, so as to flatten out the Jewish Agency contributions, and to have an adjustment in the fifth year to equate the total contributions of the two parties over the five year period. In that case the Government contributions would be approximately LP. 14,885 in the first year and LP. 4,558, LP. 4,486, LP. 4,234 and LP. 4,202 in the second, third, fourth and fifth years.

It is contemplated that the Experimental Station, with the trees thereon and all equipment, would remain the property of the Jewish Agency or, as regards the land, the Jewish National Fund, and that the Demonstration Station, with the trees thereon and the equipment, would be the property of the Government: also that the appointment of the scientific personnel for the Experimental Station would remain with the Jewish Agency.

Constitution of an Advisory Committee for the Stations. Other safeguards. 91. To supervise generally the work done at the two Stations and to advise as to the programme of future work to be carried out, an Advisory Committee consisting of the two Station Directors, representative Jewish and Arab growers, and the Director of Agriculture as Chairman would be constituted.

It would, of course, be necessary to stipulate that the estimates of the annual expenditure of the two stations should be subject to Government's prior approval; and, when sanctioned, they should not be exceeded without the previous consent of Government; and that Government should have full rights of audit.

Although/

Although the Demonstration Station would obviously not be fully developed in five years, it would no doubt be desirable to limit the agreement for a Government subsidy to that period in the first instance, in order to provide an opportunity for a review of the arrangements in the light of experience.

These Citrus Stations of benefit for both Jews and Arabs.

92. The financial assistance provided by Government for the maintenance of the stations would, it is of course understood, be for the benefit of both Jewish and Arab citrus growers.

(b) (i) <u>Cooperative Movements</u> and
    (ii) <u>Marketing</u>.

(1) Cooperative Movements and their supervision by a Registrar.

93. An appointment to the post of Registrar of Co-operative Societies not having been announced at the time of writing this Report, the position remains as described in the First Report (paragraph 110). When an officer is appointed, his work will have a dual aspect; the oversight of Jewish cooperative societies in their manifold activities, some of which are referred to below: and the formation of Arab cooperative credit and selling societies. Although it is understood that a cooperative selling society in connection with the citrus industry is under formation by prominent Arab citrus-growers in the Southern District, the work in connection with the Arab communities, whether urban or rural, will be entirely up-hill at first: and few visible results are to be expected until a considerable period of time has elapsed. Care will have to be taken that the Registrar is not saddled with extraneous duties, diversion to which would inevitably react unfavourably on his special work.

The constitution of "farms" or colonies of landless Arabs on cooperative lines has already been

discussed/

-64-

discussed in Section I of this Report.

Government's interest in citrus marketing problems.

94. There is another matter in which Government's close and practical interest is called for. In paragraph 40 above I have alluded to the marketing problems which threaten the citrus industry in the near future: and in paragraph 49 to the fact that in the state of development to which the country has already attained or is likely to attain for some considerable period, it can look only to the citrus industry as the main source of its prosperity.

Estimates of the progressive growth of the citrus industry.

95. Various estimates have been framed of the areas under citrus, and a special official survey of the groves is, I understand, being undertaken. The figures usually quoted of the existing plantations are about 130,000 dunams, of which approximately 40,000 are said to be in bearing. The estimates assume, roughly, a generaly average of 80 to 85 exportable cases per dunam; and the actual exports during the season just closed have aggregated about 3½ million cases. It would appear on this basis that in 1936/7 the total will be at least 11 millions. In an article recently published in a Jewish paper, the writer arrived at a similar conclusion by a different method. He estimates the present Jewish citrus groves in bearing as covering 10,500 dunams, with an exportable output this year of 1,400,000 cases. New Jewish plantings in the years 1926 to 1931 inclusive are given as 54,000 dunams, which in 1936/7 will yield over 5½ million cases (at over 100 cases per dunam). The writer assumes that the Arab citrus crop in the last named year will be about the same as that of the Jews: so that the total number of cases to be marketed abroad five years hence will reach at least 11 million cases. Even allowing a deduction for calamities, the produce in 1936/37 should be about, or possibly more than, three times the number of cases being exported in 1931/32.

Taking/

-65-

Taking the fruit "culled" or rejected as unfit for export, as 1/3rd to 1/4th of the gross produce, there will be also the equivalent of almost all the exportable oranges now being produced to be disposed of locally, or treated for by-products.

Increase in citrus planting. 96. Further, there is no sign of cessation in citrus planting: quite the reverse. Indeed, a prominent member of the Jewish community has expressed to me his opinion that even if 50 million cases are produced, they can all be absorbed (in addition to the dozen million cases of "rejects"). The onlooker aware of the march of events in other citrus-producing countries may well pause to wonder how all these enormous increases are to be disposed of, at home and abroad.

ii) Needs of cooperative marketing organisations. 97. The need for an effective organisation of the industry to enable this large and growing output to be marketed economically, and at the best prices, requires no emphasis; and the fullest advantages of cooperative effort must be the aim of the industry and the care of Government.

The bulk, probably 85%, of the existing output from Jewish groves is being packed and marketed cooperatively; and about three-quarters through societies dealing only with oranges. Separate orange cooperative societies are being formed out of the cooperative societies dealing with agricultural produce generally, and the aim is to have all oranges handled through separate orange societies. It is intended to form in two or three years' time a Central Fruit Growers Exchange, under expert management, whose business it will be to market the fruit of the local societies and, generally, to interest itself in the internal economy of the industry for the purpose of reducing costs and securing better profits to the growers.

With/

With the exception named in paragraph 93 above, no cooperative societies have yet been formed among the Arab growers, the bulk of whom sell their crops on the trees to brokers, who can choose their own times for picking the fruit, regardless of any effect on the succeeding year's crop. When picking is delayed the next crop suffers, and the loss falls on the grower. It is clearly most desirable in the interests of both Arab and Jewish growers that the Arab growers should lose no time in forming local cooperative societies. They would then be likely to get seasonal crop advances on better terms, and be able to avoid the uneconomical practice of selling the fruit on the trees. They could make joint purchases of packing materials on improved terms; and have the grading and packing by their members supervised, to the general advantage. The local societies could be federated - for joint purchase of packing materials on a larger scale, for selling, for shipping and other services. This would facilitate the formation of an Arab Central Fruit Growers Exchange, cooperating with the Jewish Exchange, and in time, it is hoped, amalgamating with it. Government will have to apply the stimulus, and give the movement unremitting and sympathetic oversight and guidance, working for an industry united in its efforts to obtain the best results for all growers. The greater the measure of effective cooperation, the greater are likely to be the profits of individual growers, whether Jewish or Arab.

The good work of the Agricultural Council. Need for an expanded marketing medium.

98. Among the sections of the Agricultural Council which has been formed by the Department of Agriculture, there is an Agricultural Economics and Marketing Committee that has done much valuable work in dealing with current

agricultural/

agricultural questions. It is composed of members who generously give such time as they can afford to the study of the problems to be solved: but the citrus industry is becoming so large, and is so important, that it seems to me something more than such a Committee should be established if the many wide problems likely to arise in the future are to be grappled with successfully.

The question of advertisement in connection with marketing.

99. A very able and practical representative of the Jewish community recently remarked to me that one of the country's great needs was a Marketing Board to be composed of one or two marketing experts whose sole duties would be to think out ways and means of developing new markets for the citrus and other industries: and that a second step would be the establishment in London of a Palestine House in imitation of the methods adopted by the Dominions. The situation was put in another light by a distinguished citizen of the United States of America when he expressed the opinion that the people of this country have not yet acquired even the rudiments of advertising their products. I think both these views call for the careful consideration of Government and the citrus growers.

(c) <u>Animal Husbandry</u>.

The dairy industry.

100. While I have expressed the conviction that the citrus industry must remain, at all events for many years, the principal source of the country's exports, it is necessary to consider the prospects of other rural activities.

Hopes have been entertained that a dairying industry capable of competing in foreign markets could be established. Palestine is a country with a great scarcity of natural pastures: and their extent is

steadily/

steadily being diminished with marsh reclamation and the expansion of citrus and other plantations. With this handicap and the absence of any means of disposal (other than poultry) for skimmed milk, which in other countries is fed to pigs, it is difficult to believe that Palestine dairy products can hope to compete successfully in foreign markets with those of more highly favoured countries like Australia, New Zealand, etc.

The Government Stock Farm. 101. At present the subject of animal husbandry is being pursued from two standpoints: and it is a question whether there should not be closer cooperation by the two sides than actually exists. The Government Stock Farm, Acre, is gradually being stocked with selected indigenous breeds of cattle, sheep and goats (in addition to poultry) with a view to the distribution of their progeny to farmers.

The Jewish Dairy Industry. 102. On the other hand, Jewish enterprise deals with high-grade imported cattle. The dairying industry among the Jews has developed rapidly: but its position seems to me precarious. The present costs of Jewish production, due partly to expensive methods of feeding and scarcity of pasture and fodder, and partly to faulty organisation and distribution, are too high to allow of successful competition in local markets with imported products. But Government cannot afford to let the matter rest in its present stage. It may be that time will show that, in the conditions obtaining in Palestine, the local cows, under proper feeding and other treatment, are more economical dairy animals than the high-grade and cross-bred cattle which the Jews are

now/

now using. Even so, there are about 12,000 of these latter-named cattle in the Jewish dairy farms, and it is vital that all possible steps should be taken, by experiments in feeding and fodder production, to bring down production costs.

Three main aspects of animal husbandry.
103. Animal husbandry has three main aspects - disease, feeding and breeding. Good work has been done by Government in the control and eradication of disease, but little has so far been attempted for the general improvement of feeding and breeding. The matter is of considerable importance, not only on the dairying side, but also in stock raising for meat. Tests are required with the different local breeds, to determine their capacity for both growth and milk production, and the extent to which their rate of production could be increased by improved methods of feeding and management and by selective breeding. Experiments are required also to ascertain the feeding value of local foodstuffs, so as to determine the most economic rations for different kinds of stock-cattle, sheep, goats (and poultry). A carefully-planned programme, extending over perhaps eight to ten years, should produce good results and facilitate the policy of closer settlement.

Suggestion for cooperation between Government and the Jews.
104. I suggest that Government should undertake forthwith an enquiry into the best method of carrying out the work and the funds which would be required. Should it be found that the Jewish Agency Experimental Dairy Farm at Rehoboth could usefully cooperate, if only as regards experiments designed to reduce the production costs for dairying with high-grade and cross-bred cattle, the question of a Government subvention would no doubt be considered.

(3)/

(d) Egg production.

Palestine suitable for production of turkeys and eggs.

105. An industry which shows promising prospects, and merits the sustained attention of Government, is that of egg production.

The rearing of domestic birds such as turkeys, geese, ducks and fowls in the farmyard is of particular concern to farmers under conditions of intensive cultivation: and, fortunately, climatic and other conditions of Palestine appear on the whole suited to the raising of turkeys for the table and hens for egg production.

I have been informed by a catering expert that this country can and does produce some of the very best turkeys in the world; but that, at present, while the eggs produced are generally satisfactory and superior to those which Egypt exports in such large quantities, the quality of table poultry is indifferent. No doubt, as the poultry industry progresses, this defect will be remedied. Attention is, for the time being rightly concentrated on increasing egg production.

Egg production industry requires still greater attention.

106. Popular sentiment among the Arabs (and to a certain degree among the Jews) still relegates the supervision and management of the fowl-yard to the distaff side of the house; and although ideas will probably change as the industry develops, the feeling indicated serves to retard this development. The result is that the management of fowls on scientific lines is almost entirely confined to the Jews.

Action taken by Government to promote the industry.

107. Government has already shown its interest in the poultry industry through the research into diseases conducted by the Veterinary Department and by the stocking of the Government Stock Farm, Acre, with

poultry/

poultry for the hatching eggs of which there is an unsatisfied demand.

It is hoped that production of such eggs will be largely increased in the near future.

Monograph on egg production recently published. 108. In an admirable bulletin recently published by the Palestine Economic Society an exhaustive analysis has been made of the situation as regards egg production. It is reported that between the years 1926-1930 there has been a decrease of 50% in the importation of eggs, accompanied by a fall in prices. But even in the last year named about 8 million eggs consumed in Palestine were of foreign origin. The compilers of the bulletin calculate that on the average (Jew and Arab poultry-keepers taken together) a hen in this country lays about 90 eggs per annum, which is not a high figure considering that its cost of maintenance is estimated to be equivalent to the value of 70 eggs per annum.

Conditions of a successful export trade. Results of trial shipments made to the United Kingdom. 109. Palestine being situated as it is, if the industry of egg production is to attain real prosperity it must be able to ship eggs to foreign markets in seasons of the year, i.e. between October and January, when high prices can be commanded there. During the cold weather three trial shipments to the United Kingdom were made, two by Government and one by the Jewish Selling Agency known as "Tnuva". The results surpassed expectations: and the Empire Marketing Board, with whose assistance the consignments were marketed, has in its technical report expressed the opinion that a market for Palestine eggs exists in the United Kingdom. It is noteworthy that the first Government consignment, which consisted of eggs

purchased/

-72-

purchased through "Tnuva" from Jewish settlements in the plain of Esdraelon, and the second ("Tnuva") consignment, which also came from Jewish sources, were described as very satisfactory, while the third shipment, which was composed of eggs collected from Arab villages, was generally satisfactory but the least pleasing of the three consignments.

(e) <u>Mesha'a Lands and Land Registration</u>.

The proportions of mesha'a land in various parts of the country.

110. In paragraph 32 of the First Report I quoted statistics which show how the primitive system of <u>mesha'a</u>, or land held in joint ownership, was gradually weakening: and I remarked that the proportion of mesha'a land in the country was less than 40 per cent.

It is apparent from unverified statistics kindly supplied by the Commissioner of Lands, that the position as regards partitions was at the end of last year as follows:

Villages.

	Partitioned.	Wholly or partly unpartitioned.	Unofficially partitioned.
Northern District	339	207	31
Southern "	109	168	31
Jerusalem "	131	23	-
	579	398	62

As a matter of fact, in addition to the 62 villages which are shown as unofficially partitioned, a number of the 579 villages returned by District Officers as partitioned are so probably as the result of unofficial partitioning. An analysis of the figures, as reported, reveals that in the Southern District, where much land has from climatic reasons comparatively small value, partitions have been effected to a less extent than elsewhere. In the Jerusalem

district/

district the percentage of partitioned villages is as high as 85%. This is mainly due to the congestion of the population and the consequently greater value of land in the hills. Long ago the hillmen were driven to abandon a system of ownership which prevents tree-planting, terracing, etc. On the other hand, where the population is comparatively sparse and the land provides the bare requisites of a livelihood without the labour and expense of tree-planting, manuring, etc., the mesha'a system still largely prevails.

Unofficial partitions. 111. Out of the 62 villages in Palestine which have been actually returned as unofficially partitioned, 29 lie in one District Officer's charge and 28 in another's. In 11 sub-districts no unofficial partition whatever has been carried through. It should be explained that an "unofficial" partition is one where the villagers have mutually agreed to effect partition themselves of their joint undivided lands without effecting registration in the Land Registry; and each man takes possession, with a view to permanent occupation, of the holding which is assigned to him. After 10 years of uninterrupted and unchallenged individual occupation, he obtains in any case a prescriptive right to this holding.

The excessiveness of fees levied. 112. It may be asked why, when matters have proceeded by mutual agreement as far as a partition of the village lands among the co-proprietors, steps are not taken by these owners to register their possession according to the law. One answer is that unless all the co-proprietors intimate their assent - practically an impossible condition in view of the existence of absentees and minors - the registrar refuses to register.

Even/

-74-

Even if a partition case comes before a magistrate, and he orders registration, the co-proprietors in most cases neglect to comply. In this omission is to be found the other answer to the question, viz: the exorbitance of the fees demanded by the State for validating unofficial partitions.

I reproduce below from the Report of the Mesha'a Land Commission of 1923 a summary of the fees that may be exacted from a mesha'a shareholder on partition:-

(a) the cost of a certificate of succession from the Moslem Sharia Court:

(b) 5% of the market value of his land to establish either original registration or subsequent purchase:

(c) survey charges amounting to several pounds:

(d) a registration fee for partition of ½% of the registered werko (land tax) value of his land, and

(e) in the future, an increase of 100% on his werko (land tax).

As the Committee on Economic Conditions which sat in 1930 drily remarks: "It is hardly surprising that the partition of mesha'a land has not progressed".

The ineffect- 113. Recommendations have been made to Government from iveness of the present system time to time for the encouragement of the voluntary of registration of titles. partition of mesha'a land: but until recently without success. By officers well versed in the administration it has been estimated to me that not one per cent of the land transactions in the country have, since the Occupation, been officially registered, one of the main deterrents being the exaction of the excessive fees specified above. If these fees were reduced and levied on a more reasonable scale, due regard being paid to the services rendered, I believe the fiscal gains would be considerable and the registration of title, if the system

of/

−75−

of registration in villages which I have recommended in paragraphs 43 - 54 of the First Report be set up, would become universal. At present the records of the Land Registry are popularly believed to be quite unreliable: and unless some such system as that referred to above be introduced, the work which is being done at great cost in the settlement operations for the establishment of titles will in a generation be nullified; and property records will be in as bad a state again as they were under the Ottoman administration.

Contrast of fees levied inside and outside the settlement area.

114. There is another aspect of this question of fees levied in connection with unofficial partitions.

Under revised regulations published recently for villages in the settlement area, there are payable in cases of partition carried through by the Settlement officers no fees other than a nominal survey fee for service done by the Survey Department. On the other hand, if villagers outside the settlement area seek voluntarily to partition their lands without recourse to official aid and are by any remote chance in a position to have this partition legally confirmed, they are assessed on registration to the heavy fees indicated above. It thus appears to them that they are being severely penalised for doing themselves that which Government in its own good time will do for them gratis.

A revising Committee recommended.

115. Accordingly, for the examination, and with a view to the reform, of the existing archaic system of levying fees in connection with land partitions and registrations, I recommend the appointment of a small committee.

Other benefits derivable from encouragement of partitions.

116. Further, it is well-known to those familiar with the countryside that partitions of land held in joint ownership,

whether/

whether official or unofficial, are attended by a reduction in crimes of violence, thanks to the removal of fruitful grounds of quarrel. Again, there is an educative influence in the process of unofficial partition. If, in a country where cooperation is so little in evidence among one section of the population and where internal land disputes are so common in villages, Government can encourage a spirit of solidarity and induce the people themselves to undertake work which bears in it the germs of local self-government, it should not, I submit, lose the opportunity of thus facilitating real development and progress.

Ultimate economy effected by unofficial partitions.
117. In paragraph 34 of the First Report, I referred to work already done on unofficial partitions, and recently the Commissioner of Lands has been able to depute temporarily an Assistant Settlement Officer to supervise voluntary partitions in advance of settlement operations in the Southern District. Quite apart from other benefits, one result of such partitions will be to reduce materially the work, and, consequently, the cost of survey operations.

But only a small area in one district is affected by this deputation; and similar proceedings are wanted in the other two districts so that by the time settlement operations reach them, the villages in a very large part, if not the whole, of the country, will have been unofficially partitioned.

A special staff of supervising officers suggested. Their maximum cost.
118. In paragraph 35 of the First Report I recommended the appointment of a small special staff of Palestinian officials to guide the work of partition in advance of settlement. Three District Officers or Assistant Settlement Officers it is now suggested - one for the

rest/

rest of the Southern District, one for the remaining few unpartitioned villages of the Jerusalem district, and one for the Northern District - would suffice. As soon as the work in any one district was completed, the officer of that district could be transferrd to assist in another district, or it might be found advisable to concentrate the work of all the officers at first in one district.

I estimate that the three officers (with a small staff and equipment) would cost not more than £.2500 per annum. The economies to be effected eventually on the survey side of settlement operations will be substantial: but it is not possible to frame any exact estimate.

<small>Postponement of legislation recommended.</small>
119. Finally, I have given the subject of legislation referred to in paragraph 57 of the First Report further consideration: and am of opinion that for the present the supervision of unofficial partitions should be undertaken without any enactment until further experience has been gained of the difficulties that are likely to emerge.

(f) The Hydrographic and Irrigation Surveys.

<small>The proposed hydrographic survey.</small>
120. The hydrographic survey dealt with in paragraph 77 of the First Report remains of cardinal importance to the development of the country: and its early start will be all the more necessary if the proposal made in paragraph 39 above for a village-to-village survey in the maritime plain be accepted. There are, it has been ascertained, many water supplies and resources in villages which can and ought to be developed to the benefit of the local population and of the State revenues, and which are at present either running to waste or thriftlessly used. What is required is some system of control as recommended

in/

-78-

in paragraphs 78 - 88 of that Report and contemplated in the Irrigation Ordinance under consideration, with provision of funds to be used in the form of loans. The degree of financial assistance by the State which is called for in any particular case cannot be determined until a survey has furnished the necessary data: and it is not, therefore, possible, at this juncture, to make a general estimate of sums which can usefully be spent on the objects referred to and recovered by the State in due course.

The proposed survey needs to be supplemented in another highly important direction.

Expert Irrigation Surveys also required. 121. The conclusion has been reached in paragraphs 46 - 49 that citrus growing is in existing circumstances the sole large-scale industry in sight on which Palestine can depend for its prosperity: and a caveat has been added as to the perils of attempting or encouraging its indefinite expansion in a too brief period of years.

While, however, I deprecate hasty action in pushing on with new schemes for developing the Beisan, the Huleh, the Jordan Valley and Aujha Basin areas, I am of opinion that in conjunction with, or rather as a part of, the hydrographic survey already recommended, preliminary surveys of all these projects ought to be undertaken now by an expert Irrigation Engineer and suitable staff. Sooner or later this work must be done, before a final decision can be reached as to whether development of these tracts is or is not feasible or worth attempting. What the cost of such preliminary surveys will be and within what time they can be completed, I am not at present in a position to estimate.

To my other remarks on Irrigation recorded in paragraphs 78 - 88 of the First Report I have nothing to add.

(3) /

—79—

(g) The Position of the Hill Peasantry.

The congested hill areas.

122. Among the matters enumerated as coming within the purview of the Development Scheme is the question of the congestion amongst the _fellahin_ in the hill districts of Palestine. It was contemplated that measures will be devised for the improvement and intensive development of the land, and for bringing into cultivation areas which hitherto may have remained uncultivated, and thereby securing to the _fellahin_ a better standard of living, without, save in exceptional circumstances, having recourse to transfer. In this connection paragraphs 69 _et seq._ of the First Report may be read.

Deterioration of condition of hill _fellahin_. Need of security of tenure.

123. Further and closer acquaintance with the tracts referred to leads me to the conviction that in present conditions, the condition of these _fellahin_ is steadily deteriorating. In rural communities nothing is so fatal to progress as want of security of tenure – a want which can be supplied by protecting the small proprietor and the occupancy tenant from eviction. As long as insecurity exists, there can be no incentive to the _fellah_ to improve his lands by intensive cultivation. It is not that industry is wanting. No one whose work leads him among the hill _fellahin_ can fail to be impressed with the efforts which they, under pressure of increasing population, are making to extend their lands by reclamation and terracing.

The vital wants of the _fellah_ are few: his manner of existence simple and his poverty pervading. His holding is very small: the value of the produce he raises seems almost pitiful. On the other hand his family labour on the land, and his working expenses are almost negligible. Little can be done to give him a better return from his holding, if his outlay is not at the same time to be disproportionately increased. Once more - the process of amelioration can only be a slow and lengthy one.

Existing impediments to progress in hill areas. Mewat or "dead" land restrictions.	124. There are two or three impediments to progress that, I think, could be at once removed to his advantage. Under the old Turkish law anyone who was in need of what is known as "dead land" (vacant land of a certain defined nature) might, "with the leave of the official", plough it up gratuitously and cultivate it on condition that the legal ownership belonged to the State. If anyone broke up and cultivated land of this kind without leave, the value of the land was to be exacted from him and a title deed issued to him.

Under this system, no criminal process lay against the squatter.

In 1921, however, was promulgated the Mewat (i.e. dead land) Ordinance which substituted for the Turkish law the provision that "any person who, without "obtaining the consent of the Government, breaks up or "cultivates any waste land, shall obtain no right to a "title deed for such land, and further will be liable "to be prosecuted for trespass".

Effect of restrictions.	125. The effect of this change, with its attendant penalties, has been, I am informed, to put an end to, or to curtail, the breaking up of cultivable waste in hill areas where such land might be subjected to the industry of cultivators who badly need opportunities of expansion in their home villages.

126./

Possibility of removal or partial removal of restrictions.

126. The subject is not free of complications: for the extension of cultivation in suitable areas of Mewat land is closely connected with the maintenance of forest reserves which have been brought into existence with a view to protecting tree-growth, both natural and artificial, and also to preventing the continuous denudation of soil by rain or the grazing of animals. Something could, however, be done to ease the present restrictions in favour of the hill _fellahin_: and I recommend that the Mewat Ordinance should be cancelled, or else be so modified as to remove some of the unnecessarily deterrent effects of its existing provision.

Obstacles to arboriculture in the hills.

127. Another obstacle from which the Arab peasantry suffers is the want of facilities for obtaining fruit-trees for planting. In 1928 the Director of Agriculture issued instructions that Government nurseries should continue to raise forest and ornamental trees for departmental requirements, for sale and for issue for amenity planting as before; but fruit-trees commonly raised by private nurserymen should not be produced at Government nurseries excepting olives, carobs, walnuts, mulberries and pistachios, as well as unproved fruit stocks, particularly new types the propagation of which might more conveniently be carried out at Government nurseries.

The policy of restricting issues of fruit-trees seems to have been dictated by a fear that Jewish nurserymen might suffer in their trade; but the restrictions imposed seem to have been too drastic. Arabs are not in the habit of buying common fruit-trees – other than oranges etc. – from Jewish nurserymen, very few of whom exist outside the coastal plains and the suburbs of the three larger towns, and I recommend that the rules should be modified so as to

permit/

-82-

permit of sales of any trees from Government nurseries. If the policy of producing improved varieties on a limited scale at Government stations be adopted, the question of competition with the Jewish industry will scarcely arise.

If some such order were issued, fruit-trees would at first be obtainable from Government nurseries: and, if, and when, Arab or Jew private nurseries become more general, the Government institutions would automatically be devoted to other needs. The Department of Agriculture has been making efforts to get such Arab nurseries started, and there seem good hopes of success: but it may be some years before a sufficient number of such concerns exist, particularly in the hill areas where the planting of fruit-trees is most desiderated.

Measures in being for assistance of fellahin.

128. On the positive side the Department of Agriculture is actively endeavouring to spread the advantages of good, clean seed - with such success that enough seed of the types favoured cannot yet be grown. This work too must necessarily be very gradually developed. Perhaps, one of the most astonishing features of rural economic conditions is the blindness of the moneylender, who takes so large a proportion of the fellah's grain crops, to the advantages he would derive if he assisted his clientèle in growing crops from selected seed which returns higher yields than the dirty, unselected grain to be found in the ordinary village shops.

V.
CONCLUDING REMARKS.

The matters enumerated in the Secretary of State's despatch of 26th June, 1931. How dealt with in the two Reports.

129. In the First Report and in this Supplementary Report, I have dealt with the matters which were enumerated in the Secretary of State's despatch No. 487 of the 26th June, 1931. (a copy of which is given in Appendix I to the First Report), as the initial steps to be taken to give effect to the policy of His Majesty's Government in regard to Agricultural Development and Land Settlement in Palestine.

A summary of these initial steps, and how they have been covered in the Reports, may be added:-

(a) The registration of displaced Arab families is proceeding (S.R. paragraphs 5 - 7).

(b) Schemes for the re-settlement of some of these Arab families, when registered, have been drawn up (S.R. paragraphs 17 - 36).

(c) In the First Report the pre-requisites to any large schemes of land settlement or development have been outlined (F.R. paragraphs 22-70). An enquiry has been undertaken to ascertain what State and other lands are, or properly can be made, available for the re-settlement of the displaced Arabs mentioned above and for close settlement by Jews.

The/

–C4–

The potentialities have been considered and discussed (F.R. Part II. S.R. Section I, paragraphs 8 – 43: Section II, paragraphs 44 –52: Section IV (f) paragraph 120: Appendix S.R. I).

The question of the congestion amongst the <u>fellahin</u> in the hill districts has received attention, and such measures as seem practicable for the improvement and intensive development of their lands have been indicated (S.R. Section III and Section IV (g), paragraphs 122-128).

(d) (i)   The feasibility and advisability of providing credits for Arab cultivators and Jewish settlers have been examined (S.R. Section II, paragraphs 54 – 60, and Section IV (b) paragraphs 93 – 99).

(ii)   Consideration has been given to the possibilities of draining, irrigating and reclaiming land not at present cultivated or cultivated only to a limited extent; and hydrographic and irrigation surveys have been recommended (F.R. Part II: S.R. Section IV (f), paragraphs 120 & 121, and Appendix S.R. I).

(f)   In all cases where sufficient data are available, as close an estimate as possible of the cost of the works or other measures proposed has been given.

Lastly, in Section III of this Report I have dealt at some length with the necessity of certain restrictive measures which in no way conflict with the declared policy of His

Majesty's/

Government, but which, if enacted, would serve to prevent the recurrence of many of the agrarian problems with which the country is at present and must in future, in default of such legislation, remain confronted.

Change in financial situation. The cost involved of the measures recommended in the two Reports.

130. In January last, the Secretary of State intimated that conditions had changed very much since his predecessor's despatch of the 26th June, 1931, was written, and that it could not now be assumed that it would be found practicable to make two and a half million pounds available for development purposes. His Majesty's Government would, however, give careful consideration to the Director's Reports and the High Commissioner's recommendation thereon, after receiving the observations of the Jewish Agency and the Arab Executive, so that early action might be taken, (financial circumstances permitting) to give effect to a limited scheme of development, providing first for the resettlement of landless Arabs and secondly for some assistance for Jewish settlement.

In the First and Supplementary Reports I have recommended certain measures, involving expenditure by Government, which in my opinion will facilitate development and closer settlement. These measures, with the estimated cost of carrying them out, so far as data are at present available, are:-

(i) Additional Survey staff, if found to be necessary, in order to complete the work of

settlement/

-86-

settlement at the earliest possible date:
£P. 12,000 spread over 8 years (F.R. paragraph 24).

(2) Appointment of a small special staff to undertake partitions of Mesha'a lands in advance of settlement: £P. 2,500 a year or less for, probably, three years; which would, however, ultimately effect an economy in the total cost of settlement (F.R. paragraph 35, and S.R. paragraphs ~~115~~ & 118).

Also, the appointment of a small Committee (involving no appreciable cost) to examine into the existing system of paying fees in connection with partitions and land registrations. (S.R. para. 115)

(3) The institution of a staff of Village Registrars for the proper maintenance of the record-of-rights in land and water and of records of crops etc: £P. 18,000 to £P.20,000 per annum as a maximum when the establishment has been completed. This expenditure would be offset to some extent by fees charged for copies of entries, reductions in present tax-collecting staff, closer collection of land tax or revenue and, probably, savings in other administrative services. (F.R. paragraph 53).

(4) Government control of water supplies, with the provision of loans to cultivators to facilitate the proper exploitation of water at present running to waste or thriftlessly used, as may be found to be desirable after the completion of a hydrographic survey to cost

£P.8,000/

£P.8,000 (F.R. paragraphs 77 – 39 and S.R. Section IV (f) paragraph 120).

(5) Government assistance towards the cost of Citrus Experimental and Demonstration Stations: £P. 32,365 during the first five years (S.R. Section IV (a) paragraphs 82-92).

(6) Further experiments in animal feeding and breeding over a long period: the cost to be ascertained after investigation by Government of a suitable programme of work (S.R. Section IV (c), paragraphs (100-104).

Summary of conclusions regarding re-settlement of landless Arabs and assistance for Jewish settlement.

131. In Section I of this (Supplementary) Report, I have set out the difficulties which have to be faced in effecting the re-settlement of displaced Arab families and given reasons for my conviction that progress is bound to be very slow. I have indicated that there is very little suitable land available in the dry-farming areas; and that, at present, the only other possibility is the development of small irrigated holdings on land adapted for citrus growing which is at present being cultivated extensively for cereals etc. This, I have shown, would involve the re-settlement also of the existing cultivators on the land to be acquired, and would cost about £P.800 for each displaced Arab family re-settled, spread over five or six years.

With regard to the question of assistance for Jewish settlement, I have expressed the opinion, in Section II of this Report, that even if it is found that there are no unsuperable technical obstacles to the irrigation, drainage

or/

-56-

or reclamation of the lands not at present cultivated or cultivated only to a limited extent, their exploitation would not be an economic proposition at the present stage of agricultural development in Palestine. In that Section also I have reached the conclusion that the case as presented so far to me for providing credit facilities for Jewish settlers, can scarcely win acceptance; but that some assistance might be justified later, in certain circumstances, if funds can be provided.

Cooperative Societies.

132. As stated in paragraph 93 above no appointment has, so far as I know, yet been made to the post of Registrar of Cooperative Societies. I am not, therefore, in a position to indicate what financial assistance may have to be provided, if funds are available, in order to facilitate the formation of cooperative credit societies among Arab cultivators.

133. It only remains to add an expression of the highest appreciation of the invaluable assistance rendered to me during the last two months by Mr F. Skevington, M.B.E., the Financial Adviser, first in the critical examination of the economic and financial aspects of the proposals which I have had under consideration and, secondly, in connection with the preparation of this Report; also of the careful and skilful counsel received in the preparation of parts of the Report and Appendices from Mr. A.H. Webb, K.C., Legal Adviser. I am most grateful, too, to Mr J. Dawson Shepherd, O.B.E., Irrigation Officer, and to officers of the

Department/

Department of Agriculture for much sound advice on technical and other matters: and, finally, to Mr W.A. Thorogood, the Chief Clerk, and the other members of my office staff for the cheerful energy and efficiency with which they have carried out their duties.

APPENDIX S.R.1.

In Appendix II to my First Report was given a list of State Domains, showing generally how they are at present disposed of. Detailed enquiries have been pursued with reference to the first and second major objects of the Development policy of resettling landless Arabs and ascertaining what State and other lands are or properly can be made available for close settlement by Jews. The results of those enquiries are summarised below:-

STATEMENT OF STATE LANDS.

Numbers in Appendix II of First Report.	Remarks.
1. Lake Huleh Lands	See sections 99-107 of First Report.
2. Samakh 3. Beisan Jiftlik 4. Ghor el Fara'a	See sections 93-98 of First Report.
5. Dahnuneh & Mubarakeh 6. Rakayak 7. Rushmia 8. Athlit 9. Kabbara 10. Cherkaz 11. Caesarea 12. Basset el Mullabis 13. Jaffa Sand Dunes 13a. Umm Khalid dunes (1260 dunams)	Where cultivable and not under litigation these domains are leased or conceded to the Jews.
14. Jazzair (418 dunams)	Small area leased to Arabs.
15. Mansourah (2500 dunams)	19 tenants of long standing cultivate 130 dunams each on an average. Water very scarce.
16. Subeih (7500 dunams)	An area of 2000 dunams has been taken up for the Jewish Agricultural School. 70 families of long standing cultivate about 100 dunams apiece. The people are described as very poor.
17. Kaukab El Hija (? 30,000 dunams)	The actual area of the estate is unknown. Government's share is 1/8th, or about 3000 dunams. There are 31 Government tenants of long standing cultivating about 100 dunams each.

18./

18. Kishon lands (450 dunams)	—	Small isolated plots under litigation.
19. Hedeidrin (600 dunams)	—	Under litigation.
20. Zalafe (Zafarieh) (2,700 dunams)	—	There are said to be 19 families of long standing cultivating an average of about 140 dunams. There is no well other than a "catchment" cistern.
21. Tel el Dahab (2,400 dunams)	—	50 families of long standing cultivate from 8 to 90 dunams each. No well.
22. Deir Ghazaleh (2,700 dunams)	—	Twenty-four families of long standing cultivate an average of 112 dunams each. There is a shortage of drinking water.
23. El Akrabanieh el-Gharbieh (960 dunams)	—	9 families of cultivators have been in occupation over 30 years, cultivating an average of 120 dunams each.
24. Mazra'a el Hamra (11,300 dunams)	—	154 families have been cultivating this area for 50 years: and 9 families from 15-20 years. Average holding under 70 dunams. No well exists.
25. El Farush (1,656 dunams)	—	For fifty years 70 families have been in occupation, cultivating each on an average 23 dunams. No well.
26. Sajad (7,000 dunams)	—	There are 32 families with rights cultivating normally some 230 dunams each. There are, in addition, over 100 persons who work on the land without actual rights. The people are all very poor and eke out a livelihood by leasing, when possible, about 1,000 dunams from surrounding villages.
27. Hamadieh (500 dunams)	—	Small area leased to tenants of long standing.
28. Jericho (86,600 dunams)	—	About 28,000 dunams only cultivable. This area is cultivated by 220 families, giving an average of 127 dunams apiece. It also includes about 1,000 dunams of garden cultivated by garden-owners. More land might come under cultivation if water could be made available from the Jordan.
29. Ain Feshka (1,300 dunams)		
30. Es Seweideh (17,000 dunams)	—	Uncultivable.
31. Gharabeh (108 dunams)	—	Small area leased.

32. Jahayyer
   (20,000 dunams)
   — Small area only leased for cultivation. Rest uncultivable.

33. Zeita
   (5,350 dunams)
   — 31 cultivating families of long standing who cultivate such areas as are cultivable, giving a nominal average of 173: actually much less owing to great scarcity of water.

34. Tel Arad
   (32,000 dunams)
   — Waterless. Water boring experiments by Jews some years ago abandoned as hopeless.

35. Jaladiyah
   (4,143 dunams)
   — There are 46 families with rights cultivating each about 100 dunams. The inhabitants of the domain lease annually from surrounding villages an additional area of 400 dunams, whenever they can.

36. Kofakhan
   (9,200 dunams)
   — There are 92 families with rights cultivating each about 100 dunams. The land being insufficient for needs, the inhabitants of the domain lease in addition about 2000 dunams from neighbouring villages whenever they have the opportunity.

37. Muharraqa
   (4,580 dunams)
   — There are 44 families with rights cultivating each about 100 dunams. If they have the necessary resources, the inhabitants lease also annually from surrounding villages about 1,000 dunams, in addition, for support.

38. Rafa
   (90,000 dunams)
   — Settlement operations begun: report not yet available from Settlement Officer. Cultivable land (estimated at 29,000 dunams) said to be cultivated by 300 to 400 families giving average of less than 70 dunams apiece.

39. Anata
   (15,000 dunams)
   — Generally uncultivable owing to absence of water. Area demarcated as Forest Reserve. Also under dispute as to ownership with Anata village.

40. Kharab & Awameed
   (360 dunams)
   — Antiquity site. Small area also leased to Tiberias Municipality.

41. Tob Alti
   (2,500 dunams)
   — Government Stud Farm. (Also Experimental Agricultural Farm)

42. Acre Sand Dunes
   (12,225 dunams)
   — Uncultivable. Part leased to Iraq Petroleum Co.

43. El Burj Ta
   (145 dunams)
   — Antiquity site.

44. Basset el Yaraki
   (2,500 dunams)
   — A mere swamp. Too saline for cultivation.

45. Gaza Sand Dunes
   (6,000 dunams)
   — Sites allotted for new Gaza. Area is uncultivable.

46./

46. Khirbet el Tabaka
     (600 dunams)   ⎫
                          ⎪   – Not really a Government property
47. Tubas   ⎬   in all probability. All cultiva-
     (41,700 dunams)   ⎪   ted by owners and tenants; except
                          ⎭   the area in Jordan Valley, possibly
                                 irrigable from that river.

48. Basset es Sheikh   – A swamp. The possibility of
     Mohammad   draining this for Beduin is
     (1,500 dunams)   under investigation.

APPENDIX S.R. II

AN ORDINANCE TO REGULATE THE TRANSFER OF LAND

Short Title.	1.	This Ordinance may be cited as the "TRANSFER OF LAND ORDINANCE, 1920-21".
Definitions.	2.	In this Ordinance and in all regulations made thereunder, unless there is something repugnant in the context :-

"Disposition" means a sale, mortgage, gift, dedication of waqf of every description, and any other disposition of immovable property except a devise by will or a lease for a term not exceeding three years, and includes a transfer of mortgage and a lease containing an option by virtue of which the term may exceed three years;

"Court" includes any Civil or Religious Court competent to deal with actions concerning land, as well as any Land Settlement Court which may be established:

"Land" includes houses, buildings, and things permanently fixed in the land.

Application of Ordinance.	3.	This Ordinance applies to all immovable property the subject of the Land Law of 7th Ramadan, 1274 A.H., as well as to mulk land, all forms of waqf land, and every other form of immovable property, and shall, so far as it applies, cancel the provisions of the Ordinance of 18th November, 1918.
Disposition to comply with Ordinance.	4.	No disposition of immovable property shall be valid until the provisions of this Ordinance have been complied with.

5./

-2-

Procedure.

5. (1) Any person wishing to make a disposition of immovable property must first obtain the written consent of the Government.

(2) In order to obtain this consent, a petition must be presented to the Director of Lands through the Land Registry Office of the district in which the land is situated, setting out the terms of the disposition intended to be made, and applying for his consent to the disposition. The petition must be accompanied by proof of the title of the transferor, and must contain an application for registration of a deed to be executed for the purpose of carrying into effect the terms of the disposition. The petition may also include a clause fixing the damages to be paid by either party who refuses to complete the disposition if it is approved.

Principal to be disclosed if disposition to agent.

6. (1) If the application for registration is made by an agent or nominee on behalf of a principal, the agent or nominee shall make full disclosure in his petition of the principal for whom he is acting, and the immovable property disposed of shall be registered in the name of his principal.

(2) If at any time it appears to a Court or a Registrar that immovable property has been registered under this Ordinance otherwise than in accordance with the foregoing provision, the Court or Registrar shall inquire into the case and make a report to the High Commissioner, who may impose upon any of the parties concerned penalties by way of fine or forfeiture not exceeding one-fourth of the value of the property.

7./

Power of corporation to own immovable property.	7. The Ottoman Law of 22nd Rabi El-Awal, 1331 A.H., concerning the right of a corporation to own immovable property, shall remain in force; provided that the Director of Lands may authorise any banking company to take a mortgage of land, and any commercial company registered in Palestine to acquire such land as is necessary for the purpose of its undertaking, and may, subject to the above conditions, consent to the transfer of land to any corporation.
Provision of sufficient land for tenants of agricultural land. (Section 2 of Land Transfer Amendment Ordinance No.2, 1921.)	8. (1) The consent of the Government to a disposition shall be given by the Director of Lands or the Registrar of the district or sub-district, who shall be satisfied only that the transferor has a title; provided that, in the case of agricultural land which is leased, he shall also be satisfied that any tenant in occupation will retain sufficient land in the district or elsewhere for the maintenance of himself and his family. (2) After the title has been examined and the consent of the Government has been obtained, a deed shall be executed in the form prescribed by rules made hereunder, and shall be registered in the Land Registry. (3) No guarantee of title or of the validity of the transaction is implied by the consent of the Government and the registration of the deed.
Mortgage of immovable property.	9. No mortgage shall be accepted for registration unless it complies with the terms of the Provisional Law for the mortgage of immovable property of 16th Rabi ul-Tani, 1331 A.H., and the amendments of the said Law.

- 4 -

Unauthorised disposition to be null and void.

10. (1) Every disposition to which the written consent of the Government has not been obtained shall be null and void; provided that any person who has paid money in respect of a disposition which is null and void may recover the same by action in the Courts.

(2) Nothing in this section shall affect the operation of Public Notice No.115, dated 30th April, 1919, concerning promissory notes given on account of an invalid transaction in immovable property.

Penalties for illegal disposition.

11. If any person is a party to any disposition of immovable property which has not received the consent of the Government, and either enters into possession or permits the other party to enter into possession of the immovable property, whether by himself or any person on his behalf, he shall be liable on conviction by a Court to a payment of a fine not exceeding one-fourth of the immovable property.

Registration of immovable property received by will or inheritance.

12. When any immovable property passes by operation of a will or by inheritance, the legatees or heirs, as the case may be, shall be jointly and severally responsible for the registration of the immovable property in the name of the legatees or heirs within a year of the death of the registered owner. The registration shall be made upon the certificate of a competent Court stating that the persons acquiring registration are legatees or heirs, or upon a certificate signed by the Mukhtar or Imam and two notables.

12./

- 5 -

Sale of immovable property in execution of a judgment or satisfaction of a mortgage.

(Transfer of Land Ordinance No.2, 1921)

13. (1) Notwithstanding anything in the Proclamation of 24th June, 1918, the Courts may order the sale of immovable property in execution of a judgment or in satisfaction of a mortgage.

(2) Application for sale shall be made to the President of the District Court, who may order postponement of the sale, if he is satisfied:-

(a) That the debtor has reasonable prospects of payment if given time; or

(b) That, having regard to all the circumstances of the case, including the needs of the creditor, it would involve undue hardship to sell the property of the debtor.

Power of High Commissioner to establish Land Registry Offices.

14. The High Commissioner may establish a Land Registry Office in such places as may seem desirable; and may appoint such number of Registrars and Assistant Registrars as may be necessary.

Powers of High Commissioner to make rules.

15. The High Commissioner may from time to time make rules as to any of the following matters:-

(a) The organisation, procedure, and business of the Land Registry Office;

(b) The functions and duties of the Registrar and other officers of the Land Registry Office;

(c) The mode in which the register is to be kept;

(d) The forms to be used for deeds and documents;

(e) The requirements for attestation and official verification of the execution of deeds;

(f) The fees payable for or in connection with registration;

(g) /

- 6 -

(g) The appointment of attorneys;
(h) Any other matter or thing, whether similar or not to those above-mentioned, in respect of which it may be expedient to make rules for the purpose of carrying this Ordinance into effect.

September, 1920.

Sections 6 and 7 and part of Section 8 of the original Ordinance have been cancelled by the Transfer of Land Amendment Ordinance, No.2 of 1921.

The Land Transfer Ordinance, No.2 of 1921 and Transfer of Land Amendment Ordinance, No.2 of 1921 have been incorporated in this Ordinance.

APPENDIX S.R. III.

Draft.

HOMESTEAD PROTECTION ORDINANCE, 193-.

1. This Ordinance may be cited as the Homestead Protection Ordinance, 193-.

2. In this Ordinance:

"Cultivator" means the person in actual occupation of land as owner or occupancy tenant and his successors and assigns, but does not include a mortgagee in possession under Article 8 of this Ordinance.

"Disposition" means Sale, Exchange, Gift, Mortgage or Lease for a term exceeding one year.

"Homestead Area" means that portion of the land in the possession of a cultivator the permanent alienation of which shall not be permitted except with the consent of the District Commissioner.

"Land" means land used for the purpose of agriculture but does not include building sites within municipal areas.

"Mortgagee" and "Mortgager" include their successors and assigns respectively.

"Zone" means such area or portion of Palestine as the High Commissioner shall declare by notification published in the Official Gazette to be a Zone, and such notification shall specify what area of land in each Zone shall constitute a "Homestead Area" for an owner or an occupancy tenant.

Permanent Alienation of Homestead Area.

3. No disposition of land in a Zone by a cultivator shall be registered without the consent of the District Commissioner which shall be proved by the production to

the/

the Registrar of Lands of the Order of the District Commissioner giving such consent.

4. (1) A cultivator desiring to effect a disposition of land within a Zone shall apply in writing to the District Commissioner for his consent. Such application shall contain particulars of the proposed disposition and shall also give particulars of all land owned or occupied by the applicant.

(2) If any such application shall be false in any matter required to be stated therein the person making such application shall be liable upon conviction by a Magistrate to a fine not exceeding £.100 or to imprisonment for a period not exceeding 6 months.

5. The District Commissioner shall refuse his consent to any disposition by way of the permanent alienation of the Homestead Area of a cultivator: provided always that where the District Commissioner is satisfied:

(i) that the applicant owns elsewhere other unincumbered lands not less than the area declared to be a Homestead Area in the zone in which such lands are situated or has obtained other permanent occupation, or

(ii) that the proposed disposition is a gift made in good faith for a religious or charitable purpose,

he may grant his consent to such disposition.

6. When a District Commissioner grants his consent to a disposition of land his Order shall not be taken to decide or affect any question of title to the land or any right of pre-emption or other right or interest therein.

Mortgages/

- 3 -

Mortgages of Land in a Zone.

7. (1) Save as hereinafter provided and notwithstanding anything contained in Article 90 of the Execution Law, 1330, or Article 10 of the Law for Disposition of Immovable Property, 1331, or the Mortgage Law Amendment Ordinance, 1921, a mortgage of land in a Zone by a cultivator shall not affect so much of the property comprised therein as constitutes the Homestead Area of the mortgagor.

(2) The District Commissioner shall grant his consent to a mortgage of land in a Zone by a cultivator in the following cases:

(i) if the mortgage is/one of the forms provided by Article 8 of this Ordinance,

or (ii) if he is satisfied that the intending mortgagor owns land not less in extent than the area declared to be Homestead Area in the Zone in which such land is situated.

(3) In the second of the cases mentioned in sub-section (2), if the power of sale contained in the mortgage becomes exercisable the following provisions shall apply:

(i) The Execution Officer shall give the mortgagor and mortgagee at least seven clear days' notice before proceeding to take possession of the mortgaged property as provided in Article 93 of the Execution Law, 1330.

(ii) The Execution Officer shall exclude from the property taken possession of and put for sale so much as constitutes the Homestead Area of the mortgagor and the dwelling-house and appurtenances used in connection therewith.

(iii)/

(iii) If the mortgagor and mortgagee do not agree as to what portion of the mortgaged property constitutes the Homestead Area of the mortgagor the Execution Officer shall notify the District Commissioner who shall thereupon appoint a fit and proper person who shall inspect the land and delimit the portion thereof which constitutes the Homestead Area of the mortgagor and estimate the value of the remainder and report to the Execution Officer accordingly; and such report and delimitation shall be final and conclusive.

(iv) Upon receiving such report the Execution Officer shall proceed to sell the mortgaged property (other than the portion thereof constituting the Homestead Area of the mortgagor) in accordance with the provisions of the Execution Law for the time being in force, provided that notwithstanding anything contained in Article 108 of the Execution Law, 1330, or Article 10 of the Mortgage Law, the sale shall not be confirmed if the highest bid does not amount to two-thirds of the estimated value of the property sold.

(v) In the event of the purchase money being insufficient to pay off the amount due under the mortgage the Homestead Area of the mortgagor shall remain charged with the balance so remaining due together with interest thereon at the rate agreed upon in the mortgage, and shall be deemed to be subject to a mortgage in the form and subject to the condition mentioned in Article 8 (b) of this Ordinance.

- 5 -

8. It shall be lawful for a cultivator to make his Homestead Area a security for money in any of the following ways:

(a) By a mortgage with possession whereby the mortgagor delivers possession of the land to the mortgagee and authorises him to retain possession and to receive the rents and profits thereof in lieu of interest at the rate agreed upon and towards repayment of the principal for such period (not exceeding 10 years) as may be agreed upon, on the condition that after the expiry of the said period the land shall be redelivered to the mortgagor freed and discharged from the debt and all interest in respect thereof.

(b) By a mortgage without possession subject to the condition that, if the mortgagor fails to pay the principal and interest at the rate agreed upon in the manner and at the time provided in the contract, the mortgagee may apply to the District Commissioner to place him in possession of the land, and upon such application being made it shall be lawful for the District Commissioner, after hearing the parties, to make an Order ascertaining the sum then due for principal and interest and evicting the mortgagor and directing that the mortgagee shall be put into possession for such period, not exceeding ten years from the date of his being put into possession, as the District Commissioner by his said Order shall direct, and thereupon the mortgage shall be deemed to be a mortgage with possession for such period and on the conditions mentioned in clause (a) to secure the repayment of the principal sum so found to be due together with the arrears of interest due (if any).

(c)/

(c) By an agreement whereby the cultivator creates a contract of tenancy between himself, as tenant, and the creditor as landlord for such period, not exceeding 10 years, and at such rent, not exceeding three times the amount of the land tax payable in respect of the land, as may be agreed upon, and subject to the following conditions:

(1) on the determination of the period of tenancy, and provided that the cultivator shall have duly paid the rent agreed upon the debt and all interest thereon shall be extinguished:

(2) the cultivator shall not be entitled to dispose of the tenancy thereby created:

(3) the creditor shall not be entitled to take possession of the land save by virtue of an order of the District Commissioner made on the application of the creditor and upon notice to the cultivator:

(4) on such application being made and on its being proved:

(i) that the cultivator has left or has abandoned cultivation of the land; or,

(ii) that the cultivator has used the land in a manner contrary to the rules of good husbandry; or has without sufficient cause failed to cultivate the land in the manner and to the extent customary in the locality; or,

(iii) that the creditor has obtained a judgment against the cultivator for rent payable in respect of the tenancy and that such judgment remains unsatisfied;

it shall be lawful for the District Commissioner to make an Order evicting the cultivator from the land and putting

the/

the creditor into possession thereof, and thereupon the creditor shall be deemed to be in possession in virtue of a mortgage with possession on the conditions mentioned in Clause (a) for such term, not exceeding ten years from the date of such Order, and to secure the repayment of such sum for principal and arrears of rent (if any) as the District Commissioner by his said Order shall direct.

9. No interest shall accrue during such period as the mortgagee is in possession of the land or in receipt of the rents and profits thereof, or so long as the cultivator pays the rent payable under the agreement between him and the mortgagee.

10. In the case of a mortgage made under Article 8 of this Ordinance the following conditions may be added by agreement between the parties:

(a) A condition fixing the time of the agricultural year at which the mortgagor may resume possession of the land upon redemption of the mortgage:

(b) Conditions limiting the right of the mortgagor or mortgagee in possession to cut, sell or mortgage trees or to do any act affecting the permanent value of the land.

Any condition not permitted by this Ordinance shall be null and void.

11. Where land has been mortgaged under Article 8(a) it shall be lawful for the cultivator to dispose of the same land by way of second mortgage, provided always that if such second mortgage is a mortgage with possession it shall only authorise the mortgagee claiming thereunder to retain possession of the land for such period as, together with the period of the first mortgage, shall amount to 10 years.

Redemption./

Redemption.

12. (i) A mortgagor may redeem the land at any time by payment of the sum due for principal and interest.

(ii) In the case of a mortgage made under Article 8(a) or (c), or where an Order has been made putting the mortgagee into possession of the land, if there is a dispute between the mortgagor and the mortgagee as to the sum which is properly due in respect of the mortgage, it shall be lawful for either party to apply to the District Commissioner, and thereupon the District Commissioner, after hearing the parties and such evidence as may be produced by them, shall make an Order ascertaining what sum is properly due in respect of the mortgage having regard to the period for which the mortgagee has been in possession of the land and the profits which he has made or might reasonably have made, or to the rent which he has received, and directing that upon payment of such sum by the mortgagee together with the costs (if any) ordered to be paid by him the land shall be redeemed from the mortgage.

(iii) Upon the production of a certified copy of such Order and upon the mortgagor depositing the sum payable thereunder and paying the proper fee the Registrar of Lands shall cancel the entry of the mortgage in the Land Register.

13. If the mortgagee who is in possession under a mortgage or by virtue of an Order of the District Commissioner remains in possession after the expiry of the term for which he is entitled to retain possession, or after the redemption of the land, or after the date mentioned in an Order of the District Commissioner, made under Article 14 (2) (i), it shall be lawful for the District Commissioner, either of his

own motion or on the application of any person entitled to possession to make an Order ejecting the mortgagee and putting the person so entitled into possession, and ordering the mortgagee to pay such sum as damages or by way of Occupation rent for the period for which he has been wrongfully in possession as he shall by his said Order direct.

14. (1) From and after the date of this Ordinance a transfer of land in a Zone by way of sale with a right of re-purchase made to secure the payment of money shall not be permitted.

(2) Where land within a Zone has before the date of this Ordinance been transferred by way of sale with a right of re-purchase to secure the payment of money then, as between the transferor and his successors and the transferee and his successors, the following provisions shall apply:-

   (i) It shall be lawful for the District Commissioner, upon the application of the transferor and after hearing the parties and such evidence as may be produced by them, to make an Order ascertaining what sum is properly due by the transferor having regard to the period for which the transferee has been in possession of the land and to the profits which he has made or might reasonably have made, and directing the transferee to hand over possession of the land to the transferor upon such date as shall be mentioned in the said Order:

   (ii) Upon the making of such Order the transfer shall be deemed to be a mortgage to secure the payment of the sum so found to be due by the transferor

together/

together with interest thereon at the legal rate from the date upon which the transferee was directed to hand over possession of the land to the transferor:

(iii) If an Order shall be made for the sale of the land in payment of the sum so found to be due the provisions of Article 7 (3) shall not apply to such sale.

(3) The District Commissioner shall transmit a certified copy of the Order mentioned in sub-section (2) (i) to the Registrar of Lands who shall thereupon correct the entry in the Register regarding the land in accordance therewith.

15. If proceedings in connection with a transfer of land in a Zone by way of sale with a right of re-purchase to secure the payment of money are instituted or are pending in any Civil Court at the date of this Ordinance or if a suit is instituted in any Civil Court to enforce payment of the sum due upon a mortgage to which Article 8 applies, the Court shall of its own motion stay such proceedings and refer the case to the District Commissioner to be dealt with by him under the provisions of this Ordinance.

General.

16. As between different mortgagees of the same land their rights, including the right to be put in possession thereof under Article 8 (b) or (c), shall be determined in accordance with the dates of the registration of their respective mortgages.

17. A cultivator may make a lease of his Homestead Area for any term not exceeding ten years.

18. Every agreement whereby the owner of a Homestead Area purports to alienate or charge the produce thereof or any

- 11 -

part of the share in such produce for more than one year shall not take effect for more than one year from the date of the agreement unless the sanction of the District Commissioner is given thereto, and shall, unless such sanction is given or if such sanction is refused, take effect as if it had been made for one year.

The produce of land means:

(a) crops and other products of the earth standing or ungathered on the Homestead Area.

(b) crops and other products of the earth which have been grown on the land during the past year and have been reaped or gathered.

19. (1) No land of the Homestead Area shall be sold in execution of any decree or order of a Civil Court whether made before or after the commencement of this Ordinance.

(2) Nothing in this section shall affect the right of the Government of Palestine to recover arrears of land revenue, or any dues which are recoverable as arrears of land revenue, in any manner now permitted by law.

20. It shall be lawful for the District Commissioner on hearing any application under this Ordinance by his Order to fix the costs of and incidental to such application and to declare by whom and in what proportions the same shall be payable.

21. (1) A Civil Court shall not have jurisdiction in any matter which the High Commissioner or District Commissioner is empowered by this Ordinance to dispose of.

(2) No Civil Court shall take cognisance of the manner in which the High Commissioner or District Commissioner exercises any power vested in him by or under this Ordinance.

- 12 -

22. (1) When it appears to the District Commissioner that any Civil Court has either before or after the date when this section comes into operation passed a decree or order contrary to any of the provisions of this Ordinance, the District Commissioner may apply for the revision of such decree or order to the Court, if any, to which an appeal would lie from such decree or order or in which an appeal could have been instituted at the time when the decree or order was passed, or in any other case to the Supreme Court, and if the Court finds that such decree or order is contrary to any of the provisions of this Ordinance it shall alter it so as to make it consistent with this Ordinance. Such application shall be made within two months of the date upon which the District Commissioner is informed of such decree or order.

(2) When any such Appellate Court passes an order rejecting such application the District Commissioner may within two months after the date upon which he is informed of such order apply to the Supreme Court for the revision thereof.

(3) Every Civil Court which passes an order on any application made under this section shall forthwith send a copy thereof to the District Commissioner.

(4) No stamp shall be required upon such applications: and the procedure of the Civil Courts as regards appeals shall apply so far as may be on receipt of such application: provided that no appearance by or on behalf of the District Commissioner shall be deemed necessary for the disposal of the application.

23. The powers conferred by this Ordinance upon a District Commissioner may be exercised by any officer authorised by the High Commissioner in this behalf.

24./

24. The High Commissioner, with the previous sanction of the Secretary of State, may by notification in the Official Gazette exempt any person or class of persons from the operation of this Ordinance or of any of the provisions thereof.

25. (1) The High Commissioner may make rules for carrying into effect the purposes of this Ordinance.

(2) In particular and without prejudice to the generality of the foregoing powers the High Commissioner may make rules prescribing the officers to whom applications may be made, and the manner and form in which such applications shall be made and disposed of.

-1-

Appendix S.R. IV.

DRAFT.

OCCUPANCY TENANTS ORDINANCE, 193-

1. This Ordinance may be cited as the Occupancy Tenants Ordinance 193....

2. In this Ordinance

"Court" means the Land Court.

"Holding" means a parcel or parcels of land held by a tenant from a Landlord under a contract express or implied.

"Land" means land which is used for agricultural purposes or for purppses subservient to agriculture or for pasture and includes the sites of buildings or other structures on such land, but does not include land within a municipal area which bears an increased value over and above the ordinary value of land let for cultivation.

"Landlord" means a person from whom a tenant holds land and to whom a tenant is, or, but for a special contract, would be liable to pay rent for that land, whether such person is the owner of such land or holds the same under a contract of lease; it includes the Government of Palestine in respect of State domains and also the predecessors and successors in title of a landlord.

"Rent" means whatever is payable to a landlord by a tenant on account of the use and occupation of land by the tenant, whether such rent is payable in money or in kind or in portion

of/

-2-

of the produce of the land or in agricultural labour done by the tenant for the landlord.

"Sale" and "Sell" include gift and give with or without valuable consideration.

"Tenancy" means the interest of a tenant in a holding.

"Tenant" means a person who holds land from another person under a contract of tenancy and is, or, but for a special contract, would be liable to pay rent for such land to such other person: it includes the predecessors and successors in title of a tenant, but does not include a mortgagee of the interest of a landlord nor a person who is not in actual occupation of the land, and cultivating the same by his own labour or that of his family or servants.

A person who cultivates the land of another person under a contract of service shall be deemed to be a tenant unless the seed, animals and implements used for the purpose of such cultivation are all the property of the landlord.

3. (1) A tenant who was on the 29th May, 1931, in occupation of a holding shall have a right of occupancy therein notwithstanding that the holding may have been since that date let to some other person or may have been left unlet or may be unlet at the date of this Ordinance, and such tenant is hereinafter called an "occupancy tenant".

(2) An "occupancy tenant" who at the date of this Ordinance is not in occupation of the holding in which he has a right of occupancy under this Ordinance may apply to the landlord

by/

by notice served through the Notary Public to give him possession thereof on the 1st October next after the date of service of such notice, and if the landlord shall fail to comply with such notice or if the holding has been let to some other person the "occupancy tenant" may apply to the Court for an order putting him into possession of the holding.

(3) Upon the hearing of such application. the Court, after hearing the "occupancy tenant" and the landlord and the person (if any) who is then in occupation of the holding, shall make an Order directing that the "occupancy tenant" be put into possession of the holding upon such date as, having regard to the rights of the person (if any) then in occupation of the holding, the Court shall fix.

(4) Where in the opinion of the Court the failure of the landlord to give the "occupancy tenant" possession of the holding was unreasonable the Court may order the landlord to pay to the "occupancy tenant" such sum by way of damages as it may award.

4. In the absence of a custom to the contrary no one of several joint owners shall acquire a right of occupancy against the other or others of them in the land jointly owned by them.

5. (1) Save as hereinafter provided a tenant who has acquired a right of occupancy in a holding shall not be compelled to pay a higher rent than that which was payable in respect

thereof/

-4-

thereof, at the date when he acquired such right.

(2)   It shall be lawful for the Court on the application of a tenant who has acquired a right of occupancy to reduce the rent payable by him on the ground that the productive powers of his holding have been decreased by a cause beyond his control, and the Court in its Order shall specify the date from which such reduced rent shall be payable, and it shall be lawful for the landlord at any time after the making of such Order to apply to the Court to alter the same, provided always that the rent payable in respect of the holding shall not be increased above the rate payable before the making of such Order.

6. (1)   A tenant who has acquired a right of occupancy shall not be liable to be evicted from his holding except by an order of the Court made upon one of the following grounds, namely:

    (a)   that he has used the land comprised in the holding in a manner which renders it unfit for the purposes for which he held it;

    (b)   where rent is payable in kind, that he has without sufficient cause failed to cultivate the holding in the manner or to the extent customary in the locality in which the land is situate;

    (c)

(c) that a decree for two years' arrears of rent in respect of the holding has been passed against him and remains unsatisfied;

(d) that he has without the consent of the landlord in writing sub-let the holding or any part thereof;

(e) that he has been declared bankrupt: or

(f) unless it is proved to the satisfaction of the Court before which any proceedings are brought that before the date of this Ordinance the landlord bought the land for the specific purpose of its development or colonisation or disposal for building purposes and that it is bona fide required by him for such purpose, and that the land was let to the tenant for the temporary necessity either of the landlord or tenant.

(2) A tenant who has been evicted from his holding upon one of the grounds mentioned in sub-section (1) (a) (b) (c) (d) (e) shall not be entitled to compensation for disturbance under the Protection of Cultivators Ordinance 1929.

(3) Where a landlord has taken proceedings for the eviction of a tenant upon one of the grounds mentioned in sub-section (1) (a) (b) or (d) the tenant may apply to the Court to stay such proceedings and if the Court is of opinion that adequate satisfaction for the matter complained of can be made by the payment of damages to the landlord the Court may make an Order staying such proceedings upon
the/

–6–

the payment by the tenant within the time fixed by such Order of such sum for damages as it shall direct together with the costs incurred by the landlord in respect to such proceedings.

(4) Where a tenant has been evicted from his holding upon one of the grounds mentioned in sub-section (1) and the landlord within two years from the date of the Order of eviction lets the holding the person to whom the holding is so let shall for the purposes of this Ordinance be deemed to be a successor in title of the previous tenant.

7 (1) A tenant who has acquired a right of occupancy may sell his tenancy subject to the following conditions:

  (i) Except with the consent of the landlord the sale shall be made to one person only:

  (ii) The tenant shall cause notice of his intention to sell his tenancy to be served on the landlord through the Court and shall defer proceeding with the sale for a period of one month from the date of service of such notice:

  (iii) Within the said period the landlord may purchase the tenancy for such sum as may be agreed upon or in the event of disagreement may be ascertained by the Court to be the value thereof:

        (iv)

–7–

(iv) Upon payment by the landlord into the Court of the value so fixed by the Court the landlord shall be deemed to have purchased the tenancy and thereupon the right of occupancy therein shall be extinguished, and the Court shall on the application of the landlord put him into possession of the holding:

(v) When the tenancy is subject to a mortgage the Court shall fix the value of the tenancy as if it were not mortgaged:

(vi) If the tenancy is subject to a mortgage it shall be transferred to the landlord discharged from the mortgage but the mortgage debt shall be a charge on the purchase money, and the Court shall pay to the person or persons entitled thereto so much of the purchase-money as is required to discharge the mortgage debt and pay the balance (if any) to the tenant:

(vii) If the tenancy is not subject to a mortgage the Court, after deducting any sums due to the landlord for arrears of rent or for damages for any breach of the contract of tenancy, shall pay the purchase-money to the tenant:

(viii)/

-8-

(viii) Where the tenant shall agree to sell his tenancy to some person other than the landlord he shall give the landlord notice in writing of the name of the purchaser:

(ix) Within 10 days after receiving such notice as aforesaid the landlord may refuse on reasonable grounds to accept the purchaser as tenant; in case of dispute the reasonableness of the landlord's refusal shall be decided by the Court:

(x) Within the said period the landlord may give notice both to the tenant and the purchaser of any sums which he may claim from the tenant for arrears of rent or for damages for any breach of the contract of tenancy, and (a) if the tenant does not within ten days after receiving such notice give notice to the purchaser that he disputes such claims or any of them, the purchaser shall out of the purchase money pay the full amount thereof to the landlord; and

(b) if the tenant disputes such claims or any of them, the purchaser shall out of the purchase-money pay to the landlord so much (if any) of such claims as the tenant admits, and pay the residue of the amount claimed by the landlord into Court.

Until/

Until the purchaser has satisfied the requirements of this sub-section it shall not be obligatory on the landlord to accept him as his tenant:

(xi) Where any purchase-money has been paid into Court it shall be lawful for the landlord and tenant and purchaser respectively to make applications to the Court in respect thereof, and the Court shall hear and determine such applications and make such order or orders thereon as to the Court may seem just:

(xii) Where several persons constitute the landlords of a holding any one of them may be deemed to be the landlord for the purposes of this section.

(2) A disposition of his tenancy by a tenant to one person by way of mortgage or where marriage forms part of the consideration shall be deemed to be a sale but the conditions mentioned in sub-section (1), other than condition (ii) and (ix) shall not apply thereto.

(3) Where proceedings are taken by a mortgagee of a tenancy to sell the tenancy the sale shall be made subject to the provisions of this section so far as the same are applicable as if the mortgagee were the tenant.

(4) Any sale or disposition of a tenancy made otherwise than in accordance with the provisions of this section shall be voidable at the option of the landlord.

(5) The provisions of the Homestead Protection Ordinance, 193- shall apply to any sale or disposition made under this Article.

8. Save as is provided in this Ordinance a tenancy
shall/

-10-

shall not be attached or sold in execution of a judgment.

9. When a tenant has sold or disposed of his tenancy to a person other than the landlord, that person shall have the same rights and be subject to the same liabilities in respect of the tenancy as the tenant had and was subject to.

10. Where a tenant has with the consent of the landlord sub-let his holding or any part thereof to another person such person shall in respect of the holding or part thereof sub-let to him be subject jointly with the tenant to all the liabilities of the tenant to the landlord under this Ordinance.

11. Where the immediate landlord of a tenant who has acquired a right of occupancy is not the owner of the lands which include the holding but holds the same under a contract of lease, then the determination of the interest of such immediate landlord shall not affect the tenancy of the tenant in his holding, and the tenant shall be deemed to be a tenant to the person from whom the immediate landlord held the lands (hereinafter called the superior landlord) upon the terms and at the rent provided in the contract between the tenant and the immediate landlord or by this Ordinance: provided always that where it is proved to the Court that the contract of tenancy between the immediate landlord and the tenant was made at a gross undervalue the Court may order that as from the date mentioned in such Order that tenant shall pay the rent which was payable by the immediate landlord to the superior landlord in lieu of the rent which was payable under such contract by the tenant to the immediate landlord.

12./

12. A tenancy shall not be determined by reason of the sale of the landlord's interest in execution of a judgment or in satisfaction of a mortgage whether such judgment was obtained or such mortgage was made before or after the date of this Ordinance and notwithstanding that such tenancy was created after the date of the mortgage.

13. Nothing in this Ordinance shall operate to prevent a landlord voluntarily granting to his tenant occupancy rights at any time on such terms as landlord and tenant shall mutually agree to.

14. If a landlord and tenant have entered or shall hereafter enter into an agreement extending over a period of not less than ten years, the provisions of th Ordinance as to the right of occupancy shall be deemed inapplicable to the tenancy covered by such agreement, as long as the agreement remains in force.

15. Notwithstanding anything contained in this Ordinance the District Commissioner may, on the application of the landlord, authorise the resumption by him of a holding or part thereof upon being satisfied (1) that such resumption is required for some reasonable and sufficient purpose having relation to the good of the holding or of the adjoining lands including development by drainage or irrigation or by closer settlement or colonisation or disposal for building purposes, and (2) that the "occupancy tenant" will retain sufficient land in the district or elsewhere for the maintenance of himself and his family or that he has obtained some permanent employment,

-12-

or that the purpose for which the resumption of
the holding is sought comprises the provision for
the "occupancy tenant" of developed land sufficient
for the maintenance of himself and his family
together with adequate subsistence for them pending
the development of such lands. Such resumption
shall be authorised upon such conditions as the
District Commissioner may think fit and thereupon
the "occupancy tenant" shall be required to sell
his tenancy in the whole or such part of the holding
to the landlord upon such terms as may be approved
by the District Commissioner including full compensation to the occupancy tenant".

APPENDIX S.R. V

ESTIMATED EXPENDITURE OVER A PERIOD OF FIVE YEARS ON A CITRUS EXPERIMENTAL STATION AND A CITRUS DEMONSTRATION STATION.

(Vide para. 90 of Report.)

1	2	3	4	5	6	7	8	9
	Capital expenditure already incurred or being incurred by Jewish Agency.	Further capital expenditure required in due course for buildings.	\multicolumn{5}{c}{Y E A R}		T O T A L.
			1st	2nd	3rd	4th	5th	
	£P.	£P.	£P.	£P.	£P.	£P.	£P.	£P.
I. EXPENDITURE WHICH WOULD BE INCURRED BY THE JEWISH AGENCY ON ITS CITRUS EXPERIMENTAL STATION WITHOUT ANY EXTENSION OF EXISTING ACTIVITIES, VIZ:								
(a) Capital	10,700	3,300						Column 2, £P.10,700;
(b) Salaries and expenses of 5 Scientific Divisions *			5,800	5,800	5,800	5,800	5,800	Columns 3 to 8, £P.32,300.
II. ADDITIONAL EXPENDITURE REQUIRED:								
Experimental Station.								
(a) Salaries and Expenses of 6th Scientific Division			1,000	1,000	1,000	1,000	1,000	
(b) Development of 100 dunams for field experiments			3,750	1,545	1,550	1,565	1,590	
(c) Experiments in selection of citrus trees.			500	500	500	-	-	
Demonstration Station.								
(a) Land, buildings, implements &c.			6,000	-	-	-	-	
(b) Development.			3,150	945	950	965	990	
(c) Salaries & Expenses of staff			550	568	586	604	622	
Total additional expenditure required:			14,950	4,558	4,586	4,134	4,202	32,430
TOTAL EXPENDITURE:	10,700	3,300	20,750	10,358	10,336	9,934	10,002	Col.2: £P.10,700; Rest £P.64,730.

* The functions of these Scientific Divisions are shown as follows:-

FUNCTIONS OF SCIENTIFIC DIVISIONS OF CITRUS EXPERIMENTAL STATION.

Five Existing Divisions:

1. Plant Pathology — For investigation of pathological diseases and their control.

2. Entomology — For investigation and control of insect pests.

3. Chemistry — For analyses and investigation of soils, water, fruit and by-products.

4. Citricultural Breeding and Plant Physiology — For selection of citrus stocks and buds, having regard to power of resistance to disease, high yields, quality and form of fruit.

5. Management and Economics of Citrus Orchards — For study of costs of production throughout the country, management of citrus groves, marketing and transport problems; and study and survey of methods of record keeping.

Proposed Sixth Division:

6. General Citricultural Research — For field experiments to determine the best methods of cultivation and tillage, irrigation, spacing, manuring and fertilising, transplanting and pruning, soil preparation, windbreaks; and for variety tests, introduction of new varieties, stock problems, soil types.

7.08

REPORT BY THE FINANCIAL ADVISER

TO THE DIRECTOR OF DEVELOPMENT

on

THE FINANCIAL ASPECTS OF THE

PROPOSALS IN THE DIRECTOR'S

FIRST AND SUPPLEMENTARY REPORTS
ON AGRICULTURAL DEVELOPMENT AND

SETTLEMENT IN PALESTINE.

Jerusalem.   20th April, 1932.

I arrived in Palestine on the 11th February, 1932, to act as Financial Adviser to the Director of Development.

2. My duties were to advise the Director from the financial aspect on any specific proposals for settlement and development which he might consider in connection with his Supplementary Report. I was instructed to prepare for the information of the Secretary of State and the Treasury a report on the financial aspects of those proposals: and I was to have an opportunity of considering and commenting upon the financial aspects of the Director's First Report.

3. A proper appreciation of the financial aspects of settlement and development proposals necessitates an understanding of the broad features of the natural resources and economic conditions of the country in their relation to its agriculture. I, accordingly, directed my attention from the outset to a study of those matters. To that end Mr. French, the Director, kindly arranged that I should accompany him on all his tours, in the course of which we visited all parts of the country. We inspected Arab villages and Jewish colonies, and discussed problems with cultivators and landowners, the leaders of Jewish colonisation organisations, Government officials and others. Mr. French placed freely at my disposal his profound knowledge of land administration and settlements in India and the results of his intensive study of those problems in Palestine.

4. It will be convenient if, before proceeding to observe on the financial aspects of the proposals

in/

in the Director's First and Supplementary Reports, I give a conspectus of the natural resources and economic conditions of Palestine so far as they affect its agriculture or agricultural development.

5. The most striking feature of the country is the smallness of the cultivable area. The total area is only some 10,000 square miles - about the size of Wales. Of this, according to the calculations of Sir John Hope Simpson, only 6,544,000 dunams[*)] outside the Beersheba region are cultivable. The Beersheba region, owing to its scanty and uncertain rainfall, can never, unless artesian supplies of water in sufficient quantity are discovered, provide more than a very precarious existence for a semi-nomadic Beduin population which in most years has to wander far afield in search of feed for its flocks. The rest of the country consists of barren, rocky hills and waterless desert.

6. Not only is the cultivable area very small: there is also a dearth of water supplies.

7. For six months, in the summer, there is no rain. When other supplies of water are not available, the crops raised in the summer are dependent for their moisture on the retention in the soil of the winter rains and on the heavy summer dews. Except in a few favoured and comparatively small districts, the winter rains are unreliable. For this reason, on the average, good crops on unirrigated lands are obtained in only two years out of five: in two they are definitely bad, and in one moderate. In a country of impecunious and, for the most part, improvident smallholders, this is less satisfactory than uniform seasons/

-----
*) Equivalent to 1,636,000 acres, or about 2556 square miles.

- 3 -

seasons of moderate crops. When, for example, the fellah (Arab peasant cultivator) has good crops he usually frivols away so much of his surplus as his moneylender creditor does not seize, and he has no resources to fall back upon when the bad seasons come round.

8. There is a scarcity of water supplies from rivers and springs available for flow irrigation; and the only considerable area where subterranean supplies from well bores have so far been obtained at an economic depth is the western side of the maritime plain, the home of the citrus industry.

9. The land in the Vale of Esdraelon, though deficient in water supplies, responds well to cereal farming; and the maritime plain contains the windblown sand which is so suitable, where water is available, for orange growing. The northern part of the Jordan Valley (the Beisan district) is very fertile; and substantial areas in other parts of the Valley would be, with irrigation. But the irrigation of this Valley, as well as the drainage of the Huleh Basin, which also contains very fertile land, would probably be very costly. The soil in the rest of the cultivable area of Palestine is either of indifferent quality or subject to precarious rainfall: in the Hills, which contain the majority of the Arab cultivators, it is shallow and not very fertile.

10. All things considered, the country must be regarded, in spite of its semi-tropical summer climate and comparatively mild winter, as poorly endowed for agriculture.

11/

11. The cultivable area of 1,636,000 acres is at present supporting a rural population of 746,000,* or 291 to the square mile (640 acres). The pressure on the land is very great; and it is steadily increasing with the rapid growth of the population. The recent census discloses that the population is increasing by natural increase alone at the rate of at least 19,000 per annum.

12. The Johnson-Crosbie Commission which, in 1930, enquired *inter alia* into the economic conditions of agriculturists in 104 representative Arab villages, established that the average holding in those villages was 75 dunams (18¾ acres) per family of, on the average, 6 persons.

It was calculated that, on the basis of the average prices prevailing in the years 1924-1927, a holding of 100 dunams produced a gross return of £P.64; and that the cost of production, including taxes, but no interest, was about £P. 29. This gave to the owner-cultivator, for the support of himself and his family, a net return of £P 35. A tenant-cultivator had to pay out of this a rent of £P. 15, making his net return only £P. 20.

The cost of living and other personal expenses for a family of 6 persons was estimated at £P.26: and it was accordingly calculated that the minimum holding required for the support of a fellah and his family was 75 dunams if he was the owner of the land, and 130 dunams if he was a tenant. Of the cultivable area in the villages concerned, about 30% was rented from

---

* The total population less that in the absentee/ towns of Jerusalem, Haifa, Jaffa, Tel-Aviv and in the Beersheba region.

- 5 -

absentee landlords or other villages; and as the average holding was only 75 dunams, it was clear that a considerable proportion of the cultivators could not live on the produce of their holdings without outside employment.

13. Allowing for probable understatement in the Commission's figure, the gross return from the fellah's farm is, nevertheless, very small, but his expenses of production are proportionately low; and it is doubtful whether his net return, exiguous as it is, could be appreciably increased (except as noted below in the matter of seed selection), at any rate by any methods already proved.

The labour is provided by himself and his family, and although all work hard when there is work to be done, there are many days in the year when they are necessarily idle. Accordingly, more costly implements which would merely save labour would add to his expenditure without increasing his gross return. His plough, though very primitive, costing only a few shillings, is the only one possible for the shallow and stony soil in the hill areas; and it is well adapted for extensive farming in the peculiar conditions - on unmanured fallows. For the plains, a heavier implement for deeper ploughing would not only be more expensive, but would also require heavier draught animals, which are more costly to buy and more expensive to feed: the holdings are so small that the value of the extra yield would not cover the extra outlay. Better seed will increase the yield of his crops without adding materially to his expenditure, and the Department of Agriculture is meeting this need as rapidly as supplies of the

suitable/

−6−

suitable varieties can be raised.

14. The Jews have claimed credit for their more intensive development of the dry-farming lands which they purchased from Arab landowners; but it is very doubtful whether that development has been economic.

It is admitted by the Jewish Agency that their settlers cannot afford, and are not asked, to pay anything like an economic rate of interest on the capital (£P.700 per holding on the average) provided out of the Palestine Foundation Fund for the equipment of their farms. And the limited investigations I have been able to make suggest that the Agency are not likely to be able to recover much of the interest which the settlers are asked to pay. Although the intention was that payment of interest should begin five years after the date of completion of equipment, nothing has in fact been recovered to date. Moreover, it is contemplated that the rent which the settlers will be called upon to pay for their land, which was purchased from the Jewish National Fund, will represent only a small fraction of what would be required to yield an economic rate of interest on the capital cost of the land.

15. It is true that the standard of living of the Jew is higher than that of the <u>fellah</u>, and that allowance was made for this in fixing the low rate of interest which the Jewish settlers should be asked to pay on the capital outlay. But even so, it is questionable whether, if an economic rate of interest had to be paid, the net return from the Jewish holdings would be any higher than that obtained by the <u>fellah</u>, if indeed as high.

---
* The most highly developed, and therefore the most attractive, colony in the Vale of Esdraelon is Nahalal, which was established in 1921. The net profit for a holding of about 100 dunams, after taking credit for the value of all farm produce consumed by the household, is said to be from £P. 60 to £P.80 per annum. These
figures/

- 7 -

16. The German (Templar) colonists - comparatively few in number - are understood to obtain a better net return from their holdings than either the Jew or the _fellah_. Their farming is of the mixed variety favoured by the Jews, but their equipment is less expensive, and they work harder, making themselves the butter and cheese which the Jews pay to have made in dairy factories.

17. The conclusion is, therefore, that, save in exceptional circumstances, agriculture in the dry-farming areas of Palestine yields a very meagre return; and holdings as small as are necessitated by the scarcity of cultivable land are not at present capable of supporting a family on a European standard of living and at the same time yielding an economic return on the capital employed.

No doubt in time, if the agricultural problems, including those of distribution and marketing, are tackled energetically, it will be possible to increase the net return to cultivators, particularly through more diversified farming; but progress will inevitably be slow.

18. With the scarcity of water and natural pastures, and the lack of any substantial outlet for skimmed milk (pig keeping being barred to both Moslem and Jew),

conditions/

---

figures allow nothing for rent or for interest on the equipment outlay, none of which has yet been paid. The "equipment" outlay debitable to the settler, after writing off more than a third on account of high prices etc., and including only a wooden house, is £P. 559. The capital cost of his land and improvements was about £P.640.

conditions are very unfavourable for dairying, an important side of mixed farming on small holdings. A good deal could be done, by feeding and other experiments over a long period and more economical distribution, to minimise the natural disadvantages, but there can be no justifiable hope of establishing an export trade in competition with more highly favoured countries: the most that can reasonably be expected is to capture in due course a larger share of the home market.

19. So much for dry-farming, which constitutes the bulk of agricultural enterprise in Palestine, measured by areas cultivated and numbers engaged.

Of the products of intensive cultivation on irrigated lands, citrus fruit, and in particular the Jaffa orange, is far and away the most important. Up to now the profits have been very considerable, but that happy position is not likely to continue indefinitely. The area planted with orange trees in recent years is more than twice the area already in bearing, and in five years' time the exportable output is likely to be about three times the quantity ($3\frac{1}{2}$ million cases) exported this year. The Jaffa orange is a luxury article, and expensive. To find new markets and new customers in old markets for the rapidly growing output will almost certainly necessitate the acceptance of substantially lower prices, as well as considerable additional advertising expenditure. And with the extension of the fruit bearing area, the risks and dangers of pests will increase and call for increasing expenditure on control and eradication.

20/

-9-

20. The industry may, and probably will, settle down eventually on a reasonable basis of prices, costs and profits, provided all the problems of research, experiment, transport and marketing are tackled with spirit. But the danger is that these problems, and particularly those of transport and marketing, will not be tackled in earnest soon enough, and that before a stable position is reached many growers will suffer losses and disappointments.

21. New planting (of which no account is taken in the Director's estimates) is proceeding apace in the maritime plain, and seems likely to continue so long as suitable land with an adequate water supply is available, until lower prices and profits serve to check the present exuberant optimism. It would be better if the pace were slower until the solution of the problem of marketing the increased output already in prospect is in sight.

22. Apart from citrus fruit, there are no products of intensive cultivation on irrigated lands which can at present be exported in any quantities at payable prices; and the home market is a limited one owing to the low standard of living of the bulk of the population. No doubt cultural and other improvements can be effected, so as to increase the possibilities of successful competition in foreign markets; and it may be that payable new crops are capable of being raised under suitable conditions. But all this will take time, and is speculative.

23. A systematic hydrographic survey and Government
control/

-10-

control of water supplies may be expected to pave the way for a fuller and more economical use of the already available water resources; and this will make possible closer settlement in some areas already under cultivation, or at least improve the amenities and agricultural resources of existing cultivators. But if the boring tests now in operation near Beersheba fail to disclose the existence of artesian supplies of water in sufficient quantity in that district, any considerable scheme of new settlement must depend on the possibilities of developing the Jordan Valley and the Huleh Basin and of the more intensive development of the Beisan tract. All these projects require in the first place a survey of the technical possibilities of irrigation or drainage. But even if it is found that there are no insuperable technical obstacles, there will be no case for further action before it has been demonstrated that crops can be grown on small irrigated holdings to compete successfully in foreign markets and at the same time provide a living for the settlers and an economic return on the Government's outlay.

24. For sound development, in Palestine as in other countries, the action required is that of the suction pump, not the forcing pump. If economic conditions are favourable, development will be to the general advantage. Any attempt to force the pace before the possibilities of economic production have been proved can only end in disaster and disappointment, inflicting suffering on the settlers and a heavy burden of unproductive debt on the taxpayers. In this connection

it is/

-11-

it is necessary to emphasise that the almost complete lack of reliable statistics of agricultural holdings and production in this country is a very serious handicap, for the gradual removal of which the institution of a system of Village Registrars, as recommended in paras 38 to 55 of the Director's First Report, will be essential.

25. The foregoing summary of the agricultural conditions and immediate possibilities of development in Palestine is not encouraging, but as a broad description of the salient facts I believe it to be fair. It suggests that development, if it is to be sound, must begin at the bottom— by removing obstacles which at present discourage independent development of individual holdings and by studying how to get the best results from the cultivation of the land. The latter will call for all the energies of a vigorous and keen Department of Agriculture.

26. I am, therefore, firmly of opinion that economic and financial considerations support the general attitude of caution which the Director has adopted in his First and Supplementary Reports.

27. I now submit the following observations on the financial aspects of the specific proposals in the Reports.

FIRST REPORT.

28. - Part I of the First Report is devoted mainly to a discussion of what are described as the five essential pre-requisites on which decisions would have to be given before any large schemes of development could be considered in detail. The remarks in the introductory chapters of that Part are explained in more

detail/

-12-

detail in the Supplementary Report, and my observations are given below against the relevant passages in that Report.

I turn to the five pre-requisites, giving a reference in the margin to the relevant paragraphs in the Report.

Paragraphs 23 - 28. (1) <u>Acceleration of Survey and Settlement operations.</u>

29. The additional expenditure, totalling £P.12,000, which would be required in order to accelerate by three years the completion of the survey work represents (i) the cost of training additional staff and (ii) the amount by which the cost of that staff during the period required after training to attain maximum efficiency would exceed the cost of fully efficient staff doing the same amount of work. Additional staff is not, however, recommended by the Director unless and until it is clear that, without acceleration, survey will not keep sufficiently ahead of settlement work. Approval has not yet, I understand, been given by the Secretary of State to the proposals referred to in paragraph 27 of the Report for speeding up the work of settlement as distinct from survey.

It is most important that settlement should be completed as soon as possible. Doubts as to boundaries and rights to land not only impede development of their holdings by cultivators, but also provide one of the main causes of village affrays and disputes, which necessitate greater expenditure on police than would otherwise be necessary. Proper time-coordination between the survey and settlement staffs is essential.

If/

-13-

If settlement parties are held up, the expenditure on them during the waiting period is wasteful.

Paragraphs 29 - 37.

(2) <u>Acceleration of partition of Mesha'a lands</u>.

30. The Director has submitted further observations on this subject in paragraphs 110 to 119 of the Supplementary Report. There can be no doubt as to the desirability on development and other grounds of pushing on with the work of partition of mesha'a lands in advance of settlement: and the cost, estimated at not more than £P. 2500 per annum, of the small special staff recommended, which might be required for three or four years, should be compensated for eventually by savings on the survey side of settlement operations. Indeed an appreciable economy in the total cost of settlement would in all probability be realised.

31. On financial grounds I strongly endorse the Director's plea for an examination of the existing system of levying fees in connection with land partitions and registrations. In my opinion it is desirable that the Development Department should be represented on the proposed committee.

Paragraphs 38 - 55.

(3) <u>Establishment of a land Administration Agency</u>.

32. I have nothing to urge from the financial aspect against the proposed institution of a staff of Village Registrars, which was recommended also by the Financial Commission. These officials are essential for a proper system of land administration, which is badly needed in Palestine. Without effective and workable arrangements for registering mutations in rights in

land/

-14-

land, the very costly Settlement operations now in progress will have to be repeated in a generation; and in the meantime the machinery for the collection of land revenue will remain defective, to the Treasury's loss. The fact that not one per cent of the transactions in land are registered is a severe condemnation of the present system.

Paragraph 53. 33. The estimate of £P. 15,000 to £P. 20,000 a year for the cost of the staff when the establishment is complete allows for supervising and inspectorial staff between the Village Registrars and the District Officer. There is no doubt that when the scheme is established the expenditure will be amply covered by fees charged (over and above those now being obtained) for copies of entries, better revenue collections and consequential savings in other administrative services.

Paragraphs 56 to 76.

(4) Government control of lands.

34. The method now indicated by the Director for enabling Government to acquire at fair market value land that may be required for re-settlement of landless Arabs is set out in paragraph 35 of the Supplementary Report. His precise proposals for restricting the power of alienation of land, in order to prevent the creation of further landless Arabs, are given in Section III (paragraphs 61 to 81) of that Report. My observations on these proposals will be found below against the relevant paragraphs of the Supplementary Report.

Paragraph 64. 35. The Director considers that if and when land is to be developed for the purpose or re-settling landless Arabs and for making available new areas for close settlement by Jews, it will be essential that Government

should/

--A15--

should take over control of both the land and the water, expropriating them where necessary, and re-settling the area by redistribution of the land and water to the best possible advantage of all, due regard being had to the legitimate interests of existing owners and tenants.

With the possible exceptions of the Beersheba district, if artesian supplies of water should be discovered there, and the Beisan tract, if cereal cultivation on irrigated holdings is found to be economic, the Director, as will be seen from Section II of the Supplementary Report, does not consider that the opening up of any new areas would be an economic proposition at the present stage of agricultural development in Palestine.

I am disposed to agree that if and when such development takes place, the only satisfactory course, in spite of the outlay involved, would be for Government to acquire the land and the water, as proposed, giving all the settlers the tenure of Occupancy Tenants on the lines of Appendix S.R. IV to the Supplementary Report. The expenditure required for purchase of the land, irrigation or drainage, and construction of roads would be considerable; and it would be essential, before embarking on any scheme, to be satisfied that the tenants could make a reasonable living from their holdings and at the same time pay rent on the scale which would be required in order to secure to Government an economic return on its outlay, including interest and sinking fund charges on any loan funds employed.

Paragraphs 77 to 89.

(5) **Government Control of Water Supplies.**

36. It is clearly desirable, in a country so deficient in water supplies as Palestine is, that the State should re-assert its right to the ownership of all water and

the/

-16-

the use of all water which is running to waste.

The terms of an Ordinance for the purpose are under consideration by Government.

37.   The hydrographic survey which has been recommended, at an estimated cost of £P. 8,000, is a necessary preliminary to the proper exploitation of the country's available water resources. As the Director indicates in para. 120 of the Supplementary Report, some funds will no doubt be required, when that survey has been completed, for the purpose of providing loans to cultivators to enable them to develop their water supplies to the best advantage. Such loans, if granted only in cases where an economic rate of interest can be obtained, as is intended, will serve a useful development purpose.

Paragraphs 92-112.

38.   Part II of the First Report gives an account of the large areas (Beisan tract, Huleh Basin and Jordan Valley) which are capable of development under certain conditions. It also refers (in paragraph 110) to the subject of cooperative credit societies. All these matters are referred to again in the Supplementary Report, where the Director's conclusions and proposals are set out. My observations will be found below against the relevant passages in the Supplementary Report.

SUPPLEMENTARY REPORT.

Paragraphs 5 - 43.

39.   Section I of the Supplementary Report deals with the subject of the re-settlement of landless Arabs.

I propose to submit some observations in due course on the questions of the cost of re-settlement per family and the return which may be expected on the

Government's

-17-

Government's outlay.

40. The extent of suitable land likely to be obtainable in dry-farming areas will be very small - probably not more than would be required for about 100 families. The rest of the landless Arabs to be re-settled will have to be provided for on irrigated holdings. As the Director points out, this means,

Paragraph 30. for the present at any rate, purchasing land suitable for citrus growing and developing it over a period of five years to provide for the re-settlement not only of landless Arabs, but also of the existing tenants on the land. The cost per holding, including simple interest at 5% per annum during the period of development (when no rent would be obtainable), is estimated at about £P. 650: and as the ratio of existing tenants to landless Arabs would probably be about one to four, the cost for each landless Arab family re-settled would be in the region of £P. 800.

41. Not only is this a very expensive form of re-settlement of landless Arabs, but the prospects of success cannot be said to be assured.

The Director has drawn attention (in Section IV (a) and (b) - paragraphs 82 to 99 of the Supplementary Report) to the serious difficulties likely to be experienced in marketing the largely increased output of oranges which will be available in 1936/37: and I have emphasised in paragraphs 19 to 21 above the dangers of the present rapid rate of expansion of plantations. It may well happen that within the next five years the industry will be in difficulties; and growers in despair. The landless Arabs who have been resettled will

have/

have no financial stake in their holdings, as all the funds will have been provided by Government. They will be tenants only, free to depart, without incurring any loss, whenever they feel disappointed with their prospects and can find other work.

Para. 40. 42. I, therefore, entirely agree with the Director in emphasising the imprudence of proceeding otherwise than slowly and cautiously with the re-settlement of landless Arabs on citrus lands before it is known whether and how the problems facing the industry can be solved.

Para. 41. 43. The Director suggests that it will be a matter for consideration, when the Irrigation survey of the Beisan tract has been completed, and provided satisfactory arrangements can be made with existing cultivators, whether it would be desirable, if not too costly, to arrange for the re-settlement of both landless Arabs and Jewish immigrants off the tract, on the basis of irri‑
Para. 42. gated cereal farming. He points out, however, that it is highly improbable that the expenditure required would yield an adequate return.

As regards landless Arabs, it may, of course, be desirable to consider re-settlement on this tract, even if the return obtainable on the outlay would not be an economic one, if the total number which it may be decided to re-settle cannot be provided for more economically in any other way. But there would be no other justification in my opinion for incurring expenditure which would not yield an economic return.

It is unlikely, I understand, that any progress with re-settlement in the Beisan tract would be possible
within/

– 19 –

within the next three years, owing, inter alia, to difficulties likely to be experienced in allaying the suspicions of the existing cultivators.

Paras 44-60   44.   Section II discusses the possibilities of facilitating fresh Jewish colonisation (a) by irrigating, draining or reclaiming certain large areas and opening them up for new or closer settlement, and (b) by the provision of long-term credit facilities.

Para. 50.   With regard to (a), I agree with the conclusion reached by the Director that even if funds could be made available for opening up the areas in question, their exploitation would not be an economic proposition at the present stage of agricultural development in Palestine. There is, therefore, no justification at present for incurring the heavy development expenditure

Para. 48.   that would be involved, for – to quote the words of the Director – "To encourage any considerable number of persons to settle on lands made available by Government at great expense, on which there is no reasonable prospect of raising payable crops, is calculated to cause hardships to the settlers, to bring discredit on the Government, and to place on the Palestine taxpayers a financial burden which they can ill afford to bear".

45.   The Jewish Agency will not in fact be in a position to colonise any substantial new areas for some years. The Palestine Foundation Fund, from which the capital for colonisation on lands purchased from the Jewish National Fund is obtained, has also heavy annual commitments for other services, e.g. education and health.*

The/

---
* According to the latest published accounts of the Palestine Foundation Fund, the distribution of the expenditure for the 8½ years to 30th September, 1929, was as follows:-

Colonisation/

-20-

The Agency are believed to be heavily in debt and, in addition, the salaries of their teachers and other employees are some months in arrear. Subscriptions to the Palestine Foundation Fund are at present reduced, owing to the world depression: and it is quite possible that they will never again attain the dimensions of past years. The stimulus has, admittedly, been the numbers of immigrants and new settlements on the land to which the Agency could point; and the economic outlook in Palestine suggests that the numbers will make a much less imposing showing in the future than in the last twelve years of abnormal activity.

46. When the Agency have got out of their financial difficulties, the first charge on any funds that may be available for colonisation will presumably be the completion of the necessary equipment of existing colonies which, I understand, will be likely to require nearly £P. 250,000. And then there are at least 40,000 dunams of land already purchased by the Jewish National Fund to be colonised.

Many thousands of pounds have been wasted by the Agency in past years through pushing on with new colonisation before they had in sight the funds required to complete the necessary equipment of the holdings.

47./

	£P
Colonisation	1,179,027
Education	725,111
Public Works	513,168
Immigration	355,496
Health	263,482
Urban Colonisation, National Organisations, Investments, Religious Institutions, etc.	752,668
	£P.3,788,952

-21-

Paragraphs 56-59.

47. There is nothing I need add to the reasons given by the Director for being unable to recommend the scheme submitted in tentative outline by the Jewish Agency for the establishment, with Government financial support, of a Jewish Agricultural and Settlement Bank, beyond inviting reference to the remarks in paras. 14 and 15 above, which suggest the probability that the Bank would get little, if anything, in the way of interest on its loans.

Para. 60.

48. I agree that if at some future date any available Government funds could be used with advantage in providing additional credit facilities for improving the productivity of Jewish lands, the right course would be for Government to place the funds at the disposal of a commercial bank at such a rate of interest as would enable the bank to undertake the full financial responsibility of granting the credits.

Paras 61-81.

49. It is not, of course, within my province to comment upon the precise measures which are proposed in Section III for the prevention of the creation of further landless Arabs. The general question has, however, as the Director points out, a very important financial aspect.

It has been considered desirable that Government should undertake the resettlement of those Arabs who have been dispossessed of the holdings which they cultivated before the Jews superseded them. That resettlement, it has now been ascertained, will be not only very costly, but also burdensome to the Palestine taxpayers, since the return likely to be obtainable in the form of rent will not suffice to cover the interest charges on the funds which Government will have to

provide/

-22-

provide.

There would be no justification for incurring uneconomic expenditure to retrieve the mistake which permitted the Arabs in question to be displaced from their holdings unless at the same time effective steps are taken to prevent similar displacements in the future. And it would be manifestly absurd to allow displacements to go on if it is really the intention of His Majesty's Government that the obligation to undertake re-settlement will not be limited to those

Para. 62. Arabs who have been displaced in the past: as the Director indicates, this would mean that for every 1000 dunams (250 acres) purchased by the Jews in the future, involving the displacement of 10 Arab cultivators, Government would have to expend an additional £P.8000.

Paras. 82-128. 50. Section IV contains a number of proposals designed to promote or facilitate development.

Paras 82-92. (a) <u>Citrus Experimental and Demonstration Stations.</u>

51. In view of the situation in the citrus industry, and the prominent place which the industry holds in the economic life of the country, it is clearly essential that there should be an active and efficient Experimental Station and that every effort should be made by, <u>inter alia</u>, the establishment of a Demonstration Station to secure that the best cultural, picking and packing methods are practised by all growers.

I am advised, and can well believe, that in present circumstances there is no hope of inducing the Arab growers, who represent about half the industry, to cooperate with the Jewish Agency in maintaining and financing the stations.

The Agency are doing very good work at their

Experimental/

-23-

Para. 87. Experimental Station, but they have not the funds for the expansion now required or for providing a Demonstration Station. The Station appears to be efficiently and economically managed; and I agree with the Director that the most satisfactory and economical arrangement for Government would be to cooperate with and subsidise the Agency.

Para. 90. I agree also that the pound for pound basis proposed for the subsidy, which would call for contributions by Government to a total of about £P. 32,000 during the first 5 years, would be suitable. It would ensure economical administration; and it need not involve the Agency in any greater expenditure than is now being provided by that Body. The Advisory Committee, and the stipulations proposed in paragraph 91 of the Report, would give Government adequate protection.

Details of the estimated expenditure on the two stations are available, and can be supplied when desired.

(b) Cooperative Movements and Marketing.

Paras. 93-99. 52. It is highly important that no time should be lost in appointing the Registrar of Cooperative Societies. The fellahin are oppressed by a burden of debt which, for the reasons given by the Director in paragraph 68 of the Supplementary Report, is altogether abnormal. Many of them are in a despondent mood. They see no advantage to themselves in working harder to improve their holdings, since any extra returns they might obtain would be seized by their watchful moneylender creditors. Consideration has been given to the possibilities of easing the burden, but the difficulty is that the fellahin must have new credit to enable them to carry on, and must

look/

-24-

look to the moneylenders for it until alternative credit facilities can be provided through cooperative credit societies. Any drastic action to scale down existing debts would be likely to dispose the moneylenders to refuse necessary new credit: they would see in it a precedent for similar action as regards debts contracted in the future.

Para 97.   53.   I entirely agree with the Director in stressing the importance of forming without delay orange cooperative societies among the Arab growers; and personally I am disposed to consider that efforts should be made to start the movement at once, without waiting until the new Registrar is ready to tackle the problem. The difficulty would be to get the Arabs to work together, but if that reluctance could be overcome the formation of societies of this nature would be less difficult than starting cooperative credit societies. The Jews have some very able and experienced men directing their cooperative activities, and they have given close attention to the particular matter of orange societies. I have reason to believe that they would be willing, and indeed anxious to render every assistance to Government in facilitating the formation of such societies among the Arab growers: it would be to the advantage of the Jewish, as well as the Arab growers.

54.   It is not possible to say at this stage whether it will be necessary for Government to provide any funds for making loans to Arab cooperative credit societies outside the £P. 22,000 odd already in the Treasury, representing recoveries from debtors of the old Ottoman

Agricultu:

−25−

Agricultural Bank (see para. 5 of Mr. Strickland's Report). Progress with the formation of these societies is likely to be very slow, and if any further funds are required it will not be for some years.

Arab orange cooperative societies should be able to obtain all necessary finance from commercial sources.

Paras. 100 – 104.   (c) **Animal Husbandry.**

55.   In principle I have nothing to urge from the financial aspect against the proposal that Government should provide further funds for experiments in animal feeding and breeding. Unfavourable as the conditions are in Palestine for dairying and stock raising for meat, there is no doubt that much could be done to improve the position of those industries by a carefully planned series of experiments, which would probably not cost more than £P. 2000 to £P. 3000 a year in addition to a few thousand pounds for capital outlay.

Paras. 105 – 109.   (d) **Egg Production.**

56.   I have no remarks.

Paras. 110 – 119   (e) **Mesha'a Lands.**

57.   I refer to this in paras. 30 and 31 above.

Paras. 120 and 121.   (f) **Hydrographic and Irrigation Surveys.**

58.   As indicated in para. 37 above, I agree that a hydrographic survey is necessary.

In view of the possibility of re-settling landless Arabs on irrigated cereal holdings in the Beisan tract (see paras. 41-42 of the Supplementary Report), an Irrigation survey of that tract will be desirable.

I see/

-26-

I see no objection to the survey being extended also to the Huleh, Jordan Valley and Auja Basin areas; but if the cost is likely to be considerable, and if the funds which will be available for development will not allow of all desirable development schemes being undertaken, the survey of these areas could be postponed, since there are no possibilities at present of economic development.

Paras.122-128.   (g) The Position of the Hill Peasantry.

59.   I have nothing to urge on financial grounds against the Director's proposals under this heading.

Reference	Commitments	Remarks
	for ever. He realised, however, that it would go a long way to meet Dr Arlosoroff's point if it could be said that the (land) legislation proposals had been abandoned to a certain extent for the present, and were not required in connection with Mr French's immediate task."	

7.09

MEMORANDUM.

PALESTINE - LAND LEGISLATION.

1.   The Jewish Agency are already suggesting (without having seen the reports - or, at any rate, the supplementary report-of the Director of Development) that Mr French has transgressed his terms of reference and has made recommendations which conflict with the expressed policy of His Majesty's Government in the matters of land and immigration.

The reference (in the Jewish Agency's recent letter) to immigration can be ignored, since the reports contain no recommendations on the subject. It will, however, be desirable to examine Mr French's proposals for land legislation (supplementary report) in the light of the past history of the subject and of the pledges which have been given.

I. HISTORY.

2.   The history of land legislation in Palestine, especially in recent years, is a jungle of detail. I have endeavoured to confine the following outline to essentials:—

Land legislation has been enacted or proposed with two main objects (a) the protection of the Arab cultivator and

(b) - since 1930 - the prevention of interference with the development scheme.

N.B. It may be noted here that general control of transfers of agricultural land has been advocated for both of these purposes.

3.   The Transfer of Land Ordinance 1920-1921 was intended to protect the Arab cultivator. The main provision was that the approval of the Government was

required

required for any disposition of immovable property, and that consent would not be given in the case of any leased agricultural land unless the Director of Lands was satisfied that any tenant in occupation would retain sufficient land in the district or elsewhere for the maintenance of himself and his family.

The Ordinances of 1920-1921 failed to achieve the object in view, viz., to retain the cultivator on the land, the reasons being (a) that in many cases tenants disposed of their rights for a money payment and (b) that where land was transferred by the landlord while the tenants were still in occupation, the tenants had no legal protection from eviction however long they might have cultivated the land on which they were living.

4. The provision of the Transfer of Land Ordinance requiring that, before approving a transfer of agricultural land, the Director of Lands should satisfy himself that tenants would retain sufficient land for the maintenance of themselves and their families was repealed in 1929 and replaced by the Protection of Cultivators Ordinance. This Ordinance provided for the payment to certain classes of tenants of compensation for disturbance or for improvements on their receiving a valid notice to quit. It also provided for the constitution of boards to decide disputes as to compensation, and in the case of tenants who had cultivated their holdings for a period of 5 years and more, provision was made for additional compensation.

On page 36 of his report, Sir J. Hope Simpson pointed out that this Ordinance was of little value in

preventing

preventing the displacement of tenants and that what was required was not compensation for disturbance, but provision against disturbance.

5. In January 1930 Lord Passfield interviewed the members of the Shaw Commission who had returned to England but had not yet reported. He was impressed by their statements as to the serious plight of the Arab cultivator and telegraphed to Sir J. Chancellor asking whether he had any proposals to make for remedying the position. The High Commissioner replied that he fully realised the gravity of the problem and that he was preparing legislation restricting the transfer of Arab lands to non-Arabs and amending the Protection of Cultivators Ordinance.

In March 1930 two draft Ordinances were received from Sir J. Chancellor: (a) the Transfer of Agricultural Land Ordinance and (b) an Ordinance to Amend the Protection of Cultivators Ordinance 1929.

(a) conferred upon the Government control over all dispositions of agricultural land and provided that a disposition of agricultural land belonging to a person who was an Arab in favour of a person not an Arab should not be operative unless made in writing and approved by the High Commissioner.

(b) provided that no order for eviction should be made unless the landlord satisfied the Court that the tenancy had been validly determined and (subject to certain exceptions) that adequate provision had been made for the livelihood of the tenant.

6. The Secretary of State was inclined to approve of the enactment of these two Ordinances (subject to the removal of the discrimination between Arabs

Arabs and non Arabs) as a temporary measure pending a final decision on land policy, which was to be taken when Sir J. Hope Simpson's report had been received, and suggested, that an explanatory statement on the subject should be issued by the Government of Palestine.

7. In the statement to be made to the Permanent Mandates Commission by the British Accredited Representative, published as Cmd. 3582 in May 1930, it was mentioned that legislation was to be introduced with the object of controlling the disposition of agricultural lands in such a manner as to prevent the dispossession of the indigenous agricultural population, and that these temporary measures would be superseded in any case by such permanent enactments as might be decided upon when future policy was determined in the light of Sir J. Hope Simpson's report.

8. In June 1930 representations were received from Zionist sympathisers in this country in favour of the postponement of the projected land legislation until the general policy of the Government had been announced, and Sir J. Chancellor was instructed, much against his will, to shelve the Ordinances. He referred to the statement recently made to the Permanent Mandates Commission (Cmd. 3582) and urged that the Arabs would regard postponement of the land legislation as a breach of faith.

9. In October 1930 the Statement of Policy (Cmd. 3692) was issued, in paragraph 23 of which occurs the following passage:-

> "Only by the adoption of such a policy" (i.e. more methodical agricultural development) "will additional Jewish agricultural settlement be possible consistently with the conditions laid down

down in Article 6 of the mandate. The
result desired will not be obtained except
by years of work. It is for this reason
fortunate that the Jewish organisations are
in possession of a large reserve of land not
yet settled or developed. Their operations
can continue without break while more general
steps of development in the benefits of which
Jews and Arabs can both share are being worked
out. <u>During this period, however, the control
of all disposition of land must of necessity
rest with the authority in charge of the
development.</u> Transfers of land will be permitted
only in so far as they do not interfere with the
plans of that authority. Having regard to the
responsibility of the mandatory power, it is
clear that this authority must be the Palestine
Administration."

It will be noted that in the above passage for the
first time the second main object of land legislation
comes into play, viz., the prevention of interference in
the development scheme.

      In paragraph 24 of the Statement of Policy occurs
the following passage:-

"Consideration must also be given to the
protection of tenants by some form of occupancy
right or by other means to secure them against
ejectment or the imposition of excessive rental."

      In the Statement of Policy, therefore, the
control of land transfers is contemplated specifically
for the purpose of facilitating the development scheme.
Such control is not excluded for the purpose of protecting
the cultivator, but is not suggested for that purpose, in
                                                              spite

spite of the fact that both the High Commissioner and Sir J. Hope Simpson had regarded control of land transfers as a necessary element in legislation for the protection of cultivators.

10. The High Commissioner had already been asked to have ready revised drafts of the legislation required to carry out the recommendations (with regard to land) of Sir J. Hope Simpson, in order that no time might be lost in enacting the legislation as soon as the Statement of Policy had been issued and the following six draft ordinances had been received:-

    The Transfer of Agricultural Land Ordinance.
    The Protection of Cultivators Amendment Ordinance.
    The Registration of Agriculturists Ordinance.
    The Law of Execution Ordinance.
    The Land Courts Ordinance.
    The Land Settlement Ordinance.

For the purpose of this note the first two only need be considered, the other four being ancillary or of subordinate importance.

In accordance with the Secretary of State's instructions the High Commissioner on the 14th November, 1930, forwarded these draft ordinances to the Jewish Agency and the Arab Executive in Palestine for their comments. The Arab Executive contended that the sale of land to Jews should be entirely prohibited, not merely controlled, and that the Transfer of Agricultural Land Ordinance should not apply to transactions between Arabs. The Jewish Agency in Palestine refused to comment, having received instructions to that effect from

from the Agency's head office in London, who were at that time embarking on discussions with regard to the White Paper with a Cabinet committee. In these discussions the Jewish Agency raised the strongest objections to the Transfer of Agricultural Land Ordinance, the main provisions of which were:-

(a) That no disposition of land should be operative unless in writing and unless approved by the High Commissioner.

(b) That the High Commissioner might refuse approval to the foreclosure of a mortgage or to a sale under a mortgage provided that in that event the amount due under the mortgage should be paid out of the revenues of Palestine.

11. As a result of discussions between the Cabinet Committee and the Jewish representatives, the Prime Minister's letter to Dr. Weizmann was written. Paragraphs 12 and 13 of this letter deal with the land legislation question as follows:-

"12. In giving effect to the policy of land settlement, as contemplated in article 11 of the Mandate, it is necessary, if disorganisation is to be avoided, and if the policy is to have a chance to succeed, that there should exist some centralised control of transactions relating to the acquisition and transfer of land during such interim period as may reasonably be necessary to place the development scheme upon a sure foundation. The power contemplated is regulative and not prohibitory, although it does involve a power to prevent transactions which are inconsistent with the tenor of the

scheme

scheme. But the exercise of the power will be <u>limited</u> and in no respect arbitrary. In every case it will be <u>conditioned by considerations as to how best to give effect to the purposes of the Mandate</u>. Any control contemplated will be fenced with due safeguards to secure <u>as little interference as possible with the free transfer of land</u>. The centralised control wi<u>ll take effect as from such date only as the authority charged with the duty of carrying out the policy of land development shall begin to operate</u>. The High Commissioner will, pending the establishment of such centralised control, have full powers to take all steps necessary to protect the tenancy and occupancy rights, including the rights of squatters, throughout Palestine.

"13. Further, the statement of policy of His Majesty's Government did not imply a prohibition of acquisition of additional land by Jews. It contains no such prohibition, nor is any such intended. What it does contemplate is such <u>temporary</u> control of land disposition and transfers as may be necessary not to impair the harmony and effectiveness of the scheme of land settlement to be undertaken. His Majesty's Government feel bound to point out that they alone of the Governments which have been responsible for the administration of Palestine since the acceptance of the Mandate have declared their definite intention to

initiate

initiate an active policy of development which it is believed will result in substantial and lasting benefit to both Jews and Arabs."

Following the sense of the Statement of Policy (see paragraph 9 above), the Prime Minister's letter definitely regards control of land transfers as intended to facilitate the development scheme, and makes no reference to such a measure in connection with legislation for the protection of the position of tenants.

In accordance with the terms of the Prime Minister's letter it was decided to defer the enactment of legislation dealing with control of land transfers until the development authority had begun operations. In the meantime further discussions were initiated between the Colonial Office and the Jewish Agency with regard to the form of the legislation dealing with the protection of cultivators which was to be introduced immediately.

The High Commissioner's draft ordinance amending the Protection of Cultivators Ordinance 1929 contained a provision (Clause 3) to the effect that "a disposition of land on which there were tenants etc. should not be valid <u>unless approved by the High Commissioner</u>, who, before approving the disposition, should be satisfied that adequate provision had been or would be made for the livelihood of the tenants etc. either by reserving an area of the land or by conferring on such persons rights on other land similar to those enjoyed by them on the land which is the subject of the disposition".

At the first discussion with the Colonial Office

Office, the Jewish Agency took strong exception to this provision, arguing that it had been definitely agreed to postpone all legislation affecting the disposition or transfer of land until the creation of the proposed centralised control in connection with the development scheme.

Sir J. Shuckburgh, who presided, referred this point to the Secretary of State for decision and in doing so expressed the view that there was nothing in paragraph 12 of the Prime Minister's letter to bear out the Jewish contention. It was eventually decided to omit the clause in question from the Protection of Cultivators Amendment Ordinance, and the High Cr was inf. that the Jewish contention could not easily be refuted. The Ordinance was enacted in May 1931 as a temporary measure for a period of one year in the first instance. It supplemented the Protection of Cultivators Ordinance 1929 by (a) extending the definition of tenant, (b) providing that no tenant should be evicted (except for certain specified defaults) unless the High Commissioner was satisfied that equivalent provision had been secured towards the livelihood of the tenant and (c) giving to persons who had exercised for 5 years a practice of grazing, watering animals, cutting wood or reeds etc. the same rights in the matter of eviction as had been given to "tenants".

12.   Discussions with the High Commissioner continued on the subject of the permanent land legislation which was to be introduced when the development authority should begin to operate i.e. Sir J. Chancellor's six draft ordinances referred to in paragraph 10 above. The Jews persisted in their campaign against any general control of land transfers, and when the

Director

Director of Development was appointed in August last they declined the invitation to appoint a Jewish adviser so long as the hated draft ordinances (particularly the Transfer of Agricultural Land Ordinance) were still under active consideration. The matter was reviewed in September last and it was decided to defer the enactment of the permanent land legislation until the report of the Director of Development had been received and considered. It was thought that the enactment of legislation for the control of land transactions (presumably for the purpose of facilitating the development scheme) would be difficult to justify until the position with regard to the possibility of any scheme of development had become clearer. At an interview with Dr. Brodetsky on 10th October last, endeavour was made to reach agreement on the following procedure:-

No.34 in 87072/1.

That the O.A.G. and the Director of Development should be instructed to discuss with the Palestine Executive of the Jewish Agency with a view to reaching agreement on

(1) control of land transactions as described in the Prime Minister's letter on the understanding that it would be bound up with the development scheme and discussed when that scheme was submitted:

(2) some intermediate localised limited control pending the submission of the development scheme, in order to ensure that the development plan should not be prejudiced in advance and with reference also to the problem of displaced Arabs.

Hopes of a settlement on these lines did not mature.

mature, the Jewish Agency holding that they could not face Jewish public opinion if they agreed to co-operate with the Palestine Government with a view to the enactment of any kind of restrictive legislation when it was possible that the development scheme might for financial reasons have to be postponed for an indefinite time.

13.   Mr French's first report was received early in January. This report, which contained no proposals for immediate action, dealt with certain prerequisites of any development scheme, including the general control of transfers of land. The proposed control of land transfers was justified by Mr French both as a preventive of land speculation against the Government in connection with the development scheme and as a preventive of further "displacements" of Arab cultivators. The High Commissioner informed the Secretary of State that he was not satisfied that any general control of land dispositions was immediately required and he asked for approval of the enactment of legislation to control dispositions of land in defined areas.

C.O. despatch of 17th Feb. on 97072/32.

In reply, the Secretary of State remarked that he was strongly opposed in principle to the enactment in connection with land development or the settlement of displaced Arabs of any restrictive legislation which would be general in its scope. He would, however, be prepared to consider the enactment of restrictive legislation to apply to defined areas in which it is intended to carry out definite schemes of development or settlement. The Secretary of State suggested that the enactment of the limited legislation to control dispositions of land should be deferred
                                                            until

until it was possible to consider it in direct relation to concrete schemes in definite areas to which it would be applied.

As regards prevention of speculation against the Government, the Secretary of State suggested :-

(a) that this object might be attained by an extension of the scope of the Expropriation of Lands Ordinance 1926.

(b) That it might be possible to ensure, by means of stipulations in the leases, that persons settled on government-owned land should remain government tenants, and that there should be no further disturbance of the occupancy rights of tenants in areas, (e.g., the Beisan area,) which were to be resettled.

(c) That, for the prevention of any increase in the class of landless Arabs in the hill districts and the coastal plains, he would not be prepared to consider any extension of government control of land transactions beyond the limits of areas selected for development until, at any rate, the results of the proposed comprehensive enquiry into land transactions referred to in the Prime Minister's letter were available.

At an interview with the Jewish Agency at the end of January last, Sir A. Wauchope stated that while he could not give any guarantee that legislation imposing general control of land transfers would not be introduced, he himself saw no necessity for any such legislation in connection with such development measures as were at present in contemplation.

II. PRESENT POSITION WITH REGARD TO LAND LEGISLATION.

14. The present position then is that to meet the

first

first main object mentioned in paragraph 2 we have the Protection of Cultivators Ordinance 1929 and the amending ordinance of 1931, the life of which has been extended until May, 1932, subject to the improvement of certain provisions.

To meet the second main object, viz., the facilitation of the development scheme by prevention of speculation, the High Commissioner recently proposed to amend the Expropriation of Land Ordinance 1926 so as to make it clear that land could be expropriated by Government for development purposes. The question whether this amendment should be immediately enacted is under consideration. If enacted it should place the Government in a position to obtain land at a reasonable price in spite of anticipatory purchases on the part of speculators.

[margin note: It was decided that it should not yet be enacted.]

The Protection of Cultivators Ordinance as amended is still deficient in two important respects:-

(a) It does nothing to prevent the Arab cultivator† from making himself "landless" by selling the whole of his land, ~~whether freehold or leasehold~~.

[margin note: †whether 'owner' or 'occupancy tenant'.]

(b) While providing for due notice and payment of compensation, it still allows of the eviction of a tenant when the landowner requires the land for his own purposes. It is true that, except where the eviction is for some default, the High Commissioner must be satisfied that equivalent provision has been secured towards the livelihood of the tenant, but in nearly every case the shortage of suitable land results in the payment of money to the evicted tenant who thus becomes landless.

III. MR FRENCH'S PROPOSALS.

15. In his supplementary report Mr French submits for

for consideration and discussion two draft ordinances: (a) the Homesteads Protection Ordinance and (b) the Occupancy Tenants Ordinance, which are designed to meet the deficiencies of the Protection of Cultivators Ordinance to which attention has been drawn in paragraph /4. above.

The latter Ordinance confers "a right of occupancy" on any tenant who was ~~cultivating~~ occupying a holding at the date of the enactment of the Protection of Cultivators Ordinance of May 1931, and provides against the eviction of any "occupancy tenant" except for certain specified defaults. An occupancy tenant can sell or lease his rights, subject, however, to the provisions of the Homesteads Protection Ordinance, as to which see below.

[† 86 (1)(f)]

N.B. It is expressly provided that the provision prohibiting eviction shall not apply in the case of landowners who purchased their lands for purposes of colonisation and development before the date of the introduction of the Ordinance. This means that the Jewish organisations will not be saddled forever with the Arabs whom they have permitted temporarily to cultivate the reserve estates on which Jewish colonists have not yet been established.* (The Jews admit that these reserve lands amount to 40,000 dunums, but Mr French suspects that this figure is an underestimate).

[* These Arabs will, however, be entitled to the compensation payable to evicted tenant under the Prot. of Cultivators Order.]

16.   The Homesteads Protection Ordinance provides for the gazetting of "zones" in which dispositions of land by a "cultivator" (i.e. an owner or an occupancy tenant) may be registered with the consent of the District Commissioner, and that the District Commissioner shall

shall refuse his consent to any disposition by way of the permanent alienation of the "homestead area" of a cultivator unless he is satisfied that the applicant owns elsewhere other unencumbered lands not less than the area declared a homestead area in the zone in which such lands are situated, or has obtained other permanent occupation, or that the proposed disposition is a gift made in good faith for a religious or charitable purpose.

x
The area of "homesteads" will vary in the different "zones".

The approval of the District Commissioner will also be required for a mortgage of land in a zone by a cultivator, and if the mortgage includes the homestead area foreclosure will not affect the mortgagor's occupancy of the homestead. The mortgagee will be put into "possession", but the mortgagor will remain in occupation and pay a limited rent to the mortgagee.

A cultivator will be able to lease his homestead area for any term not exceeding ten years. In such circumstances it is to be presumed that the cultivator would live on the rent of the lease.

The High Commissioner may exempt any person or class of persons from the operation of the ordinance or of any of its provisions with the previous sanction of the Secretary of State.

17. These two draft ordinances should secure the objects (a) of preventing further evictions and (b) of preventing Arab cultivators from "displacing themselves", and should thus put a stop to the process which fills the ranks of the "landless Arab" class. Mr French points out that merely on grounds of finance it is not practical to embark on a scheme of resettlement of displaced Arabs without providing against a future

increase

increase in the class of displaced Arabs. His Homesteads Protection Ordinance involves a measure of control over dispositions of land, but, as he points out in paragraph 74 (Part 3) of his report, this Ordinance does not impose anything in the nature of a general restriction upon dispositions of land. It merely requires previous consent, which would be given as a matter of course in any case not involving permanent alienation or mortgage of the "homestead area". The Homesteads Protection Ordinance does not apply to the whole country indiscriminately but will only be applied in zones (though it seems probable that the zones will have to comprehend most of the country) as and when gazetted. Mr French does not anticipate that the provisions of the Homesteads Ordinance will create an insuperable difficulty in the acquisition of land, as he contemplates that voluntary arrangements will be made whereby homestead areas could all be reserved in one compact block separate from the areas passing under the control of the purchasers.

18. The Occupancy Tenants Ordinance (see paragraph 75 of Mr French's supplementary report) is based on paragraph 24 of the Statement of Policy, where it is laid down that consideration must also be given to the protection of tenants by some form of occupancy right, or by other means to secure them against ejectment or the imposition of excessive rental. "The Protection of Cultivators Ordinance" fulfils this object to some extent, but its deficiencies have been noted above and Mr French's new ordinance should provide a remedy. The proviso with regard to lands already purchased for colonisation and development should prevent any hardship

ship to the Jewish organisations concerned.

Both ordinances are definitely related to the development scheme in that it would be absurd to undertake the financial liabilities of such a scheme unless simultaneous steps are taken by means of legislation of this nature to prevent the creation of further landless Arabs.

19. It is difficult to see how legislation of the nature proposed by Mr French could be temporary, and the Jews will probably argue that, in accordance with the terms of paragraph 12 of the Prime Minister's letter, the life of any such legislation must not extend beyond the period of the development scheme. This objection is not, however, very serious as (1) the development scheme may last for years and (2) it is not clear that legislation for the protection of tenants (such as these) need be temporary in order to comply with the terms of the Prime Minister's letter, the relevant passage of which clearly referred to control of land transfers for the purpose of anticipating obstruction of the plans of the Director of Development.

19.5.32

7.10

Extract from a Private and Personal letter
from Sir Philip Cunliffe-Lister to
Sir A.G. Wauchope, dated 3rd June, 1932.

X   X

I said to Weizmann that I was getting really sick of White Papers, letters and reports and that, if one could only go back, how much wiser it would have been to have none of these publications and great <u>ad hoc</u> enquiries, but, having settled our policy, to let the Palestine administration go ahead, working it out; and let policy be evidenced by action, the only utterances being speeches in the House, when these were inevitable, and as few as possible of those. Weizmann entirely agreed. This rather leads me to the hope that in any further developments enquiry and action will be routine work of your administration. For example, the enquiry into all land in Palestine, to which we are committed by the Prime Minister's letter and of which I suppose one takes French's Reports as a partial stage; would it not be much wiser that this should go on as the regular work of the appropriate department in Palestine, reinforced, if need be, in personnel in order to get the work done quicker. I certainly shudder at the prospect of French or anybody else conducting another enquiry to be embodied in a special report; and I expect you agree.

7.11

S E C R E T.

REVISED DRAFT MEMORANDUM FOR CABINET.

LAND POLICY FOR PALESTINE.

1. It has become necessary to take decisions on certain important questions relating to Land Policy in Palestine. The problem with which we have to deal may be stated quite simply. The Jews have for years been buying land in Palestine for agricultural colonisation. This is part of the fundamental policy of Zionism, and is likely to continue so long as funds are available, and land can be obtained. The Jews pay market prices to Arab landowners, and in many cases generous compensation to tenants and other occupants, who are displaced from the land purchased.

2. In former years when one Arab sold land to another, the landowner changed, but the tenants remained, and those who laboured on the land for regular or seasonal wage still continued to earn that wage. To some extent this practice was, and is, maintained by such organisations as the Palestine Jewish Colonisation Association. But the Zionist Policy is different. When the Jewish National Fund purchase land, not only the landlord is changed, but the tenants and all the wage earning labourer class are compelled to move; for the Zionist policy is not only to acquire ownership, but also to ensure that all the work required on the land shall be carried out by Jews only. The right of the Zionists to take such action cannot be
questioned,

questioned, but it obviously creates a new situation for the Arab cultivator.

3. The result is the growth of a body of "landless" Arabs, who may be divided into three classes:-

 (a) Tenants,

 (b) Small owner-occupiers,

 (c) Labourers.

In a more highly developed country, one might expect such persons to be partly absorbed into other occupations, and the remainder dealt with by the Poor Law Authorities, but conditions in Palestine are peculiar. The fellah is usually heavily in debt, improvident and unfitted for urban life. Political exploitation which is active in Palestine, tends to create in the "landless" class a feeling of disaffection and unrest. Sir Arthur Wauchope is definitely of opinion that this constitutes a potential danger, which should be arrested without delay, if serious consequences are to be averted.

4. The problem falls into two parts: (a) what should be done as regards Arabs who have already become "landless"?; (b) how can the process of displacement be stopped?

5. As regards (a) the Shaw Commission on the Disturbances in 1929 expressed the definite opinion that the existence of a "landless" and discontented class constituted a potential cause of future disturbance. The late Government recognised the danger and, indeed, regarded the existence of a "landless" class as indicating neglect of the spirit, if not of the letter, of the

              Mandate.

Mandate. They accordingly accepted responsibility for re-settlement of such Arabs as could be shown to have been displaced from the lands which they occupied, in consequence of those lands passing into Jewish hands, if they had not obtained other holdings or other satisfactory occupation.

6. The undertaking of the Labour Government to re-settle such Arabs was given in very different financial circumstances. The resources of the Exchequer and of the Palestine Government are limited and it is obviously necessary to re-examine our commitments in the light of the changed conditions and to determine how far we must go towards meeting them, and how it is to be done. I recognise that the problem is a difficult one. The pledges given by His Majesty's Government were very definite. The claims of "landless" Arabs are actually being accepted for registration at the present time, and any indication that His Majesty's Government do not intend to carry out their undertaking to re-settle them would have a deplorable political effect, which would be exploited to the full by the increasingly active Arab Nationalist Party and by Communists.

7. The register of "landless" Arabs is nearly complete, and it is estimated that the total may amount to some 800 or 900 families. This figure takes no account of owner-occupiers, or of Arab villagers who have hitherto worked as labourers for Arab landowners, but who will find their means of livelihood vanish when both the ownership of the land and the work on it becomes Jewish in place of Arab. Sir Arthur Wauchope holds, and I agree with him,

that

that we are only pledged to deal with "landless" Arabs, in the sense of those who have lost their land through Jewish action, i.e. tenants. For financial reasons, if on no other grounds, the Palestine Government cannot undertake, in addition, to settle on the land, at a cost of perhaps £500 each, those Arab owner-occupiers, who have voluntarily sold their land, or Arab villagers, who have lost, not land-holdings, but their employment upon the land as a result of Jewish land purchases. It is, however, necessary that the existence of the labourer class (estimated at some 3,000 families) should be recognised.

8. I should like to inform the High Commissioner that His Majesty's Government concur with his views as to the limitation of the register to displaced tenants; and I would propose to ask him to submit his own recommendations for providing land for the 800 or 900 families who are likely to be registered, with due regard to economy. It may be found unnecessary to provide for this resettlement on such a costly scale as is suggested in Mr. French's reports. i.e. £500 for settlement on unirrigated and £650-800 for settlement on irrigated land. For example, it is hoped that the Wadi Hawareth Arabs, whose settlement constitutes the most urgent problem, will be settled at a cost of about £250 per family; in this case the land is obtainable at an exceptionally low price, and the Arabs already possess tents, agricultural implements and ploughing animals, items for which Mr. French allowed £110 to £120.

9. With regard to (b), in view of the high cost of re-settlement, it is obvious that, for financial

reasons,

reasons, quite apart from the question of policy and the preservation of order in Palestine, the process of displacement should be brought to an end as soon as possible. I have discussed the question fully with Sir Arthur Wauchope and I am satisfied that there is no half-way house between leaving things as they are and so aggravating the evil, and some form of legislation to control land transactions. I am also convinced that, in view of the opposition of the Jews to legislation of this nature, any new enactment should not transgress any of our commitments to the Jews and should involve as little interference as possible with the economic life of the country.

10. Sir Arthur Wauchope considers, and I agree with him, that the right of a tenant to a holding sufficient for the subsistence of his family must be assured, but, in conformity with the proposal not to register owner-occupiers as "landless" Arabs, we consider that the right of the owner-occupier to sell his land should remain unrestricted, at any rate for the present.

11. In paragraph 12 of the Prime Minister's letter full power was reserved (pending the establishment of temporary centralized control of land transfers in connection with the development scheme) to take all steps necessary to protect tenancy and occupancy rights, including the rights of squatters, throughout Palestine. In accordance with this policy, a temporary Ordinance with a life of 12 months was enacted on the 28th of May, 1931, which amended the Protection of Cultivators Ordinance, 1929, in several important particulars. The life

life of the amending Ordinance was extended for a further 12 months on the 28th of May, 1932.

Briefly, the present Protection of Cultivators legislation provides as follows:-

(1) No tenant of two years' standing, who has paid his rent and cultivated his holding properly and not been declared bankrupt, may be evicted without at least one year's notice, compensation for disturbance and for improvements and (if he is of more than five years' standing and goes without an eviction order) the equivalent of one year's average rent. Any dispute regarding the amount of compensation has to be decided by a Board consisting of a District Officer, one representative of the landlord and one representative of the tenant. The Board's decisions require confirmation by the District Commissioner.

(2) Unless there has been failure to pay rent or to cultivate properly, or unless the tenant has been declared bankrupt, the court will not grant an eviction order unless the High Commissioner is satisfied that "equivalent provision has been secured towards the livelihood of the tenant". (The Ordinance does not specify what this "equivalent provision" must be.)

(3) The tenant's rent cannot be raised except with the consent of a Board constituted as above.

(4) Tenants who have not paid their rent and have not cultivated their land properly may be evicted at 15 days' notice unless they apply for the matter to be referred to a Board constituted as above.

12.

12. Sir Arthur Wauchope tells me that, since the amending Ordinance came into force, few, if any, tenants have been turned off their lands. No case has been referred to the High Commissioner under (2) above and, therefore, no eviction orders can have been made except after default in regard to payment of rent, or proper cultivation, or after bankruptcy. At the same time the Ordinance does not provide complete security since it merely impedes, but does not prevent, eviction, and allows of compensation in other forms than land in the case of eviction.

13. The most important parts of the existing legislation expire in May, 1933, and some legislation will, therefore, be necessary in any case within the next few months. Sir Arthur Wauchope's proposal is that the Protection of Cultivators legislation should be made permanent and that the opportunity should be taken to simplify it and re-draft it. The legislation would be 'permanent' in the sense that the time-limit would be removed, but the Ordinance would be subject to review in the event of the establishment of the centralised land control contemplated in the Prime Minister's letter. The revision suggested by Sir Arthur Wauchope is as follows:—

(1) A tenant who has paid his rent and not neglected his holding grossly, may not be evicted unless the High Commissioner is satisfied that an equivalent provision has been made for him in land up to the minimum required for subsistence of himself and his family and unless he is given at least one year's notice

notice, compensation for disturbance and for improvements and, if of more than 5 years' standing, the equivalent of one year's average rent.

(2) A tenant's rent not to be raised except with the consent of a Board constituted as at present.

(3) A tenant who has not paid his rent not to be evicted without at least one year's notice and compensation for improvements, and even then not to be evicted from the minimum area required for subsistence provided he cultivates it fairly.

(4) The minimum area to be reserved should be such as to provide the tenant with subsistence by his existing methods of cultivation. Any question as to what is a sufficient subsistence area for any particular tenant to be settled by a Board constituted as at present and liable to review, say, every 5 years.

(5) A Board to decide, as at present, all questions regarding the amount of compensation due.

(6) A tenant not to be allowed to sell his "subsistence area" but to be allowed to raise a mortgage on his interest in it subject to certain conditions.

(7) The following clause, taken from Mr. French's Occupancy Tenant's Ordinance:-

"Notwithstanding anything contained in this Ordinance the District Commissioner may, on the application of the landlord, authorise the resumption by him of a holding or part thereof upon being satisfied (1) that such resumption is required for some reasonable and sufficient
purpose

purposes having relation to the good of the holding or of the adjoining lands including development by drainage or irrigation or by closer settlement or colonization or disposal for building purposes, and (2) that the "occupancy tenant" will retain sufficient land in the district or elsewhere for the maintenance of himself and his family, or that the purpose for which the resumption of the holding is sought comprises the provision for the "occupancy tenant" of developed land sufficient for the maintenance of himself and his family, together with adequate subsistence for them pending the development of such lands."

14. Sir Arthur Wauchope is definitely of opinion that no legislation should at present be passed preventing the owner-occupier from disposing of his land. He considers that it would be difficult to justify such an interference with the right of landowners to dispose of their property and that the inclusion of the owner-occupier in the proposed legislation would be likely to strengthen the opposition to anything which it may be decided to do for the tenant. He does not anticipate, at any rate during the next few years, a serious problem arising from the conversion of owner-occupiers into "landless" Arabs.

To sum up, he is of opinion that the most we should do to prevent the creation of "landless" Arabs in the future is to consolidate, simplify and strengthen the existing Protection of Cultivators legislation on the lines indicated above, and he does not anticipate that this will cause much trouble.

15.

15. I am in entire agreement with the High Commissioner's views on the subject of preventive legislation. I would, however, suggest with regard to head (4) that the draft Ordinance should leave the determination of the "subsistence area" in each case to the Board, in order to allow of a reduction of this area in cases where the landlord may be prepared to irrigate the land and to provide for the tenant's subsistence in the meantime.

16. Annexed to this memorandum will be found a short statement as to various legislative enactments elsewhere in the British Empire and Egypt designed to secure hereditary cultivators in the continued occupation of their holdings. It will be realised that a control of land transactions which has been adopted in Tropical Africa and other countries where the bulk of the land is state land or tribally owned, must be much more drastic in its effects in a country such as Palestine where the land with which we are concerned is for the most part in private ownership. It may, however, be argued that such interference with economic conditions in Palestine can be justified as an inevitable outcome of the artificial situation created by the establishment of the Jewish National Home.

17. Whatever may be decided as to existing commitments, it is, I think, clearly urgent to prevent these commitments from being further extended, as it is not possible to draw any logical distinction between Arabs at present displaced and those who may become displaced in the near future by the same process. It must, however, be appreciated that ~~any~~ legislation ~~controlling land transactions~~,

transactions, ~~if it is to achieve its object, must be drastic and novel and~~ will be met by very strong resistance on the part of the Jews, who will probably argue that it is inconsistent with the promises given by the Prime Minister in his letter to Dr. Weizmann, and constitutes an attack upon the fundamental principles of Zionism. This contention is dealt with in Appendix I (C) paragraph 2.

18. Both these problems are dealt with in the reports of Mr. French, the Director of Development, which have not yet been published, but have been referred as confidential documents, to the Jewish Agency and the Arab Executive for their observations. The matter is, however, urgent, and in any case Sir Arthur Wauchope and I both feel that it should be dealt with independently of the reports which we have reason to believe will be rejected both by Arabs and Jews and are likely therefore to lead to much controversy.

19. The issues are so complicated and controversial, and it is in my view so important that every aspect of this two-fold problem should be carefully examined, that I suggest that in the first place the matter should be referred to a committee of the Cabinet, who should examine the whole question in the light of the considerations set out in this memorandum and make definite recommendations to the Cabinet regarding the following points:-

(1) (a) How far His Majesty's Government must regard themselves as committed to the policy of re-settling "landless" Arabs.

(b)

(b) What measures must be taken to that end in the event of the commitment being accepted.

(b) How the cost of carrying out such measures is to be met.

(2) (a) Whether the situation which has arisen does in fact justify exceptional legislative action to prevent the continued creation of the "landless" class.

(b) If so, how such action can be reconciled with the various pronouncements of His Majesty's Government and assurances given to the Jews, with special reference to the Prime Minister's letter.

(c) What are the minimum legislative safeguards which must be introduced.

(d) Should they apply to Arabs at present still occupying lands already in Jewish hands.

(e) How soon should legislation be enacted and what preliminary measures to meet anticipated criticisms should be taken.

20. Annexed to this memorandum are:-

Appendix I;

(A) Commitments of His Majesty's Government in regard to "landless" Arabs.

(B) Some account of the problem and of the attitude adopted towards it by His Majesty's Government.

(C) Comments on certain points arising from the commitments.

Appendix II; a note as to legislation in Egypt and certain parts of the British Empire designed to safeguard the interests of agriculturists.

APPENDIX I.

A. Commitments of His Majesty's Government with regard to "landless" Arabs.

1. "Legislation is to be introduced with the object of controlling the disposition of agricultural lands in such a manner as to prevent the dispossession of the indigenous agricultural population. These temporary measures will be superseded in any case by such permanent enactments as may be decided upon when future policy is determined in the light of Sir John Hope Simpson's Report". (Paragraph 5 of Statement with regard to British Policy in Palestine, May 1930, Cmd. 3582).

2. "..........It is, however, an error to imagine that the Palestine Government is in possession of large areas of vacant land which could be made available for Jewish settlement. The extent of unoccupied areas of Government land is negligible. The Government claims considerable areas which are, in fact, occupied and cultivated by Arabs. Even were the title of the Government to these areas admitted, and it is in many cases disputed, it would not be possible to make these areas available for Jewish settlement, in view of their actual occupation by Arab cultivators and of the importance of making available additional land on which to place the Arab cultivators who are now landless". (Paragraph 15 of Statement of Policy by His Majesty's Government, October, 1930, Cmd. 3692).

3. "We may proceed to the contention that the Mandate has been reinterpreted in a manner highly

prejudicial

prejudicial to Jewish interests in the vital matters of land settlement and immigration. It has been said that the policy of the White Paper would place an embargo upon immigration, and would suspend, if not, indeed, terminate, the close settlement of the Jews on the land, which is a primary purpose of the Mandate. In support of this contention particular stress has been laid upon the passage referring to State lands in the White Paper, which says that "it would not be possible to make these areas available for Jewish settlement in view of their actual occupation by Arab cultivators, and of the importance of making available additional land on which to place the Arab cultivators who are now landless".

"The language of this passage needs to be read in the light of the policy as a whole. It is desirable to make it clear that the "landless" Arabs, to whom it was intended to refer in the passage quoted, were such Arabs as can be shown to have been displaced from the lands which they occupied in consequence of the lands passing into Jewish hands, and who have not obtained other holdings on which they can establish themselves or other equally satisfactory occupation. The number of such displaced Arabs must be a matter for careful enquiry. It is to "landless" Arabs within this category that His Majesty's Government feel themselves under an obligation to facilitate their settlement upon the land. The recognition of this obligation in no way detracts from the larger purposes of development, which

His

His Majesty's Government regards as the most effectual means of furthering the establishment of a National Home for the Jews". (Paragraphs 8 and 9 of letter from the Prime Minister to Dr. Weizmann, 13th February, 1931).

4. "It is the intention of His Majesty's Government to institute an enquiry as soon as possible to ascertain, inter alia, what State and other lands are, or properly can be made, available for close settlement by Jews under reference to the obligation imposed upon the Mandatory by article 6 of the Mandate. This enquiry will be comprehensive in its scope, and will include the whole land resources of Palestine. In the conduct of the enquiry provision will be made for all interests, whether Jewish or Arab, making such representations as it may be desired to put forward". (Paragraph 10 of Prime Minister's letter).

5. "In giving effect to the policy of land settlement, as contemplated in article 11 of the Mandate, it is necessary, if disorganization is to be avoided, and if the policy is to have a chance to succeed, that there should exist some centralised control of transactions relating to the acquisition and transfer of land during such interim period as may reasonably be necessary to place the development scheme upon a sure foundation. The power contemplated is regulative and not prohibitory, although it does involve a power to prevent transactions which are inconsistent with the tenor of the scheme. But the exercise of the power will be limited and in no respect arbitrary. In every case it will be conditioned by considerations as to how

best

best to give effect to the purposes of the Mandate. Any control contemplated will be fenced with due safeguards to secure as little interference as possible with the free transfer of land. The centralised control will take effect as from such date only as the authority charged with the duty of carrying out the policy of land development shall begin to operate. The High Commissioner will, pending the establishment of such centralised control, have full powers to take all steps necessary to protect the tenancy and occupancy rights, including the rights of squatters, throughout Palestine".

"Further, the statement of policy of His Majesty's Government did not imply a prohibition of acquisition of additional land by Jews. It contains no such prohibition, nor is any such intended. What it does contemplate is such temporary control of land disposition and transfers as may be necessary not to impair the harmony and effectiveness of the scheme of land settlement to be undertaken. His Majesty's Government feel bound to point out that they alone of the Governments which have been responsible for the administration of Palestine since the acceptance of the Mandate have declared their definite intention to initiate an active policy of development which it is believed will result in substantial and lasting benefit to both Jews and Arabs". (Paragraphs 12 and 13 of Prime Minister's letter).

6." .... the proper application of the absorptive capacity principle. That principle is
vital

vital to any scheme of development, the primary purpose of which must be the settlement both of Jews and of displaced Arabs upon the land". (Paragraph 15 of Prime Minister's letter).

7. Lord Passfield's despatch to the High Commissioner for Palestine, dated the 26th June, 1931, regarding the development scheme, lays upon the Director of Development the duty, inter alia, to prepare a register of displaced Arabs as defined in the Prime Minister's letter and to draw up a scheme of resettlement for registered displaced Arabs. The despatch goes on to say that when the scheme has been approved by the High Commissioner, resettlement will be carried out as quickly as possible. (See paragraph 5,iii (b) of the despatch).

This despatch was published at the time and has been reproduced in the Annual Report on Palestine for 1931.

B. <u>Development of the problem of "landless" Arabs.</u>

1. The Report of the Shaw Commission on the disturbances in 1929 drew attention to the existence of a "landless" Arab class, and the danger of its existence and of its continuance. It referred to various ordinances from 1920 onwards designed to protect the interests of cultivators, and pointed out that these had failed to prevent the evil to which they drew attention. The definite opinion was expressed by the Commission that unless "some solution can be found to deal with this situation, the question will remain a constant source of present discontent and a potential cause of future disturbance". (Cmd.3530, page 162, paragraph 35).

2. The Shaw Report was issued in March, 1930, and in May, 1930, His Majesty's Government announced their intention to introduce legislation to control dispositions of agricultural land so as to prevent the dispossession of the indigenous agricultural population. (See commitment No. 1 above). For political reasons, however, no action was taken to carry out the announced intention of His Majesty's Government, and it was decided to await the receipt of Sir John Hope Simpson's Report. This was published in October, 1930, simultaneously with the White Paper containing the statement of policy of His Majesty's Government.

3. Sir John Hope Simpson envisaged in his Report a two-fold problem: (a) to safeguard the position of the Arab agricultural population: (b) to permit of some further extension of Jewish agricultural colonisation. His solution was an intensive development scheme on a very large scale, involving expenditure from loan funds of several millions and a programme extending over several years. His Majesty's Government, while accepting his general conclusions, were unable to contemplate capital expenditure on a larger scale than £2,500,000, which it was realised would only deal with a fraction of the problem envisaged by Sir John Hope Simpson.

4. It was considered necessary by Sir John Hope Simpson that to enable his comprehensive scheme to be undertaken, wide powers of control over land transactions should be in the hands of the Government. If it had been possible to adopt his recommendations in full,

Arab

Arab cultivators would (at any rate, in theory) have been protected from displacement without destroying the prospect of future land acquisition and development by the Jews.

5. The very restricted scope of the scheme of development which was all that His Majesty's Government felt financially justified in initiating, gave the Jews a not unreasonable excuse for objecting to Government taking the very wide powers of control of land transactions recommended by Sir John Hope Simpson and envisaged by the White Paper of October, 1930. The controversy over the White Paper thus tended to concentrate upon the degree of government control necessary for carrying out the development scheme on the reduced scale then contemplated, and the original problem of preventing the increase of a class of "landless" Arabs, which logically should now have been treated as an independent problem, receded into the background.

6. In May 1931 (see paragraph 11 of memorandum) a temporary ordinance was enacted amending existing legislation for the protection of tenant cultivators. Owing to strong Jewish pressure, however, the protection afforded did not prevent actual eviction of tenants, but permitted compensation in cash for eviction. This, owing to the improvidence of the Fellahin, their state of indebtedness and their unfitness in most cases for other occupations, did not afford an adequate solution. No attempt was made to control the disposal of land by owner-occupiers.

7.

7. The next step taken was the appointment of Mr. Lewis French, formerly Chief Secretary to the Punjab Government, as Director of Development. Mr. French took up his duties in August, 1931. On the 23rd December, 1931 he submitted his First Report to the High Commissioner. This was followed by a Supplementary Report submitted on 20th April 1932. Both reports were communicated together, as confidential documents, to the Arab Executive and the Jewish Agency whose observations upon them are still awaited by the High Commissioner.

8. In the meantime, in deference to strong Jewish representations, His Majesty's Government decided to postpone any legislation for the control of land transactions until the development scheme envisaged in the 1930 Statement of Policy was more fully worked out, and the prospective advantages of it to Jewish interests could be estimated.

9. In view of the world-wide economic depression, it was thought advisable, in January, 1932, to envisage the abandonment of a development scheme on the scale of £2,500,000, which had been proposed at the time of the issue of the White Paper of 1930. In a telegram of 20th January, 1932, the High Commissioner was authorised to inform the Arab Executive and the Jewish Agency that His Majesty's Government would consider Mr. French's reports with their observations and the High Commissioner's recommendations "with the object of taking early action if financial circumstances permit to give effect to a limited scheme of development which will provide <u>first</u> for resettlement of 'displaced'

Arabs,

Arabs, and <u>second</u> for some assistance for Jews to settle in Palestine".

10. The Jewish Agency were quick to press the point that such a restricted scheme could not be used to justify any wide or comprehensive powers of control over dispositions of land. Nevertheless, in his second report Mr. French advocates legislation considerably more drastic than that now recommended by the High Commissioner as essential to prevent an increase in the class of "landless" Arab.

11. Mr. French's reports (as stated above) have been communicated in confidence to the Jewish Agency and the Arab Executive, whose observations upon them are at present awaited by the High Commissioner, who, on their receipt will forward them to the Secretary of State with his own recommendations. It has been publicly announced in Palestine, with the concurrence of the Secretary of State, that no decisions will be taken upon the French Reports until His Majesty's Government have received and considered the High Commissioner's recommendations, together with the observations of the Jewish Agency and the Arab Executive.

12. In the meantime the Jews continue to acquire land as funds become available, and the number of potentially "landless" Arabs, "doomed Arabs" as Mr. French calls them in his report, tends to grow. The extreme difficulty which has been experienced in dealing with the case of eviction of Arabs from Jewish land at Wadi Hawareth is a striking illustration of the importance

of

of taking remedial action without delay. The united efforts of the Jewish authorities and of the Palestine Government failed to find any suitable land to which the Arab families in question could be removed in the immediate future, and the Jewish authorities agreed to their remaining on a portion of the land from which they were to have been evicted for a period of 22 months at the end of which time the High Commissioner has undertaken to provide for them elsewhere.

C. **Points arising from commitments of His Majesty's Government.**

1. It will be seen from the foregoing account, that His Majesty's Government have not been able to preserve consistency in their policy in regard to the problem of the "landless" Arab, and the changed economic conditions of the present day may be invoked to justify some departure from the intentions of His Majesty's Government as announced towards the end of 1930. There are, however, two points on which it is likely that the Jews may concentrate when resisting the proposed legislation:

2. The first point is the contention that the action proposed will be contrary to definite assurances given by the Prime Minister. The assurance in question is that contained in paragraphs 12 and 13 of the Prime Minister's letter (see A, Commitment No. 5). The answer to such a charge would appear, however, to be as follows:- The Prime Minister's assurances were given with specific reference to the policy of land settlement and development referred to in the White Paper of

October,

October, 1930, and in the relevant paragraphs of his letter to Dr. Weizmann he was concerned to re-assure the Jews upon one special point namely, that such a policy of land settlement and development would not be used as an excuse for imposing, for an ulterior purpose, restrictions upon land transactions which would be more than what was required for the purposes of carrying out that policy. His assurance could not be interpreted as debarring His Majesty's Government indefinitely from taking any action, which, even if no development or resettlement scheme were in view, might be considered necessary in the general interests of Palestine. It will be noted that at the end of paragraph 12 of his letter, the Prime Minister does in fact make it clear that, pending the establishment of the centralised control required for the development scheme, the High Commissioner would have full powers to take all steps necessary to protect the tenancy and occupancy rights, including the rights of squatters, throughout Palestine. It seems clear that he wished to draw a distinction between measures required eventually to enable the purposes of a development scheme to be carried out, and measures of a protective character, which might be required earlier, and had no direct connection with the question of development.

3. The second point which Jewish critics may make is that legislation interfering with the freedom of disposal of land would be premature, pending the result of the comprehensive enquiry into land resources promised in paragraph 10 of the Prime Minister's letter. (See A Commitment No. 4).

4.

4. To this the only reply can be that Mr. French has conducted a preliminary investigation covering the whole country into the land resources of Palestine, that His Majesty's Government are satisfied, as the result of these investigations, that possibilities of providing additional land for settlement on a scale sufficient to have any serious effect on the problem only exist in two or three areas (e.g. Huleh and Beisan), and that in these areas it will not be possible for many years, owing to legal and financial difficulties to come to a final decision as to the amount of land, if any, which could be made available for intensive settlement.

Appendix II.

Land legislation in certain parts of the British Empire and Egypt.

The principle of the inalienability of land is already widely recognised, but, owing to the different conditions of land tenure and the different objects in view, the form of legislation, in any way comparable with what is contemplated for Palestine, varies considerably in different parts of the world. The following instances may, however, be cited as having some relevance to the present case:-

(1) INDIA.

The Punjab Alienation of Land Act 1900/1907 provides that a member of an agricultural tribe may not permanently alienate land, except to a member of the same tribe or tribal group, without the sanction of the Deputy Commissioner. The term "alienation" includes the grant of occupancy rights. Similar legislation exists in the Central Provinces and the United Provinces. So far, however, as can be ascertained there is no legislation in India which provides that a minimum area of a cultivator shall be inalienable unless it can be shown that he has elsewhere sufficient land for his maintenance or has obtained other permanent occupation.

(2) EAST AFRICA:

The problem of ensuring adequate lands for the natives in Kenya has been dealt with by the creation of land reserves. In Uganda, the bulk of the land

land is Crown land, in respect of which no freehold rights are granted. There exists, however, a very limited number of native freeholders who are precluded by law from parting with their land to non-natives without the consent in the first place of the Native Government, and in the second place of the Government of Uganda.

(3) WESTERN PACIFIC.

In Fiji, where communal conditions exist, the natives may not sell their land except to Government, and non-natives can only acquire native land through the Government. The present policy is not to allow alienation of such land except for purposes of public utility or similar strong reasons. Natives may, however, grant leases of their lands to non-natives, but the Governor in Council may refuse permission for a lease if he is satisfied inter alia that the land in question is necessary for the maintenance and support of the native owners. (Fiji Native Law Ordinance 1 of 1895).

Similar restrictions as regards the alienation of native lands exist in the Solomon Islands.

(4) EGYPT.

In 1913 a Law was passed known as the 5 Feddan Law. This, however, merely lays down the principle of exemption from seizure for debt of agricultural holdings of small farmers not exceeding 5 feddans (5.69 acres) in extent. The Egyptian peasant was left free to sell or otherwise dispose of his land voluntarily because it was believed that his love of the soil was so strongly rooted in his nature that he would not proceed to this extreme.

Copy

GOVERNMENT HOUSE,
JERUSALEM.

22nd December 1932.

My dear Sir Philip,

1 Many thanks for your letters of the 18th November and 22nd November on the subject of land legislation.

2 I have, I am afraid, taken some time to answer them. I have found a variety of opinion among my officials and considerable divergence of opinion as to the facts of the case, proportion of owner-occupiers to tenants, etc. I have kept the subject very confidential and made no mention of it to anyone except experienced officials.

3 The first six paragraphs of Williams' memorandum deal with the question "What should be done as regards Arabs who have already become landless"? I enclose a note on three points in these paragraphs where I suggest there might be some expansion or alteration, but I entirely agree with the general line of argument.

Enc.I

4 I agree also with the questions propounded in paragraph 11(1) for solution by the Cabinet Committee.

5 The remainder of the memorandum deals with the question "How can the process of displacement be stopped?". I agree with you that the right of tenant to a "lot viable" must be assured, but the right of the owner-occupier to sell his land should remain unrestricted, anyway for the present.

The

6. The question is a complicated one. Its history is clearly stated in the first five paragraphs of Appendix I(A) to Williams' memorandum. In paragraph 6 of that Appendix he states the present law and here, I think, he is not quite exact. Actually the 1931 amendment to the Protection of Cultivators' Ordinance was one of importance but it is certainly necessary to simplify and strengthen the whole Ordinance in order to protect the tenant from becoming landless.

7. I doubt whether the original Ordinance of 1929 was ever properly understood by the Arabs and now that there have been a number of amendments it has become somewhat confusing even to the official mind. Briefly the present law provides as follows:-

(1) No tenant of two years' standing, who has paid his rent and cultivated his holding properly and not been declared bankrupt, may be evicted without at least one year's notice, compensation for disturbance and for improvements and (if he is of more than five years' standing and goes without an eviction order) the equivalent of one year's average rent. Any dispute regarding the amount of compensation has to be decided by a Board consisting of a District Officer, one representative of the landlord and one representative of the tenant. The Board's decisions require confirmation by the District Commissioner.

(2) Unless there has been failure to pay rent or to cultivate properly, or unless the tenant has been declared bankrupt, the court will not grant an eviction

eviction order unless the High Commissioner is satisfied that "equivalent provision has been secured towards the livelihood of the tenant." (The Ordinance does not specify what this "equivalent provision" must be.

(3) The tenant's rent cannot be raised except with the consent of a Board constituted as above.

(4) Tenants who have not paid their rent and have not cultivated their land properly may be evicted at 15 days' notice unless they apply for the matter to be referred to a Board constituted as above.

8 This Ordinance does therefore give the tenant very definite security and my advisers say that since it came into force few, if any, tenants have been turned off their lands. Certainly no case has been referred to me under (2) above and therefore no eviction orders can have been made except after default in regard to payment of rent or proper cultivation or after bankruptcy. But the most important parts of the Ordinance expire in May 1933. Some permanent legislation will therefore be necessary in any case within the next few months.

9 My suggestion now is that the Ordinance should be made permanent and that the opportunity should be taken to simplify it and redraft it on the following lines:-

(1) A tenant who has paid his rent and not neglected his holding grossly may not be evicted unless the High Commissioner is satisfied that an equivalent provision has been made for him in land up to the minimum required for a "lot viable", and unless he is given at least one year's notice, compensation for disturbance and for improvements and, if of more than five years' standing, the equivalent of
one

one year's average rent.

(ii) A tenant's rent may not be raised except with the consent of a Board constituted as at present.

(iii) A tenant who has not paid his rent may not be evicted without at least one year's notice and compensation for improvements.

Further I feel he should not be liable to eviction even then from his "lot viable" provided he cultivates it fairly. I consider a landlord should be able to get the bulk of his rent from the sale of the tenant's crops. (Actually it is very rare for a tenant to be in arrear with his rent. Rent is usually in the form of a proportion of the crop and is collected by the landlord on the threshing floor).

(iv) A "lot viable" shall mean the minimum area required to provide the tenant with subsistence by his existing methods of cultivation.

It is impossible to order a tenant who is accustomed to earn his livelihood on 100 dunums by methods of dry cultivation to accept ten dunums of irrigated land until two things are arranged for :-

(a) Money is available for the preparation of the irrigated land.

(b) The tenant has knowledge of different farming methods, and means of subsistence while the change is being effected.

Any question as to what is a "lot viable" for any particular tenant shall be settled by a Board constituted as at present, and shall be liable to review say every five years.

A Board shall also decide as at present all questions regarding the amount of compensation due.

(v)

(v) A tenant shall not be allowed to sell his "lot viable" but I suggest he should be allowed to raise a mortgage on his interest in it subject to certain conditions.

(vi) Something on the lines of the following clause which Mr. French proposed to include in his Occupancy Tenants Ordinance:-

"Notwithstanding anything contained in this Ordinance the District Commissioner may, on the application of the landlord, authorise the resumption by him of a holding or part thereof upon being satisfied (1) that such resumption is required for some reasonable and sufficient purpose having relation to the good of the holding or of the adjoining lands including development by drainage or irrigation or by closer settlement or colonization or disposal for building purposes, and (2) that the "occupancy tenant" will retain sufficient land in the district or elsewhere for the maintenance of himself and his family, or that the purpose for which the resumption of the holding is sought comprises the provision for the "occupancy tenant" of developed land sufficient for the maintenance of himself and his family, together with adequate subsistence for them pending the development of such lands."

10. To me, it seems that there is nothing very drastic in these proposals.

11. So far I have dealt only with the question of tenants. Now I come to that of owner-occupiers with which you dealt in your letter of the 22nd November.

At

/12 At the end of your letter you asked for certain information, which I will do my best to give.

/13 The decision to exclude from the register persons who had themselves sold their land to the Jews was a provisional decision, taken by Mr. French when Director of Development and not previously brought up for confirmation by this Government, nor communicated to outside parties; thus the Palestine Government is not in any sense committed. Mr. Andrews, the Acting Director of Development, explains the decision as follows:-

"Persons who themselves sold their lands to the Jews have as a rule been excluded from the register on the ground that the function of this Department was to endeavour to provide for cultivators who had been involuntarily displaced; and not for persons who have rendered themselves landless and received the price of their lands.

It is true that the term "landless Arab" does technically include an owner-occupier. Where such an owner-occupier had sold to an Effendi, and had continued to cultivate the same lands as tenant, and was subsequently displaced owing to a sale by the Effendi to the Jews, his claim would be admitted. This in fact has been done in the case of Zarnuqa village, Ramle Sub-District. Similarly where owner-occupiers sold to the Jews and remained cultivating the same land but were subsequently displaced, the view of this Department is that their claims should be admitted, unless they come within the provisions of the Protection of Cultivators Ordinance."

These

14 These two types of owner-occupiers have therefore been included in the register of landless Arabs.

15 The number of claims by owner-occupiers (other than these two types) which have already been rejected is 111 and it is estimated that there are about 20 further such claims still pending. But of this total it is probable that over 100 would have been rejected on other grounds and that only about 6 would have been registered.

16 As regards the future, it is impossible to be precise. Mr. Stubbs, the Director of Lands, and Mr. Andrews, the Acting Director of Development, agree in thinking that, with the exception of Gaza and Hebron Sub-Districts (where there are large land-owners) 80% of the cultivators are owner-occupiers and only 20% tenants. Nevertheless I do not anticipate - anyway during the next few years - a serious problem arising from the conversion of owner-occupiers into landless Arabs. Except in the immediate neighbourhood of the larger towns small isolated parcels of land are of little use to the Jews for agricultural settlement, and they find great difficulty in buying suitable blocks of land from small owner-occupiers except where the land is undivided mesha'a. In two years' time all the mesha'a land will, I hope, have been partitioned. It is possible that if the price of land rises still higher than it is at present owner-occupiers of partitioned land may be tempted to sell in large numbers. But I do not think it likely.

17 As I have said above, I am definitely of your opinion that we should abandon the idea of passing legislation which will prevent the owner-occupier from

disposing

disposing of his land. There are many people in this country, as in other countries, who make a living by buying and selling land. Others frequently desire to get rid of a piece of poor land in an unfavourable district and to acquire a better holding in another district. Others desire to dispose of their holding and to go abroad or start business or change the nature of their occupation or investment. To my mind they should not be prevented from doing so and it would be difficult to justify the interference with their right to do as they wish with their own property. Moreover, I agree with your view that the inclusion of the owner-occupier in the "landless" category and in the legislation will be likely to strengthen the opposition to anything it is decided to do for the tenant.

18. To sum up, then, I am of the opinion that the most we should do to prevent the creation of landless Arabs in the future is to consolidate, simplify and strengthen the existing Protection of Cultivators' Ordinance, and I do not anticipate that this will cause much trouble.

19. The legislation must be completed before May, when the most important parts of the Protection of Cultivators' Ordinance expire.

20. If the whole matter can be kept confidential I hope the new law will pass without much controversy. If the Jews hear that Land Legislation is contemplated, their extremists will raise a vigorous campaign which may force the Moderates to join in opposition against any law protecting tenants rights. I do not anticipate this, but the Jews are all looking forward to the elections of next July, and seeking methods by which they can gain popular support.

I return one copy of Williams' memorandum.

Yours very sincerely,

(Sgd.) Arthur Wauchope.

COPY.

Memorandum
on Land Policy in Palestine: Comments and suggested Amendments.

1. On page 1 of the Memorandum I suggest that reference should be made to the following facts.

In former years, when one Arab sold land to another, the land owner changed but the tenants remained, and those who laboured on the land for regular or seasonal wage, still continued to earn that wage. To some extent this practice was and is maintained by such organisations as the P.I.C.A.

But the Zionist policy is different. When the Jewish National Fund purchase land, not only the landlord is changed, but the tenants and all the wage earning labourer class are compelled to move, for the Zionist policy is not only to acquire ownership but also to ensure that all the work required on the land shall be carried out by Jews only.

Though shortsighted, there is nothing unjust in such action by the Zionists, but it obviously creates a new situation for the Arab cultivator.

2. Instead of the words in paragraph 6 "that they may amount to as many as 1200 families" I suggest the following "that they may amount to some 800 or 900 families, but this figure takes no cognisance of Arab villagers who have hitherto worked for Arab landowners, but who will find their means of livelihood vanish when both the ownership of the land and all the work on it becomes Jewish in place of Arab.

We are only pledged to deal with landless Arabs in the sense of those who have lost their land through Jewish action. For financial reasons, if on

no

no other grounds, the Palestine Government cannot undertake in addition to settle on the land, at a cost of perhaps £P.500 each, those Arab villagers who have lost their employment through that action. Their numbers have been estimated at some 3000 families, an estimate certainly not over the mark. But it is necessary that the existence of this second class should be recognised".

3. For the words "at a cost of about £P.500 per family" in paragraph 6, I suggest "at a cost estimated by Mr. French at £P.500 per family for dry farming and at £P.650 to £P.800 for citrus growing. It is hoped that the Wadi Hawareth Arabs, whose settlement constitutes the most urgent problem, will be settled at a cost of about £P.250 per family, but in this case the land is obtainable at an exceptionally low price, and, moreover, the Arabs already possess tents, agricultural implements and ploughing animals, items for which Mr. French allowed £P.110 - £P.120".

Extract from a very confidential semi-official letter from Sir Philip Cunliffe-Lister to Sir Arthur Wauchope, dated 2nd December 1932.

x   x   x

I then talked to him equally frankly about the land position. I said that an impossible situation was being created by the growth of expropriated tenants who, after spending their compensation money, were landless and jobless. He knew all our commitments. We not only have to meet the commitments to the landless tenants who were now proving their claims, but further, having accepted those commitments and seeing clearly that the problem if left alone would be a continually increasing one, we were bound to insure against its continuance. There were also the Wadi Hawareth Arabs, who were cultivating Jewish land on suffereance. I then said that you and I had discussed this very fully, and that we saw no way out except a legislation which would ensure that a tenant who had no alternative land or occupation would be kept in possession of a holding sufficient to support him. Weizmann faced this most reasonably, and said it was a very real problem: nor did he personally jib at the proposed solution, but he lodged this caveat. He said it would be very unfair to say that a tenant must remain in possession of a larger holding than was necessary to support him if he farmed it efficiently, and that it would be very hard to say that a tenant who could make a good and indeed a better living out of an intensive holding should be given a statutory right to a much larger holding on which he would grow less remunerative crops.

x   x   x

7.12

PALESTINE.

HIGH COMMISSIONER FOR PALESTINE,
JERUSALEM.

DESPATCH NO. 3̸k̸2̸
REFERENCE No.CF/134/32.

1̸5̸ April, 1933.

Sir,

    I have the honour to refer to your telegram No.58 of the 17th February, 1933, in which you request that you may be furnished with my recommendations on the Reports submitted by Mr. Lewis French, C.I.E.,C.B.E., on the problems of Agricultural Development and Land Settlement in Palestine, together with any comments offered on those Reports by the Arab Executive Committee and by the Executive of the Jewish Agency in response to the invitation in that sense which was extended to them, by your direction, in July, 1932.

Enclosure I.
Enclosure II.

    2.   I transmit for your information copies of the memoranda, dated the 10th March, 1933, which have been forwarded to me by the Arab Executive Committee and by the Executive of the Jewish Agency in response to that invitation, together with the comments made by the Acting Director of Development thereon.

Enclosure III.
Enclosure IV.

    3.   Before I submit my recommendations on the French Reports, it may be convenient to recapitulate the circumstances in which Mr. French was appointed by His Majesty's Government to investigate and to report on the problems of Development and Land Settlement in Palestine.

4./

The Right Honourable
   Sir Philip Cunliffe-Lister, G.B.E., M.P., etc., etc.,
     His Majesty's Principal Secretary of State
               for the Colonies.

- 2 -

4. The development of the policy of His Majesty's Government for the establishment of a National Home for the Jews in Palestine has naturally resulted in large purchases of land by the Jewish National Fund, by the Palestine Jewish Colonization Association and by individual Jewish buyers, for agricultural colonization. This is a part of the fundamental policy of Zionism, and may be expected to continue so long as funds are available and land can be obtained. The Jewish purchasers pay market prices to Arab landowners and, in many cases, generous compensation to tenants and other occupiers who are displaced from the land purchased.

5. It is an essential principle of Zionist policy not only to acquire ownership but to ensure that all the work required on the land shall be performed by Jews as far as possible, and, in the case of the official land-purchasing agency of the Zionist Organization, namely the Jewish National Fund, by Jews only, and it follows, as the result of this policy, that when land is purchased by Jews not only is the landlord changed, but the tenants and practically all the wage-earning class are compelled to move also. The right of the Zionists to follow this policy cannot be called in question, but it obviously creates a difficult problem in relation to the displaced Arab cultivator.

The upshot has been the growth, during recent years, of a body of landless Arabs who may be divided into three categories :-

(i) tenants;
(ii) small owner-occupiers;
(iii) labourers.

6./

6. The attention of His Majesty's Government was drawn to this problem by the Report of the Shaw Commission on the disturbances of 1929 (Cmd.3530, March, 1930) and by the Report of Sir John Hope Simpson (Cmd.3686, October, 1930).

In the Statement of Policy issued by His Majesty's Government in October, 1930 (Cmd.3692) and in the Prime Minister's letter to Dr. Weizmann of the 13th February, 1931, His Majesty's Government accepted responsibility for the settlement of such Arabs as could be shown to have been displaced from the lands which they occupied in consequence of those lands passing into Jewish hands, and who had not obtained other holdings on which they could establish themselves or other equally satisfactory occupation.

His Majesty's Government also accepted generally the proposals made by Sir John Hope Simpson for making further land available for Arabs (including Arabs already landless) and for Jews by means of a development scheme, and meanwhile reserved full power to take all necessary steps to protect tenancy and occupancy rights, including the rights of squatters, throughout Palestine.

For this purpose the Protection of Cultivators (Amendment) Ordinance was enacted in May, 1931, with a life of twelve months. The operation of this Ordinance was extended for a further period of twelve months in May, 1932. A summary of the provisions of this Ordinance will be found in paragraph 19 of this despatch.

7. In August, 1931, Mr. French was appointed Director of Development with the following duties :-

    (1) to prepare a register of landless Arabs;

(ii) to draw up a scheme for resettling such Arabs; and

(iii) to investigate the methods which should be adopted to give effect to the policy of land settlement adumbrated in the Statement of Policy issued by His Majesty's Government in October, 1930 (Cmd.3692) and in the Prime Minister's letter to Dr. Weizmann.

Mr. French presented a Report in December, 1931, and a Supplementary Report in April, 1932.

8. It will be recalled that the policy of His Majesty's Government as formulated in 1930 after the presentation of Sir John Hope Simpson's Report, contemplated the initiation of a comprehensive development scheme to be financed from a guaranteed loan of £2,500,000, and that, during the first years of that scheme, provision should be made from British Votes of such annual amounts as might be required to meet the interest and sinking fund charges upon the loan.

Mr. French's proposals are largely based on the assumption that financial conditions would in fact permit the initiation of a comprehensive development scheme on the lines envisaged in Sir John Hope Simpson's Report and the provision of the necessary funds therefor.

As you are aware, this is not now the case. While the financial and economic conditions of Palestine show distinct signs of improvement, world economic conditions remain uncertain, and the financial stringency in the United Kingdom still remains acute.

You have, moreover, recently emphasized the fact that while the estimated revenue of the Palestine Government for 1933/34 greatly exceeds the original estimated yield for 1932/33, it is not possible to rely upon the

continuance/

continuance of the present level of revenue for an indefinite period, and that it is of the utmost importance, having regard to the uncertainty of the future revenue position, to keep expenditure within such limits as will enable the Palestine Government to build up a free reserve of one million pounds to meet the emergency of a sudden shrinkage.

I should therefore hesitate to request His Majesty's Government to authorise the issue of a guaranteed loan of two and a half million pounds for the objects which Mr. French was instructed to consider, particularly since if the situation with regard to Palestine revenues were to change for the worse, a burden might be imposed upon the British tax-payer as a consequence of a guarantee by His Majesty's Government or the Imperial Treasury.

9. But apart from the financial aspect of Mr. French's proposals, it will be seen from the memoranda submitted by the Arab Executive Committee and by the Executive of the Jewish Agency (Enclosures I and II) that both Arabs and Jews reject the substance of the proposals, and in these circumstances it is clearly inadvisable, if not impossible, to pursue measures which are unwelcome to the very interests which they have been designed to serve.

10. Should you decide, in the light of these representations, that it is impracticable to put the French Reports into effect, it will at once become essential to take alternative measures to settle two of the most urgent problems which Mr. French set out to solve, namely:-

> (a) What action should be taken as regards Arabs who have already become landless; and

(b)/

(b) What measures should be adopted to stop the present process of the displacement of Arab cultivators?

11. Since my arrival in Palestine I have, as you are aware, made a particular study of the peculiar problems relating to agricultural development in this country.

As a result of this personal survey of the situation, I am satisfied that it is desirable to adopt certain administrative and certain legislative measures which, on the one hand, are within the limits of such financial assistance as His Majesty's Government may fairly be asked to afford and, on the other, are such as to discharge the obligations of His Majesty's Government in Palestine, to both Arabs and Jews in accordance with the general policy under which the country is governed, and to satisfy the legitimate requirements of all sections of the population.

12. As I have observed in paragraph 10 the two urgent problems which call for immediate decision are :-

(i) What action shall be taken to resettle those Arabs who are already landless, or liable to become so, as a result of Jewish colonisation to date; and

(ii) What measures should be adopted to put an end to the process of the displacement of Arab cultivators ?

The solution of the former problem can be approached by administrative measures; the second problem requires legislative action.

13. Resettlement of Landless Arabs.

The landless Arabs to be resettled may be divided into three categories, namely :-

(i)/

	No. of families
(i) Displaced claimants already admitted to the Register	584
(ii) Arabs at present cultivating land for Jewish owners for whom provision will have to be made when they are displaced	237
(iii) The Zubeid tribe in the Safad sub-district (Vide Enclosure V to this despatch).	68

Enclosure V.

I propose to make every effort to settle these families in accordance with the following programme :-

1933-34	367 families
1934-35	300 families
1935-36	222 families.

So far as possible, the families will be resettled in blocks of about one hundred, and it is expected that, for the most part, the resettlement will be confined to the sub-districts of Jenin, Beisan, Tulkarm, Tiberias, Safad and Jerusalem, where at the moment land is available.

The resettlement will be effected by the use of the two methods described hereunder :-

(i) <u>By purchase</u>. Government will purchase land, and will place the settlers thereon as Government tenants;

(ii) <u>By Lease</u>. Government will lease land, and place the settlers thereon as its sub-tenants. The owner will pay tithe and werqo, and the settler will pay rent to Government; the total of tithe, werqo and rent to equal the rent payable by Government to the landowner.

In addition to these principal methods, Government has reason to believe that the issue of long term loans to approved landowners may induce them to employ a certain number of landless Arabs and, at a later date,

to/

- 8 -

to provide them with an allotment of land.

14. It is estimated that the cost of the scheme outlined in paragraph 13 will be at least £P.250,000, made up as follows :-

	£P.
Capital cost	150,000
Advances recoverable	65,000
Reserve	35,000
	250,000.

Enclosure VI.

Detailed estimates of cost are forwarded as Enclosure VI to this despatch, and I trust that it will be possible to make provision of at least £P.250,000 for this purpose in the schedule of the proposed new Palestine Government Guaranteed Loan.

15. I propose that the resettlement scheme should be carried out under the control of a Director of Development, and the Department of Development will therefore, if my recommendations are approved, continue to exist as a separate Department of this Government until the completion of the scheme. It is not at present practicable to determine whether, when the resettlement of the 889 Arab families has been completed, the Development Department should be abolished, or whether there will be justification for its continued existence for the initiation and supervision of development measures generally.

16. The measures so far contemplated deal with a legacy from the past. I now turn to measures designed to meet the contingencies of the future.

17. Displacement of Arab cultivators.

I am satisfied that it is essential for financial, as well as for political and economic reasons to do all

in/

in our power to stop, or if that is not possible, to minimize the process of the displacement of Arab cultivators, and I have reached the conclusion that for this purpose it is necessary to strengthen the existing legislation for the protection of tenants. It is obvious that any such legislation must not transgress any of the existing commitments of His Majesty's Government, and that it must involve as little interference as possible with the economic life of the country.

18. I have carefully considered the legislation which Mr. French proposed to deal with this problem, namely, the Occupancy Tenants Ordinance and the Homestead Protection Ordinance, and I am of opinion that the terms of this legislation are too drastic in view of the mandatory obligations of His Majesty's Government.

I consider that the situation can best be met not by the introduction of new restrictive legislation but by the amendment of the existing Protection of Cultivators Ordinances.

As I have noted in paragraph 6 of this despatch, the Protection of Cultivators (Amendment) Ordinance, which is at present in operation, was enacted in May, 1931, with a life of twelve months, and was renewed for a further twelve months in May, 1932.

19. The present Ordinance provides as follows:-

> (i) No tenant of two year's standing who has paid his rent and cultivated his holding properly and not been declared bankrupt, may be evicted without at least one year's notice, compensation for disturbances and for improvements and (if he is of more than five year's standing and goes without an eviction order) the equivalent of one year's average rent. Any dispute regarding the amount of compensation has to be decided

by/

- 10 -

        by a Board consisting of a District Officer, one representative of the landlord and one representative of the tenant. The Board's decisions require confirmation by the District Commissioner.

(ii)   Unless there has been failure to pay rent or to cultivate properly, or unless the tenant has been declared bankrupt, the court will not grant an eviction order unless the High Commissioner is satisfied that "equivalent provision has been secured towards the livelihood of the tenant" (The Ordinance does not specify what this "equivalent provision" must be).

(iii)   The tenant's rent cannot be raised except with the consent of a Board constituted as above.

(iv)   Tenants who have not paid their rent and have not cultivated their land properly may be evicted at 15 days' notice unless they apply for the matter to be referred to a Board constituted as above.

20.   Few, if any, tenants have been evicted since the amending Ordinance came into force. No reference has been made to me under Section 3(A)(1) of the Ordinance, and no eviction orders can therefore have been made except after default in regard to either payment of rent or proper cultivation, or after Bankruptcy.

Nevertheless, the existing Ordinance does not provide complete security, since it merely impedes, but does not prevent, eviction, and allows of compensation in other forms than land in the event of eviction.

21.   The most important parts of this legislation will expire in May this year. I recommend that it should now be made permanent, by the removal of the existing time limit, and that it should at the same time be simplified and redrafted.

The Ordinance, amended and simplified as I now propose, would of course be subject to review in the event of the establishment of a centralized land control

as/

as contemplated in the Prime Minister's letter to Dr. Weizmann.

22. I propose that the new legislation should contain the following provisions :-

 (i) A tenant who has paid his rent and not neglected his holding grossly may not be evicted unless the High Commissioner is satisfied that an equivalent provision has been made for him in land up to the minimum required for subsistence of himself and his family, and unless he is given at least one year's notice, compensation for disturbance and for improvements and, if of more than 5 years' standing, the equivalent of one year's average rent.

 (ii) A tenant's rent will not be raised except with the consent of a Board constituted as at present.

 (iii) A tenant who has not paid his rent may not be evicted without at least one year's notice and compensation for improvements. Where a tenant has applied to the Board in accordance with Section 3(3) of the existing Protection of Cultivators Ordinance, he shall not be evicted unless the Board gives a decision against him and he fails to pay his rent within the time fixed by the Board, and even then only on an Order of the Court.

 (iv) Any question as to what is a sufficient subsistence area for any particular tenant will be settled by a Board constituted as at present, and liable to review, say, every 5 years.

 (v) A Board will decide, as at present, all questions regarding the amount of compensation due.

 (vi) A tenant will be allowed to sell or mortgage his tenancy interest in the "subsistence area".

 (vii) It is proposed to add the following proviso :-

  Notwithstanding anything contained in this Ordinance, the District Commissioner, may on the application of the landlord, authorize the resumption by him of a holding or part thereof upon being satisfied:

- 12 -

(a) that such resumption is required for some reasonable and sufficient purpose having relation to the good of the holding or of the adjoining land, including development by drainage or irrigation or by closer settlement or colonization or disposal for building purposes; and

(b) that the "occupancy tenant" will retain sufficient land of such nature as to enable him to maintain his customary means of livelihood in occupations with which he is completely familiar; the land being, as far as possible, in the vicinity of the home from which the transfer may cause his displacement; or

(c) that the purpose for which the resumption of the holding is sought comprises the provision for the "occupancy tenant" of developed land sufficient for the maintenance of himself and his family, together with adequate subsistence for them pending the development of such land.

23.   In paragraphs 13 to 22 of this despatch I have indicated the administrative and legislative policy which I propose, with your approval, to initiate, as an alternative to the relevant suggestions in the French Reports, with a view to solving the immediate problems with which His Majesty's Government are confronted in relation to the resettlement of landless Arabs and the stoppage of displacement.

I pass now to a consideration of those measures relating to the general agricultural development

of/

of Palestine some of which have already been taken independently of Mr. French's proposals, while others are in process of completion.

24. The Palestine Government has already acquired 5,740 dunums of irrigated land in the Beisan sub-district at a cost of £P.25,364 on which to resettle the displaced Arabs belonging to the northern section of the Wadi Hawareth tribe. Meanwhile these Arabs are continuing to cultivate some 3,000 dunums of land in the Wadi Hawareth as sub-tenants of the Government which is lessee to the Jewish National Fund.

Another tribe, the Arab Infiat, has been declared by the Settlement Officer to possess no title to lands adjoining the Jewish village of Hedera on which it has subsisted for many years. Government proposes to conclude with the Jewish village an exchange of Government sand-dunes for cultivated lands belonging to the village so as to secure the continued subsistence of the tribe in its accustomed place.

An economic survey has been carried out in a number of villages in the coastal plain in order to ascertain what areas in these villages might be capable of closer settlement. The results indicate, however, that no appreciable absorption of landless Arabs is likely to be possible in this direction.

- 14 -

25. Mr. French deals at length with the possibility of development in the Huleh Basin and on Jiftlik lands near Beisan.

The Huleh region is subject to a pre-war concession having the drainage of marshes and development of reclaimed areas as its objects. Apart from the existence of the rights of the concessionnaires, I consider that it would require so large a sum to develop the Huleh Basin, that I could not advise that the Palestine Government should undertake direct responsibility at present.

The Ghor Mudawwarah lands in Beisan are subject to a special Agreement concluded in 1921 in the interests of the habitual occupants discovered at that time as having rights of cultivation and grazing in the area, and I do not now regard it as possible to amend that Agreement.

In the Negeb, or arid region of Beersheba, experimental drillings have been carried out by means of special plant in the hope of tapping underground water fit for purposes of irrigation. Success here might mean the cultivation of a large area at present unproductive and underpopulated. The water which has been reached, however although of considerable quantity, shows a high salinity. In future years further experiments may be carried out, but at present the evidence is such as to render it quite unsafe to anticipate success in the next few years.

Reconstruction of the irrigation system at Jericho at the instance or under the supervision of Government is bringing about some increase in the area of intensive cultivation; and the Baisan system has been partially reconstructed with satisfactory results, but these affect very limited areas and only a small number of cultivators.

26./

26. Following the recommendations contained in the Report which was made by Mr. C.F. Strickland, C.I.E., on the cooperative movement in Palestine, the office of Registrar of Cooperative Societies has been reorganized under a specially trained Registrar whose primary task it is to organize cooperative societies among Arab farmers. The Registrar expects to be able to make a beginning in some twelve villages during the first two years of his work. I hope that this activity may be the means of bringing about improvement of Arab methods of cultivation and hence augmenting the sources of livelihood of the ordinary cultivator, and that in time dependence of the fellah on the usurer will give place to borrowing from cooperative societies on reasonable terms.

I refer subsequently to the provision of credits by Government to cooperative societies.

27. A measure of direct practical value in improving the condition of the Arab cultivator is the partition of land hitherto held in undivided ownership by a village or a large number of co-owners, who draw lots each year for the share to be cultivated. Under such a system, uneconomic holdings and indifference of tenure militated against progressive and industrious husbandry: the benefits of the division of common land in the process of settlement are becoming visible already in improvement of cultivation under the stimulus of individual effort and interest. I propose to enact legislation which should have the effect of accelerating this process, by means of which about 1,151,000 dunums have been partitioned up to the end of 1932. Although possibly three or four times that area still remains in common ownership, nevertheless the extent to which advantage has been taken of the facilities

for/

-16-

for partitioning by Government has far exceeded expectations.

The settlement of title which is now proceeding in itself furthers agricultural development, for it provides that security of tenure without which the cultivator cannot advance. I have no doubt, also, that the substitution of a single Land Tax for the Commuted Tithe and Werko, which has been decided upon, will be a further encouragement and aid to the rural population in their striving towards better economic conditions. As it is, the Commuted Tithe is reduced from 10% to 7½% in years of bad harvests and poor prices, and substantial additional remissions are granted to cultivators in genuine cases of hardship and inability to pay. Equally generous principles of relief are applied in respect of arrears of rural taxation, and of agricultural loans of various kinds.

28. The proposed new legislation for the Protection of Cultivators allows for dispossession in bankruptcy. But I have decided that in any sale by execution which is conducted in bankruptcy proceedings the following exemptions shall apply, corresponding to exemptions to be allowed in execution of judgments generally :-

(1) Provision for three months for the debtor and his family and seed grain sufficient for sowing the extent of land normally cultivated by the debtor.

(2) One pair of oxen, mules or donkeys, at the option of the debtor.

(3) Fodder for the exempted animals for three months.

(4) So much land as shall in the opinion of the Court be necessary for the support of the debtor and his family.

29. As you are aware, the Palestine Government has

made/

made available year by year, as necessity arose, considerable sums of money for distribution in short term agricultural loans to farmers, at low rates of interest, for purchase of seed, plough oxen and other requisites for winter and summer sowings.

I have now made tentative recommendations to you separately in regard to the provision of agricultural credits on a permanent and wider basis. The need for such credits is an integral part of any scheme of development and it is in my opinion urgent that they should be provided.

The question of agricultural loans resolves itself into three principal divisions as under :-

(a) short term crop loans;

(b) long term development loans in the plains;

(c) long term development loans in the hills;

and the methods by which these credits may be available are now under consideration by you with reference to a proposal that £150,000 be included in the schedule of the proposed new Palestine Government Guaranteed Loan.

30. Besides these arrangements, I intend to place a sum not exceeding £P. 20,000 a year at the disposal of the Registrar of Cooperative Societies, out of the funds of the Ottoman Agricultural Bank which are held on deposit by the Public Custodian, for the purpose of making advances to cooperative societies, so that they in turn may assist their members by loans. The following would be the conditions of these advances :

such credit to be used only where the Registrar is able to convince the Treasurer that Cooperative Societies cannot otherwise be financed by commercial banks;

loans granted from this source to Cooperative
Societies/

Societies to bear interest at the rate of 1% above bank rate with a maximum of 7%;

the maximum length of such loans to be five years and the maximum amount of any loan to be £P. 1,000, provided that no Society shall issue a loan to any of its members from such funds for a period exceeding two years.

31. A statement of the steps already taken by Government to assist the Arab cultivator will not be out of place.

The Department of Agriculture directs its attention to improving the quality of stock, of seed and of fruit-trees throughout the country and to encouraging better methods of husbandry, especially in the hill districts, so that by increasing his production and decreasing his purchases of foodstuffs the fellah may become more nearly self-supporting.

In the last fifteen months a number of school gardens have been established. Here the boys are taught simple farming practice by teachers many of whom have had special agricultural instruction at the Kadoorie Agricultural School at Tulkarm.

Since my arrival in Palestine, the size of the Government farm at Acre has been doubled, and new agricultural stations have been established at Ferradie and Majdal. This has made it possible for Government to distribute a greatly increased amount of selected seed. Further various improvements have been made at the stations already existing at Beisan, Jericho and Jerusalem.

At some or all of these stations, Government is engaged on general agriculture, animal husbandry, horticulture, poultry-keeping and bee-keeping. In addition, forest nurseries and demonstration plots for cereals and

leguminous/

-19-

leguminous crops have been established throughout the country. Thus there is now at least a nucleus for the work of agricultural improvement in each of the different climatic regions of the country. I am convinced that work is proceeding on the right lines : at the same time there is much need for further development and I intend that this further development should take place.

At the present time, Government is taking steps to acquire land for a citrus demonstration grove in the orange belt near Jaffa and in connection therewith a grant of £P. 3,000 is to be made to the Agricultural Experimental Station of the Jewish Agency at Rehovot to supplement the annual expenditure of £P. 5,000 by the Agency on experiments and research designed to improve the output and value of what is the most important industry of the country. The Jewish Agency is also being assisted by a grant of £P. 300 to maintain plots for demonstrating methods of intensive farming and a second grant of the same amount for horticultural experiments in a hillside settlement near Jerusalem.

The Government Department is undertaking feeding experiments with oats and vetch and is importing selected bulls from Syria with a view to improving the local breed of plough oxen. Experiments in improving natural pasturage and in growing maize as fodder are also contemplated.

A series of 31 observation stations has been established in the coastal plain between Ras el Naqura and Rafa on private and municipal wells, yielding valuable information as to the seasonal fluctuation of the level of the underground water-table. The observation stations are so placed that a check can be kept on subterranean water conditions in their relation to the rapid annual increase in the area under citrus culture.

For/

For the protection of the local cereal farmers, the import duties of wheat and flour have been so modified that the duty on wheat is high when the local crop is harvested and on the market, and low during the season when no Palestinian wheat is available.

The importation of acid and olive oils is regulated under a system of licences so that while manufacturers of acid oil soaps can obtain the supplies which they need, the market for local olive oil is preserved.

32. I have dealt in the preceding paragraphs with certain of the minor recommendations in the French Reports namely :-

    The establishment of Citrus Experimental and Demonstration Stations.

    The Co-operative Movement.

    Animal Husbandry.

    The partition of land held in common ownership (Meshaa land).

I now turn to further minor recommendations in the Reports, namely :-

    The appointment of Village Registrars.

    Government control of water supplies.

    Co-operative marketing.

    Hydrographic and Irrigation Surveys.

    Repeal of the Mewat Lands Ordinance.

    The sale of fruit trees to the public.

The Appointment of Village Registrars.

I have carefully considered this suggestion, but I am unable to recommend it for adoption at the present time, as I feel it would add too greatly to the cost of administration. I should prefer to await the result of the steps which I am taking to improve the traditional system of village management by means of village headmen, known as Mukhtars. It is evident that this improvement can only

be/

be brought about by inducing villagers of a better class
to accept the responsibility of this office, and with this
object in view I have authorized the increase of the re-
muneration of Mukhtars for the punctual collection of
tithes from 2 per cent to 5 per cent.

(a) <u>Government control of water supplies</u>.
(b) <u>Hydrographic and Irrigation Survey</u>.

The draft of an Irrigation Ordinance which was
prepared by Mr. French is now under final revision by a
departmental committee, after examination by the Irrigation Sub-Committee of the General Agricultural Council.
In general terms, the draft Ordinance provides for the
effective control of water supplies by Government. An
essential preliminary to the application of such an Ordinance is the carrying out of a hydrographic survey of
Palestine and the investigation of the possibilities of
irrigation. A series of deep-boring experiments is already
being carried out in suitable areas; and I agree that a
hydrographic survey should be undertaken as soon as practicable.

<u>Co-operative Marketing</u>.

The private interests concerned are fully alive
to the necessity for discovering new markets for the agricultural produce of Palestine and have already been successful, for example, in developing a considerable export
trade in citrus fruits to the Continent of Europe which
before the War purchased practically no oranges from this
country. I consider that the further development of
markets abroad may at present be left to private enterprises.
The Government on its part will continue freely to offer
its technical advice, in consultation with the Agricultural
Economics and Marketing Committee of the General Agricultural Council, and to provide facilities for the opening

of/

of new markets by means of experimental consignments of produce, and by means of visits of Trade Delegations. Successful consignments of eggs, grapes, raisins, and poultry have already been placed on the English market under arrangements supervised by the Department of Agriculture, in conjunction with Empire Marketing Board. A Committee has been appointed by Government consisting of official and non-official members, to enter into conversations with the Egyptian Authorities in order to arrive at a mutually favourable modus vivendi as regards trade relations; and the Government has agreed to sponsor Trade Delegations which may be organized by local interests to investigate the possibilities of increasing the sales of oranges, bananas and vegetables in Eastern Europe.

In the Estimates for the current financial year special provision has been made to meet the cost of further experimental consignments of agricultural produce to various countries.

Repeal of Mewat Lands Ordinance.

The Mewat (Dead Lands) Ordinance provides that any person who without obtaining the consent of the Government breaks up or cultivates any waste land shall obtain no right to a title deed for such land and further will be liable to be prosecuted for trespass.

Although in practice it has not been found necessary to exercise the powers under this Ordinance, its very existence on the Statute Book provides a salutary check upon indiscriminate cultivation and in this sense the Ordinance has its advantage; and I apprehend that to repeal it will lead to greater evil than good.

Sale of fruit trees to the public.

Mr. French recommended that the restriction of the issues of fruit trees to the public should be modified

-23-

so as to permit of sales of any trees from Government nurseries.

Within three months of my arrival in Palestine, I cancelled the order prohibiting the sale of fruit trees and the Department of Agriculture now raises many fruit trees for sale. The villagers are taking full advantage of the opportunity offered.

33. In conclusion, having regard to the considerations adduced in this despatch, I recommend that as an alternative to implementing the French Reports, I should be authorized to initiate as soon as possible the administrative and legislative measures described in paragraphs 13 to 22 which, together with the measures summarized in paragraphs 24 to 32 will, I trust, prove to be of great and lasting benefit to all sections of the people of Palestine.

I have the honour to be, Sir,
Your most obedient, humble servant,

Arthur Wauchope.

HIGH COMMISSIONER
FOR PALESTINE.

Arab Executive Committee
Jerusalem,
10th March, 1932.

His Excellency
    The High Commissioner
        Government Offices,
            Jerusalem.

Your Excellency,

The Arab Executive Committee has read the two reports which Mr. Louis French has submitted to the Secretary of State for the Colonies on Agricultural Development and Land Settlement in Palestine and has given careful study to the contents thereof. It has endeavoured, in vain, to trace, in these reports, any measures which may check the dangers with which the Arab population of this country are threatened in consequence of the Jewish Colonisation, but found out that these reports, at their best, contain nothing in the interest of the Arabs, except the re-settlement of families of Arab cultivators whose number ranges between 1,000 to 2,000 although enquiry has revealed the fact that 29.4 per cent of the Arab families are landless.

2. Your Excellency is aware that in its letter dated the 16th August, 1931, the Arab Executive Committee notified Government that it will not participate in the proposed development scheme if His Majesty's Government insists on taking the letter of Mr. MacDonald, the Prime Minister, to Dr. Ch. Weizmann, dated the 13th February, 1931, as the basis for the application of this scheme.

Middle nat
No.39.

The Arab Executive Committee observes, with regret, that His Majesty's Government is still insisting on the application of a policy in Palestine which is

- 2 -

calculated to enable the Jews to acquire what little remains in the hands of the Arabs of the agricultural lands and that the reports of Mr. French appear as if intended to apply to this policy.

3. The Arab Executive Committee cannot, nevertheless, deny that Mr. French endeavoured, in those two reports, to show the defects of the land policy which the Palestine Administration has pursued, since the Occupation, and to suggest some means which may protect the administration from falling into similar mistakes in future.

Supplementary Report, para. 61.

Indeed Mr. French has considered the decision arrived at by the Palestine Administration with regard to the re-settlement on the land of Arabs who were dispossessed if the holdings which they were cultivating before the Jews purchased them as a recognition of, and a move to retrieve, the mistake which permitted the displacements to occur. "It needs no arguments to prove," he asserts, "that the repetition of the error can only lead to a recurrence of the present situation, under which the Arabs are now labouring." Mr. French tried here to be extremely patient towards this policy and contented himself by describing it as a defective policy only.

4. Indeed, the lands of Palestine, after its separation from its sister countries, Syria and Iraq, could not be sufficient to meet the needs of the Arab cultivators who have lost, after its separation and as a result of this policy, over 1,200,000 dunums of their fertile lands. It is true that the Palestine Administration enacted, in the years 1920 and 1921, some ordinances which were designed to protect the Arab cultivator from the dangers with which he may be threatened as a result of the acquisitions of land by Jews, but when asked as to

- 3 -

number of cases in which the provisions of these Ordinances were applied, Mr. Stubbs, Director of Lands to the Government of Palestine in his evidence before the Shaw Commission replied that "he did not think that there was any case and that the Ordinances had in fact proved unworkable," and resulted in no benefit to the Arab fellah.

<small>Shaw Report page 115.</small>

5. His Majesty's Government delegated Mr. French to Palestine for the purpose of considering the following objects :

<small>First Report para. 2(i) and Palestine despatch No. 487 of 26th June,1931, para. 5(iii)(a).</small>

(i) The re-settlement of Arabs who were displaced from the lands which they occupied in consequence of the lands falling into Jewish hands, and who have not obtained other holdings in which they can establish themselves or other equally satisfactory occupation, and the improvement and intensive development of lands in the hill districts.

<small>First Report para 2(ii).</small>

(ii) The ascertainment of what state or other lands are or properly can be made available for close settlement of Jews.

As regards the first object, 4,500 claims were preferred by Arab cultivators, but Mr. French expressed the opinion that the number of claims which will be eventually accepted will range between 1,000 and 2,000. The Jews on the other hand, contend that none of these claims could properly fall within the interpretation of Arab cultivator as defined in Mr. MacDonald's Despatch. It is a source of surprise, however, that the Legal Assessor adopted the practice, in verifying claims of Arabs, of sending papers dealing with Arab claims to the Jewish Agency for the purpose of expressing their views

- 4 -

thereon. The Arab Executive Committee feels it incumbent upon itself to express its strong protest against this express partiality towards the Jews.

6. The Arab Executive Committee have observed that Mr. French endeavours in his scheme not only to arrange for the re-settlement of landless Arabs, but also for the settlement of Jewish immigrants as recommended by the Jewish Agency. The Committee is unaware of the power which enables Mr. French to find land for such Jews as, to its knowledge, Mr. French was asked to ascertain as to the state lands and other lands for the purpose of "encouraging" Jewish settlement thereon. The word 'encourage' does not mean that the Palestine Administration will be placed under an obligation to contract loans, on behalf of the whole population of Palestine, for the purpose of purchasing Arab lands and placing such lands at the disposal of Jewish immigrants which may be recommended by the Jewish Agency. On the other hand, neither the British Government nor the Palestine Administration is entitled to make the Arabs liable for the re-payment of any such loans which may be contracted for this purpose. It should be remarked that the floating of loans for the purpose of purchasing Arab lands and the development of such lands for the settlement of Jewish immigrants is not only prejudicial and unjust, but is unprecedented in history. Sir Herbert Samuel, the first High Commissioner, dismissed the claim which was made by certain quarters that Government owns vast areas of state lands in Palestine. He even went further and asked the Jewish bodies which made representations to him in connection with such lands to make a search

– 5 –

themselves so that he may be able to place at their disposal any land which they may be able to find. These bodies, however, were unable to find any such land.

Report of Sir John Hope Simpson pages 50 – 60

Sir John Hope Simpson has confirmed the view taken by Sir Herbert Samuel and dismissed, as an illusion, the current belief that Government has command of large areas of land. Notwithstanding all this, however, His Majesty's Government instructed Mr. French to inquire into the matter once again. Mr. French also confirmed,

First Report paras 13 and 14.

in his turn, that Government does not own any land, which may be placed under the disposal of Jewish settlers and to Jewish settlement, recommended to the High Commissioner the acceleration of the operations of land settlement with a view to discovering whether any unoccupied lands would be available for allotment to new settlers. The Settlement Officers, acting on this recommendation, carried out advanced settlement operations in two plots of state lands, with a not satisfactory result to the Jews. Mr. French did not hesitate to predict that what is true of these two estates will be found to be true of all other Government domains and suggested that "if it was is desirable to arrange for settlement of Jews, it will be inevitable for Government to buy land for this purpose from existing individual owners" (Arabs).

7. In his letter to Dr. Ch. Weizmann, to which reference is made above, Mr. MacDonald agreed with the Zionist Organisations that Jewish labour only will be employed in economic or agricultural works which are dependent on Jewish capital, but does His Majesty's Government feel justified in allotting state lands, which are exclusively Arabs lands, to Jews, and in acquiring, in addition and with Arab funds, lands from Arab owners for the purpose of

– 6 –

Jewish settlement? It is true that Mr. French recommends the purchase of land from Arabs and not from Jews for the purpose of re-settlement of landless Arabs of the category specified in Mr. MacDonald's letter, but the number of these landless Arabs is too small in proportion to the number of the Arabs who have been displaced from lands which they occupied in consequence of the lands falling into Jewish hands, especially when it is remembered that the number of Arab cultivators who do not own land in Palestine are estimated at nearly one-third of the whole Arab cultivators. It may be assumed, therefore, and rightly so, that the cultivators who were displaced from the lands which they occupied in consequence of the lands falling into Jewish hands and who were compelled to work as labourers in factories, as stone cutters on public roads or in similar works, will not revert back to the land for ever.

Cmd. 3692 of Oct. 1930 Para 16.

8. The Arab Executive Committee has endeavoured to ascertain the benefits which the Arabs may derive out of this scheme, should it at any time be put into execution, but failed to find therein anything which may realise any of the objects of the Arabs with regard to the lands of the country. The Arabs desire to retain what little lands remain in their possession, and to develop such lands for their maintenance and the maintenance of their descendants after them. Inquiries which have been conducted by British experts in Palestine have revealed the fact that there is no margin of land in the possession of Arabs which may be disposed of in favour of the Jews, that what lands remain in the hands of the Arabs are insufficient for their agricultural needs and that 29.4 per cent of the Arab cultivators

- 7 -

Supplementary Report, para. 9

are now landless. Mr. French, in admitting this fact stated that "in reality there are at the present time no cultivable lands at all which are surplus" and added: "if there were available areas of such lands, there would either be no problem of landless Arabs to solve or no difficulty in solving it, for the Arabs who were displaced from their lands by Jews would already have transferred themselves there in the search for the only means of livelihood familiar to them, or they could easily have been re-settled thereon by the Government".

9. It follows, therefore, that the 1,500,000 dunums of land which were required by Jews from Arabs, since the Occupation, were not "surplus lands" in excess of the needs of the Arabs and that there is no "surplus lands" at present in Palestine which can be used for Jewish settlement. Mr. French nevertheless, desires to create such "surplus land" in Palestine for the settlement of Jewish immigrants from Russia, Poland and other countries and suggests a courageous, but dangerous, method for this purpose which he illustrates by the following example:-

Supplementary Report para 11.

"An Arab land owner may hold in the coastal belt an area of, say, 500 dunums, where at present the traditional dry-farming is carried on by, say, five families of tenants. On the theory that this area is peculiarly adaptable to citrus growing, and so capable of yielding at present prices an annual net profit of , say, £P.10-12 per annum after allowing for interest and amortisation of capital expenditure on development, as against a maximum return of 500 mils per dunum under dry-farming'.

Mr. French concludes from this example that it will be possible, in this case, to allot 20 dunums of this land after development and intensive cultivation, to the five families referred to above and thus the remaining 400 dunums which will be lands "surplus" to the needs of the Arabs could be made available for closer settlement by Arab cultivators and Jewish immigrants.

10. The Arab Executive Committee, if at all it can attach any meaning to the settlement on such lands of Arabs who were displaced from the lands which they occupied in consequence of the lands falling into Jewish hands, it cannot interpret the unlimited carving of lands in the possession of Arabs to small plots for the purpose of the close settlement of the Arabs thereon and the settlement of Jewish immigrants on such lands, which, Mr. French alleges, would thus be "surplus" to the requirements of the inhabitants.

11. Mr. French overlooked the fact that the question of land, in every nation, is not one which affects the individual citizen only, but the community as a whole, especially in a country like Palestine where, as investigations revealed, the lands is insufficient for the requirements of the population which is rapidly increasing. The example given by Mr. French cannot, therefore, be taken as a concrete one, as the remaining 400 dunums to which he refers, cannot be considered as "surplus" or be made available for settlement of Jewish immigrants without prejudicing the "rights and

- 9 -

and position of the Arabs. Indeed, Sir John Hope
Simpson emphasized the fact that the land remaining
in the hands of the Arabs is insufficient for their
needs and that 29.4 per cent of the rural Arab
families are now landless. Mr. French on the other
hand admits that there is no "available surplus" land
in Palestine within the meaning attached to this term
in other countries. "In large or not fully exploited
countries, where lands are spacious and population
relatively scarce, surplus lands" Mr. French asserts,
"are those lying uncultivated and unpeopled, which can
by pioneer colonisation be brought for the first time
within history under the plough and developed for
settlement". Accepting, therefore, this interpretation
surplus lands should mean lands which are uncultivated
and which could be cultivated and developed for the
first time.

Supplementary Report para 8.

12. Mr. French further asserts that: "leaving aside
a few insignificant areas in the hills, temporarily
abandoned because the owners have lost their cattle or
other simple resources and are too much indebted to
be able to replace them in reality there are at the
present time no cultivable lands at all which are
"surplus.

Supplementary Report para 9.

Should this be the case, and there is no doubt
that it is, how can lands which are taken from the
Arabs, through development and citrus growing, be considered as "surplus" and allotted to immigrants from
Poland and Russia so long as nearly one-third of the
Arab cultivators are landless. The phrase "surplus
lands" should not be considered to mean in Palestine
the "uncultivated" part of the land of any one person

—10—

which is in excess of his needs, but those lands which may be considered to be in excess of the needs and requirements of all the Arab population of the country. An Arab land owner may hold an area of thousands of dunums although one hundred or, say, hundred and fifty dunums may be sufficient for his own cultivation. In this case the remaining part of this land cannot be considered as "surplus", unless it is in excess of the needs and requirements of the Arab community as a whole.

Supplementary Report para.10.

13. In these circumstances, the phrase "surplus lands" should not mean in Palestine "those lands which are at present devoted to extensive or cereal farming, and which in the opinion of colonising experts can be devoted to more intensive farming" but those lands which are at present devoted to extensive or cereal farming and which, in the opinion of colonising experts, can be devoted to more extensive farming, and then made available to new immigrants without prejudicing the "rights" of the other landless cultivators in the country.

14. After careful enquiry into what state lands are or can be made available for (i), re-settlement of landless Arabs and (ii) new Jewish Colonisation Mr. French states that he found no such land at all and found it necessary therefore, to search for such lands elsewhere. He preferred, however, to deal first with the more urgent of the two problems - the re-settlement of the landless Arabs, because the Jewish Organisations had reserves of land which cannot be less, and may be more, than 40,000 dunums still waiting development by colonisation." It should be noted, however, that the problem of finding land for the Arab

-11-

cultivators to which Mr. French tend his energies is comparatively insignificant as it only affects the re-settlement of a number of Arabs which may range between 500 to 1,000 cultivators, while he aims in his scheme, at the close settlement of Jewish immigrants in the lands of the country without any qualification or limitation. In other words, Mr. French's task in connection with this scheme will be limited to the re-settlement of Arab cultivators who are displaced from Arab lands in consequence of the lands falling into Jewish hands and who have not obtained other holdings on which they can establish themselves or other equally satisfactory occupation. All his energies, however, will be devoted, thereafter, to the application and enforcement of the Zionist land policy.

Mr. French is of the opinion that the important tracts which may be used for close settlement are:

(1) Certain fields of the coastal plain;
(2) The Beisan tract;
(3) Part of the Jordan Valley; and
(4) The Beersheba District, where investigations have shown that large amounts of water exist.

Mr. French nevertheless, expresses his fears lest the rapidity of the growth of the citrus industry in these areas may result in many calamities to Palestine as was the case in other countries in view of the excessive production of the crop which dumped foreign markets and frustrated the hopes of the producers. He therefore asserts that it would be imprudent to proceed otherwise than slowly and cautiously with the re-settlement of landless Arabs in these areas so that when these Arabs are re-settled it would be possible to embark on the

Supplementary Report - Para 44.

-12-

settlement of Jewish immigrants. He also recommends that Government should create entirely a new settlement of water and land at Baisan for the benefit of the existing settlers and orderly development by introduction of new settlers. As regards the Huleh Plain, Mr. French suggests that this plain which covers an area of 165,000 dunums, should be taken as integral and recommends that Government should take a complete control of the land and water of this area. This, of course, cannot be attained except by compulsory expropriation in the interests of the community at large or by buying out the interest of the concessionaires in an area which covers 55,415 dunums.

Mr. French further asserts that Jewish settlement in this area necessitates the acceleration of its development.

15. In these circumstances the Arab Executive Committee feels it incumbent upon itself to express its protest against the recommendation of Mr. French which make provision for the settlement of an unlimited number of Jewish immigrants in these areas and for the re settlement of a limited number of Arabs only.

16. The Committee is of the opinion that this scheme contains nothing which will ensure to the Arabs any rights in the lands of the country, as, at its best, this scheme makes provision for the purchase of large tracts of lands now in possession of Arabs, the curving of such lands into plots and the allotment of such plots to a very limited number of Arab cultivators. Granted, however, for the sake of argument, that the number of Arab cultivators who will benefit under the scheme will

-13-

be 1,000 and that Government will allot to each cultivator a parcel of land of 20 dunums, the whole area which will be allotted to the Arabs will not exceed 20,000 dunums. In other words, the advantages of the scheme will be limited to 1,000 Arab cultivators who were displaced from the lands which they occupied in consequence of the lands falling into Jewish hands and who have not obtained other holdings in which they can establish themselves or other equally satisfactory occupation. The land problem in Palestine, however, will continue to be as difficult, intricate and dangerous as it is at present. The Committee believes that this problem will even be more intricate if the development scheme, as outlined by Mr. French, is put into execution. The problem which now engages both the Arabs and the Jews will not be solved by the mere re-settlement of a limited number of Arab cultivators who were displaced from their holdings by the Jews as the real problem which is of concern to both these two sections of the population in this country is centered upon the whole of the lands of Palestine. Palestine is a small country the large part of which consists of hilly land and valleys. Its lands are, indeed, insufficient for the Arabs whose number is increasing by 1,800 a year. The inquiry conducted by Sir John Hope Simpson, the British Expert, in the year 1930, into the questions of land and immigration, has revealed the fact that nearly one-third of the Arab cultivators in Palestine have become landless and that what little lands remaining in the hands of the Arabs are insufficient for their maintenance. The Jews, nevertheless, continue in their endeavours to acquire what little lands remained in the hands of the Arabs.

-14-

For this reason the land problem in Palestine from an Arab point of view is becoming now more and more intricate and dangerous. The re-settlement of a few Arab cultivators who were evicted of the land by the Jews on another Arab owned land is not a solution to this problem, but the protection of what land remains in the hands of the Arabs for the Arabs themselves. Granted, however, that Government was able under this scheme, to re-settle the Arab cultivators who were dispossessed of the lands which they were cultivating as a result of its purchase by the Jews and the Jews continued to acquire other Arab lands while Government undertook to re-settle any Arab who may become dispossessed of his land in the future owing to his land falling into Jewish hands, the result will be that the Arab cultivators will either become a burden on the state or state tenants and the Jews will gradually become the owners of all the lands of Palestine on the assumption that Government will re-settle all such Arab cultivators on lands purchased from the Arabs themselves. But would not such a result be a destructive blow to the communal rights of the Arabs and disasterous to their political status?

17. Mr. French states that "the decision of Government to re-settle on the land Arabs who have been dispossessed of the holdings which they were cultivating before the Jews purchased them is a recognition of, and a move to retrieve, the mistake which permitted the displacements to occur, as they did". He also refers to the danger which will threaten the Arabs in future as a result of the continual sale of their land and asserts, in this connection, that the scheme of re-settlement of Arabs on the land by Government would not be

Supplementary Report Para. 21.

-15-

Supplementary
Report para 62.

advantageous "unless a simultaneous attempt is made to avoid a repetition of this error." He adds that "if it be intended that Government should re-settle any Arabs who may become dispossessed of their holdings in the future owing to their lands falling into Jewish hands, the solution of this problem, will, as time goes on, be rendered more and more arduous". Indeed, should this be the intention of Government in its endeavours to solve this problem, Government will require an area of 1,729,600 dunums of land for citrus growing and an outlay of £P.64,864,000, irrespective of the increase of the Arab population since the year 1930 when the Arab cultivators in Palestine were estimated at 86,980. The outlay required for the re-settlement of one dispossessed Arab family on 20 dunums of citrus land is estimated at £P.800. Government will thus be required to provide sufficient lands for such dispossessed cultivators of an area not less than 1,729,600 dunums and at an outlay of £P.64,864,000 on settlement, as stated above. Such a scheme will not be practicable for the following two reasons:

1) The Arabs will never agree to remain landless in the country, and
2) Government will not be able to provide the necessary lands and expenditure.

19. The above observations lead to the conclusion that the Development Scheme which the Government desires to carry out is not likely to solve the land problem in Palestine and that the only means for the solution of this problem will be the enactment of a law which will definitely prohibit the sale of lands to the Jews.

-16-

Mr. French himself admits the state of unrest which is prevalent among the Arabs as a result of the present land policy and refers to the various land disputes which cropped up and led to breaches of the peace between Arabs and Jews, with threats of more serious troubles should the old land policy continue to be so applied. He gives the following picture of events as an illustration of the need for a limited control over land transfers:

Supplementary Report para. 63.

"An Arab of the effendi class acquires at auction or by other means, under the Ottoman administration, proprietary rights in a large tract in return for a comparatively trivial outlay; and is content to collect such rents as he can from some occupiers. Others, being illiterate and cut off from common sources of information, do not recognise the existence of an alleged owner who himself is certainly quite unable to identify the boundaries of his own supposed property. Those limits are described in his title deeds only in such vague terms as are possible in an unsurveyed area with few distinctive topographical features, and so may be to-day, practically, unidentifiable.

"A Jewish Organisation buys this land from the owner, and, as entitled under the law, proceeds to take possession for development of its property. That proceeding involves eviction of a number of men who have possibly heard of the late owner merely as a neighbouring effendi, and who have grazed a more or less indeterminate local area for generations without paying the alleged owner any rent. The eviction displaces them from land of which, to all intents and purposes, they are, and have been for generations, hereditary occupiers. Monetary compensation is no

-17-

solace for such men as those who can find no other pied-à-terre; and who can recognise no reason for the change of circumstances which deprives them of the only form of livelihood known to them. And the offers by organisations to provide money for the purchase of land elsewhere for the re-settlement of evicted tenants represent simply the familiar device of transferring a nuisance from oneself to one's neighbour." 19. // But there are other injustices which are being committed in Palestine against the simple Arab fellah under the sight of the Government. The Arab fellah in Palestine is habitually attached to his land similar to peasants of other countries. He does not sell his land of his own free will and accord. The Jewish Organisations adopt the practice of employing/mean Arabs, in consideration of an insignificant sum of money, for the purpose of inducing the simple fellah, through various devilish means to sell his land to the Jews at, in most cases, a comparatively low price, much beyond its real value. The Arab fellah who is so deceived does not, in most cases, properly invest the money paid to him in consideration for his land and spends it in no time, and then loses his only source of livelihood and becomes a burden on others. There are, however, other factors which has facilite the activities of these agents in convincing the fallah to sell his land such as the, high taxation, the low prices of products and natural calamities. Add to this the encroachment of the Jewish Organisations on the lands of the neighbouring Arabs under the pretext of the correction of the boundaries of the land which they bought from the Arabs. It is the practice of these

—18—

Organisations to prepare plans of the land which they buy and then obtain a new title deed from the Land Registry, based on the new boundaries shown in the plan which, in most cases, include large portions of the neighbouring land. The activities of these Organisations are facilitated by the Adviser to the Land Department, who is a Russian Jew and an ardent Zionist.

19. In his observations quoted above, Mr. French desired to illustrate the position of the Arab fellah and the consequential effect on him of the sale of his land to the Jews, but there is another aspect to this question which effects the "rights and position" of the Arab nation as a whole and is more important than the problem of the Arab fellah. To this important aspect this question, however, Mr. French paid not the least consideration.

First Report Page 5.

20. In his first Report on Agricultural Development and Land Settlement in Palestine, Mr. French stated, in Part I, under the title "General Remarks" that one of the major objects which he was instructed to consider was "the ascertainment of what state and other land are or properly may be made available for closer settlement by Jews under reference to the obligation imposed upon the Mandatory by Article 6 of the Mandate." Detailed

Supplementary Report para.

investigations into the question of Government Domains have led to the conclusion that there are no such lands at all in Palestine which may be made available either for re-settlement or colonisation, as all domains are either earmarked for special purposes or already fully leased to Jewish or Arab cultivators. The Arab Executive Committee appreciates the circumstances under which no such land was allotted to the Jews and takes this opportunity

-19-

to express its strong protest against the principle of encouraging the close settlement of Jews on Government Domains. It must be stated here that these domains are Arab lands. The Ottoman Government in olden days, had usurped part of these lands, by various means, while large tracts devolved upon the State upon the death of their owners without any heirs. It is exceedingly unfair that such domains which were usurped from the Arabs through such means be alletted to the Jewish immigrants who emigrate to Palestine, par excellence, from Poland and Russia. As regards, however the stipulation made in Article 6 of the Mandate with regard to the encouragement of close settlement of the Jews on the land, this stipulation, should be borne in mind, is qualified by the condition that the "rights and position" of other sections of the population are not prejudiced. This condition relates, as it does, to the "rights and position" of the Arabs, as a whole and not to the rights of the Arab cultivators, in particular. That this interpretation is correct is borne out by Article 2 of the Mandate which sets out the obligations imposed upon His Majesty's Government as the Mandatory over Palestine and makes His Majesty's Government responsible for placing the country under such political, administrative and economic conditions as will secure the safeguarding of the civil and religious rights of all the inhabitants irrespective of race and religion, including the Arab cultivators. It is, no doubt, the duty of every civilised Government to safeguard the rights of all its citizens. Should this be the case there remains no necessity for this

-20-

specific stipulation which appears to have been considered necessary in the case of Palestine in order to avoid any prejudice being done to any one of the two sections of the population, the Arabs and Jews, owing to the probability of conflict arising between these two sections in matters relating to the immigration, lands, etc. This Article of the Mandate which is intended to safeguard the rights of all sections of the population, followed, however, by Article 6 under which the Mandatory is under an obligation to facilitate Jewish immigration and to encourage close settlements by Jews on the land, provided that "the rights and position of the other sections of the population are not prejudiced". The Mandatory is, by virtue of this Article, under two distinct obligations, both towards the Jews and the Arabs. It is under an obligation, only under this Article, to facilitate Jewish immigration on the one hand and to encourage close settlement by Jews on the land on the other. This obligation is qualified, however, by the condition which imposes upon the Mandatory to insure that "the rights and position of other sections of the population are not prejudiced". In his letter to Dr. Ch. Weizmann dated the 13th February, 1930, Mr. MacDonald, the Prime Minister, emphatically stated that the words 'rights and position' of other sections of the population, occurring in Article 6, plainly refer to the non-Jewish community, i.e. the Arab nation. "The rights and position" he stated, "are not to be prejudiced, that is, are not to be impaired or made worse". Indeed the word 'rights' occurring in this Article relate to the Arabs, as a distinct nation and not to the whole

Middle East
No.39.

-21-

population of Palestine. This interpretation is borne by the fact that Article 2 of the Mandate makes His Majesty's Government "responsible for safeguarding the civil and religious rights of all the inhabitants, irrespective of race and creed", while Article 6 applies to the Arab communities the existence of which, as independent nations, was recognised by Article 22 of the Covenant of the League of Nations. This Article, therefore, together with Article 2 of the Mandate should be interpreted to mean:

> Treaty of Peace signed at Versailles on June 28, 1919, Page 16 of H.M. Stationery Office publication.

1. that the Government is debarred, when facilitating Jewish immigration and close settlement of Jews on the land, from taking any action which may prejudice the civil rights of the Arab cultivators, and

2. that the Government is restrained, when facilitating Jewish immigration and close settlement of Jews on the land, from taking any action which may prejudice the "rights and position" of the Arab communities in their capacity as an independent nation.

21. In view of the above it should have been the duty of the Government which is restrained, under these two Articles of the Mandate, from taking any action which may prejudice the rights of Arab individuals and communities, to consider whenever its approval is sought for the admission of new immigrants or the purchase of Arab land, whether the admission of the immigrants applied for and the transfer of the Arab land to the Jews will prejudice the rights of the Arabs as individuals and the "rights and position"

-23-

Cmd. 3692
of October
1930 para. 8

of the Arab nation, or threatens their economic existence and then decides whether or not the admission of the immigrants or the transfer of the land should, in the circumstances, be allowed. It is, therefore, incorrect to state that the obligations laid down by the Mandate in regard to the two sections of the population are of equal weight" and that "the two obligations imposed on the Mandatory are in no sense irreconcilable", because, in fact, His Majesty's Government is under one obligation only by virtue of the Mandate, namely, to facilitate Jewish immigration and encourage close settlement of Jews on the land", but this obligation is qualified by a condition precedent that His Majesty's Government must insure that "the rights and position" of the Arabs, both as individuals and as a nation, are not prejudiced.

22. In his two reports now under discussion Mr. French dealt only with the "rights" of the Arab cultivators and ignored the "rights and position" of the Arab communities in their capacity as an independent nation, although the difference between the two classes of these rights is distinct. Indeed, the rights of the Arab cultivators concern only the cultivators themselves and are intended to protect their rights as individuals, and to secure for them a reasonable livelihood, but the "rights and position" of the Arab communities, in their capacity as an independent nation, relate to the Arab lands as a whole and are intended to secure the retention of sufficient areas of such land as purely Arab land.

-23-

It is fallacious to state that the word 'position' which occurs in Article 6 of the Mandate means the 'political' position of the Arabs in relation to the 'position' of the Jews in future, and that the intention of Article 6 was that, no matter what degree of development the Jewish National Home may reach through Jewish Immigration and close settlement of Jews on the land, it will be essential to safeguard the political position of the Arabs vis-a-vis the Jews. In other words, the Jews, no matter how large their numbers will be or how vast the area in their possession in Palestine, should not be allowed to subordinate the Arab communities or to enjoy a position superior to the position of such communities. This interpretation has no justification whatsoever as the obligation with regard to the "position" of the Arabs, which is stipulated in this Article, refers to the "position" of the Arabs at the present moment. In other words, this Article does not make His Majesty's Government responsible for safeguarding the "position" of the Arabs at such time as the Jews will become a majority in the country, and owners of all its lands but makes it incumbent upon His Majesty's Government to see to it that, in facilitating Jewish Immigration and close settlement of Jews on the land it will take no step which may prejudice that 'position'. Article 22 of the covenant of the League of Nations recognised the present Arab communities in Palestine, in principle, as an independent nation, but no nation will have any "position" unless it owns sufficient lands for its needs. This is a fundamental condition for any independent nation and every individual of such nation enjoys a right in the lands of the country whether he actually owns a part

—24—

thereof or not. In the circumstances no individual, a member of any nation, can dispose of any land which he independently holds in a manner which may prejudice the "rights and position" of the nation to which he belongs. It cannot be said, in this connection, that every person should be at liberty to dispose of his property at his own discretion and free will, and that no person should interfere with the exercise of his personal liberty, because it is the duty of every Government to make the exercise of the personal liberty of an individual dependent upon the public interest. Every Government which neglects this public good is considered as failing in its fundamental duties as a Government and it will then be the duty of every one of its citizens to call upon it to live up to its duties. Mr. French, however, was content in his two reports, to recommend the safeguarding of the "rights" of the individuals only. In paragraph 64 of his Supplementary Report he states:

Supplementary Report para. 64.

"It is, of course, impossible to make the world stand still, or to stay the march of progress, but the inequity of the present system which suffers such changes as I have depicted, will not, I imagine, be disputed. If the extensive and ill-defined rights of the literate and powerful are on the one side maintained, care should be taken that similarly extensive and ill-defined rights of the poor and uneducated on the other side are not over-ridden. Provided that a via media doing justice to both parties can be found, it ought to be adopted as a solution. Some provision should be made whereby the occupiers of the land described above can, at least, be left in undisputed possession of a minimum

-25-

area of land sufficient to allow of their continuing to earn their living; and of their learning in due course from progressive neighbours how to develop that minimum to the best advantage. Such a policy can be put into operation if such limited restriction is imposed on the free alienation of land as is compatible with the attainment of the object in view".

88. Had Mr. French been fair, he would have stated that this policy has prejudiced not only the rights of the Arab cultivators, but the rights and position of the Arab communities, in their capacity as an independent nation. On the other hand, the solution suggested by Mr. French does not solve the land problem in Palestine, because the Homestead Protection Ordinance which he recommends, relates to the small Arab cultivator and insures to such small holder the retention of his land. It deals, therefore, with the landless class of the Arab cultivators. Mr. French recommends that a minimum or 'Homestead' area of a cultivator should be made inalienable unless the vendor of such area shall satisfy the District Commissioner that he has a "lot viable" elsewhere or has obtained permanent occupation of the land and that the minimum area would vary in every zone to which the country would be divided

-26-

Supplementary Report para. 72

and suggests, as an illustration, that "in the coastal zone the minimum being an unirrigated area would be comparatively low, in the hills or dry-farming areas the minimum area must be much higher". Granted that Government will enact such an Ordinance and that this Ordinance will design at preventing the land-owner from selling a minimum piece of land sufficient for his maintenance(which we do not admit would be the case for the reasons stated below) the danger which threatens the Arabs will not disappear for if we reckon the area of this Homestead inalienable area, the permanent alienation of which will be prohibited, at, say, 100 to 150 dunums in the hills or dry-farming zones, and at, say, 30 to 40 dunums in irrigated zones and at 20 dunums in the citrus growing areas and the Jews took possession of all the other lands of Palestine the Arabs, who are increasing at 25,000 annually in accordance with the census taken in the year 1931, will be threatened at a no distant future, with starvation as, in that event, they will have no sufficient land for their maintenance, or otherwise, will be compelled to emigrate from the land of their fathers and ancestors in the search for their daily bread. This is borne by the fact that Palestine is a hilly country and the Jews have, since the British Occupation, already acquired its most fertile plains, little as they are, while the hilly districts which remained in the possession of the Arabs are not fit for citrus growing and could not, consequently, be made available for close settlement of Arabs after development and improvement. It should also be remarked, in this connection, that the development of such lands, not only requires large capital,

-27-

but necessitates as well that the land itself should be capable of such development. To this point, it is observed, Mr. French paid not the least attention.

23. The British experts, who have investigated the problems of land and immigration in Palestine were forced to the conclusion that there is no surplus land in Palestine which could be made available for close settlement of Jewish immigrants. This fact, moreover, was asserted by His Majesty's Government in its Statement of Policy of October, 1930, where it stated definitely that "at the present time there remains no margin of land available for agricultural settlement by new immigrants" and that "the provision of a margin available for settlement depends upon the progress made in increasing the productivity of the land already occupied (by the Arabs]". His Majesty's Government, however, were more explicit on this point and said: "as a result of recent investigations, His Majesty's Government are satisfied that, in order to attain these objects, a more methodical agricultural development is called for with the object of ensuring a better use of the land." Again His Majesty's Government asserts here that "only by the adoption of such a policy will additional Jewish agricultural settlement be possible consistently with the conditions laid down in Article 6 of the Mandate. The result desired will not be obtained except by years of work. It is for this reason fortunate that the Jewish Organisations are in possession of a large reserve of land not yet settled or developed. Their operations can continue without break while more general steps of development......are being worked out". This statement,

Cmd. 3992 para. 15.

Cmd. 3992 para. 22.

-28-

it is submitted, leads to one conclusion, namely, that the transfer of Arab lands to Jews should be prohibited until such time as it will be possible to settle Jews on other additional land without causing any detriment or prejudice to the Arabs. There is not the least reference in this Statement which will show that the intention was to safeguard the rights of the Arab cultivator or the small holder only. On the contrary, it clearly shows that the intention was to safeguard the rights and position of the Arabs, in their capacity as an independent nation. It explains the scarcity of the lands which remained in the possession of the Arabs and the availability of surplus lands in the hands of the Jews and suggests that no additional Jewish Agricultural settlement should be made unless a more methodical agricultural development is worked out and its results are known.

24. Mr. MacDonald, the Prime Minister, found it necessary, however, to interpret this statement in his letter to Dr. Ch. Weizmann, then President of the Jewish Agency, dated the 13th February, 1930, in order to remove the causes of the general uproar which was caused by the Jews in all countries in the following terms:

"In giving effect to the policy of land settlement, as contemplated in Article 11 of the Mandate, it is necessary, if disorganisation is to be avoided, and if the policy is to have a chance to succeed, that there should exist some centralised control of transactions relating to the acquisition and transfer of land during such interim period as may reasonably be

Middle East
No 39
Para 12.

necessary to place the development scheme upon a sure foundation".

Mr. MacDonald added:

"Further, the Statement of Policy of His Majesty's Government did not imply a prohibition of acquisition of additional land by Jews. It contains no such prohibition, nor is any such intended. What it does contemplate is such temporary control of land disposition and transfers as may be necessary, not to impair the harmony and effectiveness of the scheme of land settlement to be undertaken". This interpretation, it should be observed, by Mr. MacDonald lacks the explicity which is characteristic of the statement of policy and, although it was intended, in the first place, to allay the state of excitement which then prevailed in Jewish circles, in consequence of the publication of the statement of policy, it did not fail to contain and admission of the defects of the present land policy and an expression of the necessity for some form of centralized control of dispositions and transfers of land. Mr. MacDonald's letter, it should not be overlooked, leads also to the conclusion that the lands which now remain in the hands of the Arabs are insufficient for their maintenance as, admittedly, if there were surplus lands in the hands of the Arabs there would remain no necessity for any control of dispositions and transfers of land.

[Margin: Middle East No. 39 para. 13.]

25. Mr. French, however, as it has been observed elsewhere, failed to touch upon this aspect of the problem and dealt with the protection of the small Arab cultivator. In paragraph 74 of his Supplementary Report, he states that the District Commissioner, whose consent to a disposition or mortgage of the land is sought, will grant his consent, as a matter of course,

[Margin: Supplementary Report para. 74]

-30-

in any case not involving permanent alienation or mortgage of the Homestead area." Taking, for example, the Homestead Area necessary for the Arab cultivator at 100 dunums in dry-farming areas, or 40 dunums in irrigated areas or 20 dunums in the coastal zone, the Arab cultivator will be at liberty, under this stipulation, to sell to the Jews any part of this land which is in excess to that area. The Homestead Protection Ordinance, authorises the permanent alienation of the Homestead Area of a cultivator if the cultivator satisfies the District Commissioner that "he owns elsewhere other unincumbered lands in any other zone, or has obtained other permanent occupation." It appears, therefore, beyond any doubt, that Mr. French was only anxious to protect the cultivator as such, but it never occurred to him to provide for the retention of sufficient land for the Arab communities as a whole in their capacity as an independent nation. The Arabs will thus continue to be threatened with the loss of their lands and will have no other alternative but to work as stone-cutters, house-servants, or labourers in public works. "The principle of inalienability of land is not a novel one", Mr. French, states, "it existed in the old English system of entail, and also in India". On the other hand, the draft Ordinance prepared by Mr. French which is designed to protect a Homestead Area for the cultivator does not guarantee the permanent retention of this area in the hands of the cultivator. Indeed, a cultivator can easily sell it to the Jews as soon as he becomes a labourer in towns or a stone-

Appendix S.R. III Section (5) (1)

Supplementary Report, Para 73.

-31-

cutter on public roads or else he can make his Homestead Area a security for money. Mr. French has authorised the mortgage of the Homestead Area with possession believing, of course, that such a course will enable the cultivator to obtain easy credit. The Jews will always find various means to retain possession of the Homestead Area no less so then, for example, by renewing the mortgage once every ten years.

26. All Civil Governments, it is submitted, consider it as their fundamental duty to insure that the small holders should remain, as far as it is practicable, on the land and are always reluctant to encourage the emigration of such cultivators to the towns where they will inevitably join the labour class. The unnatural circumstances now prevalent in Palestine should serve as a stimulant to the Government to pay particular care towards the permanent settlement of the Arab cultivators on the land, as on their settlement depends the existence of the Arabs in this country as an independent nation or, otherwise, the destruction of their national entity.

Appendix
S.R. 11.
Section 7.

27. Section 7 of the Transfer of Land Ordinance 1920-21 provides that "the Ottoman Law of 22nd Rabia al Awal, 1331, A.H. concerning the right of a Corporation to own immovable property shall remain in force provided that the Director of Lands may authorise any Banking Company to take a mortgage of land, and any commercial company registered in Palestine to acquire such land as is necessary for the purpose of its undertaking". This Article enables Jewish Corporations, of whatever description, to acquire land in Palestine although the acquisition of land by such Corporations may be detrimental to the population, especially to the Arabs, both as individuals

and as a community. The Jewish National Fund Limited, for instance, will be enabled, by virtue of this provision, to continue to acquire thousands and even millions of dunums of land in Palestine, although the constitution of this body is inconsistent with the public interest and prejudices the rights and position of the Arabs. Under its constitution this Company purchases the land on behalf of the 15,000,000 Jews scattered all over the world and the lands which it acquires remain the property of the Jewish people and are inalienable. Under the lease granted by the Jewish National Fund it is provided that the holding shall never be held by any but a Jew and the lessee undertakes to execute all works connected with the cultivation of the holding only with Jewish labour. This and similar organisations make it a condition upon the settlers, in the agreement for payment of advances which they make to them, that they will not employ in their orange groves except Jewish labour. This practice, there is not the least doubt, is inconsistent with public interest in general and detrimental to the interests of the Arabs in particular. His Majesty's Government in its statement of policy of October, 1930, declared that the constitution of this organisation is unlawful in that it takes no account of the provisions of Article 6 of the Mandate. Indeed, the organisation has greatly prejudiced the interests of the Arabs and the detrimental effect of its enterprise is increasing day after day. It

Report of Sir John Hope Simpson page 53.

Cmd. 3992 para. 20.

-33-

is fallacious to state, in these circumstances, that the Arabs have profited by the Jewish Colonisation. His Majesty's Government, notwithstanding its express partiality in favour of the Zionist policy, admitted this fact in paragraph 18 of its statement of policy. It may be observed, in addition, that this Organisation which already owns hundreds of thousands of dunums of land in Palestine continues, until now, in its endeavours to deprive the poor Arab cultivator of his only source of livelihood, by the payment of insignificant sums of money which, it makes, as stated above, to some low persons for the purpose of inducing the Arab cultivator, by various means to sell his land. It is most surprising that these Organisations, are sometimes, unreluctantly resort to the Courts for the purpose of enforcing the eviction of the poor Arab cultivator. The following example may be quoted as an illustration:

Ottoman Land Laws by R.C., Tute page 46.

23. Article 41 of the Ottoman Land Code provides that the owner of an individed share cannot transfer his share without the leave of the persons jointly interested. If he does so, the latter have the right to claim from the transferee the restitution of his share.

This provision is not only of a social advantage to the land-owners in general but is also designed to give a priority to the co-owner in an undivided land over others. Many cases were heard by the Palestine Courts where this wealthy organisation endeavoured, by clinking to this provision, to deprive a poor Arab of a few dunums of land which he bought for his maintenance.

28. To recapitulate, it is considered that this organisation and similar other Jewish agencies are unlawful institutions and should be restrained from acquiring any land in Palestine. It may be argued that the constitution of those bodies is similar to the Waqf which is established in the country, but the difference between the two institutions is very great. A Waqf is always dedicated for charitable purposes and is an act of an individual which does not have the same effect as the act of such corporate bodies. On the other hand, it cannot be said that the law of Awqaf is detrimental, because (it does not allow the dedication of agricultural lands as Waqf as the "Raqaba" of the land is vested in the State. Agricultural lands cannot be converted into Waqf, although, in olden days, Ottoman Princes and Sultans dedicated the tithes of certain agricultural lands as Waqf for charitable purposes. This category of Waqf is commonly known as "Takhsisat" Waqf, or, untrue Waqf, and does not prevent the occupiers from selling the land as is the case with any other agricultural land. Most of the Awqaf in this country falls under this category. There is another category of Waqf which is commonly known as the "Sahih" or "true" Waqf but such Waqfs are, in most cases, houses and shops and are insignificant in number. But there are houses no agricultural lands which are Waqf of this category.

29. As regards, however, the constitution of the Jewish agencies referred to above, their constitution is placed on a political basis. They are restrained from selling the lands which they acquire and are under an obligation to lease the land to Jews only. It may be added, in this connection, that there are provisions

-35-

in the law of Awqaf which allows, in special cases, the transfer or the lease of Waqf property.

The Waqf building in Jerusalem, commonly known as the Grand Waqf Hotel, to quote a concrete example, was recently let by the Supreme Moslem Council to a Jew. The Ottoman Government prohibited corporations from acquiring any immovable property and allowed such corporations to acquire such land as may be necessary for the purpose of their undertakings only. On the 29th Rajab 1327 H.J. the Ottoman Government enacted a law which, in its 6th Article, prohibits such bodies from holding immovable property, but a few years afterwards, it amended this law and permitted such bodies to hold immovable property subject to certain prescribed conditions and restrictions which include, inter alia, the safeguarding of the interests of the rural population. In the year 1912, the Ottoman Government enacted a law under the title of "Provisional Law concerning the right of certain corporate bodies to own immovable property" dated the 22nd Rabi'al Awwal 1331, which allowed corporate bodies to own immovable property provided that "the immovable property is not to be situated within the boundaries of an inhabited village namely, agricultural lands (see Article 2 of this law). This restrictive provision was explained in the Explanatory Note which was published simultaneously with the enacted law as follows:-

"No Government allows such corporate bodies to hold immovable property, unconditionally. In all laws dealing with immovable property such corporate bodies are allowed to hold immovable property subject to certain conditions and restrictions which are pre-

The Ottoman Land Laws by C.R. Tute page 165.

-36-

cribed in special laws. Societies and Institutions are allowed to hold immovable property within the boundaries of villages but are prohibited from holding property outside the boundaries of such villages in order to avoid the detriments which may be caused by the purchase of large tracts of land by these societies, who have at their disposal large capital, and then convert the cultivator-owners into the class of agricultural tenants".

30. It appears from the above that the Ottoman Government prohibited, at first, corporate bodies from holding any agricultural land and later, permitted them to hold immovable property within the boundaries of inhabited villages. The intention, of course, was to safeguard the rights and position of the cultivators whom the Government felt that it was its duty to secure their permanent settlement on the land as owners. The Arab cultivator, however, after the Ottoman Government, not only was disturbed and dispossessed of his land, but was also denied the right to remain on the land as a tenant and was compelled to join the landless class on eviction by the Jewish Organisations. There is no other Government which permits such bodies to hold agricultural land, as is the case in Palestine. The French law, to quote an example, does not allow any society or corporate body to hold land in excess of what it requires for the purpose of its undertaking. No society is allowed, under this law, to hold land partly for its use and partly for leasing purposes (see Article 6 and 11 of the French Law dated the 1st July, 1901).

31. The Jewish organisations in Palestine have acquired until now the most fertile lands in the country and are still endeavouring to acquire what little lands remain in the possession of the Arabs. In addition to the detriments which may be caused to the interests of the Arab cultivators, to which reference was made above, as a result of the acquisition of land by those organisation, there is the danger, which is not less important, that all the lands of Palestine, or the greater part thereof, will, as time goes on, be vested in one or two Jewish Organisations with the result that the Arabs will become landless and will be unable either to own new lands or to obtain such land on lease. This will be an inevitable result, should His Majesty's Government continue to pursue the present land policy and to allow the Jewish Organisations to acquire land.

32. Mr. French produces in Appendix R.3 of his Supplementary Report a draft Ordinance under the title of "Homestead Protection Ordinance" which is designed to prohibit the permanent alienation of a small area of the land of a cultivator. This law deals with the small holder and prevents this holder from disposing of a piece of land called the Homestead Area, which is considered sufficient for his maintenance and the maintenance of his family. This Ordinance, as stated elsewhere, is insufficient alone to check the danger of eviction from the land which threatens the Arabs, as it only deals with the small holder and does not protect the Arabs in their capacity as communities against the danger of eviction, with which they are threatened. It may be observed, in this connection, that the Ottoman Law of Execution dated the 20th April,

—38—

1330, prohibits the sale of a piece of land which is sufficient for the maintenance of the cultivator and his family in settlement of a debt or in execution of an order of a Court. Mr. French recommends that this prohibition should include all kinds of dispositions in accordance with the last part of Article 2 of the Mandate which makes the Mandatory "responsible for placing the country under such political, administrative, and economic conditions as will secure.... the safeguarding of the civil and religious rights of all the inhabitants of Palestine." But it should be noted that Article 6 of the Mandate prohibits the Palestine Administration from doing anything which will facilitate Jewish Immigration and encourages close settlement by Jews on the land, unless in doing so, nothing will be done which will prejudice the "rights and position" of the Arabs. Mr. French, however, failed to include in his Reports any recommendations in connection with that Article. It may, therefore, be concluded that the draft Homestead Protection Ordinance is incomplete and does not protect the Arab cultivator from the danger of eviction from the land.

83. Section 5 of this draft Ordinance enables the District Commissioner to grant his consent to any disposition by way of the permanent alienation of the Homestead Area of a cultivator, if he is satisfied :

"(i) that the applicant owns elsewhere other unencumbered lands not less than the area declared to be a Homestead Area in the zone in which such lands are situated....or

-39-

(ii) that the proposed disposition is a gift made in good faith for a religious or charitable purpose.

Paragraph (i) of this Section carries in its wake a special danger in that it may result in compelling the cultivators to leave the *invermoant* where they have always lived and to join a different *invermant*. As regards paragraph (ii) not only the stipulations contained in this para are without any value but are imbued with many dangers, because "good faith" is an esoteric matter. It cannot be proved to the District Commissioner whose consent to the disposition is required. This may also apply with reference to the religious or charitable purposes". It would not be easy for the District Commissioner to determine whether the gift was made for a religious or a charitable purpose, while, on the other hand, it cannot be reasonably assumed that a small cultivator will dispose of his small piece of land, on which his maintenance and the maintenance of his family depends, as a gift for religious or charitable purpose. In explaining this draft Ordinance, Mr. French, states that the District Commissioner may grant his consent to any disposition by way of the permanent alienation of the Homestead Area of a cultivator if he is satisfied that the applicant has obtained other permanent occupation. It is submitted that should such a power be vested in the District Commissioner, the draft Ordinance, to use a figurative expression, will be a still-born. In other words, the Jews will always find means to convince the District Commissioner that the applicant has become a permanent labourer in a factory or a workshop or that he has obtained a suitable occupation and thus the cultivator will be liable to lose his land.

-40-

In dealing with the insuperable difficulty which will be caused to any organisation in the acquisition of a village, Mr. French suggests the following as a solution : "If there were a scheme by an organisation to buy a village for development, it would be possible in the future, as in the past, for voluntary arrangements to be made whereby homestead areas could all be reserved in one compact block of land, seperate from the areas passing under the control of the purchasers".

Supplementary Report para. 72.

In this way, Mr. French makes the Arab cultivators liable for transfer from one place to another in order to facilitate the acquisition of land by Jewish Organisations, but the important social danger which will ensue in consequence of the continual migration of Arab cultivators from one Zone to another in Palestine, and the consequential detriments which may thus be caused to the Arabs as a whole, were completely ignored by Mr. French.

34. The Arab Executive Committee has notified His Majesty's Government, on a previous occasion, that it will not accept the proposed development scheme unless and until His Majesty's Government abandons the policy laid down in Mr. MacDonald's letter to Dr. Ch. Weizmann, dated the 13th February, 1930, and as it now appears that His Majesty's Government does not propose to depart from that policy, this Committee is of the opinion that Mr. French's reports contain nothing which may move it to change the decision it took in this respect. The Executive Committee, believes, nevertheless, that Mr. French has exceeded the limits of his fundamental duties which are to find the necessary means for the application of Article 6 of the Mandate which provides,

-41-

inter alia, as follows :

Palestine Mandate Article 6.

"The Administration of Palestine, while ensuring that the rights and position of other sections of the population (the Arabs) are not prejudiced, shall facilitate Jewish immigration,...and shall encourage...close settlement by Jews on land (surplus to the needs of the Arabs) including state land and waste lands,..." It is unnecessary, at this juncture, to reiterate that the Arabs have refused the Mandate in which they had no say, but it must be observed that this Article of the Mandate does not entitle the Palestine Administration to acquire land for Jewish settlement or to advance loans to Jewish Organisations in order to assist them in the establishment of the Jewish National Home, from funds contributed by the Arab nation, as recommended by Mr. French in his Supplementary Report, because the word "encourage" which occurs in this Article means as explained elsewhere, the "encouragement" of Jewish settlement and could not be taken to mean that the Administration is under an obligation to allot lands to Jews even if it will be necessary to purchase such lands from the funds of a loan to be raised by the Government, in the name of Palestine, or to make advances to the Jewish Organisations for this purpose. In the light of the above observations Mr. French's Reports may be summarised as follows :

1. The re-settlement of landless Arabs who have been displaced from the lands which they occupied in consequence of the lands falling into Jewish hands, but who have not obtained other holdings on which they can establish themselves.

It is not expected, on the basis of Mr. French's

-42-

Reports, that the number of such Arabs will exceed 1,000 to 2,000. It will be necessary to purchase the land required for settlement purposes from Arab landowners and to settle those Arabs on small pieces of such lands (20 dunums to each Arab family).

2. The allotment of the Hulsh land to the Jewish immigrants after the termination of the concession granted to Selim Aff. Ali Salem, or the purchase of this concession under the pretext that the Jews are well able to exploit these lands which are considered to be the most fertile lands in Palestine.

3. To review the agreement between the Government of Palestine and the cultivators of the Ghor lands which is commonly known as the Baisan agreement, and to place the lands and water of this area under the complete control of the Government for the purpose of close settlement of Jewish immgrants and Arabs on the land.

4. Mr. French has carefully investigated the question of Government domains and dismissed, as an illusion, the current belief that Government has command of large areas of land which it could use for settlement purposes unless it purchases such land from the occupancy tenants, but recommends, nevertheless, that settlement operations should continue on these lands so that if any surplus land is found as a result of such settlement, Government may allot such land to the Jews.

5. Mr. French was unable to prove, until now, the existence of sufficient water in the Ghor lands or in Beersheba plain but recommends, nevertheless, that Government should continue to explore this land and to dig wells for the purpose of Jewish settlement on these lands.

6. Mr. French did not see his way to recommend the

the acceptance of the proposal submitted to him by the Jewish Agency for the establishment, with Government financial support, of a Jewish Agricultural and Settlement Bank, but was able, nevertheless, to recommend the grant of financial assistance to this Bank in some other way.

7. The Jewish Agency will inform the Government of the names of the Jewish settlers which it recommends for settlement on the land purchased by loan funds. It should be remarked, here, that the number of the Arab cultivators which will be re-settled on the land is approximately known, but the number of Jewish immigrants which it is desired to settle on the lands is not known and unlimited.

8. To promote and develop the orange growing in the country in order to make additional land available for Jewish settlement.

9. Government will not be able to carry out these schemes except in a long period which, as predicted by Mr. French, will cover tens of years.

35 In view of the above, it is considered that the fundamental object of the development scheme, will be to allot additional lands to Jewish immigrants and to continue the present "direct rule" for tens of years.

In these circumstances, the Arab Executive Committee feels it incumbent upon itself to reject the proposed scheme.

I have, etc.

(sgd). Awni Abdul Hadi
for Arab Executive Committee

הסוכנות היהודית לארץ ישראל
THE JEWISH AGENCY FOR PALESTINE

Telegrams: "JEVAGENCY JERUSALEM"
Telephone: 671 (4 LINES)
Codes: BENTLEY'S

OFFICE OF THE EXECUTIVE.
P. O. Box 92,
Jerusalem

Ref. No. Pol/236/33

10th March, 1933.

His Excellency,
   The High Commissioner for Palestine,
      Government Offices,
         Jerusalem.

Your Excellency,

I have the honour to refer to Your Excellency's letter No.CF/134/32 of June 13, 1932, transmitting a copy of the Reports on Agricultural Development and Land Settlement in Palestine submitted by Mr. Lewis French, C.I.E., C.B.E., formerly Director of Development in Palestine, on December 23, 1931 and April 20, 1932, respectively, and to offer the following observations of the Executive of the Jewish Agency upon them.

2.   These Reports are the fourth in a series of documents devoted mainly to the subject - the first three being the Report of the Shaw Commission, the White Paper 1930, and the Report of Sir John Hope-Simpson - which have appeared since the disturbances of 1929. The common denominator of all these reports and statements is a measure of agreement with regard to the increasing pressure upon the land resources of Palestine resulting from Jewish immigration and settlement, the dangers supposed to threaten the well-being of the non-Jewish peasantry and, in consequence of both, the social and political crisis with which Palestine is alleged to be permanently confronted. The reply of the Jewish Agency repudiating this basic thesis has been given repeatedly and in considerable detail in its

Page 2. דף

הסוכנות היהודית לארץ ישראל
THE JEWISH AGENCY FOR PALESTINE

memoranda submitted, respectively, to the League of Nations following the publication of the Shaw Report and the White Paper 1930, and to Sir John Hope Simpson prior to the submission of his Report. The French Reports, however, prove conclusively that such argument in detail and the accumulating mass of evidence adduced have failed to deflect the trend of thought of these official investigators, none of whom, in fact, has stayed in Palestine beyond some weeks or, at most, months, and may not, therefore, have had time to acquire an adequate knowledge of local conditions. Our data thus stand neither accepted nor refuted. It is, therefore, the intention of the Executive to confine this letter to the analysis of some fundamental principles underlying the Reports submitted by the Director of Development rather than attack isolated statements. Our observations with regard to such individual clauses of the Reports as may call for criticism or correction are embodied in a separate memorandum attached to this letter.

3.   In summing up in advance the main conclusions of this analysis, the Executive is bound to state that it cannot see in the policy presented in Mr. French's Reports an outline of a scheme such as His Majesty's Government appeared to contemplate when, through the Prime Minister's letter addressed to Dr. Weizmann on February 13,1931, it referred to "the larger purposes of development which His Majesty's Government regards as the most effectual means of furthering the establishment of a national home for the Jews." The Reports of Mr. French appear to be founded upon mistaken premises. They continually substitute apprehensions for facts. They are, on the whole, sterile on the constructive side and thoroughly ill-advised in their proposals for restrictive legislation. They are based on the fallacious assumption that a policy

הסוכנות היהודית לארץ ישראל
THE JEWISH AGENCY FOR PALESTINE

shackling Jewish initiative would relieve its advocate from the duty to devise positive ways and means for the advancement of either Jew or Arab. This Executive is, therefore, forced to the conclusion that these Reports cannot be accepted as a basis of land and development policy in Palestine in the execution of which the Jewish Agency would find itself in a position to cooperate.

4. The first and most serious premise of Mr. French's Reports, which has been at the base of the controversy of the last few years, is that of the alleged large-scale displacement of Arab cultivators owing to their land passing into Jewish hands. It should be borne in mind that in the first instance this issue was presented not as an economic problem pure and simple, but as a grave political and social danger to which, in the last analysis, the unrest in the country, culminating in the disturbances of 1929, had to be attributed. This indictment figures prominently in the Report of the Shaw Commission, the majority of the members of which were of the opinion that

> "there can be no doubt that a continuation, or still more an acceleration, of the process which results in the creation of a large, discontented and landless class is fraught with serious danger to the country."

(Report of the Commission of Inquiry p.124)

Ever since, the allegation of the existence of a "landless proletariat" of Arabs, due to displacement by the Jews and doomed to vagabondage and misery, has not disappeared from the discussion of the Palestine situation. The Zionist movement was thus charged with trying to work out the destiny of the Jewish people at the expense of the welfare of the non-Jewish population of Palestine. A cloud of suspicion was cast on Zionist work and, in the eyes of outside observers, the whole policy of the Jewish National Home seemed, on moral grounds, to have been put on trial.

5. Sir John Hope Simpson in his Report went so far as to suggest, with a figure importing mathematical precision, that 29.4% of the Arab rural population were landless, leaving in the reader's mind a vague impression that it was owing to Jewish settlement activities that landlessness had reached such alarming proportions. Upon these statements was based the land policy defined in the White Paper, 1930, the conclusions of which were regarded by the Jewish people as liable to bring Jewish work in Palestine to a virtual standstill. It was for this reason that, in the subsequent discussions with the Cabinet sub-Committee, the representatives of the Jewish Agency requested that this matter be made the subject of a careful investigation so that the truth or falsity of the displacement charge might be authoritatively established. The instruction given to the Director of Development to prepare a register of so-called "displaced Arabs" was dictated not only by the need for such a register for purposes of a re-settlement scheme, but also by the necessity for testing the validity of the contentions of the Shaw and Hope Simpson Reports. In the light of the facts as presented in the French Reports it may be said without fear of over-statement that the allegations of "displacement", as a problem of such proportions as would in any way justify its being called a political danger or a source of social unrest, stands clearly refuted.

6. With regard to the actual extent of "displacement", as established by Mr. French's enquiry, the following facts should be stated:

    (a) The sum total of claims as quoted by Mr. French is not correct. The Development Authorities explain that by mistake the number of claims as given in the Reports at 3,700 exceeds by 1,000

Page 5.　　דף　　　　　　　　הסוכנות היהודית לארץ ישראל
THE JEWISH AGENCY FOR PALESTINE

The number actually received by that time. The actual number was only 2,722 - a difference, by mistake, of 27%. Out of these 2,722 over 1,000, it is reported, were not filed by the claimants at all, but based upon information received from Mukhtars of villages. Later on 466 new claims were added, bringing the final total to 3,188.

(b) Out of the 3,188 claims 3,005 have been examined by the Legal Assessor with the result that 2,520 have been rejected and 570 accepted, while 83 are still pending. The inclusion of the accepted claimants in the register of displaced Arabs is provisional and subject to further scrutiny. This Executive has reason to believe that of the claims provisionally approved a substantial proportion may ultimately have to be rejected, particularly if the definition laid down in the Prime Minister's letter were fully and strictly applied, namely if not only the past possession of land by the claimants, but also their present occupation and source of livelihood were thoroughly enquired into. At any rate, even on the present figure only 14.7% of a not impressive total of the claims preferred have been provisionally approved.

(c) Out of the 570 claims provisionally accepted about 200 relate to the cases of Bedouin at Wadi Hawareth, a tract of land the purchase of which was effected only in the course of the last few years, in fact after the disturbances of 1929. An analysis of each of these claims (which this Executive has made an effort to carry through in view of the malicious propaganda centering on this particular land transaction) shows that the majority of these claimants derive their livelihood at present (as they have done for a number of years), in one way or another, from occupations connected with the neighbouring Jewish village of Hederah, whether as wage-earners, carters, camel drivers, or as vegetable growers and milkmen. This fact is one of the reasons for the reluctance of a good many claimants to be moved to any other place, however attractive from the agricultural point of view, where they would have to revert to their former mode of life as graziers or ploughmen.

7. It may be of interest to add that among the applications put forward and not accepted by the Director of Development there were found, inter alia, the following classes of claims:-

(i) 1,000 cases of information from Mukhtars, as mentioned above, referring to transfers of from 3 to 5 dunams each;

(ii) cases of applicants who stated that they held relatively large areas of land elsewhere in Palestine, including members of wealthy land-owning families confessing to the ownership of as much as hundreds of dunams of land under citrus.

(iii) applicants who held land in Transjordan and had been living there for many years.

(iv) 70 claims from the Jerusalem District, all referring to transfers of less than one dunam, apparently building-plots;

(v) applicants reporting sales to other Arabs, and basing their claim on the assumption that the buyers may intend to resell the land to Jews;

(vi) redundant cases appearing in a number of files

These facts, it is submitted, throw an interesting side-light upon the character which the landless Arabs enquiry came, to a large extent, to assume.

הסוכנות היהודית לארץ ישראל
THE JEWISH AGENCY FOR PALESTINE

8. The displacement of some 500 graziers and cultivators covering a period of twelve years, since the establishment of the British Administration in Palestine, or, or an average, about 50 families a year, cannot in any way be regarded as representing that ominous process which is described or foreshadowed in the documents referred to. Even if Mr. French's forecast of the number of "displaced" Arabs as given (on p.60) at 1,000 to 8,000 had proved correct - which it has not - the position would have not changed substantially. Suppose Sir John Hope Simpson was right in placing the number of landless Arabs in Palestine at above 29% of the village population, which would mean some 30,000 families. The 570 families, the landlessness of which is attributed to the purchase of their land by Jews, would then make out 1.9% of the total landless class. It is thus clear that the principal thesis upon which recent official reports (including those of Mr. French) were based, has been definitely disproved by the results of this enquiry.

9. The more surprising becomes Mr. French's attitude in prejudging, as a matter of fact, the issue of "displacement". At the very beginning of his Report (p.6) he states:-

> "It was obvious that....the acquisition for permanent settlement by immigrants could not have been effected without considerable displacement of existing cultivators."

He further refers to the decision of the Government to resettle displaced Arabs as "a move to retrieve the mistake which permitted the displacements to occur as they did" (p.75), and then goes on to say that "it needs no argument to prove that a repetition of the error can only lead to a recurrence of the present situation." Such issues are clearly no matter for conjecture alone. They can only be decided in the light of carefully established facts. Yet the Director of Development commissioned to investigate the

Page 8.   הסוכנות היהודית לארץ ישראל
         THE JEWISH AGENCY FOR PALESTINE

facts begins his report with, and bases a series of restrictive measures, upon these assumptions. Since, however, on the strength of his own figures, the author must have had the feeling that the scope of the displacement problem had been out of all proportion overstated by his predecessors as far as the past was concerned, he could not but project it from the past into the future. The centre of gravity is therefore conveniently shifted from facts to expectations, from existing dangers to vague apprehensions, a plane into which it is easy for human imagination to follow. But if Mr. French then proceeds to make provisions in law in order to prevent a process from recurring in the future, which has not been proved to have occurred in the past, it must at once be said that no case has been established for such a course.

10.   The issue which was, it may be said, tacitly implied in the thesis of displacement and which is only another aspect of it, is that of land shortage which - so the argument runs - must be considered a main factor limiting the possibilities of expansion of the Jewish National Home. It is not intended to restate here the facts submitted to Sir John Hope Simpson in this Executive's memorandum of July 1930, nor to enter upon any controversy concerning statistics. It may be sufficient to say, in summarising these facts, that, without taking into account the possibilities of settlement in the hill districts and in the wide and sparsely populated Southern part of Palestine, the final resume of our account was and remains that on the basis of present technical knowledge and methods of cultivation the room available in Palestine for additional settlement is as follows:

Page. 9.   דף   הסוכנות היהודית לארץ ישראל
THE JEWISH AGENCY FOR PALESTINE

(a)	Maritime Plain	800,000	dunams	37,000	families
(b)	Huleh District	100,000	"	4,400	"
(c)	Beisan Lands	200,000	"	3,600	"
(d)	Lower Jordan Valley	210,000	"	9,900	"
		1,310,000	"	54,900	"

This computation was based upon the assumption of a lot viable varying according to the different agricultural zones of the country. It is important to state that Mr. French accepts, in theory as well as in practice, this principle of variation. In this respect, as further explained in the attached memorandum under para. 18, the French Report represents an important advance upon Sir John Hope Simpson's analysis in the discussion of the absorptive capacity of Palestine agriculture.

11.   What, however, is most relevant in this connection is that, whatever degree of urgency the problem of land shortage in Palestine may at present be assigned - in accordance with the varying points of view of the investigators - it cannot be dissociated from three major facts, all of which have their root in developments which have taken place since the establishment of the British Administration. These are: first, the administrative separation of Transjordan; second, the misallocation of the Beisan lands; and third, the alienation of the State Domain.

12.   If nowadays the contention of a scarcity of land in Palestine can altogether be raised, it is to a very large extent due to an administrative act of the Mandatory Government whereby Transjordan was in practice barred to Jewish economic and settlement activities. Without entering on this occasion into a discussion of the questions of political expediency and legal status connected with this act, it cannot be overlooked that, when the Mandatory Government undertook the administration of Palestine, the two provinces forming the Mandated territory were one. The density of population in the whole western province is given today at 32.5 per square kilometre, and in

the eastern province at 5.1 per square kilometre. The ratio of 1 to 6 must be modified in the light of the fact that in certain districts of Western Palestine the density of population has reached over 80 per square kilometre while, in order to arrive at a fairly correct notion of the relative density of population on either side of the River, the desert region of Transjordan should be left out of account. When the figures are so corrected, the relative density of population as between Eastern and Western Palestine will probably be found to be, 1 to 3, or perhaps 1 to 4. The separation of two areas which are not divided by any natural barrier has increased the difficulties in the Palestinian land market, raised the price of land and added to the pressure on the country's land resources, and left at the same time Transjordan in a state of misery and stagnation. Whatever the political status of Transjordan, or the intentions of the Mandatory Power in its regard, its exclusion from the scope of a Palestine development policy and from the terms of reference of Mr. French - or, for that matter, Sir John Hope Simpson - cannot be accepted as warranted. It is contrary to the interests of the Jewish National Home and of the entire population of Western Palestine no less than of the inhabitants of Transjordan themselves.

13. As to the Beisan lands, Mr. French endorses the statement made by Sir John Hope Simpson in his Report (p.85) by stating (p.25):

> "How is it possible to deal with this tract, the permanent settlement of which with the original cultivators has only just been brought to completion, but which is clearly susceptible of development on more intensive lines? Development is proceeding, as I have stated....but wide spaces of demarcated and partitioned land are lying untilled....It is certain that speaking generally the present holders, if left to themselves, can never develop this fertile tract. They have neither the education nor the resources.....Mr. Shepherd,

Page 11

הסוכנות היהודית לארץ ישראל
THE JEWISH AGENCY FOR PALESTINE

> who examined the whole tract in the light of his great experience in Egypt, and made the most detailed calculations, came to the conclusion that, in theory at any rate, close settlement of about 3,500 in an irrigable area of 100,500 dunams was possible. The expenditure was put, for the whole scheme, at a conservative estimate of over half a million pounds. Given a thriving community, he believed the value of the land would multiply perhaps five-fold...the latest estimates of families actually resident on the irrigated lands is about 950. If there is room for 3,500 families in all... the number of new families that could be introduced on about 110,000 dunams (not 100,500) of irrigable land, will be approximately 2,500."

As there are altogether about 570 "displaced" Arabs, it appears that Beisan alone would still, according to Mr. French, after providing for all of them, have room for 2,500 less 570 i.e., for about 1,900 new settlers.

14. The statement quoted above supports the case made by the Jewish authorities for many years past, and long disputed by official experts. The memorandum submitted by the Jewish Agency to Sir John Hope Simpson, dividing the whole area of the Semakh and Beisan Jiftlik into the categories of un-irrigable, partly irrigable, and irrigable land, and fixing the farm-unit at 130, 100 and 25 dunams respectively, arrives at an estimate of room being available for the establishment of additional 3,600 farms. This computation was, moreover, based on a figure of 1,585 families assumed to be living on the Beisan irrigable lands, which now stands refuted as an over-estimate in the light of the figures supplied by Mr. French.

If, however, the Director of Development, in summing up the Beisan position confines himself to the final statement that "the political repercussions among the Arabs" of any disturbance of the status quo must be considerable, it should be pointed out that he does not work out the conclusions of his own analysis and fails to present an adequate plan for the re-allocation of the Beisan lands. As to those "political repercussions" it is well known that many of the present holders of land rights at Beisan continue to be willing sellers of the surplus tracts which they cannot utilise.

15. With regard to State/lands in general, Mr. French repeats the negative verdict of official opinion by saying: "The answer then of the careful enquiry made into the question that State lands are or can, in existing conditions, be made available for (1) re-settlement of landless Arabs, or (2) new Jewish colonisation, must be restated as, none at all."

It is very difficult to ascertain in how far the position on the two Government estates referred to may be used as a basis for generalisation. It is equally difficult to see how the Development Authorities could have verified statements made by the present occupants of State Domain as to the period of their occupancy. It is well known that in the first few years of the civil administration, squatting on State lands went on on a considerable scale and, in the conditions prevailing in Palestine, it would seem almost impossible today to distinguish the squatter from the occupancy tenant of long standing. The Annual Report of the Palestine Government, 1920/1921 states (p.114) that in addition to the Mewat lands already demarcated as State Domain (which must also have amounted to a considerable area) the Palestine Government possessed at that time approximately:

```
889,978 dunams of cultivable land
 43,242    "    "  marshes
  9,900    "    "  pasturage
  2,685    "    "  orchards and groves
```

It further states (p.115) that "the alienation of State lands by sale has not generally been permitted, and in most cases since the Occupation leases for one year only have been entered

THE JEWISH AGENCY FOR PALESTINE

הסוכנות היהודית לארץ ישראל

into." Long leases have only been granted where the drainage of swamps or other considerations of public utility were pressing.

The present position concerning State lands as it emerges from an analysis of figures contained in the French Report, is as follows. The total of State lands accounted for in Mr. French's appendices is, excluding the Beisan lands, roughly 600,000 dunams. Out of this area, 338,255 dunams are in the hands of Arab tenants or occupiers who claim various rights of long term occupancy. Additional 118,000 dunams are allocated to various holders (Iraq Petroleum Company, Antiquity sites, Town Planning sites, etc.). About 170,000 dunams are in the hands of Jewish lessees while the remaining 83,500 are under litigation. The bulk of the disputed lands has also been assigned to Jewish interests (sand dunes at Rishon-le-Zion, PICA Concession at Caeseria, etc.). How in the circumstances described in the Government Report 12 years ago, a state of affairs has been allowed to develop in which at present occupancy rights on more than 400,000 are claimed by Arab occupiers remains unexplained. If, however, Government now maintains that little or no land of any cultural worth in any State Domain is available for settlement, it cannot be absolved from responsibility for a process which has taken the State lands out of the scope of rational development policy and barred them to close settlement provided for in Article 6 of the Mandate.

16. It should further be emphasised that the paramount importance which the Reports of the Director of Development attach to the land problem, in judging the capacity of Palestine to absorb new immigrants, should not prevent the prospects of manufacturing industries from receiving the full consideration which they in this connection deserve. While it is true that the positive obligations imposed upon the Government by the Mandate refer in particular to land and close settlement policies, this should not be taken to imply that other possible avenues open

to Jewish enterprise in Palestine can be disregarded. It may be said that the Jewish people themselves were, in a sense, surprised by the important part which secondary industries have come to play as centres of absorption for immigrant workers.

As a matter of fact manufacturing industries have by no means lagged behind agriculture from the point of view of their absorptive capacity. Tel-Aviv alone has, as far as employment of labour is concerned, nearly kept pace with the whole of the plantation belt. At the present moment the number of Jewish workers with a fairly steady employment in the factories and workshops of Tel-Aviv, which have grown up almost unnoticed, amounts to about 6,000. The promising industrial prospects of Haifa are well known and in Jerusalem, too, the labour force is steadily, if more slowly, growing. Out of a total permanent investment of at least twenty million pounds made by Jews in Palestine in the course of the last decade, at least five million pounds have been invested in manufacturing industries and workshops. It should, moreover, be observed that a significant change in the composition of the urban working class has been produced by the growth of manufacturing industries. Ten years ago the building trade accounted for the bulk of the Jewish labour force in the towns. No one would perhaps have been able to foretell what new openings these building workers would find the moment building activities would slow down. Yet when the slump came, the great majority of these workers, struggling hard and passing through a strenuous process of re-adjustment, found their way into new channels of industrial employment. Today, although building activities are proceeding on a relatively large scale in the three principal towns, according to the records of the Labour Federation, building workers do not represent more than 1,600, or 13%, out of about 12,000 men,

Page 15.   דף   הסוכנות היהודית לארץ ישראל
                              THE JEWISH AGENCY FOR PALESTINE

employed in manual labour in the towns. In assessing the
prospects of development and defining the basis of a future
policy with regard to immigration and colonisation these
tendencies must by no means be overlooked or underrated.

17.   It is by such facts that a Palestine development
policy, which really aims at raising the standards of the
population at large, and promoting modern methods in agriculture and industry, will have to be guided. It might have
been assumed that no expert investigator could overlook the
plain fact that Jewish activities as such, the untiring
initiative, enterprising courage and scientific spirit of
the Jewish settlers as well as the continuous influx of Jewish
capital, public and private, are in themselves the most powerful agent at work in the general development of Palestine.
Yet one looks in vain for a reference in Mr. French's Reports
which would assign this factor its due weight. The author of
the Reports, it is true, here and there mentions some isolated
fact illustrating the point. In speaking of the development
of the Huleh area he says that "a leavening of Jewish colonists
in this district would tend to an acceleration of the desired
development after the marshes have been drained." On another
occasion (p.64) he writes: "The only prudent and effective
method for the re-settlement of the great majority of the
landless Arabs seem to be similar to those which have been
adopted by the Jewish organisations." However, what is the
general effect, reflected in these isolated facts, of the
persistent working of this force upon the development of
Palestine? The amount invested by Jewish agencies and individuals
in the course of the last half century in agriculture, industries, building, etc., may reach fifteen or twenty times
the two-and-a-half-million pounds which it was originally
contemplated to raise as a development loan. Although even

Page 15.   הסוכנות היהודית לארץ ישראל
         THE JEWISH AGENCY FOR PALESTINE

an investment of this size has not been sufficient to change the face of the country as a whole, its effects have been manifest in a variety of ways in many spheres of the country's economic life.

The results of the recent census are, from this point of view, most instructive. They would appear to indicate that the growth of the non-Jewish population has been most marked in just those areas which are closest to the districts of Jewish development. While the Arab rural population throughout the country has increased by 34.4% between 1922 and 1931, it has grown by 98% in the Jaffa sub-district, by 80% in the Haifa sub-district and by 44% in the Ramleh sub-district. It is in these districts that Arab peasantry shows the greatest progress in the application of modern methods of agriculture. The newly acquired skill is reflected in higher yields of crops, better housing and improved technical equipment applied on the model of Jewish farming. The results reached in the Jewish agricultural research service as far as cross-breeding, seed selection, and the study of marketing methods is concerned, make themselves felt throughout the country. Jewish industrial areas offer a market of considerable purchasing power for agricultural produce by which Arab producers benefit to a large extent. The absorptive capacity of urban areas for Arab labour, skilled and unskilled, has been constantly increasing. Standards of living and, in consequence, wage-levels of Arab labour are, in normal times, slowly but noticeably rising. The increased revenue of the Palestine Government to which Jews contribute per head three times more than non-Jews results in an increased expenditure on public works and social service with the consequent fall in infant mortality and improvement in communications. Particular attention is here drawn to our

Page 17.   דף   הסוכנות היהודית לארץ ישראל
THE JEWISH AGENCY FOR PALESTINE

observations under Para. 72 of the First Report in the memorandum, describing the effects on the Arab population of Jewish development in the Maritime Plain, the main scene of progress in recent years.

18.   If, nevertheless, it remains true that many Arab cultivators, particularly in the hill districts, have to endure severe economic hardship, and are crushed by the burden of debts, disease, illiteracy, feuds and litigation, in the Director of Development's account it would appear that it is the advance of Jewish immigration and settlement which are somehow to blame. Jewish agricultural settlement has scarcely touched the hills; it has been almost entirely confined to the Maritime Plain, the Emek and some parts of Galilee. It is very difficult to see what nexus it is proposed to establish between development in those areas and the wretched conditions of the fellahin in the hills of Samaria and Judea. The general question is whether the lot of the Palestine fellah as a class has, on the balance, been worsened or improved during the period of Jewish activities. A reference to the plight of his fellow peasant in Transjordan, Syria, Iraq or even Cyprus would provide the most adequate answer to the query. On the other hand, upon reading Mr. French's Reports one cannot help wondering what might have been his answer had he been asked ten years ago whether there was room in Palestine for another 120,000 immigrants and what would be the effects of immigration on such scale. It is fairly certain that, in the light of his present theory, he would have predicted complete and irretrievable catastrophe. In the meantime, while this number of immigrants have actually come and settled, emigration of Arabs from Palestine has fallen below pre-war levels and the rural Arab population - again, according to the census - has grown even more rapidly than the urban.

19. It is self-evident that no economic development and progress is possible without a certain amount of dislocation. The relevant question is only how this dislocation works out in its ultimate results, and whether it is not counter-balanced or even outweighed by the tapping of new and more remunerative sources of livelihood. A conception such as appears throughout to underlie Mr. French's presentation of the problem, which would favour the introduction of the railway without any of the coachmen losing any of their earnings or having to change their mode of life, is obviously untenable. If the railway has to come there must be a certain amount of dislocation. Coachmen will have to become conductors, linemen, engine-drivers; many coach routes will be changed. Over 100,000 Jews have immigrated into Palestine in the course of the last decade, establishing agricultural settlements and industries. A certain dislocation must inevitably ensue. As far as agricultural cultivators and graziers are concerned, approximately 570 of them, who have previously, either as freeholders or as tenants cultivated their lands, or grazed their flocks, may have been left landless. Many others have changed their mode of life. The answer, however, to the question whether this fact is not more than a hundred times outweighed by what the country as a whole gained in wealth and health does not seem open to any doubt.

20. There is in the French Reports one other argument which, already faintly discernible between the lines of the Hope Simpson Report, recurs here time and again, explicitly and implicitly. It is the idea of the tremendous impact of Jewish financial power upon the weak structure of the "native" economy - mighty Jewish corporations, in their sinister operations defying all safeguards and restrictions. This line of argument appeals not only to prejudices current throughout the Christian world as regards the power of Jewish "finance" and its effects upon

הסוכנות היהודית לארץ ישראל
THE JEWISH AGENCY FOR PALESTINE

non-Jewish "poverty" but also to notions prevailing in various quarters as regards the effect of modern well-equipped European capitalism upon the backward economy of the natives of undeveloped regions. Applied to Palestine, it is in both directions a profound misunderstanding.

21. It is of course true that, in spite of a policy of strict economy supported by our settlers themselves, the standard of living in Jewish settlements - buildings, cultural opportunities, capital outlay per head - is considerably higher than in the fellah's villages. This is an inevitable result of the fact that the Jewish settler is a European immigrant of a certain cultural standard. A hospital providing for maternity cases and children's diseases is not a luxury but part of his civilised minimum of existence. A Jewish settlement can hardly do without a reading room or a shower bath. In comparison with Arab peasants an impression is produced of people living on a level of relative comfort, which, for its explanation, requires a reference to Jewish finances. Seen, however, in the light of the conditions in which the masses of the Jewish people are living and the tasks in consequence, imposed upon those who are responsible for the establishment of the Jewish National Home nothing can be further from the truth.

The mass of the Jewish people are in the throes of a merciless struggle for existence. Pauperised in Soviet Russia, thrown out of their economic position in the States of Eastern Europe, confronted with a tidal wave of violent anti-semitism in Central Europe, endangered by the rationalisation crisis in the United States, there is hardly anywhere a ray of light for them. Out of the rank and file of this mass come, by tens and hundreds of thousands, the penny contributors to our national funds.

Page 20.   דף

הסוכנות היהודית לארץ ישראל
THE JEWISH AGENCY FOR PALESTINE

Measured by the needs of the Jewish people, the distress of the masses, the economic urge for migration and settlement, Zionism has always been and remains a poor and struggling movement. At present about 7000 agricultural workers who have been employed on private plantations for from five to ten years await settlement. 40,000 young men and women are organised in the Hehalutz organisation in various countries, training for Palestine without any definite prospect of being provided here with land and equipment. If they could be absorbed new tens of thousands would appeal for the same assistance. In relation to a task of such scope our "corporations" and institutions are not "rich and powerful", but rather inadequate and hard up. On the other hand, it should not be overlooked that Jewish colonising agencies are not the profit-hunting enterprises of chartered companies based upon the exploitation of cheap native labour, but are serving purposes of public utility in the highest sense of the term, providing land for people without means, supplying farm equipment and offering housing and credit facilities for immigrant labourers and artisans.

22.   The Director of Development, in attempting to outline a Palestine development policy, did not take advantage of the accumulated experience of two generations in achieving some remarkable economic progress in Palestine. He did not approach the Jewish aspect of the problem from the point of view of the Mandate which lays upon the Mandatory Power the positive obligation of securing the establishment of the Jewish National Home, a term which does not figure in Mr. French's vocabulary. Instead of realising, in the light of objective facts, that there is nothing self-contradictory or inconsistent in the task of the Mandatory in actively promoting the establishment of the Jewish National Home while furthering the well-being of all of Palestine's inhabitants, Mr. French's point of departure seems

הסוכנות היהודית לארץ ישראל
THE JEWISH AGENCY FOR PALESTINE

to remain the alleged antagonism between the two parts of the Mandate. This fundamentally erroneous idea cannot but lead to barren arguments. With it as basis, a constructive policy can never be worked out. A conception that whatever may benefit the Jewish settler must necessarily turn out to be harmful to the Arab cultivator, while whatever restricts the enterprise and progress of the Jew would automatically protect his Arab neighbour, can only lead to a programme which instead of being an instrument of development must become a means of obstructing it. Finally, superimposed upon this mistaken theory of a permanent conflict inherent in the Palestine Mandate there appears, again and again, in Mr. French's Reports, a peculiar faith in elaborate administrative engineering which must be termed truly bureaucratic. If a system of survey and land settlement operations, partition of musha', training of the local village registrar, enactment of highly technical legislation, mostly restrictive, exploration of new markets and safeguarding a commercial rate of profit on all funds invested are one and all necessary pre-requisites to any attempt at a successful operation of a development scheme, the natural process of development drawing its life-blood from the initiative, enterprise and unceasing effort of the people themselves, will certainly not wait for the administrator.

23. It is not then surprising to find that the main impression produced by the practical recommendations embodied in the Reports is that of utter sterility and absence of a constructive programme. In adumbrating such a programme Sir John Hope Simpson in his Report wrote:

> "A methodical scheme of agricultural development should be thought out and undertaken, which will ensure the use of the land of the country to better purpose than has been the case hitherto. This development should have two distinct aims: In the first place, to improve the method of cultivation of the Arab fellah in the dry tracts, and also to extend

הסוכנות היהודית לארץ ישראל
THE JEWISH AGENCY FOR PALESTINE

> irrigation wherever that is possible, so that the fellah will be able to obtain a reasonable livelihood from a smaller area of land than that which has been essential hitherto. In the second place, so as to rearrange holdings of land, that there will be a margin of further settlement in accordance with the terms of Article 6 of the Mandate." (p.143).

24. All that remains of these positive intentions in Mr. French's recommendations on issues of major policy is, as far as the Arabs are concerned, a rather elaborate and singularly expensive scheme for the re-settlement of a number of those registered as "displaced" in accordance with the terms of the Prime Minister's letter. While this Executive does not wish to say anything against a proposal to settle on the land such Arabs as are proved to come under the category of "landless" defined in the Prime Minister's letter, it should be clear that the expenditure of Government funds, as proposed by Mr. French, to the amount of about £800 per family for the purpose of settling these people in the orange belt, must be taken exception to as both extravagant and precluding any possibility of its becoming reproductive. Moreover, it is self-evident that such a scheme would in no way benefit the Arab peasant class as such. One could imagine all the families approved as "landless" being resettled at what must be called an exorbitant cost (assuming sufficient funds were available) without the villagers in other districts even noticing the performance. Mr. French may be genuinely anxious to devise a policy for the general improvement the position of the Arab peasantry, in the hill districts and elsewhere, but there appears nothing in his Report - beyond a vague and strangely misplaced warning against the perils of Jewish encroachment upon the hills - which can be interpreted as a scheme serving that purpose. On the other hand, it may be safely stated that if/development funds of such

Page 23.

הסוכנות היהודית לארץ ישראל
THE JEWISH AGENCY FOR PALESTINE

scope were available, methods might well be devised to ensure the benefit of such expenditure - through the extension of adequate credit facilities, promotion of cooperation, the improvement of live-stock, the provision of fruit nurselings or the supply of selected seed - to a much wider area of Arab agriculture.

25. As to Mr. French's proposals in connection with the provision of further facilities for Jewish settlement they are even more nebulous; in fact, practically worthless. The Prime Minister's letter referred to the close settlement of Jews on the land as being "a primary purpose of the Mandate" and declared that "the obligation to facilitate Jewish immigration and to encourage close settlement by Jews on the land remains a positive obligation of the Mandate, and it can be fulfilled without prejudice to the rights of other sections of the population." Mr. French, it is true, makes a number of proposals, embodied in paras. 88 to 121 of his Supplementary Report, relating to minor schemes, like that of an establishment of a citrus experimental station or certain measures for the promotion of export of agricultural produce, with some of which the representatives of the Jewish Agency on the General Agricultural Council have agreed, and several of which they themselves indeed put forward as a means of Government assistance in the development of the country's agricultural resources. If these proposals, all or any, were carried into effect, Jewish agriculture, along with the rest of the country, might possibly share in the benefits resulting. With regard, however, to the major problems of Jewish agricultural development, Mr. French's general conclusion appears to be that there is nothing, for the time being, that Government could do for its assistance or encouragement - a conclusion doubly amazing in view of the unceasing effort on the part of Jewish settlers themselves to

work out new ways and means of raising their efficiency and output, improving the quality of produce, developing markets and expanding the absorptive capacity for labour in Jewish farming. Although Mr. French admits possibilities of new settlement in the Beisan area - as has been mentioned above - and in the Huleh District, in respect of which he concurs with the opinion of this Executive in that the Turkish pre-War concession is holding up development, and although he recommends the undertaking of a hydrographic survey of the Beisan and Huleh districts and of the Jordan Valley, his final summary of the situation (p.70) is that "even if funds could be made available for our opening up these areas, their exploitation would not be an economic proposition in the present stage of agricultural development in Palestine." As far as the Beersheba district and other parts of the Jordan Valley are concerned, the problem of an adequate water supply appears to be, in his eyes, an insurmountable obstacle. As to this Executive's proposal for the investment of funds for purposes of Jewish development in an Agricultural and Settlement Bank, Mr. French does not recommend its adoption expressing his conviction (p.74) that there is not "sufficient justification, at this stage, for the Government supplementing the funds already available for this purpose from other sources." He assures us that "the position may be different later when marketing difficulties and other obstacles to the profitable export of payable crops have been removed." Having rejected the Jewish Agency's proposal, Mr. French does not consider himself called upon to produce on his part such alternative proposals as might, all doubts and scruples notwithstanding, commend themselves to him for acceptance. All Mr. French has in the last analysis to contribute to the advancement of Jewish settlement on the land, described by the Prime Minister as a "primary purpose of the Mandate", and to "the

הסוכנות היהודית לארץ ישראל
THE JEWISH AGENCY FOR PALESTINE

larger purposes of development which His Majesty's Government regard as the most effectual means of furthering the establishment of a National Home for the Jews" appears to be a set of proposals for the enactment of restrictive legislation.

25. The system of checks and brakes on Jewish agricultural progress so suggested is as far-reaching as the positive content of the French Reports is insignificant. In Para.129(e) of the Supplementary Report Mr. French expresses his conviction that these measures "in no way conflict with the declared policy of His Majesty's Government." Mr. French is mistaken. These proposals are not only inconsistent with the obligations placed upon the Mandatory Power in the Mandate, but are entirely incompatible with the assurances contained in the Prime Minister's letter. In the same measure they are contrary to the interests of economic progress and development of the country as a whole. Moreover, it should never be overlooked that the legislative programme contemplated in the Prime Minister's letter had its origin in a situation in which the displacement issue appeared to be of such scope as to warrant the taking by Government of special powers, however strictly defined. The circumstances in which conclusions were then reached appear now in a different light, with the result that the premises have to be revised. Mr. French, in advocating his measures chooses to ignore these developments and his recommendations thus can in no way be reconciled with the requirements of the situation. He urges the necessity for the establishment of a centralised control of land transactions adding that, in his opinion, the only effective way a Transfer of Land Ordinance can be used is to apply it to the whole country with power to the High Commissioner to exempt therefrom such districts as do not come within the orbit of any development scheme. He proposes an Occupancy Tenants Ordinance and a Homestead Protection Ordinance.

He further makes a vague suggestion with a view to restricting the free transfer of land from Arabs to Jews in the Maritime Plain. He desires to protect cultivators in the hills against Jewish purchases (although Jewish settlement has so far certainly had no effect whatever on the position of those cultivators). In short, he advances a number of proposals which, if enacted, would pile up obstacles in the way of Jewish colonisation and would, rather than promote the development of Palestine agriculture as a whole, obstruct its natural progress.

26.   With regard to the Transfer of Land Ordinance, such as appears to be contemplated by the late Director of Development, the general objections of this Executive to legislation of this kind were fully set forth in a letter addressed to the Under Secretary of State for the Colonies on the subject of a similar draft Ordinance, dated August 31, 1931. The numerous arguments advanced on that occasion would seem to hold equally good with regard to the draft Ordinance attached to Mr. French's Second Report. Special attention is invited to the following passage which occurs in the letter under reference:

> "The draft Ordinance would, if enacted, produce injury to the economic life of Palestine and retard its development by discouraging the application of capital to the improvement of agricultural land. In accordance with the proposed legislation the owner of land could be deprived for an indefinite period of the power of disposing of his land to a buyer who is willing to invest in the improvement of the land the capital which the owner has not at his disposal. By including mortgages within its scope, the Ordinance would discourage the lending of money by banks and individuals, so that landowners would not be able to secure loans for the improvement of their property. But the draft Ordinance goes even further. It proposes to give the High Commissioner power to refuse approval of foreclosure or sale in the case of mortgages already in existence at the time of the enactment of the Ordinance, burdening the general revenues of Palestine with the obligation to pay out sums of money to mortgagees. This interference with the credit basis of economic life in Palestine cannot but be detrimental to progress, and must also

הסוכנות היהודית לארץ ישראל
THE JEWISH AGENCY FOR PALESTINE

> tend to place Palestine outside the scope of the possible benefits of international mortgage credit."

27. Again, in defining the necessary measure of co-ordination in land policy so as to "place the development scheme upon a sure foundation", the Prime Minister stated:

> "The power contemplated is regulative and not prohibitory, although it does not involve a power to prevent transactions which are inconsistent with the tenor of the scheme. But the exercise of the power will be limited and in no respect arbitrary. In every case it will be conditioned by considerations as to how best to give effect to the purpose of the Mandate. Any control contemplated will be fenced with due safeguards to secure as little interference as possible with the free transfer of land. The centralised control will take effect as from such date only as the authority charged with the duty of carrying out the policy of land development shall begin to operate. The High Commissioner will, pending the establishment of such centralised control, have full powers to take all steps necessary to protect the tenancy and occupancy rights including the rights of squatters, throughout Palestine.
>
> Further, the statement of policy of His Majesty's Government did not imply a prohibition of acquisition of additional land by Jews. It contained no such prohibition, nor is any such intended. What it does contemplate is such temporary control of land disposition and transfers as may be necessary not to impair the harmony and effectiveness of the scheme of land settlement to be undertaken."

Apart from Mr. French's proposals being incompatible with the rulings laid down in this paragraph, it must be emphasised that, if it is calculated to prevent interference with development operations and ensure the success of re-settlement schemes, it must be regarded as entirely out of proportion to the purposes which it aims at. Mr. French suggests for the next 12 to 18 months a beginning of the re-settlement of 100 to 200 landless Arabs. But even if the re-settlement of about 500 families were to be carried out within a comparatively brief period of time, the total area involved would be relatively

insignificant. This Executive is firmly convinced that
activities of such limited extent would in no way warrant
the institution of a system of land control to be applied to
the country as a whole with the resulting serious interference
with economic life and a widespread obstruction of agricultural
progress. If, however, Mr. French's intention is to be interpreted as "the recongition of, and move to retrieve, the
mistake which permitted the displacements to occur as they did"
and as a measure to prevent a repetition of the error which
"can only lead to a recurrence of the present situation", it
must be once more said that "the present situation" seems to
have been thoroughly misinterpreted by the author of the Reports.

28. As to the Homestead Protection Ordinance and Occupancy
Tenants Ordinance foreshadowed in the Reports, some observations
on their major provisions are included in the attached memorandum.
In the view of this Executive these projects bear all the
characteristics of legislation which would work out to be in
many cases ineffective, and economically harmful in those cases
where it would be made effective. Such legislation is liable
to affect adversely agricultural mortgages; it may easily
jeopardise important agricultural reforms such as the substitution
of normal short-term credit for usurers' debts, the development
of rational farming and the intensive cultivation of surplus
lands. Although (on p.76) Mr. French reaches the conclusion
that "it is of course impossible to make the world stand still
or to stay the march of progress", his preventive measures are
nothing but an attempt at enforcing the maintenance of an
economic and social status quo in Palestine which is neither
in the interests of the Arab village population nor in keeping
with the policy of the establishment of the Jewish National Home.

Page 29.   הסוכנות היהודית לארץ ישראל
            THE JEWISH AGENCY FOR PALESTINE

29.   The Executive of the Jewish Agency has always been anxious to cooperate with His Majesty's Government and the Administration of Palestine in working out a development policy based upon the principles laid down in the Mandate. It remains prepared to lay before His Majesty's Government its proposal for such a scheme, and would appreciate an opportunity of discussing with Government the details of a programme, of which the larger objects would be the promotion of Jewish immigration and settlement as well as the advancement of the general welfare of all the inhabitants of the country. The Jewish Agency continues to maintain that there are no conflicting interests which would render such a policy impossible, and that it need not, therefore, be based upon restrictive measures and interference with the progress of Jewish activity in Palestine which is in harmony with the general progress of the country. It finally desires to record its conviction, sufficiently argued on various occasions in the past, that any work undertaken by His Majesty's Government in connection with land development in Palestine should be so directed as to offer equal benefits to the Jewish National Home on the one hand, and to the Arab population on the other, and that, in point of time, such benefits should, on the whole, accrue simultaneously to both sections of the population.

The Executive trusts that His Majesty's Government and the Government of Palestine may see their way to give sympathetic consideration to the arguments advanced in the foregoing observations and in the attached memorandum, and look forward to a period of close and fruitful cooperation

Page 30.　　　　　　　　　　　　　　הסוכנות היהודית לארץ ישראל
　　　　　　　　　　　　　　　　　THE JEWISH AGENCY FOR PALESTINE

between the representatives of His Majesty's Government
and the representatives of the Jewish Agency.

　　　　　　　　　　　　I have the honour to be
　　　　　　　　　　　　Your Excellency's
　　　　　　　　　　Most obedient servant,

　　　　　　　　　　　　[signature]
　　　　　　　　　　　　Dr.Ch.Arlosoroff
　　　　　　　　EXECUTIVE OF THE JEWISH AGENCY

CHA/RH

Page............ דף

הסוכנות היהודית לארץ ישראל
THE JEWISH AGENCY FOR PALESTINE

MEMORANDUM

ON THE REPORTS ON AGRICULTURAL DEVELOPMENT AND

LAND SETTLEMENT IN PALESTINE

by Lewis French, C.I.E., C.B.E.

(formerly Director of Development)

הסוכנות היהודית לארץ ישראל
THE JEWISH AGENCY FOR PALESTINE

       The Executive of the Jewish Agency presents herewith seriatim the following observations relating to the respective paragraphs of the Reports of Mr. French:

FIRST REPORT +

Appointment of Jewish Adviser

<u>Para.7.</u> The statement that "the Jews, on their part, have taken no positive steps to make an appointment" of an Adviser to the Director of Development, as originally contemplated, calls for an explanation. The non-appointment of the Jewish Adviser is not to be attributed to any tactics implying lack of co-operation. On the contrary, in the negotiations with both the Cabinet Sub-Committee in 1930-1931 and the Inter-Departmental Committee presided over by the Lord Advocate in 1931, the positive attitude, in principle, of the Jewish Agency towards a Palestine development policy was repeatedly expressed, and a programme of work was outlined which, in their view, presented an adequate basis for the execution of such a policy. Parity and simultaneity were laid down as guiding principles for the application of development funds for purposes serving Jewish and Arab interests respectively. Despite the fact that H. M. Government did not, at that preliminary stage, see their way to consider these fundamental principles as accepted, this Executive did not adopt a generally negative attitude with regard to the appointment of the Jewish Adviser. At the time, however, when the Director of Development arrived in Palestine, the Land Transfer Bill, to which strong exception had been taken in November 1930, was again proposed for enactment in its original form. The possibility of this Bill becoming law,

+ Abbreviations: First Report - F.R. Supplementary Report - S.R.

Page 8 דף   הסוכנות היהודית לארץ ישראל
THE JEWISH AGENCY FOR PALESTINE

which was regarded as definitely prejudicial, prevented the Executive, for the time being, from proceeding with the appointment of an Adviser. Later on, the measure was deferred, but not withdrawn. In the meantime, conditions and prospects had so much changed that - as Mr. French points out in S.R. para.130 - "it could not be assumed that it would be found practicable" to make the proposed loan available for Palestine development purposes. In these circumstances, it did not appear advisable for the Jewish Agency to proceed with an appointment the purpose of which would have necessarily been confined to purely non-constructive functions, namely, the participation in the "displaced Arabs" enquiry.

Preliminary Results of Displaced Arabs Enquiry

Para.8. Mr. French states, with reference to the registration of the landless Arabs, that "it was obvious that, whether this extensive area (held by Jewish organisations) has been bought from large Arab proprietors or from small landholders, the acquisition for permanent settlement of immigrants could not have been effected without considerable displacement of existing cultivators." Against this sweeping statement the facts should be set. The Table communicated to this Executive by the Acting Director of Development under No.DC/1/33 of 6th March, 1933, gives the following summary of the "displaced Arabs" enquiry:

	Claims	Accepted	Rejected	Pending
Tul Karm	718	239	478	-
Nazareth	304	69	235	-
Safad	102	16	18	68
Haifa	430	107	297	2
Beisan	127	22	105	-
Jenin	6	-	6	-
Jerusalem	71	-	68	3
Jaffa-Ramleh	913	109	799	10
Gaza-Beersheba	149	4	145	-
Tiberias	378	4	374	-
	3198	570	2520	83

Page 3 דף

הסוכנות היהודית לארץ ישראל
THE JEWISH AGENCY FOR PALESTINE

Note: The small discrepancy in the numbers for Tul Karm, Nazareth, Haifa, Beisan and Jaffa is explained by the fact that in some cases one claim was put forward in the name of two or three individuals.

The figure of 3,700 in the paragraph under reference, as representing the total number of claims forwarded up to the date of the Report, should, as explained in the covering letter, be reduced by 1000 or about 30%. The reason is that, according to a statement of the Department of Development, an error had occurred in the calculation. In the meantime, a few hundreds of fresh claims have reached the Development Department, bringing the final total of claims to 3188. The bulk of these new claims came from the Tiberias district where, as the Table shows, out of 378 claims preferred 374 stand now rejected. It should further be pointed out that not less than one half of the 570 claims so far provisionally accepted do not refer to cultivators, as Mr. French's above-quoted reference may seem to imply, but to Beduin (the bulk of them from the Wady Hawareth and the Haifa Bay tracts). The Beduin's grazing and watering rights are, of course, of a more precarious character than those of a tenant cultivator. His use of the land is more wasteful and backward. Here, indeed, we have a classic example of the issue of goat versus man - swamp pasture against orange plantation.

Mr. French's reference to the apprehensions which were expressed at the political results of the preliminary enquiries and to the "vague accusations of pressure" which were advanced may allude to correspondence which passed between him and the Jewish Agency during the early stages of the registration. It should be observed that, at the time, this Executive submitted facts to show that some District Officers were inviting claims from people who did not

חסוכנות היהודית לארץ ישראל
THE JEWISH AGENCY FOR PALESTINE

otherwise appear to have considered themselves qualified. According to our information the total of claims which reached the Development Offices included over 1,000 which were not put in by the claimants themselves, but by the village Mukhtars without authority from the persons concerned. This procedure may be justified as a means of disposing once and for all of the "displaced Arabs" issue. This Executive is not in any way interested in leaving any possible claim untested. It is satisfied that whoever had a claim to put forward, flimsy as it may have been, has made use of the chance offered to him. Whether, however, the term "pressure" is so entirely out of place in relation to the procedure adopted by some local officers, is open to argument.

Procedure in scrutiny of claims

Para. 9. It is stated that "the process of converting Arab cultivators into landless Arabs does not necessarily cease with the receipt of claims already put in." This is one of those sentences frequently recurring in Mr. French's Reports which, without necessarily being based upon facts, produce a vague effect of fear in the reader's mind. In reality, the volume of land transfer which took place during the last few years is almost insignificant (not by any means because of lack of offers of land). In 1930 the nett physical area acquired by Jews was 19,566 metric dunams; in 1931, 12,585 metric dunams. The only case of an impending Jewish National Fund purchase which may have been brought to the attention of Mr. French at the time of writing the Report was that of Shatta. The village of Shatta recently purchased by the Jewish National Fund was inhabited by 17 tenants and 16 harrathin (agricultural labourers, paid in kind who, Mr. French's remarks in S.R.83 notwithstanding, do not qualify as "displaced" under the term of the Prime Minister's Letter).

These tenants and labourers were all transferred to other lands in the same district.

With regard to the procedure agreed upon for our participation in the scrutiny of the claims, reference is made to the following extract from a letter addressed to this Executive by the Acting Director of Development, under No.DC/1/33 dated 4th March, 1933:

> "The name of each individual who has been recommended for inclusion in the Register of Landless Arabs has, however, been submitted to the Jewish Agency together with a copy of his application (if that had not been already sent), and each case has been and will be reconsidered in the light of their observations. I understand that this procedure has been found preferable by the Jewish Agency as involving less labour for their staff....
>
> "Whenever any further observations are received they will be considered and the Legal Assessor is ready to discuss any individual case or cases with the representative of the Jewish Agency and to hear such evidence as they may wish to submit ...."

This procedure will be applied in respect of those claims out of the 570 provisionally accepted which have not yet been examined.

Control of Land Transfers in Interests of Development

Para.10. This paragraph introduces the first reference to legislation restricting land transfers. The need for such control is here argued on grounds of the necessity of preventing the artificial inflation of land prices "if acquisition of private lands is not to be hampered by the speculation which will inevitably follow the knowledge that Government is in the market for such property." In the course of discussions relating to the proposed Land Transfer Ordinance this Executive all along maintained that, for the purpose of controlling prices, there is no need to establish a centralised control of land transfers. It has been submitted to the High Commissioner

Page 6 דף   הסוכנות היהודית לארץ ישראל
THE JEWISH AGENCY FOR PALESTINE

that, to achieve that end, it would be sufficient to give the Development authorities powers to purchase land either at a valuation price or at the price current at a certain date prior to the actual commencement of development activities in the district concerned. This Executive concurs with the suggestion, referred to in S.R. para.35, that the best solution would be to extend to development activities the powers conferred upon Government for purposes of public utility under the Expropriation Ordinance.

Encroachment on State Lands

Para.14. The current belief that "the Government has at its command large areas which it could transfer to colonists" is, in corroboration of the Hope-Simpson Report, here and in S.R. para.15, dismissed as an illusion. Mr. French is inclined "to the belief that little or no land of any cultural worth of any State Domain is now likely to be discovered which is not already subject to hereditary or analogous tenancy rights." This inclination is based upon the results of advanced settlement operations in two Government estates, in connection with which Mr. French "ventures to predict that what is true of these two estates will be found to be true of all Government Domains." As far as our knowledge goes, such operations have hitherto been carried out only in the State lands of Jaladiyeh, Muharraqa, Kofakha and Sajad. Whether these estates are typical of the rest is an open question to which Mr. French's predictions may or may not provide the correct reply. In the event, however, that they do not prove to have been correct, the question arises, as has been pointed out in the covering letter, whether and to what extent occupancy rights on State lands have been allowed to grow up in the course of the period of the British Administration. In S.R. para.111 it is stated that, after

Page 7

הסוכנות היהודית לארץ ישראל
THE JEWISH AGENCY FOR PALESTINE

ten years of uninterrupted and unchallenged individual occupation, the cultivator obtains in any case a prescriptive right to his holding. Failure on the part of Government to challenge in time the claims of squatters or to undertake settlement of all State lands in advance of the general settlement programme must therefore have resulted in continuous encroachments on State Domains. It would be worth while ascertaining in how many cases such prescriptive rights have been acquired between 1920 and 1932.

Close Settlement and Markets

Paras.16 and 17. With regard to the general policy aiming at closer settlement in Palestine, Mr. French says that "the aims a priori are admirable, but idealism must not blind us to the more grave risks that hover round this policy", and winds up by saying that on account of gloomy marketing prospects for oranges and bananas, the exclusion of melons from Egypt, the threatened raising of the Egyptian tariff against Nablus soap and its adverse effect upon olive production, this policy "raises apprehensions in thoughtful minds as to the future." This sentence, recurring in many variations throughout the Report, goes far to reveal the general frame of mind of its author which may be defined as apprehensive of development rather than concerned with development. If apprehensions raised in thoughtful minds had been allowed to prevail, many of the achievements of man, in Palestine and elsewhere, would not have seen the light of day. Neither the development of the citrus belt, nor the introduction of grape-fruit in the heavy soil zone, nor the improvement of the local banana and other fruit (to the extent to which they have developed), nor the establishment of modern industries or the export of their produce would ever have been possible in such a spirit.

Page 8 דף   הסוכנות היהודית לארץ ישראל
                                                         THE JEWISH AGENCY FOR PALESTINE

Such statements as that "there have already been failures in banana-growing in the Beisan tracts owing to unsuitability of soil or water", or that the oranges grown in the Upper Huleh Basin are not at present exportable, do not prove anything. Dozens of products with which the home market is now supplied, and which, if in limited quantities, are already shipped abroad, either did not exist at all only a few years ago or were then in their infancy, going through failure after failure without accepting defeat, until they have reached their present promising stage. The "Tnuva" Cooperative Association which markets the bulk of the Jewish dairy, poultry and vegetable produce and supplies a large part of the daily needs of the town population with European tastes, is itself only a few years old. As regards the dangers attending the future of the citrus industry, further reference will be made to the subject under S.R.46.

Lot Viable and Intermediate Types

Para.18. The provisional adoption of an average farm unit for irrigated land of 30 dunams and for unirrigated land of 130 dunams represents an important advance upon the Hope-Simpson Report, which, although in theory admitting the possibility of differentiating between farm units in various zones, bases its final computations on a uniform lot viable of 130 dunams. This is a decisive step forward in the discussion of the absorptive capacity of Palestine agriculture. In practice, of course, a variety of intermediate types exists between the extremes. This intermediate type, of which one specimen is referred to in S.R. para.42, is described by Dr. Ruppin with regard to the coastal belt in the following terms:

> "On the other hand, Mr. French leaves completely out of account an intermediate type which is based upon 50-60 dunams of unirrigable and 5-20 dunams irrigable land. In

הסוכנות היהודית לארץ ישראל
THE JEWISH AGENCY FOR PALESTINE

so doing he blocks for himself the road to that type of settlement which we proposed for the coastal plain in our memorandum to Sir John Hope-Simpson.... This omission on Mr. French's part is the more regrettable as this method does not call for any outlay of funds on the part of Government, but only for a helpful attitude. It has a further advantage in that it avoids the abrupt transition from an entirely extensive to a fully intensive method of farming and makes possible a gradual transformation during which the fellah retains partly his extensive mode of cultivation while at the same time going in for irrigated crops on the remaining portion of his lands."

The system so described fits in better with the facts of actual development (for instance, of Arab farming in the coastal belt where surplus lands have been made available for Jewish settlement) than the abstract presentation of two extreme types.

Cost of Jewish and Arab Settlement

Para.19. The cost of settlement is here estimated at no less than LP.350-LP.400 per unit farm in the case of the Arab settler, while "in the case of a Jewish colonist, assisted by one of the Jewish organisations, who would build his house and stock his farm, the cost may be taken as LP.60 per family less." Prima facie the conclusion that it should cost less to settle a Jewish family which is known to have higher requirements for household and equipment than the Arab, is certainly surprising. The explanation of the puzzle is found in Mr. French's reliance on some anonymous "Jewish organisations" which would step into the breach and provide the balance. At the root of this reliance seems to be the general confidence in Jewish wealth to which reference is made in the covering letter. It goes without saying that an assumption that the Jewish settler, who contributes much more than the average share to public revenue from which Development expenditure will ultimately be defrayed, is not entitled to equal benefits from such expenditure cannot be allowed to stand unchallenged.

Page 10 דף   הסוכנות היהודית לארץ ישראל
THE JEWISH AGENCY FOR PALESTINE

Productivity of Settlement Expenditure

Para.20. The constructive plans which the Director of Development has in mind are here described as based on the assumption "that the funds are to be provided from a loan and that any scheme advocated must show that it will be ultimately reproductive." While in general this basis need not be disputed, it should be borne in mind that national development and State colonisation cannot always be expected to yield immediately a commercial rate of interest, but almost any close settlement scheme is ultimately reproductive, even if the returns which can be shown in the balance-sheet may fall below the current rate of profit. If, therefore, Governments have in many cases raised money for purposes of colonisation, without charging high rates to the newly-established settlers, and supplementing the sinking fund from general revenue on the assumption that the progress of the settlement will in the long run lead to an increase of public revenue which will at least make up for such a direct contribution, this policy appears, in the light of experience, economically and financially sound. Agricultural colonisation on the basis of a commercial rate of interest has hardly ever been or hardly ever will be feasible. Considerations of economic productivity vary according to whether they are viewed from the angle of private or of national economy. On the other hand, it would appear from S.R.62 that Mr. French does not in earnest expect an economic return on the capital outlay from the Arabs to be resettled.

Jewish Land Reserve

Para.21. Reference is made here to reserves of land which the Jewish Agencies held and "which they will want to colonise on lines similar to those hitherto followed." This question is dealt with in the observations to S.R. para.14 below.

Page 11

הסוכנות היהודית לארץ ישראל
THE JEWISH AGENCY FOR PALESTINE

Land Transfer Control Countrywide or Limited?

Para. 22. Among the prerequisites for a Palestine development policy which Mr. French here enumerates, he includes Government control of lands "in the areas coming under development" and Government control of water "in similar areas." This definition stands obviously in contradiction to F.R. para. 60 which states that in the Director's opinion "the only effective way in which a Land Transfer Ordinance can be used is to apply it to the whole country."

Effects of Partition and Survey

Para. 32. The importance for the general progress of Palestinian agriculture of the acceleration of survey and settlement operations and of the partition of undivided lands is not disputed. Mr. French's presentation of the problem, however, betrays a thorough misconception of the actual process at work. On the one hand, the theory that survey and settlement operations, partition of undivided lands, the establishment of local land agencies, and elaborate land legislation, must necessarily precede close settlement and economic development is not borne out by the facts. The sun will not stand still at Gibeon until the battle of the careful and punctilious administrator is fought and won. In reality, close settlement and development seems to go hand in hand with the introduction of a modern land regime, and with good administration in general. Close settlement and development promote good administration at least in the same degree as good administration promotes close settlement and development. As Mr. French himself points out, where Arabs want to plant trees or irrigate their lands they partition the mesha'. On the other hand, Mr. French ascribes to the partition of mesha' lands, and to the progress of settlement and survey operations miraculous effects which cannot be

Page 12 דף   הסוכנות היהודית לארץ ישראל
THE JEWISH AGENCY FOR PALESTINE

understood save by reference to quite different causes. An illustration of the naive over-emphasis of the effects of partition is supplied by Mr. French himself in F.R. para.33:

> "In two small tracts of the Maritime Plains, out of 250,000 dunams covered by settlement operations, one sixth of the whole area has already been devoted to citrus plantations by Arab and Jewish cultivators. One half of this total is attributed by the Settlement Officer directly to his official labours, while in the case of the other moiety progress has been helped by security of title and credit facilities, thanks to settlement."

It will be noted that Mr. French's examples are drawn from a sphere where settlement operations and Jewish colonisation happen, more or less, to go hand in hand and to coincide in time, with the proviso that while Jewish colonisation has there been in progress for some fifty years, settlement operations have been taking place for perhaps five years. The wholesome effects of settlement are fully appreciated. But agricultural revolutions are not wrought within a couple of years, as Mr. French points out elsewhere. Settlement operations were carried out, not only (under Camp and Lowick) near the Jewish colonies, but also (under Reading) near Gaza, and (again under Camp) in the Beisan sub-district, without similar results becoming manifest, and, consequently, similar conclusions being warranted. It thus becomes evident that Mr. French, in attempting to isolate the effects of partition of land on agricultural development, not only mistakes to a large extent cause for effect and a secondary factor for a prime agent, but, in particular, disregards the decisive part played in the process by the supply of capital. In many cases the prospect of obtaining the capital required for development through the sale of surplus lands was in itself a powerful stimulant to partition.

Page 13 דף

הסוכנות היהודית לארץ ישראל
THE JEWISH AGENCY FOR PALESTINE

A series of illustrations is here given of villages in the vicinity of Jaffa, some of which have not developed on account of lack of means and initiative in spite of settlement and survey operations having been completed there some time ago, while others, where these operations lagged behind, rapidly expanded their plantations.

(i) Village of Mghar. Area: 20,000 dunams. Settlement completed in October 1932. No lands sold to Jews until 1931 (and then only a few hundred dunams). This village has only some tens of dunams planted.

(ii) Village of Naaneh. Area: 15,000 dunams. Settlement completed in September 1931. Only began to sell land in the course of the last three years (2000 dunams sold up till last summer). Position similar to that of Mghar.

(iii) Village of Aqer. Settlement completed in January 1933 but started selling surplus land several years ago. Has now some hundreds of dunams of excellent groves.

(iv) Village of Zarnuqa. Settlement completed in 1930. Sold prior to settlement 6000 dunams out of a total area of 13,000. Has now about 2000 dunams of orange groves.

(v) Village of Sarafand el Kharab. Settlement completed at the same time as in Naaneh. Sold 5000 out of 10,000 dunams; position now similar to that of Zurmqa - 2000 dunams of oranges with almost every villager sharing.

(vi) Village of Kubeibeh. Settlement completed one year after Naaneh but development similar to that of Sarafand el Kharab.

(vii) Village of Bashid. Did not sell a single dunam. Settlement in process of completion. No plantations.

(viii) In the vicinity of Petah Tikwah. Villages of Yehudieh, Salama, etc. - settlement completed only two or three years ago; possess hundreds of dunams of fruit-bearing groves, planted at least six years ago. The reasons for this development are sale of surplus land, income from wages for work in Petah Tikwah and training in citriculture.

Page 14   הסוכנות היהודית לארץ ישראל
THE JEWISH AGENCY FOR PALESTINE

Land Sales and Unofficial Partitions

<u>Para.34.</u> In addition to the part admittedly played by especially energetic and interested District Officers in effecting unofficial partitions in advance of settlement, the inducement for such partitions offered by prospects of Jewish land purchases, particularly in certain districts of the coastal belt, is self-evident and well-known to anyone with local experience.

The Mukhtar

<u>Para.44.</u> The description of the incapacity of the Mukhtar as "the only local agency between the land and headquarters" is very vivid and impressive. It is particularly noteworthy that "local village records of transactions in land, or of crops, or of rights and changes therein do not exist." This statement throws light upon the value of the information which some Mukhtars supplied for the "displaced Arabs" enquiry. Although the overwhelming majority of the cases reported by them has presumably been <u>prima facie</u> dismissed as irrelevant, it is interesting that they were included in the total of claims quoted by the Director of Development.

Occupancy Rights on State Lands

<u>Para.46.</u> Mr. French here assumes, without further explanation, that occupancy rights for tenants "in fact exist in State Domains at any rate." It would be interesting to learn whether the intention is that seizure of Government lands without any authority by squatting and encroachment should be covered by these legal terms. This question is particularly in place since we are informed by S.R. para.77 that Government are now - perhaps too late - appealing in the Civil Court against the assignment of rights of occupancy "as hitherto occupancy rights are believed not to have existed under Ottoman, i.e., current law."

Page 15   הסוכנות היהודית לארץ ישראל
                                      THE JEWISH AGENCY FOR PALESTINE

Aspects of Land Control

Para.56. The problems connected with Government control of land are here divided into four heads, Mr. French adding that the two first-named subjects (Re-settlement of Landless Arabs and Close Settlement of Immigrant Jews) and the two-last named (Relief of the Congestion among the Hill Fellahin and Prevention of the Creation of Fresh Landless Arabs) have in some aspects to be considered together. This statement, in so far as it may be taken to imply any definite nexus between Jewish land purchases on the one hand and either the existence of a landless Arab class or the congestion among the hill fellahin on the other, is entirely unfounded. Although an analysis in detail of these contentions will be given under the relevant clauses, the implication as such has to be here repudiated.

Punjab and Palestine

Para.57 Mr. French here compares the task of rewsettling landless Arabs in the conditions of Palestine with the position in the Punjab Canal Colonies where "millions of acres of such waste lands were available inhabited only by nomad tribes similar to the Beduin." Although he utters a warning against being "misled by memories of pioneer colonists in vast virgin lands," his ensuing picture of the problem in Palestine is apparently tinged by his own mental associations with his past experience. The statement that here "virtually every cultivable dunam is already subject to proprietary or tenancy rights" should not be confounded with the assumption that every cultivable dunam is actually cultivated, let alone put to its best use. Mr. French's own exposition of the possibilities existing in the Huleh basin, the Beisan tract, the Jordan Valley and the Beersheba district is the best comment on the point.

הסוכנות היהודית לארץ ישראל
THE JEWISH AGENCY FOR PALESTINE

Proposals for Land Transfer Ordinance

Paras. 59 and 60. The argument for a restrictive Land Transfer Ordinance is in this paragraph again based upon the dangers of speculation. In order to obviate them a measure is proposed which is intended to apply to the whole country. If this argument is set against S.R.para.27, where the programme for the next twelve to eighteen months is outlined in the terms of a plan to re-settle, or to begin to re-settle, about 100 to 200 displaced Arabs (for whom, roughly speaking, some 3000 to 6000 dunams of irrigable, or 13,000 to 26,000 dunams of entirely unirrigated land would be required) it at once becomes clear how entirely out of proportion the proposed legislation is to the object in view. The explanation is, of course, that Mr. French wants the Transfer Ordinance for the purpose of putting the brakes on land transfers in general (allegedly in order to protect the present holder of land) no less than for the purpose of preventing speculators from getting the better of the Development Authorities. The main arguments in criticism of this proposal have been put forward in the covering letter and in the Memorandum of this Executive on the draft Land Transfer Ordinance, 1931.

Mr. French's alternatives to the countrywide application of a Land Transfer Ordinance such as he contemplates seem to be in themselves proof of his recognition that a restrictive measure of such a sweeping character could never commend itself to any Government which has the interests of economic progress at heart. He therefore suggests that the High Commissioner be given the power either to exempt from the centralised control "such districts as do not come within the ambit of any development scheme," or "to apply the Ordinance district by district as appears at the time needed." He expresses his preference for the former method because the latter, in his view, "invites protests and embitterment." There is no doubt in the mind of this Executive that if such legislation were at all contemplated, the second of the two alternative proposals will be preferable inasmuch as it would come to affect only those districts in which development operations will actually be in progress, leaving the rest of the country untrammelled by bureaucratic interference. It should be borne in mind that the High Commissioner would have to delegate his powers to subordinate officials who would not, even with the best will, be able to cope with the mass of transactions and who might, with a worse will, successfully obstruct any land transfer. If the first alternative were adopted only a few specifically-named districts would escape this danger. The apprehensions expressed by Mr. French with regard to the second alternative appear unwarranted since the operation of the measure would, as a rule, affect only strictly limited areas. Besides, the proposal should not be to apply the Ordinance "district by district" as Mr. French formulates it - implying that ultimately all districts would come to be affected - but to make it cover only those districts where development operations would actually take place.

If the object of the proposed measure were merely to prevent outside interference with development activities, this could be achieved by one of two other measures which appear to be preferable to either of Mr. French's suggestions. The one would be the control of land prices by applying the Expropriation Ordinance to development purchases as explained above; the second - a plan contemplated by Sir John Hope-Simpson - to give Government the right of pre-emption in the case of land transactions interfering with development operations. These would be the only effective safeguards which would make the powers given to the High Commissioner

Page 18   הסוכנות היהודית לארץ ישראל
                          THE JEWISH AGENCY FOR PALESTINE

regulative, limited and in no respect arbitrary, as the
Prime Minister's letter explicitly provides.

Exception should be taken to the inclusion of Jewish
Corporations among the speculators threatening the normal
course of development activities. Even if Jewish land purchasing agencies were to appear in the market as competitors
against the Government, it should be borne in mind that they
would not be doing so for purposes of speculation and profit,
but in order to throw these lands open for close settlement.
Anyone with the outlook of a coloniser should not disregard
the difference.

Private Initiative in Jewish Development

Para.61. Jewish settlement in Palestine is here described
as "effected by the Palestine Jewish Colonisation Association
and the Zionist Organisation." It should not be overlooked
that in point of fact private initiative of hundreds of
individuals and associations, large and small, has contributed its share in a very marked degree to the development
of Jewish agriculture.

The State And the Organisation of Settlers

Para.62. That "the State which undertakes the provision of
land on which the settler .... is to be placed should retain
its control of the land" would seem to be unexceptionable as
a matter of general policy. Such a policy, however, has
nothing to do with Mr. French's further argument that the
State "should not allow any third party to be interposed
between itself and the beneficiary." In various countries
where State colonisation has been carried out with some
measure of success, a representative organisation of settlers
has received official encouragement as fostering among them
the spirit of self-reliance and educating them in self-
government. If settlers organise and form one representative
body which, on the one hand, is intimately familiar with their

Page 19. הסוכנות היהודית לארץ ישראל
THE JEWISH AGENCY FOR PALESTINE

needs and feelings, and, on the other hand, undertakes to deal on their behalf with the colonising authorities, it is all to the good of colonisation. The experience of the Jewish Agency Colonisation Department in dealing with its settlers confirms this opinion, it being understood, of course, that the authority of the Department in charge is fully maintained. Should the State embark upon colonisation activities in Palestine, the autonomous organisation of the settlers and the formation of a body representing them officially vis-a-vis the Government should, if anything, be encouraged.

Developments in Beisan and Huleh

Para. 64. In discussing the possible results of free transfer of land with reference to the areas "where possibilities exist" (Beisan, Huleh, etc:) the statement is made that, unless the "chaotic conditions" which "allow each and all to buy and sell at will" be replaced by a regime under which Government would take over control of the land and water, there would be "re-created once more - and then too late - the problem of the landless Arab" with which Government is at present attempting to grapple. This façon de parler must not only be taken as supporting the inflated conception of the "displaced Arabs" issue but, more specifically, as liable to create the impression as if displacement were going on in the districts here considered. No facts are given on which such an impression could be based.

Alleged transfers of land from Arab cultivation at Beisan

Para. 65. As to Mr. French's statement that "in the Beisan area, for example, symptoms of this process may already be detected" - implying a continued process of displacement - the facts are as follows: the total of claims preferred in the Beisan District is 127 out of which 105 have been rejected, and 22 provisionally approved. These claims, however, do not refer to the Jiftlik area altogether, but to the Eastern Emek (the villages of Nuris, Naoura, Kumie, etc.). Purchases and options in the Beisan Jiftlik area affect, as a rule, surplus and waste lands owned by absentee transferees who have been awarded by Government large areas of land running into many hundreds of dunams and exceeding by far the working capacity of any bona fide cultivator.

With regard to the concluding sentences of this paragraph it should be said that they represent one of the most striking instances of Mr. French's argument liable to produce or strengthen the Arab fear complex by hinting at vague possibilities without taking the trouble of presenting facts. Mr. French says: "The next step will certainly be acquisition of the essential water-rights; resulting in, not the extrusion of the present owners from their lands, but the silent reduction of these lands to unirrigated, which in the Beisan district practically means uncultivable areas. A similar sequence of events is to be feared in the Jericho State domain." It will be observed that all this is mere conjecture. No instance is given where such events have taken place, nor can such instances, in the opinion of this Executive, be given. Nothing has actually happened and yet the reader's mind becomes imperceptibly permeated with an indefinite impression of grave dangers lurking in the dark.

Moreover, it does not appear from Mr. French's statement that in a number of important cases, if not in all, Government has not transferred property rights in water in the Beisan area to the beneficiaries of the Gher al-Mudawwara agreement, but has retained the title to the water sources. In such circumstances, Mr. French's assumption becomes even less comprehensible.

הסוכנות היהודית לארץ ישראל
THE JEWISH AGENCY FOR PALESTINE

Mr. French further refers to options alleged to have been taken in the Beisan area as "areas of a considerable proportion of certain villages where the transferees have fulfilled the conditions of the Agreement of 1921." This statement should be confronted with what Mr. French has to say with regard to the self-same transferees in F.R. para.96. There we read:

> "Some two years ago the Director of Lands reported that in no case had a transferee, even under the modified terms of the 1921 Agreement, been able from his own resources to discharge his financial obligations. The local authorities were of opinion that while the terms of the Agreement were not unduly severe, the indebtedness of the transferees prevented them from paying up the capital sums due. If a prize were offered to the cultivator who had done best, it would fall to one who still required twenty-two years to pay off the capital sum, quite apart from any interest. For villages to clear off the original capital sums due for the land, without interest, periods ranging from 45 to 143 years will be required. It is added that the 'transferees are fully aware of their obligations under the Agreement and that the land will revert to Government at the end of the fifteen years, if the total amount due is not paid, and are merely trusting that Government will, in due course, solve the problem for them.'"

The obvious conclusion is that where the transferees have fulfilled the conditions of the Agreement of 1921 they have only been enabled to do so by disposing of their surplus land at a good price.

Differentiation between Jewish and Arab settlers

Para.66. The displaced Arab here is described as "a son of the soil to be replaced on the land of his country"; the Jewish immigrant is not described as the son of a scattered and persecuted people returning as of right to the country of his National Home. This is only literary criticism, but, it is suggested, pointing to a feature of some significance.

Taken as a whole, this paragraph is truly amazing. Mr. French repeats his suggestion that a displaced Arab

Page 22

הסוכנות היהודית לארץ ישראל
THE JEWISH AGENCY FOR PALESTINE

should be placed on the soil and provided with a house, farm and stock; the Jewish immigrant, with the occupancy rights of the developed land on equal terms, while all the requisites of his home and farm would be supplied by the Jewish Organisations. This piece of discrimination has already been commented upon under Para.19. Mr. French then goes on to say: "The only differentiation here will be that Government will surely recover in due course all its expenditure from the Arab settler; while from the Jewish colonist it will recover only the cost of the developed land, leaving the Jewish bodies to recover their share." It cannot be disputed that the style of this statement is extraordinary. The effect is produced as if there actually was a "differentiation" and as if Government was likely to recover less from the Jewish than from the Arab settler. Is there, in fact, any such differentiation? Would Government not recover from either exactly what it gives him? Or would Mr. French expect the Jewish settler to pay Government for the farmhouse and equipment which he would not get from Government?

Jewish Scientist's Estimate

Para.67. If here "a prominent Jewish agricultural scientist" is invoked, credited with "some sense of possibilities", in support of the opinion that "a development policy worth the name would cover three decades", it is suggested that a development policy so described was no doubt meant to encompass a constructive programme of wide scope with regard to both Jewish and Arab agriculture of which, it is regretted, hardly a trace can be found in the present Report.

Average Size of Arab Village Household

Para.69. According to a statement in this paragraph, "enquiries show that in many Arab villages the computation of an average of five persons per family living on the lot

Page 23

הסוכנות היהודית לארץ ישראל
THE JEWISH AGENCY FOR PALESTINE

viable is now far exceeded." The provisional results of the 1931 Census, which are now available, show the opposite. The following figures for the average size of a household in certain districts, entirely or predominently Arab, are based upon these results:

Place	Average number of persons per household
Gaza	4.7
Hebron	4.9
Bethlehem	4.5
Jerusalem (without suburbs)	4.3
Ramallah	4.4
Tulkarm	4.7
Nablus	4.8
Jenin	4.8
Acca	4.5

Jewish Development in Hill Districts:

Para. 70: With regard to the hill country, Mr. French states that in some parts unrestricted transfer of land means the advance of the Jews in this area "without such noticeable progress of development as in the coastal plains, but with similar results in reinforcing the class of landless Arabs." He adds that there is further taking place a process of absorption of the Arab peasant proprietor by the Arab capitalist landlord or effendi, which may lead to the same evil "as is anticipated from excessive expropriation by the Jews". It would indeed be very interesting to find out to what facts Mr. French alludes. It is to be regretted that he does not try to adduce a shred of evidence in support of his statement. He surely cannot have meant either Kiryat Anavim (Dilb) or Atareth (Kalandiah). Dilb was purchased from the Sheikhs of Abu Gosh and a few Jerusalem effendis (Jawdat Nashashibi, Zaki Nasibi, etc.) in 1912 and 1921. The land had not been cultivated before. Part of it had turned Mahlul, and this was bought from the Government. The

Page 24

הסוכנות היהודית לארץ ישראל
THE JEWISH AGENCY FOR PALESTINE

settlement is now cultivating some 500 dunams, the remainder being rocky hillsides partly re-afforested. Kalandiah was bought before the War from fellahin, each selling a small part of his land. High prices were paid, calculated according to the number of trees and vines on each dunam; the purchase money was used for debt settlement. In the case of both settlements land was wrested from the stony wilderness and put under cultivation. In neither case has there been any displacement. (In the whole of the Jerusalem district to which practically all Jewish hill settlements belong, 71 applications of Arabs claiming to be landless were filed, of which 68 have been rejected by the Director of Development and 3 are pending). Since, however, Dilb and Kalandiah are the only two Jewish land purchases in the hill country of any appreciable size that have taken place in the course of the last twenty years, the case which Mr. French tries to make out on this point fades out altogether.

To call the progress in development in these settlements less noticeable than in the coastal plain does not seem to be quite fair. The difficulties of development are infinitely greater on the rocky hillsides, where the very humus has to be recreated by terracing, than they are in tried-out and infinitely more favourable conditions of the citrus belt. The achievements, especially in the growing of fruit and the introduction of new varieties, are, it is submitted, from the coloniser's point of view, not less striking.

Fellah Development in the Hill Districts.

Para.71: It would appear that with regard to the hill districts the real danger in the mind of Mr. French was the absorption of the peasant proprietor by the effendi or Arab

הסוכנות היהודית לארץ ישראל
THE JEWISH AGENCY FOR PALESTINE

capitalist landlord. This, at any rate, would be the only explanation suggesting itself for the statement that "if the process of dispossession continues, in another three or four decades the Arab peasant proprietor will become almost extinct". Although prima facie such a prophecy sounds highly exaggerated, it should be clear that if such a process of wholesale absorption of the hill fellahin by effendis is really going on, it must be the product of economic forces, and the remedy against it should be sought not in restrictive legislation but in a programme of constructive relief which would enable the hill fellah to hold his own. Attention may here be drawn to the following passage from Dr. Ruppin's memorandum:

> "In the hill districts in which approximately two-thirds of all the Palestine fellahin are to be found, the plan of co-ordination between the settlement of Jews and the transition of the Arabs to intensive cultivation would not, for the time being, seem feasible. Jewish colonisation has so far to a large extent been based upon the application of modern agricultural machinery which suits only the conditions of the plains. In the hills, where manual labour plays a more important part in cultivation, we have not yet worked out an adequate technical method. The Jews, therefore, do not for the time being purchase land in this region. A reform of fellah farming in the hill tracts, where water for irrigation purposes is scarce, must aim at an improvement and increase of livestock and draught animals and the planting of fruit trees which need no artificial irrigation (olives, figs, vines, apples, pears, apricots, etc.). The fellah has so far planted only few fruit trees because it takes at least four years until such a tree bears fruit and he has found it difficult to incur the cash outlay required (seedlings, fencing, etc.) and for a number of years to forego the crop yield from the area to be planted. If, however, he were supplied with seedlings from a Government nursery, either free of charge or on an instalment basis, and granted a special planting credit of LP.4 to LP.5 per dunam in order to make up for the deficiency in income resulting from crops on the area put under fruit trees, this might prove a strong stimulant for him to plant. Such planting credits,

Page 26 דף   הסוכנות היהודית לארץ ישראל
                                        THE JEWISH AGENCY FOR PALESTINE

just as the loans for the purchase of better livestock and poultry and the irrigation of vegetable plots, should be given through the medium and under the supervision of local co-operative societies. With a credit of LP.30 - LP.40 per family fairly good results would probably be achieved. The loan might be repaid in 15 to 30 yearly instalments plus a low interest, repayment to begin with the bearing of fruit."

Further reference to the problem is made under S.R. para.123.

Development in the Maritime Plain.

Para.72: This is one of the pivotal paragraphs of the First Report. The conclusion is here reached that "in the maritime plains where the settlement of the Jews is most marked, some restriction of free transfers of land from Arab to Jew is also highly desirable." This observation does not appear among the specific recommendations of the Reports. Moreover, it is, in a certain sense, contradicted by S.R.Para.45, where Mr. French states that "the coastal plain is being actively developed for citrus fruit growing, and in my opinion the rate of progress will probably continue to be fully as rapid as the circumstances warrant." Mr. French seems here to have resigned himself to the recognition that no restrictive measures are likely to commend themselves to Government with regard to the coastal plain, which has in recent years been the main scene of Palestine's agricultural development, pushing forward with remarkable force and changing completely the face of that part of the country.

Since, however, on this occasion the control of land transfers is no longer argued from the point of view of danger or interference with development operations, but by reference to the necessity of protecting the native cultivator - and this just with an eye to the coastal

Page 27   דף

הסוכנות היהודית לארץ ישראל
THE JEWISH AGENCY FOR PALESTINE

plain - it is necessary to describe in some detail the real process of development which is going on in that region and in the analysis of which Mr. French has so distinctly failed. The development of the whole Sharon Plain, from Rehoboth up to the new P.I.C.A. colonies in Samaria, which has resulted in the opening of these tracts for intensive cultivation and close settlement, has not only not brought about any noticeable displacement of Arab cultivators but has caused a striking development of fellah citrus growing in holdings of the "intermediate type". According to the data collected by the Tel Aviv Office of the PICA, the area of orange groves laid out by Arab smallholders in villages near Jaffa with the proceeds of the sale of surplus land to Jews, was conservatively estimated in 1929 at 10,000 dunams. It should be noted that this whole process is a feature of recent growth. Only ten years ago there was no fellah citriculture in Palestine.

The case of the following villages may serve as an illustration of this development:

(1) In the village of Safriyeh, which sold part of its lands to various individuals through the Bnei Benyamin Bank, twenty fellahin planted an average of 30 dunams each, or a total of not less than 600 dunams.

(2) In the village of Sarafand al Kharab, about one-half of which was sold to Rishon, Ness Ziona and Beer Yaacov, thirty-two peasants planted between them 1032 dunams. In many of these groves up-to-date electric irrigation plants had been put up and the current of the Palestine Electric Corporation is in use. In addition, 1120 dunams were planted by four wealthier landowners who had sold part of their land to the Anglo-Palestine Bank, the Jewish National Fund, and other Jewish organisations.

(3) In the village of Zarnuga, 31 villagers planted 1176 dunams with the proceeds of the sale of land to Rehoboth. A number of them received the price of land partly in the form of motors and pumps in the selection of which they consulted the Jewish orange growers of Rehoboth. In some cases even the deep ploughing in preparation for planting was carried out with Jewish tractors, and expert

advice was liberally given.

(4) In the village of Qubeibeh, 14 fellahin planted 670 dunams of orange groves. In this case, however, a good part of the money went to various brokers of the effendi type who out of their profits and commission again planted groves in the neighbourhood.

It is of interest to note that not only did the fellahin use the proceeds of these land transactions for buying machinery and planting oranges, but in many cases young men from Jewish colonies were employed in laying out the groves and, later on, in grafting the trees; even the budwood was to a large extent supplied from Jewish groves in the neighbourhood. The total planted by 1929 in the Arab villages of the Rishon-Rehoboth block, in addition to what was planted by effendis, was over 4,000 dunams. At least an equal area had by that time been planted by fellahin in the Petach-Tikvah area.

As to the Sharon block, the following illustrations may give a picture of what has been and is taking place there.

(1) The village of Sheikh Muwannas. Area 19,000 dunams, of which 7000 are Wakf. Out of the miri land 1500 dunams was sold to Jews since 1924. Prior to that year part of the land of the villages was being left untilled. Methods of cultivation were primitive - an Arab plough drawn by bullocks or a camel; The normal annual rental was 2 to 3 Piastres per dunam. Those who grew vegetables by the Yarkon (Auja) River irrigated them either by primitive canals or from barrels; The income from a dunam of vegetables was £6 to £8 a year: There were no plantations excepting an orange grove of about 200 dunams owned by one family.

Between 1924 and 1932 the village underwent a complete transformation. A number of the fellahin sold part of their land to Jews and invested the proceeds in orange groves; A list of hand shows groves varying from 10 to 125 dunams owned by villagers. All of them have enlarged the areas under vegetables by means of modern pumping installations, which enabled them to cultivate up to 80 dunams and more where formerly only 10 dunams could be managed. They also began to use chemical fertilisers with the result that yields have been rising. At present a dunam of vegetables brings in £20 to £25 a year. The rental per dunam of land leased for growing cereals or melons has risen to 200-300 mils, while payments in kind have given way to cash payments.

The vegetables found a ready market at Tel-Aviv and Jaffa, as well as in the colonies of Petach-Tikvah, Herzliah and Ir Shalom. A number of villagers make at present their living as vegetable dealers and some of them have in their turn begun to lay out orange groves of their own. The total area under vegetables in this village amounts to 2000 dunams, all irrigated by modern plant and worked by European ploughs and other implements. All lands without exception are now cultivated. Not only is there no unemployment in the village - those who have no land of their own being steadily employed as labourers - but bedouin and villagers from the neighbourhood are attracted by the opportunities of work available.

All along, housing conditions have been improving: new houses being continually put up to take the place of dilapidated buildings. The sanitary position, as measured by infant mortality and the incidence of malaria, is also showing marked progress thanks, inter alia, to the draining of the Birkat Katuriya swamp (on the lands of the neighboring village of Jalil) which has been carried out by the American Zion Commonwealth.

It goes without saying that the proximity of the village to Tel-Aviv and Jaffa and the good communications provided through the regular motor-bus services connecting Tel-Aviv with the neighbouring Jewish colonies have contributed in a large degree to the relative prosperity of Sheikh Muwannas. In former times a whole day would be spent in carrying the local produce to the town market.

(2) The Arab al-Auja lands. This is a special case in so far as the 20,000 dunams comprised in this tract belonged to the head family of a Bedu tribe (Abu Kishk). Half of this area was sold to Jews and served for the establishment of the three smallholders' settlements of Ein Hai, Hadar and Ramataim. The proceeds of the sale were used by Sheikh Shakir Abu Kishk and his brothers (a) to settle their debts and mortgages, amounting to £10,000; (b) to plant an orange grove of 145 dunams; (c) to rebuild their residence; (d) to lay out by the Yarkon River two vegetable fields of 70 and 40 dunams respectively. The whole tribe benefitted from the transaction, nearly all using the gratuities paid to them to replace their tents by houses or huts. Means were also found after the sale for the establishment of a school.

The whole area is at present cultivated, supporting, in addition to the newly-established Jewish colonies, an Arab population of 1007 souls according to the 1931 census while ten years earlier the whole population was much smaller.

Page 30 דף

הסוכנות היהודית לארץ ישראל
THE JEWISH AGENCY FOR PALESTINE

Some of the Beduin are also working as hired labourers in orange groves, Jewish and Arab. Formerly, drinking water used to be drawn by the Beduin directly from the river where the herds and cattle were also being watered, with all the harm for the tribe's health. Since wells were drilled for irrigation, Sheikh Shakir distributes water from those wells to the whole tribe. The state of health has considerably improved.

(3) The village of Miska contains an area of 16,000 dunams in one block, between Kalkilieh and the sea, about one half of which is Musha'. Practically every villager of Miska has a share in this tract, so that no question of rent or payment of a portion of the produce arises. Out of the partitioned half of the land about 2,500 dunams were sold to Jews, most of it by the villagers themselves with the exception of a few hundred dunams sold by Omar Eff. El Bitar of Jaffa and the sons of Musa Kazim Pasha al Husseini, and served for the establishment of the estates of Gan Haim and Kalmaniah. The portion of the land sold small as compared to other villages. The development of Miska is, also relatively, slow. The population was 433 according to the census of 1922 and 635 according to the recent census. With the proceeds of the sale, again, debts were settled and olive groves planted and farming methods improved. In the past, it is true, there were already small plots planted with trees, but the main development has taken place in the course of the last few years.

Here again the same features may be observed - people benefitting by the market for vegetables, eggs and poultry created by Jewish settlements, part of them eking out their income by working for wages in the neighbouring orange groves, the improvement of health conditions, better education facilities and an improved water supply.

A survey village by village of the district in which the typical coastal plain development has been going on - a survey such as Mr. French himself, in accordance with S.R.39, promised to undertake in the autumn of 1932 - would result in a monotonous repetition of the same set of characteristics. This applies, for example, to such villages as Bir-Adas, Jalil, Al-Haram, Kufr Abush, Um Khalid, Kufr Saba, Tireh, Azzun, Taiba Tahta, etc.

Practically in every village where land was sold there are people who were not affected by the transfer; others who have retained sufficient land for their

Page 31 הסוכנות היהודית לארץ ישראל
THE JEWISH AGENCY FOR PALESTINE

maintenance in the village; others still, who moved elsewhere and again established themselves on the land; a number who changed their occupations without being any the worse for the change; and a residue, whose position appeared to have deteriorated.

As to the extent of this deterioration called "displacement", the following official figures characterise the situation:

Village	Claims Filed	Rejected	Provisionally Accepted
Kufr Saba	37	33	4
Miska	54	54	-
Um Khalid	91	73	18
Azzun	53	52	1
Tireh	26	26	-
Taiba Tahta	30	30	-
Qaqun	14	14	-

It follows that out of the 305 claims preferred in the seven villages enumerated, which represent the bulk of claims put forward in the area of Jewish development in the Sharon, only 23 have been found to have any basis in fact. In the area of these villages about 50,000 dunams passed into Jewish hands. It may be left to the judgment of any unbiassed investigator whether this extent of dislocation is or is not overwhelmingly outweighed by the achievements described.

A few more data relating to the new PICA colonies in Samaria where a similar process may be observed:

(1) Pardess Hannah. Prior to the purchase of this tract by the PICA the lands were partly waste and partly marshy. As much as was cultivated was put for the winter under melons or kursan. The better part of the inhabitants left the land

הסוכנות היהודית לארץ ישראל
THE JEWISH AGENCY FOR PALESTINE

before it was purchased by the PICA on account of malaria. After the purchase the sellers partly moved into town (Tul Karm and Haifa) where they bought houses, partly to new land holdings in Transjordan and Syria. A group of people of Circassian and Bosnian origin, settled on the land by the Turkish Government, returned to Anatolia.

(2) Fukra. Sold by Beduin graziers. Part of the land had in the past been used for winter crops, the remainder for pasture. The former occupants stayed in the district, partly as workers in the newly laid out orange plantations and at Hederah, partly as dairymen, purchasing improved stock and selling dairy produce.

(3) Sindyana. Surplus land of the village sold by fellahin. Most of the land had in the past been untilled on account of lack of means. The yields were very unsatisfactory because of the marshy character of the soil prior to drainage. The sellers remained in the village, using the proceeds of the sale in a way similar to that practised in the Sharon block.

An illustration from the Jordan Valley, near the Lake of Tiberias.

At present, Arab villagers lead here a precarious existence by growing cereals. Owing to scanty rainfall they can only grow winter crops. For lack of means they do not go in for large scale irrigation and intensive farming. The recurrent droughts threaten them continually with starvation. In those cases where they find a purchaser with an eye to the potential value of the land under irrigation, they can, with the price received for one dunam, buy two or three dunams across the Lake in the Syrian territory, where better rainfall permits of the growing of both winter and summer crops, and, in addition, pay off their debts.

The economic mechanism of the process of development which is taking place in the maritime plain as a result of the coordination of Jewish settlement activities and Arab transition to methods of intensive cultivation is described by Dr. Ruppin in the following instructive analysis:

Dr. Ruppin's Scheme

He assumes for the sake of illustration a village of a cultivable area of 10,000 dunams, of which (according to the conditions actually prevailing in the coastal zone) about 5,000 are capable of irrigation, including 2,000 dunams suitable for citrus. This village, it is further assumed,

Page 33 דף   הסוכנות היהודית לארץ ישראל
THE JEWISH AGENCY FOR PALESTINE

sells 3000 dunams, so that the average area of a holding which was 95 dunams prior to the sale (the actual average in the Maritime Plain) decreases to 67 dunams, of which 19 would be irrigated after the sale.

The Arab cultivators would utilise these remaining 67 dunams according to the following scheme:-

For citrus	3 dunams
" vegetables, fodder and reserve for additional plantations in the future	16 "
" cereals	47 "
" building plot, garden, etc.	1 "
	67 "

Out of the sale of 28 dunams at an average price of LP.4.500 per dunam, the fellah would have received about LP.125, which amount would be used to effect the transition of his farm from extensive to intensive cultivation, based upon the smaller area.

This amount would be invested in some such way as the following:

LP.30	to repay the debts (which according to Sir John Hope Simpson reach an amount of LP.30 on an average).
LP.30	for his share in proper irrigation plant for the irrigation of six dunams.
LP.36	as contribution to his upkeep during the three years before his plantation bears fruit. (It is assumed that the manual labour in the grove must be carried out by the fellah himself).
LP.30	cost of deep ploughing of three dunams and of planting them with grafted trees which would bear fruit at the end of three years.

The following is a comparison between the income and expenditure in a fellah's holding under the former system of cultivation and under the proposed scheme during

Page 34 דף

הסוכנות היהודית לארץ ישראל
THE JEWISH AGENCY FOR PALESTINE

the initial period after planting.

I. Old System (95 dun.)	II. New System (67 dun.)
Income from 95 dun. cereals after deducting the expenses for draught animals, at PT.40 per dunam........ LP.38	**Income** from 3 dunams of oranges......LP.0.-
Income from one cow, poultry, etc..... 5	**Income** from 3 dunams irrigated (vegetables and fodder at LP.2);. 6.-
LP.43	**Income** from 60 dunams of cereals at LP.40 per dun.... 24.-
Expenditure.	Contribution to the upkeep (1/3 of LP.36) (see above).......... 12.-
18% interest on LP.30 debts......LP.5.400	LP.42.-
Taxes, purchase and repair of agricultural implements...... 4.500	**Expenditure.**
LP.9.900	Taxes and repair of agricultural implements....LP. 6.-
Balance for upkeep, clothing, etc.......... 33.100	Balance 36.-
LP.43.000	LP.43.000

III.

The New Farm after the Grove Bears Fruit.

Net Income from 3 dunams of oranges at LP.10.....LP.30

" " from 3 dunams of irrigated land placed under vegetables and fodder............................. 6

Income from 60 dunams of cereals at PT.40 per dunam.......................... 24

LP.60.-

Expenditure.

Taxes and repair of agricultural implements..................... LP. 8.-

Balance...................... LP.52.-

During the first three years the fellah's income gradually increased from LP.33.100 up to LP.36, and at the

הסוכנות היהודית לארץ ישראל
THE JEWISH AGENCY FOR PALESTINE

end of these three years to LP.52. Moreover, it is left to the fellah to increase the net return of his holding by developing into citrus plantations the additional three dunams which were temporarily put under vegetables. This would result in an additional net income of LP.24, i.e., an increase of the total earnings to LP.76. The fellah would be able further to add to this income by extending the area under irrigation from 6 to 19 dunams.

On the 3000 dunams sold out of a total area of 10,000 dunams, including 1200 dunams irrigable, about 100-150 Jewish families would in the meantime be settled and placed in a position to make a satisfactory living.

Applying this reasoning to the whole of the Maritime Plain a scheme would emerge which is here presented in its broad outline. The four million dunams which make up what is termed "the coastal plain" are composed as follows:

1. Light irrigable soil (particularly suitable for citrus) 500,000 dunams
2. Heavier irrigable soil (less fit for oranges but suitable for grape-fruit, vegetables, etc.) 750,000 "
3. Unirrigable but suitable for cereals 1,250,000 "
4. Uncultivable (sand dunes, etc.) 1,500,000 "

Out of the cultivable 2,500,000 dunams (1, 2 and 3) the following approximate areas are at present in Jewish and Arab possession, respectively:

	Arab	Jewish
Orange plantation	80,000	80,000
Irrigable land fit for oranges	280,000	60,000
Irrigable land more fit for grape-fruit, vegetables, etc.	700,000	75,000
Unirrigable land fit for cereals	1,040,000	185,000
Total:	2,100,000	400,000

Page 36

הסוכנות היהודית לארץ ישראל
THE JEWISH AGENCY FOR PALESTINE

It follows that each of the 22,000 fellah families living in the coastal plain has at its disposal approximately 95 dunams of cultivable land, partly irrigable. The possibilities of irrigation, however, are exploited either in a very limited degree or, as is the case of many villages outside the sphere of Jewish settlement, not at all. The policy suggesting itself in the light of this analysis to anyone anxious to harness economic forces and natural potentialities for the development of the Maritime Plain is self-explanatory. Some such policy seems to have been in the mind of Mr. C.F. Strickland who in his Report on Agricultural Co-operation in Palestine expresses the following opinion:

> "There is in general much to be said for encouraging the fellah to sell a part of his irrigable land through the agency of the Loan Fund Committee, and to repay the reasonable claims of his creditors from the sale of such proceeds and develop the remainder of his irrigable land with any surplus remaining and with such additional money as the Fund will advance."

To reach the conclusion, in the name of Development, that "in the Maritime Plains, where the settlement of Jews is most marked, some restriction of free transfers of land from Arab to Jew is highly desirable" is to work in an exactly opposite direction to the aim professed.

Small Cultivator in Citrus Belt

Para.73. Mr. French, again referring to orange growing in the Maritime Plain, maintains that "the chief risk - an ever-present one - that the progress of comparatively large growers, backed by plentiful financial resources, which weight the scale so heavily against the independent small Arab proprietor, will mean the entire and permanent displacement of the latter from the soil." For the time being the process is the other way round. Orange cultivation by

הסוכנות היהודית לארץ ישראל
THE JEWISH AGENCY FOR PALESTINE

Arab smallholders, the outcome of recent development, is at present steadily expanding.

Alleged Need of Restrictive Ordinance

Para.74. Mr. French's ceterum censeo with regard to the alleged need for a Land Transfer Ordinance collapses in the light of a closer analysis of the dangers he depicts.

Punjab Land Alienation Act

Para.75. With regard to the usefulness of the Land Alienation Act in force in the Punjab opinions do not seem to be unanimous by any means. In point of fact, thirty years after its coming into force in the Punjab it was initiated only on a very modest scale elsewhere. The Royal Commission on Agriculture in India, which undertook a thorough study of the problem on the spot, did not find itself in a position to recommend a sweeping extension of this Act to other provinces. (Cf. Report of the Royal Commission pp.421/422).

State Control of Water Supply

Paras.77 to 89. These paragraphs as well as S.R. para.14 deal with proposals for a government control of the water supply. It is not proposed to enter here into a detailed discussion of the problem which forms at present the subject of special consideration in connection with the proposed Irrigation Ordinance. Jewish experts have actively co-operated on the Irrigation Sub-Committee of the General Agricultural Council in working out and amending the draft Ordinance and it is assumed that the Jewish Agency will have an opportunity of expressing its views on such legislation as may be proposed.

In the meantime, it should be borne in mind that the problem which the present generation in Palestine is facing is the fullest possible development of the country's potential water resources rather than the mere control or

Page 38 דף   הסוכנות היהודית לארץ ישראל
THE JEWISH AGENCY FOR PALESTINE

the distribution of existing supplies, important as that may be in itself. It may be noted that the year 1932 has witnessed the tapping of sub-surface supplies in various parts of the country by means of deep drilling which were not foreseen by those inclined to err on the side of undue pessimism (Karkur, Yavneel, Yagur, Tel Adashim). For a pioneer settler's story of water development without official interference reference may be made to the following vivid account supplied by Mr. Smilansky:

> "Forty years ago, when we started planting oranges, the wells then existing were as a rule yielding 10 to 15 cubic metres per hour and it was not possible to work on without a break so as not to pump up sand together with the water and thereby undermine the well shaft. The upper level of Palestine's water table being characterised by a strong admixture of sand, the area which under technical conditions then prevailing could be served by one well had to be kept within narrow limits, not to exceed 10 to 15 dunams. As there was no official control to ensure that no more than a proper quantity of water be drawn, that the well shaft be not exposed to any risks and that the area of the grove should not exceed the working capacity of the well, we went in for planting larger groves.

> "When it become clear that the supply was inadequate we were forced to find a way, and, necessity being the mother of invention, we hit upon the device of using a filter which prevented the pumping up of the sand. This enabled us to pump water day and night, the wells did not collapse while the orchards grew in size. Thus it came about that even the working capacity of the filter-equipped wells was outgrown by the size of the plantation. There was still no control and necessity again compelled us to further exertion. We dug more deeply and resorted to the use of pipes of a wider diameter. We put up more powerful engines and pumps. Little by little we reached a yield of 60 and 70 cubic metres per hour, as a rule, and 100 to 150 cubic metres with particularly good machinery.

> "Today we are irrigating 200 dunams from one well. If we are asked: What would have happened if by chance you had not succeeded to find a sufficient water supply in time to save your enlarged plantation? Our reply would be: What does it matter? Had not

הסוכנות היהודית לארץ ישראל
THE JEWISH AGENCY FOR PALESTINE

orange growing in Palestine in any case remained within its narrow confines if we had not ventured into more daring experiments? Unless you run a risk, you cannot expect to succeed."

Legislation by Regulations

Para. 91. It is here suggested that "much travail and confusion would be saved if legislation concerning development and land settlement were in the future to be directed to the embodiment of the main principles, leaving the rest to rules and regulations duly gazetted under the Ordinance." If the term "duly gazetted" simply implies publication after approval by the High Commissioner, then such a procedure, which is all too usual with regard to rules and regulations, is doubly dangerous in a country where there is no public control over the Administration. Even in England there is a continuous complaint about encroachment of legislative privilege by departmental orders and regulations. In a country like Palestine, the opportunity offered to the population of commenting upon proposed legislative measures cannot be renounced.

Beisan Lands

Paras. 93 to 98. The special case of the Beisan lands dealt with in these paragraphs and in Appendix III(a) has been referred to in the covering letter and, in greater detail, in the Memorandum submitted by this Executive to Sir John Hope Simpson. In supplementing our statements there made, attention is invited to the following:

In reporting to the Permanent Mandates Commission on the question of State lands in Palestine, in June 1926, the late M. Freire d'Andrade stated:

"If the Arab farmers have received larger plots than they can cultivate, it will be open to the Jewish organisations to acquire such surplus lands and the Mandatory Power will certainly afford them every facility in accordance with the provisions of the Mandate."

Page 40 דף   הסוכנות היהודית לארץ ישראל
THE JEWISH AGENCY FOR PALESTINE

Huleh Basin

<u>Paras. 99 to 107.</u> In these paragraphs the problem of the Huleh area and concession is discussed. This Executive has nothing to add on this subject to its observations embodied in the memorandum submitted to Sir John Hope Simpson.

In para.107, however, Mr. French, referring to further settlement prospects in the Huleh, remarks that "settled as Government tenants, a leavening of Jewish colonists in this tract would tend to an acceleration of the desired development after the marshes have been drained." This statement is indeed illuminating. Jewish colonisation on Huleh lands does not appear as a purpose in itself, still less as one of the primary purposes of the Mandate, let alone as a positive obligation of the Government. It is supposed to serve as a device (to be applied in small doses only) for the stimulation and enlightenment of Arab agriculturists. The area of Jewish settlement is to be used as a Government experimental farm or demonstration field to promote the agricultural progress of others. If one chooses at all to enter into the field of ideology, this conception of Mr. French appears as a new (Oriental) edition of the old (European) "mission theory" of the liberal era which bade the Jews be a "light unto the nations." It is worth pointing out that out of the failure and defeat of that theory there was borne the idea of Jewish self-emancipation which is the very essence of Zionism.

History of Beisan Tract

<u>Appendix III(a) Para.3.</u> Mr. French states here that "in general it may be said that the tenants who were cultivating the Beisan area in 1921 were the original owners or descendants of the original owners of these lands." This statement is seriously called in question by the general tenor of the

Page 41. דף   הסוכנות היהודית לארץ ישראל
                                THE JEWISH AGENCY FOR PALESTINE

introductory paragraphs of the Appendix. The picture of
the Beisan area as here presented is composed of such
elements as fellahin "living in mud hovels", "if not themselves cattle-thieves - ready to harbour these and other
criminals", neighbouring Beduin making the fellahin's lot
"an alternation of pillage and blackmail", "wild and lawless
by nature constantly at feud with their neighbours on both
sides of the Jordan", "raids and highway robberies forming
their staple industry, while such cultivation as the Beduin
were capable of filled in the intervals of more exciting
occupation", "the individual plots of cultivation, such as
it was, changing hands annually", "raids by marauding
tribes and exactions by corrupt tax collectors." That in
such conditions of anarchy unchecked "the original owners
or descendants of the original owners of these lands" should
have been able to maintain settled rights of occupancy in
a stable succession of generations sounds, at the least,
surprising. As far as historical knowledge goes, the area
has during the last few decades been recurrently swept by
raiding tribes, destroying villages and again and again
reducing cultivated land to wilderness.

Status of Beisan Occupiers

Para.11. Mr. French here tries to support by legal argument
his contention that the ab antiquo rights to the land of the
occupiers of the Beisan tract were, at least tacitly, admitted by Government. He refers to the wording of the
indenture of the Ghor el Muduwwara Agreement which defines
the settlement of rights as "permanent". As against that,
Article 13 of the Agreement itself should be quoted:

> "13. If the transfer price (Badal Tatweeb)
> is not fully paid by the end of the
> fifteenth year, the transferee shall
> be deemed to have forfeited his right
> to his title deed and to have been a
> tenant of the Government. He shall pay

Page 42   הסוכנות היהודית לארץ ישראל
THE JEWISH AGENCY FOR PALESTINE

to the Government a rental of ten per cent on the gross yield of the area cultivated during the fifteen years, less the total of the instalments of the transfer price which he shall have paid; and he shall forfeit any interest prescribed in Article 12 which he may have paid on any instalment. He shall, however, retain his rights to any buildings erected or trees planted by him on the land, subject to the power of the Government to purchase the same from him at a fair compensation to be determined by arbitration."

Since Mr. French seems anxious to invest the claims of the Beisan occupiers with a halo of legal sanctity, it is necessary to point out that the text of this article clearly defines them as what they in fact are, namely, beneficiaries of an act of grace on the part of Government.

"Wealthy Corporations

Para.12. If in referring to the Beisan cultivators, Mr. French says that "they were not backed by wealthy corporations, and they were compelled to rely in their struggle with nature on their own impoverished resources, unassisted by any outside help, technical or financial", this allusion to the supposed opulence of Jewish colonising agencies is dealt with at some length in paras. 20 and 21 of the covering letter.

Progress in Beisan Villages Reported

Para.15. Reference is here made, on the authority of the Chairman of the Demarcation Commission, to the "remarkable progress" noticeable in a few of the villages of the Beisan area "considering the short time which has elapsed since the parcellation of the lands." It would have been greatly appreciated if more precise information had been given as to which villages this statement refers to. The growing of bananas on scattered plots by capitalist planters, Arab, German or British, has unfortunately very little to do with the agricultural development of the land retained by the transferees.

Page: 43

THE JEWISH AGENCY FOR PALESTINE
הסוכנות היהודית לארץ ישראל

SUPPLEMENTARY REPORT.

Summary of Displaced Arabs Enquiry

Para.7: Mr. French's forecast concerning the eventual result of the displaced Arabs enquiry as given here is that while Jewish estimates range from 800 to 1200 he "puts the figure between 1000 and 2000." To summarise once more the actual position, out of 3188 claims, 570 have been provisionally accepted and 2520 rejected, with 83 pending.

Surplus Land

Para.8: Mr. French's theory of surplus land does not acknowledge that lands other than virgin or waste lands should be genuinely termed "surplus" lands. Let us disregard for the moment that in fact there have been and still are in Palestine, especially along the seashore, here and there tracts of soil capable of development which could not and are not to this day worked at all by fellahin, while other tracts have been reclaimed by drainage. Theoretically speaking, however, the problem of surplus land belongs to the category in which we have to class the problems of over-population and over-production. Economic science knows — and has known for a long time past — that in the use of such terms as "over-population" or "over-production" the difference between an "absolute" and a "relative" application of the term has not to be lost sight of. Over-production of shoes does not necessarily mean that mankind is over-supplied with shoes; but only that in relation to the existing purchasing power there are more shoes in the market than can profitably be disposed of. A statement that a country is over-populated does not mean that a given number of inhabitants cannot by any means be supported on its territory; but only that in relation to the present economic and technical organisation there is a pressure of the population on the means of subsistence. Similarly, in speaking of surplus lands, we have not in mind absolute surplus, but surplus in relation to the carrying capacity of the land, if the technical and economic equipment at present available were properly applied in its development. It may be very convenient indeed to dismiss this usage of the term as a result of a "confusion of thought and imperfect acquaintance of the facts".

The carrying capacity of land.

Para.9: In the light of the foregoing remarks Mr. French's statement that there "are at the present time no cultivable lands at all which are surplus, in the sense that they are not already subject to cultivation or occupancy by tenants or owners" calls for examination. The term "subject to cultivation or occupancy" is very elastic and "relative indeed. If there are tracts (such as in the Haifa Bay area and elsewhere) capable of being used for plantation, suburban vegetable gardening, or similar purposes, on which a few score half-starved Bedu families are at present grazing goats and cutting reed-grass (hilfe) - the returns of the latter industry being estimated at 3 to 5 pence per dunam a year - it is difficult to see how it can be maintained, especially from the point of view of a Director of Development, that these tracts are "subject to cultivation".

Every Jewish settlement in the country may serve to illustrate the point at issue. At Rehoboth an area of 20,000 dunams supports 4,000 Jews and 1,000 Arabs; on the "Sidra" tract near Rehoboth, where the soil is even

הסוכנות היהודית לארץ ישראל
THE JEWISH AGENCY FOR PALESTINE

better, 7,000 dunams support 150 souls of a Bedu tribe - a possible "surplus" of at least 6,000 dunams. At Petach Tikvah, 30,000 dunams support 8,000 Jews and 2,000 Arabs. A tract of 20,000 dunams near Jalil supports 300 persons only - a possible "surplus" of 18,000 dunams. To cite a case from a different zone of settlement, in the Nuris Block (Eastern Emek) where prior to the purchase of the land by the Jewish National Fund an Arab population of 39 tenant families found its livelihood, there are at present, in the villages of Ain Harod, Tel Yosef, Kfar Yehezkiel, Geva, Hugim, Beit Alfa and Hefzi-Ba, according to the last census, over 1500 souls settled on a Jewish standard of living.

Another illustration of major importance is Wadi Hawareth. The Shaw Report puts this area at 30,826 dunams (it is, in fact, considerably larger) and its settled population at about 1200 souls. According to the Report the tract was used for grazing and, in part, for melon-growing. The tithe assessment for 1928 estimates the value of its yield as "at least £P.7,000". As far as expert opinion goes, not less than half the area in question is good plantation land. Divided rationally into small holdings of 20 dunams each, the Wadi Hawareth area can and will support 1500 families of settlers (about 7,500 souls) or more than six times the present population, on a European standard of living, and not in destitution as to-day. Adding the population which will indirectly derive its livelihood from this land, such as workers, artisans, teachers, merchants, physicians, chauffeurs, and officials, the number should be three times as large, or 4,500 families, which is about 20,000 souls. The 15,000 dunams of plantation land may yield no less than £300,000

Page 46   הסוכנות היהודית לארץ ישראל
                 THE JEWISH AGENCY FOR PALESTINE

or £P. 20 per dunam, instead of less than five shillings per dunam as in 1928. The revenue of the Government from the plantation area only can therefore be increased eighty-fold. To the figure of £P.300,000 should be added the proceeds of dairying, poultry-raising and vegetable growing on the remainder of the area. Whether, in such circumstances, the Wadi Hawareth land is now rightly considered a relative surplus area should be left to the judgment of those interested in the intensive development of Palestine.

The Mechanism of Development.

Para.12: As against the "simple arithmetic" used by Mr. French in describing the mechanism of development on relative surplus land, we point to our observations under F.R.72 where this process is analysed not in terms of abstract calculation but on the basis of actual experience.

Fellah's Transition to intensive cultivation.

Para.13: The difficulties which the Arab fellah has to face in exchanging his traditional methods of extensive farming for the limitations imposed by intensive cultivation (as described in this paragraph) are, no doubt, real. That this process cannot be completed overnight is equally true. On the other hand, it should be kept in mind that a very large number of small-holders in the citrus zone have had a more or less extended period of training in orange growing as wage-labourers in Jewish or Arab groves. This is not an exception, to be mentioned parenthetically, ("if the means of livelihood cannot be obtained by casual labour in the neighbourhood") but to a very large extent the rule. Moreover, on Mr. French's own showing, the argument should not be in favour of an abrupt transition from the extensive type of cereal growing to the extreme type of small orange grove, but of the gradual development of intensive holding through an intermediate type of farming such as described by Dr. Ruppin. In this way, the Arab peasant would add gradually, year by year, a few more dunams to the planted area, while his income would be made up from wages for labour in a larger grove, plus the yield of a small but growing plantation, plus the return of a correspondingly decreasing area under cereals. This sort of development has been going on for years in the coastal plain without there having occurred to any one the extraordinary suggestion that Government ought to pay the fellah a maintenance allowance for five years, until his grove reaches the bearing stage, as Mr. French seems to advocate.

Jewish Land Reserve.

Para.16: Mr. French here tries to make out a case for treating the two problems of the re-settlement of landless Arabs and of Jewish colonisation not as deserving equal consideration but as if the former was the more urgent of the two. This may have seemed so to Mr. French, particularly since he was labouring under a misapprehension as regards the real dimensions of the "landless Arabs" problem. It did not appear so in the Prime Minister's letter which referred to the close settlement of Jews on the land as being "a primary purpose of the Mandate" and spoke of the larger purposes of development regarded by His Majesty's Government as the most effectual means of furthering the establishment of a National Home for the Jews.

Mr. French's argument is, inter alia, based upon the fact that Jewish organisations hold reserves of land still awaiting development. In S.R. para.53 he once more emphasises that in view of this reserve the provision of immediate aid to Jewish organisations becomes a matter of secondary importance. If the area of this land reserve is

Page 48 הסוכנות היהודית לארץ ישראל
THE JEWISH AGENCY FOR PALESTINE

correctly stated by Mr. French to be something like 40,000 dunams, it should be pointed out that in the meantime additional 10,000 dunams (at Wadi Hawareth) have been allotted out of this area to applicants of the working and middle-class type, in holdings of 20 dunams each. As to the balance, part of it has until recently been under litigation, another part has likewise been handed over to settlers, so that the remainder is essentially not large enough to justify a dilatory handling of the Jewish settlement problem.

Harrathin.
Para.23: It should be clear that the problem of the harrathin, or agricultural labourers paid in kind, mentioned in this paragtaph does not in any way come within the purview of the displaced cultivators enquiry. In every agricultural country of the world there are hired farm labourers who, strictly speaking, must be called "landless". In countries which are yet backward, such labourers are usually paid in kind. Most of them move from place to place, staying only perhaps a couple of years in any particular area. If the Government were out to provide every inhabitant of every village in Palestine with land, the problem would become inseluble - quite apart from any Jewish settlement policy. Besides, the working of larger farm units would become impossible unless a rural labourers' class were "recreated".

Immediate Development Programme.
Para.27: Mr. French's constructive contribution to the fellah's problem is a programme of re-settling, or beginning to re-settle, 100-200 "displaced Arabs" within the next twelve to eighteen months. Our opinion on this programme, standing as it does against the background of 90,000 peasant families, has been offered in para.24 of

הסוכנות היהודית לארץ ישראל
THE JEWISH AGENCY FOR PALESTINE

the covering letter.

Cattle and Implements owned by Claimants.

Para.29: In a critical remark concerning Sir John Hope Simpson's suggestion that in case the resettled Arab family will already have cattle and implements, the provision of maintenance will be unnecessary, Mr. French declares that if the person concerned "has still his cattle and implements and sufficient resources for maintenance it will seem that he will have obtained satisfactory occupation and needs no re-settlement." Mr. French's assumption is, in fact, borne out in the case of many claimants under the "displaced Arabs" enquiry.

Exclusion of Dry Farming Areas from Programme.

Para.30: The statement that the greater part of the displaced Arabs "will have to be replaced on the land under conditions of intensive cultivation", there being no sufficient land for extensive or dry-farming, can only be understood in the light of the exclusion from the scope of the Director of Development's practical recommendations of the areas eminently suitable for dry farming such as the southern region/(Negeb), Transjordan, etc., where many of the difficulties anticipated in para.31 (connected with the adaptation of the bedouin to intensive cultivation) would not arise.

Cost of Settlement compared to Thousand Families Scheme.

Para.36: The final conclusions as to the cost of resettling an Arab family on the assumptions of Mr. French's plan is here given as "£P.600 to £P.700 per family unit allowing simple interest at 5% on the outlay during the period of six years before the holding can be self-supporting", or £P.800 if the cost is charged to the registered landless families only. Without entering into any discussion of this conclusion or the data upon which it is based, it is worth

הסוכנות היהודית לארץ ישראל
THE JEWISH AGENCY FOR PALESTINE

Page 50

while confronting them with the following estimate of the cost of settlement of one family unit under the Thousand Families Plan at present in the process of execution, which is based upon a combination of wage-income and the gradual development of the settler's own farm, and which is ultimately designed to make the settler self-supporting as an independent small-holder on a European standard of life:

Unit Cost in Thousand Families Plan (area - 10 dunams).

1. A two-room house of reinforced concrete with kitchen and veranda; reinforced concrete out-buildings: stable, chicken coop, W.C. and shower . . . £P 120
2. Cow and chickens 25
3. Water installation for irrigating the plot, fencing and deep ploughing of 2½ dunam vegetable plot   25
4. Central Water Installation 30
5. For developing seven dunam oranges, including entire installation. 192

                                                       £P 392

Note:- All costs based on use of organised Jewish labour.

Reference to F.R. Para.72.

Para.45: The contradiction between the general tenor of this paragraph and that of F.R. para.72 has already been emphasised.

Marketing Prospects of Citrus Fruits.

Paras.46-51: The gloomy exposition of the dangers threatening the future of the citrus industry in connection with the problem of marketing oranges and grapefruit, would seem to hold good in an equal degree (particularly at a period of an economic world depression) in respect of every kind of goods, whether of primary production or of manufacturing industries. A certain risk is involved in the development of whatever productive resources one might attempt to tap. He who fears the wolf should not go near the forest. The reflection that the world may supply itself with all the goods it needs without having recourse to the Palestinian producer offers only slight comfort to that producer himself. To suggest, however, that he should defer the development of his production until markets had been offered ready-made to absorb his goods is to advocate a thoroughly fantastic and red-tape conception. No example is known in world economics of markets having been prepared in advance of production. Market expansion has always been the result of expansion of production. It is the pressure of the volume of goods produced that opens markets. The fall in prices following upon relative over-production in most cases opens markets. Relative over-production enforces improvements of organisation, of shipping, packing and grading, and stimulates marketing propaganda. This should not be taken as a plea against adopting all precautionary measures which may appear practicable in order to increase, as quickly as possible, the absorptice capacity of markets so as to keep pace with the gradual expansion of production, and to explore new channels of demand. As a matter of fact, Palestine growers and shippers have for some time past been engaged in such activities. It is only a plea against an attempt to check or stop development (if that were at all possible) until markets are explored. If there is anyone who puts the cart before the horse, it is Mr. French, and it is very curious indeed to find him accusing us of so erring.

In this connection attention may be drawn to the following extract from a letter of Sir John Russell, the Head of the Rothamsted Experimental Station:

> "Any forecast as to the future of the orange trade is necessarily purely hypothetical. More than anything else it depends on economic recovery in England and America. The rapid development of the trade in summer oranges, lemons and grape fruits show that western European people enjoy citrus fruits and will consume them at all times of the year. The taste is not confined to one class but is widespread: the recognition of

הסוכנות היהודית לארץ ישראל
THE JEWISH AGENCY FOR PALESTINE

> the value of the Jaffa orange is universal. My own opinion is that an improvement in the economic position would see an expanding demand for citrus fruits.
>
> The potential supply is not to be gauged entirely by acreage: some of the plantations in other parts of the world being on unsuitable stock are not likely to give full yields or high quality. "

Settlement Bank Scheme Upheld.

<u>Para.56</u>: The criticism levelled in paragraphs 56 to 59 against the proposed scheme by the Jewish Agency of a Jewish Agricultural and Settlement Bank is in no way convincing. This Executive begs to uphold its original project in full, although the discussion of the details of the scheme may, it is feared, have lost its practical value because the Development Loan Scheme has apparently been abandoned. Should Government at any time choose to resume negotiations with regard to such a scheme, a re-examination of the technical aspects of the plan submitted would be possible.

The argument that - in contra-distinction to, say, the Central Bank of Cooperative Institutions - the proposed Settlement Bank could not do what Mr. French terms "selective business" seems altogether unfounded. The same careful investigation which is made by the Central Bank into "the circumstances of the prospective borrower, not only as to the adequacy of the security he has to offer, but also as to the likelihood of his having an income sufficient to enable him to meet the interest and repayment without difficulty" can be undertaken by the Settlement Bank. There is no doubt that there could be no difficulty in finding suitable applicants among the settlers of the Jewish Agency colonies and elsewhere with whom the risk of loss would be reduced to the same minimum as in the case of similar banks. In fact,

הסוכנות היהודית לארץ ישראל
THE JEWISH AGENCY FOR PALESTINE

the class of clients to which the Settlement Bank would cater would be to a very large extent identical with the present clientele of the Central Bank.

Criticism of the Bank's Scheme Refuted.

Para. 57: The argument that the settler would have to pay £P.20 per annum, which according to our contention, he is capable of paying in interest and amortization of principal in respect of the bank's loan of £P.300, and, remaining indebted to the Jewish Agency for the balance of the original £P 700 loan, would not be able to carry the burden, is not conclusive. Neither the amount of £P.20 nor that of £P.300 are sacrosanct figures. If it should become evident that the annual instalments payable by the settlers according to their contract with the Jewish Agency are not sufficient to cover interest and amortisation of a loan of £P.300, they would have to content themselves with a smaller loan from the Bank. There is, at any rate, no reason to make the whole bank scheme hinge upon amounts adduced as mere illustration.

The contention that the settler in the Zionist colonies would not, in the circumstances described, be "a willing borrower from the Bank" shows how little Mr. French is familiar with the frame of mind of our people. The urge for a further advance in colonisation, that is, for a chance for more men to be settled on the land, is most powerful among the members of Zionist settlements and there is no doubt, that they would spare no effort in shouldering their own liabilities in order to facilitate, in the manner described in our project, the promotion of Jewish land settlement.

The last point made here by Mr. French is that in view of the fact that "the land in all Jewish Agency colonies is owned by the Jewish National Fund and is let to the settlers on long term leases with certain restrictive condi-

Page 54

הסוכנות היהודית לארץ ישראל
THE JEWISH AGENCY FOR PALESTINE

tions, notably that the land must never be occupied by a non-Jew", the Bank would, in case of foreclosure, have difficulties in finding "other suitable Jewish candidates who would be prepared to assume all the obligations of the lease and of the Jewish Agency and bank loans." It is submitted that this is a purely theoretical handicap. In practice, the number of suitable candidates - even candidates with moderate means of their own with which to make their start - has hitherto always been far in excess of the number of homesteads available. In abstracto Mr. French may be right, because every qualification limits the market. In actual fact there is not a less reasonable amount of certainty that the Bank would find a suitable man to take the defaulter's place in a Jewish National Fund settlement, than in the open market.

The Bank's Prospects of Profit.

Para.58: The statement made here by Mr. French with regard to the relative prospects of profit for the bank and of the payment of interest on its debetures - again as compared with the Central Bank - is misleading. It is not correct to assume that in the case of the Central Bank "the margin between the rates of interest paid by the Bank and charged to the borrower, available for expenses and losses, is four per cent." The Central Bank borrows money at six per cent from Barclay's to an amount, it is believed, running at times up to £50,000. Evidently, this is considered a profitable transaction - otherwise it would not be entered into - although the margin it leaves to the 8 per cent charged by the Bank for intermediate and longer-term loans is only 2 per cent. As to the money which is loaned to the Central Bank by the Palestine Economic Corporation at four per cent, this argument is not quite in point, because the Palestine Economic Corporation owns 75 per cent of the share capital of the Bank, and, accordingly, shares in the profits accruing. Furthermore, the bank sets aside, it is believed, 1½% for reserve, and to this extent the value of the share capital which the Palestine Economic Corporation owns increases from year to year. There is, of course, a difference between a principal shareholder lending money to his own institution at 4 per cent, and any ordinary lender charging the market rate.

The crux of the argument, however, is that Mr. French does not agree that business with new settlers is an advisable programme for an Agricultural Settlement Bank, "as there would be no satisfactory evidence of the settler's ability to farm his holding efficiently and to meet his loan obligations". This assumption that banking operations cannot be adjusted to the specific requirements of colonisation is as erroneous as it is out of place in a Development Report. At the same time it is true that it may hardly be possible, as already pointed out, to base State colonisation on a commercial rate of interest. On the other hand it would be highly interesting to learn how it is proposed to recover the high charges to which Mr. French refers on the outlay for the settlement of Arabs by the Development Authorities. Is not this expenditure, too, supposed to come vrom loan funds?

The settlement Bank and the Taxpayer.

Para.59: The contention that, if Government would take up debentures of a Jewish Settlement Bank it would mean "to impose extra taxation on agriculturists generally, in order to provide uneconomic credit facilities for a limited number" is, to use Mr. French's own words, "manifestly unfair". The term "uneconomic", as explained, does not reveal an adequate understanding of either the economics or the national productivity of colonisation. In Palestine, of course, unlike the Punjab, there is no Canal Company paying an annual net profit of 40% on its capital. On all ventures of State colonisation the taxpayer in general is supposed to bear taxation,

Page 56

הסוכנות היהודית לארץ ישראל
THE JEWISH AGENCY FOR PALESTINE

pro tempore benefiting only those directly concerned, but for which the whole community will in due course be recouped with compound interest in an indirect way. Furthermore, it has to be borne in mind that, although Palestine is predominantly agricultural, the percentage of taxation borne by the rural population by no means corresponds to its numbers. As far as the Jewish section of the population is concerned, they are admittedly contributing to public revenue a percentage more than double their ratio to the population.

Funds for Jewish Development Delayed.

Para.60: Even with reference to a plan of providing long term credit for Jewish agriculture which Mr. French in principle approves he does not feel satisfied "that there is sufficient justification at this stage for Government supplementing the funds already available for this purpose from other sources. The position may be different later when marketing difficulties and other obstacles to the profitable export of payable crops have been removed." In the light of this statement it does no longer appear surprising that the Jewish Agency's proposal for the establishment of a Settlement Bank with the help of Development funds should have been turned down by the author of the Report. Mr. French may rest assured that after "marketing difficulties and other obstacles to the profitable export of crops" will have been removed, there will be other, no less serious, difficulties to cope with. If Government intends to wait with the investment of development funds until a situation free of difficulties may present itself, there can be no Development policy in Palestine or elsewhere. Besides, in such a case there would be no need for public development funds, since private investment capital would be forthcoming.

הסוכנות היהודית לארץ ישראל
THE JEWISH AGENCY FOR PALESTINE

Growth of Population and Forces of Development.

Para.68: Here, in a striking reversal of other statements in the Report, it is at long last admitted that Government "is not likely to obtain an economic return for its outlay on the resettlement of Arabs and that the heavy expenditure connected therewith will be a burden imposed on the tax-payers of Palestine." This inevitable conclusion has already been referred to in the observations to F.R. Para.66. The renewed reference to the problem of the "displaced Arabs" contained in that paragraph as being rendered more and more serious as time goes on "by reason of the high rate of increase in the Arab population (which on the figures disclosed by the recent census cannot be less than 18,000 per dunam) and the steady shrinkage of the areas of land available for Arab cultivation" is another instance of Mr. French's way of making general statements calculated to strengthen the fear complex in the mind of his readers.

In general it should be pointed out that if development experts seriously intend to take into consideration the factor of the steady increase of the non-Jewish population and to provide for the third and fourth generation, they have, by their own showing, no solution as long as they adhere to their traditional line of argument. All the calculations of these investigators go to show that, even if the Jews did not from now on purchase one more dunam in Palestine, the increase of the Arab population amounting to hundreds of thousands would not be absorbed by Palestinian agriculture. The truth, of course, is that once the growth of population reaches the rate which it has reached in Palestine, the choice before the country is clear: either relative over-population and mass emigration, or modern economic development based upon heavy capital investment and up-to-date technical equipment, the establishment of manufacturing industries, the expansion of

הסוכנות היהודית לארץ ישראל
THE JEWISH AGENCY FOR PALESTINE

the scope and purchasing power of the home-market, and a transition to intensive and diversified cultivation also involving a heavy capital outlay. Those who are anxious to provide for the future of the growing Arab population of Palestine can, therefore, from the economic point of view, do nothing better than promote Jewish immigration, capital import, and the technical advancement of manufacture and agriculture. The smaller Jewish immigration and influx of capital will be, the larger Arab emigration from Palestine is bound to become. Conversely, the more rapid the pace of economic progress, the greater the total population which will be finally absorbed and maintained in the country.

Land Disputes.

Para.62 (continued): As evidence for the agrarian unrest caused by the past policy of laissez-faire with regard to displacement, Mr. French refers to "the various land disputes which are constantly cropping up and leading to breaches of the peace between Arabs and Jews, with threats of more serious trouble." This statement is highly misleading, and requires a very strong rebuttal. First of all, it should be made clear that - as Mr. French himself states (S.R.para.116) - land disputes are, in fact, more frequent among Arab peasants than they are between Jews and Arabs. This is a feature common to all agricultural countries at a backward stage of development. It is authoritatively estimated that about one-third of all cases of Arabs murdered by Arabs in Palestine have their root in land disputes. If cases of clash between Jews and Arabs have become more frequent in the course of recent years, the objective investigator/ should seek the reasons on a plane quite different from that on which Mr. French argues. It should be observed that in no Arab petition to the League of Nations or the British

Page 59   הסוכנות היהודית לארץ ישראל
                                          THE JEWISH AGENCY FOR PALESTINE

Government prior to the presentation of the Arab Executive's case before the Shaw Commission, did the issue of displacement and land disputes figure at all. Since the riots of 1929 and the Shaw Report the following three factors have been in operation, all tending to stimulate inter-racial land conflicts:

(a) The trend of recent land legislation, with its definite bias in favour of the possessor and occupant as against the legal owner, and the incidental effect of which is to encourage and, to some extent, protect the trespasser and squatter.

(b) The continuous public agitation centering on the displacement issue in its most exaggerated version, in speech and writing.

(c) The registration of "displaced" Arabs with its inevitable tendency to awaken unrestrained appetites, and encourage fantastic hopes of free distribution of Jewish lands to all and sundry.

An analysis of recent cases of land conflicts between Jews and Arabs (Kuskus Tabun, Haifa Bay, Tulkarm district, etc.) would provide ample evidence in support of this reading of the events.

Transplantation of tenants.

Para.63: The suggestion that offers by Jewish land purchasing agencies "to provide money for the purchase of land elsewhere for the re-establishment of evicted tenants represents simply the familiar device of transferring a nuisance from oneself to one's neighbour" does not appear to be to the point. There are districts in which Jewish settlement is being carried on, and there are others in which Jewish colonising agencies have so far been relatively less interested, or the conditions of which are not equally suited to Jewish colonisation. If a transplantation of tenants from a zone of Jewish settlement into such relatively "indifferent" areas is feasible, it helps to provide land for Jewish settlers without doing a damage to the transferred cultivators. If even such a policy does not

הסוכנות היהודית לארץ ישראל
THE JEWISH AGENCY FOR PALESTINE

appear in the eyes of the Director of Development as meeting the case, it is difficult to see on what terms any change of the status quo would meet with his approval.

Rights to be Protected.

Para. 64: Here Mr. French says very clearly that, although he does not believe he will be able to stop the railway from coming in ("it is, of course, impossible to make the world stand still") he does want to keep the coach-drivers' economy absolutely intact. Moreover, he represents the rights of the coach-drivers as being endangered by the over-powering force and the sinister working of progress, and raises, in the hearts of the "poor and uneducated", the fear of what their fate may be in the new order of things:

> "if the extensive and ill-defined rights of the literate and powerful are on the one side maintained, care should be taken that similarly extensive and ill-defined rights of the poor and uneducated on the other side are not overridden."

The facts of the Palestine situation as it has developed in recent years - with the series of measures of land legislation, displaced Arabs enquiry, etc. - would justify a statement to the contrary. If the extensive and ill-defined rights of the poor and uneducated, the nomadic and improvident, are so scrupulously guarded, the rights of the forward-looking and enterprising elements, carrying with them the promise of ultimate well-being for all, should not be overridden only because they <u>are</u> literate, and happen to be considered "powerful" by the Director of Development.

Is His Majesty's Government's Declared Policy a handicap?

Para. 65: The opening sentence of this paragraph is again highly illuminating. Mr. French says: "Given the physical limitations of a poorly endowed country such as Palestine and given the declared policy of His Majesty's Government as regards future colonisation", as if he were speaking of the

Page 61

הסוכנות היהודית לארץ ישראל
THE JEWISH AGENCY FOR PALESTINE

two great handicaps by which Palestine is beset. If one of these two handicaps did not exist, it is to be inferred, the whole necessity for a development policy would not have arisen. The true development outlook, in the view of this Executive, would be to say: "Given the physical limitations of a poorly endowed country such as Palestine, the declared policy of His Majesty's Government with regard to Jewish colonisation is the only course which holds out a promise of a better future for the existing and the prospective population of the country."

To say that "the last policy has demonstrably entailed what is felt to be harshness and injustice towards part of the indigenous population" stands refuted by the results of the investigation inaugurated under Mr. French's terms of reference. This sentence, again, bears witness to the current, but none the less erroneous, belief, to which reference is made in the covering letter, that the two parts of the Palestine Mandate inevitably clash.

Homestead Protection Ordinance.

Para. 72: The principle underlying the proposed Homestead Protection Ordinance is not denied sympathy. The question, however, arises whether the obstacles on the road to its application in practice would not prove insuperable. Mr. French's proposed legislation may, in a certain sense, be described as an attempt to re-establish the medieval institution of glebae adscripti. This class of people permanently attached to the soil and denied the freedom of movement cannot be made to fit in with the economic order which has developed in the world in the last few centuries. Mr. French himself rightly observes that the Five Feddan Law of Egypt is not comparable with the Ordinance he advocates, since the Egyptian measure does no more than provide for exemption from seizure for debt of small agricultural holdings. Extracts from

from comments which appeared at the time of the enactment of the Five Feddan Law may show how its probable economic effects were judged by quarters upon which the peasant depended for his credit:

> "Jusqu'ici il (le paysan egyptien) trouvait facilement un prêteur, parce qu'il avait un gage serieux, a offrir, sa terre. Avec le regime de l'insaississabilité il perd ce moyen. S'il rencontre encore un prêteur qui consente à lui avancer l'argent indispensable, il aura à accepter les conditions onereuses exigees en pareil cas comme compensation à la diminution des garanties, c'est à dire qu'il aura à payer un interêt beaucoup plus élevé. L'usurier, contre lequel on a voulu proteger les fellahs, y trouvera son avantage sans compter qu'il saura trouver le moyen de reprendre les garanties que le legislature a pretendu lui enlever."
>
> (Correspondence d'Orient, 1912, III).

> "We should not be surprised if the effect of the new law would be that, at the same time as the conditions under which the fellah is able to get money will become more onerous owing to the new law, his creditors will deal more harshly with him when he does not meet his engagements, and he may be worse off under the new regime under the old."
>
> (Monthly Bulletin of British Chamber of Commerce of Egypt, 1912).

The working of the law seems to have borne out these forecasts, for in 1932 the legal position was again altered. The "Times" of August 2, 1932, reports from Cairo:

> "The Government is now enabled to seize smallholdings in order to recover debts owing to the Agricultural Credit Bank. The Five Feddan Law, passed in 1912 at the instigation of Lord Kitchener, made agricultural holdings of less than this area exempt from distraint for debt, but the law has now been altered. The effect of this change will apparently be to place the smallholder as entirely in the hands of the Government as he was in the hands of the usurer before the passing of the Five Feddan Law, and to turn the Agricultural Bank into a handy instrument for exerting political influence."

That a law going even beyond the scope of the Five Feddan Law should be practicable appears, prima facie, more than doubtful. Mr. French's own proposals, if closely examined, will show that inalienability is, strictly speaking, unattainable. It is recommended that " a minimum of homestead area of a cultivator should be made inalienable, <u>unless the vendor of such shall satisfy the District Commissioner that he has a lot viable elsewhere or has obtained permanent occupation off the land.</u>" It should be made clear that all that Mr. French's proposed legislation will amount to in practice is an administrative "enquiry before the completion of the transaction instead of a subsequent action to upset it." As against that possible advantage there have to be weighed the economic risks and legal entanglements arising from the constitution of numerous legally inalienable minimum parcels of land. If a cultivator and his family are bent upon selling out and leaving the land and farming and taking up/any job in the city, or working for wages in a plantation, or emigrating, no District Commissioner in the world can stop them. If the law does not give them sufficient freedom, it will be circumvented until it is changed.

Criticism of Major Features of the Draft.

Para. 74: An analysis of the individual clauses of the Homestead Protection Ordinance, a draft of which is attached to Mr. French's Report, does not appear to be called for, as it is not known that any such measure is actually contemplated.

Among the points of principle which may require consideration are the following:

(i) The provisions of Section 7 (2) and (3) as well as those of Section 19 (1) are bound entirely to destroy such credit as the small cultivator may possess, since no remedy will be available against him in a Civil Court. The consideration that such provisions "would tend to restrict easy rural credit - a desirable consummation", is, it is submitted, purely theoretical. In practise, the effect of the proposed legislation would be to drive the cultivator back into the arms of the usurer and tighten the moneylender's grip on him.

הסוכנות היהודית לארץ ישראל
THE JEWISH AGENCY FOR PALESTINE

(ii) In general, the provisions with regard to mortgages as contained in Sections 8 to 16 seem to bear this theoretical character and are not in keeping with the actual conditions of the country.

(iii) The powers given to the District Commissioner under Sections 12 (2) and 20 to 22 exceed those at present exercised by a President of a District Court in foreclosure proceedings. The District Commissioner is accorded the final authority of a Court and in view of the delegation of powers which is inevitable and is, in fact, expressly provided for in Section 23 of the Draft Ordinance, the powers at present refused to a competent judge of long-standing will be granted to an Administrative Officer. Even the High Court of Justice will not be able to interfere with a District Commissioner who may be exercising his powers unreasonably and unjudicially.

Occupancy Tenants Ordinance.

Para. 75: In introducing his recommendations for an Occupancy Tenants Ordinance, Mr. French quotes the Report of the Shaw Commission to the effect that similar measures "were designed to avoid the danger which appears to be imminent, namely, that large numbers of tenants and cultivators for whom no alternative land is available would be deprived of their holdings." No better illustration could be cited for the inflationist presentation of the displacement problem, and no weaker argument for further restrictive legislation.

Difficulties anticipated.

Para 79: The following statement of Mr. French is noted:
"That the fulfilment of any scheme to give protection of tenants by some form of occupancy rights bristles with difficulties cannot be gainsaid."

Criticism of Major Provisions of the Draft.

Para. 81: Comments on tenancy legislation in general have been presented to Government by the Jewish Agency in the memoranda submitted in connection with the different stages of the Protection of Cultivators Ordinance and its Amending Ordinances. As to the draft Occupancy Tenants Ordinance attached to Mr. French's Report, the following major points should be observed:-

הסוכנות היהודית לארץ ישראל
THE JEWISH AGENCY FOR PALESTINE

(i) Section 3 lays down the 29th of May, 1931, as the date of establishing rights of occupancy, "notwithstanding that the holding may have been since that date let to some other persons, or may have been left unlet." This provision, in granting rights to people who may have left the land and in disregarding the rights of others who may have obtained leases in the meantime, is quite extraordinary. The new lessee is left without any security of compensation although he may have incurred considerable expense in moving on to the land and in improving it. He is not offered any remedy. Why a tenant who may have left the holding of his own free will should still possess occupancy rights as against the new tenant is incomprehensible.

(ii) Section 5 provides that "a tenant who has acquired a right to occupancy in a holding shall not be compelled to pay a higher rent than that which was payable in respect thereof at the date when he acquired such right." It shall, however, "be lawful for the Court, on application of the tenant who has acquired a right of occupancy, to reduce the rent payable by him on the ground that the productive powers of his holding have been decreased." This provision, apparently fixing the rent for an indefinite future, does not give the owner any opportunity of applying for an increase for whatever reason it may be. The building of roads or railways, the establishment of new settlements in the vicinity or changes of currency may all be legitimate causes to ask for an increase of rent. On the other hand, the tendency of the proposed clause is to perpetuate uneconomic use of the land and obstruct development.

(iii) If the provisions of the Occupancy Tenants Ordinance are to be coordinated with those of the Homestead Protection Ordinance, a legal situation will arise second to none in complexity. In the conditions of the Palestine peasantry, uneducated and apt to quarrel, such a situation must lead to endless litigation. If, for example, the provisions of the Homestead Protection Ordinance - as laid down in Section 7(5) - will apply to any sale of tenancy rights, much confusion is to be expected. The old tenant, who may have left on his own account and may want to waive his tenancy rights, may be refused permission to do so by the District Commissioner.

(iv) Section 12 opens the door wide to mortgagors to defeat the mortgagee by creating tenancies after the date of the mortgage, thus making it impossible for the mortgagor to collect his debt. This provision must be very harmful to the development of mortgage credit in Palestine and will, in particular, hit Arab landowners of all classes.

הסוכנות היהודית לארץ ישראל
THE JEWISH AGENCY FOR PALESTINE

It is not considered necessary to go into further detail in analyzing the proposals of Mr. French. Should Government really have any intention of amending existing legislation for the protection of cultivators on the lines recommended in the Report, this Executive will certainly seek another opportunity to express its full views on the subject.

Improvement of Hill Fellah's Farming.

Para. 123: The statement that in the case of the hill fellah, whose condition is described as "steadily deteriorating", "little can be done to give him a better return from his holding if his outlay in not at the same time to be disproportionately increased" is definitely rejected by our agricultural experts. Mr. Elazari Volcani, Head of the Jewish Agency Agricultural Experiment Station, has, on the basis of prolonged researches and tests, worked out plans for the increase of the hill fellah's net income by means of a few none too costly improvements in the internal organisation of his farm, such as the provision of stronger draught animals, the supply of suitable fruit trees and better seed, and similar measures.

DC/297/33.

DEPARTMENT OF DEVELOPMENT,
P. O. B. 649,
JERUSALEM.

24th March, 1933.

~~CONFIDENTIAL~~.

CHIEF SECRETARY.

        Subject : Observations of Arab Executive Committee on Report by Mr.L.French,C.I.E., C.B.E.

        Reference: Your file CF/134/32.

    I do not think that any useful purpose will be served by attempting any detailed criticism of the observations of the Arab Executive Committee. Their attitude is quite frankly described in para. 34: "The Arab Executive Committee has notified His Majesty's Government on a previous occasion that it will not accept the proposed development scheme unless and until His Majesty's Government abandons the policy laid down in Mr. Mac Donald's letter to Dr. Weizmann dated the 13th February, 1930, and as it now appears that His Majesty's Government does not propose to depart from that policy this Committee is of the opinion that Mr. French's Reports contain nothing which may move it to change the decision it took in this respect". (Please see your file CF/58/31.)

    2. The only concrete suggestion contained in the observations of the Committee is that a law should be enacted which will definitely prohibit the sale of lands to the Jews (par.18) at all events "until it

will be possible to settle Jews on other additional land without causing detriment and prejudice to the Arabs" (par.23), which presumably means never. From this point of view two objections are raised to the proposed Homestead Protection Ordinance: (i) that it will not provide for the natural growth of the Arab population (which no land legislation is likely to do)(par.22), and (ii) that it does not prohibit sales to the Jews, nor provide for the retention of sufficient land for the Arab communities as a whole in their capacity as an independent nation". (par.25)

3. The Committee return again and again to the assertion that 29.4 per cent of the Arab families are landless, but when one turns to the Report of Sir John Hope Simpson (p.26), on the authority of which this assertion is made, it is plain that the figure, which is only an estimate based on returns from 104 villages, includes shopkeepers, artisans, agricultural labourers and herds - in fact the whole class who, even in a purely agricultural community, do not live directly by cultivation - as well as those who were formerly cultivators but have lost their land whether by sales to the Jews or otherwise. But the Committee seem to be of opinion that it is the duty of Government to provide every Arab family with land (par.9-17).

4. In par.5 it is stated that 4,500 claims as landless Arabs were preferred by Arab cultivators and the Committee allege that the practice adopted by the Legal Assessor of sending papers dealing with Arab

claims to the Jewish Agency for the purpose of their expressing their views thereon amounted to "an express partiality towards the Jews". The figure 4,500 is an error, due to a miscalculation; the actual number of claims received is 3,188.

It is true that in the case of some villages copies of the applications were submitted to the Jewish Agency for their observations before the applicants were interviewed and their claims investigated by the Legal Assessor, but this procedure was found to involve so much unnecessary labour that it was abandoned, and in the case of the remaining villages the names of those only who, after such investigation, had been recommended for inclusion in the Register of Landless Arabs were submitted to the Jewish Agency. In fact, replies or comments by the Jewish Agency were received before investigation in 748 cases, of which 245 have been recommended for acceptance. In the case of applications which were clearly unsustainable, as, for example, showing that the applicant still has ample land, the applicant was notified that it was proposed to reject his application, but that if he had any further representations to make they would be considered. The number of replies received to such notifications has been only fractional. In all other cases, and in those in which the replies received showed that further consideration was desirable, the Legal Assessor attended at the nearest convenient centre and heard the applicants personally and examined such evidence as was available. When the observations of the Jewish

- 4 -

Agency had already been received he naturally compared them with the evidence produced to him, but in the great majority of cases there has been singularly little controversy as to matters of fact.

6. The statement contained in par.18 that "Jewish organisations adopt the practice of employing certain mean Arabs in consideration of an insignificant sum of money for the purpose of inducing the simple fellah to sell his land....", and that contained in par.33 that "the Arabs one and all receive with indignation and repudiation the sale of even one foot of Arab land to the Jews", are interesting in view of the fact that amongst the number of those who have sold or acted as agents in connection with the sale of land to Jewish organisations are:

    Omar Eff. Bittar - Member of the Arab Executive.
    Shucri Eff. Taji - Member of the Arab Executive.
    Selim Eff. Abderrahman - Member of the Arab Executive.
    Abdul Rahman Bey Taji - Member of the Supreme Moslem Council.
    Abdul Raouf Bittar of Jaffa.
    Dimitri Tadros of Jaffa,

L. Andrews
ACTING DIRECTOR OF DEVELOPMENT.

Comments

of the

Department of Development

on the

Memorandum of the Jewish Agency

on the

First and Supplementary Reports on Agricultural

Development and Land Settlement in Palestine by

Lewis French, C.I.E.,C.B.E.

FIRST REPORT.

Appointment of Jewish Adviser.

Para. 7: The only correspondence I have on this subject is your telegram No.216 dated 7.9.31 addressed to the Secretary of State, and a copy of your "Secret" Despatch (B) dated 30.1.32. also addressed to the Secretary of State, attaching notes of interviews with the Executives of the Jewish and Arab Agencies.

Preliminary Results of Displaced Arabs Enquiry.

Para. 8: Exception is taken by the Jewish Agency to the statement that "the acquisition of the land bought by Jewish Organisations for permanent settlement of immigrants could not have been effected without considerable displacement of existing cultivators", and the number of claims submitted by persons claiming to be landless Arabs is referred to as showing that this figure (3118) represents the highest at which the number could be put.

2. While it is not suggested that every person displaced because or is a "landless Arab", the number of persons who were displaced must have been considerable as the following instances will show:
(1) as a result of the sale of the Sursock property in Nazareth S.D. six villages (Waraqani, Jabata, Ikhnaifes, Affula, Jinujar and Tel el Adas), which in 1922 had a population of 1359, have disappeared:
(2) the villages of Dar el Beida, Jidru, Harbaj, Jeida and Tall esh Shummam in Haifa District, which in 1922 had a population of 722, have also ceased to exist.

3. All these people must have been "displaced" though in fact those of them who were cultivators, for the most part, found other land or employment.

4. It is true that the Landless Arab problem, if its extent is to be judged merely by the number of claims lodged and approved, appears to be less acute than was apprehended, but in this connection I should like to repeat the observation contained in the Report of the Legal Assessor, which I forwarded with my DC/17/31 confidential of the 25th January, 1933; he stated (with reference to the sales of the Sursock properties in Nazareth S.D.):

> "It may be noted that out of 155 former cultivators in the villages sold earlier 68 appear to have been able to obtain land, while of the 52 cultivators at Sulam (1930), only four have obtained land elsewhere. This fact, and the difficulty experienced in finding land for the people of Wadi Hawarith, support the view expressed at p.125 of the Report of the Shaw Commission: 'In the past persons dispossessed have in many cases been absorbed in the neighbouring villages: we were, however, told that this process, though it may have been possible four or five years ago, is no longer possible today'".

On the Arab side the number of landless Arabs has, no doubt, been exaggerated and no account has been taken of the sources of employment opened to displaced tenant-cultivators by the development of the larger towns and the increase of the area under citrus, but in my view the real basis of the outcry was not so much the existing state of affairs as apprehension for the future.

5. Of the 574 claims rejected from Tiberias

- 5 -

District, 158 were rejected because the applicants are still tenants in lands bought by the P.I.C.A. or other Jewish purchasers in this District which have not yet been taken up by them. Others were tenants in the same lands but have given up cultivation.

6. Of the applicants from Wadi Hawarith and Haifa Bay only 45 were mere graziers, the remainder appear from Tithe Records or other evidence to have been tenant cultivators.

Procedure in Scrutiny of Claims.

Para. 9: In his letter No.CF/25/33 of 5.3.33. the Chief Secretary confirms the conclusions of Mr. French, as para. 2 of this letter reads as follows:

> "In giving the brief statistical record of the classification of the claims of landless Arabs, you should draw attention to the fact that there may be many Arabs who have not submitted claims, but who nevertheless have not gained other equally satisfactory occupation and consequently that the number of registered landless Arabs at the closure of the register may be less than the total number of landless Arabs in Palestine".

2. According to records of the Director of Lands the areas bought by Jews from non-Jews during the last three years are as follows:

Year	Area	
1930	19,370	dunams
1931	18,590	"
1932	18,893	"

3. As regards Shatta, the following number of claims were received from this village:

No. of Claims:	20
Accepted:	Nil.
Rejected:	All: most of them received compensation and left since their applications were lodged.

- 4 -

Litigation is still going on as regards some 36 persons from Shatta who claim that they have rights under the Protection of Cultivators Ordinance, 1929.

4. If the agricultural labourers referred to in Mr. French's remarks in para. 23 of the Supplementary Report could prove that each was given a piece of land by his employer, the produce of which constituted his wages, he would qualify as "displaced" under the terms of the Prime Minister's letter.

Control of Land Transfers in Interests of Development.

Para. 10: I do not think that any special legislative action is called for to ensure that lands are acquired at reasonable prices for the settlement of landless Arabs, as I have so far succeeded in finding land at reasonable prices. Of course, it is to be remembered that I am keeping away from the orange belt on the coast.

2. Up to time of writing I have purchased some 6,000 dunams of land and hold options on another 1,600 dunams, besides which I have been offered at least 50,000 dunams of land at prices in the region of LP 3 per metric dunam and, in some cases, this even includes the cost of fellaheen abodes.

3. It is stated that these lands are free from tenants or at all events are cultivated by persons who have other land. I have not yet had an opportunity to confirm this. As regards some of this land, I have been given to understand that the

- 5 -

reason for its being untenanted is owing to the fear of owners that tenants may acquire rights under the Protection of Cultivators Ordinance.

4. Your attention is also drawn to the notes of a meeting between His Excellency and Dr. Arlosoroff on the 27th January, 1932. At that meeting His Excellency and the Chief Secretary made the following statements as regards proposed land legislation:-

His Excellency said he could not give a guarantee that the proposed Land Ordinance restricting purchases and lease of land over the whole country would be abandoned, because His Majesty's Government had not given such a guarantee. But he could say that he had no intention at present of asking for permission to enact such an Ordinance, as he saw no necessity for it in connection with the work at present on hand. Nor did he think such an Ordinance to be necessary for Mr. French in his present task of finding immediate remedies to deal with the present situation.

His Excellency said he understood the point to be that it would be a satisfaction to the Jewish Agency if a statement could be made that the Palestine Government did not consider the legislation at present necessary.

The Chief Secretary agreed that there appeared to be no necessity for such legislation in connection with the immediate work the Commission had in hand.

His Excellency said that Government could not bind itself for ever; he realised, however, that it

- 6 -

would go a long way to meet Dr. Arlosoroff's point if it could be said that the proposals had been abandoned to a certain extent for the present and were not required in connection with Mr. French's immediate task.

Encroachment on State Lands.

Para. 14: The position as far as I know has not altered since Mr. French wrote this paragraph.

2. The remarks of the Jewish Agency in this connection might well be referred to the Commissioner of Lands for comment. As far as I know there are no large tracts of State Domain Lands available for settlement.

Close Settlement and Markets.

Paras. 16 and 17: The Jewish Agency seem to have assumed that Mr. French, because he drew attention to certain risks in a change from extensive to intensive cultivation, was hostile to all development. It is submitted that this criticism is not justified having regard to the fact that any loss arising out of the closer settlement of landless Arabs must necessarily fall on Government. It is not denied that courage and persistence have often turned failure into success and will do so again. The object of the report was to attempt to place all relevant facts before Government.

Lot Viable and Intermediate Types.

Para. 18: No comments, the figures mentioned in para. 18 are merely provisional.

– 7 –

Cost of Jewish and Arab Settlement.   *Para.19:* I have no fault to find with the figures given by Mr. French for the settlement of an Arab family. In fact, the Wadi Hawarith (North) settlement at Tall esh Shauk and Ashrafiyat Rushdi is working out at LP.267 per family unit. The question of whether or not the Jewish settler is to be supplied with a house by Jewish organisations is one of policy.

2. In this connection I would refer you to para.8 of the Secretary of State's telegram dated 21.1.32. which reads:

> "We must be careful not to imply admission of Jewish claim to parity in share of the Fund or land, and language should not be used which might be taken to imply such admission".

Productivity of Settlement Expenditure.   *Para.20:* I see no reason why an economic return should not be expected on the capital outlay in connection with the re-settlement of landless Arabs. In the Wadi Hawarith (North) scheme, it is proposed to settle some 90 families on lands at Beisan, on which Government is expected to recover 5% per annum on the total outlay. It may be that in some cases the return will only be indirect in the form of increased revenue.

Jewish Land Reserve.   *Para.21:* See remarks under Special Report (Para.16).

Land Transfer Control Countrywide or Limited?   *Para.22:* Please see Memorandum attached to your CF/451/31 of 25.1.32. and my remarks under para.10.

- 8 -

Effects of Partition and Survey.

Para. 52: Undoubtedly partition of mesha'a land and settlement does to a great extent open the way to development, but little can be achieved without money and example, both of which, anyhow in the area around Jaffa, have been provided by the Jewish people.

2. The villages which remain unpartitioned are probably, as pointed out by Mr. French, the most stubborn cases.

3. As regards the illustrations from villages in the vicinity of Jaffa, given on page 15 of the Jewish Agency's memorandum, I have only to remark that in the case of El Qubeiba, while the villagers have benefitted, a result of the sale has been the displacement of a settled tribe of bedu who were formerly tenant cultivators; out of 90 claims submitted by them 66 have been provisionally approved.

Land Sales and Unofficial Partition.

Para. 54: Voluntary partition of mesha'a is now proceeding under the direction of the Commissioner of Lands, with very satisfactory results. It would not be fair to attribute the desire of all fellaheen to have their land partitioned to the prospects of Jewish land purchases, although this may hold good in the coastal belt.

2. The remedy suggested in para. 55 is being carried out by Assistant Settlement Officers specially deputed for this work. Please see letter No. LS/14 of 10.5.32. from the Commissioner of Lands (C.S. file L/111/31).

The Mukhtar.

Para. 44: Particulars of sales furnished to District

- 9 -

Officers by Mukhtars (unaccompanied by actual claims) are not included in the number of 3185 claims, though they were erroneously included in the number mentioned by Mr. French in para.8 of his First Report.

Occupancy Rights on State Lands.

Para.45: The appeal mentioned in para.77 of the Supplementary Report is still pending.

Aspects of Land Control.

Para.56: Where land is bought and taken up for the purposes of colonisation the inevitable result is that the former cultivators are displaced; it is true that they may be able to find other holdings elsewhere; it is also true that, if they, and others, can forthwith change to intensive or partly intensive cultivation, the remaining land in the locality may be sufficient to support them; but unless and until one of these alternatives happens a certain number of former cultivators are rendered landless. To this extent there would seem to be a definite nexus between Jewish land purchasers and the existence of a landless Arab class.

Punjab and Palestine.

Para.57: Undoubtedly the question of re-settling landless Arabs is a difficult one, as land must in every case be purchased, and every care taken that additional landless Arabs are not created. It is true that every cultivable dunam is not actually cultivated, nor put to its best use, but even the lands in the Huleh will most likely have to be

- 10 -

eventually purchased; this will also be the case in the Beisan tract. Even in the so-called waste tracts of Beersheba every dunam of land has a claimant.

Proposals for Land Transfer Ordinance. <u>Paras. 59 and 60</u>: I agree with the Jewish Agency that no restrictive legislation is required, and that if the Expropriation Ordinance could be made applicable in case of necessity, it would meet any difficulties which may arise.

Please see comments under para.10.

Private Initiative in Jewish Development. <u>Para. 61</u>: No comments.

The State and the Organisation of Settlers. <u>Para. 62</u>: It is agreed that a body representative of the Settlers would be most desirable, provided that, as the memorandum points out, Government retains control.

Developments in Beisan and Huleh. <u>Para. 64</u>: It must be understood that land without water in Beisan is of little value for settlement purposes. If displacement is not already going on it will take place in the following manner: a capitalist purchases a plot of land and in his deed of purchase has it stated that it includes the "water appertaining to the land". He proceeds to cultivate intensively and uses so much water that the neighbours take measures against him. In order

- 11 -

to keep his banana grove profitable he purchases or hires water from neighbours. But it may be that affairs become so chaotic that the Government is petitioned by the inhabitants to divide the water in accordance with the areas it feeds. This is done and the capitalist with his 100 dunams of bananas finds that he gets only water sufficient for 50. If he wishes to keep his grove intact he must then buy 50 dunams of land, leave it uncultivated and use the water appertaining to it on his banana grove. I am informed this purchase or hire of water or purchase of land for the sake of its water is practised in Beisan. As a matter of fact during the last few years field cultivators in Jericho have disposed of about 1/6th of their water supply to garden cultivators. Those who have disposed of their entire right are virtually landless.

Alleged Dangers of Land Transactions at Beisan.

Para. 65: At the time Mr. French wrote the paragraph Jewish buyers were certainly making every effort to obtain land in Beisan S.D., to wit the purchase of one-tenth of the Tall esh Shauk estate. The purchase of the other 9/10ths was stopped as the result of instructions from the Headquarters of the P.I.C.A. in Paris, and the drop in the pound sterling. (This estate has since been purchased by Government.)

2. Quite recently the Jewish National Fund has purchased approximately 5,000 dunams of land from the Arab Sagr at Sakhina, leaving this section of the tribe with only some 500 dunams of land. They have

- 12 -

not so far put in claims as landless Arabs, but they will certainly be hard put to it to obtain sufficient grazing for their animals. (The population of this tribe as per the Census of 1931 is 374 persons.)

3. The Jewish National Fund have also recently purchased 1,000 dunams of the lands of Ashrafiyat Rushdi. (No Arabs displaced as far as is known.)

4. The J.N.F. also hold options on 3,264 dunams of the lands of the Arab Ghazzawieh, 2,500 odd dunams at Nasil el Jizl, and several thousand in the Bawati area.

5. With regard to water-rights: spring areas and main canals are Government reservations, but this does not mean that adjoining lands have not the same rights of irrigation which they have enjoyed ab antiquo, and, as the law stands at present, such rights are disposed of, often apart from the land to which they appertain, in the manner and with the results described in my comments on para.64: for example, I am informed that one considerable banana grove is irrigated in part with water hired from Jewish owners who are not at present cultivating their land. It is submitted that in such areas as Beisan the control of disposition of land and water-rights is desirable in the interests of the community.

Differentiation between Jewish and Arab Settlers.

Para.66: Mr.French's statement appears to have been misunderstood: if Government provides the Arab settler with house farm and stock, it looks to recover

- 13 -

the cost of the whole; if the Jewish colonist gets from Government only the land, while Jewish organisations supply the house and stock, Government recovers only the price of the land. This is the exact contrary of "expecting the Jewish settler to pay Government for the farm and equipment".

3. Please also see my remarks at para.19.

Jewish Scientist's Estimate.

Para.67: Please see C.S.letter No.CF/481/31 of 20.1.32. wherein instructions were issued to the Director of Development to put forward definite proposals for

    (a) the re-settlement of displaced Arabs and
    (b) development with a view to Jewish colonisation,

both to be regarded as an immediate palliative and to be on the smallest scale compatible with effectiveness.

2. On the present lines of settlement it should not take many years to deal with those Arabs whose claims have been admitted. At the time Mr. French wrote this paragraph a large scheme of development was contemplated.

3. Please see remarks under para.19.

Average Size of Arab Village Household.

Para.69: Perhaps the Superintendent of Census will check. It is quite true that in certain of the hill districts the reduction in the size of holdings is nearing a self-supporting minimum. The District Officer of the Ramallah Sub-District states that in in his sub-district the average holding is 7 dunams of land; on the other hand, the increased planting of orange-groves by Arabs and the growth of towns with

- 14 -

their accompanying industries have provided sources of employment which did not exist formerly, i.e. during the Ottoman administration.

Jewish Development in Hill Districts. Para.70: Protection of the small-holder will be provided by the proposed Amendments to the Protection of Cultivators Ordinance.

2. While it is true that purchases by Jews have not taken place to any great extent in the hill country, I presume Mr. French had in view villages with land both in the plain and the hill, which by the sale of their plain lands, were being forced to fall back on the areas owned by them in the hills.

3. I must say that the achievements of the Jewish colonists in Kiryat Anavim (Dilb) are commendable.

4. The commencement of Cooperative Societies and the legislation proposed by Mr.C.F.Strickland for the summary relief of indebted cultivators will also tend no doubt to prevent land passing from Arab peasants to Arab capitalists.

5. Mr. French had in view the Nablus Sub-District when he wrote this paragraph.

Fellah Development in the Hill Districts. Para.71: Please see remarks under para.70.

Development in the Maritime Plain. Para.72: Dr. Ruppin's scheme is based so far as I can judge on reliable figures. The paragraphs 71 to 76 give an opportunity for its introduction. It postulates a complacent attitude of the fellah with a wholesale interference with his liberty of action and in effect

- 15 -

requires to a marked degree the restriction of free transfer advocated by Mr. French and taken exception to as likely to work in an exactly opposite direction to the aim professed. Indeed I should have thought that control was an essential accompaniment of the Ruppin scheme.

2. See also remarks under para.52.

Small Cultivator in Citrus Belt. Para.73: In the past Jewish purchases of land have been chiefly from big landowners or from villagers with musha'a. There are now few large landowners except in the Gaza Sub-District and as the partition of musha'a proceeds Jews will find it hard to buy land from small owner-occupiers. I do not share the fears envisaged by Mr. French in this paragraph.

Alleged Need of Restrictive Ordinance. Para.74: See remarks under paragraphs 10 and 70.

Punjab Land Alienation Act. Para.75: Mr. Strickland, to whom I referred this point, has commented as follows:

> "The opinions of the agriculturists in the Punjab are quite unanimous that the Alienation of Land Act, which prohibits a sale or permanent mortgage of land by an agriculturist in favour of a non-agriculturist, has been their salvation. It has turned back the tide of transfers, and in normal years for the last two decades the Government returns have shown a net gain of land by the agriculturists from non-agriculturists. The non-agricultural buyers were almost always moneylenders or their relatives. Where this was not the case, the sale by an agriculturist was generally due to indebtedness, and the peasant tribes were being progressively reduced to the position of rack-rented tenants under moneylender landlords, who seldom (except in a few districts on the Indus) improved the land.

> "The Act is habitually denounced by the

"moneylending classes, including many lawyers, journalists and politicians. Mr. M.L.Darling, I.C.S. in his "Punjab Peasant" also expresses doubt as to its value in advanced and irrigated areas. I strongly disagree with him, so do almost all British officers in the Punjab, and all agriculturists of the areas to which he refers.

"Government (the District Officer) authorises a sale by an agriculturist to a non-agriculturist for good reasons, e.g. extension of a town etc. The limitation of the right of alienation restricted credit at first, but moneylenders now lend freely on future produce or on general character. So do cooperative societies. Cooperative Societies are not exempt from the provisions of the Act.

"A non-agriculturist may take a lease not exceeding 20 years in satisfaction of his debt, which is then extinguished at the end of the term. I have never heard of such a lease being taken. The moneylender does not want full payment: he wants an annual tribute.

"The Act has been extended to the North West Frontier Province and Delhi Province, and similar acts apply to the Bundelkhand area of the United Provinces, the aboriginal tribes of the Central Provinces and elsewhere, and (in a less effective form) to the Deccan area of the Bombay Province.

"The Royal Commission on Agriculture (pp.420-2) could not make a general recommendation as to the extension of the Act, but invited local Governments to consider the question. The report was issued in 1928. The United Provinces raises the question from time to time, but no action has, I think, been taken.

"Similar legislation is in force in the Federated Malay States, prohibiting the transfer of large areas of Malay land to non-Malays (e.g. Chinese). The same prohibition of transfers to non-indigenous persons is maintained in Siam, Java, Egypt (I think) and of course the whole of tropical Africa.

"But the problem is not comparable in those cases to that of Palestine, except perhaps the Malayan case."

-----

2. I also attach an extract of the relevant paragraph from the Report of the Royal Commission on Agriculture in India dated 1928.

- 17 -

State Control of Water Supply.	**Paras. 77 to 89:** An Irrigation Ordinance is at present under discussion by Government and the General Agricultural Council, on which Council the Jewish Agency is represented.
Legislation by Regulations.	**Para. 91:** This is entirely a question of policy.
Beisan Lands.	**Paras. 93 to 98:** This question is at present under consideration by Government. This Department will shortly have purchased some 10,000 dunams of the irrigable lands, besides which the Jews have bought and hold options on large areas. Cultivators from Ramallah, Bethlehem, Sarona, and Jerusalem, have also bought large areas.
Huleh Basin.	**Paras. 99 to 107:** Please see letter DC/3/31 of 23.12.31. from Mr. French and my DC/3/32 of 9.3.33.
History of Beisan Tract.	**Appendix III(a) Para. 3:** I agree with the Jewish Agency that it is very doubtful if any of the present-day cultivators were the original owners or descendants of the original owners of these lands. 2. In 1870 a Commission of Enquiry visited Beisan, as did another Commission 50 years later, to report on the land situated there. The Commission appeared to have reported that they found the lands in disorder, exposed to raids by marauding Bedouin from across the Jordan, abandoned by the cultivators and only scantily cultivated. 3. There is, then, evidence for assuming that it is

- 18 -

doubtful if any of the present-day cultivators can prove their occupation before 1870.

4. Your attention is drawn to para.2 of the High Commissioner's Despatch No.247 (Ref. Adm. 305) dated 23.7.21. which would appear to confirm that the original cultivators of the lands had forfeited their rights by deserting them and leaving them without cultivation for a period of between 20 and 30 years. In 1870/2 the Commission found that the few cultivators who were in the area had not been established long enough to acquire rights or possession.

Status of Beisan Occupiers.
: Appendix III(a) Para.11: No comments. The Commissioner of Lands can no doubt comment on this paragraph as the Agreement was negotiated by him.

Wealthy Corporations.
: Appendix III(a) Para.12: No comments.

Progress in Beisan Villages Reported.
: Appendix III(a) Para.15: I agree with the Jewish Agency that very little progress is to be noticed in the villages included in the terms of the Agreement. In certain villages a few fruit-trees are being grown, and there progress ends.

- 19 -

SUPPLEMENTARY REPORT.

Summary of Displaced Arabs Enquiry.	Para.7: No comments necessary.
Surplus Land.	Para.8: It is true that there are lands in the possession of both Arabs and Jews which are not being properly cultivated, but these cannot be called surplus lands. Of course, if you divide the country up into small intensive farms, and transfer the inhabitants from one place to another, surplus land will be available.
The carrying capacity of land.	Para.9: It is true that there are areas of land in Palestine not properly cultivated, but I fail to see how it is possible to dispossess the present holders. 2. The Jews also have large areas of land which they are not at present fully cultivating. The P.I.C.A. alone has some 26,352 dunams of land which it leases out to Arabs. Other Jewish owners and bodies also have apparent surplus lands. I would not be far wrong in saying that in Tul Karm Sub-District alone there are at least 50,000 dunams in Jewish hands which were not being cultivated last year. Then there is the glaring case of Affula.
The Mechanism of Development.	Para.12: See remarks under para.22 of First Report.
Fellah's Transition to intensive cultivation.	Para.13: The Memorandum suggests that the transition from extensive to intensive cultivation can be tided over by one of two methods: (1) by the experience which

- 20 -

the cultivator will gain as a labourer in an orange-grove, and (2) by the cultivation of a holding of the semi-intensive type.

2. An orange-grove provides employment for about one labourer per 15 dunams, and displaced fellaheen must look for employment mainly, if not entirely, in Arab-owned groves: the field for additional labour in citrus groves is therefore limited.

3. As regards the second method suggested, it is not easy to see where a number of displaced cultivators are to find the requisite 60 dunams each, unless, by reason of some general scheme of development, a number of other cultivators are turning from extensive to semi-intensive cultivation.

4. The adoption of citrus growing by Arabs in the coastal plain is hardly typical: most of the sales in this district were sales of portions of their land by owner-occupiers, who as a result obtained capital to develop the remainder. The real problem is how to provide for tenant-cultivators who are without capital.

5. With regard to the suggestion of a maintenance allowance to the fellah, in Dr. Ruppin's scheme for settlement in the Coastal plain (Para. 72), a sum of £36 is allowed for the upkeep of the settler during the transition period, and in para. 71, referring to hill districts, he suggests an advance of £2 to £3 per dunam "to make up for the deficiency in income resulting from crops on the area put under fruit trees".

Jewish Land Reserve.

Para. 16: It is true that Jewish Institutions hold surplus lands, and from the daily press it would appear

- 21 -

that they are finding difficulty in obtaining the requisite number of workers to cultivate same.

2. I do not agree with the Jewish Agency that the surplus lands in their hands are so small that they do not justify a dilatory handling of the Jewish settlement problem. I should say that a conservative estimate of 75,000 dunams would not be far off the mark.

3. According to the instructions contained in Despatch No. 487 of 26.6.31. it is the first duty of Government to provide land for registered displaced Arabs, and this Department is now endeavouring to purchase sufficient lands for the settlement thereon of the 200 families from Wadi Hawarith.

4. Please see comments under para. 19 of the First Report.

Harrathin.   Para. 23: Please see sub-para.(d) of the remarks at para. 9 of the First Report.

Immediate Development Programme.   Para. 27: Please see Mr. French's "Secret" letter No. DC/153/32 of 20.4.32.

2. Government are in possession of the estimated cost of the proposed settlement at Tall esh Shauk (DC/14/33 of 11.3.33.) and it may be possible either by taking lands on lease or by granting loans to provide for the settlement of other landless Arabs more cheaply (see my DC/208/33 of 12.3.33.)

Cattle and Implements owned by Claimants.   Para. 29: I agree with the remarks of Mr. French.

- 22 -

Exclusion of Dry Farming Areas from Programme.	Para. 30: Trans-Jordan did not come within the scope of the Director of Development. The Negeb can only be made suitable for successful farming by the finding of water in large quantities. A Government plant is already working in the Beersheba area. It must also be remembered that every piece of land is claimed by some member of the tribes which roam in that area.
Cost of Settlement compared to Thousand Families Scheme.	Para. 36: Cost of land is not included in the Jewish Agency's estimate, and it must be remembered that, under their scheme, the small-holder is more or less guaranteed permanent employment by the neighbouring capitalist grove-owner during the period that elapses before his own farm becomes productive. 2. Government has at present in contemplation the adoption of a similar scheme at Nathaniya with the cooperation of Mr. Mohl and the Hanotaiah Company.
Reference to F.R. Para. 72.	Para. 45: No comments.
Marketing Prospects of Citrus Fruits.	Paras. 46-51: The warning, and it is no more than a warning, for the need of caution in view of marketing problems could not be more emphasised than by the very recent measures taken by the Government of U.S.A. to curtail the production of various crops.

- 25 -

Settlement Bank Scheme Upheld.	Para. 56:	I do not feel competent to comment, and would refer you to paras 47 and 48 on page 21, of the Report of the Financial Adviser dated 20.4.32., and which was forwarded to you by the Director of Development under cover of his DC/153/32 of 20.4.32.
Criticism of the Bank's Scheme Refuted.	Para. 57:	
The Bank's Prospects of Profit.	Para. 58:	
The Settlement Bank and the Tax-payer.	Para. 59:	
Funds for Jewish Development Delayed.	Para. 60:	

Growth of Population and Forces of Development.

Para. 62: Please see Mr. French's Confidential letter addressed to Government No. DC/153/32 of 20.4.32. in which it is stated that the cost of settling "landless Arabs" has been rendered intentionally vague.

Agrarian unrest: It is suggested that the explanation of the matters stated under this heading is that given in my observations on F.R. paragraph 8.

Transplantation of Tenants.

Para. 65: I do not agree with the remarks of the Jewish Agency. Even today the same process is taking place at Umm Khalid where the founders of Nathaniya Colony are paying away large sums, even as much as £20 per dunam, in order to get rid of the Arabs who worked for the landowner. It is true that in some cases the money will be put to proper use, but unfortunately in the majority of cases it is frittered away and the tenant is then liable to become a burden on the tax-payer.

- 24 -

Rights to be protected.	Para. 64: The proposed amendments to the Protection of Cultivators Ordinance will deal with the point raised by Mr. French in this paragraph.
Homestead Protection Ordinance.	Para. 72: The quotation from the "Times" seems rather to be an argument for the necessity of the Five Feddan Law than against it. 2. The proposed law will not prevent "a cultivator, who is bent upon selling out and leaving the land", from doing so.
Criticism of Major Features of the Draft.	Para. 74: (1) There is ground for believing that the alteration of the law regarding imprisonment for debt has already restricted easy rural credit with the effect of increasing the activity of the fellaheen in the cultivation of their land. 2. Recently a very intelligent Arab landowner made the following observation to me: "I believe that the Imprisonment for Debt Ordinance and the new Execution Law were not only a comfort to the fellah but an inducement to capitalists to employ their money in works productive to the country. Also the fellah, finding no moneylenders to lend to him, began to depend upon himself in earning his money". 3. The statements that the proposed legislation will "entirely destroy such credit as the small cultivator may possess" and that "the effect of the proposed legislation would be to drive the cultivator back into the arms of the usurer and tighten the moneylender's grip on him" appear to be contradictory.

- 25 -

Occupancy Tenants Ordinance.	Para. 75: Please see remarks on First Report para. 8.
Difficulties anticipated.	Para. 79: Agreed.
Criticism of Major Provisions of the Draft.	Para. 81: (i) It is suggested that the anomaly is apparent rather than real: a tenant who had left a holding of his own free will would not be likely to claim occupancy rights. The section as drafted only purports to be an attempt to avoid the difficulty proved to be a real one by the history of the Protection of Cultivators Ordinance 1929, that making the right conferred by the law dependent upon some qualifying period renders the law nugatory and places tenants in a worse position than before, because landlords refuse to grant leases and tenants are driven from place to place.

(ii) It seems equitable that a landlord should have the right to ask the Court to increase the rent of a holding when changed circumstances justify it.

(iii) It is suggested that it may be assumed that District Commissioners will use their powers reasonably.

(iv) It would be easy to provide expressly that any tenancy created by a mortgagor after the date of the mortgage which in the opinion of the Court is calculated to delay or defeat the rights of the mortgagee should be voidable. By English law a mortgagor in exercising his powers of leasing is a trustee for the mortgagee and any lease made by him must be at the best rent that can be obtained.

Improvement of Hill Fellah's Farming.	<u>Para. 125</u>: It is not disputed that the condition of the hill fellaheen is susceptible of improvement. Larger draught animals, however, would be useless save upon exceptional holdings.